Bill Garcia
Dept. of
Psychology

A History and Theory
of Informed Consent

A History and Theory of Informed Consent

RUTH R. FADEN

TOM L. BEAUCHAMP

in collaboration with

NANCY M. P. KING

New York   Oxford

OXFORD UNIVERSITY PRESS

1986

Oxford University Press

Oxford   New York   Toronto
Delhi   Bombay   Calcutta   Madras   Karachi
Petaling Jaya   Singapore   Hong Kong   Tokyo
Nairobi   Dar es Salaam   Cape Town
Melbourne   Auckland

and associated companies in
Beirut   Berlin   Ibadan   Nicosia

Library of Congress Cataloging in Publication Data
Faden, Ruth R.
A history and theory of informed consent.
Bibliography: p.   Includes index.
1. Informed consent (Medical law)—History.
I. Beauchamp, Tom L.   II. King, Nancy M. P.   III. Title.
K3611.I5B43   1986   344'.041'09   85-13858
ISBN 0-19-503686-7   342.44109

Printing (last digit): 9 8 7 6 5 4 3 2

Printed in the United States of America
on acid free paper

to our parents
Anita, David, Honey, and Tom
with gratitude and respect

and to our
Karine

Preface

Our primary goal in writing this book has been to provide a satisfactory answer to the question "What is informed consent?" Our subject matter is the origin and nature of this concept. We therefore concentrate on conceptual issues, with special attention to the conditions under which an informed consent is obtained.

In Chapters 1 and 2 (Part I), we set the stage for our analysis by discussing basic concepts and structures of reasoning in moral philosophy and law. Fundamental questions about informed consent have been framed from the perspective of these two disciplines, each of which has contributed an influential literature on the subject.

Moral philosophy and law do not exhaust, however, the perspectives brought to bear on issues of informed consent in subsequent chapters. In Chapters 3 through 6 (Part II), we employ historical methods to examine the origins and status of informed consent in clinical medicine (Chapter 3), in the law (Chapter 4), in research involving human subjects (Chapter 5), and in federal policy (Chapter 6). Ours is an interpretative history: We are primarily concerned with when and how developments in informed consent occurred in these domains.

In Chapters 7 through 10 (Part III), we move from history to a theory of informed consent. We begin with the concept of autonomy. An analysis of autonomous action is presented (in Chapter 7) that serves as the basis for an analysis of the meaning of "informed consent" (in Chapter 8). Our answer to the question "What is informed consent?" is developed in Chapters 9 and 10, where we bring perspectives from philosophy and psychology to bear in an expanded treatment of the conditions of autonomy and informed consent.

Throughout this volume we address questions of public policy and professional ethics, but this book is not about the proper role of informed consent in medical care and reaserch. We do not provide an analysis of the desirability of participation by patients or subjects in decisionmaking, nor do we identify the conditions under which health care professionals and research investigators should obtain informed consents. Our primary goals are historical and conceptual rather than normative. We discuss the nature of informed consent, its conditions, and the ends it serves, but not whether and when informed consent obligations should be imposed.

Although our effort is essentially nonnormative, it is directly relevant to practical affairs. The development of satisfactory policies and practices of informed consent requires an understanding of the concept and its history. Here, as elsewhere, there is a need to be clear concerning that about which we speak before reaching conclusions about how things ought to be.

August 1985   ❧   R.R.F.
Talloires, Lac D'Annecy, France   T.L.B.

Acknowledgments

This volume has benefited from an extensive array of constructive and critical comments by scholars from various disciplines. We owe an overwhelming debt of gratitude to our collaborator and legal consultant Nancy M. P. King. Without her dedication and contribution, every chapter would have been diminished. She is the primary author of Chapter 4, our constant guide to legal insights and legal materials, and our major critic on all else.

Many scholars influenced the arguments in Parts II and III (Chapters 3 through 10). For improvements in the historical arguments presented in Chapter 3, we owe a deep debt of gratitude to Kathryn Olesko, Ed Pellegrino, and Martin Pernick. For similar service on legal materials—especially Chapter 4—we, together with Nancy King, must thank Stewart Jay, John Robertson, and Steve Teret. Each expended a sustained effort to help us develop a legal framework and an accurate history. In Chapters 5 and 6 our arguments were improved through critical comments and historical materials provided by Gert Brieger (and his colleagues at the Institute for the History of Medicine at Johns Hopkins), Larry Bachorik, Joe Brady, Donald Chalkley, Stuart Cook, James Jones, Herbert Kelman, Patricia King, Charles McCarthy, William McGuire, Charles McKay, Barbara Mishkin, M. Brewster Smith, Robert Veatch, and LeRoy Walters.

For comments, data, and telephone discussions regarding *all* of the above chapters—and some below—we owe a special acknowledgment to our friend and inspiration, Jay Katz. Our criticisms of his work on informed consent must not be interpreted as a repudiation of his general contribution. Our arguments—critical and constructive—are everywhere indebted to him; no one in the literature on informed consent has taught us as much or presented such a clear challenge to our views.

Chapters 7 through 10—on the relation of autonomy and informed consent—were markedly improved by philosophically and psychologically minded critics Jason Brandt, James Childress, Wayne Davis, Gerald Dworkin, Terry Pinkard, Dan Robinson, Alex Rosenberg, and R. Jay Wallace. The criticisms by Davis and Wallace were invaluable, as they altered the very character of the theory and its underlying argument.

Many research assistants also helped make this volume possible. Two stand out: Deborah Kohrman, who helped organize the voluminous literature on informed consent, and Bettina Schöne-Seifert, who assisted us with structuring and improving the entire volume. We also thank Sarah V. Brakman, Kathy Buckley, Timothy Hodges, Sara Finnerty Kelly, Donna Horak Mitsock, Kim Quaid, and Tina Kotek for research assistance that improved the accuracy and detail of every chapter.

Our historical research tapped the services of several libraries, private and public offices, and data retrieval systems. Judy Mistichelli of the Kennedy Institute of Ethics Library was faithful in executing our research objectives and ingenious in devising new strategies of her own design. We also were assisted by librarians at the History of Medicine rooms at the Johns Hopkins University (Welch Library–Institute for the History of Medicine), Georgetown University (Dahlgren Medical Library), and the National Library of Medicine (N.I.H.). Similarly, we must acknowledge the assistance of the keepers of the files and records at the American Medical Association, the American Psychological Association, and the Office of the Director of N.I.H. Each helped us find data that otherwise would have remained locked away.

Superb assistance was provided through our university offices, where for years drafts were faithfully prepared in what must have seemed an endless flow of rewriting and proofing. We are indebted for this assistance to Denise Brooks, Caren Kieswetter, Gwen Thomas, and Mary Ellen Timbol.

Finally, we must thank the National Library of Medicine and our project officer, Peter Clepper, for a grant [NLM-EP (K10 LM 0032-01, 01S1, 01S2)] which generously supported this work. This financial assistance was augmented by sabbatical leaves from Johns Hopkins and Georgetown universities which facilitated the writing of the final chapters and their redrafting. We are sincerely grateful to those who made these leaves possible.

Contents

I
FOUNDATIONS

1

Foundations in Moral Theory

The history of informed consent is rooted in multiple disciplines and social contexts, including those of the health professions, law, the social and behavioral sciences, and moral philosophy. In recent years, the most influential fields have been law and moral philosophy; the central problems of informed consent have been framed in their vocabularies. Yet these disciplines, each with distinct methods and objectives, serve strikingly different social and intellectual functions. The aim of our first two chapters is to present analytic frameworks of the distinctive forms of reasoning found in moral philosophy and law, in order that the history and theory found in the ensuing eight chapters may be more easily understood.

Although these two foundational frameworks are both intricate and controversial, the essences of the legal and the moral approaches to informed consent are not difficult to understand. The law has focused almost exclusively on clinical rather than research contexts. From the legal point of view, a physician has a duty both to inform patients and to obtain their consent. If a patient is injured as a result of a failure on the part of a physician to disclose information about a procedure, then the patient may collect money damages from the physician for causing the injury. This legal vision of informed consent is more focused on financial compensation for unfortunate medical outcomes than on either the disclosure of information or the consent of the patient in general.

For this reason, many have been suspicious about the adequacy of the law as a vehicle for defining or setting requirements of informed consent, and have increasingly come to regard the major issues as moral rather than legal. From the moral point of view, informed consent has less to do with the liability of professionals as agents of disclosure, and more to do with the autonomous choices of patients and subjects. In Chapters 7 and 8 we argue that, in one important sense of the term, an "informed consent" is an autonomous authorization by a patient or subject. This definition is more suited to discussion from the moral point of view than the legal point of view.

3

We can oversimplify and drastically abbreviate the differences between law and moral philosophy as follows: The law's approach springs from a pragmatic theory. Although the patient is granted a right to consent or refuse, the focus is on the physician, who holds a duty and who risks liability by failure to fulfill the duty. Moral philosophy's approach springs from a principle of respect for autonomy that focuses on the patient or subject, who has a right to make an autonomous choice.

Thus expressed, these frameworks are disarmingly simple, but their interpretation and comparison have proved difficult, and numerous scholarly controversies surround them. Indeed, it would be fatuous to suggest that in moral philosophy and law there is firm agreement as to either the appropriate methods of analysis or structures of reasoning. Any defensible position will need an argued statement of its basic premises. A statement of the premises of moral theory is our immediate goal.

Principles, Rules, and Rights

Moral deliberation and justification rest on principles, rules, and rights, understood as abstract action-guides. These general guides and their relationships will be the focus of our attention in this section. However, before we turn directly to them, some background assumptions regarding the words "ethics," "morality," and "moral philosophy" deserve mention.

The Concept of Morality

The word "morality" has meanings that extend beyond philosophical contexts and professional codes of conduct. Morality is concerned with practices defining right and wrong that are usually transmitted within a culture or institution from generation to generation, together with other kinds of customs and rules. Morality denotes a social institution, composed of a set of standards pervasively acknowledged by the members of the culture. In this respect, it has an objective, ongoing status as a body of action guides. Like political constitutions and natural languages, morality exists prior to the acceptance (or rejection) of its rules and regulations by particular individuals. Its standards are usually abstract, uncodified, and applicable to behavior in many diverse circumstances.

The terms "ethical theory" and "moral philosophy," by contrast, suggest *reflection* on the institution of morality. These terms refer to attempts to introduce clarity, substance, and precision of argument into the domain of morality. Moral philosophers seek to put moral beliefs and social practices of morality into a more unified and defensible package of action-guides by challenging presuppositions, assessing moral arguments, and suggesting modifications in existing beliefs. Their task often

centers on "justification": Philosophers seek to justify a system of standards or some moral point of view on the basis of carefully analyzed and
defended theories and principles, such as respect for autonomy, distributive justice, equal treatment, human rights, beneficence, nonmaleficence, and utility—some of the principles commonly employed in contemporary moral philosophy.

Despite these rough distinctions, we shall use the terms "moral" and
"ethical" as synonymous, and "moral philosophy" and "ethical theory"
will also be used interchangeably. "Morality," however, will be confined
to social practice.

Reasoning by Principles

Philosophers try to exhibit how to avoid confusing a merely personal attitude or religious dogma with a reasoned and justified moral position.
Accordingly, moral philosophy offers principles for the development and
evaluation of moral arguments. Rights, duties, obligations, and the like
derive from these principles. ("Values" is a still more general term, and
one we shall rarely employ.) Such principles—the choice and analysis of
which are controversial—constitute the heart of modern ethical theory.
They are the key to understanding the structure of moral reasoning
employed so frequently in discussions of informed consent. Most of these
principles are already embedded in public morality and policies, but
only in a vague and imprecise form. The job of ethical theory is to lend
precision without oversimplification. It should always be remembered
that moral debate about a particular course of action or controversy is
often rooted not only in disagreement about the proper interpretation of
applicable moral principles, but also in the interpretation of factual
information and in divergent assessments of the proper scientific, meta-
physical, or religious description of a situation.

Although it is neither possible nor necessary to outline a full ethical
theory in this volume, three moral principles relevant to our subject matter need to be addressed and briefly analyzed: respect for autonomy,
beneficence, and justice. These broad principles provide the basis for the
more specific rules and requirements found in professional codes of medical and research ethics. The first two principles are already widely
employed, however imprecisely, in discussions of informed consent,
and—when joined with justice—they are sufficiently comprehensive to
provide an analytical framework through which many moral problems
surrounding informed consent may be understood and evaluated. We
shall not here debate whether these three principles jointly form a *complete* moral system nor whether other moral principles are distinct or
derivative from these three principles.

Problems of informed consent have often been addressed in codes and
regulations specific to clinical and research contexts. These prescriptions

are composed of rules of conduct directed at the amelioration of specific professional problems, and usually are formulated by professional associations or government agencies. There are two principal ways of construing the relationship between these documents and the general principles found in ethical theory: First, such statements may be viewed as individual, self-contained systems of ethical rules fashioned for specific contexts but unrelated to externally valid principles. Alternatively, they may be viewed as having a justification in broader ethical principles that are required for or presupposed in their own formulations of rules.

According to the latter conception—which we accept throughout this volume—codes and regulations can and should be evaluated in terms of general ethical principles. Even if it could rightly be argued that codes have been written in the past without direct reference or appeal to basic principles, these codes can be both criticized and defended by appeals to such principles. The principles discussed below are intended to serve as such a basis for critical analysis of moral codes, policies, and regulations that traditionally have been used to address informed consent.

In using the language of "principles" we do not mean to evade the important question of whether *principles* are more fundamental to a basic moral framework than *virtues* or *rights*. Nowhere in this volume do we address the virtues or virtue theory, because this is not the orientation we bring to the analysis of informed consent. We do, however, draw on rights language, as does the informed consent literature generally. We shall now see that rights are correlative to duties, both of which derive from principles. We shall maintain that for every duty there exists at least one correlative right, and that duties and rights are grounded in principles.

Rights as Correlative to Duties

Only recently has Western society emphasized the importance of human rights, and only recently have rights come to play an important role in public policy discussions, such as those involving informed consent. Rights are powerful assertions of claims that demand respect and status, and they occupy a prominent place in moral theory and political documents. If someone appeals to rights, a response is demanded. We must accept the person's claim as valid, discredit it by countervailing considerations, or acknowledge the right but show how it can be overridden by competing moral claims.

Legal rights are widely acknowledged and codified, but the status of moral rights is more puzzling. Some thinkers are skeptical of their validity; others find absurd the profusion of rights and the conflicts resulting from their various claims. Absurd or otherwise, rights language has been extended to many controversial arenas—rights to privacy, rights to health care, rights of children, rights of animals, rights of the elderly, rights to confidential information, rights to shelter, and so on. How, then, are we to understand the language and basis of rights in moral discourse, and what is the relationship between one person's rights and another's duties?

A plausible claim is that a right always entails the imposition of a duty on others either not to interfere or to provide something, both the duty and the right being justified by the same overarching principle. Thus, if as a matter of justice a state promises or otherwise incurs a duty to provide such goods as influenza shots or other medical care to needy citizens, then citizens can claim an entitlement or right to that care if they meet the relevant criteria. The right to die, the right to privacy, the right to be free to make a decision, and all other so-called negative rights, which are often grounded in respect for autonomy, may be treated as entailing someone else's duty to abstain from interference with one's intended course in life.

If our treatment of the "correlativity thesis" is correct, little is distinctive about rights as a moral category. As with duties, the moral basis for their assertion simply rests in moral principles. Although it remains controversial in contemporary ethical theory whether rights are based on duties, duties based on rights, or neither based on the other, we have tried to circumvent this controversy by holding that the principles in a moral system both impose duties and confer rights. We presume this analysis throughout this volume for both moral *and* legal rights. The rights most central to our arguments, the right to make an autonomous choice and the right to perform autonomous actions, will be treated as strictly correlative to the duty not to interfere with the autonomous choices and actions of others and, in special relationships, correlative to the duty to enable others to make autonomous choices. These rights and duties derive from the principle of respect for autonomy.

Three Principles

Respect for Autonomy

Respect for autonomy is the most frequently mentioned moral principle in the literature on informed consent, where it is conceived as a principle rooted in the liberal Western tradition of the importance of individual freedom and choice, both for political life and for personal development. "Autonomy" and "respect for autonomy" are terms loosely associated with several ideas, such as privacy, voluntariness, self-mastery, choosing freely, the freedom to choose, choosing one's own moral position, and accepting responsibility for one's choices. Because of this conceptual uncertainty, the concept of autonomy and its connection to informed consent needs sustained analysis, which we provide in Chapters 7 and 8.

Historically, the word "autonomy" is a legacy from ancient Greece, where *autos* (self) and *nomos* (rule or law) were joined to refer to political self-governance in the city-state. In moral philosophy personal autonomy has come to refer to personal self-governance: personal rule of the self by adequate understanding while remaining free from controlling interferences by others and from personal limitations that prevent choice. "Autonomy," so understood, has been loosely analyzed in terms of external nonconstraint and the presence of critical internal capacities integral to self-governance.[1] But, again, major confusion can emerge over the precise analysis of autonomy if we move beyond the core idea that the autonomous person is not bound by controlling constraints and is in control of personal affairs.

Almost all existing analyses of autonomy focus on the autonomous *person*. Our central interest, however, is in autonomous *choice*—or, more generally, autonomous *action*. This distinction is between (1) persons who have the capacity to be independent and in control, and (2) the actions that reflect the exercise of those capacities. This distinction may be thought trivial because it might seem by definition that only autonomous persons act autonomously. However, as we shall see in Chapters 7 and 8, the criteria of autonomous choices are not identical with the criteria of autonomous persons. Autonomous persons can and do make nonautonomous choices owing to temporary constraints such as ignorance or coercion. This is a matter of significance for a theory of informed consent. It is no less important that some persons who are not autonomous can and do occasionally muster the resources to make an autonomous choice under circumstances calling for informed consents and refusals.

It is one thing to be autonomous, and another to be *respected* as autonomous. Many issues about consent concern failures to respect autonomy, ranging from manipulative underdisclosure of pertinent information to nonrecognition of a refusal of medical interventions. To respect an autonomous agent is to recognize with due appreciation that person's capacities and perspective, including his or her right to hold certain views, to make certain choices, and to take certain actions based on personal values and beliefs. Such respect has historically been connected to the idea that persons possess an intrinsic value independent of special circumstances that confer value. As expressed in Kantian philosophy, autonomous persons are ends in themselves, determining their own destiny, and are not to be treated merely as means to the ends of others.[2] Thus, the burden of moral justification rests on those who would restrict or prevent a person's exercise of autonomy.

The moral demand that we respect the autonomy of persons can be formulated as a *principle of respect for autonomy*: Persons should be free to choose and act without controlling constraints imposed by others. The principle provides the justificatory basis for the right to make autonomous decisions, which in turn takes the form of specific autonomy-related rights. For example, in the debate over whether autonomous, informed patients have the right to refuse self-regarding, life-sustaining medical interventions,[3] the principle of respect for autonomy suggests a morally appropriate response.

Although the obligation to obtain informed consent in research and clinical contexts is generally understood to be grounded in a principle of respect for autonomy, several issues about the proper limits of the obligation remain unsettled. Whether the principle is the exclusive or even the primary justification of consent requirements is controversial, as we shall see in later chapters. More important is the question of the exact demands the principle makes in the consent context—for example, as to requirements that certain kinds of information be disclosed. Another question concerns the restrictions society may rightfully place on choices by patients or subjects when these choices conflict with other values. If choices might endanger the public health, potentially harm a fetus, or involve a scarce resource for which a patient cannot pay, it may be justifiable to restrict exercises of autonomy severely, perhaps by state intervention. If restriction is in order, the justification will rest on some competing moral principle such as beneficence or justice. This issue of *balancing* the demands made by conflicting moral principles will be addressed later in this chapter.

Many unsettled issues also surround the *scope* of the principle of respect for autonomy. In particular, the number and kinds of duties it entails are unresolved. For example, are duties of disclosure derived from respect for autonomy, or are they derived from an independent principle? Is there a connection to the right of privacy,[4] which has often been linked directly to both autonomy and informed consent? (See pp. 39–43.)

We take the view that a broad moral framework adequate for the analysis of informed consent does not need to postulate either a "right to privacy"[5] or a "principle of veracity" in addition to a principle of respect for autonomy, because the latter alone will suffice as a basic principle. Wherever a moral right to privacy or the principle of veracity is invoked in the specific context of informed consent, we will treat it as either reducible to or derivative from an autonomy right (although we do not suggest that the *meaning* of "privacy" or "veracity" can be reduced to the meaning of "autonomy"[6]). As we shall see in Chapter 2, the legal right to privacy also has roots in respect for autonomy, which is expressed in the law as respect for self-determination. (See pp. 27–28.)

Beneficence

The welfare of the patient is the goal of health care and also of what is often called "therapeutic research." This welfare objective is medicine's context and justification: Clinical therapies are aimed at the promotion of health by cure or prevention of disease. This value of benefiting the person has long been treated as a foundational value—and sometimes as *the* foundational value—in medical ethics. For example, a celebrated principle in the history of medical codes of ethics is the maxim *primum non nocere*—"above all, do no harm"—commonly viewed as the fundamental maxim of the Hippocratic tradition in medicine. Recent scholarship has shown that in the Hippocratic writings the more precise formulation of the primary moral injunction is "help, or at least do no harm,"[7] thus demanding the provision of benefit beyond mere avoidance of harm.

The principle of beneficence includes the following four elements, all linked through the common theme of promoting the welfare of others:[8] (1) one ought not to inflict evil or harm; (2) one ought to prevent evil or harm; (3) one ought to remove evil or harm; (4) one ought to do or promote good. Many philosophers have held that the fourth element may not, strictly speaking, be a duty; and some have claimed that these elements should be hierarchically arranged so that the first takes precedence over the second, the second over the third, and the third over the fourth.

There is a definite appeal to this hierarchical ordering internal to the principle of beneficence. In particular, good philosophical reasons exist for separating passive nonmaleficence (a so-called negative duty to avoid doing harm, as expressed in 1) and active beneficence (a so-called positive duty to afford assistance, as expressed in 2–4). Ordinary moral discourse and many philosophical systems suggest that negative duties not to injure others are more compelling than positive duties to benefit others.[9] For example, we do not consider it justifiable to kill a dying patient in order to use the patient's organs to save two others. Similarly, the duty not to injure a patient by abandonment seems to many stronger than the duty to prevent injury to a patient who has been abandoned by another (under the assumption that both are moral duties).

Despite the attractiveness of this hierarchical ordering rule, it is not firmly sanctioned by either morality or ethical theory. The duty expressed in (1) may not *always* outweigh those expressed in (2–4). For example, the harm inflicted in (1) may be negligible or trivial, while the harm to be prevented in (2) may be substantial. For instance, saving a person's life by a blood transfusion justifies the inflicted harms of venipuncture on the blood donor. One of the motivations for separating nonmaleficence from beneficence is that they themselves conflict when one must *either* avoid harm *or* bring aid. In such cases, one needs a decision rule to prefer one alternative to another. But if the weights of the two principles can vary, as they can, there can be no mechanical decision rule asserting that one principle must always outweigh the other.

In concrete cases, the conceptual distinctions between 1–4 begin to break down, at least in application. For example, if a physician prescribes morphine for a patient in extreme pain, is she providing a benefit (4) or removing a harm (3) or both? Similarly, when the state provides certain needed medical treatments to citizens, it can be argued that the state is not only providing a benefit (4), but also preventing and removing the harms of illness and death (2 and 3). To avoid running down a child playing in the street—that is, to refrain from doing harm (1)—requires positive steps of braking, turning, warning, and the like.[10]

Such problems lead us to unify the moral demands that we should benefit and not injure others under a single principle of beneficence, taking care to distinguish, as necessary, between strong and weak requirements of this principle. The strength of these requirements corresponds only in some cases to the ordering of 1–4. In its general form, then, the principle of beneficence requires us to abstain from intentionally injuring others, and to further the important and legitimate interests of others, largely by preventing or removing possible harms.

There are several problems with the principle, so understood. For example, to what extent does the principle require the benefactor to assume personal risk or to suffer harm? Although it is widely agreed that we are obligated to act beneficently only if we can do so with minimal personal risk or inconvenience,[11] are there no conditions—special circumstances or role relationships—in which we are obligated to act beneficently even in the face of significant personal risk? Are not parents morally bound to sacrifice time and financial resources for their children? But would a stranger to the child be so bound?

A related problem is determining in any given instance to whom duties of beneficence are owed. Whose interests count, and whose count the most? The principle of beneficence should not, as a *principle*, be restricted to single parties even in special contexts such as the patient-physician or subject-researcher relationship. Thus, the principle itself leaves open the question as to whom one's beneficence should be directed. For example, in the soliciting of consent to therapeutic research, there may be duties of beneficence to numerous third parties (future patients, employers, the state, endangered parties, etc.), even if the patient-subject's interests are the primary reason for an action. But third parties may not always have interests that should count.

Another vexing problem in ethical theory concerns the extent to which the principle of beneficence generates moral *duties*. Any analysis of beneficence that includes element (4) potentially demands severe sacrifice and extreme generosity in the moral life—for example, giving a kidney for transplantation or donating bone marrow. As a result, some philosophers have argued that this form of beneficent action is virtuous and a moral *ideal*, but not a duty. From this perspective, the positive benefiting of others is based on personal ideals that are supererogatory rather than obligatory: We are not morally *required* to promote the good of persons, even if we are in a position to do so, and even if the action is morally *justified*. The underlying problem is that actions such as sacrificing bodily parts and loving one's enemies may be more costly to the agent than morality demands.

Several proposals have been offered in moral philosophy to resolve this problem by showing that beneficence *is* a principle of duty, but these theoretical ventures are extraneous to our concerns here.[12] The scope or range of acts required by the duty of beneficence is an undecided issue, and perhaps an undecidable one. Fortunately, our arguments do not depend on its resolution. That we are morally obligated on *some* occasions to assist others is hardly a matter of moral controversy. Beneficent acts are demanded by the roles involved in fiduciary relationships between health care professionals and patients, lawyers and clients, researchers and subjects (at least in therapeutic research), bankers and customers, and so on. For example, physicians on duty in an emergency room are obligated to attend to injured, delirious, uncooperative patients, sometimes at considerable risk both to themselves and to the patient.

We will treat the basic roles and concepts that give substance to the principle of beneficence in medicine as follows: The positive benefit the physician is obligated to seek is the alleviation of disease and injury, if there is a reasonable hope of cure. The harms to be prevented, removed, or minimized are the pain, suffering, and disability of injury and disease. In addition, the physician is of course enjoined from *doing* harm if interventions inflict unnecessary pain and suffering on patients. While these considerations are all included under beneficence, we view the idea of a lexical ordering of sub-principles as an expendable overgeneralization.

In therapeutic research, the benefits and harms presented to subjects parallel those in medicine—the cure, removal, or prevention of pain, suffering, disability, and disease. In nontherapeutic research, the subjects' interests are less at center stage, because the positive benefit sought by the scientist is new knowledge. Often (but not necessarily) this knowledge is desired because it is expected to contribute to the resolution of important medical or social problems. Therapeutic and nontherapeutic research thus differ in the kinds of benefits each hopes to achieve. Although in both there is an equally strong imperative to avoid harming the subject, therapeutic research may legitimately present increased potential for harms if they are balanced by a commensurate possibility of benefits to the subject.

Those engaged in both medical practice and research know that risks of harm presented by interventions must constantly be weighed against possible benefits for patients, subjects, or the public interest. The physician who professes to "do no harm" is not pledging never to cause harm but rather to strive to create a positive balance of goods over inflicted harms. This is recognized in the Nuremberg Code, which enjoins: "The degree of risk to be taken should never exceed that determined by the humanitarian importance of the problem to be solved by the experiment."[13] Such a balancing principle is essential to any sound moral system: Beneficence assumes an obligation to weigh and balance benefits against harms, benefits against alternative benefits, and harms against alternative harms.

Health care professionals and research investigators often disagree over how to balance the various factors, and there may be no objective evidence that dictates one course rather than another.[14] In clinical contexts, this balancing can also present situations in which health care professionals and patients differ in their assessments of the professional's obligations. In some cases, benefit to another is involved—as, for example, when a pregnant woman refuses a physician's recommendation of fetal surgery. In other cases the refusal may be exclusively self-regarding. Some health care professionals will accept a patient's refusal as valid, whereas others are inclined to ignore the fact that an informed consent to treatment has not been given, and so try to "benefit" the patient through a medical intervention.

This problem of whether to override the decisions of patients in order to benefit them or prevent harm to them is one dimension of the problem of medical paternalism, in which a parental-like decision by a professional overrides an autonomous decision of a patient. Although not central to our concerns, the issue of paternalism is at the core of many discussions of informed consent. Much of the literature in the field focuses on such fundamental moral questions as when consent need not be obtained and when refusals need not be honored. Paternalism and antipaternalism hide in every corridor of these discussions.

The issue of proper authority for decisionmaking is an implicit theme throughout this volume. In health care, professionals and patients alike see the authority for some decisions as properly the patient's and authority for other decisions as primarily the professional's. It is widely agreed, for example, that the choice of a birth control method is properly the patient's but that the decision to administer a sedative to a panicked patient in an emergency room is properly the physician's. However, many cases in medicine exhibit no clear consensus about legitimate decisionmaking authority—for instance, who should decide which aggressive therapy, if any, to administer to a cancer victim or whether to prolong the lives of severely handicapped newborns by medical interventions? Similar disputes appear in the research context—for example, as to whether the researcher has the authority to use persons without their knowledge as subjects in low-risk research.

Decisions regarding who ought to serve as the legitimate authority—
patient, subject, or professional—can turn decisively on what will maximally promote the patient's or subject's welfare. Standing behind the
position that authority should rest with the patients or subjects may be
the goal of benefiting patients and subjects by enabling them to make
the decision that best promotes their welfare. Promotion of the value of
autonomous choice in medical decisionmaking by patients is often justified by arguments from beneficence to the effect that decisional autonomy by patients enables them to survive, heal, or otherwise improve
their own health. These arguments range from the simple contention
that making one's own decisions promotes one's psychological well-
being to the more controversial observation that patients generally know
themselves well enough to be the best judges, ultimately, of what is most
beneficial for them. Similar arguments are also used in research contexts
where it is maintained that requiring the informed consent of subjects
will serve as a curb on research risks. Here autonomous choice is valued
extrinsically for the sake of health or welfare rather than intrinsically for
its own sake.

Justice

Every civilized society is a cooperative venture structured by moral,
legal, and cultural principles that define the terms of social cooperation.
Beneficence and respect for autonomy are principles in this fabric of
social order, but *justice* has been perhaps the subject of more treatises
on the terms of social cooperation than any other principle. A person has
been treated in accordance with the principle of justice if treated
according to what is fair, due, or owed. For example, if equal political
rights are due all citizens, then justice is done when those rights are
accorded. Any denial of a good, service, or piece of information to which
a person has a right or entitlement based in justice is an injustice. It is
also an injustice to place an undue burden on the exercise of a right—
for example, to make a piece of information owed to a person unreasonably difficult to obtain.

Many appeals to "justice" present a confused picture because they are
not appeals to a *distinctive principle* of justice that is independent of
other principles such as beneficence or respect for autonomy. These
appeals to "what is just" use the term "just" in a broad and nonspecific
sense to refer to that which is generally *justified*, or in the circumstances
morally *right*. Claims of justice tend to emerge in literature on informed
consent when it is believed that someone's legal or moral rights have
been violated, and sometimes these claims also confuse justice with justification. For example, articles on psychological research involving
deception often denounce the research as *unjustly* denying subjects
information to which they are entitled. Yet, as the argument develops, it

often turns out that the controlling moral principle in such a judgment is less one of justice per se than respect for autonomy. (The argument could, of course, involve appeal to both principles.) Similarly, proponents of a physician's obligation to withhold potentially harmful information from patients for therapeutic reasons sometimes argue that it would be *unjust* for the physician to provide less than the best possible medical treatment. Here the moral concern is one of beneficence rather than justice. Many complaints of "injustice" in the informed consent literature can be linked in this way to alleged violations of the principle of respect for autonomy or of the principle of beneficence.

However, not all issues of justice in biomedical ethics can be entirely accounted for by appeal to other principles. How to allocate scarce medical resources and the validity of claims to possess a right to health care are staple examples of justice-based problems. Although more difficult to isolate, various problems that plague the literature on informed consent also seem justice-based. For example, much of the controversy surrounding the use of prisoners as subjects in research centers less on whether prisoners can give valid informed consent in the coercive environment of incarceration than on whether justice permits creation of a ready pool of human volunteers out of the class of those incarcerated by the state, especially when the same pool of persons might be repeatedly used. This question turns on the just distribution of the burden of the risks of research participation in society and thus is *centrally* a problem about justice rather than beneficence or respect for autonomy. The issue is whether this burden could be warranted even if the public welfare is enhanced by the practice (a consideration of beneficence in the form of public utility) and even if the prisoners are capable of giving, and *do* give, a voluntary informed consent (a consideration of autonomy). The point of many analyses of research involving frequently used and vulnerable subjects is whether autonomous consent is sufficient to *override reservations based on justice* about approaching such persons to be research subjects in the first place.

It has also been argued that rules of informed consent can be motivated less by a concern to promote autonomous choice than by a concern to promote justice. Charles Lidz and his associates maintain that some who have argued for rules governing informed consent in psychiatry, including rules promoting increased disclosure in such areas as consent to electroconvulsive treatment (ECT), have been motivated by a concern over the *fairness* of subjecting patients to a potentially harmful treatment because of administrative convenience. They note that the advocates of strict disclosure "sought to use informed consent as a technique to minimize the use of ECT by using premises of equity and justice." However, as so often occurs, the persons Lidz has in mind were probably motivated by a *mixture* of moral concerns of respect for autonomy, beneficence, *and* justice. Lidz and others describe their *own* concerns in studying multiple problems of informed consent as motivated by the question whether a "more equal and mutual participatory relationship" can be established between health professionals and patients. They too seem motivated by a mixture of considerations of respect for autonomy, justice, *and* beneficence.[15]

We, like many writers in ethics, will make reference to all three of these principles, but in our analysis justice will have nothing like the prominence of the other two principles. The major moral and conceptual problems about informed consent are not justice-based and do not directly confront issues of social justice.

Balancing Moral Principles and Rights

Controversial problems about abstract moral principles such as "respect for autonomy" and "beneficence" inevitably arise over how much these principles demand and over how to handle situations of conflict with other moral principles, such as justice. Whatever the prominence of these principles, we must acknowledge that if they conflict—as they do on occasion—a serious weighting or priority problem is created. Successful novels and dramas often depict these moral principles in their baldest forms of conflict: A person steals in order to preserve a life, lies in order to protect a sworn secret, or breaks a duty to keep confidentiality in order to protect a person endangered by its maintenance. Under such conditions it must be decided which (if either) moral consideration has priority—a problem known in ethical theory as how to "weigh and balance moral principles." Many problems about informed consent, especially informed refusals, take this form. For example, these problems include involve whether to override refusals of treatment by patients, as when Jehovah's Witnesses refuse blood transfusions but the transfusions are given nonetheless.

The philosopher W.D. Ross is celebrated for his attempt to handle this problem of conflict.[16] Ross provides a list of several valid moral principles, including principles similar to the three we have had under examination. According to him, we must find "the greatest duty" in any circumstance of conflict by finding "the greatest balance" of right over wrong in that particular context. This metaphor of weights moving up and down on a balance scale is vivid, but crude and potentially misleading. Ross sought to give as much precision as possible to his ideas through a fundamental distinction between *prima facie* duties and *actual* duties: "Prima facie duty" refers to a duty always to be acted upon unless it conflicts on a particular occasion with an equal or stronger duty. A prima facie duty is always right and binding, all other things being equal. Although a firm duty, it is nonetheless conditional on not being overridden or outweighed by competing moral demands. One's actual duty, then, is determined by the balance of the respective weights of the competing prima facie duties.

Consider the following example:[17] A seventy-three-year-old man was mortally ill in a hospital and required a mechanical respirator. Although he had been judged competent, his request to have the respirator disconnected was refused. He then disconnected it himself, only to have the hospital staff reconnect it. The matter wound up in court. The patient contended that the hospital and his physicians had an obligation to allow him to make his own choices, even though his choice entailed his death. His physicians and legal representatives of the state of Florida argued that they had a duty to preserve life and to prevent suicide. Here the duty to preserve life is in direct conflict with the duty to respect the autonomous decisions of another person. Both are prima facie duties. A Florida court then had to fix the *actual* duty of the hospital and physicians. In a complicated balancing of the conflicting obligations, the court concluded that the patient's choice should be overriding because considerations of autonomy were *here* (though not *everywhere*) weightier. The court reasoned that "the cost to the individual" of refusing to recognize his choice in a circumstance of terminal illness could not be overridden by the duty to preserve life.

Partially as a result of Ross's arguments, moral philosophers have generally come to regard both duties and rights not as absolute trumps but, rather, as strong prima facie moral demands that may be validly overridden in circumstances where stringent opposing demands are presented by a competing moral principle. To call lying prima facie wrong means that if an act involves lying it *is* wrong, *unless* some more weighty moral consideration prevails in the circumstances. Moral principles and statements of rights thus have far greater moral importance than mere rules of thumb, which do not have the same force of standing obligations.

As Ross admits, neither he nor any moral philosopher has yet been able to present a system of rules free of conflicts and exceptions. He argues that the nature of the moral life simply makes an exception-free hierarchy of rules and principles impossible. Contemporary moral philosophy has proved incapable of providing a solution to this problem of weighing and balancing that improves on Ross's approach. The metaphor of "weight" has not proved amenable to precise analysis, and no one has claimed to be able to arrange all moral principles in a hierarchical order that avoids conflicts.

Ross's thesis also applies to circumstances in which a single principle directs us to two equally attractive alternatives, only one of which can be pursued. For example, the principle of beneficence, when applied to problems of disclosing information to patients, could require both disclosure *and* nondisclosure; both options could lead to equally *beneficial*, albeit *different*, outcomes. Whether the conflict is of this sort or between two different principles, there may not be a *single* right action in some circumstances, because two or more morally acceptable actions may be unavoidably in conflict and prove to be of equal weight in the circumstances.

We assume throughout this volume that respect for autonomy is but a prima facie principle, and that it therefore has the same *but only the same* prima facie claim to override as other valid moral principles of comparable significance, such as beneficence or justice. Neither respect for autonomy nor any moral principle has an absolute standing that allows it on every occasion to override conflicting moral claims. Our analysis presupposes, as an inherent feature of the moral life, a pluralism of moral principles equally weighted in abstraction from particular circumstances. (Ross does not entirely accept this thesis of "equal weight.") Therefore, we hold that the moral principles of beneficence and justice—as well as more particular role responsibilities such as providing the best professional care—can have sufficient weight under *some* conditions to override respect for autonomy.

The moral view underlying this claim is not meant to diminish the standing of autonomy. Autonomy gives us respect, moral entitlement, and protection against invasions by others. Few matters of morals could be more important. But we should step back and ask, as Daniel Callahan has put it, "what it would be like to live in a community for which autonomy was the central value . . . [and] sole goal."[18] There is an historical and cultural oddity about giving a standing of overriding importance to the autonomous individual. Moral communities—indeed morality itself—was founded at least as much on the other principles we have mentioned, and usually in a context of strong commitment to the public welfare.

Callahan has argued that making autonomy *the* moral value rather than *a* moral value, weighting it to trump every other moral value, buys the luxury of autonomy at too high a price, and we would agree. However, we would be well advised not to depress the value of autonomy relative to the other principles in our framework. Autonomy is almost certainly the most important value "discovered" in medical and research ethics in the last two decades, and it is the single most important moral value for informed consent and for the argument in this book. The pertinent point is that autonomy not be either overvalued or undervalued, although both evaluations have presented serious problems for informed consent.

This analysis of plural prima facie *duties* applies to *rights* as well. It has often been assumed, owing perhaps to political statements about fundamental human rights, that certain rights are absolute trumps. However, decisive counterexamples can be mounted against this thesis. For example, it is sometimes proclaimed that the right to life is absolute, irrespective of competing claims or social conditions. The dubious validity of this

thesis is evidenced by common moral judgments about capital punishment, international agreements about killing in war, and beliefs about
the justifiability of killing in self-defense. Most writers in ethics now
agree that we have an *exercisable right* not to have our life taken only if
there is not a *sufficient moral justification* to override the right. The right
to life—like the right to make an autonomous decision, the right to give
an informed consent, or a parent's right to decide for a child—is legitimately exercisable and creates actual duties on others if and only if the
right has an overriding status in the situation. Rights such as a right to an
informed consent, a right to die, and a right to lifesaving medical technology thus must compete with other rights in many situations, producing protracted controversy and a need to balance with great discretion
the competing rights claims.

Numerous authors in biomedical and research ethics believe that if a
person is acting autonomously and is the bearer of an autonomy right,
then his or her choices morally ought *never* to be overridden by considerations of beneficence or proper care. This is not our assumption.
Although the burden of moral proof will generally be on those who seek
to intervene in another's choice, as the need to protect persons from
harm becomes more compelling, thereby increasing the "weight" of
moral considerations of beneficence in the circumstances, it becomes
more likely that these considerations will validly override demands to
respect autonomy. Similarly, because some autonomy rights are less significant than others, the demands to protect those rights are less weighty
in the face of conflicting demands.

The literature in biomedical and research ethics reveals how
entrenched and difficult these conflicts among principles and rights can
be. However, in our book these problems, including the aforementioned
problem of paternalism, take a back seat to problems of conceptually
analyzing informed consent and establishing its relationship to the principle of respect for autonomy. We shall be arguing for the priority of
enabling autonomous choice as the goal of informed consent requirements. However, we shall *not* argue that either this goal or the underlying principle of respect for autonomy always or even generally outweighs other moral duties or goals in either medical care or research.

Conclusion

We encounter many unresolved moral problems about informed consent
in this volume. We must not expect too much in the way of final moral
solutions from the framework of philosophical ethics outlined in this
chapter. Philosophy can provide a reasoned and systematic approach to
moral problems, but it does not supply mechanical solutions or definitive
procedures for decisionmaking. Practical wisdom and sound judgment

are its indispensable allies in applied contexts. However, this lack of finality is no reason for skepticism. Moral philosophy can still yield well-constructed arguments and criticisms that advance our understanding. Moral dilemmas require a balancing of competing claims in untidy circumstances, and moral philosophy can make a significant if not decisive contribution. In these respects philosophy is neither surpassed by nor superior to legal reasoning and legal solutions, as we shall see in Chapter 2.

Notes

1. See Isaiah Berlin, *Four Essays on Liberty* (London: Oxford University Press, 1969), 130.
2. For some reflections on what Kant's views do and do not show, see Arthur Flemming, "Using a Man as a Means," *Ethics* 88 (1978): 283–98.
3. See, for example, President's Commission for the Study of Ethical Problems in Medicine and Biomedical and Behavioral Research, *Deciding to Forego Life-Sustaining Treatment* (Washington, D.C.: U.S. Government Printing Office, 1983), 244ff; and, for the theoretical grounding of this claim in autonomy, *Making Health Care Decisions* (Washington, D.C.: U.S. Government Printing Office, 1982), Vol. 1, 44ff, esp. 47.
4. These issues are treated in Tom L. Beauchamp and James F. Childress, *Principles of Biomedical Ethics*, 2nd ed. (New York: Oxford UniversityPress, 1983), esp. Chaps. 3, 7.
5. As we shall see in Chapter 2, *legal* commentary in the United States appealed to a right of privacy at the end of the nineteenth century in order to protect individuals against intrusions into zones of private life through newspaper gossip or telephone wiretapping. The "new right" was to serve as a tool for something that had not until then been explicitly protected legally. This legal concept was later broadened, according to a theory of constitutional law, to protect not only against the exploitation of personal information, but also against interference with certain forms of personal decisionmaking.

Analysis of the moral right to privacy that builds on ordinary language meanings of "privacy" as well as on the several legal notions of privacy has led to a complex array of different rights. In some respects, privacy has served in recent moral theory as a catch-all right, in part as a result of futile attempts to "translate" legal privacy rights into a directly corresponding, but more neatly formulated, moral right.

Part of the confusion about privacy results from different writers who attempt to explicate privacy as at once (1) an independent moral right (one that does not overlap with other well-established moral rights, such as the right to freedom from intrusion or the right to autonomous choice), (2) a moral concept that basically accords with the common law's concept of privacy, and (3) a notion that does not depart significantly from ordinary language meanings of "privacy." It is doubtful that these three conditions can all be met by a single moral concept of privacy.

Compare W.A. Parent, "Recent Work on the Concept of Privacy," *American Philosophical Quarterly* 20 (1983): 341–55; Stanley Benn, "Privacy and Respect for Persons: A Reply," *Australasian Journal of Philosophy* 58 (March 1980): 54–61; Gerald Dworkin, "Autonomy and Informed Consent," in President's Commission, *Making Health Care Decisions*, Vol. 3, 63–81, esp. 66–70; Robert Gerstein, "Intimacy and

Privacy," *Ethics* 89 (October 1978): 76–81 and "Privacy and Self-Incrimination," *Ethics* 80 (1970): 87–101; Tom Gerseky, "Redefining Privacy," *Harvard Civil Rights-Civil Liberties Law Review* 12 (1977): 233–96; Arthur Caplan, "On Privacy and Confidentiality in Social Science Research," in Tom L. Beauchamp, et al., eds., *Ethical Issues in Social Science Research* (Baltimore: The Johns Hopkins University Press, 1982), 315–25; Judith Jarvis Thomson, "The Right to Privacy," *Philosophy and Public Affairs* 4 (Summer 1975): 295–314; and Thomas Scanlon, "Thomson on Privacy" and James Rachels, "Why Privacy is Important," both in *Philosophy and Public Affairs* 4 (Summer 1975): 315–33.

6. On this point see Dworkin, "Autonomy and Informed Consent," 66–71.

7. See Ludwig Edelstein, "The Hippocratic Oath: Text, Translation, and Interpretation," *Supplements to the Bulletin of the History of Medicine* 30, Supplement 1 (Baltimore: The Johns Hopkins University Press, 1943); reprinted in Owsei Temkin and C. Lilian Temkin, eds., *Ancient Medicine: Selected Papers of Ludwig Edelstein* (Baltimore: The Johns Hopkins Press, 1967). The translation provided here of the benefit injunction is from *Epidemics*, 1:11, in W.H.S. Jones, trans., *Hippocrates*, 4 vols. (Cambridge, MA: Harvard University Press, 1923), 1:165.

8. See William K. Frankena, *Ethics*, 2nd ed. (Englewood Cliffs, N.J.: Prentice-Hall, Inc., 1973), esp. 47.

9. Perhaps the most important philosophical statement of this position is found in W.D. Ross, *The Right and the Good* (Oxford: Clarendon Press, 1930), 21.

10. For a discussion of such problems, see Joel Feinberg, *Harm to Others: The Moral Limits of the Criminal Law* (New York: Oxford University Press, 1984), 136–41; Richard Trammell, "Saving Life and Taking Life," *Journal of Philosophy* 72 (1975): 131–37, and "Tooley's Moral Symmetry Principle," *Philosophy and Public Affairs* 5 (1976): 305ff.

11. A widely held view is that one has a duty of beneficence only if one can prevent harm to others at minimal risk to oneself and if one's action promises to be of substantial benefit to the other person. This analysis of beneficence can be more tightly formulated as follows: X has a *duty* of beneficence toward Y only if each of the following conditions is satisfied: (1) Y is at risk of significant loss or damage, (2) X's action is needed to prevent this loss or damage, (3) X's action would probably prevent this loss or damage, (4) the benefit that Y will probably gain outweighs any harms that X is likely to suffer and does not present significant risk to X. This formulation is indebted to Eric D'Arcy, *Human Acts: An Essay in Their Moral Evaluation* (Oxford: Clarendon Press, 1963), 56–57.

Provision of benefit beyond these conditions would be to act generously but beyond the call of duty. Our formulation is only one plausible construal of the general duty of beneficence, but we believe it suffices for our purposes in this volume. For contrasting views, see Earl Shelp, "To Benefit and Respect Persons: A Challenge for Beneficence in Health Care," Allen Buchanan, "Philosophical Foundations of Beneficence," and Natalie Abrams, "Scope of Beneficence in Health Care," all in Earl Shelp, ed., *Beneficence and Health Care* (Dordrecht, Holland: D. Reidel Publishing Co., 1982).

12. See, for example, Frankena, *Ethics*, 47; Peter Singer, "Famine, Affluence, and Morality," *Philosophy and Public Affairs* 1 (1972): 229–43, and *Practical Ethics* (Cambridge: Cambridge University Press, 1979), 168ff; Marcus G. Singer, *Generalization in Ethics* (New York: Alfred A. Knopf, Inc., 1961), 180–89; and Michael A. Slote, "The Morality of Wealth," in William Aiken and Hugh LaFollette, eds., *World Hunger and Moral Obligation* (Englewood Cliffs, N.J.: Prentice-Hall, Inc., 1977), 125–47.

13. Nuremberg Code, Principle 6, from *Trials of War Criminals Before the Nuremberg Military Tribunals Under Control Council Law No. 10* (Military Tribunal I, 1947; Washington, D.C.: U.S. Government Printing Office, 1948–49).

14. A comprehensive treatment of this problem in the context of research is found in Robert J. Levine, *Ethics and Regulation of Clinical Research* (Baltimore: Urban & Schwarzenberg, 1981), Chapter 3.

15. Charles W. Lidz, et al., *Informed Consent: A Study of Decisionmaking in Psychiatry* (New York: The Guilford Press, 1984), 7–8.

16. Ross, *The Right and the Good*, 19–42.

17. *Satz* v. *Perlmutter*, 362 S.2d 160 (Florida District Court of Appeals, 1978).

18. Daniel Callahan, "Autonomy: A Moral Good, Not a Moral Obsession," *The Hastings Center Report* 14 (October 1984): 40–42.

2

Foundations in Legal Theory

We maintained in Chapter 1 that moral principles are to be understood as principles of duty and that these duties are correlative to rights. Although no structure of principles in law corresponds directly to moral principles, moral principles are expressed and enforced by the law in the form of rights and duties devised for the specific purposes of a legal framework. In these respects the law is shaped by and established to protect moral interests, and the criteria of evidence and argument are often similar in the two disciplines.

In this chapter, we first examine various relationships between moral principles and legal rights and then turn to the so-called "legal doctrine of informed consent." Two areas of the law are relevant to this doctrine. They represent different legal traditions through which requirements to obtain informed consent can be defined. The first and most important for the current legal doctrine of informed consent is *tort law*. A "tort" is a civil injury to one's person or property that is intentionally or negligently inflicted by another and that is measured in terms of, and compensated by, money damages. Civil injuries can be contrasted with criminal injuries, which are punishable by imprisonment or by fines not intended as compensation but paid as penalties to the state. At common law, an unjustifiable failure to obtain informed consent is a tort. In this chapter we examine the following dimensions of tort law: the theory of liability, disclosure requirements, causation, and valid exceptions to the obligation to obtain consent.

The second relevant area is the legal right to privacy, a right embedded in American *constitutional law*. Privacy, like many constitutional rights, serves as a check on the authority of the state over individuals' lives. In many instances, harmful state intrusions on privacy can be legally prevented rather than merely recompensed. The right of privacy has been applied to various kinds of medical choices, including treatment refusal, but there is as yet no developed constitutional doctrine of "informed consent."

23

Moral Principles and Legal Rights

The law relies on moral principles to delineate rights and duties in both case law (judge-made law expressed in court decisions) and statutory law (federal and state statutes and their accompanying administrative regulations). The same correlativity of rights and duties appears in law as in morality: If one person has a legal right and another the corresponding duty, the latter may be held legally responsible, and so liable, for violating the person's right by failure to fulfill the duty.

In law, many factors besides commonly shared moral principles influence theories of legal liability. Although they may be loosely spoken of as legal principles, these other factors are not true principles; they are a set of paradigms, constructs, and provisos unique to law and the institutions of law. Included are such diverse considerations as the basic structure and goals of the adversary system, theories of individual and governmental accountability, problems of enforcement and remedies, practical issues arising from the use of case-by-case adjudication, and, finally, the traditional division of law into different categories, which differ in content and in the operative influences that shape legal theories of liability.

American law is divided, first, into the common law—the tradition of judge-made law that began in medieval England—and, second, into law derived from the Constitution and statutes that supplant or supplement the common law. Although it has been substantially reconstructed by statute, the legal doctrine of informed consent is essentially a common law development. The common law is further divided into criminal and civil law, and civil law again into sub-categories, including tort, property, and contract law. Within these broad common-law categories, legal problems are classified according to "causes of action," or, in modern terminology, "theories of liability." These consist of sets of "elements," each of which must be pleaded in court and proved true by a preponderance of the evidence in order for the complaining party to prevail.

In English and early American law, the common law causes of action were rigid and formal. Every claimed wrong had to be fitted into one of the "writs" that laid out the procedures and argument for each cause of action. Although modern common law is more flexible, the influence of its history is still felt. The theory of liability under which a case is pleaded is vital not only in shaping the proof of a case at trial but also in determining the theoretical understanding of many legal issues. To detach the law from this fundamental structure is impossible, even within the purest legal analysis. The need to fit facts and principles into a framework of trial proof affects the legal understanding of those facts and principles in every instance. Moreover, if a single moral principle—such as respect for autonomy—underlies several different theories of liability, it may emerge in each theory in different garb.

Informed consent is interpreted in the legal tradition as grounded in, and justified by, the moral principle of respect for autonomy. However, in the legal context, informed consent is not precisely about how best to respect autonomy or to enable autonomous decisionmaking. Legal language is oriented more toward specific (correlative) rights and duties that are derived from principles than toward the principles themselves. Thus, in case law the justification for informed consent is couched in rights language—the patient's right to self-determination—and the primary concern of the law is to prescribe the duties that devolve upon physicians in order that this right be protected.

Common Law and the Legal Doctrine

A legal "doctrine" is a body of legal theory applied to a particular topic. Legal scholarship often focuses on doctrines rather than on theories of liability, in part because there may be more than one relevant theory of liability according to which a particular issue can be discussed. The legal doctrine of informed consent derives from the common law and includes the entire body of law dealing with the general obligation to obtain informed consent, specific requirements by which to meet these obligations, and the exceptions to both.[1]

The legal doctrine derives in American case law almost exclusively from the physician-patient relationship in therapy, as contrasted with the researcher-subject relationship in research. The discussion in this chapter, together with the history in Chapter 4, presents the framework of informed consent law in the clinical context. The regulatory history of informed consent in biomedical and social research is reviewed in Chapters 5 and 6.

Much of the legal scholarship on informed consent addresses the legal doctrine by delineating its exceptions and boundaries. Detailed inquiry into these topics is beyond the scope of our volume, although we outline them below. We do not address the doctrine as a whole; instead, we focus almost exclusively on the most crucial and controversial aspect of informed consent in the law, which is the scope and configuration of specific requirements that define consent in case law. These requirements are shaped by the exigencies of translating morality into social practice through the adversary legal system and its theories of liability.

The failure to obtain informed consent in situations where it is legally required is a tort. The linking of informed consent to a financial remedy and the other constraints of civil law is crucial to understanding the legal doctrine. A general civil right of individual integrity, expressed not as a single theory but through various doctrines of tort, property, and contract law, protects an individual's freedom of action, ownership, and

decision from certain kinds of interference by others. Legal requirements of informed consent fasten on one aspect of this general right,
namely, the protection from physical intrusions by others.

Within the physician-patient relationship, the right of bodily integrity
is supplemented by what the law considers to be the fiduciary duty of
physicians to respect and promote the patient's interests and well-
being.[2] A fiduciary relationship exists because patients and physicians
are unequal in possession of information and power to control the circumstances under which they meet. One party is fit and medically
knowledgeable, the other sick and medically ignorant.[3] In law the right
to self-determination and the fiduciary duty restrict the physician's role
and protect the patient from unwarranted intrusions such as surgery
without consent.

The key issues in case law and legal literature on informed consent can
be divided into four categories: choice of the theory of liability, disclosure requirements, causation, and the exceptive case.

Theory of Liability

The law imposes duties on members of society, requiring either action
or abstention from action. One who fails to fulfill a legal duty is liable to
punishment (in the criminal law) or is obligated to make compensation
for the misdeed (in the civil law). The theory of liability under which a
case is tried determines the civil (or the criminal) duty that must be fulfilled. In recent informed consent cases, negligence is the theory of liability almost always applied. However, the informed consent doctrine
originally developed and flourished under the battery theory of liability.
Courts in some states still apply the battery theory exclusively, and other
states that primarily apply negligence law to informed consent cases continue to use battery under some circumstances. As a result, no fundamental and unified legal theory underlies all informed consent cases. In
Chapter 4 we will discuss the historical development of the informed
consent doctrine in battery, the shift to negligence theory, and the relationship of this shift to the difficult legal issues raised by informed consent. Here we compare the battery and negligence theories of liability
and the way informed consent is treated by each.

The choice between battery and negligence has been the focus of
much legal scholarship about the doctrine of informed consent. There is
reason to think that this distinction is not as significant as the volume of
legal commentary about it suggests, but some understanding of the difference between the theories is needed to appreciate the prominence of
this distinction in legal theory.

Under *battery* theory the defendant is held liable for any intended
(i.e., not careless or accidental) action that results in physical contact—
contact for which the plaintiff has given no permission, express or

implied, and which the defendant therefore knew or should have known was "unauthorized." The defendant need not have an evil intent, nor must injury result; the unpermitted contact is itself considered offensive. Evil intent, injury, or both are usually alleged, however, because if neither is present, the plaintiff's recovery, if any, will be of a small sum. In practical reality these damages are rarely worth the trouble of bringing a suit. Under *negligence* theory, on the other hand, unintentional, "careless" action (or omission) is the source of liability. The carelessness occurs in regard to some activity in which the defendant has a socially or legally imposed duty to take care or to behave reasonably toward others, and injury is caused by failure to discharge the duty. The injury must be translatable into money damages or the plaintiff cannot win in court.

The foregoing descriptions seem to imply that battery and negligence describe starkly different types of conduct. This is often true; however, in some circumstances, and in informed consent law in particular, the battery and negligence theories can be viewed as distinct but not mutually exclusive. We now turn to a fuller delineation of the two theories and their differences.

Battery. The civil law definition of a battery is simple: It is an intentional and legally unpermitted physical contact with ("touching" of) another person. Because the essential purpose of the battery theory of liability is the protection of a so-called dignitary interest—the individual's bodily integrity—no injury need result from violation of this interest. Treatment without consent is *itself* an actionable wrong in battery law. The defendant (the party against whom the complaint is lodged) who intentionally causes an unpermitted contact with the plaintiff (the party who complained) has committed a "technical battery" and is liable for damages that usually are "token" or "nominal"—a small sum not meant as compensation for measurable harm. The plaintiff need not even be aware of the event at the time contact has taken place (for example, he or she may be anesthetized). The defendant may act in good faith, without any desire to harm, perhaps in the mistaken belief that the plaintiff has consented, or even in such a way as to benefit the plaintiff, yet nevertheless be guilty of a battery.[4]

Still, battery traditionally has antisocial connotations. Because it is expensive to bring a lawsuit, few persons will file suit unless they can plausibly claim substantial damages. Therefore, most cases brought to court do allege malice or serious injury. However, all the plaintiff must show to win in court is that the defendant intended a contact that a reasonable person would find offensive under the circumstances, or one that the defendant should have known would be offensive to that particular plaintiff.[5] There is no requirement that the plaintiff demonstrate that the defendant intended to cause physical or psychic harm.

To defend against a charge of battery, the defendant can show that the plaintiff consented to the touching, or that the plaintiff's dissent could not have been anticipated. In ordinary social interactions, consent to many harmless contacts is assumed by the law because reasonable people deem such contacts inoffensive. However, if the defendant actually knows or reasonably should know—for example, through personal knowledge of the plaintiff—that the plaintiff objects "unreasonably" to some accepted social contact such as social kissing, then an act by the defendant such as kissing the person on the cheek is a battery.

The battery theory of liability protects the right to choose whether to permit others to invade one's physical integrity, and thus is based on the general right of self-determination in the law. It is well captured by the following passage from a 1914 case that became a powerful rallying symbol in the informed consent literature: "Every human being of adult years and sound mind has a right to determine what shall be done with his own body; and a surgeon who performs an operation without his patient's consent commits an assault."[6] This right of self-determination is the legal equivalent of the moral principle of respect for autonomy discussed in Chapter 1. Patients are considered in law to know that physicians must obtain consent, and physicians are expected by law to know that patients are owed this form of respect. A physician who performs an invasive procedure (regardless of its medical benefit) without the patient's permission may thus be found guilty of a battery even if a reasonable person would have authorized the procedure if asked.

The physician may be found to have committed battery if no consent at all was obtained, if consent was obtained for a procedure different in scope or kind from the one actually performed, or if the physician failed to inform the patient adequately about potential consequences of the procedure.[7] In general, if the physician performs a particular procedure the basic nature[8] of which has not been communicated to the patient, whether by virtue of omission of important information or by misrepresentation, then what appears to be a "consent" is "vitiated" and rendered invalid.[9] The central issue for the battery cause of action is thus whether an *effective* (or *valid*) consent—not merely some consent—was given. Battery requires that consent be based on an adequate but not necessarily extensive understanding of the nature of the contemplated procedure.[10]

Negligence. The negligence theory of liability rests on premises different from those of battery. Negligence is, in effect, the failure to use due care; negligence is the tort of *unintended* harmful action or omission. It is analyzable in terms of five essential elements: (1) a legally established *duty* to the plaintiff must exist; (2) the defendant must *breach* that duty; (3) the plaintiff must experience an *injury* (measurable in monetary terms as *damages*); (4) this injury must be *causally* related, by a direct causal chain, to the defendant's breach of duty; and (5) the causal relationship between the act or omission and the injury must be *proximate*.

Proximate causation (5) is a limitation on responsibility that can be invoked in negligence cases in order to preclude liability for remote or unforeseeable causation of injury.

The duty breached by a negligent act or omission is based in a general duty to exercise reasonable care in interacting with others. This duty is measured in law by the standard of the reasonable person, an imaginary actor who represents the community consensus of acceptable or appropriate behavior. This consensus establishes neither a standard of what average persons do nor an aspirational ideal beyond the reach of most persons, but a minimum threshold below which the ordinary person may not fall without being found deficient under the law. (See the discussion of the reasonable person standard in the sections on Disclosure and Causation, pp. 32–33.)

Professional negligence, or malpractice, is a special instance of negligence in which professional standards of care have been developed for persons possessing or claiming to possess special knowledge or skill. Medical malpractice is but one type of professional negligence. The physician found to have committed malpractice is held liable for violation of a duty to exercise the requisite skill and care of the ordinary qualified member of the medical profession. Fellow professionals represent the peer group, whose standards and testimony at trial are necessary to establish the scope of that duty. The theory of medical negligence, as applied to informed consent, assumes that there is a professional duty of due care to provide to patients an appropriate disclosure of information before obtaining an authorization for treatment. Lack of informed consent is treated as professional negligence in essentially the same respect as is careless performance of a surgical procedure.

The informed consent action in negligence has five elements, corresponding to the above five elements of general negligence: (1) the physician has a *duty* to give information to the patient (under the appropriate standard of disclosure), which is part of the professional duty of due care; (2) the physician *breaches* the duty; (3) there is an *injury* to the patient that makes the patient worse off (in financially measurable terms) than if the procedure had not been performed; (4) the injury is the *materialization* of an undisclosed outcome or possible outcome (risk); and (5) had the plaintiff been informed of the outcome or risk, he or she (or a reasonable person) would not have consented. Underlying (5) is the crucial premise that the injury was *caused* by the nondisclosure.

Courts and commentators have offered numerous reasons for the contemporary trend toward negligence and away from battery as the preferred theory of informed consent liability.[11] A widespread view is that battery—as the cruder and more drastic theory—is useful only in limited situations where the nature of the procedure has not been disclosed at all or an action intentionally exceeds the scope of the consent. Some courts see physicians as invariably acting in good faith to benefit the patient, and therefore do not interpret failures to inform as intentionally antisocial acts such as those typically found in assault and battery.

However, some legal commentators have argued that the battery action, in recognizing the dignitary importance of individual bodily integrity and self-determination, is closer to the spirit of the informed consent doctrine than is negligence, which has the effect of lessening the expectations imposed by law on the medical profession. Accordingly, several commentators have proposed "hybrid" or modified theories of liability that are fashioned from combinations of the law of battery and that of negligence, accommodating features of both.[12]

Disclosure Requirements

Questions regarding the nature and amount of the information that must be disclosed to a patient are central to the legal doctrine of informed consent and have evoked voluminous commentary.[13] Many controversies surround the amount of information that must be disclosed about the procedure's risks and negative consequences. Other disagreements exist regarding what must be disclosed about the nature and purpose of the procedure, its benefits, and alternative procedures. Two competing disclosure standards have evolved as attempts to resolve these problems: the professional practice standard and the reasonable person or objective standard. A third standard, the subjective or individual standard, has also been proposed, largely in legal commentary.

The Professional Practice Standard. This first standard holds that both the duty to disclose and the criteria of adequate disclosure, its topics and scope, are determined by the customary practices of a professional community. Proponents of this standard argue that the physician is charged professionally with the responsibility of protecting the health of the patient and must use proper professional criteria for determining the information that should be disclosed and withheld. Disclosure, like treatment, is from this perspective a job belonging to physicians by virtue of their professional expertise, role, and commitment. Custom in the profession establishes the standard of care for disclosure, just as custom establishes the standard of care for treatment. The patient, subject, reasonable person, or any person without expert knowledge is unqualified to establish what should be disclosed. In the most influential of the early informed consent negligence cases, *Natanson* v. *Kline*, the court held: "The duty of the physician to disclose . . . is limited to those disclosures which a reasonable medical practitioner would make under the same or similar circumstances."[14] This is the rule applied in all ordinary malpractice cases to determine the duty of due care in the performance of medical procedures.

The professional practice standard remains the dominant rule in informed consent law.[15] All the courts adopting the professional practice rule require expert testimony from members of relevant professional groups to determine whether a physician has violated a duty to disclose the risk in question. The decision in a 1972 case in which radiation therapy for Hodgkin's disease led to paralysis provides a typical expression of this standard: "Generally the duty of the physician to inform and the extent of the information required should be established by expert medical testimony."[16]

Despite its popularity, the professional practice standard has been criticized severely as a disclosure rule for informed consent law. It has been questioned whether a customary standard of disclosure actually exists within the medical profession, and how much consensus is required for the establishment of such a standard. A second objection is that truly negligent care might be perpetuated if relevant professionals generally offer the same inferior information, whether through ignorance, as a genuine conviction, or for reasons of professional solidarity.[17]

Another more fundamental objection centers on a basic assumption of the medical practice standard—that physicians have sufficient expertise to know what information is in the best interests of their patients. This assumption is empirical, yet there are no reliable data on these issues, and current research on the effects of detailed disclosure is both sketchy and inconclusive. Although the bulk of available data suggests that detailed disclosures are either harmless or beneficial for patients, this conclusion is not much more adequately grounded than the contrasting hunches of experienced physicians who appeal to anecdotal evidence.[18] There is some evidence to support the claim that because of the value patients place on information, they would support a disclosure standard requiring more detailed information than physicians typically give.[19] Related data suggest that physicians believe that the additional information desired by patients often would in fact be harmful to them. Physicians' concerns over these negative consequences clearly affect their norms and practices of disclosure.[20] Not yet established is whether this additional information is *in fact* harmful to patients.

Although these empirical issues raise important questions about the professional practice standard, the principal objection to this standard is that it undermines individual autonomy, the protection of which is the primary function and moral justification of informed consent requirements. Several courts have held that granting priority to the judgment of physicians gives an unjustifiable weight to professional standards in Anglo-American jurisprudence. These courts argue that a standard of medical practice applies only to specifically medical judgments and that, ultimately, decisions for or against medical care, being *nonmedical* judgments, are reserved to the patient alone.[21]

The Reasonable Person Standard. These objections to the professional practice standard have prompted some courts to adopt a different standard for determining the scope of disclosure, one designed to protect more adequately the patient's right of self-determination. This standard focuses on the information the "reasonable person" needs to know about risks, alternatives, and consequences. The legal litmus test under this standard for determining the extent of disclosure is the "materiality," or significance, of information to the decisionmaking process of the patient. The patient, rather than the physician, is the judge of whether the information is material. Thus, the right to decide what information is pertinent is shifted away from the physician to the patient. The reasonable person standard requires a physician to divulge any fact that is material to a reasonable person's decision; there is no need for expert testimony about many matters, because the jury itself can determine the reasonableness of the disclosure.[22] Physicians may therefore be found guilty of negligent disclosure, according to this standard, even if their behavior conforms perfectly to recognized and routine professional practice.

Because the reasonable person standard asserts that the applicability and scope of the fiduciary duty of disclosure are determined not by professionals (as is characteristic of professional negligence) but by the court and jury (as in battery), commentators have argued that courts that apply this standard have created a hybrid cause of action, combining elements of negligence with elements of battery theory.[23] The implications of this standard for physicians are significant: Physicians cannot assume that, simply because they have patients under their care, they are at liberty to pursue the best interests of these patients, as the profession of medicine defines "best interests." To do so would unduly constrict the patient's role in the patient-physician relationship.

In 1972, three appellate decisions—*Canterbury* v. *Spence, Cobbs* v. *Grant,* and *Wilkinson* v. *Vesey*—firmly established this reasonable person standard in the jurisdictions of Washington, D.C., California, and Rhode Island.[24] Other courts that subsequently addressed the problem of disclosure have, on occasion, switched to the reasonable person standard.[25] However, many courts that had already adopted the professional practice standard have declined to change their position. In addition, recent statutes have invalidated this new common law standard in several jurisdictions.[26]

Despite its popularity with legal commentators and courts, the reasonable person standard has been subjected to stern criticism. Many critics—largely within the medical community—have maintained that the reasonable person standard is not in the best interests of either patients or physicians, and is in any case impossible to satisfy.[27] Others raise questions about the interpretation of the standard, and thus about the standard's ability to specify a sufficiently precise duty for physicians. For example, the concept of the materiality of information is only ambiguously defined in *Canterbury* and related cases, and the central concept of the reasonable person goes altogether undefined.[28]

The courts have not specifically tackled the special problems attendant upon invoking these concepts in the informed consent context, which leaves their practical impact somewhat indeterminate. If no specific duty of disclosure follows from the reasonable person standard, the standard may project a false sense of improvement over older standards.[29] Some empirical evidence suggests that in clinical settings it makes no difference to physicians' disclosure practices whether the professional practice standard or the reasonable person standard is operative in the relevant legal jurisdiction.[30] Also, because the needs of the reasonable person depend on surrounding circumstances, there seems no way to predict how each court will treat the specific facts of each case, thus presenting difficulties for physicians in their attempts to determine what information a reasonable person "in the same or similar circumstances" as those of the patient would want.

It can therefore be asked whether the reasonable person standard more adequately captures the legal doctrine's intent to protect the patient's right of self-determination than does the professional practice standard.[31] Because application of the abstract reasonable person standard to a concrete case requires the incorporation of specific facts of the case, the pressing question is always what the reasonable person would need to know "under the same or similar circumstances." How liberally should the standard's consideration of the patient's peculiar circumstances or position be construed? Can it be successfully argued that the more the reasonable person standard is interpreted as taking into account the patient's particular position, the closer this standard comes to the intent of the underlying right of self-determination?

The extent to which the reasonable person standard can and ought to be tailored to the individual patient (i.e., made subjective) is an unresolved problem in informed consent law. A continuum of interpretations exists, at one end of which is found the third, the "subjective" disclosure standard.

The Subjective Standard. A body of thoughtful legal commentary favors the subjective over the objective disclosure standard.[32] The subjective standard would require the physician to disclose whatever information is material to the *particular* patient.[33] Opponents of this standard argue that it places an unfair legal burden on physicians to intuit the idiosyncratic values and interests of their patients,[34] and then leaves physicians at the mercy of their patients' self-serving hindsight in court.[35]

By contrast, proponents of the subjective standard argue that the patient's right to make decisions for personal reasons is not adequately protected by any other standard. If patients have a right to make idiosyncratic choices, they may need information that would not be considered material by reference to the standard of a reasonable person or the standard of a professional consensus.[36] Moreover, risks of unfairness to physicians can be minimized, according to the subjective standard's proponents, because the jury's assessment of the patient's credibility serves as a check against self-serving testimony. Physicians would not be expected under the standard to do more than make a reasonable effort to determine their patients' desires—although again it cannot be made precise how much effort would be deemed "reasonable" under any given circumstance.

Causation

From a legal perspective—but probably from no other perspective—causation is a topic of the same importance as disclosure. The importance of causation lies in its connection to responsibility: Causation in the law, unlike causation in science, is a concept structured to identify *causal responsibility* for an outcome. Legal causation is a means of ascribing liability to a person whose act or omission is responsible for an event. Under the negligence theory of liability, a patient attempting to recover in an informed consent case must show a causal connection between the physician's failure to make adequate disclosure and the patient's injury.[37] This condition of causation is not met if the patient would have consented to the procedure had the injury-producing risk been disclosed.

A problem for this causation requirement in informed consent law is the selection of an acceptable method of proof that the patient would not have elected treatment if a proper disclosure had been made. Plaintiffs usually testify that they would not have consented if the risks had been disclosed, but their view might be distorted by the experience of a negative outcome. In early cases, courts addressing the issue applied a subjective rule, asking whether the particular patient-plaintiff would have consented or withheld consent had he or she been adequately informed. A jury would make this finding by assessing the credibility of the patient's testimony.

Few informed consent cases have been decided by this subjective guideline, because nearly all jurisdictions that adopted or hinted at a subjective causation rule applied it in conjunction with a professional practice standard for disclosure. For these courts, the dispositive factor was not causation, but rather the extent of the disclosure duty as established by expert testimony. The subjective causation rule has thus largely been neglected in judicial opinions and in legal commentary. However, in jurisdictions in which the reasonable person standard of disclosure has been adopted, causation has become dispositive in some cases. As a consequence, the subjective causation rule, like subjective disclosure, has come under attack for placing the physician at the mercy of the patient's hindsight, anger, and resentment. In order to protect the physician, the 1972 landmark opinion in *Canterbury* v. *Spence* turned to an objective standard for causation, based on what a reasonable person in the patient's circumstances would have decided if an adequate disclosure had been provided.[38]

Commentators—and a few courts—criticize this objective causation standard for the same reason they criticize the objective disclosure standard, namely, its inconsistency with the right of self-determination underlying the informed consent doctrine.[39] Legal commentators who support the subjective approach correspondingly maintain that physicians will not be unduly penalized by its adoption,[40] because the mechanisms of cross-examination and argument by defense counsel are sufficient to permit the jury to make a reasonable judgment as to the credibility of the patient's claim that treatment would have been refused.

Proponents of subjective causation argue that the jury should evaluate testimony in light of the patient's unique position, because the jury must judge whether the patient's contention is reasonable and credible, given his or her professed beliefs and assessment of the situation. To date, however, very few post-*Canterbury* court decisions regarding informed consent have adopted an exclusively subjective causation rule.[41] The statutory and common-law trend has been toward the objective standard.[42]

Exceptions

All courts passing on the issue have ruled that a patient's right to self-determination, as protected by the legal doctrine of informed consent, is not absolute in the sense of always validly overriding every competing claim. Several legally justified exceptions are recognized. In general, legal duties and rights, like moral duties and rights, have no more than prima facie value. A prima facie legal duty such as the duty to obtain informed consent is therefore not always an *actual* duty. Valid exceptions are admitted in law if promotion of the best interests of society or of the individual demands them.

There are five recognized exceptions to the informed consent requirement: the public health emergency, the medical emergency, the incompetent patient, the therapeutic privilege, and the patient waiver.[43] All but one of these exceptions, the controversial therapeutic privilege, are commonly taken as both morally and legally valid, and thus as being consistent with—or placing a valid limit on—the duty to respect individual autonomy. By contrast, the therapeutic privilege has elicited a particularly furious exchange over whether autonomy rights can be validly overridden for paternalistic reasons.

Public health emergencies are crisis situations in which the health of an identified population may be dependent on the adoption of a mass health program. Interventions by public health officials are authorized by law. Typical examples of justified governmental disregard of informed consent include the restriction of individual movement by quarantine in order to prevent the spread of infectious disease and the imposition of fines and other penalties to assure mass vaccination to control epidemics.

Medical emergencies, by contrast, refer to crises in which an individual patient is at imminent risk of significant injury, decline, or death if treatment is withheld or postponed. If a delay in time required to obtain consent might result in substantial harm to the patient, and no evidence exists to indicate that the person would refuse the treatment or would reject the benefits provided, the courts have ruled that a physician is relieved of the duty to obtain informed consent. If the patient in an emergency is unconscious, delirious, or otherwise incompetent to consent, but the time factor is not so crucial as to prohibit discussion altogether, the case falls under the incompetence exception, where the physician is generally required to secure a guardian's or relative's consent.[44]

Consent to treatment is often said to be "implied" in an emergency, but this "implication" is based on a standard of the reasonable person, not the particular individual. This language and strategy are evasive, because the implicit claim is that consent has been obtained when in fact no authorization has occurred. The courts have also generally evaded defining or establishing precise conditions for an emergency by reference to the significance of the harms at stake. The range of conditions recognized as valid has included everything from the preservation of life and limb to the alleviation of pain and suffering.[45]

The incompetent person is one who, for one or more of a number of reasons, is unable to give an informed consent. Competence can be either a factual or a presumptive, categorical determination. Minors, for example, are presumed incompetent in law, whereas adults can generally be declared legally incompetent only on the basis of some "factual" determination. The age of majority for consent varies by state law and by type of medical treatment. Some state laws essentially declare that minors achieve majority by engaging in certain activities, such as marriage, or by seeking certain forms of medical care, such as treatment for venereal disease. However, all jurisdictions agree that except in special cases a minor is unable to give effective or valid informed consent and thus that the informed consent of a parent or legal guardian is required before the minor may be treated. The issue of legal capacity is more complex for adult patients, for whom an individualized determination normally must be made. If a person is incompetent, the physician is usually required, absent an emergency, to secure some form of third-party consent from a guardian or other representative legally empowered to give it.

There is no widely agreed-upon standard, test, or definition of incompetence. In Chapter 8 we address these problems, although our conceptual treatment only partially removes the considerable ambiguity and confusion that surrounds the incompetence exception.

The therapeutic privilege of a physician to withhold part or all of the material information from a patient, because of the harmful effects of disclosure, is the most controversial and interesting exceptive case. It brings directly into conflict the principles of respect for autonomy and beneficence—the recipe for paternalism. Unfortunately, the precise formulation of the privilege varies among the jurisdictions. If framed broadly, it can permit physicians to withhold information if disclosure would cause *any* countertherapeutic deterioration, however slight, in the physical, psychological, or emotional condition of the patient. If framed narrowly, it can permit the physician to withhold information if and only if the patient's knowledge of the information would have *serious* health-related consequences—for example, by jeopardizing the success of the treatment or harming the patient psychologically by critically impairing relevant decisionmaking processes.

The *Canterbury* decision represents a narrow account:

> The [therapeutic privilege] exception obtains [if] risk-disclosure poses such a threat of detriment to the patient as to become unfeasible or contraindicated from a medical point of view. It is recognized that patients occasionally become so ill or emotionally distraught on disclosure as *to foreclose a rational decision*, or complicate or hinder the treatment, or perhaps even pose psychological damage to the patient.[46]

The narrowest possible formulation is narrower still; it is analogous to the incompetence exception, because it can be validly invoked only if the physician reasonably believes disclosure would render the patient incompetent to consent to or refuse the treatment, that is, would render the decision nonautonomous. To invoke the therapeutic privilege under such circumstances does not conflict with respect for autonomy, as an autonomous decision could not be made in any event. However, broader formulations of the privilege that require only "medical contraindication" of some sort do operate at the expense of autonomy. These formulations may unjustifiably endanger autonomous choice altogether, as when the invocation of the privilege is based on the belief that an autonomous patient, if informed, would refuse an indicated therapy for what the medical community views as incorrect or inappropriate reasons. Such paternalism is sometimes resolutely contested, because it risks capsizing the normal duty of disclosure and the requirement to obtain consent, and thus unduly threatens the basic values underlying the informed consent obligation.

Beyond the question of the privilege's scope, the courts have also varied over the formulation of an acceptable standard for determining what information may be withheld. As with disclosure, the basis of the standard could be professional, objective, or subjective. In addition, confusion reigns over appropriate measures of rationality, psychological damage, and emotional stability under any such standard. It has been argued that unless the therapeutic privilege is tightly and operationally formulated, the medical profession can use it to deprive the unreasonable but competent patient of the right to make decisions, especially in light of the physician's commitment to the patient's best interest, as defined by medicine. Loose standards can permit physicians to climb to safety over a straw bridge of speculation about the psychological consequences of information. According to the "beneficence model" of the physician's responsibility for the patient, which, as we will see in Chapter 3, has dominated medical practice throughout its history, almost any invocation of the privilege to withhold or distort information can be "justified" in order to avoid some anxiety for a patient.

Some courts and commentators, recognizing these difficulties, have argued that the therapeutic privilege must be formulated narrowly.[47] They have also called for disclosure to third parties whenever reasonable. These courts and commentators caution against potential abuse of the privilege because of its inconsistency with the patient's right to know and to decline treatment. *Canterbury* is among the most explicit: "The privilege does not accept the paternalistic notion that the physician may remain silent simply because divulgence might prompt the patient to forego therapy the physician feels the patient really needs."[48] This attempt to contain physician discretion has important implications beyond its function in shaping the concept of therapeutic privilege: As we shall see in Chapters 3 and 4, it is no less than an attempt to reorient medical practice away from a beneficence model toward an autonomy model that emphasizes the patient's right of self-determination.

Waiver is the final exceptive case. It is strikingly different from the others because it entails an informed choice by the patient or subject. The exercise of a waiver allows patients to relinquish their right to an informed consent—that is, they may excuse the physician from the obligation to obtain informed consent. The patient may delegate decision-making authority to the physician, or request not to be informed, thus freeing the physician from the disclosure duty.[49] In effect, the patient may make an informed decision not to make another informed decision.

Although the patient waiver exception may conform to entrenched ways in which many patients actually interact with their physicians, it has never been carefully delineated in law, and commentators have noted several problems. According to well-established case law in such diverse areas as tort, contract, and fourth amendment search-and-seizure law, a person can effectively waive a legal right only if the waiver is informed, reasoned, and voluntary. On the level of moral reasoning, too, a waiver—as a decision about a decision—is not necessarily in conflict with respect for a patient's autonomy. But under what conditions can a patient make a voluntary and informed decision to waive the right to hear relevant disclosable information?

This question presents a conceptual problem about whether such a decision could be informed and voluntary, but there are also empirical and moral issues. One empirical question is whether potential abuse of the waiver by physicians can be prevented, given the disadvantageous bargaining position of the patient and the admittedly fine line between a voluntary waiver after an honest suggestion and a nonvoluntary waiver after intimidation. An attached moral problem concerns how much the physician must disclose about the possible consequences of a waiver. Should waivers be discouraged, on grounds that they are difficult to bring in line with the basic purpose of informed consent requirements, which is to allow for autonomous decisionmaking?

These and other problems attending the waiver exception remain unresolved in case law on informed consent and in legal commentary.

Constitutional Law and the Right to Privacy

The constitutional right of privacy serves to protect individual autonomy; it has been invoked to prevent governmental interference with various areas of personal health care decisionmaking from abortion and contraception to treatment refusal. This right thus potentially affords a means of autonomy protection that is an alternative to the common law informed consent doctrine. The concept of autonomy expressed in the legal theory underlying the right of privacy has some characteristics that make a promising avenue for further development of the law of informed consent. For this reason we briefly examine privacy law even though it has not, in the strict sense, addressed issues of informed consent.

The common law basis of informed consent requirements has classically protected autonomy by a retrospective evaluation of decisions already made. Cases have recently appeared in which patients seek to assert autonomy rights prospectively, by obtaining court authorization to make a disputed medical decision in the face of opposition from physicians, institutions, or families. Because the common law doctrine of informed consent usually lacks the power to do more than compensate for injuries already suffered, these prospective cases are brought under the Constitution and are not informed consent cases per se, despite a noticeable similarity in their subject matter. Some constitutional cases address the question in terms of religious freedom, under the first amendment. Other cases are cast in federal constitutional terms as "privacy" cases.

Although not explicitly enumerated in the Bill of Rights, the right of privacy is now generally thought to arise from the "penumbra" of the first, ninth, and fourteenth amendments.[50] (Justice Brandeis relied in early cases on the fourth amendment as well.) An individual holds the right, like other constitutional rights, only against the state and against parties acting on behalf of the state—not against other individuals or nongovernmental entities.[51]

The Supreme Court early in the 1920s employed an expansive "liberty" interest to protect family decisionmaking about various issues, including childrearing and education.[52] The Court later switched to the term "privacy" and expanded the individual's and the family's protected interest in family life, childrearing, and other areas of personal choice.[53] The clearest and most modern expression of this privacy right has come in the Court's family planning decisions. *Griswold* v. *Connecticut* (1965),[54] a case dealing with contraception, was the first to discuss the right of privacy as not merely shielding *information* from others but as creating a zone of *protected activity* within which the individual is free from governmental interference. According to this modern interpretation, the right to privacy protects liberty by delineating a zone of private life—including, for example, family planning decisions—within which the individual is free to choose and act.

It may seem inapposite to denominate this personal right as one of privacy, rather than liberty pure and simple, but it can be understood as a right to maintain certain activities as private in the sense that they are not subject to *governmental* oversight or intrusion.[55] The constitutional right of privacy shields certain personal information, choices, and activities from such governmental imposition. This right is still an inchoate notion, no doubt in process of further development.[56] The direction of its development until now, however, indicates that the account of rights of individual liberty on which it is based could conceivably have important implications for informed consent.

Informed Consent as a Privacy Claim

As is plain from the Supreme Court's contraception and abortion decisions,[57] some forms of intimate personal decisionmaking similar to those addressed by informed consent requirements, especially rights to refuse medical treatment, are protected by the constitutional right to privacy. These are matters of the protection of self-determination. Justice Douglas' concurring opinion in *Doe* v. *Bolton* enumerates categories of activities that fall within the privacy right, indicating that the broad range of interests encompassed by this constitutional right include several categories more accurately captured by the terms "liberty" or "autonomy":

> First is the autonomous control over the development and expression of one's intellect, interests, tastes, and personality. . . . Second is freedom of choice in the basic decisions of one's life respecting marriage, divorce, procreation, contraception, and the education and upbringing of children. . . . Third is the freedom to care for one's health and person, freedom from bodily restraint or compulsion, freedom to walk, stroll, or loaf.[58]

In *Whalen* v. *Roe*,[59] the Supreme Court acknowledged that the right of privacy protects an "interest in independence in making certain kinds of important decisions." Decisions regarding medical treatment have been specifically acknowledged by lower courts as falling within that cat-

egory. The courts in the leading "substituted judgment" decisions dealing with incompetent patients, the Karen Quinlan case[60] and the Joseph
Saikewicz case,[61] relied on the right of privacy in introducing the idea of
the *competent* patient's right to make medical decisions:

> There is implicit recognition in the law of the Commonwealth, as else-
> where, that a person has a strong interest in being free from noncon-
> sensual invasion of his bodily integrity . . . . One means by which the
> law has developed in a manner consistent with the protection of this
> interest is through the development of the doctrine of informed
> consent. . . .
> Of even broader importance, but arising from the same regard for
> human dignity and self-determination, is the unwritten constitutional-
> right of privacy found in the penumbra of specific guarantees of the
> Bill of Rights. . . . As this constitutional guaranty reaches out to protect
> the freedom of a woman to terminate pregnancy under certain condi-
> tions, . . . so it encompasses the right of a patient to preserve his or her
> right to privacy against unwanted infringements of bodily integrity in
> appropriate circumstances.[62]

This right of privacy is not an absolute trump, however. For example,
there is no absolute right to abortion on demand. Even within the zone
of privacy the state can override a patient's treatment decision if it has a
compelling reason for so doing. "Compelling" is a legal modifier referring to governmental interests needed to overcome "fundamental" but
not "absolute" constitutional rights like the right of privacy. Thus, fundamental constitutional rights are similar to prima facie moral rights (as
"prima facie" is discussed in Chapter 1). Although generally binding,
they can be validly overridden.

The compelling interests most commonly invoked by the state and by
courts to override patients' treatment choices are (1) the interests of particular third parties, such as the viable fetus's interest in life in the abortion decisions, or a surviving infant's interest in the mother's care if the
mother seeks to refuse lifesaving treatment for herself, and (2) the
health, safety, and welfare of society at large—for example, protection
of others' health if an individual refuses vaccination or protection of the
public from the high costs of caring for unhelmeted persons who sustain
head injuries from motorcycle accidents.

The Prospective Character of Privacy Actions

Historically, as we shall see in Chapter 4, informed consent has been
addressed predominantly through the common law. Several important
differences between common law and constitutional law are responsible
for the paucity of privacy cases addressing problems of medical decisionmaking. Foremost among these is that the Constitution only protects
individuals against governmental intrusions, or "state action." By means

of a constitutional claim, an informed consent statute adopted by a state legislature can be challenged, and patients can ward off court-ordered treatment, but individual physicians who are not agents of the state cannot be directly compelled to obtain informed consent.

The other major difference is also potentially the greatest strength of constitutional theory for informed consent: its power to order parties to act or to refrain from action. Common law tort theory is based on the fundamental premise that tortious injuries can be compensated by means of money damages. Courts are not permitted to exercise their extraordinary remedies such as issuing injunctions if an adequate financial remedy exists. Thus, under the common law of informed consent, patients cannot compel physicians to disclose information; they can only sue for damages after there has already been a failure to disclose.

By contrast, constitutional privacy actions directed toward protecting individual freedom to act without governmental interference are inherently *prospective* in nature. It is an axiom of constitutional theory that preventing constitutional violations is preferable to assessing damages after violations take place. The constitutional consent and refusal cases that have arisen thus far have established the individual's right to make certain medical choices, and to refuse treatments in the face of the opposition of physicians and others.

Patients who have not received information they need to give an informed consent are unlikely to detect any violation of their rights until injury results (if it does). However, with an awareness of a right to an informed consent and of the kinds of disclosures physicians must make to fulfill their corresponding duty, a patient could constitutionally compel a physician acting as an agent of the state to satisfy a court that the requirements of informed consent have been met *before* the proposed procedure is undertaken. This prospective involvement by the court would make possible the effective protection of the purely dignitary autonomy interest that is violated by failures of disclosure that do not result in physical injury. For this reason a constitutional model that uses premises of privacy has been suggested by some commentators as a promising resource for constructive development of the law of informed consent.[63]

Conclusion

In this chapter and the previous chapter we have noted important similarities between moral and legal reasoning in the various rights and principles they mutually endorse. We have found the principle of respect for autonomy, which is generally cast in law as the right of self-determination, to be basic to both frameworks and to their support for rules of informed consent. This discovery is unsurprising because the purpose of these principles is to protect bodily integrity and choice by denying others a right to intrude without consent. The right to privacy also functions to protect such personal interests, as do rules that limit the scope of exceptions such as the therapeutic privilege. In all these matters, legal and moral theory tend to cooperate like a pair in the motions of a dance.

However, neither of these frameworks is reducible to the other, and it does not follow from the moral acceptability of an act that law should permit it. For example, a refusal to disclose information may be courageous and praiseworthy in some circumstances, but law and policy need not sanction such acts, and there might be sound reasons of policy for legally prohibiting them. The judgment that an act is morally wrong also does not entail that it should be legally prohibited or punished. Issues of the symbolic value of law, legal liability, costs to the system, practicability within the litigation process, and questions of compensation may demand that legal requirements be different from moral requirements.

In Chapters 3 through 6, we move beyond these foundational frameworks to a review and interpretation of the history of informed consent in clinical medicine and research. We argue that the moral and legal principles introduced in these first two chapters have been at the forefront of the historical development of informed consent requirements, with respect for autonomy or the right of self-determination occupying a central justificatory role in framing rules governing consent. Any theory of the nature of informed consent, such as the one we present in Chapters 7 through 10, must begin with an appreciation of its historical roots, not merely its conceptual foundations.

Notes

1. A different definition is provided by Alan Meisel and Loren Roth, who define the doctrine of informed consent as "the legal model of the medical decisionmaking process." See their "Toward an Informed Discussion of Informed Consent: A Review and Critique of the Empirical Studies," *Arizona Law Review* 25 (1983): 272.

2. Many persons are considered fiduciaries in law. Persons who deal, in business relationships or otherwise, with others who rely on their superior knowledge, place confidence in them, and trust that they are acting in the best interests of the other parties are held to a fiduciary standard. Thus, realtors, stockbrokers, and other advisors may be fiduciaries; so may parents, guardians, physicians, attorneys, trustees, and estate executors.

3. For a sensitive treatment, see Drummond Rennie, "Informed Consent by 'Well-Nigh Abject' Adults," *New England Journal of Medicine* 302 (April 17, 1980): 917.

4. In battery, the physician can be held liable even if the plaintiff has benefited from the intervention, though the amount of damages may be adjusted to reflect benefits conferred. See Leonard Riskin, "Informed Consent: Looking for the Action," *University of Illinois Law Forum* 1975 (1975): 580–84; James E. Ludlam, *Informed*

Consent (Chicago: American Hospital Association, 1978), 25; Jay Katz, "Informed Consent: A Fairy Tale? Law's Vision," *University of Pittsburgh Law Review* 39 (1977): 144–45.

5. See below for explanation of the reasonable person concept and standard. Although nonconsensual contact of the sort encompassed by battery theory is referred to in the law as "offensive," the term is meant to be synonymous with "nonconsensual," having no additional negative connotations. Their equivalence is the essence of the legal understanding of battery as addressing *dignitary* injury.

6. *Schloendorff* v. *Society of New York Hospitals*, 211 N.Y. 125, 126, 105 N.E. 92, 93 (1914).

7. See, for example, *Schloendorff* v. *Society of New York Hospitals* (cite above); *Bang* v. *Charles T. Miller Hospital*, 251 Minn. 427, 88 N.W.2d 186 (1958); *Berkey* v. *Anderson*, 1 Cal. App. 3d 790, 82 Cal. Rptr. 67 (1969); *Bryson* v. *Stone*, 190 N.W.2d 336 (Mich. 1971).

8. See, for example, Brazier, "Informed Consent to Surgery," *Medicine, Science, and the Law* 19 (January 1979): 49; Ludlam, *Informed Consent*, 21 n. 10, 26; Riskin, "Informed Consent: Looking for the Action," 584; Alan Meisel, "The Expansion of Liability for Medical Accidents: From Negligence to Strict Liability by Way of Informed Consent," *Nebraska Law Review* 56 (1977): 80.

9. See, for example, *Cathemer* v. *Hunter*, 27 Ariz. App. 780, 558 P.2d 975 (1976); *Wall* v. *Brim*, 138 F.2d 478 n. 7 (5th Cir. 1943); *Hunt* v. *Bradshaw*, 242 N.C. 517, 88 S.E.2d 762 (1955).

10. The definitive treatment of this problem is still that found in Marcus Plant, "An Analysis of Informed Consent," *Fordham Law Review* 36 (1968): 650. See also the valuable argument in Katz, "Informed Consent: A Fairy Tale?" 144, 168.

11. See, for example, *Natanson* v. *Kline*, 186 Kan. 393, 350 P.2d 1093, 354 P.2d 670 (1960); *Trogun* v. *Fruchtman*, 58 Wis.2d 596, 599–600, 207 N.W.2d 297, 313 (1973); Allan McCoid, "A Reappraisal of Liability for Unauthorized Medical Treatment," *Minnesota Law Review* 41 (1957): 423–25; Riskin, "Informed Consent: Looking for the Action," 585–94; and Katz, "Informed Consent—A Fairy Tale?" 165–66.

12. See Alexander M. Capron, "Informed Consent in Catastrophic Disease Research and Treatment," *University of Pennsylvania Law Review* 123 (1974): 364–76; McCoid, "A Reappraisal of Liability for Unauthorized Medical Treatment," 381, 434; Angela Holder, "Commentary" (on Alan Stone), in D.M. Gallant and R. Force, eds., *Legal and Ethical Issues in Human Research and Treatment* (New York: SP Medical & Scientific Books, 1978), 44–45; Plant, "An Analysis of Informed Consent," 639, 650–56; Riskin, "Informed Consent: Looking for the Action," 600–604; *Trogun* v. *Fruchtman* (cite above); and *Hales* v. *Pittman*, 118 Ariz. 305, 576 P.2d 493, 497 (1973).

13. See David W. Louisell, *Medical Malpractice* (New York: Matthew Bender Co., 1973). See also Meisel, "The Expansion of Liability for Medical Accidents," 80–99. A controversial recent case, *Truman* v. *Thomas*, 165 Cal. Rptr. 308, 611 P.2d 902 (1980), has held the physician's duty to include disclosure of the risks of refusal of a routine diagnostic procedure (here a Pap smear). See Chapter 4.

14. 186 Kan. 393, 409 (1960).

15. See Annotation, "Necessity and Sufficiency of Expert Evidence and Extent of Physician's Duty to Inform Patient of Risks of Proposed Treatment," 52 ALR 3d 1084 (1977); Annotation, "Modern Status of Views as to General Measure of Physician's Duty to Inform Patient of Risks of Proposed Treatment," 88 ALR 3d 1008 (1978); Ludlam, *Informed Consent*, 29; Plant, "The Decline of Informed Consent"; David Seidelson, "Medical Malpractice: Informed Consent Cases in 'Full-Disclosure' Jurisdic-

tions," *Duquesne Law Review* 14 (1976): 309–11, nn. 1 & 2. George Annas has suggested, in a private communication with the authors, that many courts may interpret the professional practice standard more flexibly in informed consent cases than in other malpractice cases.

16. *ZeBarth* v. *Swedish Hospital Medical Center*, 81 Wash.2d 12, 18, 499 P.2d 1, 9 (1972).

17. Jon R. Waltz, "The Rise and Gradual Fall of the Locality Rule in Medical Malpractice Litigation," *DePaul Law Review* 18 (1969): 408.

18. See, for example, R.J. Alfidi, "Informed Consent: A Study of Patient Reaction,"*Journal of the American Medical Association* 216 (1971): 1325–29; M.K. Denney, et al., "Informed Consent: Emotional Responses of Patients," *Postgraduate Medicine* 60 (1975): 205–209; S.H. Rosenberg, "Informed Consent: A Reappraisal of Patients' Reactions," *California Medicine* 119 (1973): 64–68; G.T. Roling, et al., "An Appraisal of Patients 'Reactions to 'Informed Consent' for Peroral Endoscopy," *Gastrointestinal Endoscopy* 24 (1977): 69–70; J.W. Lankton, et al., "Emotional Responses to Detailed Risk Disclosure for Anesthesia: A Prospective, Randomized Study," *Anesthesiology* 46 (1977): 294–96; B.M. Patten and W. Stump, "Death Related to Informed Consent," *Texas Medicine* 74 (1978): 49–50; A.F. Lalli, "Urographic Contrast Media Reactions and Anxiety," *Radiology* 112 (1974): 267–71; E.D. Schwarz, "Use of a Checklist in Obtaining Informed Consent for Treatment with Medication," *Hospital and Community Psychiatry* 92 (1978): 97–98; and Ronald Katz, "Informed Consent: Is It Bad Medicine?" *Western Journal of Medicine* 126 (May 1977): 426–28.

19. See, for example, Ruth R. Faden, et al., "Disclosure of Information to Patients in Medical Care," *Medical Care* 19 (July 1981): 718–33; Charles Keown, Paul Slovic, and Sarah Lichtenstein, "Attitudes of Physicians, Pharmacists, and Laypersons toward Seriousness and Need for Disclosure of Prescription Drug Side Effects," *Health Psychology* 3 (1984): 1–11.

20. Faden, et al., "Disclosure of Information to Patients," 728.

21. E.g., *Canterbury* v. *Spence*, 464 F.2d 772, 785 (D.C. Cir. 1972); *Wilkinson* v. *Vesey*, 295 A.2d 676, 688 (R.I. 1972); *Cobbs* v. *Grant*, 8 Cal. 3d 229, 104 Cal. Rptr. 505, 502 P.2d 1 (1972).

22. See Capron, "Informed Consent in Catastrophic Disease Research," 346–47; Jon R. Waltz and T.W. Scheuneman, "Informed Consent to Therapy," *Northwestern University Law Review* 64 (1970): 618ff; Riskin, "Informed Consent: Looking for the Action," 581.

23. See sources cited in n. 12. But some commentators see no real inconsistency in this use of the reasonable person standard in a negligence framework. See Lawrence W. Kessenick and Peter A. Mankin, "Medical Malpractice: The Right To Be Informed," *University of San Francisco Law Review* 8 (1973): 261.

24. *Wilkinson* v. *Vesey* 295 A.2d 676; *Canterbury* v. *Spence*, 464 F.2d at 786–87; *Cobbs* v. *Grant*, 502 P.2d 1. These cases gradually assembled a set of consideratons used to explicate the concept of the reasonable person in this context.

25. Seidelson, "Medical Malpractice: Informed Consent Cases in 'Full Disclosure' Jurisdictions."

26. Plant, "The Decline of Informed Consent"; Alan Meisel and Lisa D. Kabnick, "Informed Consent to Medical Treatment: An Analysis of Recent Legislation," *University of Pittsburgh Law Review* 41 (1980): 423–26; Alan Meisel, "The Law of Informed Consent," in President's Commission, *Making Health Care Decisions*, Vol. 3, 206–45.

27. See, for example, R.P. Bergen, "The Confusing Law of Informed Consent," *Journal of the American Medical Association* 229 (July 15, 1974): 325; B.B. Markham,

"The Doctrine of Informed Consent—Fact or Fiction," *Forum* 10 (Spring 1975): 1073–79; Marcus Plant, "The Decline of Informed Consent"; and Robert B. Howard, "More on Informed Consent," *Postgraduate Medicine* (January 1979): 25.

28. The failure to analyze the reasonable person in this context is understandable and perhaps pardonable. The concept of the reasonable person has a long tradition in the law. First mentioned in English common law in 1738, the reasonable man standard is applied in particular cases by the factfinder (the jury or sometimes the judge) in circumstances where an actor's behavior should be judged objectively.

The reasonable person concept is "objective" in a dual sense. First, the standard personifies the common behavioral assumptions that members of society must make about their fellows in order to interact efficiently. Thus, the reasonable person presumably can serve as a basis on which parties to contracts may conduct business without fear of hidden misunderstandings. Second, the reasonable person is prescriptive as well as descriptive, serving as a standard that individuals must meet or risk liability. The reasonable person is to be understood as a composite of reasonable persons, and not as the individual actor in the case being considered. As Prosser puts it:

> The courts have gone to unusual pains to emphasize the abstract and hypothetical character of this mythical person. He is not to be identified with any ordinary individual, who might occasionally do unreasonable things; he is a prudent and careful man who is always up to standard. Nor is it proper to identify him even with any member of the very jury who are to apply the standard; he is rather a personification of the community ideal of reasonable behavior, determined by the jury's social judgment.

Thus, the reasonable person is to be distinguished both from identifiable actors and from statistical norms or averages, such as empirical findings of what the *average* person would do. See William L. Prosser, *The Law of Torts*, 4th ed. (St. Paul: West Publishing Company, 1971), 151.

29. See Jay Katz, "Informed Consent—A Fairy Tale?"

30. See the two studies by Faden, et al., "Disclosures of Information to Patients" and "Disclosure Standards and Informed Consent."

31. Jay Katz has argued for the superiority of the subjective standard in his *The Silent World of Doctor and Patient* (New York: Free Press, 1984), e.g., 75–76, 78. See also Alexander M. Capron, "Informed Consent in Catastrophic Disease Research and Treatment," esp. around 408.

32. See, for example, Capron, "Informed Consent in Catastrophic Disease Research"; Jay Katz, *The Silent World of Doctor and Patient*, 76; Theodore J. Schneyer, "Informed Consent and the Danger of Bias in the Formation of Medical Disclosure Practices," *Wisconsin Law Review* 1976: 124; and Riskin, "Informed Consent: Looking for the Action."

33. *Wilkinson* v. *Vesey*, 295 A.2d at 687 (paraphrasing Harper and James, *The Law of Torts* [1968 Supp.], 60–61).

34. The subjective disclosure standard is essentially a creature of legal commentary rather than case law. The California Supreme Court appeared to adopt it in *Cobbs* v. *Grant*, but only opaquely. See Capron, "Informed Consent on Catastrophic Disease Research and Treatment," 406–407. Subsequent California decisions have declined to follow *Cobbs*. See *Truman* v. *Thomas*, 611 P.2d at 902 and 905 (citing *Sard* v. *Hardy*, 281 Md. 432, 444, 379 A.2d 1014 (1977), and *Wilkinson* v. *Vesey*, 295 A.2d at 676, in support of its application of the reasonable person standard). It has been argued that *Scott* v. *Bradford*, 606 P.2d 554, 556 (Okla. 1980) applies a subjective disclosure standard (see Meisel, "The Law of Informed Consent," 195 n. 9). How-

ever, this reading is dubious (see n. 41 below). The foremost proponent of the reasonable person standard over the subjective standard is *Canterbury* v. *Spence*, 464 F.2d at 787 (citing Waltz and Scheuneman, "Informed Consent to Therapy," 639–40).

35. E.g., President's Commission, *Making Health Care Decisions*, Vol. I, 26.

36. It is arguable that the reasonable person standard allows more scope for the individual's peculiar circumstances than proponents of the subjective standard are willing to admit. The potential exists in every case for considering the patient's distinctive circumstances, while still requiring a reasonable decisionmaking process. The difficulty for the jury lies in determining *which* of the patient's circumstances the reasonable person standard—or the subjective standard—requires them to take into account. How flexible the former standard is in *practice* is disputable. Untapped potential for a highly individualized determination using either standard seems to exist.

37. This requirement of causation, which has no parallel in the battery theory, is analyzable into two distinct causal elements: a harm-inducing physical or psychological cause and a (causally connected) nondisclosure cause. First, the patient's injury must result not from poor care but simply from the occurrence of a foreseeable risk of the procedure—a risk that should have been disclosed to the patient in accordance with whatever disclosure standard is to be applied. Second, a causal relationship must be established between the physician's nondisclosure and the patient's injury.

38. *Canterbury* v. *Spence*, 464 F.2d at 791:

> Better it is, we believe, to resolve the causality issue on an objective basis: in terms of what a prudent person in the patient's position would have decided if suitably informed of all perils bearing significance. . . . The patient's testimony is relevant on that score of course but it would not threaten to dominate the findings. . . . Such a standard would in any event ease the fact-finding process and better assure the truth as its product.

39. See Capron, "Informed Consent in Catastrophic Disease Research," 407–408; Jay Katz, *The Silent World*, 79; Meisel, "The Expansion of Liability"; Riskin, "Informed consent: Looking for the Action," 588, 602. See also *McPherson* v. *Ellis*, 305 N.C. 266, 287 S.2d 892, 896 (1982).

40. Capron, "Informed Consent in Catastrophic Disease Research,"420. See also Meisel, "The Expansion of Liability for Medical Accidents," 111–13.

41. *Scott* v. *Bradford*, 606 P.2d 554 (Okla. 1980) and *Wilkinson* v. *Vesey*, 295 A.2d 676, utilize a subjective *causation* test in conjunction with a reasonable person *disclosure* standard, a combination that arguably undercuts the value of the subjective test almost as much as combining it with a professional standard. These courts permit the patient to make an idiosyncratic decision. However, they also hold that the only information the physician is obligated to disclose is information material to a reasonable person, rather than the information desired by that patient.

42. Plant, "The Decline of Informed Consent"; Meisel and Kabnick, "Informed Consent to Medical Treatment: An Analysis of Recent Legislation," 441–43; and President's Commission, *Making Health Care Decisions*, Vol. 1, 23.

43. See generally Alan Meisel, "The 'Exceptions' to the Informed Consent Doctrine: Striking a Balance Between Competing Values in Medical Decisionmaking," *Wisconsin Law Review* 1979 (1979): 413–88.

44. *Canterbury* v. *Spence*, 464 F.2d at 789. Questions have been raised, however, regarding the legal authority of relatives under these circumstances. See, for example, *Nishi* v. *Hartwell*, 52 Haw. 188, 198, 473 P.2d 116, 122 (1970).

45. See Charles W. Lidz, et al., *Informed Consent: A Study of Decisionmaking in Psychiatry* (New York: The Guilford Press, 1984), 16 (includes case references).

46. *Canterbury* v. *Spence*, 464 F.2d at 789 (emphasis added). For a broad formulation, see *Wilson* v. *Scott*, 412 S.W.2d 299, 301 (Tex. 1967).

47. See President's Commission, *Making Health Care Decisions*, Vol. 1, 95–96; M.J. Myers, "Comment: Informed Consent in Medical Malpractice," *California Law Review* 55 (1967): 1396–1410; E.S. Glass, "Restructuring Informed Consent: Legal Therapy for the Doctor-Patient Relationship," *Yale Law Journal* 79 (1970): 1533; Comment, "Informed Consent—A Proposed Standard for Medical Disclosure," *New York University Law Review* 48 (1973): 548–63; Capron, "Informed Consent in Catastrophic Disease Research and Treatment," 387–92; and Meisel, "'Exceptions,'" 467–70 (recommending its abolition).

48. *Canterbury* v. *Spence*, 464 F.2d at 789. See also *Cobbs* v. *Grant*, 8 Cal. 3d at 233.

49. *Cobbs* v. *Grant*. See Meisel, "'Exceptions,'" 459.

50. The origin, nature, and extent of the right of privacy are subjects of debate among legal scholars. Widely invoked in court decisions of the late 1960s and early 1970s, the right may have declined in popularity in subsequent years.

51. Historically, the earliest expression of the privacy right was derived from two common law doctrines, libel and copyright law, and not from the Constitution. At that time, the right was limited to protecting individuals from those who would pry into, observe, or publicize personal matters. In an influential 1960 article, William Prosser argued that the common law of privacy protects not one but four different privacy interests: (1) An interest in *freedom from intrusion* into solitude and personal affairs; (2) An interest in *freedom from disclosure* of potentially embarrassing facts about one's person; (3) An interest in *freedom from publicity* that falsely represents one's views or conduct; and (4) An interest in *freedom from appropriation* of one's name or likeness for the advantage of another. The constitutional right developed from these inherently subjective privacy interests. See Samuel Warren and Louis Brandeis, "The Right to Privacy," *Harvard Law Review* 4 (1890): 193–220; William L. Prosser, "Privacy," *California Law Review* 48 (1960): 383–423. For a critique of the latter, see Edward J. Bloustein, "Privacy as an Aspect of Human Dignity: An Answer to Dean Prosser," *New York University Law Review* 39 (1964): 962–1007.

52. *Pierce* v. *Society of Sisters*, 268 U.S. 510 (1925); *Meyer* v. *Nebraska*, 262 U.S. 390 (1923).

53. E.g., *Wisconsin* v. *Yoder*, 406 U.S. 205 (1972); *Stanley* v. *Georgia*, 394 U.S. 557 (1969); *Loving* v. *Virginia*, 388 U.S. 1 (1967); *Skinner* v. *Oklahoma*, 316 U.S. 535 (1942).

54. 381 U.S. 479 (1965). In this case, Justice William O. Douglas, in writing the majority opinion for the court, rested his decision on privacy, but four separate opinions by members of the majority cited different grounds to justify their concurrence in the result. Not all were based on a "right to privacy."

55. Similarly, the common law privacy right protects an individual's right to restrict, to some degree, the flow of information about himself or herself against the intrusions of anyone having an interest in this information. (See n. 51 above.) Common law privacy has not been extended to protect against decisionmaking interference, however, and thus is of no use to informed consent.

56. See, for example, Tom Gerseky, "Redefining Privacy," *Harvard Civil Rights-Civil Liberties Law Review* 12 (1977): 233; Jeffrey Reiman, "Privacy, Intimacy and Personhood," *Philosophy and Public Affairs* 6 (1976): 26; Comment, "A Taxonomy of Privacy," *California Law Review* 64 (1976): 1447. See also Laurence Tribe, *American Constitutional Law* (Mineola, N.Y.: The Foundation Press, 1978), 886–96.

57. Especially *Carey v. Population Services Int'l.*,431 U.S. 678 (1977); *Whalen v. Roe*, 429 US 589 (1977); *Roe* v. *Wade*, 410 U.S. 113 (1973); *Doe* v. *Bolton*, 410 U.S. 179 (1973); *Eisenstadt* v. *Baird*, 405 U.S. 438 (1972); and *Griswold* v. *Connecticut*, 381 U.S. 479 (1965). In *Planned Parenthood of Central Missouri* v. *Danforth*, 428 U.S. 52 (1976) and *Bellotti* v. *Baird*, 443 U.S. 622 (1979), the Court invalidated state statutes requiring parental consent, consultation, or notification in cases of abortions for minors.

58. *Doe* v. *Bolton*, 410 U.S. at 211–13. In *Roe* v. *Wade*, Doe's 1973 companion case, the language used is "the concept of personal liberty embodied in the Fourteenth Amendment's Due Process Clause," 410 U.S. at 129 (1973).

59. 429 U.S. 589, 599–600 (1977).

60. *In re Quinlan*, 70 N.J. 10, 355 A.2d 647 (1976).

61. *Superintendent of Belchertown State School* v. *Saikewicz*, 370 N.E.2d 417 (Mass. 1977).

62. Ibid., at 424, citing, inter alia, *In re Quinlan*. See also *Severns* v. *Wilmington Medical Center, Inc.*, 425 A.2d 156, 159 (Del. 1980).

63. Meisel, for example, has proposed "a common-law analysis for the right of the individual to make medical decisions, paralleling the analysis based on a constitutional right of privacy." See "Exceptions," 431 n. 70. See also Riskin, "Informed Consent: Looking for the Action," 603 n. 129; and Note, "Informed Consent and the Dying Patient," *Yale Law Journal* 83 (1974): 1646.

II

A HISTORY
OF INFORMED
CONSENT

3

Pronouncement and Practice in Clinical Medicine

This chapter initiates Part II, which is an attempt to understand historically how disclosure and consent have been implemented in the clinic,
the laboratory, and the courts. This history is essential for understanding
the contemporary concept of informed consent and for evaluating the
practice of informed consent in the different settings in which it has
developed, with their characteristic limits and concerns.

In this chapter we begin with a brief intellectual history of classical
oaths, codes, and treatises in medical ethics. We then examine nineteenth-century social developments and medical case reports before
turning to the twentieth-century literature in medical ethics and medical
practice that first examined problems of informed consent. In Chapter 4
we extend this treatment by tracing the development of the legal doctrine of informed consent, which developed from a conception of the
legal duties of the physician. In Chapters 5 and 6 we turn from the bed-
side to the laboratory by tracing the history of informed consent in
research and in federal policy governing research. In Part III, Chapters
7 through 10, we analyze the concept of informed consent less as an historical product than as a form of autonomous action. The analysis in these
final four chapters is a *theory* rather than a *history*.

The historical focus of the next four chapters invites a statement of
certain problems involved in interpreting historical writings and practices, and we begin with such a statement.

Problems of Historical Interpretation

Interpreting the History of "Consent": Some Perils of the Project

Before we can confidently infer that what appears to have been a consent
practice or policy qualifies for the term *informed* consent, we need to

know what we are seeking. This inquiry requires criteria of what will qualify for the label of "informed consent" in this and the next three chapters.

Overdemanding criteria would render it impossible to find any theory or practice of informed consent at any time. We shall avoid this problem by using the following criteria, which we believe are neither unreasonably demanding nor so loose as to encompass all discussions and arrangements between professional and patient or subject: (1) a patient or subject must *agree to* an intervention based on an *understanding* of (usually disclosed) relevant *information,* (2) consent must *not be controlled* by influences that would engineer the outcome, and (3) the consent must involve the intentional giving of *permission* for an intervention. Together, these conditions specify what we will label "informed consent" when looking at *historical* evidence of consent practice, policy, and theory in this and the following three chapters. (However, as we argue in Chapters 7 and 8, these conditions do not form an adequate conceptual analysis of the *meaning* of "informed consent.")

If all three criteria are satisfied at a given time, we conclude that we have found an instance, practice, or policy of informed consent. If there is good and sufficient evidence that one or more of the criteria was *not* satisfied, while the others were, an interpretation of whether meaningful consent was at work will depend on some exercise of judgment about specific criteria at issue and about the proper label to be attached. Depending on the circumstances, we might infer, for example, that there was indeed a practice, policy, or instance of consent or refusal, or of disclosure, but not one that qualifies as *informed* consent. Generally, we will not have the data base—sufficient evidence—to frame well-confirmed hypotheses or judgments, and we will rarely mention or make specific appeal to these criteria. We present them more as an advance notice of what we are attending to when we judge whether informed consent was in place at a given time.

An important distinction is that between a *failure to satisfy criteria* and a *failure of evidence.* It is sometimes tempting to hold that there was no practice of informed consent during a given period because our criteria are not satisfied, when all we can say in fairness to the facts is that we do not have good and sufficient evidence for saying that at the time informed consent either did or did not exist. The paucity of available evidence of consent practices and consent-seeking behavior by physicians is apparent in some of the periods we will be examining, and may therefore evoke considerable interpretative dispute.

For example, in the diaries of nineteenth-century surgeons, statements may be found that the surgeon *advised* amputation of an infected leg and that the patient *agreed* or *consented.* Without more evidence, we cannot discern whether this reported "consent" was based on accurate and adequate information. The patient may have been given pitiful information about the painfulness of the amputation, or perhaps the bleakness of the case was contrived to make acceptance of the operation inevitable. There are also many possible reasons for a physician's obtaining consent. For example, certain procedures cannot easily be performed without a freely cooperative—and, in this sense, consenting—patient.

It would be a mistake to infer from evidence of this sort that true "consent" was obtained for certain procedures at some time during the history of medicine, or that it was routinely obtained, or that there existed at that time some policy or practice of obtaining informed consent. Furthermore, evidence of *truthfulness* in disclosure does not permit any inference about the existence of *consent* practices; total physician control over decisionmaking is not incompatible with truthtelling. In short, the data available about "consent" in earlier periods may provide scant evidence about the actual nature and quality of "consents" obtained and virtually nothing about the justification that may have been invoked for the practices or policies of the period.

Much of the evidence regarding the existence or nonexistence of consent practices in a given period is of questionable generalizability—a physician's diary here, some published case reports there, and so on. Often missing is any way of inferring whether the available experience represents the mainstream of medical practice or mere accident or idiosyncracy. We still have but poor information about the extent to which consent practices were diffused through the medical community in any period prior to the 1960s.

Finally, there is the related question of what can be reasonably inferred from oaths, prayers, codes of ethics, published lectures, and general pamphlets and treatises on medical conduct, usually written by individual physicians or medical societies for their colleagues. In the absence of more direct data about actual consent practices, these documents have been relied on heavily in numerous writings on informed consent. However, it is not always clear whether the statements made in these documents were primarily exhortatory, descriptive, or self-protective. Some writings describe, for educational purposes, conduct that was in accordance with prevailing professional standards. Other documents aim at reforming professional conduct by prescribing what should be established practice. Still others seem constructed to protect the physican from suspicions of misconduct or from legal liability.

Thus, to view prescriptions in codes and similar material at face value, as reflective of prevailing professional opinion in their epoch, may cause serious distortions. "Informed consent" is a creature of a broad range of social practices and institutions in the twentieth century. To remove the notion from contemporary cultural and historical contexts in which it was nourished in order to test retrospectively for its presence in other cultures is a dangerous undertaking requiring special precautions. We thus should be hesitant to claim conclusiveness for the evidence from which historical theses often must be fashioned.

Two Competing Historical Interpretations

Two recently framed and competitive historical analyses illustrate the difficulty of amassing historical evidence about informed consent and its historical justifications. The two theses have been ably defended by historian Martin S. Pernick and psychiatrist Jay Katz.

Pernick concludes, after a thorough examination of a wide variety of nineteenth-century sources, that "truth-telling and consent-seeking have long been part of an indigenous medical tradition, based on medical theories that taught that knowledge and autonomy had demonstrably beneficial effects on most patients' health." However, he also acknowledges that nineteenth-century views differed in both *content* and *purpose* from those entailed by "modern concepts of informed consent."[1] The nineteenth-century social context was not rights-oriented, and Pernick cautions that consent practices were commonly justified by considerations of therapeutic benefit rather than individual rights.

Whatever their justification or reason, Pernick believes it is unassailable that meaningful consent practices existed in nineteenth-century American medicine. His thesis has received tangential support in application to the twentieth century in an article published nearly simultaneously by theologian John Fletcher, who holds that "the moral obligation of informed consent in medicine and research was reasonably clear before 1939," and that the courts had already been active before that time in "establishing the validity of the principle."[2]

These two interpretations seem supported by the well-entrenched belief in *legal* writings that the law of informed consent can be traced at least to the early days of the twentieth century. Thus, in *Canterbury* v. *Spence*, Judge Spottswood Robinson writes as follows: "Suits charging failure by a physician to adequately disclose the risks and alternatives of proposed treatment are not innovations in American law. They date back a good half century."[3] The next few sentences of this seminal opinion on informed consent note the many disagreements and unresolved points of controversy that surround the law, but enlist numerous cases dating as distantly as 1914 as precedent cases of "informed choice" and "true consent".

By contrast to these charitable perspectives on the history of law and medicine, Katz argues that:

> The history of the physician-patient relationship from ancient times to the present . . . bears testimony to physicians' inattention to their patients' right and need to make their own decisions. Little appreciation of disclosure and consent can be discerned in this history, except

negatively, in the emphasis on patients' incapacities to apprehend the mysteries of medicine and therefore, to share the burdens of decision with their doctors.

It is the history of silence with respect to patient participation in decision making that I wanted to document. . . .

When I speak of silence I do not mean to suggest that physicians have not talked to their patients at all. Of course, they have conversed with patients about all kinds of matters, but they have not, except inadvertently, employed words to invite patients' participation in sharing the burden of making joint decisions.[4]

Katz dismisses the currents of generosity in the above sources. For example, he spurns Pernick's portrayals as "contentions [that] attempt to prove too much, for none of the celebrated proponents of truthfulness based their arguments on a felt need that patients should understand their situation so that they could participate in medical decision making." Katz holds that Pernick fails to appreciate that the sources invoked were *not* aimed at disclosure "for purposes of gaining patients' consent."[5]

As for court decisions and legal scholarship, a tradition to which Fletcher implicitly appeals, Katz either rejects the cited evidence as inconclusive or regards the declarations of courts as overoptimistic rhetoric: Any meaningful *legal* pronouncement on informed consent, he says, "is only 25 years old." The problem, in his view, is that the law has little to do with fostering real communication in the clinic and has suffered from what he calls the "low status of disclosure and consent." He agrees that "*consent* to *surgical* interventions is an ancient legal requirement." He holds, however, that the consents thus obtained were not meaningful consents, because "there was no right for patients to decide, after having been properly informed, whether an intervention was agreeable to them in light of its risks and benefits as well as available alternatives." The early cases noted in *Canterbury* "merely reaffirmed a citizen-patient's elementary right to be free from offensive (uninvited) contact"; these were not findings that "broke new legal ground," because they did not establish any real right to "thoroughgoing self-determination." In Katz's view, judges have only "toyed briefly" with the idea of informed consent since 1957, "bowing" in its direction largely to set it aside. Like physicians, judges always defer to a model of medical care rather than a model of the right to make one's own informed decisions, and thus both have failed to appreciate that "autonomous decision making requires two-way conversation."[6]

Where Katz sees no informed consent, Pernick finds it in abundance. Nonetheless, it is tempting to think that with sufficient diligence in interpretation, Pernick's thesis can be reconciled with Katz's. The basis of this presumption is that these two interpreters are writing at cross purposes, and leaving a cloud of uncertainty in the wake of their separate paths.

Whereas we and Katz start with a present-day understanding of "informed consent" and use history to ask whether this concept existed in the past, Pernick's purpose is to trace viewpoints on medical decision-making found in former decades on their own terms. For Pernick to say that "truth-telling and consent-seeking have long been part of an indigenous medical tradition" is not something that, on a careful reading, Katz would wish to deny. Katz's theses are all about *"meaningful* conversation." "A history of silence" in the relationship of doctors and patients does not preclude either disclosure or consent. His view in fact acknowledges such a history: "Disclosure in medicine has served the function of getting patients to 'consent' to what physicians wanted them to agree to in the first place," in light of their ideals of "caring custody."[7] Katz and Pernick also agree that the *"current controversy"* about "informed consent"—as we now use the term—is 25 years old,[8] and to support their theses, these writers use as evidence many (but not *all*) of the same historical sources, including codes of medical ethics ranging from ancient Greek medicine to contemporary documents by the American Medical Association (AMA).

Unless one supposes Pernick to mean that there *has* been a *meaningful* dialogue in the historical practices of consent to which he refers, there is no reason to think that he need disagree with Katz. And yet both Katz and Pernick believe that they *do* disagree. Pernick believes that conflicts between Katz's views and his own derive from Katz's methodology of tracing the history of "informed consent" as if it were an isolated entity that could be abstracted from its historical context.[9] He argues that "by the late eighteenth century, in Europe and America" a tradition had arisen in medicine that "promulgated a vision of the doctor-patient contract in which the patient's informed deference to the physician's scientific knowledge would be reciprocated by the physician's respect for the informed patient's autonomy. They did not write specifically about 'informed consent.' . . . But these physicians did develop an influential indigenous medical tradition that encourages the doctor to *share information and decisionmaking with his patients.*"[10] This thesis is exactly the one Katz rejects. The two views are thus rivals in their entirety, although—predictably—the extent to which these two writers agree on the *meaning* of the basic notions of "consent" and "autonomy" is somewhat unclear. Katz seems to apply more stringent standards for what could qualify under these labels than does Pernick.

The historical claims we make in this chapter tend to favor Katz's in this struggle to understand history, but we resist accepting the strength of his thesis that (in *Salgo*, see pp. 125–129 in Chapter 4), "the doctrine of informed consent surfaced, seemingly out of nowhere." We also think he overreaches for his thesis in asserting that "disclosure and consent . . . have no historical roots in medical practice." Katz, unlike Pernick, most often has the legal doctrine in mind. In a part of his thesis that we resist in Chapter 4, he holds that this legal doctrine is like the "deus ex machina" in Greek plays; we shall try to show that this claim is overstated in light of legal history.[11]

In the present chapter, we largely agree with Katz's views about pre-twentieth-century practices and beliefs. What Katz most forcefully denies regarding Pernick's perspective is that "indigenous medical traditions" of disclosure and consent amount to anything meaningful down to the present day in the way of autonomous decisionmaking. Because our book is, in the end (see Chapters 7–10), primarily about what it *means* for a patient or subject to choose and consent meaningfully, this historical (and indeed sociological) claim by Katz is of profound importance to our ultimate objectives. In this chapter we shall show not only why we think he is in considerable measure correct, but also how the ideas of truthtelling, disclosure, and consent have been handled in medicine throughout the ages.

Until recently—roughly the 1957 date engraved on the birthstone of informed consent by both Katz and Pernick—the justification of practices of disclosure and consent-seeking were strictly governed by what we shall call a *beneficence model* rather than an *autonomy model* of the physician's responsibility for the patient.[12] The "autonomy model," as we use the term, is the view that the physician's responsibilities of disclosure and consent-seeking are established primarily (perhaps exclusively) by the principle of respect for autonomy. (See pp. 7–9.) The "beneficence model," as we use the term, depicts the physician's responsibilities of disclosure and consent-seeking as established by the principle of beneficence, in particular through the idea that the physician's *primary* obligation (surpassing obligations of respect for autonomy) is to provide *medical* benefits. (See pp. 9–14.) The management of information is understood, on the latter model, in terms of the management of patients ("due care") generally. That is, the physician's primary obligation is to handle information so as to maximize the patient's medical benefits. Here, the principle of beneficence is used to provide clinical-specific meanings for the benefits and harms to be balanced by the physician.[13]

Because these two models embrace distinct perspectives on responsibilities to patients, they can emerge in conflict in precisely the same way we witnessed conflict among principles in Chapter 1. We shall maintain that the beneficence model in medicine has traditionally been understood as requiring provision of a medical benefit that serves the best medical interests of patients and that this requirement may indeed conflict with respect for the patient's autonomy. Pernick's thesis is not incompatible. He sees physicians as respecting autonomy in the eighteenth and nineteenth centuries *because of the beneficial therapeutic out-*

come of such respect. In effect, we are in agreement that physicians operated out of a beneficence model in the consent context. The beneficence model not only traditionally dwarfed any nascent autonomy model in medical practice but led to an environment in which autonomy figured insignificantly or not at all in reflections about disclosure. The consent practices emerging from this context were *not meaningful exercises of autonomous decisionmaking*, despite the bows in the direction of respectfulness and truthtelling found in a few codes, treatises, and practices.

Codes and Treatises from Hippocrates to the AMA

The history of "informed consent" can no more be reduced to a linear narration of social events and practices than can the history of major concepts in Western thought such as "democracy," "autonomy," or "scientific law." An *intellectual* history of the major writings of prominent figures in ancient, medieval, and modern medicine is the natural beginning point for our history, because of its rich and telling storehouse of information about cultural and theoretical commitments to disclosure and discussion between physician and patient. But it is also a disappointing history from the perspective of informed consent. It shows primarily how inadequately, and with what measure of hostility and insularity, problems of truthfulness, disclosure, and consent were framed and discussed prior to the twentieth century. The paramount issue is *truth telling*; consent and autonomy are scarcely mentioned in the traditional writings. Accordingly, we shall witness more a history of the concept of information management than of informed consent.

Our discussion is confined largely to secular Western sources, and later in the chapter is restricted to the United States. This orientation is not intended as a denial either of national traditions of medical ethics in Japan, China, the Mideast, India, etc. or of important religious traditions of medical ethics in Christianity, Judaism, Islam, and Confucianism.[14] However, their influence on the history we are writing is generally indirect and seldom paramount. While religiously rooted notions such as that of the Christian gentleman influenced various epochs in medical ethics, it is doubtful that the moral positions that developed internally within the profession of medicine received a theological justification or grew from distinctly *religious* traditions. For example, Thomas Percival's medical ethics reflects the Christian gentleman conception, yet very little in his pragmatic volume is directly traced or traceable to doctrines of *Christian* ethics. To be a Christian gentleman really meant for Percival that a doctor should be virtuous: reasonable, considerate, temperate, informed, self-critical, and the like. Likewise, Benjamin Rush often proposes that in certain situations of conflict between physician and patient, Christianity should determine what is to be done. Yet Rush's medical ethics has no real basis in religion or theology, even though he was a student of that discipline; moreover, he will recommend the study of philosophy in order not to be misled by "Schoolmen and divines."[15] The point of direct appeals to the Christian religion in early American medicine seems to have been to instruct practitioners to act virtuously: "to be Christians *and* gentlemen in their interactions with each other and with patients."[16]

Some have wished that the impact of these traditions might have been greater than it was, so that entrenched Hippocratic authoritarianism would have been subdued, but such wishes can only be entertained as contrary-to-fact conditionals: speculations about how things might have been had historical circumstances been different.[17]

Ancient Medicine

A primary historical source for our understanding of the physician's responsibility for the patient derives from the Hippocratic physicians in ancient Greece. The ancient Greek religious sect known as Pythagoreanism—not secular Greek philosophical ethics—appears to have been the inspiration underlying Hippocratic thinking, although this has never been conclusively demonstrated and discernible religious commitment is minimal.

The Hippocratic Oath (or Oaths, as some prefer to say) developed from this environment into a public pledge to uphold professional responsibilities. It fails, however, to address what are now considered fundamental issues of responsibility, including the roles of communication, disclosure, and the giving of permission in the patient-physician relationship.[18] Consent by patients goes unmentioned, and most topics and problems in modern medical ethics are ignored or given but passing notice.

The *Corpus Hippocraticum* is, nonetheless, the first set of Western writings about medical professional conduct, and remains among the most influential today. Despite its failure to mention solicitation of patients' permissions or respecting patients' decisions, the *Corpus* does discuss various problems of truthtelling, bluntly advising physicians of the wisdom of "concealing most things from the patient, while you are attending to him . . . turning his attention away from what is being done to him; . . . revealing nothing of the patient's future or present condition."[19] It is usually unclear how many contexts fall under such rules, but the physician is often portrayed as the one who commands and decides, while patients are conceived as persons who must place themselves fully in physicians' hands and obey commands.[20] If consent to treatment was solicited at all in ancient Greece—an historical uncertainty—Hippocratic documents suggest that a consent might not have been based on accurate, disclosed information.[21] Hippocratic physicians were also trained to look carefully for the lies that would be told to them by the patient!

Some writers have differentiated in the Hippocratic texts between problems of medical *ethics* and those of medical *etiquette*, the latter applying to rules of conduct found chiefly in the works *Decorum* and *Precepts*, by contrast to the Oath. These rules govern speech, dress, calmness of manner, appearance, personal nourishment, and interprofessional conduct.[22] The rules were viewed less as moral responsibilities than as means of "gaining reputation."[23] It has been skillfully argued that some core Hippocratic principles—for example, "administer no poison"—were formulated not from ethical conviction but to alleviate prevalent societal mistrust and to obtain more patients.[24] Consent appears to have played no significant role in these considerations.

In any event, etiquette need not be discounted or disparaged. In times when physicians lacked both social reputation and financial security, when no licensure system controlled entry into the profession or monitored professional quality, medical etiquette was one of the physician's major tools for acquiring potential patients' trust and to dissociate physicians from medical quacks.

Hippocratic authoritarianism is best understood through what we earlier dubbed the beneficence model. The purpose of medicine is expressed in the Oath as that of benefiting the sick and keeping them from harm and injustice.[25] This pledge, together with other Hippocratic writings, presupposes that the physician has special skills and moral commitments to the use of those skills in treating patients. This medical beneficence is the proper goal of medicine, and professional dedication to it makes one a physician. In the *Epidemics* we find perhaps the best, and certainly the most famous, expression of this beneficence model of responsibility: "Declare the past, diagnose the present, foretell the future; practice these acts. As to disease, make a habit of two things—*to help, or at least to do no harm.*"[26]

These are the primary goals for patient care and professional responsibility framed in the Hippocratic writings. Skilled communication in care and deference to the patient's preferences are foreign ideas, except insofar as dialogue could be used to instill confidence and "persuade" of a therapeutic regimen. This orientation is made more surprising than it otherwise might be by Hippocratic views on medical education and commitment, which insist that voluntary obedience to rules and the dictates of conscience must be one's guide as a teacher, learner, and professional.

The Hippocratic orientation is also an historical curiosity: Medical ethics throughout the spheres not under Hippocratic dominance—that is, most of ancient Greece—appear less authoritarian and beneficence-based. Non-Hippocratic physicians were permitted, for example, to engage in activites forbidden by Hippocrates, such as aiding in suicide and infanticide. In the Ancient period, Hippocratic views were shunned for generations in favor of other traditions. The first reference to the Oath in extant classical literature (that of Scribonius Largus) is hundreds of years later, in the first century A.D. It was at least as late as the rise of Christianity, and probably several centuries later, before the Oath and practices of Hippocratic physicians gained serious attention, let alone preeminence.[27]

Medieval Medicine

Christian monastic physicians traditionally held to the Hippocratic traditions, where medical authoritarianism and obligations of obedience by patients were strengthened further by theology. Writings in medical ethics were often simply *dicta* pulled directly from the Hippocratic writings, and laced with the etiquette and theology of the times. With the arrival of secular liberal arts universities and medical facilities, secular prescriptions emerged from the writings of late medieval physicians. Perhaps the most significant of these for our purposes was Frenchman Henri de Mondeville (ca 1260–1325), a surgeon and teacher of anatomy who transplanted a number of important medical traditions from Bologna to France. His writings, and also the views of most of the figures of the period, appear to be traceable directly to the Hippocratic texts.[28]

With regard to truthtelling, Mondeville overtly embraced the beneficence model, in full acceptance of traditional Hippocratic authoritarianism. For example, he advised his colleagues to "[P]romise a cure to every patient, but . . . tell the parents or the friends if there is any danger."[29] Mondeville appears to have considered the maintenance of hope to be of sufficient therapeutic benefit to justify deception.[30] He was often blunt. As Henry Sigerist humorously paraphrased Mondeville on the topic of lying in order to keep the patient in good spirits: "The surgeon must not be afraid to lie if this benefits the patient. For instance, if a canon is sick, tell him that his bishop has just died. The hope of succeeding him will quicken his recovery."[31] Mondeville also required that "patients, on the other hand, should obey their surgeons implicitly in everything appertaining to their cure."[32] The surgeon should even compel obedience by threatening them with the consequences of disobedience and by selectively monitoring and exaggerating information.[33] Mondeville neither advised physicians to solicit patients' decisions nor found it appropriate that patients dissent from their physicians' opinions.

Mondeville did, however, reflect on the "unfortunate" case in which the patient violently refuses a vital medical intervention. He advised the physician that it would be prudent not to accept the case, because a patient who is screaming or fighting is unlikely to enhance the physician's good reputation.[34] Citing Mondeville's injunction that "if the patient is defiant, seldom will the result be successful" and his advice that if the physician should not obtain the patient's confidence he "must not accept the case,"[35] Pernick concludes that "Mondeville cautioned *not to treat* patients *without obtaining their consent.*"[36]

This interpretation is overreaching. Although Pernick may mean "acquiescence" by this use of "consent," Mondeville never mentioned consent, and does not appear to have had even intentional acquiescence in mind. He merely said that one must not treat a patient without obtaining the patient's *confidence.* Mondeville did indeed recommend, in therapeutically unimportant matters, that "[the surgeon] ought to . . . fall in with [patients'] lawful requests so far as they do not interfere with the treatment."[37] But even this benevolent tolerance of patients' requests is a far distance from advocating consent or decisionmaking by patients. It is a distant conceptual journey from confidence to consent—almost as distant as the beneficence model from the autonomy model. Pernick concludes that consent was sought in early medicine only *for reasons of* beneficence. We think further evidence is needed even of this thesis. In any event, we are in agreement with Pernick that to interpret Mondeville's recommendation as invoking an autonomy model is incorrect.

Mondeville lived and wrote during a crucial period of social transformation in European medicine. By the end of the fifteenth century, medical schools and rules of licensing and practicing were under rapid development. Rudimentary ethical rules and prescriptions of etiquette were also in place—for example, rules governing the conditions under which a prognosis could be disclosed and what a physician could disclose in public about other physicians. But informed consent's time was yet to come.

Enlightenment Medicine

The Hippocratic tradition was carried forward from medieval to modern medicine as an ideal of moral commitment and behavior. Medical schools were quick to train students in Hippocratic principles, despite their somewhat archaic form. But a less authoritarian flavor, with more attention to actual practice, gradually emerged. A small but influential sample from what may be called Enlightenment medicine is found in the writings of both Benjamin Rush (1745–1813), a committed revolutionary and signer of the American Declaration of Independence affectionately referred to as the "American Hippocrates," and John Gregory (1724–1773), a prominent Scottish physician and one of Rush's teachers. Both wrote and lectured on medical ethics, and both were profoundly influenced by the intellectual ambience of the Enlightenment's commitment to progress and reason in the conduct of human affairs.

Rush was no typical representative of the late eighteenth century physician. He wrote hundreds of essays on social issues such as slavery, and was a man of wide classical learning. For example, he grappled seriously with philosophers such as Locke, Descartes, Hutcheson, Smith, Beattie, and Shaftesbury; he also lectured on the philosophy of mind and on moral psychology.[38] He used his background in philosophy both as a means to a constructive medical ethics and as a tool to criticize his fellow physicians for such "vices" as avarice, false statement, and inhumanity.[39]

Rush believed that doctors ought to share a rich body of information with their patients. His reasons were rooted heavily in an Enlightenment philosophy that saw happiness and freedom of choice as causal conditions of health. In anticipation of later developments that would move medicine and public health into close alliance, Rush advocated the demystification of medicine—the enlightenment of the public—by giving the public access to medical information and educating patients about their conditions. This program was recommended with the expectation that medical benefits would flow from increased comprehension and reflection by patients and the public, as in other areas of human life.[40] Rush also believed that harm might be caused by an unchecked commitment to Hippocratic beneficence. This belief was similarly rooted in the Enlightenment belief that disorders could be remedied or prevented by, among other things, maintaining conditions of liberty and reason.

The provision of truthful and comprehensive information, as well as the education of patients and the public, were recommended by Rush, as was the value of an informed decision to accept medical therapy.[41] Nowhere in Rush's writings, however, is there evidence that he advocated *consent*-seeking, or that decisions diverging from medical advice would be uniformly respected. Rush was not advocating informed consent; he wanted patients to be sufficiently educated so that they could understand physicians' recommendations and therefore be motivated to *comply*.

Rush was not even optimistic that patients would often form their own opinions about appropriate medical choices, and distinct echoes of the beneficence model are found throughout his writings. For example, he advised physicians to "yield to them [patients] in matters of little consequence, but maintain an inflexible authority over them in matters that are essential to life."[42] In a telltale lecture "On the Duties of Patients to their Physicians," Rush argued: "The obedience of a patient, to the prescriptions of his physician, should be prompt, strict, and universal. He should never oppose his own inclinations nor judgment to the advice of his physician."[43] He also admitted the need for deception, especially in dealing with unenlightened patients.

The goal of Rush's Enlightenment ethics was not a principle of respect for patients' decisions, but a principle of truthtelling fashioned for the sake of medically beneficial outcomes. This expectation of beneficial outcomes was not widely shared by the physicians of the period, who tended to see medical harm, rather than benefit, as the frequent outcome of truthtelling; this *empirical* belief was Rush's real target in writing about the education of patients.

A no less important figure in the Enlightenment was Rush's contemporary and teacher, Dr. John Gregory, Professor of Medicine in the University of Edinburgh. His *Lectures on the Duties and Qualifications of a Physician* (1772) was deeply influenced by the writings of Francis Bacon. It was published in several editions in various Western nations and influenced medical ethics across the Atlantic for decades thereafter.[44] In these lectures Gregory recognized duties of physicians to educate the public and duties of educated laypersons to learn about medicine. He viewed the physician's *role* in traditional terms of beneficence to patients, but he also saw a duty, albeit prima facie and measured by practical judgment, of truthfulness and disclosure in carrying out that role:

> A physician is often at a loss when speaking to his patients of their real situation when it is dangerous. A deviation from truth is sometimes in this case both justifiable and necessary. It often happens that a person is extremely ill; but yet may recover, if he be not informed of his danger. It sometimes happens, on the other hand, that a man is seized with a dangerous illness, who has made no settlement of his affairs, and yet perhaps the future happiness of his family may depend on his making such a settlement. In this and other similar cases it may be proper for a physician, in the most prudent and gentle manner, to give a hint to the patient of his real danger, and even solicit him to set about this necessary duty. But in every case it behooves a physician never to conceal the real situation of the patient from the relations. Indeed justice demands this; as it gives them an opportunity of calling for further assistance.[45]

In effect, the principle of beneficence is invoked to develop the idea that the physician has a prima facie obligation of *beneficence*—not of respect for autonomy and not of "justice" as we would use this term today—to be truthful to some among the dying.

Gregory discussed the importance of openness and honesty with patients in the same terms. Obligations to respect autonomy independent of medical benefit played no role in his reflections. Gregory was also quick to underscore that the physician must be keenly aware of the harm that untimely revelations might cause, while attending carefully to the style and timing of disclosures that would present dismaying or tragic information to the patient, so as to mitigate the impact of these disclosures.[46] More generally, Gregory called for those virtues that enable the physician to be a person of "humanity" who feels, with sympathy, the misfortunes and distress of patients.[47] Here we find the convergence of a beneficence-oriented conception of medicine with an ideal of gentlemanly and humane conduct.[48]

Pernick attempts to enlist Gregory, Rush, and other Enlightenment figures in defense of his historical thesis about early consent practices.

He traces their perspectives on the patient-physician relationship to "an Enlightenment version of informed consent," a view "increasingly circumscribed by later nineteenth-century physicians who viewed autonomy as a danger to the health of most patients."[49] Gregory was brilliantly iconoclastic in his attacks on the indifference, insensitivity, ignorance, and excessive self-interest of physicians, but "informed consent" and "autonomy" are too liberally employed in Pernick's wording to be fair to the facts of history and contemporary usage, even when qualified by the phrase "an Enlightenment version." There was as yet no informed consent, in our previously introduced sense, and no promotion of autonomous decisionmaking for the sake of autonomy. Moreover, the physicians of Gregory's own beloved Scotland paid little attention to his admonitions. The beneficence model remained triumphant in "the Enlightenment" even after Gregory's proposals for patient/physician equality.

Gregory and Rush were thoughtful and reflective physicians with keen insights into the virtues appropriate to the physician. They appreciated the value of information and dialogue from the patient's point of view, but the idea of informed consent was yet to take more than primitive shape in the writings of these the most insightful and reflective physicians of the Enlightenment period. On the matter of truthtelling and deception, Katz sums it up well: "Like Gregory, though somewhat more insistently, Rush too favored deception whenever enlightenment was not equal to the task of managing the physician-patient relationship."[50]

Modern British and American Medicine

Percival's Medical Ethics. Gregory was a major figure in rethinking the physician's character and responsibility in mid-to-late-eighteenth-century Britain. As that century drew to a close, a former student at Edinburgh emerged south of the Scottish border, in Manchester, as a preeminent figure in the history of medical ethics. Thomas Percival (1740–1804) published his landmark work, *Medical Ethics*, in 1803—although it had first been drafted in 1794 for hospitals and medical charities. A broad work on both ethics and etiquette, this volume too, in its sections on "professional conduct" in encounters with patients, is aligned with Hippocratic beneficence.[51]

Percival represented a coalescence of Enlightenment medicine and the ideal of the Christian gentleman. Written in its initial 1794 form as a response to a request that he act as referee of serious intraprofessional quarrels at a hospital in Manchester, his work often focused on issues of "medical etiquette" such as fees, consultations, seniority among colleagues, and the like. His preoccupation with "gentleman-like behavior"—rather than what we might today consider moral philosophy or moral conduct in the doctor-patient relationship—is paradigmatic of other writings on medical ethics that appeared at the time.

Percival's *Medical Ethics* makes a pointed and specific appeal to benevolence and contains a short list of recommended virtues that are associated with benevolence and special responsibility. The work makes no more mention, however, of consent solicitation and respect for decision-making by patients than had previous codes and treatises. The Enlightenment made its impact on Percival, but he was in partial retreat from it at exactly the time Rush was at the peak of his power and influence.

Like the Hippocratic physicians and Gregory, with whose works he was intimately familiar, Percival moved from the premise that the patient's best medical interest is the proper goal of the physician's actions to descriptions of the physician's proper deportment, including traits of character that maximize the patient's welfare. Recognizing the dependence of patients, physicians were counselled to discard feelings of pride and dignity, attending strictly to the patient's medical needs. Authority directs the physician to role responsibilities, dictated by the profession's understanding of its obligations—which are invariably *beneficence*-based in Percival's work. Again we see the triumph of the beneficence model as the broad framework for fashioning a medical ethics.

Percival's book is not a philosophical work, but it is philosophically competent. It is in part a reaction to the Enlightenment philosophy behind the writings of Rush and Gregory, and Percival sought to balance the openness recommended by Gregory with ancient Hippocratic principles. His style is a set of aphorisms and guidelines, in which he neither advocated disclosure nor said much about communicating with patients. On the one hand, Percival counseled physicians in bleak cases "not to make gloomy prognostications . . . but to give to the friends of the patients timely notice of danger . . . and even to the patient himself, if absolutely necessary."[52] On the other hand, he warned specifically, as Rush had, that to silence a patient with blunt authority may only result in a worsening of the patient's condition in less grave situations.

Percival tried to examine the issue of truthtelling dispassionately, without introducing a physician's bias. Nonetheless, he held that the balance of truthfulness yields to beneficence in the critical cases. He recognized that the patient's *right* to the truth clashed with his own recommendation of benevolent deception in medicine, but rights never achieved the same status as virtues in his ethics, where he looked to the "characteristic excellences" of "the virtuous man." In an overt attempt to balance veracity against beneficence—with the balance tipped sharply toward a beneficence model—he argued that

> To a patient, therefore, perhaps the father of a numerous family, or one whose life is of the highest importance to the community, who makes inquiries which, if faithfully answered, might prove fatal to him, it would be a gross and unfeeling wrong to reveal the truth. His right to

it is suspended, and even annihilated; because, its beneficial nature being reversed, it would be deeply injurious to himself, to his family, and to the public. And he has the strongest claim, from the trust reposed in his physician, as well as from the common principles of humanity, to be guarded against whatever would be detrimental to him. . . . The only point at issue is, whether the practitioner shall sacrifice that delicate sense of veracity, which is so ornamental to, and indeed forms a characteristic excellence of the virtuous man, to this claim of professional justice and social duty.[53]

Percival was here struggling against his friend and the inspiration for many of his views, the Rev. Thomas Gisborne, who opposed giving false assertions intended to raise patients' hopes and lying for the patient's benefit.[54] Percival held that the physician does not actually *lie* in acts of deception and falsehood, as long as the objective is to give hope to the dejected or sick patient. The role of the physician, after all, is primarily to "be the minister of hope and comfort."[55]

Percival was deeply concerned about both the appearance and the consequences of lying, because, as a practice, it affected the gentlemanly image of the physician, the potential recovery of the patient, and the character of the physician as a moral agent. Moreover, he was well aware of the moral arguments against lying found in Augustine, Gisborne, Dr. Johnson, and others.[56] Partially under their influence, he insisted that honesty, including honest disclosure, must be the gentlemanly norm *except in* emergency situations, terminal situations, and situations where harm would be caused by truthfulness. The viewpoint is clear: Preventing harm in the hard cases justifies deception; only *otherwise* should rules of disclosure govern conduct. Percival is simply not compelled by the weight of moral arguments to the contrary conclusion; but at least he was aware of those arguments.

There is also a different opposition, of which Percival was aware, between his views on truthtelling and those found in Rush and Gregory. Their differences are not over moral principles. Rather, the differences are to be accounted for by empirical controversy over the *consequences* of truthfulness. Rush claimed that truthtelling *promotes* health; Percival saw it as *detrimental* if the truth was "gloomy" and the circumstances dire. This essentially empirical controversy died down in the nineteenth century but arose again early in the twentieth and still persists among modern physicians, although it was not then and is not now based on adequate empirical data.

The AMA and Its Legacy. Percival's work served as the model for the American Medical Association's (AMA) first Code of Medical Ethics in 1847. Many whole passages were taken verbatim from Percival, including the prescription for beneficent deception of patients "with gloomy prognostications."[57] One passage was not: A striking segment of the official Introduction to the Code by committee member John Bell, who presented the Code to the convention, asserted that "veracity, so requisite in all the relations of life, is a jewel of inestimable value in medical description and narrative, the lustre of which ought never to be tainted for a moment, by even the breath of suspicion." This statement—ostensibly about *all* the relations of life—was located in the section of the Introducton on physicians' intercourse *with each other*. There is no comparable passage about their relations with their patients.

Before the passage of this code, which had been drafted by a committee and passed unanimously, there had been no national or nationally recognized code, although many state and local societies had their own codes. However, the chairman of the drafting committee for the code, Isaac Hays, wrote in a note accompanying the committee report: "On examining a great number of codes of ethics adopted by different societies in the United States, it was found that they were all based on that by Dr. Percival, and that the phrases of this writer were preserved to a considerable extent in all of them." But it was also noted that some of the sections in the new code were "in the words of the late Dr. Rush."[58] Nathan Davis later noted that the AMA's code was "copied" chiefly from Percival, with several paragraphs coming from both Rush *and* Gregory. However, the literal wording of their work was often recast to fit a broader medical context more appropriate to mid-nineteenth-century America. For example, Hays was a Jew who found it easy to keep the essence of Percival while deflecting the AMA code from the *Christian* gentleman orientation that Percival emphasized.[59]

More than Percival's language survived: His viewpoint on medical ethics gradually became the living creed of professional conduct in the United States. Its already authoritarian standpoint was, if anything, enhanced, and Rush's native enlightenment viewpoint diminished, by Percival's publication from a distant continent. However, the enlightenment tradition was not erased by Percival's influence. The publication of the AMA code was quickly followed in 1849 by a brilliant and ingenious work by Connecticut physician Worthington Hooker that included commentary on the Code. Entitled *Physician and Patient*, Hooker's book merits attention as the most original contribution to medical ethics by an American author in the nineteenth century.[60] The book was billed by Hooker as an attack on quackery and on all who "unjustly cast aspersions" on the medical profession. But he was also determined to attack abuses by physicians "with an unsparing hand."[61]

Paradoxically, in the act of *defending* the AMA's ethics in general, Hooker felt compelled to *attack* the AMA's moral views on truthtelling in particular. His first book stands out above all others in the history of medical ethics as a ringing, uncompromising denunciation of lying and deception in medicine; moreover, it demonstrates an extraordinary sensitivity to the feelings of patients and their needs for information. Two years later, in his *Inaugural Address as Professor of the Theory and Practice of Medicine in Yale*, Hooker expanded his attack, criticizing physicians for deceiving patients, providing unnecessary services as if necessary, and studying "the science of patient-getting, to the neglect, to some extent at least, of the science of patient-curing."[62]

Hooker was well aware of the beneficence model operative in Percival and the AMA code. While he praised the "benevolence" of physicians, he simply did not accept either benevolent deception or the philosophy of Hutcheson on which his predecessors relied. He argued that "the good, which may be done by deception in a *few* cases, is almost as nothing, compared with the evil which it does in *many* cases. . . . The evil which would result from a *general* adoption of a system of deception [shows] the importance of a strict adherence to truth in our intercourse with the sick."[63] By the same token, Hooker allowed suppression of information if the physician is uncertain or the information to be disclosed is certain to confuse the patient. Disclosure in these circumstances, he reasoned, would amount to deception, and the physician's task is to *prevent* deception.[64]

Hooker mounted both an empirical and a moral attack on the adequacy of his predecessors' and peers' views on truthtelling, and specifically attacked the presuppositions of benevolent deception at work in Percival. One conclusion in his chapter on truth is paradigmatic: "There are cases in which [withholding information] should be done. All that I claim is this—that in withholding the truth no deception should be practised, and that if sacrifice of the truth be the necessary price for obtaining the object, no such sacrifice should be made."[65]

Hooker followed his book on *Physician and Patient* with another on *Lessons from the History of Medical Delusions*, which was based on the earlier book. It was a probing indictment of the delusions underlying many "conjectures" in medicine and the remedies of quackery, which can be believed by well-meaning physicians and patients alike. This book, together with an earlier pamphlet on why the community of physicians is not respected, presented a theory of error and truth in medical belief as well as "a true and full picture of medical delusions" and arguments against medical secrecy.[66] In effect, Hooker presented a philosophical attempt to protect patients from the delusions that were (often quite honestly) presented as if they were medical truths.

He argued that even the most informed patients and physicians are at times blinded by the hope of a remedy, even though prudent judgment suggests its inefficacy. His chief example was Bishop Berkeley, one of the great minds of the eighteenth century who somehow committed even elementary inductive fallacies in his enthusiasm for the virtues of Tar Water.[67] Hooker made the valuable observation that the judgment of physicians in making recommendations, no less than the patient's in

receiving them, are subject to serious distortions and need to be checked
by sober sources whenever there is an underlying enthusiasm for a remedy. One of the many "dispositions" to error that he catalogued is
expressed as follows:

> *The disposition to adopt exclusive views and notions* . . . gives to its pos-
> sessor the character of a *one idea man.* . . .
>   The way in which this disposition leads to error is this. A physician
> has his attention directed to a particular set of facts. He becomes
> intensely interested in them. They fill the field of his mental vision, and
> he becomes in a measure blind to other facts. He now not only gives to
> his favorite facts an undue importance, but his imagination invests
> them with hues that do not belong to them.[68]

Hooker defended his views with more exacting and extensive argument than any writer in medical ethics in the nineteenth century.
Though by far the best-argued of all the major treatises, his may have
also been the least listened to on the subject. Katz's neglect of the Rev.
Gisborne and of Hooker is not surprising because their impact was slight.
However, his omission of them is unfortunate, because they better than
any other figures fit few of his generalizations about the nineteenth century. Hooker is a compelling counterexample to any claim that a Percivallian beneficence model entirely controlled the great works of the
nineteenth century. Hooker is, indeed, strikingly reminiscent of Katz in
his eloquent championing of patients' rights.

Unlike Hooker's, Percival's ideas had met with early and widespread
approval by others in the profession in the United States, even prior to
1847. By 1833 his code had been accepted as the basis of medical conduct in medical societies in Boston, Washington, New York, Ohio, and
Maryland.[69] By 1855 many state societies had voluntarily adopted the
AMA code, and the goal of making it a truly national code was nearly
achieved.[70] There were dissidents, however. As we shall establish in the
next section, American medicine was facing a challenge of credibility at
the time as a result of impostors and quacks, and the gentlemanly code
of Percival was not uniformly viewed as the most efficacious way to
achieve credibility. State medical societies had therefore often written
codes that dissented from the AMA's in at least modest ways.

In the 1870s the Massachusetts Medical Society appointed a commission to work on its code of ethics over a two-year period. In 1880, two
versions were presented. The *minority* version—written by Henry J.
Bigelow of Boston—was approved. Bigelow stated that the majority
code, which was modeled after the prevailing AMA code, contained

> sections from every code which ever existed. It is mediaeval, prehis-
> toric. . . . It includes sections taken from codes written in times of
> rapacity between medical men; in times when doctors fought in the
> consultation room. It contains no appeal to high motives.[71]

Despite the provocative rhetoric, Bigelow's code also failed to address the *moral rights* of patients, other than their right to skillful professional treatment. It contained, moreover, but one sentence about veracity: The physician "should neither permit needless apprehension, nor fail to give seasonable notice of danger."[72] This purportedly progressive code was far from revolutionary, but in this respect it is typical of the nineteenth-century codes, in which there is little more than an unanalyzed general recognition that truthtelling can both inflict and prevent harm, but without recognition of *informed consent* issues.

The Medical Society of the State of New York was also at this time in partial revolt from the AMA and drafted its own simplified system of medical ethics, which was adopted by the membership. But as a consequence in June 1882 delegates from this Medical Society were refused admission to the AMA National Meetings in St. Paul. Partially as an attempt to persuade the New York Society to reenact the national code, in 1883 Austin Flint published an incisive and constructive commentary on this code.[73] His *Medical Ethics and Etiquette* shines as the most carefully reasoned work in the late nineteenth century, more probing than any since Hooker.[74] He introduced careful distinctions between moral rules with "moral weight" and medical etiquette, which is merely a matter of convention.

Although a little gem of a treatise in its own right, Flint's commentary also exhibits the capture of the nineteenth century by Percival's vision. Flint argued that all members of the AMA were morally bound to the AMA code, which he viewed as "but justice to the memory of an excellent English physician."[75] In a comment on Section 4 of the code, which deals with disclosures to patients and family, Flint reiterated the typical nineteenth-century view that physicians should err, if a judgment must be made, "on the bright side," and that "it is a duty always to encourage patients as much as the circumstances of the case will allow." He maintained further that "unfavorable events which may be apprehended should not be referred to in the hearing of the patient, although it may be judicious to mention them to friends, in order that they be not taken by surprise, and attach blame to the physician for concealment." If asked a blunt question, Flint counseled, it should be answered correctly, but wrapped in such wording as "not to exclude hope." He also argued that the physician must not shrink from the duty to disclose, with discretion and tact, serious danger and possibility of death. Neither the consent of nor consultation with the patient is anywhere mentioned.[76]

In the same year that Flint's book was published, Nathan Davis—perhaps the most renowned exponent of the AMA code—predicted that Percival's principles, lasting as they had for almost 100 years, "will probably continue to be the guide of the great mass of intelligent medical men through the centuries to come."[77] His statement turned out to be remarkably accurate. It may be that today's medical students have never heard of Percival, but from that it does not follow that they are not immersed by their training in his general point of view. Although the American Medical Association revised its code in 1903, 1912, 1947, 1957, and 1980, up until the 1980 revision the viewpoint on the patient-physician relationship remained largely unchanged. Even the 1957 revision, which represented a substantial departure in *format* from the code accepted by the AMA in 1847, was described by the AMA's Council on Constitution and Bylaws as preserving every basic principle of the earlier code.[78]

The extent to which the 1980 revision of the AMA code represents a departure from the main lines of Percival's legacy is not easy to determine. This revision includes injunctions to physicians to deal honestly with patients and to respect the rights of patients. It was intended in part "to seek a proper and reasonable balance between professional standards and contemporary legal standards in our changing society,"[79] a goal undoubtedly influenced by the emergence of the legal doctrine of informed consent and related currents in medical ethics. We will return to this issue in later sections of the chapter that focus on the interaction between legal developments and contemporary medical ethics. As we note in these sections, it is unclear whether the aforementioned injunctions in the 1980 code are interpreted by physicians as Percival interpreted the obligations of disclosure and truthfulness or as genuine autonomy rights. What is clear is that Percival's views enjoyed remarkable staying powers.

The Tradition of Medical Beneficence

We can now draw this examination of traditional codes and treatises to a conclusion. We have used the language of "disclosure" and "truthfulness" in order to interpret admonitions and guidelines in the works surveyed. Writers such as Pernick use the same texts as evidence of *consent*. We have resisted this inference, because these documents do not appear to contemplate consent. Certainly Katz is correct in judging that *informed* consent has always been an alien notion in influential writings in the history of medicine and medical ethics. More pervasive are Hippocratic and Percivallian principles that physicians ought not harm patients by revealing their condition too abruptly and starkly, a clear appeal to the beneficence model. Although consent-seeking practices and rudimentary rules for obtaining consent in surgery have been present throughout at least the last 150 years of American history, the more parsimonious explanation for these practices would appeal to practical and clinical necessity, medical reputation, and the demands of decency more than an overt moral concern for the *autonomy* of patients. Informed consent as a practice of *respecting autonomy* has *never* had a sure foothold in medical practice, as both Katz and Pernick would agree.

The writings of pre-twentieth century medical ethics may today seem like curious relics, indefensible under the scrutiny of pure distanced reason. This would, however, be an intolerably provincial point of view if it were directed specifically at medicine, as though that profession were simply wrapped in a cocoon of isolated self-protectionism. The greatest British moral philosophers of the period were locked in moral harmony with the physicians.When Percival was examining the Rev. Gisborne's stern admonitions on truthfulness, he consulted the leading British moral authority of the eighteenth century in philosophy, Francis Hutcheson. (Hume and Reid had yet to achieve a similar status in British philosophy.) Percival was delighted to find Hutcheson teaching that deception is often the manifestation of a virtue rather than an injury:

> No man censures a physician for deceiving a patient too much dejected, by expressing good hopes of him; or by denying that he gives him a proper medicine which he is foolishly prejudiced against: the patient afterwards will not reproach him for it.—Wise men allow this liberty to the physician in whose skill and fidelity they trust: Or, if they do not, there may be a just plea from necessity.[80]

Lest it be thought that this was a convenient moral idiosyncrasy of Hutcheson, we may turn to the most careful and probing British moral philosopher of the nineteenth century, Henry Sidgwick, in whose writings we find a similar, though less sweeping, opinion: "Where deception is designed to benefit the person deceived, Common Sense seems to not hesitate to concede that it may sometimes be right: for example, most persons would not hesitate to speak falsely to an invalid, if this seemed the only way of concealing facts that might produce dangerous shock; nor did I perceive that any one shrinks from telling [certain] fictions to children."[81] Hooker, a physician whose *general* moral theory was strikingly similar to Sidgwick's, would have been shocked by the "any one." He had devoted a large section of his work on truthfulness to rebutting this very point (as applied to children). But we have seen that Hooker's views were overshadowed by the towering figures and embedded practices of his time.

Before we reach to condemn the opinions of any of these figures in light of contemporary views about the moral necessity of informed consent, it is well to remember that informed consent was not then and is not today a matter whose necessity should be insisted upon in *all* contexts or whose justification is easily established. Much that a physician does, to many a patient's eternal gratitude, is to benefit the sick. It is therefore understandable why physicians have always been greatly under the influence of the beneficence model in determining obligations of truthfulness and disclosure. The autonomy model is, in the light of history, still a novel, provocative, and even radical idea. Yet we shall see that it *is* the idea that underlies the movement to informed consent.

In the works we have examined there was not a single recommendation to obtain *consent* or to respect autonomy for the sake of autonomy. Although Hooker came close, even he did not fall fully under what we have called the *autonomy* model, for he was concerned with disclosure and truthtelling rather than autonomous decisionmaking and consent-seeking. While Percival used the language of "respect," he inverted its present-day use in medical ethics: The virtues of the physician were aimed at instilling the *patient's* respect, gratitude, and confidence in the physician. Percival was devoted to the *welfare* of the sick patient, but the *autonomy* of the patient was not his objective.

American Medical Practices in the Nineteenth and Early Twentieth Centuries

The nineteenth century and the early twentieth century witnessed a rapid expansion in medicine. However, little that was imaginative in the way of published codes and writings or theoretical reflection on the ethics of the profession or the doctor-patient relationship appeared other than the codes and writings examined above. During this period physicians were preoccupied with professional standards of care and with fending off threats to their reputation presented by medical "quackery," which many in the *public* believed no more dangerous than regular medicine. The focus on quackery had from the beginning of the AMA been intentionally packaged as part of its medical ethics. Thus, John Bell, in presenting the first original Code of Ethics to the 1847 AMA Convention, stressed the importance of the obligation "to bear emphatic testimony against quackery in all its forms." The preceding years had been a time when few methods of treatment were standard and open skepticism prevailed about American medicine. Sects advocating different treatment philosophies abounded, as did public confusion about medicine. In response, practitioners of "regular" or "allopathic" medicine sought to shore up both its public standing and its professional standards.[82]

The turn of the century coincided with an active period for the publication of ideas about proper conduct in medical journals, debates in medical societies, and the fashioning of appropriate ways for physicians to relate to patients and the public. Percival, the 1847 code, and the support of medical societies, as well as such writers as Flint, had produced some degree of unity and self-regulation in the profession, and more was to come.[83] Perhaps the safest generalization about medicine at this time is that although routine consent to consequential interventions such as surgery existed, practices of benevolent deception and nondisclosure shaped the professional norm of standard practice, and benevolent deception in the obtaining of consent was not unusual. The connection between *consent* and *autonomy* had yet to be made.

Cases of Consent and Refusal

Pernick has provided evidence from routine medical and surgical case records to show that patients' desires to undergo or not undergo surgery were routinely acknowledged, and that many refusals to give consent to surgery were heeded.[84] This, together with case law, is his primary evidence of "indigenous" consent-seeking practices. This evidence merits special review.

Available Documentary Evidence. Pernick sets out to study the "behavioral values that were transmitted through the example of daily medical practice."[85] His evidence is drawn from the following: (1) Surgical Records of the Massachusetts General Hospital from 1840–41, 1845–47, 1854–55, 1859–60, and 1866–67; (2) Surgical Records of the New York Hospital, 1845–46, 1847–48, 1854–55, 1859–60; (3) the Fracture Books of the Pennsylvania Hospital, 1852–69. From an examination of these materials—all surgical—and related nineteenth-century materials such as case law, Pernick concludes that: "Even when the surgeons judged an operation essential to save a life, a patient's objections could usually prevent the procedure."[86] Furthermore, "nineteenth-century doctors and judges . . . concurred that surgeons should be held to a medically [i.e., beneficence-] based standard of informed consent."[87] "Surgeons" is an important restriction, because Pernick does not extend his thesis about surgical consent to consent in internal medicine. Pernick apparently means no more than that patients could refuse treatments and that they had legal rights to compensation for malpractice.

Pernick also studies the introducton of anesthesia as a medical procedure. He maintains that "the mid-nineteenth century introduction" of surgical anesthesia "clearly violated nineteenth-century standards of informed consent" and reveals many cases of surgeons operating "without the patient's knowledge or consent." But he also holds that "some surgeons opposed these infringements of patient autonomy" and that patients did in some cases have their "own way."[88]

These arguments are valuable, although we must be cautious in weighing the claims about autonomy. In order to test further the prevalent practices in medicine in the nineteenth century, we surveyed medical case reports during the same period Pernick surveyed hospital records. The value of this body of evidence has gone largely unappreciated in contemporary biomedical ethics, but information about actual *consent practices* or lack thereof in the nineteenth century can probably be better inferred from medical records such as those surveyed by Pernick and by published medical case reports, medical commentary on malpractice, and legal counsel offered to doctors than from the broad, general pronouncements in the various medical codes and writings surveyed in the previous section.

We cannot here provide a comprehensive survey of these sources, and legal considerations are put off until Chapter 4. Instead we shall confine attention to early cases reported in the *Boston Medical and Surgical Journal*, which had been published since 1828 by the Massachusetts Medical Society—a body with considerable influence in the nineteenth century because of the prominence of the New England medical establishment. The Massachusetts Society's pronouncements were widely disseminated through this journal, which a century later would become the *New England Journal of Medicine*. (This *Journal* was the *New England Journal of Medicine and Surgery* until 1828, when it was continued as Vol. I of the *Boston Medical and Surgical Journal*. We shall hereafter refer to it in abbreviated form as the *Boston Journal* or the *Journal*.)

The detailed case descriptions disseminated in this *Journal* were predominantly taken from records of patients admitted to the Massachusetts General Hospital. Some case reports, however, came from private practitioners or were reprinted from foreign publications. These reports, which would over the years yield in the pages of this *Journal* to more theoretical and empirical essays about medical science, were distinguished from the beginning by their presentation of detail. Often they consisted of transcriptions from the treating physician's diaries, containing daily and even hourly notes. Editorial selection of cases published in the journal was made in accordance with criteria such as the peculiarity of symptoms and the novelty of therapeutic effects. A search for evidence of how treatment recommendations and decisions were made reveals that the style of handling problems of consent was not fixed or routine. On the one hand, physicians did not generally ignore questions from and decisions reached by patients concerning treatment; on the other hand, they did not appear to proceed in accordance with any established formal or informal practices of informing or obtaining consent.

Case Reports in the Boston Journal. In the following representative collection of cases, published between 1829 and 1837 in the *Boston Journal*, striking examples of this variation in practice are found. Some generalizations, which generally accord with Pernick's empirical conclusions, may be offered about these cases. Still, we shall argue that any inference of a practice of informed consent is tenuous both *conceptually* and *empirically*. Our method was to survey every issue of this *Journal* during these years, after which detailed case reporting became progressively less common. We examined the medical and surgical cases, with an eye to procedures of agreement and consent.

The majority of cases in these volumes reveals nothing whatever about the way treatment decisions were made, even in the case of surgical case descriptions. The evidence often reveals little or nothing about disclosure and consent practices, although some cases explicitly indicate a consent solicitation, and others an entire dismissal of disclosure and consent, such that the decision was made by the physician without consulting the patient.

An example of the latter is the following case: A "very heavy" woman had fallen and severely fractured both bones of her right leg. A question arose regarding the necessity of amputation. The *Journal* reported: "Dr. W. therefore resolved to take the responsibility of allowing the limb to remain, without suggesting to the patient the question of amputation; and this opinion was concurred in by Dr. S." The patient was an adult who was described as "of much fortitude, and a strong religious confidence." Nonetheless, her physician explicitly assumed decisional authority. As Pernick properly notes, this behavior may be explained in part by the nineteenth-century view that women patients were less capable of making reasoned decisions about medical treatment.[89]

Other cases, however, provide evidence that physicians sometimes respected their patients' preferences, and in particular, their decisions to refuse medical treatment. Although no conclusion is possible about whether these decisions were solicited or whether they were based on true and adequate information, these cases provide persuasive evidence both of attempts to gain consent and of disagreement between patient and physician.[90] In one case, the patient "showed [a small tumor below her right knee joint] to a physician . . . who . . . proposed to remove it, but patient would not consent. He made some applications and left her."[91] In another report: "As the young man [presenting with a strangulated hernia] did not readily consent to an operation, a bag of pounded ice and salt was directed to be applied. . . . About sunrise, on Monday morning, he consented to an operation, as I had repeatedly advised through the night."[92]

Many case reports conclude with language like the following: "I advised her to go into the Hospital. She did not do this . . . I lost sight of her."[93] "[A]s I could not in any way overcome her objections," treatment was not performed,[94] and "as the patient . . . persisted in returning to her service, she was discharged."[95] These passages afford evidence that some patients received information and made decisions that were at least *tolerated*.

Better evidence of consent-*seeking*, as opposed to merely respecting patients' refusals, is given by the following example: A hydrocephalic baby, whose head circumference had continuously increased in size since birth, was seen at two months as "a fair case for the operation advised and practiced by continental surgeons. It was early proposed to the parents, but I could not obtain their consent without the promise that an improved state of health would follow from its performance. I visited the child occasionally until its death, which took place six months from the birth."[96] This example is interesting because it deals with a parental decision on behalf of a child, so that there could be no claim that deception was beneficial to the patient's health. In addition, although deception would apparently have induced parental consent, it was not attempted.

Fully developed informed consent language, evidencing both purposeful disclosure of information and an invitation to autonomous choice by the patient, seems to be found in other cases. These cases involve not only a discussion of the nature and consequences of the proposed treatment, but also the risks, benefits, and possible alternatives—three disclosure categories that were not explicitly recognized in literature on medical disclosure until legal decisions in the mid-twentieth century.

In one case, a young butcher and horse dealer presented with an aneurism of the carotid artery. "The nature of the disease was fully explained to the patient, who, fortunately, was a man of strong sense and most determined resolution, and, from his employment leading him to study the diseases of horses, there was no difficulty in making him comprehend the dangerous tendency of the disease. He therefore submitted, with perfect confidence, to the proposed plan of treatment." This included bleeding, diet, application of leeches, and digitalis. Several weeks later, under circumstances of continuous deterioration, "the operation was recommended, as the only remaining chance. Its advantages and disadvantages were fairly stated, and the chance of success, although small, made him anxious that it should be performed."[97]

To a man whose nose was destroyed as a result of an accident and who was considered a good candidate for rhinoplastic surgery:

> [T]he difficulties of such an operation as would be required were distinctly stated to him, the improbability of its succeeding so as to restore the organ in such a manner that the deformity should not be known, that the new nose might become very flattened, and perhaps on the appearance of cold weather gangrene might take place, and finally, that even his life might be endangered by it. I felt it my duty to state the case plainly, having seen all these accidents occur from the operation and death in two cases. . . . Notwithstanding all these objections, he said that he was ready to incur any risk which would give him the least chance of having the deformity under which he labored obviated, as life in this present state was hardly desirable.[98]

In another case, a 38-year-old mother of ten children presented with vaginal discharge and abdominal pain: "An examination was made per vaginam, and the source of all the trouble [cancer] at once detected. She was apprised of her situation, and of what she might expect to ensue. . . . The patient, after being fully apprised of the *danger* and *uncertainty* of an operation, was left to consult her own feelings, and submit or not as she chose."[99]

Finally, consider a case of a woman with polypous disease of the vagina: "I informed the patient of the nature of the case; that the foundation of her difficulties was the diseased structure in the vagina, and that no plan of general treatment would be successful until that was removed; that it was possible something might be done by astringent and stimulating applications to the part, but that the ligature afforded the most probable chance of success. The former mode, being most congenial to the patient's feelings and those of her friends, as well as my own present views of the case, was adopted." Four weeks later, the physician states, "I now . . . urged the removal of the polypous by ligature. To this the patient's friends were opposed and she would not submit. I was therefore forced to abandon the object."[100]

Although sketchy, these case reports of actual practice reveal that at least some sincere, and detailed, attention was paid to consent-seeking. However, nothing can be fairly concluded about the perceived *justification* for these practices. Was the patient's choice respected for the sake of autonomy, or because disclosure provided some medical benefit for the patient, or because the proposed intervention required the patient's active cooperation, or because disclosure was commonly practiced or consent legally required? As we noted earlier, in light of the near exclusive influence of the beneficence model in the medical etiquette and ethics of the period, the more parsimonious explanations for these consent practices would not include respect for the autonomy of patients as a likely justification. Other explanations, more consonant with the prevailing viewpoint of organized medicine and with the pronouncements of leading figures of medical authority, are readily available and more plausible.

Still, in most examples we found, respect for the patient's refusal outweighed medical concern about the harms and risks of the choice made—that is, the beneficence model was not always employed to *override* the patient's wishes. Indeed, respect for the patient's refusal led, quite foreseeably, to a fatal outcome in several cases. Whether it was beneficence, patients' demands, rules of etiquette, physicians' public welfare concerns, or respect for autonomy that shaped these early consent practices, at least one conclusion seems supportable about formal policies: Neither the AMA nor the courts had so affected practice that a uniform policy pervaded the clinic.

Later Cases and Commentary. After the period examined thus far, case reports, though still an important constituent of medical publications, became briefer and less personal. They took on a more technical character as the influence and success of scientific knowledge in medicine began to increase; as a result, they provided much less information about the character of doctor-patient interactions and consent practices. At about this same time, *Boston Journal* articles reflecting major developments related to medicine and current professional concerns began to complain about the growing problem of malpractice lawsuits.[101] It was even suggested that surgeons, who were victims of the most common suits for orthopedic injuries, should refuse to treat strangers without obtaining from them "a bond covenanting not to sue for damages if deformity or permanent loss of use in a limb should follow. . . ."[102]

Journal articles in the first third of the twentieth century continued to complain regularly about the still-increasing number of suits against physicians. A 1929 legal commentary in the *New England Journal of Medicine* reported that "about once every four days some patient makes a

claim against a physician, seeking legal redress for alleged malpractice."[103] This was a first wave of the "malpractice crisis" that was to crest
in the 1970s.

Physicians' responses in this earlier period foreshadowed some modern views of the role of consent-seeking and communication with
patients, in an attempt at discouraging suits. In 1934 physicians were
urged to "Secure consent before you operate. . . . In major operations
the patient is under complete anesthesia. The physician may discover
conditions not anticipated before the operation was commenced and
which if not remedied will endanger life or health. In such cases he may,
and perhaps in aggravated cases must, remove the newly discovered danger, but it is always wise to get consent to this action. . . . It is a principle
of law that one's body is not to be mutilated in any manner except by
one's consent."[104] Even more explicit was Frederic Cotton's (1933)
instruction to his colleagues: "Signature of a paper stating the understanding of the kind of treatment proposed, the risks involved, the necessary limitations in case of success, even the chance of partial failure,
seems to have no argument against it, though rarely used. It would seem
wise as minimizing the chance of honest misunderstanding."[105] Cotton
also warned that "in regard to operations, the scheme of having a patient
sign away his rights as to the results is legally invalid and may be a
boomerang."[106]

In addition to the realization that consent-seeking practices can operate as a potential shield against malpractice suits by "minimizing the
chance of honest misunderstanding," the possibility of legal liability for
failure to obtain consent itself slowly dawned on American medicine. A
most interesting report from the *Boston Journal* constitutes an example
of the legal dilemma of whether consent should be treated as an ordinary
issue of medical custom or as authorizing what would otherwise be
"assault and battery." This 1848 report of a "failure to obtain consent
case" was depicted as a curiosity, a "trial of a novel character." Under
the headline "Trial of a Physician for Assault and Battery,"[107] the report
described the New Hampshire case of *Delaware* v. *Gale*, in which a
woman brought charges against her male accoucheur for touching her
during labor. At that time, the presence of men during labor and delivery
was regarded as improper and indelicate in many circles of society.[108]
Plaintiff testified that Dr. Gale

> commenced making an assault upon me by placing his hands upon my
> person. I had labor pains occasionally and at intervals of a quarter and
> a half hour, he renewed his assaults, by placing his hands upon my per-
> son. At these different times, I told the doctor to let me alone and go
> away, but he did not. . . . The doctor *did not ask my consent* to make
> an examination."[109]

Several doctors were called for the defense and testified that Dr.
Gale's conduct was "not different from the usual practice on such occa-

sions." The court found that the defendant had performed his professional duty and had not committed any "offense whatsoever," and ordered him to be discharged from criminal custody. The *Journal* viewed the "case alluded to [as] a new mode of harassing the profession . . . with not exactly the same object in view [as a malpractice suit]—as criminal punishment, instead of pecuniary damages, was the penalty anticipated." Criminal battery charges like the one brought in this case were rare, and the *Journal* concluded that such suits were "not likely to succeed, and we may therefore hardly expect a repetition of the attempt."

The *Journal's* estimate might be ascribed to the belief that medically beneficial "battery" would not appear reprehensible to juries. In a comprehensive report on malpractice by George Gay that appeared in the *Journal* in 1911, the following case report addressed this issue: A man had crushed his leg "beyond repair" but vigorously refused to consent to the advised amputation.[110] Gay reported: "Legal advice as to our duty was taken, and we were assured that so long as the patient had his senses, he had the right to refuse any and all methods of treatment of whatever nature. On the other hand, should an operation be performed in accordance with the dictates of common humanity, but contrary to the patient's consent and orders, the operator might be called upon to defend his action in court. The probabilities were that under the circumstances no jury would render a verdict for the plaintiff. . . . [N]o operation was done in this case and the man died in two or three days."[111]

This patient's physicians knew that, as the *Gale* case showed, they would be highly unlikely to *lose* a lawsuit (whether brought by the patient or by the state) if their treatment saved him. Yet they declined to treat him because even if they succeeded, charges could still be brought against them for either civil or criminal battery, and they would have to defend in court to win. The duty to obtain consent here had a double import—as a legal duty in itself and as protection against suit. Gay said: "Everyone knows it to be a well-established fact that a person in his right mind has a right to decide as to whether any operation shall be performed upon himself."

Gay also discussed an unreported case of a brakeman who sued his physician for amputation of his crushed arm. The brakeman said he had not given consent (although he had allegedly given his oral consent in the presence of "three physicians and a nurse"). The judge argued that "Consent . . . of an individual must be either expressly or impliedly given before a surgeon may have the right to operate upon his patient. But consent may be expressed or implied."[112] The patient's right to consent was paired by Gay with a set of concerns about legal protection. He suggested the need for written consent, consultation with another physician, and formal records. He also urged that "careful and explicit explanations of the nature of serious cases, together with the complications liable to arise and their probable termination, . . . be given to the patient . . . for our own protection."[113]

Secrecy, Benevolent Lying, and the Politics of Protection

Well into the first decade of the twentieth century, there were no prevalent or established canons or practices governing either the disclosure of information to or the consent of patients, let alone *informed* consent. Nonetheless, throughout this period there existed, as something of a distracting surrogate, a powerful struggle over the suppression of information. A disdainful skepticism among patients about the worth and credentials of doctors, leading to extensive physician-hopping, motivated physicians to devise methods for gaining the trust of their patients.

Whereas we might today regard honest and careful communication as the most appropriate means to the end of trust, the favored route in the late nineteenth and early twentieth centuries seems to have been the concealment of information that might give rise to questions about competence or that might lead the patient to seek another physician. The rationalizing argument was used that concealment of information was necessary because the patient's hope and consequent recovery might otherwise be seriously retarded.[114] The traditional exhortation to instill hope in patients, while concealing the bad news, was conveniently harnessed to the exigencies of protecting the physician's reputation. This was no environment in which informed consent could flourish.

In historical perspective, these practices are quite understandable. Disagreements within a bitterly divided profession of medicine resulted in constant controversy over what constituted medical knowledge. This controversy stilled the development of moral or legal requirements, because any such requirements and their enforcement entailed favoring one sect's account of what qualified as "information." The information seeker was forced to shop in the medical marketplace for information; yet, somewhat paradoxically, those very market forces encouraged physicians who valued certain medicines to suppress information about them, in order to protect both the doctor's reputation and the patient's welfare.[115]

The other side of this problem was that patients not infrequently accused their physicians of blatant deception, especially in the prescribing of drugs with undesirable side effects. These circumstances gave rise to suits for assault and battery as well as fraud and negligence, which the press regularly reported.[116] This apparent trend is counterbalanced by evidence that many physicians opposed such practices and were engaged in either moral or political campaigns to reform them.

Late in his career, Richard C. Cabot looked back on his relationships with patients as a young physician at the turn of the century: "As a young physician I tried the usual system of benevolent lying from 1893–1903. About that time a bitter experience convinced me that I could not be . . . a philanthropic liar in medicine or in any part of my life. I swore off and have been on the water wagon of medical honesty ever since."[117] This reference to the "usual system" supports, although it hardly confirms, the virtual absence of anything resembling informed consent in medicine. (Hooker said essentially the same thing in 1849.) Cabot himself is not a good example from which to generalize about standard practice, because he was well known for his independence, inflexible devotion to truth, personal disinterestedness, and pioneering spirit. He had also taken up a serious study of philosophy, where he developed a fondness for Immanuel Kant's absolutism on matters of truthtelling, although he himself never fully succumbed to absolutism.[118] Katz interprets Cabot's work as "unparallelled in the medical literature" and as constituting a "radical break" with Enlightenment figures such as Gregory and Rush, but we have seen that this thesis is questionable.[119] Gisborne a century earlier and Hooker a half century earlier had held similar views. Moreover, Cabot's recommendations no more amounted to informed consent than did theirs.

The more typical physicians of the time—especially those who were politically active—were preoccupied with serious struggles over how to handle problems of medical secrecy. Numerous issues arose regarding how to frame rules of confidentiality of information given to physicians by patients, how to monitor the prevalent practice of concealing information about fellow physicians in malpractice cases, how to foster devotion in patients, how to control misrepresentation in advertising by physicians, whether to suppress theoretical disagreements among physicians, and how much information consultants should (or should be allowed to) disclose to patients. In each of these areas, suppression of information had gained a strong foothold in practice. These were the struggles of the period over the management of information, and they were little more than surface skirmishes with problems of informed consent.[120]

In short, in the late nineteenth century and on through the period in which the AMA revised its code in 1903 and 1912, the profession was almost wholly consumed with the politics of regulation, the competition presented by quacks and sects, its public image, and its professional standards of care. The profession had tried to control its members with the 1847 moral code, an effort that had been a mixed success. In the early twentieth century the profession turned to legal regulation, where it found greater success in controlling both the practice of medicine and the marketing of drugs and "cures." Furthermore, persistent efforts at the reorganization of medical schools by the AMA and Abraham Flexner's influential 1910 study produced a major revolution in professional standards and education.

At this point, just before the Great War (World War I), the earlier emphasis on moral codes and reflective treatises on medical ethics began to wane. Legal regulation, an enhanced medical education, and specialization were ushered in as the proper ways to combat threats to the profession. The diminution in attention to "ethics" that ensued was no great loss in the minds of many persons interested in seeing regulations with teeth. After about 1912, physicians in American medicine were increasingly interested in avoiding schisms, unifying medicine, and protecting the status quo. In the wake of its near-fragmentation into fractious sects, medicine was on its way to monopoly. Codes of ethics either went unrevised or declined in influence in the process.

In medicine, as in all of the disciplines that might have made a contribution to medical ethics, interest flagged. Moral philosophy had been one of the premier courses throughout undergraduate curricula in the nineteenth-century American university; in the early years of the twentieth century, however, ethics was increasingly a specialized academic discipline within philosophy. Worse still for any impact the discipline might have had on medicine, the idea flourished of examining ethics by using a scientific, value-free methodology. One was to analyze ethics, not preach it. Academic respectability and a quasi-scientific status were thought to be achieved only by objectivity, distance, and rigorous methods of analysis that had become inaccessible to anyone outside of philosophy.

Normative ethics, then, was losing its grip on both medicine and philosophy, where value-free inquiry and professional specialization were on the rise. The two disciplines had lost significant contact after the heyday of Enlightenment figures such as Rush and Gregory. There was no longer the intellectual or social climate needed to foster an interdisciplinary effort or to encourage medical societies to continue to make carefully reasoned ethical pronouncements. The law was beginning to weave its garment of requirements of consent—ultimately of informed consent—but there was stillness in medicine and moral philosophy.

The Arrival of Informed Consent

"Informed consent" first appeared as an issue in American medicine in the late 1950s and early 1960s. Prior to this period, we have not been able to locate a single substantial discussion in the medical literature of consent and patient authorization. For example, from 1930 to 1956 we were able to find only nine articles published on issues of consent in the American medical literature.[121] Medical ethics and medical policy—as reflected in codes, treatises, and actual practices—were almost entirely developed within the profession of medicine, which was little distracted by canons of disclosure and consent. However, shortly after the middle of the twentieth century, a major transformation occurred: The influential forces and documents in ethics and policy began to take on *external* roots. Sometimes these external influences were greeted as an unwanted alien forced on medicine; but in other quarters of medicine they were greeted with open admiration.

Of these influences, the most prominent from the perspective of informed consent were case law and a revitalized, interdisciplinary medical ethics. In fairness, the emerging legal doctrine of informed consent—the term was coined in case law in 1957—must be credited with first bringing the concept of "informed consent" to the attention of the medical community. However, within short order, informed consent was lifted from this narrow legal base by a new medical ethics and placed in the center of a debate about decisional authority and the doctor-patient relationship, a debate still underway.

Many hypotheses could be invoked to explain why and how case law and medical ethics came to address informed consent in medical care beginning in the late 1950s, and also why and how law and ethics influenced each other. Perhaps the most accurate explanation is that law and ethics, as well as medicine itself, were all affected by issues and concerns in the wider society about individual liberties and social equality, made all the more dramatic by increasingly technological, powerful, and impersonal medical care. Although this thesis would be difficult to sustain without situating it in the context of a careful and extensive sociohistorical analysis of the period, it seems likely that increased legal interest in the right of self-determination and increased philosophical interest in the principle of respect for autonomy and individualism were but instances of the new rights orientation that various social movements of the last 30 years introduced into society. The issues raised by civil rights, women's rights, the consumer movement, and the rights of prisoners and of the mentally ill often included health care components: reproductive rights, abortion and contraception, the right to health care information, access to care, human experimentation, and so forth. These urgent societal concerns helped reinforce public acceptance of the notion of rights as applied to health care.

At the same time, the Nazi atrocities and the celebrated cases of abuse of research subjects in the United States raised suspicions about the general trustworthiness of the medical profession. The rise of interest in informed consent in medical care in the second half of the twentieth century may have been as much a result of complex social forces changing the role and status of American medicine as a reaction to specific legal developments. An obvious example is found in the 1972 "Patient's Bill of Rights" of the American Hospital Association. (See pp. 93–95.) This bill was passed in large part because of consumer pressures for better care and facilities, as well as for more appropriate standards of respect. This increased respect was made manifest through provisions calling for recognition of the need to obtain informed consents and to honor refusals of treatment.

In the remainder of this chapter, we refrain from further speculation about the original "causes" of the current interest in informed consent in medical care. It is doubtful that the explanatory causal lines linking informed consent with the social movements of the 1960s and 1970s, case law, medical ethics, and medical technology can be easily untangled. Instead, we concentrate on *when* and *how* informed consent emerged as an issue in medical care, to the relative neglect of *why* questions.

Becoming Informed About Informed Consent: 1957–1972

In Chapter 4 we chronicle the evolution of the legal doctrine of informed consent from its nineteenth- and early twentieth-century roots, through the landmark cases of *Salgo* (1957), *Natanson* (1960), *Canterbury* (1972), and beyond. By comparison to the rather clear lineages in this legal history, the emergence elsewhere in the mid-twentieth century of informed consent in clinical medicine is difficult to trace. There are no historical works on the subject, and, as we shall see, contemporary empirical studies of consent practices and attitudes date only from the late 1960s. It is thus from a meager data base that we attempt to reconstruct when and how informed consent emerged in medicine.

Available evidence points to the courts and the legal profession as spearheading the interest in informed consent found in medicine. Certainly the medical literature leaves traces of this line of descent. The number of articles on issues of consent picks up dramatically beginning in the late 1950s.[122] Not surprisingly, many of these early references report the opinions in *Salgo*, *Natanson*, and less well-known cases tried in other courts.[123] Generally written by lawyers, these reports functioned to alert physicians both to "informed consent" as a new legal development and to potential malpractice risk.

How physicians reacted to the reports of legal developments in the 1950s and 1960s is not well understood, but a handful of empirical studies of informed consent in clinical medicine provides some insights.[124] It is noteworthy that these studies conducted between approximately 1965 and 1970, were done at all. Empirical investigations would not likely have been undertaken if informed consent were not already perceived as a significant issue in the medical care setting. A second point worth noting is that the authors of each of these studies viewed informed consent, in whole or in part, as a *legal* issue or a legal obligation.

The first of these studies was conducted by the lawyer-surgeon team of Nathan Hershey and Stanley H. Bushkoff.[125] The purpose of the study was to determine the extent to which there existed among surgeons a medical practice standard for disclosure like that applied by the courts. As a test of this hypothesis, the study was a failure, largely because the investigators were unsuccessful in securing the cooperation of hospitals and surgeons. Hershey and Bushkoff's account of the problems they encountered in soliciting physician participation is, however, instructive in illustrating the extent to which the surgeons in their sample were suspicious of "informed consent."

Most importantly, we know from their account that the pre-operative consent form was not yet a ubiquitous feature of the practice of surgery. As part of their study, Hershey and Bushkoff required that cooperating surgeons complete a "fill-in-the-blank" consent form for each of their patients. However, surgeons at several hospitals objected to the study because they were not currently using *any* kind of consent form for surgery, a practice virtually unimaginable today. In the end, only ten surgeons, representing but three hospitals, participated in the study. Together, these surgeons provided data on "informed consent" in 256 surgical cases. From this limited sample, Hershey and Bushkoff inferred that a consistent standard of disclosure among surgeons existed and that this standard included a description of the operative procedure and its attendant risks and consequences.

Although the Hershey and Bushkoff study provides some insight into the attitudes and practices of surgeons, a second late-1960s study conducted by law professor Donald Hagman provides a somewhat richer, albeit limited slice into prevailing views and attitudes. This study presents informed consent as an ethical as well as a legal issue. In the study, 379 physicians evaluated 26 cases—some hypothetical and some based on the facts of actual malpractice cases—in terms of the following question: "Was the resolution of the case proper as a matter of good medical practice? As a matter of ethics? As a matter of law?"[126]

Although the cases frequently involved consent issues, physicians' attitudes towards general informed consent requirements were not directly addressed. Still, the physicians' responses to these cases suggest that—at very least—most of the physicians recognized both a moral and a legal duty to obtain patient consent for certain procedures and to provide some kind of disclosure. For example, although 50% of the physicians thought it medically proper for a physician to perform a mastectomy with no authorization from the patient other than her signature on the blanket consent form required for hospital admission, only 30% of the physicians regarded this procedure as ethically proper and only 38% viewed it as legally proper. Similarly, only 31% of physicians thought it was ethically proper and 22% legally proper for a physician soliciting consent to bronchoscopy to fail to tell the patient that he intends to take a biopsy as part of the examination. At the same time, however, when physicians were asked whether it was appropriate for a patient to be told only that an operation was "dangerous"—without disclosing a specific, 25% risk of injury to the mandibular nerve—over half thought that the more general disclosure was medically and ethically proper (58% and 54% respectively); only 29% thought it was legally proper. Perhaps most distressing, from the perspective of contemporary values, was the finding that more than half the physicians (53%) thought that it was ethically appropriate for a physician not to tell a cancer patient that she had been enrolled in a double blind clinical trial of an experimental anticancer drug and was currently receiving a placebo.

The two remaining studies—Ralph Alfidi's study of angiography patients and Carl H. Fellner and John R. Marshall's study of kidney donors—have become classics of the limited empirical literature on informed consent. For our purposes, most noteworthy about these two studies is the starkly different attitudes they expressed toward informed consent.

Fellner and Marshall were openly skeptical about informed consent. Their article, titled "The Myth of Informed Consent," was among the first of a string of commentaries in the medical literature that questioned the meaningfulness of informed consent in medical settings. It is not that Fellner and Marshall *resented* informed consent as a legal intrusion on medical practice. They studied kidney donors, and they clearly believed that the decision to donate is rightfully the potential donor's and that it ought to be based on solid information. Indeed, their study provided good evidence that, at least in organ donation, a process of informing and seeking consent was the conventional practice. However, because the thirty donors in their study did not base their consent decisions on a cost-benefit analysis of medical facts, Fellner and Marshall concluded— rather precipitously—that the decision to become a kidney donor is an "irrational" process that fails to meet the requirements of informed consent.

Alfidi's article, by contrast, served as an empirical "vindication" of informed consent, albeit on a different point. Over 200 angiography patients completed a short questionnaire after having read a consent form describing the risks of the procedure. Because only 2% of the patients refused angiography based on the consent form itself, Alfidi argued that physicians' fears that this new legal requirement would be bad for medicine were exaggerated. Unfortunately, we have no way of knowing how many physicians, if any, found Alfidi's arguments persuasive. We do know that at least one radiologist was outraged by Alfidi's conclusion: Shortly after the publication of Alfidi's results, N.J. Demy published a scathing response, criticizing informed consent as inimical to the moral duty of the physician to take responsibility for the patient's care.[127] Like Fellner and Marshall, Demy questioned the capacities of patients to make the rational and informed decisions necessary for informed consent.

What, then, can be said about informed consent in medicine before the 1970s? On the basis of the volume of commentary in the medical literature, it is likely that many physicians were at least dimly aware of informed consent as an "issue." As to consent practices, the empirical studies suggest that there was at least enough consent-seeking in surgery, organ donation, and angiography to warrant empirical investigation. Also during this period, the procedure-specific consent form was gaining acceptance, although it was not yet universally in use.

As to whether physicians regarded informed consent as a legal nuisance or a moral problem, the picture is partial and unfocused. However, the patterns were soon to become better defined in at least some quarters, in what amounted to an explosion in commentary on informed consent in the medical literature in the early 1970s, with over 250 relevant articles published between 1970 and 1974.[128] This explosion of literature was at least partially stimulated by the 1972 *Canterbury* case and two other cases—*Cobbs* and *Wilkinson*—also decided in 1972 (see pp. 132–137).[129]

Predictably, much medical commentary in the 1970s was negative: Physicians saw the demands of informed consent as impossible to fulfill and—at least in some cases—inconsistent with good patient care. In tone the articles ranged from serious critique[130] to caustic parody.[131]Dire predictions were voiced that fearful patients would refuse needed surgery after disclosure.[132]

In much of this commentary the *moral* dimensions of the legal question of informed consent were not recognized.[133] This began to change in the 1970s. With the ascendancy of a new form of and approach to medical ethics, informed consent in medicine was to become no less a moral than a legal issue.

The Development of a New Medical Ethics

At about the same time that complex developments in case law on informed consent were provoking reactions in the medical community, events at Nuremberg, Helsinki, NIH, and FDA began cumulatively to have a revolutionary impact on research ethics. We do not here recount these developments; they are the staple items in Chapters 5–6. However, they also have an important role in the history now under consideration. Together with *Canterbury* and the other major legal decisions, they were the events, perhaps more than any others, that turned the attention of scholars in law, philosophy, theology, history, and the biomedical and behavioral sciences to issues of informed consent.

During approximately this same period, there were parallel events of importance in medical technology, some with far-reaching implications for public policy. For example, dialysis emerged in Seattle in 1962 with widespread publicity surrounding moral problems in the selection of subjects. This issue spread, later in the 1960s, to kidney and heart transplantation, and was joined with an increasing focus on problems of the right to health care and Medicare. These spectacular biomedical and political developments retrospectively appear to have been necessary although not sufficient conditions of a new era of moral reflection on medicine.

These early eye-catching issues in medical ethics were largely focused on what we called in Chapter 1 issues of *justice*—that is, social justice—rather than issues of autonomy. By contrast, the Nuremberg Code and the whole research tradition, as we shall see in Chapter 5, had been more concerned with autonomy and beneficence; issues of informed consent had therefore quickly surfaced. Clinical medical ethics was slower in coming to this set of concerns, which it absorbed from the literature of research ethics and the emerging legal literature on informed consent and medical malpractice. Thus, informed consent emerged and developed in clinical medical ethics as a set of reflections on the rights of patients that used as its data base legal case materials in malpractice, research ethics materials that emerged after Nuremberg, and new federal policies and regulation.

Once the flood was flowing in the direction of a new medical ethics there seemed no way to stop it, as issues arose from every quarter. Not only the problems already mentioned—that is, the just allocation of medical resources, informed consent, and patients' rights generally— but also abortion, the definition and determination of death, euthanasia and the prolongation of life, the use of behavior control techniques, and genetic intervention and reproductive technologies, all exploded into a massive tangle of problems with special literatures. In the decade from 1962 to 1972, the old ideas of medical ethics began to undergo transformation, so much so that terms like "bioethics," "moral problems in medicine," "biomedical ethics," and the like drowned the term "medical ethics," as if to signal the dawning of a new subject matter in a new era.[134]

The new discipline received its imprimatur with the founding of two institutes of bioethics between 1969 and 1971, and with a resurgence of the teaching of biomedical ethics in this new form in medical schools.[135] In one major respect the new "bioethics" was genuinely new: It was an interdisciplinary field uncontrolled by and heavily distanced from professional medicine.[136]

Contemporary medical ethics and its concerns over consent are the offspring of these recent historical developments, only incidentally descended from older traditions. By the benchmarks we established at the beginning of this chapter (and shall tighten and elaborate in Chapter 8), informed consent was *never* the concern of the great writings and teachings in medicine, theology,[137] or any discipline traditionally addressing the search for moral truths in medicine. Informed consent is a creature originally of law and later snatched from the courts by interdisciplinary interests and spearheaded by an ethics driven more philosophically than theologically.

Ethical treatises directed toward physicians prior to the years around 1972 were less oriented toward anything approximating informed consent than were works that emerged in later years. Although Joseph Fletcher's pioneering *Morals and Medicine* (1954) exhorted physicians to afford patients not only freedom of choice but also "the fullest possible knowledge" of the medical facts and available alternatives, the focus of Fletcher's book was more on the dying patient's "right to know the truth" than on questions of disclosure, consent, or decisional authority. Paul Ramsey's important 1970 volume, *The Patient as Person*, devoted substantial space to the theme of consent as a canon of loyalty, but the focus was dominantly on guardian consent and on the physician's duties of loyalty, fidelity, and mutuality.[138]

Prior to *Canterbury* (1972; see pp. 132–137) and the National Commission for Protection of Human Subjects (1974–78; see pp. 215–219), the ethics community was napping. Books in this field that moved beyond legal issues to a greater focus on the connections between autonomy and informed consent were not to appear for four or five years after *Canterbury*. In 1980, K. Danner Clouser wrote: "During the last ten years, and particularly in the last five, a surprising phenomenon has taken place. There has been an incredible surge of interest in biomedical ethics." This is an entirely accurate statement by one who witnessed the entire flow of developments. Yet Clouser, like most of us, finds it deeply puzzling *why* this phenomenon occurred.[139] What is clear is that informed consent became a major moral problem when it did because it was swept along with a tide of interest in morals and medicine—including issues of disclosure and consent—that began around 1974.

As this "phenomenon" was forming, there occurred a not unrelated social development of importance for informed consent—the adoption of a bill of rights for hospital patients.

The Language of Rights. In 1969 the Joint Commission on Accreditation of Hospitals, a highly influential nongovernmental hospital accrediting association drawing its membership from various medical and hospital groups, issued a new revised policy statement. Little was said in this policy about problems of patients, and the organization was asked by various consumer groups to redraft the statement with an eye toward the concerns of patients. Leading these efforts was the National Welfare Rights Organization, which in June 1970 drafted a statement with 26 proposals for the rights of patients. This seems to have been the genesis of the so-called patients' rights movement. After several months of deliberation and negotiation, some of the 26 proposals were accepted by the Joint Commission on Accreditation of Hospitals as parts of a new preamble statement in its 1970 *Accreditation Manual*. The American Hospital Association then began to debate the issue of patients' rights and adopted "A Patient's Bill of Rights" in late 1972. Shortly thereafter, in January 1973, a commission from the U. S. Department of HEW (now HHS) recommended that health care facilities adopt and distribute such statements in a manner that would "effectively communicate" with patients.[140]

The AHA Patient's Bill of Rights was published in 1973. It was only one, albeit the most influential, of several patients' rights statements to appear in the 1970s.[141] These statements served two distinct functions:

(1) They were a means of reducing the incidence of malpractice claims by reducing the impersonality of, and consequent dissatisfaction of, patients with the modern hospital experience; (2) they met the demands of consumer groups for more accountability from providers.[142] We can only speculate that the reaction by providers to malpractice litigation was the dominant influence on the moves made by hospitals.

Prominent in the various rights statements that appeared are a number of provisions intended to address concerns of informed consent. For example, the AHA Patient's Bill of Rights includes the following statements:

> The patient has the right to obtain from his physician complete current information concerning his diagnosis, treatment, and prognosis in terms the patient can be reasonably expected to understand. . . .
>
> The patient has the right to receive from his physician information necessary to give informed consent prior to the start of any procedure and/or treatment. . . .
>
> The patient has the right to refuse treatment to the extent permitted by law and to be informed of the medical consequences of his action. . . .
>
> The patient has the right to obtain information as to any relationship of his hospital to other health care and educational institutions insofar as his care is concerned.[143]

Documents like this one were potentially reputation builders for their subscribing institutions, providing evidence of their humane concerns to patients whose newly aroused consumer sentiments were making them alert to their rights.[144] To the extent attention was paid by physicians to the various prescriptions concerning patients' rights to disclosure, consent, refusal, confidentiality, and privacy, a near revolutionary departure from traditional Hippocratic benevolence was presented by this document, at least on the surface. For perhaps the first time in any influential document of medical ethics, the physician was compelled, by claim of right, to incorporate patients into the decisionmaking process and to recognize their right to make the final authoritative decision.

Although confined to hospitals and other institutions, the AHA Bill of Rights was one of the earliest signals of the place of an autonomy model in medical practice. The language of this Bill—and generally of the newer, rights-based writings in bioethics—is itself important in this respect. Medical codes and didactic writings had traditionally emphasized the physician's obligations or virtues. Trust rather than commerce was the theme of the relationship. A paternalistic or authoritarian ethics easily flowed from this approach in the context of medicine. But the language of rights abruptly turned the focus in a different (albeit, we argue in Chapter 1, *correlative*) direction. The language of rights is the language of valid entitlement—a demand by some upon the conduct of others.

This emphasis is a new kid on the block in medical ethics. Its tone and connotation carry a message, usually reserved for law, that has never before been a part of physicians' thinking about patients. When turned in the direction of medical decisionmaking, it literally invites the replacement of the beneficence model with the autonomy model.

Curricula and Literature. Although the rights language of the AHA's Bill of Rights was alien to traditional medical ethics, it fit well with the orientation of the newer "biomedical ethics" boom of the 1970s. In the late 1970s, 11 texts in biomedical ethics were published; most of these were targeted for use in courses in the new bioethics and in medical schools, and most had sections or chapters on informed consent.[145] The texts were produced because the market was already growing. Surveys of medical ethics teaching show that nearly all medical schools had some form of medical ethics teaching—however abbreviated—by the mid-to-late 1970s.[146] There are no data on how much teachers' time is actually devoted to informed consent, but this medical ethics instruction—even if minimal—began to present to young physicians the view that informed consent is not merely a legal doctrine, but also a moral right of patients that generates moral obligations for physicians.

The legal perspective on informed consent was also presented to many medical students in the classroom beginning in the 1970s. In a 1978 survey, the overwhelming majority of medical schools reported offering some kind of instruction in medicolegal areas,[147] and informed consent was reported (perhaps with exaggeration) to be the hottest topic in the general area: 66 schools reported offering some form of instruction in "informed consent" in their medicolegal teaching, far more than in any other topic. Moreover, 52 listed themselves as teaching students about the "nature of informed consent" and 51 gave instruction in the related area of the right to refuse treatment.

It is difficult to assess the real magnitude and impact of this exposure to ethics and law. Sometimes, the instruction is limited to a few hours and requires little or no class preparation or participation. Nonetheless, by the 1970s, medical students were at least being told that informed consent exists and that it imposes certain moral and legal responsibilities upon physicians.

At the same time word is spreading in the classroom, it is also surfacing in the medical literature. Earlier we noted that the National Library of Medicine (NLM) had identified 272 citations on informed consent through its computerized retrieval system (MEDLARS) in the period from January 1970 to April 1974. In the next two years (May 1974 to June 1976) NLM identified a whopping 403 citations, and in the years between July 1977 and July 1982, an additional 403 citations.[148] Another computerized literature retrieval system—BIOETHICS LINE—whose data base was expanded beyond MEDLARS to include more periodicals in law, philosophy, theology, and the social sciences, catalogued between 300 and 400 citations in informed consent *every year* in the period from 1974 to 1979. Only one-third of these citations are about informed consent in human experimentation.[149]

An AMA Position. Among the most important of the citations to informed consent in the medical literature to appear during this period was a statement by the Judicial Council of the American Medical Association published in 1981.[150] Earlier we noted that the AMA's code of ethics had undergone a major revision the preceding year (1980). Although this revision for the first time acknowledged the physician's obligation to respect patients' rights, the code did not include any specific reference to informed consent. The AMA's official policy on informed consent appeared the next year, in the form of an opinion from the Judicial Council, which functions as the AMA's core ethics committee.[151] This opinion is particularly noteworthy because it recognizes informed consent as "a basic social policy" necessary to enable patients to make their own choices even if the physician disagrees.[152] Moreover, the opinion is a testament to the impact of the law of informed consent on medical ethics. Closely copying much of the language of *Canterbury* v. *Spence*, the landmark 1972 court decision (see pp. 132–137), the Judicial Council took the following position:

> INFORMED CONSENT.
>
> The patient's right of self-decision can be effectively exercised only if the patient possesses enough information to enable an intelligent choice. The patient should make his own determination on treatment. Informed consent is a basic social policy for which exceptions are permitted (1) where the patient is unconscious or otherwise incapable of consenting and harm from failure to treat is imminent; or (2) when risk-disclosure poses such a serious psychological threat of detriment to the patient as to be medically contraindicated. Social policy does not accept the paternalistic view that the physician may remain silent because divulgence might prompt the patient to forego needed therapy. Rational, informed patients should not be expected to act uniformly, even under similar circumstances, in agreeing to or refusing treatment.[153]

The President's Commission for the Study of Ethical Problems in Medicine and Biomedical and Behavioral Research: 1980–1983. As further evidence of the climate of interest in informed consent one need look no further than the authorization by the U.S. Congress in November 1978 of the President's Commission for the Study of Ethical Problems in Medicine and Biomedical and Behavioral Research.[154] The President's Commission was first convened in January 1980, with informed consent as a main issue. The President's Commission was established to continue the type of work done by the earlier National Commission for the Protection of Human Subjects of Biomedical and Behavioral Research (see Chapter 6, pp. 215–221), which had not considered many ethical issues about medicine and research that were of interest to the general public. The

President's Commission rarely made recommendations about federal policies, which had been the overriding goal of the National Commission. Instead, the President's Commission studied the ethical implications of a number of issues that arose more in the realm of treatment than in research.

The President's Commission ultimately published its findings and conclusions in nine reports, each on a special subject. Other activities and a summary volume were also published. In writing these volumes, "the Commission was instructed to bring ethical analysis of the implications of medical practice and research out of the classrooms, the hospital wards, and the scholarly journals and into a public forum in Washington."[155] These reports stand as model documents in the integration of scholarship and public policy, although they are framework documents rather than attempts to put problems into the language of regulation.

The President's Commission produced one report that dealt directly with informed consent, and another indirectly on the subject: *Making Health Care Decisions: The Ethical and Legal Implications of Informed Consent in the Patient-Practitioner Relationship* (with two appendix volumes of documents, scholarly papers, and empirical research) and *Deciding to Forego Life-Sustaining Treatment*. As its title suggests, the first report focused as much on general issues in medical decisionmaking as on informed consent. The Commission argued that although informed consent has emerged primarily from a history in law, its requirements are essentially moral and policy-oriented, rather than legal. It held that informed consent is ultimately based on the principle that competent persons are entitled to make their own decisions from their own values and goals, but that the context of informed consent and any claim of "valid consent" must derive from active, shared decisionmaking.[156] The principle of self-determination was described as the "bedrock" of the Commission's viewpoint.[157]

In the second report, the Commission built on these conclusions. It used, as an axiomatic premise, the position that decisions about health care must finally rest with competent and informed patients. This premise led straight to the conclusion that the right to autonomous choice includes the choice to forego life-sustaining treatment, thus defeating the normal "presumption in favor of sustaining life." The Commission hypothesized that recognition of this fact could have a pervasive and unsettling effect on hospitals, where such behavior is generally viewed as suspect and disruptive—a view the Commission found an indefensible undermining of "patient self-determination."[158]

The autonomy model seems here to be gaining ascendancy over the beneficence model. Yet, in both volumes the Commission cited two basic values as *fundamental*: self-determination (autonomy) and well-being (beneficence). The Commission never explicitly stated—as did the National Commission—that the *sole* or *primary* value underlying its first-party consent provisions is respect for autonomy, but it repeatedly hinted that this was the case. The following summarizes the Commission's official view:

> The primary goal of health care in general is to maximize each patient's well-being. However, merely acting in a patient's best interests without recognizing the individual as the pivotal decisionmaker would fail to respect each person's interest in self-determination. . . .
> When the conflicts that arise between a competent patient's self-determination and his or her apparent well-being remain unresolved after adequate deliberation, a competent patient's self-determination is and usually should be given greater weight than other people's views on that individual's well-being. . . .
> Respect for the self-determination of competent patients is of special importance. . . . [T]he patient [should have] the final authority to decide.[159]

Practices and Attitudes of Physicians. The efforts of the President's Commission testify to the status informed consent had achieved in moral thinking about medicine. Yet, neither the presence of a federal commission, a statement by the AMA, nor the sheer volume of commentary provides direct information about physicians' actual consent practices or opinions, or about how informed consent is viewed or experienced by patients. Since the 1950s and 1960s, several empirical studies of informed consent in medical care have been conducted, some sponsored by the President's Commission.[160] As might be expected, these studies vary considerably both in terms of the kinds of questions they ask about informed consent and their quality and methodology. They also vary in their findings. Although they do not provide an entirely consistent picture of current consent practices, these studies yield some insights that, duly qualified, are worth noting.

From the perspective of our history, the most important study is the national survey conducted by Louis Harris and Associates in 1982. This survey, commissioned by the President's Commission, interviewed a carefully drawn representative sample of 805 physicians and 1,251 members of the general public.[161] Its results give the impression that obtaining informed consent has become a routine component of American medical practice, particularly for invasive medical procedures. Almost all of the physicians surveyed indicated that they obtained either written consent (over 80%) or *both* written *and* oral consent (about 15%) from their patients before inpatient surgery or the administration of general anesthesia. (Compare these figures with Hershey and Bushkoff's findings or lack thereof in the late 1960s.) At least 85% said they usually obtain some kind of consent—written or oral—for minor office surgery, setting of fractures, local anesthesia, invasive diagnostic procedures, and radiation therapy. Only blood tests and prescriptions appear to proceed frequently without patient consent, although even here about half of the physicians reported obtaining oral consent.[162]

The statistics are almost as impressive on the matter of informing patients, as opposed merely to obtaining their consent. Over 75% of physicians reported that they always or usually explain to their patients the nature and purpose of the recommended treatment, the pros and cons of this treatment versus alternative treatments, the likely side effects, the risks of death or serious disability that have (at least) a 1:100 probability of occurrence, and the probable impact of the treatment on the patient's family life and job. These physician reports differ slightly from patients' perceptions of the informing practices of their own physicians, as assessed in the sample of the general public; 77% of "the public" said their doctor usually or always explains the nature and purpose of the recommended treatment, whereas 68% credit their physicians with regularly disclosing the pros and cons of alternative treatments and likely side effects.[163]

The overall impression conveyed by this survey is that the explosion of interest in informed consent in recent years has had a definite and important impact on medical practice. Although there are no earlier surveys possessing the scope of the Harris study with which its findings can be directly compared, it seems overwhelmingly likely that this amount of informing and consent-seeking was not as characteristic of medicine ten years earlier, or even five years earlier.

It would be inappropriate, however, to exit from these comments without two qualifications: First, there is evidence in the survey data that when physicians report widespread seeking of patient consent, they may have in mind something quite different from what is suggested by the three criteria of informed consent with which we began this chapter. Second, the overall flavor of the results of the Harris survey conflicts in important respects with the findings of other informed consent studies.

Regarding the first point, the most telling data are physicians' responses in the Harris survey to the question "What does the term informed consent mean to you?" In their answers, only 26% of physicians indicated that informed consent had anything to do with a patient's *giving permission, consenting,* or *agreeing* to treatment; only 9% indicated that it involved the patient's making a *choice* or stating a *preference* about his or her treatment. Like lawyers and courts, the overwhelming majority of these doctors appeared to recognize only the information-giving component of informed consent, viewing informed consent as explaining to a patient the nature of his or her condition and treatment, having the patient understand what is taking place.[164] But if informed consent means only *telling* things to a patient, not asking anything (such as permission) of the patient, how are we to interpret claims by physicians that they regularly "obtain consents" from patients before medical procedures?

Perhaps all these physicians understand by "informed consent" is that the patient's signature is obtained on a consent form; perhaps also they mean that some kind of disclosure has been made. This interpretation fits better with the results of other studies of informed consent, which have been more negative. Some studies have failed to find any sizeable evidence of "informed consent" in clinical medicine;[165] other studies have found little evidence that the consents being obtained are meaningful exercises of informed choice by patients.[166]

Conclusion: Everything's Changed, and Nothing's Changed

The findings of the latter studies tend to support Katz's view that informed consent in clinical medicine has more the quality of fairy tale, myth, or mirage than reality.[167] As he sees it, informed consent has done nothing to *change* historical medical practice because informed consent has never really *arrived* in medicine, never really taken hold. Katz is probably both right and wrong about informed consent and clinical medicine. Discounting problems in the evidentiary base, Katz seems right in his thesis that informed consent has not changed the fundamental character of the physician-patient relationship. The lines of authority and control seem roughly to be what we saw them to have been in Percival's time: The beneficence model is overwhelmingly predominant. Patients routinely acquiesce to medical interventions rather than autonomously authorizing them.[168] From this perspective all the changes are surface displays, while below the surface there are no more real "informed consents" than in the past.

At the same time that nothing has changed in medicine, everything has changed. Every day, in hospitals and clinics all over the United States, patients are giving their "informed consents" to surgery, diagnostic procedures, anesthesia, and the like. True, these may be less than substantially autonomous exercises of decisional authority; nevertheless, the practice of medicine has been changed, at least on the surface. Physicians must, at the very least, pay lip service to the rights of their patients to be informed and to consent; they (or the nurses) must introduce the subject and get the form signed. Moreover, we suspect that *many* health care professionals pay more than lip service. In taking their moral and legal obligations to obtain informed consent seriously, they are obtaining *informed consents* that are substantially autonomous decisions.

We have seen in this chapter that basic changes in consent rules and practices are remarkably recent. Informed consent did not become an issue in medicine until the twentieth century, although we have seen evidence of consent-seeking and the respecting of patient refusals in the nineteenth century. Nevertheless, before the mid-twentieth century, the beneficence model, in roughly the form Percival defended in 1803, was the only operative model of the physician's responsibility to the patient. There was no place for informed consent within its domain. As long as the beneficence model remained the unchallenged model for medical ethics—and we have seen that proficient critics such as Worthington Hooker never succeeded in disturbing Percival's vision of the model— physicians were able to rely almost exclusively on their own judgment in the medical management of their patients.

Gradually, external forces began to challenge various assumptions in this model. These forces worked in tandem with widespread social developments. Thus, for example, the Patient's Bill of Rights was connected to various consumer and civil-rights movements that were everywhere demanding increased rights to make free and informed decisions. The result of such developments has been to introduce both confusion and constructive change in American medicine as that profession struggles to meet unprecedented challenges to traditional medical ethics. At the same time, responsibility for fixing the terms of consent requirements has shifted from the physician's turf to that of the wider society.

Amid the convergence of complicated social causes and reasons that may never be properly sifted by historians, it was case law that *introduced* the concept of informed consent to medicine in the mid-twentieth century using the language of "self-determination." Shortly thereafter, informed consent was transformed in a social context beyond law from a malpractice issue to a moral duty incumbent on physicians, one straightforwardly linked to the principle of respect for autonomy. In the next chapter we chronicle the steps in this *legal* history.

Notes

1. Martin S. Pernick, "The Patient's Role in Medical Decisionmaking: A Social History of Informed Consent in Medical Therapy," in President's Commission for the Study of Ethical Problems in Medicine and Biomedicial and Behavioral Research, *Making Health Care Decisions*, (Washington: U.S. Government Printing Office, 1982), Vol. 3, 3.

2. John C. Fletcher, "The Evolution of the Ethics of Informed Consent," in Kare Berg and K.E. Tranoy, eds., *Research Ethics* (New York: Alan R. Liss, 1983), 204. Surprisingly, Jay Katz is cited as one of three supporting references for this claim. No source prior to 1941 is cited by Fletcher in defense of this claim.

3. *Canterbury* v. *Spence*, 464 F.2d 772, 779–80 (D.C. Cir. 1972).

4. Jay Katz, *The Silent World of Doctor and Patient* (New York: Free Press, Macmillan Inc., 1984), 28, 3–4.

5. Ibid., 15, 18.

6. Ibid., 2, 49–50 (emphasis added), 79.

7. Ibid., 28, 1–2.

8. Pernick, "The Patient's Role in Medical Decisionmaking," 3; Katz, *The Silent World*, 60, 82.

9. Pernick, personal communication; see also "The Patient's Role in Medicial Decisionmaking," 2–3, 14, n. 34, 34, n. 100.

10. Ibid., 5. (Italics added.)

11. Katz, *The Silent World*, 60, and "Disclosure and Consent in Psychiatric Practice: Mission Impossible?" in Charles K. Hofling, ed., *Law and Ethics in the Practice of Psychiatry* (New York: Brunner-Mazel, Inc., 1980), 98.

12. Here and in later chapters the discussion of these models is derived from the formulations of them in Tom L. Beauchamp and Laurence McCullough, *Medical Ethics: The Moral Responsibilities of Physicians* (Englewood Cliffs, NJ: Prentice-Hall, Inc., 1984), esp. Chapter 2.

13. Cf. Katz, *The Silent World*, 16f.

14. For a qualification on this claim, see n. 137 below on religious traditions and theological pronouncements.

15. Benjamin Rush, *Medical Inquiries and Observations*, 2nd ed. (Philadelphia: Thomas Dobson, 1794), 1:332. Rush does *not*, however, take the view that the doctrines of religion are either overridden by or properly explicated by philosophy. See, for example, his essay "A Defence of the Bible as a School Book," in *Essays, Literary, Moral and Philosophical* (Philadelphia: Thomas & Samuel F. Bradford, 1798), 105. See also George W. Corner, ed., *The Autobiography of Benjamin Rush* (Princeton: Princeton University Press, 1948), 162–66.

16. Chester R. Burns, "Medical Ethics, History of: North America: Seventeenth to Nineteenth Century," in Warren Reich, ed., *Encyclopedia of Bioethics*, 4 vols. (New York: The Free Press, 1978), 3:963.

17. See Robert M. Veatch, *A Theory of Medical Ethics* (New York: Basic Books, 1981), Part I, esp. Chapter 2.

18. For an analysis of these features, see Ludwig Edelstein, "The Hippocratic Oath: Text, Translation, and Interpretation," *Supplement to the Bulletin of the History of Medicine* 30, Supplement 1 (Baltimore: The Johns Hopkins University Press, 1943); reprinted in Owsei Temkin and C. Lilian Temkin, eds., *Ancient Medicine: Selected Papers of Ludwig Edelstein* (Baltimore: The Johns Hopkins Press, 1967). [Also reprinted in book form as *Hippocrates: The Oath* (Chicago: Ares Publishers, 1943).]

19. Selections from the Hippocratic Corpus, *Decorum*, XVI, in W.H.S. Jones, trans., *Hippocrates*, 4 vols. (Cambridge, Mass.: Harvard University Press, 1923–31), 2:297, 299.

20. For a useful collection of the critical passages, with commentary, see Paul Polani, "The Development of the Concepts and Practices of Patient Consent," in G.R. Dunstan and Mary J. Seller, eds., *Consent in Medicine: Convergence and Divergence in Tradition* (London: King Edward's Hospital Fund, 1983), 59–62; and Edmund D. Pellegrino, "Toward a Reconstruction of Medical Morality: The Primacy of the Act of Profession and the Fact of Illness," *Journal of Medicine and Philosophy* 4 (1979): esp. 35–37.

21. Several authors have noted that the physicians who served free citizens did not treat patients without having persuaded them of the necessity of the proposed intervention, while the physicians of slaves granted their patients no such courtesy. Thus, some consent-seeking practices are thought to have existed during the classical period, although we believe the evidence too tenuous to be reliable. For support of this classical consent hypothesis, see Mark Siegler, in "Searching for Moral Certainty in Medicine: A Proposal for a New Model of the Doctor-Patient Encounter," *Bulletin of the New York Academy of Medicine* 57 (January-February 1981): 56–69. He refers to Plato's *Laws*. A similar view is found in P. Lain Entralgo, *Doctor and Patient*, trans. F. Partridge (New York: McGraw-Hill, 1969), esp. 36ff.

22. See Ivan Waddington, "The Development of Medical Ethics—a Sociological

Analysis," *Medical History* 19 (1975): 36–51. Percival drew similar distinctions. See below.

23. Ilza Veith, "Medical Ethics Throughout the Ages," *AMA Archives of Internal Medicine* 100 (1957): 504–12. William Frankena has argued that the Greeks were not concerned with a "moral" way of life at all, as we now understand the term. Rather, they were interested in "the *rational* way to live." See his *Thinking About Morality* (Ann Arbor: University of Michigan Press, 1980), 11.

24. Fridolf Kudlien, "Medical Ethics and Popular Ethics in Greece and Rome," *Clio Medica* 5 (1970): 91–121.

25. Edelstein, "The Hippocratic Oath," 3.

26. Jones, *Hippocrates*, 1:165 (emphasis added). This text does *not* say "first—or 'above all'—do no harm," or *primum non nocere*, to use the later Latin formulation, which is of unknown origin.

27. In making this claim we rely in part on unpublished work by Robert Veatch and Carol Mason. For basic documents and an influential analysis, see W.H.S. Jones, *The Doctor's Oath: An Essay in the History of Medicine* (Cambridge: Cambridge University Press, 1924). See also Darrel W. Amundsen,"Medical Ethics, History of: Ancient Greece and Rome," *Encyclopedia of Bioethics*, 3:930–38, esp. 930,934.

28. See Mary Catherine Welborn, "The Long Tradition: A Study in Fourteenth-Century Medical Deontology," in Chester R. Burns, ed., *Legacies in Ethics and Medicine* (New York: Science History Publications, 1977), on whose extensive quotations from Mondeville's untranslated work we have heavily relied. On the influence of theology and the connections to Hippocratic writings, see Katz, *The Silent World*, 7–9.

29. Henri de Mondeville, "On the Morals and Etiquette of Surgeons," as entitled and reprinted from a 1910 source, in Stanley J. Reiser, Arthur J. Dyck, and William J. Curran, eds., *Ethics in Medicine: Historical Perspectives and Contemporary Concerns* (Cambridge, MA: MIT Press, 1977), 15. (This "essay" is a string of quotations artificially placed together.)

30. Henri de Mondeville, from passages in Welborn, "The Long Tradition," 213.

31. Henry E. Sigerist, *On the History of Medicine* (New York: MD Publications, Inc., 1960), 145.

32. De Mondeville, "On the Morals and Etiquetteof Surgeons," in *Ethics in Medicine*, 15.

33. Welborn, "The Long Tradition," 213.

34. Ibid., 213.

35. Ibid., 213.

36. Pernick, "The Patient's Role in Medical Decisionmaking," 5 (emphasis added).

37. De Mondeville, "On the Morals and Etiquette of Surgeons, in *Ethics in Medicine*, 15.

38. Rush, *Medical Inquiries and Observations*, Vol. 2, Chap. 1. Published as a single essay entitled *An Oration . . . An Enquiry into the Influence of Physical Causes upon the Moral Faculty* (Philadelphia: Charles Cist, 1786). See also notes from lectures on the subject by Rush: "Lecture Notes on the Human Mind: Manuscript" (Philadelphia: Bound, unpublished, 18—), esp. 16–30, 35–38, 74, 80, 97–101. On deposit, Maurice H. Givens Rare Book Room, Welch Library, Johns Hopkins University.

39. Benjamin Rush, "On the Vices and Virtues of Physicians," a lecture delivered Nov. 2, 1801 and published in his *Sixteen Introductory Lectures* (Philadelphia: Bradford and Innskeep, 1811), 123–25.

40. "On the Causes Which Have Retarded The Progress of Medicine, and the Means of Promoting Its Certainty and Greater Usefulness" (Delivered Nov. 3, 1801), in Rush, *Sixteen Introductory Lectures*, 154–55. See also his lecture, "On the Causes of Diseases, that are not Incurable," esp. 66–69.

41. Rush, "On the Vices and Virtues of Physicians," 124f.

42. Rush, *Medical Inquiries and Observations*, 1:323.

43. Rush, *Sixteen Introductory Lectures*, 324.

44. John Gregory, *Lectures on the Duties and Qualifications of a Physician* (London: W. Strahan and T. Cadell, 1772). This volume is a "corrected and enlarged" volume published anonymously in 1770 as *Observations on the Duties and Offices of a Physician and on the Method of Prosecuting Enquiries in Philosophy* (London: W. Strahan and T. Cadell, 1770). This earlier volume contains a useful abstract in its "Advertisement" that is not found in the later edition.

45. Ibid., 34–35.

46. Ibid., 61–63, 34–36.

47. Ibid., 19–23.

48. See the interpretation by Laurence B. McCullough, "Historical Perspectives on the Ethical Dimensions of the Patient-Physician Relationship: The Medical Ethics of Dr. John Gregory," *Ethics in Science and Medicine* 5 (1978): 47–53. We are indebted to McCullough for private discussions about Gregory's work.

49. Pernick, "The Patient's Role in Medical Decisionmaking," 10.

50. Katz, *The Silent World*, 16.

51. Thomas Percival, *Medical Ethics; or a Code of Institutes and Precepts, Adapted to the Professional Conduct of Physicians and Surgeons* (Manchester: S. Russell, 1803). The now more readily available edition is Chauncey D. Leake, ed., *Percival's Medical Ethics* (Huntington, NY: Robert E. Krieger Publishing Company, 1975). This edition, which is not entirely reliable, will be cited in brackets for page numbers. Our work on Percival has been aided by a pre-publication copy of the introductory essay to a new reprint edition of Percival's book, written by Edmund Pellegrino. We are also indebted to him for personal conversations about Percival.

52. Ibid., 31 [91].

53. Ibid., 165–66 [194–95]. The full title placed by Percival on this "Note" (dropped by Leake, in part) is, "A Physician Should Be Minister of Hope and Comfort to the Sick.—Enquiry, how far it is justifiable to violate Truth for the Supposed Benefit of the patient." (xv).

54. Ibid., 156ff [186ff].

55. Ibid., 31 [91], 159–60 [189–90].

56. Ibid., 164f [193]. See also Chester R. Burns "Historical Introduction" to the 1975 Leake reprint edition, xxiiif.

57. See American Medical Association, *Proceedings of the National Medical Conventions, Held in New York, May 1846, and in Philadelphia, May 1847* (Adopted May 6, 1847 and submitted for publication in Philadelphia, 1847), 94.

58. American Medical Association, "Code of Medical Ethics," 92; and see also Morris Fishbein, *A History of the American Medical Association 1847 to 1947* (Philadelphia: W.B. Saunders Co., 1947), 35–36; and Austin Flint, *Medical Ethics and Etiquette: The Code of Ethics Adopted by the American Medical Association, with Commentaries* (New York: D. Appleton and Co., 1883), 5; first published in *New York Medical Journal* 37 (1883).

59. Nathan Davis, *History of Medicine, with the Code of Medical Ethics* (Chicago: Cleveland Press, 1903), 190; and Fishbein, *A History of the American Medical Association*, 35–40.

60. Worthington Hooker, *Physician and Patient; or a Practical View of the Mutual Duties, Relations and Interests of the Medical Profession and the Community* (New York: Baker and Scribner, 1849).

61. Ibid., viii-ix, and Chap. 4.

62. Worthington Hooker, *Inaugural Address: The Present Mental Attitude and Tendencies of the Medical Profession* (New Haven: T.J. Stafford, 1852), 27.

63. Hooker, *Physician and Patient*, 357f, 378–81, and see 375, 377.

64. Ibid., 381.

65. Ibid., 380.

66. Worthington Hooker, *Lessons from the History of Medical Delusions* (New York: Baker & Scribner, 1850), iv, 11, 102–105; and *Dissertation, on the Respect Due to the Medical Profession, and the Reasons that It is not Awarded By the Community* (Norwich, Conn.: J.G. Cooley, 1844), 10–18, 20–21.

67. Hooker, *Lessons from the History of Medical Delusions*, 12–16, 20, 22, 31.

68. Ibid., 33–34.

69. Donald E. Konold, *A History of American Medical Ethics 1847–1912* (Madison, WI: State Historical Society of Wisconsin, 1962), 9; Burns, "Medical Ethics, History of: North America: Seventeenth to Nineteenth Century," 965–67; Davis, *History of Medicine*, 189–91.

70. Chester R. Burns, "Reciprocity in the Development of Anglo-American Medical Ethics, 1765–1865," in Burns, ed., *Legacies in Ethics and Medicine*, 305.

71. "Winter Meeting of the Councilors of the Massachusetts Medical Society," *Boston Medical and Surgical Journal* 102 (1880): 156.

72. "The New Code of Ethics of the Massachusetts Medical Society," *Boston Medical and Surgical Journal* 102 (1880): 256.

73. Fishbein, *A History of the American Medical Association*, 38.

74. Flint, *Medical Ethics and Etiquette*.

75. Flint, *Medical Ethics and Etiquette*, 5. The dominance of Percival is everywhere evident in the late nineteenth century. Considerable feeling for the pervasive sense of the code's adequacy is found in an influential treatise on *The Physician Himself*, published (in the *second* edition) in 1882:

> Dr. Thomas Percival['s code] . . . until now has governed our whole profession throughout this broad land. . . . [It] stands like a lighthouse to guide and direct all who wish to sail in an honorable course. . . .
>
> By its justness this code remains as fresh and beautiful to-day as when Percival penned it seventy-five years ago.

D.W. Cathell, *The Physician Himself* (1882; modern reprint, Arno Press—The New York Times, 1972), 42–43.

76. Flint, *Medical Ethics and Etiquette*, 23, 24.

77. See Konold, *A History of American Medical Ethics*, 13, referencing an editorial by Nathan Davis, "Do Moral Principles Change?" *Journal of the American Medical Association* 1 (1883): 57. Davis was Dean and Professor of Medicine at Northwestern University, a politically active member of the AMA, and perhaps the foremost historian of American Medicine, the AMA, and medical ethics of his times. He personally witnessed developments in the code for over 50 years. The historical view that he took, in lectures from 1892–1897, published in 1903, was that "It was not until the end of the eighteenth century that the Hippocratic Code was more fully *discussed, revised, and extended* by Sir Thomas Percival" and became the living code of the AMA through its conventions, which simply lifted material from Percival, Rush, and Gregory. Davis, *History of Medicine*, 189–91 (italics added).

78. See Judicial Council of the American Medical Association, *Current Opinions of the Judicial Council of the American Medical Association* (Chicago: American Medical Association, 1984), vii–viii for a history of these revisions.

79. Ibid., viii.

80. Percival, *Medical Ethics*, 160–61 [191].

81. Henry Sidgwick, *The Methods of Ethics*, 7th ed. (Indianapolis: Hackett Publishing Co., 1981), 316.

82. Konold, *A History of American Medical Ethics*, Chapters 2–3; Fishbein, *A History of the American Medical Association*, 36, 31–34.

83. American physicians had been out to regulate their fellows by the erection of professional standards at least since a set of influential moral rules modeled on Percival and published by Boston physicians in 1808 as *Boston Medical Police*. See Konold, *A History of Medical Ethics*, 2. See also Burns, "Reciprocity in the Development of Anglo-American Medical Ethics," 302, and "Medical Ethics, History of: North America: Seventeenth to Nineteenth Century," 965.

84. Pernick, "The Patient's Role in Medical Decisionmaking," 11.

85. Ibid., 3.

86. Ibid., 11, 12.

87. Ibid., 16.

88. Ibid., 22–26. See also Martin S. Pernick, *A Calculus of Suffering: Pain, Professionalism and Anesthesia in Nineteenth Century America* (New York: Columbia University Press, 1985), esp. 228–34.

89. "Hospital Report. Fractures of the Limbs," *Boston Medical and Surgical Journal* 2 (1829): 84. See Pernick, "The Patient's Role in Medical Decisionmaking," 23.

90. Occasionally physicians would even perform treatments that, in their professional judgment, were contraindicated or futile but were sought by patients. A patient with severe, constant pain in his foot "entertained the idea, from which nothing could divert him, that if the toe were removed within the part pained, he should certainly be relieved. ... It did not seem probable to any of the physicians who visited him, that amputation would cure him. He was therefore constantly advised against it. ... " But finally his physician gave in and amputated his toe—reportedly without removing the pain. Z.B. Adams, "Fatal Corn," *Boston Medical and Surgical Journal* 2 (1829): 242.

91. William Parker, "Hospital Report," *Boston Medical and Surgical Journal* 2 (1829): 67.

92. Jonathan S. Millet, "Successful Operation for Hernia," *Boston Medical and Surgical Journal* 12 (1835): 186.

93. John C. Warren, "Cases of Neuralgia, or Painful Affections of Nerves," *Boston Medical and Surgical Journal* 2 (1829): 130.

94. J.B. Brown, "Remarkable Disease of the Kidney," *Boston Medical and Surgical Journal* 2 (1829): 155.

95. Walter Channing, "Collections in Morbid Anatomy," *Boston Medical and Surgical Journal* 2 (1829): 52.

96. J. Wood, "Case VII—In Which A Hydrocephalic Head, Eighteen Inches in Circumference, Passed Through A Common-Sized Pelvis; Together With An Account of Its Admeasurements at Different Periods," *Boston Medical and Surgical Journal* 11 (1834): 275.

97. D. Evans, "Aneurism of the Innominata and Root of the Carotid," *Boston Medical and Surgical Journal* 2 (1829): 88–89.

98. J. Mason Warren, "Rhinoplastic Operation," *Boston Medical and Surgical Journal* 16 (1837): 70.

99. "Cancer Uteri-Operation," *Boston Medical and Surgical Journal* 2 (1829): 289–90.

100. D.H. Bard, "History of a Polypous Excrescence in the Vagina, Attended with Unusually Severe Symptoms," *Boston Medical and Surgical Journal* 2 (1829): 434.

101. E.g., "Editorial: Accusation of Malpractice," *Boston Medical and Surgical Journal* 31 (1846): 123–24.

102. Alexander Young, "The Law of Malpractice," *Boston Medical and Surgical Journal* (New Series) 5 (June 1870): 441.

103. "Why Are Malpractice Suits?" *New England Journal of Medicine* 200 (1929): 93.

104. Halbert G. Stetson and John E. Moran, "Malpractice Suits: Their Cause and Prevention," *New England Journal of Medicine* 210 (1934): 1383–84.

105. Frederic Jay Cotton, "Medicine, Ethics and Law," *New England Journal of Medicine* 208 (1933): 589.

106. Ibid., 589.

107. *Boston Medical and Surgical Journal* 38 (1848): 528–29.

108. See, for example, *De May* v. *Roberts*, 46 Mich. 160, 9 N.W. 146 (1881), where plaintiff won an action for deceit and assault against her physician and a "young unmarried man with no medical training whom she allowed to lay hands upon her in her extremity," thinking he was a medical assistant trained in childbirth. The court was eloquently indignant that this stranger had deceptively intruded upon an occasion "most sacred" to the plaintiff.

109. As reprinted in *Boston Medical and Surgical Journal* 38 (1848): 528–29. [Emphasis added.]

110. George W. Gay, "Suits for Alleged Malpractice," *Boston Medical and Surgical Journal* 165 (1911): 353–58, 406–11.

111. Ibid., 357.

112. Ibid., 356–57.

113. Ibid., 411, 357.

114. See Konold, *A History of American Medical Ethics.*

115. Pernick, "The Patient's Role in Medical Decisionmaking," 17–18, citing in part John J. Elwell, *A Medico-Legal Treatise on Malpractice and Medical Evidence*, 3rd ed. rev. and enl. (New York: Baker, Voorhis & Co., 1871), 112–15, 29. On the free-market nature of the period, see Paul Starr, *The Social Transformation of American Medicine* (New York: Basic Books, 1982), 22–24, 61–64, 77–78.

116. Ibid., 16–18.

117. Richard Clarke Cabot, *Honesty* (New York: Macmillan, 1938), as quoted in Fletcher, "The Evolution of the Ethics of Informed Consent," 201. A predecessor comment is found in Cabot's better known, early essay "The Use of Truth and False-hood in Medicine," *American Medicine* 5 (1903): 344–49. See also his historically interesting *Adventures on the Borderlands of Ethics* (New York: Harper & Brothers, 1926), Chapter 2, and *The Meaning of Right and Wrong* (New York: Macmillan, 1936), which contains his essay "Honesty."

118. See Thomas Franklin Williams, "Cabot, Peabody, and the Care of the Patient," in Burns, *Legacies in Ethics and Medicine*, esp. 307–308, 313. See also Ralph Barton Perry, "Richard Clarke Cabot," *Harvard Alumni Bulletin* (May 19, 1939), and Paul D. White, "Obituary: Richard Clarke Cabot," *New England Journal of Medicine* 220 (1939), 1049. Cabot majored in philosophy, lectured in Josiah Royce's courses in logic, and became Professor of Social Ethics.

119. Katz, *The Silent World*, 25.

120. Konold, *A History of American Medical Ethics*, Chapter 3, esp. 44–57.

121. The *Quarterly Cumulative Index Medicus* was searched every year from 1930 through 1956, under three headings: (1) jurisprudence, medical; (2) ethics, medical; and (3) physicians: relations to patients. In the 1930s, we were able to find only two articles on consent, both in Michigan, and two articles on the general topic of disclo-

sure: C.C. Purdy, "Legal Consent to Operations," *Journal of the Michigan Medical Society* 34 (1935): 621–22; H.V. Barbour, "Get Complete Consent in Writing Before You Operate," *Journal of the Michigan Medical Society* 35 (1936): 572–73; R.E. Stifel, "How Much Should the Patient Be Told?" *Hygeia* 8 (1930): 818–19; and W.A. White, "Should the Doctor Tell?" *Southern Medicine and Surgery* 94 (1932): 362–67.

In the 1940s, we found three articles on consent: E. Hoyt, "Courts Value Consent for Surgery on Minors," *Hospitals* 19 (1945): 54–58; E. Hoyt, "Shadowy Form of 'Consent' in Emergency Operations," *Hospitals* 19 (1945): 68, 71; and J. Turners, "Is Practice of Obtaining Consent for Operation Protection or Risk?" *Modern Hospital* 73 (1949): 73–74. And, we found three articles on disclosure: M.G. Selig, "Should Cancer Victim Be Told Truth?" *Journal of the Missouri Medical Association* 40 (1943): 33–35; L.E. Hamlin, "Should Worker With Silicosis be Informed of His X-ray?" *Industrial Medicine* 14 (1945): 190–92; and C.C. Lund, "Doctor, Patient and the Truth," *Annals of Internal Medicine* 24 (1946): 955–59.

Also during the 1940s we found a series of three articles on consent published in a British medical journal by S.R. Speller: "Consents to Operations and Other Surgical Procedures: Patients Other than Mental or Mental Deficiency Cases," *The Hospital* 42 (1946): 21–24; "Consents to Operations and Other Surgical Procedures: Mental Patients," *The Hospital* 42 (1946): 59–61; and "Consents to Operations and Other Surgical Procedures: Mental Deficiency Cases and Note on Illegal Operations," *The Hospital* 42 (1946): 97–99.

By contrast, during these same two decades, 27 articles specifically on patient consent were published in the European, foreign language medical literature—17 in German periodicals. Most of the European articles discussed developments in the courts.

From 1950 through 1956, we found four articles on consent in the American literature, one of which was in a Canadian journal: J. Turner, "Consent for Operation," *Journal of the Mt. Sinai Hospital* 17 (1951): 373–76; P.R. Overton, "Consent Necessary for Uncontemplated Surgery," *Texas State Journal of Medicine* 52 (1956): 692–93; L.L. Minty, "Unlawful Wounding: Will Consent Make It Legal?" *Medico-Legal Journal* 24 (1956): 54–62; and T.L. Fisher, "Permission (to administer treatment or to operate)," *Canadian Medical Association Journal* 74 (1956): 480–482. Also during this period we found ten foreign language articles on consent in medicine.

122. The data base for the period 1957–1959 is the *Current List of Medical Literature*; from 1960 forward the reference is the *Cumulated Index Medicus*. Using the same methodology discussed in n. 121, we found 12 articles on consent issues published in the three-year period 1957–1959 (in the American medical literature). By contrast, only nine articles on consent appeared in the American medical literature in the preceding 27 years (see n. 121.). This can also be compared with the decade of the 1960s, when over 50 consent articles were published. See also nn. 148 and 149 and surrounding text.

123. See, for example, E.C. Bryson, "Malpractice: Recent Trends," *Postgraduate Medicine* 25 (1959): A-52 passim; W.A. Kelly, "Physician, Patient, and Consent: A Discussion of Some Cases Involving Consent," *Journal of the Kansas Medical Society* 62 (1961): 4–17; B.D. Hirsh, "Informed Consent to Treatment: Medico-Legal Comment," *Journal of the American Medical Association* 176 (1961): 436–38; K.W. Dale, "Court Decision: Kansas Receives a Ruling on Informed Consent," *Journal of the Kansas Medical Society*, 62 (1961): 2–3 and R.W. Baldwin, "Consent in Medical Practice," *Maryland Medical Journal* 11 (1962): 647–51.

124. Nathan Hershey and Stanley H. Bushkoff, *Informed Consent Study* (Pittsburgh, PA: Aspen Systems Corporation, 1969); D.G. Hagman, "The Medical Patient's Right to Know: Report on a Medical-Legal-Ethical, Empirical Study," *U.C.L.A. Law*

Review 17 (1970): 758–816; Carl H. Fellner and John R. Marshall, "The Myth of Informed Consent," *American Journal of Psychiatry* 126 (1970): 1245–50 and Ralph J. Alfidi, "Informed Consent: A Study of Patient Reaction," *Journal of the American Medical Association* 216 (May 1971): 1325–29. There were also during this period a few studies of informed consent in human experimentation; see, for example, L.C. Park, L. Covi and E.H. Uhlenhuth, "Effects of Informed Consent on Research Patients and Study Results," *Journal of Nervous and Mental Disorders* 145 (1967): 349–57 and L.C. Epstein and L. Lasagna, "Obtaining Informed Consent: Form and Substance," *Archives of Internal Medicine* 123 (1969): 682–88.

125. Unfortunately, Hershey and Bushkoff do not provide the precise dates within which data were collected. There is a suggestion in the text that the study was initiated between 1964 and 1966; see Hershey and Bushkoff, *Informed Consent Study*, 4.

126. Questionnaires were mailed to 300 Minnesota physicians and 400 California physicians. The response rates were 61% for the Minnesota sample and 49% for the California sample. In addition the questionnaire was administered to 146 health care professionals attending seminars on medical-legal issues at UCLA, not all of whom were physicians. Each of the 26 hypotheticals was not submitted to all subjects. The number of replies per hypothetical varied from N=34 to N=184. Percentages reported here are for the Minnesota and California physician samples only.

127. N.J. Demy, "Informed Opinion on Informed Consent," *Journal of the American Medical Association* 217 (1971): 696–97.

128. The National Library of Medicine identified 272 citations on informed consent in the period from January 1970 to April 1974 in its Medical Literature Analysis and Retrieval System (MEDLARS), NLM Literature Search No. 74–16. See also Caroline L. Kaufmann, "Informed Consent and Patient Decision Making: Two Decades of Research," *Social Science and Medicine* 17 (1983): 1657–64 for an analysis of the rate of growth of the literature in legal and social science journals as well as medical journals in the period from 1960 to 1980. Kaufmann notes that in this period less than 10% of total articles on informed consent identified from Index Medicus were written by lawyers; a few additional articles were authored by writers holding joint degrees in law and medicine.

129. In the official publication of the American Medical Association, articles appeared shortly after the 1972 cases alerting the membership to these important legal developments. The articles were written by a lawyer, prepared for the AMA Office of the General Council; Joseph E. Simonaitis, "Recent Decisions on Informed Consent," *Journal of the American Medical Association* 221 (1972): 441–42 and "More About Informed Consent," *Journal of the American Medical Association* 225 (1973): 95–96.

This was not the first series on informed consent published by a lawyer in *JAMA*. In 1970, Angela R. Holder published three articles: "Informed Consent: Its Evolution," *Journal of the American Medical Association* 214 (1970): 1181–82; "Informed Consent—The Obligation," *Journal of the American Medical Association* 214 (1970): 1383–84; and "Informed Consent—Limitations," *Journal of the American Medical Association* 214 (1970): 1611–12.

130. See, for example, D.L. Wilbur, "Editorial: Informed Consent," *Postgraduate Medicine* 54 (1973): 25, and Franz J. Ingelfinger, "Informed (But Uneducated) Consent," *New England Journal of Medicine* 287 (August 1972): 465–66.

131. See, for example, Paul E. Huffington, "Perfection of Standards, and Informed Consent in Preventing Malpractice Suits," *Maryland State Medical Journal* 19 (1970): 75–77 and Mark M. Ravitch, "Informed Consent—Descent to Absurdity," *Medical Times* 101 (1973): 184–88.

132. See, for example, J.F. King, "The Jaws of Informed Consent," *Maryland State Medical Journal* 25 (1976): 78–81.

133. For a discussion that raises the ethical issues see George Crile, Jr., "Breast Cancer and Informed Consent," *Cleveland Clinic Quarterly* 39 (1972): 57–59. Crile is advocating informed consent for breast cancer surgery. Not all physicians writing in the 1970s were critical of informed consent; see, for example, Crile and physician-lawyer Lawrence V. Hastings, "The Physician-Patient Relationship: A New Approach to Informed Consent," *Journal of the Florida Medical Association* 59 (1972): 61.

134. See Daniel Callahan, "Bioethics as a Discipline," *Hastings Center Studies* 1 (1973): 66–73; Roy Branson, "Bioethics as Individual *and* Social: The Scope of a Consulting Profession and Academic Discipline," *Journal of Religious Ethics* 3 (1975): 111–39.

135. Pennsylvania State University–Hershey was the first to create a department of medical humanities, in 1967, and Columbia College of Physicians sponsored an experimental program of integrated studies in medical ethics in 1968. But the movement to medical schools was widespread. See Robert M. Veatch, Willard Gaylin, and Councilman Morgan, *The Teaching of Medical Ethics* (Hastings-on-Hudson, N.Y.: Hastings Center Publications, 1973), and Thomas K. McElhinney, *Human Values Teaching Programs for Health Professionals* (Philadelphia, PA: Society for Health and Human Values, 1976).

136. Callahan, "Bioethics as a Discipline," 69–73.

137. If we were to thoroughly explore the history of medical ethics in religious traditions we would prove only a negative—the nonexistence of any significant writings or practices regarding informed consent. To be sure, Roman Catholic and Jewish moral writings had for centuries attempted to bring theological and philosophical principles to bear on pressing issues such as abortion, contraception, sterilization, death and dying, surgery, and so on. Catholic writers such as Edwin Healy, Gerald Kelly, Charles McFadden, and Thomas J. O'Donnell had carried on an active program of applied ethics, using the distinctive principles of Catholic moral theology. Theologians, chaplains, and hospitals had long paid careful attention to these teachings and framed practical policies to conform to them. In 1949 the Catholic Hospital Association in the United States published its Ethical and Religious Directives for Catholic Health Facilities (revised 1954, 1971), which attempted to synthesize many of the traditional and newer writings into working principles. Roman Catholic concerns with practical medical ethics were often published in the pages of the *Linacre Quarterly*, published since 1932 by the National Federation of Catholic Physicians' Guilds.

A similar story could be told about the Jewish tradition, which had been concerned with issues of death and dying and medical care since ancient times. Immanuel Jakobovits' *Jewish Medical Ethics*, first written in 1959 and published in English in 1962, rekindled a longstanding interest in this ancient tradition, especially as it might apply to newly emerging issues in biomedicine. Yet none of these writings dealt in any substantive respect with informed consent. Moreover, as we would expect from sectarian writings, the principles involved never gained currency in the interdisciplinary environment that, we contend, gave rise to moral concern about informed consent in psychiatry, medicine, the behavioral sciences, philosophical ethics, and legal theory. Immanuel Jakobovits, *Jewish Medical Ethics* (New York: Bloch Publishing Company, 1975).

138. Joseph Fletcher, *Morals and Medicine: The Moral Problems of: The Patient's Right to Know the Truth, Contraception, Artificial Insemination, Sterilization, Euthanasia* (Princeton: Princeton University Press, 1954), esp. 35–36. In the "Preface to the Princeton Paperback Edition," Fletcher wrote, in 1978, that his book "remained the only work of its kind for another fifteen years or more" (xiii), but he notes that an

extraordinary amount was done from 1968–1978 on issues such as patients' rights and truthtelling. Paul Ramsey, *The Patient as Person* (New Haven: Yale University Press, 1970), esp. Chapter 1.

139. K. Danner Clouser, *Teaching Bioethics: Strategies, Problems, and Resources* (Hastings-on-Hudson, NY: The Hastings Center, 1980), ix, 55f; and his "What is Medical Ethics?" *Annals of Internal Medicine* 80 (1974): 657–60. For the developing literature, see also LeRoy Walters, ed., *Bibliography of Bioethics* (Detroit: Gale Research Co., 1973—).

140. On the patients' rights movement generally, its origins and influences, see Annas, "Patients' Rights Movements," *Encyclopedia of Bioethics* 3:1202–5. See also Annas's discussion of the movement in *The Rights of Hospital Patients*, 4; Bradford Gray, "Complexities of Informed Consent," *Annals of the American Academy of Political and Social Science* 437 (1978): 37, 40; Bernard Barber, "Compassion in Medicine: Toward New Definitions and New Institutions," *New England Journal of Medicine* 295 (1976): 939; and Willard Gaylin, "The Patient's Bill of Rights," *Saturday Review of the Sciences* 1 (February 1973): 22.

141. Other states (e.g., Massachusetts) codified similar bills, often for their mental health facilities (see Chapter 4, pp. 139–140.) DHEW also adopted a patients' bill of rights for skilled nursing facilities participating in Medicare and Medicaid. *Federal Register* 39 (October 3, 1974): 35774–75. See also Joint Commission on Accreditation of Hospitals, *Accreditation Manual for Hospitals*, (Chicago: 1970), 1–2.

142. George J. Annas, *The Rights of Hospital Patients: The Basic ACLU Guide to a Hospital Patient's Rights* (New York: Avon Books, 1975), 25–27; and "Patients' Rights Movement," 3:1201–2.

143. American Hospital Association, "Statement on a Patient's Bill of Rights," *Hospitals* 47 (February 1973): 41.

144. According to George Annas, the thrust of the JCAH Preamble and the AHA Bill of Rights "is toward encouraging etiquette and courtesy in the doctor-patient relationship in the hospital context, not toward informing the patient of his rights." (*The Rights of Hospital Patients*, 28.)

145. Howard Brody, *Ethical Decisions in Medicine* (Boston: Little, Brown and Company, 1976); Paul Ramsey, *Ethics at the Edges of Life* (New Haven: Yale University Press, 1978); Robert Veatch, *Death, Dying, and the Biological Revolution* (New Haven: Yale University Press, 1976); Tom L. Beauchamp and LeRoy Walters, eds., *Contemporary Issues in Bioethics* (Encino, CA: Dickenson Publishing Co., Inc., 1978); Samuel Gorovitz, et al., eds., *Moral Problems in Medicine* (Englewood Cliffs, NJ: Prentice-Hall, 1976); Robert Hunt and John Arras, eds., *Ethical Issues in Modern Medicine* (Palo Alto, CA: Mayfield Publishing Co., 1977); Reiser, Dyck, and Curran, *Ethics in Medicine*; Thomas A. Shannon, ed., *Bioethics: Basic Writings on the Key Ethical Questions that Surround the Major Modern Biological Possibilities and Problems* (New York: Paulist Press, 1976); Robert M. Veatch and Roy Branson, eds., *Ethics and Health Policy* (Cambridge, MA: Ballinger Publishing Co., 1976); Tom L. Beauchamp and James F. Childress, *Principles of Biomedical Ethics* (New York: Oxford University Press, 1979); Ronald Munson, ed., *Intervention and Reflection: Basic Issues in Medical Ethics* (Belmont, CA: Wadsworth Publishing Co., 1979).

146. Robert M. Veatch and Sharmon Sollitto, "Medical Ethics Teaching: A Report of a National Medical School Survey," *Journal of the American Medical Association* 235 (1976): 1030–33. There were 112 AAMC-member medical schools in 1974; 107 responded to the survey, and of those 97 (91%) reported offering some form of medical ethics teaching. See also Robert C. Cassidy, et al., "Teaching Biopsycho-Ethical Medicine in a Family Practice Clerkship," *Journal of Medical Education* 58 (1983): 778, referring to 1981 studies. Historically, an earlier survey by Veatch is illuminat-

ing: "National Survey of Medical Ethics in Medical Schools," in *The Teaching of Medical Ethics*, 97–102.

147. Barbara Grumet, "Legal Medicine in Medical Schools: A Survey of the State of the Art," *Journal of Medical Education* 54 (1978): 755–58.

148. National Library of Medicine, Public Health Service, NIH, Literature Searches No. 76–35 and No. 82–14.

149. Computer search, BIOETHICSLINE, conducted in November 1984 by Judith Mistichelli, Kennedy Institute of Ethics Library.

150. Judicial Council of the American Medical Association, *Current Opinions of the Judicial Council of the American Medical Association* (Chicago, IL: American Medical Association, 1984), 29–30. (This opinion was first published by the Judicial Council in 1981.)

151. For a history of the Judicial Council and its role as the AMA's ethics committee, see Fishbein, *A History of the American Medical Association*, 948–60; see also Judicial Council, *Current Opinions—1984*, 37–47.

152. The Judicial Council's opinion does not exhaust the AMA's current activities in informed consent. The Health Policy Agenda Project—a project charged with developing a philosophical framework for the American health care system, sponsored by the AMA (but including representation from 150 organizations and groups)—has presented two very strongly worded "working principles" on informed consent to the AMA House of Delegates for consideration:

> PRINCIPLE 5–8—Health care professionals have the responsibility to communicate with patients in a frank and informative manner that encourages both informed decision-making by patients and a relationship of trust between patients and professionals.
>
> PRINCIPLE 5–9—Informed consent to diagnostic procedures and treatment should include the following elements:
>
> 1. Ensuring of the patient's right of self-determination;
>
> 2. The legal capacity as well as the actual ability of the patient or his her representative to give consent to the particular procedure or treatment;
>
> 3. Disclosure of the purpose and the potential effects on the patient of the procedure, treatment and alternatives to permit an informed decision; and
>
> 4. The voluntary decision of the patient regarding the procedure or treatment.
>
> The duty and responsibility for providing the information to be disclosed and for obtaining the informed consent should rest with each individual who initiates or directs the procedures involved in the particular case.

These working principles were endorsed by the House of Delegates in June 1984. However, the AMA is not expected to adopt these principles officially until they are presented in final form in the Health Policy Agenda's final report sometime in mid-1986. Personal communication, Gail Sheehy, American Medical Association, January, 1985, and American Medical Association, Proceedings of the House of Delegates, 123rd Annual Meeting (June 17–21, 1984), 72.

153. Judicial Council, *Current Opinions—1984*, 29–30.

154. President's Commission, *Summing Up*, 1–2.

155. Ibid., 3; see also Alexander M. Capron, "Looking Back at the President's Commission," *The Hastings Center Report* (October 1983): 7–10.

156. President's Commission, *Making Health Care Decisions*, Vol. 1, Chapter 1, esp. 30; President's Commission, *Summing Up*, 20.

157. President's Commission, *Making Health Care Decisions*, Vol. 1, *Report*, 50–51.

158. President's Commission, *Deciding to Forego Life-Sustaining Treatment* (Washington, D.C.: U.S. Government Printing Office, March 1983), 2–4, and Chapters 1–2.

159. Ibid., 26–27, 44; see also President's Commission, *Summing Up*, 34.

160. The precise number of studies depends on how one counts them—some studies have been specifically on informed consent in clinical medicine; other studies—not precisely focused on informed consent—have been on related topics, for example, patients' and physicians' attitudes towards disclosure of medical information or models of medical decisionmaking. In addition, studies of informed consent in research also often have implications for the clinical setting. Unfortunately much of this literature does not tell us anything about physicians' actual consent practices, or the related experiences of patients.

For a review of the empirical literature up to 1982, see Alan Meisel and Loren H. Roth, "Toward an Informed Discussion on Informed Consent: A Review and Critique of the Empirical Studies," *Arizona Law Review*, 25 (1983): 265–346. See also Charles W. Lidz, et. al., *Informed Consent: A Study of Decisionmaking in Psychiatry* (New York: The Guilford Press, 1984); W.D. White, "Informed Consent: Ambiguity in Theory and Practice," *Journal of Health Politics, Policy and Law* 8 (1983): 99; William M. Strull, Bernard Lo, and Gerald Charles, "Do Patients Want to Participate in Medical Decision Making?" *Journal of American Medical Association* 252 (1984): 2990–94; Ruth Faden, et. al., "A Survey to Evaluate Parental Consent As Public Policy for Neonatal Screening," *American Journal of Public Health* 72 (1982): 1347–51; Charles Lidz and Alan Meisel, "Informed Consent and the Structure of Medical Care," in President's Commission, *Making Health Care Decisions*, Vol. 2, 317–410; Paul S. Appelbaum and Loren H. Roth, "Treatment Refusal in Medical Hospitals," in President's Commission, *Making Health Care Decisions*, Vol. 2, 411–77; and Barbara Rimer, et. al., "Informed Consent: A Crucial Step in Cancer Patient Education," *Health Education Quarterly* 10 (1983): 30–42.

161. The methodology and results of this survey are described in detail in Louis Harris, et. al., "Views of Informed Consent and Decisionmaking: Parallel Surveys of Physicians and the Public," in President's Commission, *Making Health Care Decisions*, Vol. 2, 17–316.

162. President's Commission, *Making Health Care Decisions*, Vol. 1, 108.

163. President's Commission, *Making Health Care Decisions*, Vol. 1, 79.

164. Common responses given by physicians include: (1) "generally informing patient about condition and treatment" (59%); (2) "disclosing treatment risks to patients" (47%); and "patient understanding his or her condition and treatment" (56%). See President's Commission, *Making Health Care Decisions*, Vol. 1, 18, and Vol. 2, 302.

165. The best study on this point is Lidz and Meisel, "Informed Consent and the Structure of Medical Care," 317–410. But see also Sue Fisher, "Doctor Talk/Patient Talk: How Treatment Decisions are Negotiated in Doctor-Patient Communication," in Sue Fisher and Alexandra D. Todd, eds., *The Social Organization of Doctor-Patient Communication* (Washington, D.C.: Center for Applied Linguistics, 1983), 135–57.

166. See Meisel and Roth, "Toward an Informed Discussion of Informed Consent," 333–40.

167. Katz, *The Silent World*, 83–85.

168. It is a separate issue whether patients prefer the beneficence model or the autonomy model. See, for example, Strull, Lo, and Charles, "Do Patients Want to Participate in Medical Decision Making?"

4

Consent and the Courts:
*The Emergence of the Legal Doctrine**

The history in Chapter 3 gave but a crow's nest view of the role that law has played in identifying and developing consent issues. In this chapter we telescope that view to follow more closely the gradual development of the law of informed consent. Although the eighteenth and nineteenth centuries produced a few "consent" cases, informed consent is a more recent phenomenon. Only in the twentieth century did the "legal doctrine of informed consent," as displayed in Chapter 2, assume recognizable shape.

Our history has a chronological structure. We begin, however, with a brief prolegomenon about legal history and case law that is meant to facilitate interpretation and understanding of the events that form the history.

Reading Law

The legal history of informed consent in this chapter should be distinguished in methodology and scope from the histories delineated in Chapters 3, 5, and 6. The histories in these chapters would be considered narrow by some historians because of a lack of attention to the impact made on informed consent by broad cultural influences such as the civil rights and consumer protection movements. Our goal in these three chapters is principally to understand *when* and *how* (and less *why*) informed consent developed and was modified in various institutions. In the present chapter the history is still narrower in scope and disciplinary affiliation. We largely confine our attention not only to a single discipline, law, but also to the reasoning of selected court opinions. Case law is the near-exclusive domain of our inquiry.

°Nancy M. P. King is the principal author of this chapter.

114

Any attempt to understand the history of a common law doctrine like informed consent by using the perspective on cases that is taken *by the law itself* is certain to be a more specialized enterprise than the histories written in the other chapters. Although legal historians can trace—and have ably traced—the social and political factors that influence the emergence and history of a legal theory or doctrine, including influences on judicial formulation of opinions, "the law" can also be isolated from these sources and shown to grow from within itself. The law, we might say, has its own internal history. Not infrequently, a theory is given initial shape in the lower trial courtroom, is made precedential (and available to other lawyers) by publication of the decision of the higher appellate court (and occasionally by publication of lower court opinions as well), and is influential insofar as it appears and is acknowledged in later decisions. Much can be learned both from studying the case precedents—as contrasted with cases that are not relied upon—and from studying how they are read and misread by other courts and by commentators.

The kind of history in which we engage in this chapter, then, treats the cases and their connections as they are formed *internal to law*. Care must be taken in analyzing the development of the judicial doctrine of informed consent to understand how the logic and structure of case law affects its history. Case law emerges from courtrooms, where the past is reconstructed, primarily by the spoken word, in an adversarial setting.[1] Some fact situations are more easily dealt with through the court process than others; thus, court decisions often hinge on discrete, factual matters. This is important for informed consent, where, for example, the courts have been more readily able to address questions about the disclosure of particular risks than about the overall quality and atmosphere of an open-ended exchange of information between patient and physician.

Courts are, of necessity, preoccupied with the cases before them. Their primary goal is the secure, after-the-fact resolution of narrow and concrete questions of duty, responsibility, blame, injury, and damages in specific cases. Unprecedented judicial theorizing often endangers this process, and so is avoided. The slow, conservative development of emerging doctrine is ensured by the courts' desire to follow past precedents whenever possible, rather than to break new ground. The result, for informed consent, is a body of decisional law that tends to be both repetitive and incomplete, with its theory strikingly unsettled.[2] In interpreting the history of the law of informed consent, Justice Oliver Wendell Holmes' famous observation cannot be overemphasized: "The law did not begin with a theory. It has never worked one out. The point from which it started and that at which it has arrived are in different planes."[3]

The ensuing history may appear to make the distinction between the battery and negligence themes of liability excessively important (See

Chapter 2, pp. 26–30.) It is not our desire to harp upon distinctions that have comparatively little modern significance for informed consent. But in the attempt to understand what the courts said they were doing and believed they were doing, the language and labels that the courts employed are of considerable importance, enabling us to identify and to trace the justifications underlying informed consent.

Consent Before the Twentieth Century

Late Eighteenth-Century England: The Slater Case

It is sometimes claimed by writers with historical interests that the first case to make consent to medical care an issue was the 1767 English decision *Slater* v. *Baker and Stapleton*.[4] Although *Slater* was occasionally cited by nineteenth-century American courts, it has had little or no precedential effect on informed consent in twentieth-century American law. In this respect, there is no direct, or even indirect, line between *Slater* and the modern legal doctrine. Still, *Slater* is an important illustration of how judicial reasoning can be influenced by practical as well as by theoretical concerns, resulting in the kind of unclarity that has hindered understanding of informed consent law since its earliest development.

In *Slater*, the plaintiff hired Drs. Baker and Stapleton to remove the bandages from a partially healed leg fracture. Instead, the defendants, over the plaintiff's protests, refractured the leg and placed it in an apparently experimental apparatus to stretch and straighten it during rehealing. Slater claimed that the defendants had, in essence, breached the contract they had made with him by "ignorantly and unskillfully" breaking his leg and injuring him. To prove this claim, the plaintiff adduced evidence about orthodox practice through the use of expert witnesses. These physician-witnesses all testified that the unorthodox apparatus that had been used was contrary to standard practice, and that it was also contrary to standard practice to refracture a leg unless the bone was setting very badly. Two of the physicians also testified that, in any case, they would not refracture a healing bone without the patient's consent.[5]

Slater was complicated, however, by the position argued by the defendants, who maintained that, because Mr. Slater appeared to be complaining that they had refractured his leg without his consent and indeed over his protests, the proper action should have been trespass *vi et armis*—a cause of action very close to what we would now call battery. The allegation made in a trespass case is not one of ignorance or lack of skill. The court, to avoid the necessity of dismissing the action because it had technically been brought under the wrong "writ," held that defendants were liable under the contract theory pled by the plaintiff.[6] In its explanation, the court used reasoning that would in subsequent centuries fall under malpractice law:[7]

> In answer to this, it appears from the evidence of the surgeons that it was improper to disunite the callous [bony material in healing] without consent; this is the usage and law of surgeons: then it was ignorance and unskillfulness in that very particular, to do contrary to the rule of the profession, what no surgeon ought to have done; and indeed it is reasonable that a patient should be told what is about to be done to him, that he may take courage and put himself in such a situation as to enable him to undergo the operation.[8]

Battery and Malpractice in Nineteenth-Century American Cases

Martin Pernick, a historian of nineteenth-century medicine whose views we examined in Chapter 3, has identified a handful of what he terms "informed consent" cases from the nineteenth century that were tried as malpractice cases. Because he found no case before 1889 where a physician was charged with battery, Pernick concludes that the American legal system in the nineteenth century enforced informed consent requirements only if "medical experts testified that such consent comprised an ordinary and beneficial part of medical therapy." Thus, Pernick sees consent as enforced in nineteenth-century courts on grounds of (medical) beneficence—that is, because consent was part of the therapeutic process—rather than from a principle of respect for autonomy that might have been expressed legally through a battery finding. Pernick argues that it was not "until 'the polarization of 'science' and 'values' at the turn of the century [that] American courts attempt[ed] to enforce informed consent as an independent legal and moral right. . . . "[9]—that is, for autonomy-based reasons.

Pernick finds more in the nineteenth-century courts than we judge significant for the evolution of the legal doctrine of informed consent. The history of precedents and reasoning in the courts is such that although some potential for informed consent's later flowering can be readily located in the nineteenth-century cases, no more than in *Slater* is there a direct doctrinal or precedential link between these cases and the emergence of requirements of the legal doctrine of informed consent as outlined in Chapter 2. Indeed, in some instances it is questionable whether the cases turned, in other than minor respects, on *consent* issues.

As an illustration, consider *Carpenter* v. *Blake*,[10] in which the defendant physician had treated a dislocated elbow by unorthodox means. The court found negligence in the defendant's failure to inform the patient of the care and precautions she needed to take for successful healing according to this method, and also found that the patient's consent to the physician's withdrawal from the case was procured by a misrepresentation that the arm was healing properly. The misrepresentation vitiated the consent on which the physician sought to rely. Pernick sugggests that *Carpenter* may be viewed as an informed consent case brought in negligence—a decision, as he puts it, that "upheld the patient's right to information and choice, but only insofar as informed consent constituted good medical practice and helpful therapy."[11]

Carpenter is not about informed consent, however. The plaintiff had complained that the physician's treatment of her arm was medically negligent, because the treatment did not correct the dislocation and because the physician abandoned her care while assuring her that her arm was healing properly. The defendant answered, first, that his treatment was medically acceptable, and second, that the plaintiff had consented to his cessation of treatment. The court replied to the defendant's first argument as follows:

> If . . . it is enough for the physician to put the arm on a pillow [resting at a certain angle, rather than the usual practice of putting it in a sling,] . . . it would seem proper, if not necessary, that the attending surgeon should inform the patient, or those having charge of him or her, of the necessity of maintaining that position. . . . [T]he danger [of the joint's straightening improperly if moved from that angle] should be disclosed to the end that all proper precaution may be taken to prevent it.[12]

The court was here maintaining that due care may sometimes require physicians to give information to patients in order to alert them to side effects of medication, to elicit their assistance in home care, to educate them about possible complications, and the like. This view of the due-care obligations of physicians as including duties to issue appropriate warnings and instructions was not uncommon in the law and was to be mentioned with approval in later consent cases.[13] So interpreted, *Carpenter* is an *information* case but not a *consent* case.

Consent was introduced into the case only in connection with the physician's second argument in his defense. At issue was the validity of the plaintiff's consent to the *cessation* of treatment, not her consent to *treatment*. Thus, it is inappropriate to use this case, as Pernick appears to do, to illustrate the preference of nineteenth-century courts for malpractice over battery, because the case could never have been tried in battery: There was never any question of a nonconsensual touching. Instead, the relevant claim made by the plaintiff was of fraud: Consent to the cessation of treatment—rather than consent to any touching—had been fraudulently obtained.

One nineteenth-century opportunity to face the issue of consent to treatment head on was lost because the plaintiff's case was weak. The plaintiff in *Wells* v. *World's Dispensary Medical Association*[14] claimed that defendants had falsely and fraudulently told her that she had a uterine tumor so that they could profit by operating to remove it. The court held that the plaintiff's counsel failed to prove that no tumor had existed at the time of the surgery, so that she could not prevail on the charge of fraud. But the jury had delivered a verdict in favor of the plaintiff, which the court sought to uphold, if possible. Presumably because the plaintiff's attorney had attempted, without being very clear about it, to make a last-ditch alternative argument of malpractice, counsel for both parties had extensively litigated not only the question of the tumor's *existence*, but also the malpractice question of whether the removal of such a tumor, if it existed, was good medical practice under the circumstances. This battle was waged even though the complaint was never amended to include a claim of negligence. The court then upheld the jury's verdict as a finding that defendants were negligent not for fraudulently obtaining "consent," but for removing the tumor. Thus, on our interpretation, Pernick's reading of the decision as holding that "surgeons who performed operations without obtaining an informed consent were held to have committed malpractice" is not supported by the facts or the reasoning of the decision.[15]

In general, the difficulty encountered in reading and interpreting these and the few other available relevant nineteenth-century cases is twofold. First, they are few in number, with all of the malpractice cases reported in the century amounting to a short list.[16] Second, and more significantly, the cases that deal with consent and information do so in only incidental, rudimentary fashion, usually in contexts where the primary claim of the lawsuit was a clear instance of medical negligence. From a legal perspective, consent issues simply never found a proper voice at this early stage.

The Early Twentieth-Century Cases: The Birth of Basic Consent

Although nineteenth-century case law touching on consent is scarce, the few nineteenth-century cases available were not as different in theory from early twentieth-century cases as Pernick evidently believes. Nor, for that matter, were the early twentieth-century cases as unsympathetic to consent concerns as Jay Katz has claimed.[17]

In 1923, American Law Reports (ALR), a compiler of cases on topics of interest as an aid to the practicing attorney, published an "annotation" surveying all twentieth-century cases to date on the "Character and Extent of Surgical Operation Authorized by Patients."[18] These consent cases turned on a determination of the existence or nonexistence of actual or implied *authority* given to the physician by the patient under the circumstances. That determination was based, in large part, on judgments regarding the extent of the deference to expert skill that is implied in the initiation of the physician-patient relationship and on the physician's expert knowledge concerning the need for and urgency of the contested medical intervention. As a result, these cases were often tried as

negligence cases, by appeal to a professional practice standard.[19] However, the cases generally recognized that once the nature and scope of
the patient's authorization is established, extension *beyond* it is a technical battery.

Almost ten years later, in 1932, ALR published a related compilation
of medical consent cases—an "annotation" on consent to surgery that
also surveyed all of the American twentieth-century cases to date. It
opened with this statement of the "general rule":

> The general rule seems to have become well established that, before a
> physician or surgeon may perform an operation upon a patient, he must
> obtain the consent either of the patient, if competent to give it, or of
> someone legally authorized to give it for him, unless immediate oper-
> ation is necessary to save the patient's life or health, although under
> exceptional circumstances the consent may be regarded as having been
> impliedly given. (The action for operating without consent seems usu-
> ally to be regarded as one for assault or trespass, rather than for
> negligence.)[20]

Thus, early twentieth-century cases applied a malpractice standard to
determine the scope of express and implied consent without intent to
contradict the basic principle that to proceed with no consent was a classic instance of battery.[21] The landmark consent cases of the twentieth
century, as we will now see, more explicitly examined the principles
underlying the physician-patient relationship, and applied that understanding to develop and illuminate the nature and scope of consent.

Four battery decisions between 1905 and 1914 are almost universally
credited with formulating the basic features of informed consent in
American law.[22] In these cases—the most famous of which is the oft-
cited *Schloendorff* v. *Society of New York Hospitals*—the consent
requirement is justified through the right of self-determination, which is
the legal equivalent of the moral principle of respect for autonomy. The
language and reasoning of these early decisions will be readily seen to
anticipate later developments in the informed consent doctrine. The first
two of these cases, *Mohr* v. *Williams* (1905) and *Pratt* v. *Davis* (1906),
are intertwined in reasoning and chronology. Although *Mohr* was the
first of the two to come to the lower courts, the final opinion in that case
came down *after* the first lower court ruling in *Pratt*, which it cites extensively. Thus, the chronologically earlier case (*Mohr*) cites a previous
lower court opinion in a "later" case (*Pratt*) as precedent.

Pre-Schloendorff Cases

The Mohr Case. In *Mohr* v. *Williams* (1905),[23] a physician obtained his
patient Anna Mohr's consent to an operation on her right ear. In the
course of the procedure he determined that the left ear was actually the

one that needed surgery in the first place, and operated upon it instead. When the hearing in her left ear was further impaired by the surgery, Mrs. Mohr sued her physician for operating on that ear without her consent. The basis of the action was battery.

The court found that the physician should have obtained the patient's consent to the surgery on the left ear:

> The free citizen's first and greatest right, which underlies all others—
> the right to himself—is the subject of universal acquiescence, and this
> right necessarily forbids a physician or surgeon, however skillful or
> eminent, who has been asked to examine, diagnose, advise and pre-
> scribe (which are at least necessary first steps in treatment and care),
> to violate without permission the bodily integrity of his patient by a
> major or capital operation, placing him under anaesthetic for that pur-
> pose, and operating on him without his consent or knowledge.[24]

Thus, the physician has no "free license respecting surgical operations,"[25] and a patient's consent to any procedures cannot be implied from the mere fact that he or she has consulted the physician's expertise regarding what treatment will be most beneficial. Express consent to a particular surgery is required. A single narrow exception provides that consent may be implied—but only if an emergency were to arise in the course of an operation or if some unforeseen condition were to come to light that was within the scope of a consent that had already been expressly given by a now-unconscious patient. Operating on the other ear, the court found, was not within the scope of the consent already given—not simply because it was a different ear (that is, physically outside the zone of operation), but because the ear was in a different condition and therefore the dangers and risks involved were different:

> If a physician advises a patient to submit to a particular operation, and
> the patient weighs the dangers and risks incident to its performance,
> and finally consents, the patient thereby, in effect, enters into a con-
> tract authorizing the physician to operate to the extent of the consent
> given, but no further.[26]

The court did not anywhere use the magical words "self-determination" or "autonomy," but clearly "the free citizen's . . . right to himself" is the functional equivalent of the right of self-determination. The basic right to protect one's bodily integrity from unauthorized intrusions forms the justification for battery liability. However, more than mere bodily integrity was at issue even in this early, simple case. The court in *Mohr* assumed that a valid consent requires that the patient have knowledge of "dangers and risks" and the opportunity to weigh them in the course of reaching a decision. Although the facts required no more than a decision as to whether the patient had consented to the procedure that was performed, the *Mohr* court analyzed consent as a full decisional process and not merely as a bare permission to touch.

This interpretation is supported by the sources on which the court relied in reaching its decision. One source was a torts treatise recognizing that the purpose of a consent requirement is not simply to authorize what would otherwise be a battery, but to ensure that the patient makes an effective treatment decision: "The patient must be the final arbiter as to whether he shall take his chances with the operation, or take his chances of living without it. Such is the natural right of the individual, which the law recognizes as a legal right."[27] The court also drew an analogy between consent in the physician-patient relationship and entering into contracts in other trades and occupations, thus suggesting that consents, like contracts, are products of informed deliberation.

The Pratt Case. In *Pratt* v. *Davis* (1906),[28] the physician had performed a hysterectomy without first obtaining the patient's consent. In its earlier (1905) decision, the lower court could find no previous English or American cases in which a physician was held liable for operating without consent, nor any that held that consent was *not* required; but prior cases had held that consent could be *implied*.[29] The physician's attorney argued that "the employment of the physician or surgeon gives him implied license to do whatever in the exercise of his judgment may be necessary."[30] The lower court rejected that view using ringing and memorable language that was quoted soon afterward in that same year by the appellate court in *Mohr*.

In 1906, after the *Mohr* case had been decided, the Illinois Supreme Court affirmed the lower court's decision in the *Pratt* case. The higher court decision in *Pratt* was an influential precedent for later cases in the courts of other states. This decision discussed the consent requirement at some length. Like *Mohr*, *Pratt* specifically limited "implied" consent to emergencies and cases where the patient actually knows the consequences of submitting to the physician's exercise of professional judgment. The court rejected the argument that the patient was necessarily incompetent to give consent because she was epileptic. It also noted that the defendant had admitted deceiving the patient in order to obtain her consent to a prior, related procedure.

The *Mohr* and *Pratt* decisions, intertwined in reasoning and in chronology, are often cited in tandem. These cases are memorable for requiring physicians to obtain consent to particular procedures, for holding so-called "implied" consent an insufficient substitute except in limited exceptional circumstances, and for their strong language regarding the nature and importance of self-determination.

The Rolater Case. The plaintiff in *Rolater* v. *Strain* (1913)[31] had consented to a foot operation to drain an infection, but had specifically instructed her physician not to remove any bone. Despite her instruction, he removed a bone from her toe.

Defense counsel attempted to distinguish this case from *Pratt* and *Mohr* on the ground that the patient had in fact consented to foot surgery, which was performed on the correct foot. The court held, however, that because the operation was not performed in the manner agreed upon and consented to, there was no distinction in principle between the cases. Thus, the reasoning of the two earlier cases was extended to different facts. *Mohr* had suggested that some procedures not specifically consented to might nonetheless be within the scope of the consent already obtained; *Rolater* strengthened the patient's control by honoring a carefully circumscribed consent that expressly forbade, against the physician's professional judgment, a procedure within the operative field.

The Schloendorff Case

In 1914, the eminent Justice Benjamin Cardozo applied the reasoning and precedents of the cases cited above in his celebrated opinion in *Schloendorff* v. *Society of New York Hospitals.*[32] In *Schloendorff* the physician had removed a fibroid tumor after the patient had consented to an abdominal examination under anesthesia, but had specifically requested "no operation." Ironically, because the case focused on the liability of the defendant hospital for torts committed by surgeons using its facilities, the court neither found a violation of informed consent nor said anything about the information a patient needs in order to exercise the right of self-determination.

Nonetheless, Justice Cardozo's opinion is the most widely quoted in the current informed consent literature, and stands as a classic statement of the patient's right to self-determination: "Every human being of adult years and sound mind has a right to determine what shall be done with his own body; and a surgeon who performs an operation without his patient's consent commits an assault, for which he is liable in damages."[33] This brief, eloquent formulation drew considerable attention to the proposition that patients have the right to protect the inviolability of their persons by choosing how they will be treated medically, and that interference with this right may constitute unauthorized bodily invasion—a battery—regardless of the skill with which the treatment was administered and even if it was ultimately beneficial.

The Role of the Early Cases

It is the nature of legal precedent that each decision, relying on earlier court opinions, joins a chain of authority that incorporates the relevant language and reasoning from the cited cases. In this way, these early consent cases built upon each other to fill out the battery theory of liability as grounded in a right of self-determination. *Schloendorff*'s pioneering use of the term "self-determination" developed meanings found in the earlier three decisions. Subsequent cases that followed or relied upon

Schloendorff implicitly adopted its justificatory rationale, although many failed to offer explicit analysis. By this chain of legal reasoning, "self-determination" came to be the primary rationale or justification for the legal requirement of informed consent.

In these early cases, physician behavior was often egregious, and courts did not shrink from using ringing language and sweeping principles to denounce it. The same language was then applied as precedent in later cases in which physicians' behavior was less outrageous. As the informed consent doctrine developed and the problems grew more subtle, the law could have turned away from the language of self-determination, but instead came increasingly to rely on this rationale as its fundamental premise.

Schloendorff is the most frequently cited case in later cases. Several reasons may be offered for its popularity: "Self-determination" is a ready catchphrase, Justice Cardozo a renowned jurist, and the New York court respected and influential, so that other jurisdictions were predisposed to follow such distinguished precedent. The cases preceding *Schloendorff*, however, convey a better sense of the nature and scope of judicial understanding of consent at the time. The language of those cases, especially *Mohr*, demonstrates an advanced appreciation of the decisional process, including the patient's right to weigh dangers and risks before consenting.

This understanding exceeds the "narrowly conceived" right to be free from offensive or uninvited contact that Katz ascribes to these early cases.[34] He reasons that because the early cases "neither invited nor required a sophisticated examination of the relationship between disclosure and consent, on the one hand, and self-determination, on the other," they did not establish the right of thoroughgoing self-determination that has often been claimed for them. He is right on both counts; nonetheless, his view of these cases still underestimates both their historical importance and their analytical sophistication.[35]

No legal doctrine springs full-blown from a case. The law laid down in these early cases reflects only an *incremental* process of doctrinal development. More "sophisticated" analysis had necessarily to await new facts.[36] However, the language already in the cases demonstrates that inherent in the elementary, narrow, unsophisticated battery right of freedom from bodily invasion is an understanding of the patient's authority and decisionmaking that is rich and revolutionary in potential.

For example, the *Mohr* court's attention to the need of patients to weigh "dangers and risks" before consenting or refusing (see p. 121) is evidence of the law's recognition that consent in battery is more than a bare permission to touch. Any touching may still be offensive, and thus a battery, if the one giving permission is ignorant of the nature of the touching for which the permission is given. Such ignorance is likely to be more common—or more visible—in medical contexts than elsewhere. The medical context also demonstrates that the deliberative process employed to dispel that ignorance may be complex. The court in *Mohr* reasoned that in order to ensure that the patient was not ignorant of the nature of the touching to which she consented, she was entitled to the opportunity to reflect on the particular risks and dangers associated with surgery on the ear that actually received it.

Katz correctly maintains that these early cases, despite ringing rhetoric, said—indeed, on their facts, *could say*—comparatively little. As we have noted, legal theories unfold incrementally; new cases present new wrinkles that create issues needing resolution and further refinement of precedent. As more complicated cases emerge, the legal community carries forward values from the past, adapting them to new cases. Thus, although each case on its own may have said comparatively little, taken together these early cases set forth a theory of liability based on a principle—self-determination—that stood ready to yield greater dividends. The process continued without reaching completion, as is characteristic of the common law. When later cases began to build on these early pronouncements, it became clear that they were mining a rich lode, only later to be shaped and announced as "informed consent."

1957-1972: Consent Becomes Informed

After the *Schloendorff* decision, other courts continued to decide battery cases on the basis established by the early cases just examined. No major advances in the doctrine emerged in the next 40 years, as courts in different jurisdictions took up consent issues and either decided them in battery or disposed of them as matters of malpractice. But the first two decades in the second half of the century evoked a dramatic new development: the evolution of the traditional duty to *obtain consent* into a new, explicit duty to *disclose certain forms of information* and then to obtain consent. This development needed a new term; and so "informed" was tacked onto "consent," creating the expression "informed consent," in the landmark decision in *Salgo* v. *Leland Stanford Jr. University Board of Trustees* (1957).

Salgo and Battery

The Salgo Case. After Martin Salgo suffered permanent paralysis as a result of a translumbar aortography, he sued his physicians for negligence in its performance and in failing to warn him of the risk of paralysis. The court found that physicians had the duty to disclose "any facts which are necessary to form the basis of an intelligent consent by the patient to proposed treatment."[37]

The *Salgo* court suggested, without any accompanying analysis, that this new duty to disclose the risks and alternatives of treatment was a logical extension of the already established duty to disclose the treatment's nature and consequences, rather than a duty different in kind.[38] But *Salgo* clearly introduced new elements into the law. Unlike courts in previous cases, the *Salgo* court was not interested merely in whether a recognizable consent had been given to the proposed procedures. Instead, *Salgo* latched tenaciously onto the problem of whether the consent had been informed when given. The court thus created "informed consent" by invoking the same right of self-determination that had heretofore applied only to a consent requirement in order to justify an informed consent requirement. By appeal to *Schloendorff* and other consent cases that applied the battery theory, the apparatus of justification from those earlier cases was imported into this "new" doctrine. The "new" doctrine resulted from the application, to this new factual situation, of the same theory of consent that had been applied to previous cases. *All* pertinent topics of consent—the nature, consequences, harms, benefits, risks, and alternatives of a proffered treatment—were therefore conceived as information needed by patients in order that they know what they are choosing.

Salgo is a malpractice case. Its new duty to obtain informed consent is one of a number of issues raised on appeal from a malpractice judgment in the patient's favor. There is no discussion of the legal basis of informed consent; the cases cited by the court in support of the duty are battery cases, including *Schloendorff*, but the tenor of the language follows that of the lower trial court, whose instruction to the jury on disclosure focused on the negligence-based concept of the physician's fiduciary duty to patients. The lack of analysis of the new "informed" consent leaves it uncertain whether the *Salgo* court meant to ground informed consent in battery or negligence. It is, in fact, possible that the court was drawing on both traditions, perhaps intentionally and perhaps unconsciously. In any event, the explicit shift to negligence came only later.

The decision in *Salgo* did far more than create "informed consent." In a splendid burst of obscurity, the *Salgo* court tempered its extension of traditional battery analysis with the suggestion that the "full" disclosure it required should be consistent with physician *discretion*.[39] *Salgo* appeared to find discretion by physicians necessary to make the new, extended disclosure manageable, but without giving physicians any real guidance in the use of that discretion. Jay Katz considers this invocation of discretion paradigmatic of a judicial dilemma that has lain at the heart of informed consent ever since:

> The conflict created by uncertainties about the extent to which individual and societal well-being is better served by encouraging patients' self-determination or supporting physicians' paternalism is the central

> problem of informed consent. This fundamental conflict [reflects] a thorough-going ambivalence about human beings' capacities for taking care of themselves and need for caretaking. . . . [40]

As Katz points out, *Salgo* at least began asking the right questions.[41] But perhaps it did more: *Salgo* was the first American case to bring together the two consent liability theories. On the one hand, we have seen that in some early twentieth-century cases, consent-getting was treated as one aspect of good medical care. On the other, it was treated by the *Schloendorff* line of cases as dictated by an independent duty to respect autonomy. Not until *Salgo*, when the self-determination precedents were extended explicitly to require disclosure of risks and alternatives, was medical judgment presented as a means of tempering that autonomy-based duty.[42] This clash approximates the clash between the autonomy model and the beneficence model discussed in Chapters 1 and 3. It also accounts for the ambivalence Katz sees as pervasive in the courts. In *Salgo*, autonomy and beneficence met clumsily, unexpectedly, like two figures backing into each other in a darkened room, both struggling to reach the light. In the 20–year period after that decision, this struggle would continue.

An Influential Legal Commentary. A few months before the *Salgo* case was decided, a prominent legal commentator had already advocated a choice between battery and negligence theories. In an influential 1957 article,[43] Allan McCoid surveyed the "unauthorized treatment" decisions to date with the intention of determining "whether there is a real distinction between 'negligent' malpractice and unauthorized treatment or whether the same standard of conduct may be applied in all cases involving improper action on the part of doctors." Both failure to obtain consent and negligent treatment are improper actions by doctors. Therefore, he reasoned, for reasons of "consistency of theory and appropriateness of liability," there should be a single basis of liability in all "malpractice" cases. He found that courts seemed to apply the battery theory of liability in most cases where the procedure consented to differed from the operation performed. Some courts, however, applied negligence law for consistency—especially when, as was common, the unauthorized treatment claim was joined with a negligent treatment claim—or, more often, because negligence theory afforded the plaintiff a longer time in which to bring suit (that is, a longer statute of limitations). McCoid's own reasons for choosing negligence were more philosophical than the courts'. He argued that even though the requirements for battery were met in unauthorized treatment cases, physicians merit special legal treatment because they generally act in good faith for the benefit of their patients.[44]

Informed consent cases that were decided after *Salgo* and that applied the battery theory exhibited an ability equal to that of the negligence theory to address difficult and important consent issues. Nonetheless, the perception grew in most courts that battery was unsuitable and should rarely be used—a perception that may owe more to McCoid's influence than to that of any other commentator or court. The shift in law to liability based on negligence can perhaps be traced as directly to his work as to the opinions in the courts.

Battery Theory After Salgo. As we have noted, the battery theory of informed consent continued to develop after the *Salgo* decision. *Gray* v. *Grunnagle* (1966)[45] was a major decision in a jurisdiction that still today applies the battery rather than the negligence theory of liability to informed consent.[46] In *Gray*, a patient who was paralyzed after an exploratory laminectomy successfully claimed that his consent had not been informed. The patient argued that he was unaware that anything more than a surgical examination was to be performed and was given no information about the risk of paralysis. The *Gray* court defined consent as necessarily "accompanied with deliberation"[47] and as arising from the quasi-contractual physician-patient relationship—an analysis foreshadowed in the early *Mohr* case,[48] which used a contract analogy to illuminate the nature of consent under battery theory.

Another informed consent battery case, *Berkey* v. *Anderson* (1969),[49] linked the duty of disclosure to the law of fraud and deceit, as *Pratt* had done. The patient, Mr. Berkey, consented to a myelogram without having been informed of its seriousness or the risks involved. Berkey asked Dr. Anderson whether the myelogram would be similar to the electromyograms he had undergone. Dr. Anderson responded that myelograms were diagnostic and exploratory, producing minor discomfort when the patient is strapped to a cold table. He failed to mention that a spinal puncture is involved in myelograms, which is *not* used in electromyograms, and he was otherwise reassuring about the procedure. In reviewing the sketchy information provided by the physician, the court stated that "[if] appellant was simply told a myelogram was nothing to worry about and that the most uncomfortable thing about it was being tilted about on a cold table, the jury could have concluded that under the facts the statement was actually deceptive."[50]

Deception, familiar in the early cases as a basis for invalidating consents,[51] was thus applied in *Berkey* to find consents *uninformed* and therefore invalid. The *Berkey* court also emphasized that the physician-patient relationship is fiduciary in character, and that in all such relationships the law imposes a duty of "full disclosure." The measure of this duty in the case before the court was "whether the doctor gave [the patient] sufficient information as to the nature of a myelogram so that he could intelligently decide whether he wished to have it. ... " Thus, relying on *Salgo*, the court introduced a patient-centered disclosure standard, rejecting a standard that would require expert testimony.[52]

Cooper v. *Roberts* (1971),[53] the most recent battery case of importance in informed consent law, followed the outlines of *Gray* (a decision from the same jurisdiction, Pennsylvania) and *Berkey*. The court stated that the "primary interest" of informed consent is "having the patient informed of all the material facts from which he can make an intelligent choice as to his course of treatment, regardless of whether he in fact chooses rationally."[54] In *Cooper* the patient had not been informed of the risk of stomach puncture during a diagnostic examination with a fiber-optic gastroscope. In determining how best to ensure, in *Gray*'s language, the "deliberation" that informed consent required, the court rejected the professional standard of disclosure applied in negligence cases. Instead, it chose a reasonable person standard (see pp. 32–33), as had *Berkey*. The *Cooper* court reasoned that the latter standard represented a better balance between the autonomy of the patient and "the interests of fostering the practice of responsive, progressive medicine."[55]

Here the important notion of seeking an "equitable" balance of interests emerged as an acknowledged force shaping informed consent law. These battery cases were closely linked, in reasoning and justification, to the early twentieth century cases, but they also faced the need, first identified in *Salgo*, to accommodate disclosure problems of greater complexity, particularly how to determine which risks should be disclosed. This is not to say that earlier cases ignored these problems, but only that the courts had not heretofore needed to respond to them on the facts before them.

With self-determination firmly established as the justification in the informed consent battery cases and in *Salgo*, other interests were now invoked to shape and qualify the consent requirement. *Salgo* chose to balance these interests by means of physician discretion. This discretion would eventually be embodied in a professional standard that looked to the customary practice of reasonable physicians for its definition.

At the same time that some courts were delineating the disclosure duty according to battery theory, other courts, influenced in part by McCoid, were coming to consider the duty a question of negligence law.[56] Hints began to surface in decisions and commentary that the failure to obtain informed consent might sometimes be merely a matter of neglect, error, or oversight on the part of the physician, and thus properly malpractice, rather than the *intentional* omission necessary to a claim of battery.[57]

Natanson and Negligence

Two opinions by the Kansas Supreme Court in the case of *Natanson v. Kline* (1960)[58] must be said to have pioneered the negligence theory in informed consent cases. This court was the first explicitly to ground the physician's informed consent liability in negligence rather than in battery; its two opinions predate the just-discussed battery cases, *Gray*, *Berkey*, and *Cooper*, by several years.

Mrs. Natanson sued her physician for failure to obtain her informed consent to cobalt radiation therapy, which was administered after a mastectomy. She suffered severe radiation burns and brought a malpractice claim, alleging negligence by Dr. Kline, a radiologist, both in the performance of the new method of treatment and in failure to warn of its nature and hazards. Her physicians acknowledged that, although she actually consented, she had not been adequately warned of the risks inherent in the procedure. The court established the duty of disclosure as the obligation "to disclose and explain to the patient in language as simple as necessary the nature of the ailment, the nature of the proposed treatment, the probability of success or of alternatives, and perhaps the risks of unfortunate results and unforeseen conditions within the body." Thus, the *Natanson* court required essentially the same extensive disclosure— of the nature, consequences, risks, and alternatives of a proposed procedure—as had *Salgo*.

The duty to disclose was, moreover, couched in the same strong self-determination language that surfaced in *Schloendorff* and had become identified with battery:

> Anglo-American law starts with the premise of thorough-going self-determination. It follows that each man is considered to be master of his own body, and he may, if he be of sound mind, expressly prohibit the performance of life-saving surgery, or other medical treatment. A doctor might well believe that an operation or form of treatment is desirable or necessary but the law does not permit him to substitute his own judgment for that of the patient by any form of artifice or deception.[59]

The *Natanson* court focused, as had the courts in *Mohr* and *Salgo*, on the importance of disclosure for effective decisionmaking, establishing that it was the physician's duty to disclose facts necessary for the patient's intelligent consent and invoking the same justificatory principle of self-determination found in the battery decisions.

However, the *Natanson* decision was based on *negligence* law, largely because the plaintiff had alleged only negligence.[60] The court held that the physician has a duty to make a reasonable disclosure of the risks and hazards of treatment or face possible *malpractice* liability. In this case, the physician was found by the court to have disclosed nothing about the possible risks and hazards of the new therapy; thus, he "failed in his legal duty to make a reasonable disclosure . . . to his patient *as a matter of law*."[61] The court went on to explain that even if the physician *had* made *some* pertinent disclosure, questions of the sufficiency of the disclosure might still have arisen: "The expert testimony of a medical witness is required to establish whether such disclosures are in accordance with those which a reasonable medical practitioner would make under the same or similar circumstances."[62]

Hence, *Natanson* held that mere consent of the patient does not shield the physician from negligence even if the medical performance is good. The medical practice can be flawless, but if injury results from a known risk inherent in the procedure that is undisclosed to the patient, the physician may be liable. This notion was new to malpractice, even though the battery theory had always held that flawlessly administered unauthorized treatment could give rise to liability.

Battery and negligence appeared after *Natanson* as virtually identical in their disclosure requirements for informed consent: The procedure's nature, consequences, and risks, as well as its alternatives, all had to be transmitted. The significant difference lay in the disclosure standards: "Mere consent" was found insufficient in *Natanson* because the patient was not informed of collateral hazards that any "reasonable medical practitioner" would disclose, a standard that implicitly permits discretion paralleling the physician discretion in *Salgo*.[63] By contrast, we have seen that the post-*Salgo* battery decisions chose a layperson's reasonableness standard to measure the necessary disclosure.

The *Natanson* court routinely applied all of the legal elements of negligence to the disclosure duty. The result was the first informed consent decision embodying some controversial concepts that are central features of the negligence theory of liability. These include the disclosure standard just discussed, based on the professional duty of due care, and a causation requirement that provides as follows: If the patient "would have taken the . . . treatments even though Dr. Kline had warned her that the treatments he undertook to administer involved great risk of bodily injury or death, it could not be said that the failure of Dr. Kline to so inform the [patient] was the proximate cause of her injury."[64]

Application of the negligence theory of liability, with this causation requirement, has the potential to limit severely the patient's recovery of damages if the court or jury does not believe the patient's testimony that he or she would not have consented if informed. Thus, from the viewpoint of negligence, if avoiding the breach of duty would not have prevented the injury, then the breach did not *cause* the injury. By contrast, in battery the injury *is* the touching without a valid (informed) consent itself, with no requirement of *resulting* harm in order to recover nominal damages. (Chapter 2 provides an explanation of this and other differences between battery and negligence.)

Apparently determined to avoid responsibility for legal innovation, the *Natanson* court referred to these controversial applications of negligence concepts to informed consent as merely "procedural." Nonetheless, the decision created unprecedented problems of proof and fairness for plaintiffs. These problems, which surfaced later, were responsible for the deliberate call for and creation of what has been termed a "hybrid" theory of liability. The new theory would attempt to mitigate the plaintiff's proof problems by introducing elements more characteristic of battery into the negligence theory applied to informed consent.

The immediate result of *Natanson*, however, was that by the early 1970s there coexisted two distinct lines of informed consent cases: the battery cases, following directly from the early twentieth-century cases and from *Salgo*, and the negligence cases, which followed *Natanson* by incorporating the self-determination rationale of the early cases into the negligence framework. The professional practice standard of disclosure espoused in *Natanson* represented an easy solution to the courts' dilemma of determining the extent of appropriate disclosure. The standard was already familiar to the courts in ordinary negligent treatment cases, and its application to disclosure seemed natural. In adopting it, the courts did not need to engage in either analysis or innovation. Thus it is no surprise that most courts addressing the issue after *Natanson*, and after McCoid's analysis (which *Natanson* cited with approval), should choose the negligence theory and its attached professional practice standard.

This choice did not affect the courts' acknowledged *justification* for requiring informed consent, which, as we have seen, remained self-determination in all of the battery cases and in any negligence case that relied upon them. Because the negligence cases that followed *Natanson* relied, as *Natanson* did, on the self-determination justification from the early *battery* cases to ground the duty to obtain informed consent, the negligence cases no less than the battery cases appealed to the principle of respect for autonomy as a foundational premise in the legal doctrine.

1972–Present: Informed Consent Flourishes

After *Salgo* opened the door to professional "discretion" in disclosure, controversy developed over the reconcilability of entrenched professional disclosure practices with the patient's right of self-determination. On the one hand, the *Berkey* court, applying the battery theory, had rejected Dr. Anderson's argument that the standard for determining his disclosure obligation to the patient was what physicians routinely disclose about risks. On the other hand, negligence cases, like *Natanson*, simultaneously embraced that very standard.[65]

Three 1972 negligence decisions steered a zigzag course between these extremes and came to be regarded as landmarks. These cases were *Canterbury* v. *Spence*[66] and two decisions that closely followed *Canterbury* both chronologically and ideologically: *Cobbs* v. *Grant*[67] and *Wilkinson* v. *Vesey*.[68] This trilogy of decisions led many to believe that the professional practice standard of disclosure would quickly be replaced by the patient-centered reasonable person standard. This trend was considered by some courts and commentators to be the promise and potential glory of a flourishing new doctrine of informed consent based on full protection of the self-determination right. But the promise and glory

quickly faded: The professional practice disclosure standard was not dis-
placed in American informed consent law. These three decisions established but an important *minority* trend in American courts.[69]

These three decisions and those that later followed them differ from
Natanson in that they graft some features of the battery cases—notably
an orientation toward patient-centered rather than professional disclosure standards—onto what is otherwise a negligence theory of liability.
Because professional negligence liability properly is based not on court-
and jury-determined duties but on professional custom, the resulting
blend of elements led these cases to be labeled "hybrids."

The Canterbury Case

Canterbury v. *Spence* was the first and most influential of these landmark
decisions. In this case the patient underwent a laminectomy for severe
back pain. After the laminectomy, the patient fell from his hospital bed,
and several hours later suffered major paralysis. He had not been warned
that a laminectomy carried approximately a 1% risk of such paralysis. A
second operation failed to relieve the paralysis, and an appeals court
held that risk of possible paralysis should have been disclosed before the
first procedure.

Judge Spottswood Robinson's opinion focused on self-determination,
again quoting *Schloendorff*: "The root premise is the concept, fundamental in American jurisprudence, that '[e]very human being of adult years
and sound mind has a right to determine what shall be done with his own
body'. ... "[70] Consent was held to require the informed exercise of
choice; thus, the physician's disclosure should have provided the patient
an opportunity to assess available options and such attendant risks as
paralysis. As to sufficiency of information, the court held: "[T]he
patient's right of self-decision shapes the boundaries of the duty to
reveal. That right can be effectively exercised only if the patient possesses enough information to enable an intelligent choice."[71]

Canterbury exhibited a judicial need to examine informed consent in
light of the growing disagreement over its appropriate expression. The
law's continuing emphasis on self-determination was more carefully
expounded in *Canterbury* than previously. In language much like that of
the post-*Salgo* battery cases discussed above, the opinion offered a justification for the disclosure duty that incorporated a demanding interpretation of self-determination:

> True consent to what happens to one's self is the informed exercise of
> a choice, and that entails an opportunity to evaluate knowledgeably the
> options available and the risks attendant upon each. The average
> patient has little or no understanding of the medical arts, and ordinarily
> has only his physician to whom he can look for enlightenment with
> which to reach an intelligent decision. From these almost axiomatic

considerations springs the need, and in turn the requirement, of a reasonable divulgence by physician to patient to make such a decision
possible.[72]

Because any decision determining what is to be done to his or her body
"is the prerogative of the patient," the patient must decide by means of
an acquired understanding of therapeutic alternatives and their hazards.
The physician therefore has a duty of "reasonable disclosure" of the
risks of and alternatives to the proposed treatment, a duty based in the
"fiducial quality" of the physician-patient relationship.

The court came to this conclusion by connecting the disclosure duty
to the physician's general duty of due care in malpractice law, a duty to
act in the patient's best interests. First, the court pointed out that the
duty to treat the patient with reasonable skill and due care has traditionally called for disclosure of information—for example, warnings regarding side effects of drugs, instructions as to proper self-care, information
as to conditions discovered in the course of examination, and advice
regarding the consultation of specialists if the physician finds that the
problem exceeds his own skill and knowledge. This disclosure duty is
readily understandable in terms of beneficence, because giving good
information may be as important for care as are proper diagnosis and
therapy.

The court declared that "due care normally demands that the physician warn the patient of any risks to his well-being which contemplated
therapy may involve."[73] If *only* due care is involved, then the giving of
risk information is much like telling a patient that drowsiness resulting
from medication may make it unwise to drive. In this way, information
about risks helps patients to maximize their well-being through personal
behavior that is technically outside the realm of the physician-patient
relationship. But the *Canterbury* court went further:

> The context in which the duty of risk-disclosure arises is invariably the
> occasion for decision as to whether a particular treatment procedure is
> to be undertaken. To the physician, whose training enables a self-sat-
> isfying evaluation, the answer may seem clear, but it is the prerogative
> of the patient, not the physician, to determine for himself the direction
> in which his interests seem to lie. To enable the patient to chart his
> course understandably, some familiarity with the therapeutic alterna-
> tives and their hazards becomes essential.[74]

The court looked specifically to history and precedent to support this
conclusion:

> This disclosure requirement, on analysis, reflects much more of a
> change in doctrinal emphasis than a substantive addition to malpractice
> law. . . . [I]t is evident that it is normally impossible to obtain a consent
> worthy of the name unless the physician first elucidates the options and

the perils for the patient's edification. Thus the physician has long borne a duty, on pain of liability for unauthorized treatment, to make adequate disclosure to the patient. The evolution of the obligation to communicate for the patient's benefit as well as the physician's protection has hardly involved an extraordinary restructuring of the law.[75]

Canterbury is here acknowledging that early twentieth-century consent cases such as *Pratt* and *Mohr* had indeed contained language and reasoning that formed a substantial base for the later expression of the disclosure duty so central to informed consent. Those cases began the chain of authority that developed into the body of law upon which *Canterbury* drew.

Self-determination thus provided the *Canterbury* court with its primary justification for protecting a patient's right of decision. But the court had also carefully outlined and put forward the due-care duty to disclose. The court appeared simply to graft the two duties together, and to assume that the patient's personal choices and the obligations inherent in the physician's commitment tend generally to the same end.[76] The assumption is flawed, of course; that there can be divergence between the interests and goals of patients and those of physicians is a fundamental premise of informed consent itself.[77] However, by joining the two duties and then placing a premium on the patient's decision, the *Canterbury* court went further than its predecessors in attempting a way out of the ambivalence that had so long plagued the doctrine.

In its historically most significant and dramatic finding, the *Canterbury* court rejected the professional practice standard of disclosure. *Canterbury* swam upstream against a powerful current of support for this standard, which had become firmly established in those jurisdictions adhering to the negligence cause of action—a clear majority in 1972. Although the professional practice standard is consistent with the negligence cause of action that *Canterbury* embraced, the court could not agree that "the patient's cause of action is dependent upon the existence and nonperformance of a relevant professional tradition." It reasoned that "to bind the disclosure obligation to medical usage is to arrogate the decision on revelation to the physician alone. Respect for the patient's right of self-determination on particular therapy demands a standard set by law for physicians rather than one which physicians may or may not impose upon themselves."[78]

The court held that a physician is required to disclose information to patients unless, in the physician's informed medical judgment, due care requires some degree of nondisclosure under the circumstances. That is, the therapeutic privilege can validly be invoked to override the disclosure requirement. The extent of the disclosure otherwise required is to be measured exclusively by a lay reasonable person standard of what is material to the patient's decision rather than a professional standard based on customary practice. To the *Canterbury* court, the weighing of risks and benefits for the patient is not an expert skill to be measured through a professional standard because it is not intrinsically a professional judgment.

Through its interpretation of the right of self-determination, the *Canterbury* court was thus led to reject a powerful trend toward reliance on professional judgment in favor of a fuller recognition of patients' rights. Using language and reasoning similar to that found in the post-Salgo battery cases such as *Gray* and *Berkey*, *Canterbury* recognized that although professional expertise is necessary in identifying the nature and consequences of the procedure, the feasibility of alternatives, and the severity of the risks, once the physician has exercised medical judgment in developing and presenting this information to the patient, further deference to the physician's judgment is unnecessarily in derogation of the patient's decisionmaking right.

The *Canterbury* court did not, however, require physicians to divulge whatever information the patient might deem significant, claiming that such a role "would summon the physician to second-guess the patient, whose ideas on materiality could hardly be known to the physician," and thus would "make an undue demand upon medical practitioners, whose conduct, like that of others, is to be measured in terms of reasonableness." Instead, "on the basis of his medical training and experience [the physician] can sense how the average, reasonable patient expectably would react."[79] The court agreed with Jon R. Waltz and Thomas Scheuneman that: "A risk is thus material when a reasonable person, in what the physician knows or should know to be the patient's position, would be likely to attach significance to the risk in deciding whether or not to forego the proposed therapy."[80] *Canterbury*'s chosen disclosure standard was identical with that adopted by the post-*Salgo* battery cases; its justification for adopting less than a wholly subjective standard rested not on fears about the patient's ability to decide, but on concerns of fair application and proof.

Canterbury confirmed that the negligence theory of liability requires that proximate causation be shown. The patient must prove that disclosure of a material risk would have resulted in a decision against treatment, and therefore that the disclosure failure "caused" the injury that resulted when the risk materialized. But the court, again relying on Waltz and Scheuneman, rejected the notion that mere examination of the credibility of the patient as to the quite hypothetical choice he or she *would* have made if informed could adequately protect the physician from biased hindsight by patients or from overly sympathetic juries: "Better it is, we believe, to resolve the causality issue on an objective basis: in terms of what a prudent person in the patient's position would have decided if suitably informed. . . ."[81] If a subjective standard were applied to satisfy this proximate cause issue, then a patient could recover if *that particular* patient would not have consented had an adequate disclosure been made. *Canterbury* insisted that this determination would be guesswork and would constantly place physicians in jeopardy of hindsight and even outright falsification. Hence, as it had done for disclosure, the court allowed only the "objective reasonable person" as the standard for proximate cause determinations.

Canterbury therefore succeeded in reaffirming that self-determination is the sole justification and goal of informed consent, and that the patient's needs for information rather than the physician's practices must form the basis of any adequate standard of disclosure. On the other hand, it rejected an individual, subjective interpretation of these needs and turned instead to the reasonable person, that "tired and weary old creature of tort law,"[82] to place a limit upon patients' informational claims. The court acknowledged that its choice among the possible standards was designed to protect physicians from undue burden and liability in the practical application of the doctrine to the courtroom setting. The reasonable person standard thus acted as a means of limiting physicians' liability. The standard could also be viewed, however, as entailing that only the "reasonable" person's needs for information deserve legal protection—a means of undercutting the right of self-determination. *Canterbury*'s choice of the standard therefore created as much controversy as it attempted to solve.

The courts in the other two 1972 cases intended to follow *Canterbury* closely. *Cobbs* v. *Grant*, an ulcer surgery case that relied extensively on *Canterbury*'s language, required disclosure of "all significant perils,"[83] defining those as "the risk of death or bodily harm, and problems of recuperation."[84] Both *Cobbs*[85] and *Wilkinson* v. *Vesey*[86] held that decisions whether to proceed with a therapy require reference to the values of the patient, and thus are not exclusively *medical* determinations. *Wilkinson* held that "a physician is bound to disclose all the known material risks peculiar to the proposed procedure." It defined materiality as "the significance a reasonable person, in what the physician knows or should know is his patient's position, would attach to the disclosed risk or risks in deciding whether to submit or not to submit to surgery or treatment."[87]

These three decisions thus followed the contemporary trend, begun in the early cases and firmly established after *Salgo*, of requiring disclosure of diagnosis, prognosis with and without treatment, proposed treatments, risks inherent in the treatment, and alternative treatments and their risks. However, as we have seen, there were now some important differences between the *Natanson* line of negligence cases and this new trilogy. The 1972 decisions combined features of negligence and battery theories into a new approach that attempted a fairer balance than is present in the *Natanson* line of cases between, on the one hand, the right of self-determination of patients and, on the other hand, the exigencies and demands of the physician-patient relationship and the complexities of the legal setting.

Post-Canterbury: The Truman Case

After *Canterbury*, little of historical significance emerged in the next decade in the courts regarding informed consent, with the exception of *Truman* v. *Thomas* (1980).[88] *Truman* was decided in California, by the court that had decided *Cobbs* v. *Grant* in 1972. The court in *Truman* permitted the children of a woman who died from cervical cancer to sue her doctor for failing to disclose the risks of not undergoing the Pap smear test, which she had repeatedly refused. Although her physician (and the minority of the court) argued that the duty to disclose applies only to procedures to which patients *consent*, and not to those they refuse, the court quoted *Cobbs*, which held that the patient must be apprised of "the risks of a decision *not* to undergo the treatment" as well as the "risks inherent in the procedure . . . and the probability of a successful outcome of the treatment."[89]

The duty to disclose the risks of no treatment, which the *Truman* court regarded as established by *Canterbury* and made binding upon California physicians by *Cobbs*, resembles the already established duty to disclose alternatives to a proposed procedure. In many instances, no treatment *is* an alternative to the procedure proposed. Thus, the risks of doing nothing are very likely to fall within the scope of the physician's duty to disclose information about any proffered procedure. To this extent, *Truman* had said nothing new. What was new was the application of this disclosure duty even if the patient refuses and there has been no bodily intrusion. The court held that the importance of the right to make decisions about one's body is not diminished by the kind of decision one makes, reasoning that no other result is consistent with the fiduciary nature of the physician's duty to present the proper information.

This point is legally and historically important because it is incompatible with the battery theory of liability, as traditionally understood. There is no battery without an unauthorized bodily intrusion, or "touching."[90] A disclosure requirement based on battery theory alone must have as its goal the authorization of interventions that would otherwise be instances of battery. Even when earlier battery decisions acknowledged the patient's right to *decide*—rather than the right merely to be free from unauthorized physical invasions—the choices in the cases had always been to consent to physical invasions. In *Truman* the court was envisioning no such invasion in requiring that refusals be informed.

Regardless of the nature of battery liability, however, the understanding of self-determination espoused by the early battery consent cases seemed even then to be more fundamental, to move beyond this basic physical requirement. For example, the *Mohr* court focused on the deliberative process, rather than solely on which of Mrs. Mohr's ears received surgery. But because by definition battery is about physical integrity, battery theory cannot recognize the importance and value of the patient's decision about medical treatment unless it is a decision permitting bodily invasion. This appears to be the only unassailable limitation on the use of battery theory for informed consent.

In contrast, negligence law, as *Truman* has shown, can acknowledge the value of the patient's right to decide even if the decision is one to forego some invasion. The end result of *Truman*'s reasoning was to reinforce the strength of the self-determination justification for informed consent by protecting a right to decide that is not compromised by this limitation of legal theory. It also pointed to the need for a theory of informed consent that is independent of the constraints of the battery/negligence distinction.

Strategies in Statutory Law

Informed Consent in Malpractice Statutes. The courts' role in introducing doctrinal advances like that seen in *Truman* has been sharply curtailed by the involvement of state legislatures in the informed consent arena. In the early 1970s, coincident with the *Canterbury* decision but resulting primarily from increases in the number of ordinary malpractice suits and in the size of awards, a crisis in malpractice insurance drew public notice. Skyrocketing insurance premiums pushed physician lobbying groups and state legislatures into actions designed to ease the financial impact of malpractice lawsuits on doctors,[91] and many state schemes to limit malpractice liability were enacted as a result. Legislators reasoned that informed consent was often used by plaintiffs as another way to recover in court for bad outcomes.[92] State legislatures therefore began to include informed consent provisions in liability-limiting specifications. In more than a few instances these provisions undercut the impact of the common law.[93] Only a few informed consent statutes codified the *patient-oriented* provisions suggested by the commentators and implemented by a the minority of courts.[94]

Twenty-five states enacted informed consent legislation from 1975 through 1977. The replacement of the common-law path to informed consent by statute in so many states—30 states by 1982—reflects both the doctrine's high social visibility and the political influence of physicians on state legislatures. The statutes generally adhere closely to the models supplied by the traditional negligence theory of liability, namely, the professional practice disclosure standard and the objective causation standard.

Because these standards have always been dominant in the courts, the flurry of legislative activity in this area does not indicate overall a significant retrenchment in the informed consent doctrine: A codification of the disclosure and causation standards from the traditional negligence theory would represent a change from the established common law in only a minority of jurisdictions. Informed consent legislation in most jurisdictions has had the effect of freezing the law where it already was, cutting off the possibility of further development and change through the courts. Alan Meisel and Lisa Kabnick, in a comprehensive study of informed consent legislation, concluded that, on balance, the number of jurisdictions adhering to the various possible formulations of informed consent theory was largely unchanged after the flurry of statutory reform; thus, the doctrine has remained just about as it was under the common law.[95]

Special Informed Consent Legislation. In addition to the more common informed consent statutes aimed at malpractice reform, a number of special statutes mandating informed consent for various treatments and procedures were proposed or enacted during the 1960s and 1970s. These statutes were responses to particular instances of abuse: They were usually passed to prevent the exploitation of a vulnerable patient population or to curtail the administration of a dangerous or questionably beneficial treatment or procedure. Enactments have occurred at the local, state, and federal levels, and specific provisions have sometimes appeared in regulations rather than in statutes themselves. Special statutes mandate disclosure and informed consent in such matters as sterilization,[96] electroconvulsive therapy,[97] breast cancer treatment,[98] and the administration of psychotropic drugs.[99]

These special consent laws are addressed not to the injured patient's financial recovery, as are the malpractice reform provisions, but to ensuring that the patient receives information *before* the point of decision. The statutes are thus close in spirit to the self-determination purpose of informed consent. Often, however, the statutes were enacted not simply to provide information, but to *deter* patients from consenting to the treatment in question. Thus, they were aimed ultimately at curtailing the use of various treatments. Such a linking of informed consent to the prevention of abuses of self-determination and simultaneously to the control of treatments that are considered harmful or useless is a blurring of autonomy and beneficence rationales that is characteristic of the history of informed consent in research, as we shall see in Chapter 5.

Conclusion

In this chapter we have maintained that throughout the history of the legal doctrine of informed consent in the twentieth century, self-determination has been the principle most consistently invoked to justify the obligation to obtain consent. Yet such a simple formulation will mask a considerable legal complexity unless it is qualified and substantiated by careful reference to the history of the landmark cases.

The language of justification rarely appears in case law, but specific forms of justification can be deduced from the precedents cited and the theory of liability chosen. The battery theory of liability finds a natural justification in respect for autonomy expressed as the right of self-determination. However, informed consent cases that apply the negligence theory of liability are less easy to subsume under a single justification. The law of medical malpractice in general is beneficence-based: It prescribes the medical profession's duty to do that which will promote the well being of patients by possessing and exercising reasonable care and skill in the practice of medicine. But although negligent *treatment* cases thus are firmly linked to beneficence-based concerns, modern *informed consent* negligence cases have had strong ties to the principle of respect for autonomy, as is evidenced by the role that *Schloendorff* and other battery cases have played as precedent for them. The law has a venerable history in dealing with consent cases, reaching back to well before 1957. Despite a few hints of provocative consent language in some nineteenth-century cases, the turn-of-the-century battery cases first focused attention on the importance of consent. The later decisions of major impact— *Salgo, Natanson,* and *Canterbury,* in particular—are firmly rooted in these early-twentieth-century precedents.

Although in the history we have offered in this chapter appeals to the autonomy principle have often been blundering, confused, and combined with distinguishable principles as if they were indistinguishable, respect for autonomy has never been *abandoned* in law as the justificatory basis of the right to authorize or refuse medical care. Certainly the right has often been neglected, and the courts have tempered it (and probably at times abused or ignored it) because of other concerns they must confront. Often these concerns have been beneficence-based considerations of the welfare of patients. That is, therapeutic goals for the patient have competed with and sometimes been allowed to overwhelm the patient's right to choose. At other times, the law has been diverted from the course of protecting autonomous decisionmaking for patients by the mechanics and pragmatic constraints built into the legal process. It must be remembered that compensation for past injury is the common law's means of protecting autonomy rights. Proof of an abuse can occur in court only after the fact, and that proof must fit the courtroom's procedural rules and conventions.

The legal doctrine of informed consent and the much-trumpeted legal right of self-determination have not had and are not likely ever to have a direct and deep impact on the daily routines of the physician-patient relationship.[100] This inefficacy is not surprising or a cause for alarm: Notwithstanding the societal decision to resolve certain limited kinds of problems in the courts, informed consent in clinical practice should be first a problem of medical ethics, not of legal requirements. This judgment is of course primarily normative and sociological, even though our concern in this chapter has been legal and historical.

However, as our clinical history in Chapter 3 demonstrated, case law has been extremely influential, not directly upon medical practice but rather on many disciplines in the intellectual history of informed consent—probably more influential than the writings from any other discipline. The focus of our history has been intentionally narrow in scope; a broader history of the *influence* of the law would not be confined, as ours has been, to the internal workings of the courts. Case law has stimulated philosophers, physicians, legislators, social scientists, legal commentators, and many others to reflect on the adequacy of present practices of obtaining the consents of patients (and subjects).[101] The law contributed the term "informed consent" and set others on the road to conceiving of the social institution of consent rules as a mechanism for the protection of autonomous decisionmaking. Although it is true that the law of informed consent does not now have—and perhaps never had—any significant power to effect and enforce changes in physicians' consent practices through legal sanction, it serves justice to remember the profound impact of the law and the frontiers explored by judges in authoring the landmark cases. The law's effect on thinking about the physician-patient relationship has far outstripped the effect that the small volume of informed consent cases has had in mandating particular disclosures.

The influential role of the courts in the history of informed consent may be at least partially explained by the fact that the courts already had in place a structure that was better equipped to address issues of consent than did either medicine or medical ethics. We have maintained that for decades legal theory has possessed principles that could give expression to concerns of consent. Civil liberties, self-determination, fraud, bodily integrity, battery, trespass, the fiduciary relationship, contract, and the like were all staples of the law. As soon as the cases were brought to the courts, these principles came into play and began to evolve into the framework described in Chapter 2.

In medicine, there was no ready set of internal principles that paralleled those of law. Developments in medicine therefore had to come from an external source or framework. There *was* an available moral framework in medicine, but it was entirely beneficence-based and ill-suited for grappling with problems of autonomous decisionmaking and informed consent. Chapters 3 and 4 suggest that the transition to informed consent in medicine involved a more abrupt and dramatic departure than in law. To put it in the most naked form of contrast, medicine was jolted from an exclusive preoccupation with a beneficence model to awareness of an autonomy model of responsibility for the patient. Physicians had heretofore considered the physician-patient relationship by beginning from the patient's submission to the physician's professional beneficence. The law enlarged that perspective by viewing the relationship within a wider social framework, emphasizing instead that patients voluntarily initiate the relationship and have the right to define its boundaries to fit their own ends. The goals sought by patient and physician were generally the same; but when they differed, the law was capable of demonstrating to medicine the validity of autonomy concerns.

Developments in case law were the triggering cause of medicine's changing perspective. Although we saw in Chapter 3 that moral philosophy and other disciplines joined the bandwagon and became contributing causes of change, by comparison to the contributions made by physicians and indeed writers in any field, including ethics (see Chapter 3), the courts must be said to have been the pioneers of today's concerns about informed consent.

Notes

1. When the law upholds a particular moral principle (as discussed in Chapters 1 and 2), it does so by creating corresponding rights and duties that derive from the principle. In the enforcement of these rights and duties, legal reasoning must consider a collection of factors that come into play in law: proof, enforceability, procedural fairness, and other pragmatic matters that have little or no weight in other contexts. See, for example, the discussion of these factors in President's Commission for the Study of Ethical Problems in Medicine and Biomedical and Behavioral Research, *Making Health Care Decisions* (Washington, D.C.: U.S. Government Printing Office, 1982), Vol. 1, 23–29.

2. See W.D. White, "Informed Consent: Ambiguity in Theory and Practice," *Journal of Health Politics, Policy and Law* 8 (1983): 99:

> Decisional law in the Anglo-American tradition has been, above all, eminently pragmatic, and deliberately so. Its essential genius has been its ability to respond to changing circumstances with a minimum of speculation and theorizing, thereby maintaining a firm rootage in the immediate, concrete human problems under scrutiny. Furthermore, the thrust of decisional law, as it addresses new problems under the guidance (and sometimes the control) of precedent, has been essentially conservative. A traditional view among jurists and legal scholars has therefore been that the narrower the decision, the better the holding; and the less philosophizing, the better the rationale.

3. Oliver Wendell Holmes, quoted in Charles O. Gregory, et al., eds., *Cases and Materials on Torts* (Boston: Little, Brown, 1977), 68.

4. 95 Eng. Rep. 860, 2 Wils. K.B. 359 (1767). For an analysis of the case in the nineteenth century, see Alexander Young, "The Law of Malpractice," *Boston Medical and Surgical Journal* (new series) 5 (June 1870): 432–33 (also cited as Volume 82).

5. 2 Wils. K.B. 360.

6. Several pragmatic reasons could explain why the plaintiff introduced such evidence and cast the complaint in contract terms rather than assault terms. During the eighteenth century, a case could be tried under only one writ, and not all courts were

authorized to hear cases in every writ. It is possible that the prospects for recovery in *Slater* were more favorable under a contract writ than under a trespass writ. The *Slater* court appeared unusually willing to look beyond technicalities in order to reach a fair resolution.

7. There was no distinct tort of "negligence" or professional negligence (malpractice) in Anglo-American law until after 1800, Stewart Jay, personal communication, January, 1985.

8. 2 Wils. K.B. 362.

9. Martin S. Pernick, "The Patient's Role in Medical Decisionmaking: A Social History of Informed Consent in Medical Therapy," in President's Commission, *Making Health Care Decisions*, Vol. 3, 3.

10. 60 Barb. 488 (N.Y. Supreme Court 1871), *aff'd*, 75 N.Y. 12 (1878).

11. Pernick, "The Patient's Role," 14.

12. 60 Barb. at 514–15.

13. See, for example, *Beck* v. *German Klinik*, 78 Iowa 696, 43 N.W. 617 (1889). (Here the physician was found liable in negligence for not giving the patient instructions for care of a properly set broken leg after discharge from the hospital.) See also the thorough survey of these grounds for liability in Allan H. McCoid, "The Care Required of Medical Practitioners," *Vanderbilt Law Review* 12 (1959): 549, 586–97, and the extensive citation of similar modern cases in *Canterbury* v. *Spence*, 464 F.2d 778, 781 (D.C. Cir. 1972).

14. 120 N.Y. 630, 24 N.E. 276 (Ct. App. N.Y. 1890).

15. Pernick, "The Patient's Role," 14.

16. Summaries of the cases are collected in *American Digest, Century Edition* (St. Paul, MN: West, 1901), under the Physicians and Surgeons heading, in Volume 39.

17. Pernick, "The Patient's Role," 16; Jay Katz, *The Silent World of Doctor and Patient* (New York: The Free Press, 1984), 52.

18. Annotation, "Character and Extent of Surgical Operation Authorized by Patients," *American Law Reports* 26 (1923): 1036.

19. W.E. Shipley, "Liability of Physician or Surgeon for Extending Operation or Treatment Beyond that Expressly Authorized," *American Law Reports 2nd* 56 (1967): 695, 697. The use of this standard naturally led to results like that cited by Pernick in *Twombly* v. *Leach*, 65 Mass. 397 (1853) (discussed in Pernick, "The Patient's Role," 14), and by Katz in *Hunt* v. *Bradshaw*, 242 N.C. 517, 88 S.E.2d 762 (1955) (discussed in Katz, *The Silent World*, 53–57) where it was held that withholding information could be adjudged beneficial to patients.

20. Annotation, "Consent as Condition of Right to Perform Surgical Operation," *American Law Reports* 76 (1932): 562.

21. See our discussion in Chapter 2 and see also the discussions of early twentieth-century cases in Herbert Winston Smith, "Antecedent Grounds of Liability in the Practice of Surgery," *Rocky Mountain Law Review* 14 (1942): 233–55, and Allan H. McCoid, "A Reappraisal of Liability for Unauthorized Medical Treatment," *Minnesota Law Review* 41 (1957): 381, 382–434.

22. See, for example, McCoid, "A Reappraisal of Liability for Unauthorized Medical Treatment," 381; William L. Prosser, et al., eds., *Cases and Materials in Torts*, 4th ed. (Mineola: Foundation Press, 1977), 165–66.

23. 95 Minn. 261, 104 N.W. 12 (1905).

24. 104 N.W. at 14, quoting *Pratt* v. *Davis*, 118 Ill. App. 161 (1905), *aff'd*, 224 Ill. 300, 79 N.E. 562 (1906) (discussed below).

25. 104 N.W. at 13.

26. Ibid., 15.

27. 95 Minn. at 168, citing Edgar B. Kinkead, *Commentaries on the Law of Torts: A Philosophic Discussion of the General Principle Underlying Civil Wrongs ex Delicto* (San Francisco: Bancroft-Whitney, 1903).

28. 224 Ill. 300, 79 N.E. 562 (1906).

29. 118 Ill. App. 161 (1905), esp. 166.

30. 79 N.E. at 565. See also *Application of President and Directors of Georgetown College, Inc.*, 331 F.2d 1000, petition for rehearing en banc denied, 331 F.2d 1010, Cert. denied, 377 U.S. 978 (D.C. Cir. 1964), implying that a patient who seeks emergency room services may be presumed, nothing else appearing, to consent to whatever services are deemed necessary.

31. 39 Okla. 572, 137 P.96 (1913).

32. 211 N.Y. 125, 105 N.E. 92 (1914).

33. 211 N.Y. 128, 105 N.E. 93.

34. Katz, *The Silent World*, 50.

35. Ibid., 52.

36. Katz's surprise (*The Silent World*, 52) that courts should be reminding physicians of such elementary duties as consent-getting as late as the twentieth century is curious. One could as easily argue that the courts were silent on these duties earlier because no relevant cases arose sooner, perhaps because the violations were too *few*.

37. *Salgo* v. *Leland Stanford Jr. University Board of Trustees*, 317 P.2d 170, 181 (1957). The quoted language comes directly from the amicus brief submitted by the American College of Surgeons to the court. This unattributed source was identified by Jay Katz (*The Silent World*, 60–63). According to one of the brief's authors—Paul Gebhard of Vedder, Price, Kaufmann and Kammholz, a Chicago law firm known for its work in health law—the broad-brush duty implied by the language of the brief was fully endorsed by the College at the time (personal communication, 10/10/84). That endorsement was admittedly accompanied by the naive belief that *Salgo*'s formulation was a clear and uncomplicated solution to the problem of balancing autonomy and beneficence. The College and its lawyers could not know that *Salgo* was only the next step on a long road.

38. It was early understood in battery cases that if the patient did not know the nature of the "touching" consented to, the consent was not valid and the physician was guilty of battery. See Marcus Plant, "An Analysis of Informed Consent," *Fordham Law Review* 36 (1968): 639.

39. "[I]n discussing the element of risk a certain amount of discretion must be employed consistent with the full disclosure of facts necessary to an informed consent." 154 Cal. App. 2d at 578, 317 P.2d at 181.

Thus, *Salgo* simultaneously affirmed both that patients' bodies and decisions are theirs and that the physician's decision-facilitating role might be defined by a "medical" judgment of the patient's best interests. To invoke the therapeutic privilege in this way was not new: It was mentioned in *Pratt* (and other cases) and seems to have been well established in commentary. See Alan Meisel, "The Expansion of Liability for Medical Accidents: From Negligence to Strict Liability by Way Of Informed Consent," *Nebraska Law Review* 56 (1977): 99–101. The role of the physician's discretion in disclosing risks without a specific invocation of the therapeutic privilege *is* new in *Salgo*, however. See Jay Katz, "Informed Consent: A Fairy Tale? Law's Vision," *University of Pittsburgh Law Review* 39 (1977): 150.

40. Katz, "Informed Consent: A Fairy Tale?" 138, 139ff.

41. Katz, *The Silent World*, 65.

42. The only time, it appeared, that the two views had been juxtaposed previously

was in the aforementioned English case, *Slater* v. *Baker and Stapleton* (1767), which boasted a decidedly ambiguous collection of possible theories of liability.

43. McCoid, "A Reappraisal of Liability for Unauthorized Medical Treatment," esp. 434.

44. Ibid., 424–27. McCoid reasoned that even if the requirements of battery were met, the patient had already agreed to submit to *some* form of physical invasion, whether with proper information or not. McCoid balanced the need to protect the physician's professional discretion against the plaintiff's personal integrity interest, which was lessened by the initial submission to the physician's care; on balance, it was his conclusion that negligence theory should be applied.

McCoid's position flows from his characterization of these cases as fundamentally *malpractice* cases. He essentially ignores the reasoning of factually plainer cases like *Pratt, Mohr,* and *Schloendorff*, which, as we have seen, specifically rejected the argument that physicians should be specially treated by being permitted to act with "implied" consent in their patients' best medical interests. McCoid's reasoning better accords with *Salgo*'s introduction of medical discretion directly into the apparently absolute right of self-determination that the earlier cases had identified.

45. 423 Pa. 144, 223 A.2d 663 (1966).

46. Each jurisdiction is free to choose whether to follow courts in other states regarding trends in the law. Some states have only recently begun to recognize the informed consent doctrine [see, again, *Scott* v. *Bradford*, 606 P.2d 554 (Okla. 1980)], and Georgia does not recognize it at all. Compare Alan Meisel and Lisa D. Kabnick, "Informed Consent to Medical Treatment: An Analysis of Recent Legislation," *University of Pittsburgh Law Review* 41 (1980): 407.

47. 223 A.2d at 669, quoting Justice Joseph Story's *Equity Jurisprudence* (Boston: Little, Brown, 1918).

48. *Gray* also concluded, relying solely on post-*Salgo* battery decisions [for example, *Mitchell* v. *Robinson*, 334 S.W.2d 11 (Mo. 1960); *Bang* v. *Charles T. Miller Hosp.*, 251 Minn. 427, 88 N.W.2d 186 (1958); *Scott* v. *Wilson*, 396 S.W.2d 532 (Tex. App. 1965); *Bowers* v. *Talmadge*, 159 So.2d 888 (Fla. App. 1963)], that disclosure by the physician of risks and alternatives is necessary for an informed consent. Proponents of the negligence theory sometimes argue that although *some* disclosure ought to be required to preclude battery, the failure to disclose risks and alternatives in particular can only be a matter of negligence. See Plant, "An Analysis of Informed Consent." *Gray* established, despite the unclarity in *Salgo*'s choice of theory, that the fuller disclosure requirement could be imposed under battery theory.

49. 1 Cal. App. 3d 790, 82 Cal. Rptr. 67 (1969).

50. 1 Cal. App. 3d at 805, 82 Cal. Rptr. at 77.

51. See Meisel, "The Expansion of Liability for Medical Accidents," 79–82.

52. See Chapter 2, pp. 30–34, for a discussion of the different disclosure standards and the role of expert testimony. 37 Cal. App. 3d at 805, 82 Cal. Rptr. at 77, 78. The court reasoned that disclosure is required because of the patient's medical ignorance and reliance on the physician for information. The court rejected what seemed to be a claim by the physician that the patient had *waived* disclosure. The patient testified that although he was ignorant of the nature of myelograms, "anything that they were going to do to help . . . was okay." In response, the court remarked: "The statement is subject to the interpretation that the 'anything' appellant had in mind was something far less drastic than a myelogram."

53. In *Berkey* and other cases decided after *Salgo*, the "therapeutic privilege" was introduced into the informed consent doctrine (see discussion in Chapter 2, pp. 36–38). We have not attempted an extensive historical analysis of the degree to which

the availability of the privilege undercut in the courts the application of patient-centered disclosure standards. Formally, however, limiting physician discretion to an exceptive case is different from permitting it outright, as *Salgo* seemed to do. In this respect, decisions like *Berkey* may be viewed as clarifying, if not strengthening, the patient's decisional authority.

54. 220 Pa. Super. 260, 286 A.2d 647 (1971).

55. 286 A.2d at 650. The court justified the disclosure standard as follows:

> This gives maximum effect to the patient's right to be the arbiter of the medical treatment he will undergo without either requiring the physician to be a mindreader into the patient's most subjective thoughts or requiring that he disclose *every* risk lest he be liable for battery. The physician is bound to disclose only those risks which a reasonable man would consider material to his decision whether or not to undergo treatment. This standard creates no unreasonable burden for the physician. Ibid., 650.

56. James E. Ludlam, *Informed Consent* (Chicago: American Hospital Association, 1978), 23; President's Commission, *Making Health Care Decisions*, Vol. 1, 21–22.

57. See, for example, McCoid, "A Reappraisal of Liability for Unauthorized Medical Treatment," 387; and Plant, "An Analysis of Informed Consent."

58. 186 Kan. 393, 350 P.2d 1093, *opinion on denial of motion for rehearing*, 187 Kan. 186, 354 P.2d 670 (1960).

59. 186 Kan. at 406–07, 350 P.2d at 1104, quoting without attribution Hubert Winston Smith, "Therapeutic Privilege to Withhold Specific Diagnosis From Patient Sick With Serious or Fatal Illness," *Tennessee Law Review* 19 (1946): 349f.

60. 354 P.2d at 672. See Katz, *The Silent World*, 53, 55. He comments that plaintiffs and their lawyers hindered the cause of self-determination by failing to bring all but the most timid and routine arguments before the courts.

61. 354 P.2d at 673. "As a matter of law" is a legal term of art, meaning that no individualized, factual determination (as by a jury) is necessary, but rather that the proposition stated is given as true in every case. Here it means that because *no* disclosure about risks and hazards was made, the appellate court was free to find a breach of the duty to disclose—instead of having to return the case to the lower court to determine whether some particular disclosure was sufficient.

62. 354 P.2d at 675.

63. 350 P.2d at 1103.

64. Ibid., 1107.

65. A few negligence cases had at least attempted to move away from such reasoning by the 1970s. One was *Getchell* v. *Mansfield*, 260 Or. 174, 489 P.2d 953 (1971). In *Getchell* the court distinguished neatly (although perhaps over-nicely for the practicalities of trial) between a disclosure standard based on the custom of physicians in the locality and an absolute legal duty to disclose risks and alternatives, provided that medical knowledge demonstrates that (1) the risks are material, (2) there are feasible alternatives, and (3) disclosure will not harm the patient. It rejected the professional standard, which required expert testimony to establish the duty itself, and espoused the absolute legal duty, which required expert testimony to establish its three conditions.

66. 464 F.2d 772 (D.C. Cir. 1972).

67. 104 Cal. Rptr. 505, 502 P.2d 1 (1972).

68. 295 A.2d 676 (R.I. 1972).

69. The malpractice bar had by this time largely ceased to consider cases based solely on informed consent a useful avenue of recovery. Personal communication, Ste-

phen Teret, 12/84. The trends in the courts from 1972 to 1983 are summarized in President's Commission, *Making Health Care Decisions*, Vol. 1, 23, nn. 30 and 31.

70. 464 F.2d at 780 (citing *Schloendorff*, 105 N.E. at 93).

71. Ibid., 786.

72. Ibid., 780 (footnotes omitted).

73. Ibid., 781 (footnote omitted).

74. Ibid., 781 (footnotes omitted).

75. Ibid., 782–83 (footnotes omitted).

76. McCoid makes the same assumption, which is also arguably at the heart of the *Salgo* court's contradictory language. See the analysis of the President's Commission in *Making Health Care Decisions*, Vol. 1, Chapter 2, esp. 44–45.

77. Compare President's Commission, *Making Health Care Decisions*, Vol. 1, 44–45; Katz, "Informed Consent: A Fairy Tale?" 148, 152–53, 171–72. This divergence underlies the controversies over refusal of treatment and the therapeutic privilege. Indeed, it seems unlikely that there would be much dispute over informed consent if physicians did not fear that their patients might wish to make decisions against medical advice.

78. 464 F.2d at 783, 784. Compare *Cooper* v. *Roberts*, 286 A.2d 647 (1971), and cases relied upon therein—battery cases that use almost identical language.

79. 464 F.2d at 787.

80. Jon R. Waltz and Thomas W. Scheuneman, "Informed Consent to Therapy," *Northwestern University Law Review* 64 (1970): 628, 640. This influential article referenced an extensive body of writings, especially student notes and comments.

Canterbury displayed through its footnotes considerable reliance on legal commentary for its groundbreaking ideas—from McCoid to a number of student pieces that included Comment, "Informed Consent in Medical Malpractice," *California Law Review* 55 (1967): 1396, and Note, "Restructuring Informed Consent: Legal Therapy for the Doctor-Patient Relationship," *Yale Law Review* 79 (1970): 1533. Perusal of the references in *Canterbury* paints a good picture of the influence legal scholarship had on the developing informed consent doctrine.

81. 464 F.2d at 791.

82. Meisel, "The Expansion of Liability for Medical Accidents," 21.

83. 502 P.2d at 12.

84. Ibid., 11.

85. Ibid., 10.

86. 295 A.2d at 688.

87. Ibid., 689 (citing Waltz and Scheuneman).

88. 165 Cal. Rptr. 308, 611 P.2d 902 (Cal. 1980).

89. 611 P.2d at 906, quoting *Cobbs*, 502 P.2d at 10.

90. Thus, in *Malloy* v. *Shanahan*, 421 A.2d 803 (Pa. Sup. Ct. 1980), the progressive battery jurisdiction that produced *Gray* v. *Grunnagle* and *Cooper* v. *Roberts* refused to apply the informed consent doctrine to the prescribing of drugs because no touching was involved. (Compare our discussion of the *Carpenter* case, text accompanying n. 13.) Other courts, however, might not hesitate to apply the battery doctrine to noninvasive treatments, so long as such treatments have effects upon the patient.

91. On the malpractice crisis and the related malpractice insurance crisis generally, see Andrew P. Tobias, *The Invisible Bankers: Everything the Insurance Industry Never Wanted You to Know* (New York: Simon & Schuster, 1982); Sylvia Law and Steven Polan, *Pain and Profit: The Politics of Malpractice* (New York: Harper & Row, 1978). See also Ludlam, *Informed Consent*, 41–42; Meisel and Kabnick, "Informed Consent to Medical Treatment," 414–17; Marcus Plant, "The Decline of 'Informed Con-

sent,'" *Washington and Lee Law Review* 35 (Winter 1978): 91.

92. See Meisel, "The Expansion of Liability for Medical Accidents," 51. See also n. 39 above.

93. President's Commission, *Making Health Care Decisions*, Vol. 3, 204–45. For example, the North Carolina Supreme Court, in *McPherson* v. *Ellis*, 305 N.C. 266, 287 S.E.2d 892 (1982), interpreted the common law of that state to apply a subjective causation standard in a case arising before the enactment of the state's informed consent statute, N.C. Gen. Stat. § 90–21.13 (3) (1981). Now, because of that statute, an objective standard applies. *McPherson*, 305 N.C. 273 n.2, 287 S.E.2d 897, n.2; *Dixon* v. *Peters*, No. 8214 S.C. 754 (N.C. Ct. App., filed 6 Sept. 1983) (slip op. at 8). Some of these medical malpractice acts have been held unconstitutional for reasons unrelated to their informed consent provisions. See, for example, *Carson* v. *Maurer*, 120 N.H. 925, 424 A.2d 825 (1980) (New Hampshire); *Arneson* v. *Olson*, 27 N.W.2d 125 (N.D. 1978) (North Dakota).

94. See, for example, Pennsylvania General Statutes, Title 40, 1301.103 (1975); Oregon Revised Statutes, 677.097 (1974); Washington Revised Statutes, 7.70.010–.080 (1977). See also Texas Regulations 3, 4293–96, 319.01.03.001–.003 (Dec. 12, 1978), issued pursuant to Texas Revised Civil Statutes Annotated, Article 4590; 603 (Vernon Cumulative Supplement, 1980).

95. See Meisel and Kabnick, "Informed Consent to Medical Treatment." The occasional change from a *Canterbury* model at common law to a less patient-oriented statute in one state was usually balanced by an "enlightened" statute, mandating greater disclosure, in another state.

96. The federal sterilization regulations appear in the *Code of Federal Regulations* 42, Part 50, pursuant to the United States Public Health Service Act. They were first published in the *Federal Register* on November 8, 1978, and were explicitly drafted to respond to the abuses brought to light in cases like *Relf* v. *Weinberger*, 372 F.Supp 1196 (D.D.C. 1974), *vacated and remanded*, 565 F.2d 722 (D.C. Cir 1977); see also *Stump* v. *Sparkman*, 435 U.S. 349 (1978); *Walker* v. *Pierce*, 560 F.2d 609 (4th Cir. 1977). The federal regulations mandate a 30–day waiting period and require that the informed consent interaction be specially tailored to avoid anticipated barriers of language, intimidation, understanding, class, culture, and handicap. A set of required forms and information documents is appended to the regulations. Many states in addition have their own sterilization consent laws. See, for example, Oregon Revised Statutes, 436.225 (1983).

97. California regulations provide for mandatory disclosure of information regarding side effects and controversies over ECT's effectiveness. California Welfare and Institutions Code 5326.85 (West, 1980). See Carol Levine, "Voting 'Yes' to a Ban on Electroshock," *Hastings Center Report* 2 (1982): 19.

98. Massachusetts General Statutes, Chapter III, 70E (1979), discussed in George J. Annas, "Breast Cancer: The Treatment of Choice," *Hastings Center Report* 10 (April 1980): 27. The statute requires that patients receive "complete information on all alternative treatments which are medically viable." Minnesota had a breast cancer disclosure provision in its patients' bill of rights for one year. It was deleted in 1983 and replaced by more general informed consent provisions. See Minnesota Statutes Annotated, 144.651 (West Cumulative Supplement, 1984).

99. Oregon's 1983 Senate Bill 414, which did not pass, would have required disclosure of the hazards of neuroleptic medications and ECT. As of 1977, about half the states had laws requiring that inmates of mental institutions give their informed consent to special treatments and procedures, including ECT, neuroleptics, psychosurgery, and sterilization. Usually these right-to-refuse provisions form part of the

institutional inmate's bill of rights in the state mental health code. See Joy Bennet, "Practice Manual: The Right to Refuse Treatment Under State Statutes," *Mental Disability Law Reporter* 2 (1977): 241–56.

100. The number of malpractice cases decided on informed consent grounds has been very small and is unlikely to grow in the future. In response to skyrocketing malpractice insurance premiums, in 1973 the Secretary of then-DHEW created the Commission on Medical Malpractice to study the malpractice problem and suggest solutions. In a comprehensive and influential study, this Commission determined that informed consent was the most significant issue in only 2.4% of all appellate malpractice decisions nationwide up to 1971. *Medical Malpractice: Report of the Secretary's Commission on Medical Malpractice* (Washington, D.C.: Government Printing Office—Department of Health, Education, and Welfare, 1973), 73–88, and Vol. 2: Appendix, 147, Table III-71. A few years later, the National Association of Insurance Commissioners found, after surveying all claims resolved between 1975 and 1976 (well after the impact of the 1972 *Canterbury* decision discussed in Chapters 2 and 4 was first felt), that informed consent was raised as an issue, either substantial or inconsequential, in only 3% of the cases. (Law and Polan, *Pain and Profit*, 113.) James Ludlam of the AHA, who served on the Secretary's Commission, wrote elsewhere that the *allegation* of failure to obtain informed consent was made in only 14% of malpractice suits filed in the mid-1970s. See his *Informed Consent*, 6. (As a matter of interest, there were 3,717 appellate decisions in malpractice cases up to 1971. See Secretary's Commission, op. cit.)

101. Examples of scholarly legal commentary widely cited in the law and elsewhere include the aforementioned writings of Alan Meisel, as well as: Alexander M. Capron, "Informed Consent in Catastrophic Disease Research and Treatment," *University of Pennsylvania Law Review* 123 (December 1974): 340; Joseph Goldstein, "For Harold Lasswell: Some Reflections on Human Dignity, Entrapment, Informed Consent, and the Plea Bargain," *Yale Law Journal* 84 (1975): 683; and Leonard Riskin, "Informed Consent: Looking for the Action," *University of Illinois Law Forum* (1975): 580.

An excellent example of the influence of the law and legal scholarship upon professional ethics is the AMA's Judicial Council 1981 opinion on informed consent. It closely paraphrases the language of *Canterbury*, without attribution, as noted in Chapter 3 (see pp. 96, 112n).

5

The Development of Consent Requirements in Research Ethics

Formal requirements of informed consent have primarily emerged from two contexts: standards governing clinical medicine, as examined in Chapters 3 and 4, and standards governing research involving human subjects. In this chapter and the following chapter we examine informed consent in research by looking at such mechanisms of control as the Nuremberg Code and the Declaration of Helsinki, government commissions, regulatory agencies, and professional societies.

The practice of research with human subjects is virtually as ancient as medicine itself, but concern about its consequences and about the protection of human subjects is a recent phenomenon. Unlike the accounts developed in Chapters 3 and 4, events in research ethics before the end of World War II that merit attention are few in number and without significant impact on later developments. Issues about consent and human subjects have figured most prominently in biomedical research, but there is also a rich history in the behavioral and social sciences, which we examine in the last half of this chapter. Developments in psychological research, as well as several celebrated cases in related fields of social research, consume our attention in these sections.

Our primary objective is to show how informed consent obligations and requirements, as we know them today, emerged and developed in the United States. This is accomplished by examination of influential cases, political developments, regulatory interventions, government-appointed ethics commissions, and intraprofessional developments from the end of World War II to the mid-1970s. In Chapter 6, we complete the account by examining U.S. federal policies as they have developed through the mid-1980s.

One reason for the relatively late dates in this chapter is that scientifically rigorous research involving human subjects became common in the United States only in the mid-twentieth century. Not until shortly before the outbreak of World War II was research an established and thriving concern. Thereafter, and despite the taint of Nuremberg, scientific research and health applications were enthusiastically hailed and supported by legislative initiatives until roughly the mid-1960s, when moral criticism began to arise in the United States.[1]

Throughout this history, the role of respect for autonomy in the structure of justification, as discussed in Chapters 1 and 2, has been subtle and complicated. The earliest and premier moral and legal concern about subjects has historically been to *control the risks* presented to subjects by research, not to *enable autonomous choice* about participation. More broadly conceived, the goal has been first for research with human subjects to ensure adequate levels of safety or benefit and therefore to prevent abuses of subjects. Consent requirements first appeared in research codes and guidelines without specific reference to underlying or justificatory principles. However, it has by now been firmly established in the evolution of thinking about research ethics that there are two primary goals for policies covering human subjects of research: controlling imposed risks—a beneficence-based consideration—and providing for informed consent—an autonomy-based consideration. Both forms of justification occupy a prominent place in our exposition, as in previous chapters.

Consent in the Biomedical Sciences

The ideal laboratory species for accumulating data on human functions and reactions is human, and that "animal of necessity"[2] has been widely utilized in research in the biomedical sciences in the second half of the twentieth century. Improved techniques and new technologies have made precise observation of human subjects possible without subjection to the hazardous methods often used with animals. Both the minimization of risk and the obtaining of consent have become integral to our very conception of justified research involving human subjects.

This perspective cannot, however, be claimed for earlier times. Practicing physicians have traditionally been governed by the oaths and codes of ethics surveyed in Chapter 3, as well as by licensing and regulatory boards. Similar controls for the biomedical researcher are recent phenomena.[3] Classic works in medical ethics—such as Percival's 1803 treatise (see Chapter 3)—had virtually nothing to say about medical experimentation with human subjects.[4] There was in fact no broad interest in consent to research prior to the Second World War.

It would, however, be overreaching to assert that issues in the ethics of research and consent *never* arose in earlier periods.[5] Sporadic outcries did at various points appear against the use of human subjects without their consent, as did occasional published accounts critical of the ethics of experimentation. For example, Russian physician V. Smidovich, writing under the pseudonym "V. Veresaeff," wrote an impassioned, carefully reasoned, and well-documented critique of clinical and research practices throughout the world in a book published in Russia in 1901, and then translated into English and published in London in 1904. This extraordinary work, *The Confessions of a Physician*, received considerable attention in educated circles in Russia.[6] Two other examples prior to World War II are found in public concerns about the consent practices involved in Walter Reed's research on yellow fever[7] and in American courts, which around 1935 began for the first time to recognize that properly structured and monitored human experimentation is permissible if and only if it does not deviate radically from accepted procedures and the subject has given knowledgeable consent.[8]

But to inflate such early developments as if they flowed smoothly into or had some direct causal connection with later developments in research ethics that brought about what we now understand informed consent to represent would be to abuse the facts of the historical record. Such early events, if explored by able historians, can no doubt shed light on the evolution of values in research with human subjects. However, these events had no direct causal influence on later developments in informed consent.

The modern concern with informed consent in research grew gradually after the occurrence of what is still today the most important watershed event: the unprecedented cruelties and generally inferior science, administered by what were often well-trained physicians of prominence, during the Nazi reign in Germany. This extraordinary evil was to change forever and always how we would view the involvement of human subjects in scientific research.

The Nuremberg Code

The Nuremberg Code was the first major curb on research in any nation. This brief Code was prescribed in 1948 as part of the judgment in *United States* v. *Karl Brandt*, the Nuremberg trial of Nazi physicians who engaged in "biomedical experiments" during the Second World War.[9] Although it is a common misconception that these were the earliest examples of willfully harmful, vicious research on unwilling human subjects,[10] the Nazi experiments were in many respects unprecedented in the extensiveness and extremity of the harm and suffering to which they knowingly exposed their victims. Using subjects drawn from the populations of concentration camps (Jews, gypsies, Poles, and Russians), Nazi scientists explored the effects of ingesting poisons, intravenous injections of gasoline, immersion in ice water, and the like. Infection with epidemic jaundice and spotted fever virus were typical parts of "medical" experiments.

Twenty doctors and three administrators, many occupying responsible positions within the Third Reich's medical hierarchy, were indicted before the war crimes tribunal at Nuremberg late in 1946. In its opening statement the prosecution declared:

> The defendants in this case are charged with murders, tortures, and other atrocities committed in the name of medical science. . . . In many cases experiments were performed by unqualified persons; were conducted at random for no adequate scientific reason, and under revolting physical conditions. All of the experiments were conducted with unnecessary suffering and injury and but very little, if any, precautions were taken to protect or safeguard the human subjects from the possibilities of injury, disability or death. In every one of the experiments the subjects experienced extreme pain or torture, and in most of them they suffered permanent injury, mutilation, or death, either as a direct result of the experiments or because of lack of adequate follow-up care.[11]

Dr. Andrew Ivy, who served during the trial as a consultant and expert witness on scientific and ethical questions, criticized the research for its design, relevance, and extreme cruelty. He argued that the medical tragedies were magnified by the invalidity of the experiments, which revealed nothing of use to "civilized medicine."[12]

The extreme disregard of ethics in the Nazis' exploitation and abuse of subjects is all the more remarkable in light of the fact that in 1931 Germany had enacted, on moral grounds, strict "Richtlinien" (regulations or guidelines) to control both human experimentation and the use of innovative therapies in medicine. Issued by the Reich's Health Department, these regulations remained binding law throughout the period of the Third Reich. Consent requirements formed two of fourteen major provisions in the guidelines, one dealing with "New Therapy" and the other with "Human Experimentation." It was demanded in both cases that consent (first party or proxy consent, as appropriate) must always be given "in a clear and undebatable manner."[13]

Questions of the nature of appropriate information, bona fide consent, careful research design, and special protections for vulnerable subjects were all carefully delineated in these guidelines. Human experimentation was declared impermissible without consent, and absolutely impermissible with dying patients. A special irony is that no other nation appears to have had such morally and legally advanced regulations at the time of the Nazi abuses and during the Nuremberg Trials. A second irony is that although the Nuremberg Code is widely assumed to be the first major document in the history of research ethics to deal with consent in a detailed manner, the 1931 regulations contain no less adequate provisions than those in the Code itself.

At the trial it was evident that in no respect could the victims of the Nazi experiments qualify as volunteers, much less as *informed* volunteers. The Nuremberg Military Tribunals unambiguously condemned the sinister political motivation of the experiments in their review of "crimes against humanity."[14] The defendants were found to have corrupted the ethics of the medical profession in particular and those of science in general, and to have repeatedly and deliberately violated their subjects' rights. As Ivy put it, "None [of the defendants] were motivated by the spirit of the true scientist, namely to seek the truth for the good of humanity."[15]

During testimony the accused defended their actions by an aggressive attack on the thesis that voluntary participation by human subjects *generally* occurs in medical experimentation. One defendant—formerly head of the reputed Robert Koch Hygiene Institute—stated:

> Aside from the self-experiments of doctors, which represent a very small minority of such experiments, the extent to which subjects are volunteers is often deceptive. At the very best they amount to self-deceit on the part of the physician who conducts the experiment, but very frequently to a deliberate misleading of the public. In the majority of such cases, if we ethically examine facts, we find an exploitation of the ignorance, the frivolity, the economic distress, or other emergency on the part of the experimental subjects.[16]

The tribunal forthrightly rejected this defense, thereby giving a central role to the voluntary participation and consent of research subjects, regardless of whether it was common professional practice among physician-investigators to seek consent. Specifically, the judges took responsibility for establishing the "basic principles [that] must be observed in order to satisfy moral, ethical and legal concepts" in the conduct of human subjects research.[17] This list of ten principles constituted the "Nuremberg Code."

Principle One of the Code states, without qualification, that the primary consideration in research is the subject's voluntary consent, which is "absolutely essential." It requires that consent have at least four characteristics:[18] It must be voluntary, competent, informed, and comprehending. The rest of the Code sets general bounds within which an investigator may conduct research and delineates the conditions under which a subject has the ability to volunteer.

Although these principles do not explicitly so state, informed consent requirements presumably come into play only *after* an appropriate risk/benefit assessment has been made. The Code does not attempt to describe either how the subject's consent may be secured or how the limits of experimental risk are to be defined, because the Court held that such determinations were beyond its sphere of competence. The Code also did not distinguish clearly between justificatory appeals to autonomy and to beneficence in support of consent requirements, thereby setting the stage for the continued blurring of these justifications for consent in later reflection on research ethics.

The Nuremberg Code proved more influential in the years after 1948 than might have been predicted at the time. With the profusion of biomedical research during the postwar period, researchers and their governments began to appreciate the importance of ethical principles in research. The Nuremberg Code served as a model for many professional and governmental codes formulated throughout the 1950s and 1960s.[19] However, the Code was limited in scope, and soon after its acceptance it came to be viewed, rightly, as inadequate to govern the complex variety of situations arising in the expanding fields of biomedical and social scientific research. Pressure to develop less general guidelines for specific fields began to mount.

The Declaration of Helsinki

The gross violations investigated at Nuremberg were gradually perceived by the medical community as a general threat to the reputation and integrity of biomedical research. Partially in response to this perceived threat, the World Medical Association (WMA) began in the early 1960s to draft a more suitable code to distinguish ethical from unethical clinical research. A draft of the WMA's code was produced in 1961, but the code was not adopted until a meeting at Helsinki in 1964.[20] This three-year delay was not caused by vacillation or indifference, but rather was the result of normal political processes and a determination to produce a universally applicable and useful document.[21]

Like the Nuremberg Code, the Declaration of Helsinki made consent a central requirement of ethical research. This requirement was linked to an influential distinction it proposed between therapeutic and nontherapeutic research. The former is defined in the Declaration as research "combined with patient care," and is permitted as a means of acquiring new medical knowledge only insofar as it "is justified by its potential diagnostic or therapeutic value for the patient." The latter is defined as purely scientific research without therapeutic value or purpose for the specific subjects studied. The Declaration requires consent for all instances of nontherapeutic research, unless a subject is incompetent, in which case guardian consent is necessary. Paragraph I.9 of the Declaration reads as follows: "In any research on human beings, each potential subject must be adequately informed of the aims, methods, anticipated benefits and potential hazards of the study and the discomfort it may entail [and] that he is at liberty to abstain. . . . The doctor should then obtain the subject's freely given informed consent."

By contrast, informed consent is not required in therapeutic research if it is not "consistent with patient psychology." The justification for this broad exceptive provision rests on the same beneficence-based premises that support the physician's therapeutic privilege in medical practice (as discussed in Chapters 2 and 4). Although there is a modest check on the physician's judgment—"If the doctor considers it essential not to obtain informed consent, the specific reasons for this proposal should be stated in the experimental protocol for transmission to [an] independent [review] committee"[22]—some commentators see this therapeutic loophole as a serious flaw, especially if inattentive review committees evaluate protocols.[23] Certainly the gap separating Paragraph I.9 and the beneficence-based exceptive provision ("consistent with patient psychology") is as cavernous as the parallel exception in the *Salgo* decision in the courts. (See pp. 125–127.)[24] The exceptive provision remains intact in later revisions, despite several years of scrutiny by the WMA Council and its Committees on Medical Ethics. Simultaneously, the emphasis on disclosure and consent remained strong and explicit in the 1975 revision.

Historically, the Declaration is certain to prove less significant as a consistent moral treatise than as a landmark that, despite its confusions, functions—as did *Salgo*—as a rallying point for other codes and as a source for the stimulation of reflection on informed consent and research ethics. The American Medical Association (AMA), the American Society for Clinical Investigation, the American Federation for Clinical Research, and many other medical groups endorsed the Declaration or established ethical requirements consonant with its provisions;[25] and officials at federal agencies in the United States looked first to Helsinki before developing their own provisions, some of which were close to verbatim reformulations. (For example, the FDA's policy on consent was under development shortly after the Helsinki Declaration and drew on it extensively: see pp. 202–205.)

Whatever its shortcomings, the Declaration will be remembered as a foundational document in the history of research ethics and the first significant stab at self-regulation internal to medical research itself. Without undue artificiality, it can be said that Nuremberg was the first code prescribed for medicine externally by a court system and Helsinki the first code prescribed internally by a professional body in medicine.

Influential Scholarly Publications

Stimulated by the activities at Nuremberg and by the consequent rise of concern in medical and scientific associations, individual scholarly investigations and publications on research ethics began to appear. One of the earliest—and perhaps the most significant—was Henry K. Beecher's 1959 monograph, *Experimentation in Man*. In his introduction, Beecher announced that the atrocities disclosed at Nuremberg and the continuing advance into new areas of human biomedical research called for "a long, straight look at our current practices."[26] He offered analyses of the social necessity for human experimentation, relationships between subject and investigators, the justification for clinical trials, and permissible risks, while providing an extensive review of the major existing codes. He stressed the necessity of obtaining the subject's consent to experimentation, but he cautioned that different levels of disclosure were appropriate for different forms of research. For example, a subject who is also a patient in a clinic, where treatment is the first aim, is not in the same dire need of complete information as the subject of nontherapeutic research, who anticipates no immediate benefit. Beecher thus seemed willing to allow considerations of beneficence to regulate how vigorously autonomous choice should be protected in therapeutic research.

In commenting on the various codes that had been adopted, Beecher shied away from rule-based or regulatory approaches to the control of experimentation. He held that rules and regulations, while occasionally needed, are in general "more likely to do harm than good," and will utterly fail to "curb the unscrupulous." For example, he argued that the Nuremberg Code's unqualified insistence on the consent of all subjects "would effectively cripple if not eliminate most research in the field of mental disease," as well as render impermissible all use of placebos. "[E]ven the 'obvious' matter of consent," he held, "is not so easy to live up to as it sounds."[27] The thrust of his essay was to heighten awareness of the complex character of the moral problems, to insist on the overwhelming importance of sound training in scientific methodology, and to make scientific practices consonant with moral sensitivity.[28]

The Law-Medicine Institute Study. Recognition of the importance of the kinds of problems noted in Beecher's work led the Public Health Service in January 1960 to award a three-year grant to a project at the newly established (1958) Law-Medicine Research Institute at Boston University. The project's objective was to investigate the practices of medical researchers and research institutions in the United States with regard to ethical problems in the conduct of human subjects research. The results of a 1962 survey by the Institute were of special significance. A questionnaire was sent to 86 departments of medicine, 52 of which responded. The research indicated that few institutions had procedural guidelines governing clinical research. Some had criteria covering specific aspects, such as experimentation with drugs; others replied that they used only informal guidelines for review. A majority indicated that they viewed even self-regulation by committees to be undesirable and preferred to leave these procedures entirely to the investigators. Only 16 institutions had special consent forms for research projects. The report concluded that internal institutional regulation of research was generally insensitive and sporadic.[29]

The Institute also published an anthology, *Clinical Investigation in Medicine,* in 1963. Edited by Irving Ladimer and Roger Newman, this book assembled 73 selections from scholars in multiple disciplines in an attempt to provide a manageable review of the legal and moral aspects of human biomedical research. Central throughout are questions of informed consent,[30] and Ladimer broaches the subsequently influential idea of prior examination of specific research protocols by a review group.[31] But historically the book's contribution came through its facilitation of high quality discussion of ethical problems confronting biomedical research.

Beecher's Later Articles. In 1966 Beecher made another landmark contribution, this time an article in the *New England Journal of Medicine* in which he published detailed cases of research containing serious or potentially serious ethical violations. That the consent of subjects was obtained was mentioned in only two of 50 cases Beecher collected, from which he selected 22 for publication for "reasons of space." Several of these experiments were performed with a high ratio of risk to benefit, and involved vulnerable or disadvantaged subjects who were unaware of their participation in research. In one experiment, physicians substituted placebos for an established and effective treatment. In another case, physicians administered chloramphenicol, a known inducer of (potentially fatal) aplastic anemia, to patients without their knowledge. Beecher argued that the ease with which he had collected samples from published articles in medical journals meant that "if only one quarter of them is truly unethical, this still indicates the existence of a serious situation."[32]

In the same year, Beecher brought further attention to problems of informed consent through an insightful and critical editorial on the topic in the *Journal of the American Medical Association.*[33] He argued that informed consent refers to an ambitious goal, but one to which physician-investigators must aspire in order to discharge their basic responsibilities to patients. Beecher again criticized rigid codes and appealed to the virtuous physician as the appropriate standard for ensuring that informed consent will be obtained. He maintained that most of the transgressions he had detected stemmed from investigator "thoughtlessness and carelessness," and he advised that the most "dependable safeguard" against abuse is the "truly *responsible* investigator."[34] We will see in Chapter 6 that Beecher's work made an immediate and vital contribution to U.S. federal policy in what was perhaps its most formative and receptive period.

Pappworth's Human Guinea Pigs. Beecher cited ongoing work by Englishman M.H. Pappworth, who had collected more than 500 papers involving allegedly unethical experiments. A year later Pappworth published his findings under the flashy title *Human Guinea Pigs.* This book revealed numerous cases in which subjects were exposed to procedures not intended for their benefit. The experiments were performed on newborn infants, children, pregnant women, surgery patients, the mentally handicapped, and the dying. They generally involved persons whose consent was difficult or impossible to obtain.

Pappworth argued that researchers commonly take risks with uninformed patients for nontherapeutic research to which informed patients would not consent. He concluded that researchers often showed little concern for their subjects and that "the voluntary system of safeguarding patients' rights has failed and new legislative procedures are absolutely necessary." He recommended prior review of research, compulsory reporting during the conduct of the experiment, and disclosure to subjects of any injury or complications, even if minor.[35] For Pappworth, *principles* and *rights* were an issue in a way they were not for Beecher. However, it was again unclear whether these were envisioned as autonomy rights or welfare rights or both.

Katz's Anthology. In 1972 psychiatrist Jay Katz, with the assistance of Alexander Capron and Eleanor Swift Glass, published an exhaustive anthology and casebook, *Experimentation with Human Beings.* Drawn from sociology, psychology, medicine, and law, it was then, and is still today, the most thorough collection of materials on research ethics and law ever assembled between two covers. Originally inspired by his disgust over the fate of Holocaust victims, Katz, like Beecher, had become convinced that only a persistent educational effort could bring about real change in the practice of research using human subjects:

> As I became increasingly involved in the world of law, I learned much that was new to me from my colleagues and students about such complex issues as the right to self-determination and privacy and the extent of the authority of governmental, professional, and other institutions to intrude into private life. Although these issues affect the interactions of physician-investigators with patient-subjects and of the professions as a whole with the research process, they had rarely been discussed in my medical education. Instead it had been all too uncritically assumed that they could be resolved by fidelity to such undefined principles as *primum non nocere* or to visionary codes of ethics.[36]

Katz presented readings from original documents edited to stimulate discussion of tensions between principles of free scientific inquiry and protection of subjects' rights. Failure to resolve these issues, he maintained, could retard or stifle the progress of research, because reaction to violations of human rights fosters a reluctance to undertake the burden of research in the face of public dissatisfaction.

Katz's anthology is an encyclopedic resource on informed consent and other topics in research ethics throughout the formative years of the research codes and regulations discussed below. By including materials from both the biomedical and the social sciences, the book also bridged an interdisciplinary gap that no other publication had attempted to cross. Coincidentally, it was published on the eve of the disclosure of what has become perhaps the most celebrated of all the cases of research abuse in the United States: the Tuskegee syphilis experiments. We now turn to a discussion of this and other cases of alleged abuse of consent and of other ethical obligations in resesarch.

Controversy over Cases

After a decade of discussion over the place of codes in the regulation of human biomedical research, several incidents involving consent violations moved the discussion of post-Nuremberg problems into the public arena. Thus began a rich and complex interplay of influences on research ethics: scholarly publications, journalism, public outrage, legislation, and the case law discussed in Chapter 4. Often these incidents motivated scholarly writings, which in turn influenced public discussion, which led finally to new codes and reforms of older ones.

The Jewish Chronic Disease Hospital Case.[37] One of the first incidents to achieve notoriety involved a study conducted at the Jewish Chronic Disease Hospital (JCDH) in Brooklyn, New York. The chief investigator, Dr. Chester M. Southam, was a physician at the Sloan-Kettering Institute for Cancer Research who had been conducting research for ten years on the role the body's immune system plays in defense against cancer. In July 1963, Dr. Southam persuaded hospital medical director Emmanuel E. Mandel to permit research involving injection of a suspension of foreign, live cancer cells into 22 patients at the JCDH. The motivation was to discover whether in cancer patients a decline in the body's capacity to reject cancer transplants was caused by their cancer or by debilitation. Patients without cancer were needed to supply the answer. Southam had convinced Mandel that although the research was entirely nontherapeutic, it was routine to do such research without consent. Some patients were informed orally that they were involved in an experiment, but it was not disclosed that they were being given injections of *cancer* cells. No written consent was attempted, and some subjects were incompetent to give informed consent.

Previous studies had indicated that cell implants are promptly rejected by healthy individuals, and the investigators allegedly believed that every patient must, as a matter of biological law, finally reject the injected cells (though at different rates) because they are foreign. Thus, it was argued that no patient was at increased risk of developing cancer by virtue of the injections. It was decided not to inform even the competent subjects of the use of cancer cells because to do so might agitate them unnecessarily. The physicians defended their actions by precedents in case law: They argued that it was customary in the profession that consent not be documented even in far more dangerous research.

When he learned of the research from some young physicians who objected to it, attorney William Hyman, a member of JCDH's Board of Directors, brought suit to obtain access to hospital records in order to learn the extent of the study.[38] He was concerned not only about the abuse of the patients and damage to the hospital's reputation, but also about the institution's possible liability for having given the experimental injections without consent. Review proceedings indicated that the study had not been presented to the hospital's research committee and that several physicians directly responsible for the subjects' care had not been consulted before the injections were given. Three physicians who *had* been consulted by Dr. Mandel had argued that the investigators should *not* perform the research because the subjects were incapable of giving appropriate consent.

In 1966 the Board of Regents of the State University of New York censured Drs. Southam and Mandel for their role in the research. They were found guilty of fraud, deceit, and unprofessional conduct. The Regents particularly deplored the physicians' assumption that they could perform any act they wished without a patient's consent so long as the research stands to benefit scientific inquiry. The Regents' Committee on Discipline held that they were guilty of unprofessional conduct not only in *what* they did, but in the *way* they did it, namely, without disclosure of the fact that cancer cells were used and without obtaining consent:

> A physician has no right to withhold from a prospective volunteer any fact which he knows may influence the decision. It is the volunteer's decision to make. . . . There is evidenced in the record in this proceeding an attitude on the part of some physicians . . . that the patient's consent is an empty formality.
>
> Deliberate nondisclosure of the material fact is no different from deliberate misrepresentation of such a fact. . . . The alleged oral consents that they obtained after deliberately withholding this information were not informed consents and were, for this reason, fraudulently obtained.[39]

This strong language appears to indicate that the Board of Regents recognized that informed consent is necessary to protect subjects' rights of self-determination, even if the level of risk is low and the potential benefit high. Beecher, for his part, denounced the activities of the physicians involved as a straightforward failure to put consideration of patients' interests first.[40]

Mandel and Southam were placed on a year's probation by the Board of Regents. There were no immediate repercussions at either Sloan-Kettering or the Public Health Service, which, together with the American Cancer Society, had funded the original research. However, this case was destined to function as a profoundly important precedent in the subsequent development of federal guidelines.[41] As one official of the Public Health Service later reported, the JCDH case "made us aware of the inadequacy of our procedures and it clearly brought to the fore the basic issue that in the setting in which the patient is involved in an experimental effort, the judgment of the investigator is not sufficient as a basis for reaching a conclusion concerning the ethical and moral set of questions in that relationship."[42] As we shall see, this case served to bring to consciousness at PHS the existence of a gap in moral responsibility in scientific research as well as an uncertain legal position.

Willowbrook. Another major controversy about consent developed at Willowbrook State School, an institution for "mentally defective" children on Staten Island, New York. Willowbrook was originally designed to house 3,000, but its population had soared to over 6,000 in 1963. Approximately two-thirds of the children were severely retarded, with I.Q.s below 20. A large percentage of them were not toilet trained. These conditions facilitated the rapid spread of fecally borne infectious hepatitis of a relatively mild strain. By 1954, virtually all susceptible children contracted the disease within six to twelve months of residence at the institution.

In their attempts to develop an effective prophylactic agent, Saul Krugman and his associates began a series of experiments in 1956. They deliberately infected newly admitted patients with isolated strains of the virus. Of the 10,000 admissions to Willowbrook after 1956, approximately 750–800 children were admitted to Krugman's special hepatitis unit. These groups included only children whose parents had given their written consent. Children who were wards of the state were never included in the studies. Originally, information was conveyed to parents by letter or personal interview. In later years a group technique, involving discussion of the project with a group of parents of prospective patients, was employed.

These experiments were well known in circles of experimental medicine, and had been listed by Beecher in 1966 as one among his 22 "ethically dubious" experiments. There was little reaction at the time to Beecher's pointed finger, and the work continued. These studies finally reached the public's attention after further questioning by Beecher in his 1970 book *Research and the Individual,* after criticism in the same year by theologian Paul Ramsey, and after publication in April 1971 of a sharply critical and controversial letter by Stephen Goldby in *The Lancet.*[43] (The editors of *The Lancet* supported this letter and apologized to its readership for not having faced the issues previously.)

The researchers involved in the experiments were then forced to defend their actions publicly. They argued that because the majority of children contracted hepatitis anyway as a result of conditions in the institution (later, in 1980, Krugman said that susceptible children *inevitably* would become infected), they were therefore placed in no more danger than the other institutionalized children. The investigators asserted that they would only be watching the course of a natural disease, not actively intervening. They also maintained that the studies benefited the children. By being placed in a special, well-equipped, and well-staffed unit with optimum isolation and attention, the children would be at less risk from other infectious diseases in the institution and would be administered the best available therapy for hepatitis. By causing in them what was likely to be only subclinical infection, the researchers hoped to immunize them against the particular hepatitis virus.

Krugman and his associates argued that "the strictest conditions of informed consent" had been maintained in obtaining permission from the parents, including provisions for "meticulous explanations" and an environment of free choice.[44] They stressed that the studies had been reviewed and sanctioned by various local, state, and federal agencies. Several influential editors of prestigious medical journals concurred with them, arguing that the research was valuable for understanding hepatitis, was of potential value to the children at the institution, had adequate consent provisions, did not expose the children to unusual risks, and was performed by competent investigators.[45]

Critics questioned these arguments, including the defense based on free consent and meticulous disclosure. They argued that the study increased the child subject's risk of later developing chronic liver disease, and noted that the subjects did not receive protective doses of gamma-globulin, as had other residents of Willowbrook.[46] Both the methods by which parental consent was obtained and the legitimacy of the "consent" acquired were challenged. The consent forms used for the injection read as though the children were to receive a *vaccine* against the virus, and some parents had only been contacted by letter. Moreover, in late 1964, when overcrowding forced Willowbrook to cease admission of new patients, Krugman's special research unit still accepted children whose parents "volunteered" them for the studies. Critics maintained that parents were coerced by an implicit threat into volunteering their children as a means of procuring placement at Willowbrook.

In a commentary on the Willowbrook experiment, and in subsequent debate with Krugman, Louis Goldman questioned both the thoroughness of disclosure and the freedom of the consent. He doubted whether Krugman had ever actually *informed* parents about "the acute mortality of one or two children in a thousand, the development of chronic hepatitis, the possible link to cirrhosis in later life," and about alternative treatments. He held that the facts of the case indicated that the "explanation" by investigators to parents might have shaded from "persuasion" into "coercion"—especially after late 1964 when admissions to the institution were made only for children "voluntarily" assigned to the special hepatitis unit.[47]

Krugman admitted that the consent procedures had been "inadequate" prior to 1964, a year in which he claimed that significant strides were made to provide personal counseling and "more informed" consent.[48] Other critics suggested that financial considerations and social pressures arranged during the group meetings in which parental consent was solicited might have undermined the parents' ability to act in their children's best interests. Krugman's research unit was later closed, but closure on the debate about the ethics of the studies conducted in the unit has never been achieved.[49]

The Tuskegee Syphilis Study. The most notorious case of prolonged and knowing violation of subjects' rights to emerge in the 1970s was a Public Health Service study initiated in the early 1930s. Originally designed as one of the first syphilis control demonstrations in the United States, the stated purpose of the Tuskegee Study was to compare the health and longevity of an untreated syphilitic population with a nonsyphilitic but otherwise similar population. Although physicians of the 1930s often had confidence in the treatments used and were familiar with the consequences of the disease, there was no highly effective therapy and much remained unknown about the severity of untreated syphilis well into the 1950s.[50]

While some historical uncertainties surround the origins of the research, there was no clearly defined protocol and the decision to make it a long term study came later.[51] However, it is known that a loss of funding led PHS physicians to shift their focus from treatment to mere observation. Beginning in 1932, they traced the pathological evolution of syphilis in approximately 400 black males. Another 200 without syphilis served as controls.

These subjects knew neither the name nor the nature of their disease. That they were participants in a nontherapeutic experiment also went undisclosed. They were informed only that they were receiving free treatment for "bad blood," a term local blacks associated with a host of unrelated ailments, but which the white physicians allegedly assumed was a local euphemism for syphilis.[52] No attempt was made to explain what "bad blood" meant, presumably because the physicians believed that the subjects were incapable of comprehending any complex explanation. The investigators assumed that the subjects would comply without question; their deference to authority and desire to receive medical attention made them readily available subjects. The subjects were also misinformed that research procedures such as painful spinal taps were a "special free treatment," a patently false statement.[53] As historians James Jones and David Rothman have both argued, theirs was a "manipulated" consent, extracted from subjects in such "social deprivation" that manipulation came effortlessly.[54]

Although the experiment was designed to last only six to eight months, a few investigators believed—evidently with some scientific warrant—that it had unrivalled potential. They pushed to extend it indefinitely. (Smidovich, or Veresaeff, had found the most egregious abuses at the turn of the century in venereal disease research.) Meanwhile, untreated subjects were systematically blocked from receiving available treatments. Whatever treatment the men received prior to 1973 came from physicians who were not connected with the study. The PHS gave them treatment only after the experiment was exposed. To counter vague protests from subjects during the course of the research, the physicians maintained that proper treatment was being administered and that the experiment, because of the new "wonder drugs," was a "never-again-to-be-repeated opportunity."[55]

By 1936 it was evident that complications beset many more infected subjects than controls, and a decade later it became apparent that the death rate for those with syphilis was twice as high as for controls. Although the study was reviewed several times between 1932 and 1970 by PHS officials and medical societies, as well as being reported in 13 articles in prestigious medical and public health journals,[56] it continued uninterrupted and without serious challenge. One justification offered (several evolved over time), as at Willowbrook, was that researchers were only observing the course of a natural and inevitable disease. However, in 1972, a reporter, Jean Heller, published an account of the study on the first page of the *New York Times*, and thereafter the old "justifications" seemed not to work.[57]

The Department of Health, Education, and Welfare then appointed an ad hoc advisory panel to review the study as well as the Department's policies and procedures for the protection of human subjects in general. The panel found that neither DHEW nor any other government agency had a uniform or adequate policy for reviewing experimental procedures or securing subjects' consents. Research practices were regulated largely by those in the biomedical professions who conducted the research. The panel, although sharply divided at times, recommended that the Tuskegee study be terminated at once, and that the remaining subjects be given the care necessary to treat whatever could be treated of the disabilities that resulted from participation.[58]

The panel mentioned the need for improvements in resolving conflict between "two strongly held values: the dignity and integrity of the individual and the freedom of scientific inquiry." It also recommended that Congress establish "a permanent body with the authority to regulate *at least* all Federally supported research involving human subjects."[59] With respect to obtaining adequate informed consents, the panel recommended that a committee be appointed with the mission of educating subjects about their rights and ensuring the quality of consent statements. While consent was viewed as a moral principle for biomedical experimentation, with the burden of moral proof falling on those who would depart from this obligation, the panel left many questions to be answered by another body:

> [A National] Board will have to find answers to such policy questions as: Under what circumstances can what benefits to individuals or society justify modifications in the informed consent requirement? Should certain groups or potential subjects be excluded from participating in research or high-risk investigations be proscribed unless informed consent can be obtained? When is third party consent permissible, and what safeguards should be introduced whenever the consent of a third party is invoked? . . .

> The policies we have in mind cannot be formulated overnight or without serious study of the problems inherent in this field.[60]

In its conclusion, the panel proposed that "society can no longer afford to leave the balancing of individual rights against scientific progress to the scientific community alone. . . . Therefore, we have urged throughout a greater participation by society in the decisions which affect so many human lives."[61] The panel report signaled that despite Nuremberg, Helsinki, and the Jewish Chronic Disease Hospital Case, informed consent mechanisms and the committee review process were still in a primitive condition in the United States, and that more effective provisions were needed to protect the rights of subjects.

Aftermath. It is striking that a panel that revealed as many problems as the Tuskegee panel could have reported its findings as late as 1972–1973. Yet, as the final touches were put on the ad hoc advisory panel's report, and while national attention was focused on the Supreme Court's impending decision on abortion, newspapers began to publish reports that PHS-supported investigators were using decapitated fetuses in metabolism research sponsored by NIH (when in fact they took place in Scandinavia). Other controversies mushroomed over psychosurgery and research on prisoners, children, and the mentally retarded. It became apparent that the Tuskegee panel had opened rather than resolved the debate over "human experimentation." Congress responded in 1974 by appointing a National Commission, whose deliberations and conclusions we shall examine in Chapter 6. This commission was charged to examine *behavioral* as well as *biomedical* research, and we shift at this point to the topic of the history of informed consent in behavioral research prior to 1974. Only then will we be adequately prepared for the federal policy developments traced in Chapter 6.

Consent in the Behavioral Sciences

Informed consent has emerged as an issue in virtually all of the social and behavioral sciences. Methodological differences across these disciplines have resulted in different perspectives on, and problems with, informed consent. We cannot trace the history of consent in each of these distinct disciplines, and we have therefore elected to treat only psychology in detail. This discipline has the richest and lengthiest history of struggle with the problem of consent within the behavioral and social sciences.

Psychology Gets a Code

The precise beginning of a concern with research ethics in American psychology is difficult to date, but a general interest existed as early as

1938,[62] when the American Psychological Association (APA), then with
2,318 members, created a special Committee on Scientific and Professional Ethics.[63] This committee was instructed in 1939 to consider
whether the APA should develop a code of ethics for its members. One
year later, a verdict was reached: The committee "did not feel that the
time was ripe for the Association to adopt a formal code."[64] However,
the Committee did recommend that a standing body be appointed to
investigate charges of unethical behavior against individual psychologists. This task had been undertaken informally by this special committee
since its inception. It is unlikely that early cases of alleged misconduct
included issues involving *consent* in research. However, by the time the
investigatory activities of the by-then standing committee were formal-
ized, relations between psychologists and their research subjects was
recognized as one of the areas in which complaints were to be
considered.

By 1947, after almost ten years' experience in investigating allegations
of misconduct, the Committee on Scientific and Professional Ethics concluded that the rapid growth of psychology warranted the development
of a code of ethics. This task was delegated to a new APA committee, the
Committee on Ethical Standards for Psychology, which began its work
that same year. The impetus for this code seems to have come more from
problems in the practice of clinical and consulting psychology than from
issues in research, but the code was fashioned to include research involving human subjects as well.

Perhaps most unique and interesting about this code was the process
by which it was developed, a process that relied on empirical and participatory methods. The members of the APA—7500 in number by
1948—were asked by letter to submit a report of any situation known
to them personally in which a psychologist had encountered a moral
problem. They were also asked to describe what they viewed as the relevant ethical issues. Over 1,000 reports were received and classified into
six areas, one of which was research.

Based on these incidents, committee members prepared draft statements of standards, which were circulated to subcommittees of psychologists with special expertise. Revised statements were then published in
the APA's official publication, the *American Psychologist*, for comment
by the membership. The draft of the section covering ethical standards
in research was published in 1951.[65] Neither "consent" nor "informed
consent" appears anywhere in section 4.3, the section titled "The Psychologist's Relation to his Research Subjects." However, under provision 4.31, which bears the noteworthy heading "Protecting the Subject's
Welfare," the following principle (4.31–1) was proposed:

> Only when the problem being investigated is significant and can be
> studied in no other way is the psychologist justified in withholding
> information from or temporarily giving misinformation to research sub-

jects or in exposing them to emotional stress. He must seriously consider the possibility of harmful after-effects, take all necessary steps to
remove the possibility of such effects when they may be anticipated,
and deal with them if and when they arise. *Where there exists a danger
of serious after-effects, research should not be conducted unless the subjects are fully informed of this possibility and volunteer nevertheless.*[66]

How this proposed principle was received by the membership is
uncertain, as is the extent to which psychological research of the period
actually relied on informed volunteers of the sort called for by 4.31–1,
rather than on naive or unwitting subjects. There is little discussion of
draft principle 4.31–1 in published comments on the 1951 drafts.[67]
However, in this environment, there emerged a full code of ethics, perhaps the first *published* code of ethics in the behavioral sciences. It was
written by a psychologist for the Cornell Studies in Social Growth
research program.[68] This code, "Principles of Professional Ethics,"
included a consent requirement far stricter than that proposed by the
APA committee:

> 3. To the maximum degree possible, the free consent of persons (sub-
> jects) involved is secured at each stage of research activity.
> a. In requesting verbal consent, persons are given as direct and
> explicit an account as possible of research objectives and purposes. In
> requesting consent the investigator does not attempt to evoke or capi-
> talize on feelings of obligation or desires to please.
> b. Consent can be secured only in relation to those experiences the
> consequences of which the person is in a position to appreciate; that is,
> consent to an unknown experience is not regarded as true consent.[69]

The Cornell code suggests that at least some psychologists were both
soliciting and worrying about free and informed consent from their subjects. Yet, the incidents reported by correspondents and published with
the draft standards (and by reference to which principle 4.31–1 was proposed) suggest that other psychologists were using research methods
that ignored or grossly violated what we would today probably consider
minimal requirements of consent, voluntary participation, and respect
for the autonomy of subjects. Consider the following examples:[70]

> [Example #1]
> In order to develop a scoring system for the TAT,[71] I have frequently
> used the technique of giving subjects false information with the pur-
> pose of creating in them a state of mind, the effects of which I could
> then measure on their TAT productions. For example, I have told a
> large class of subjects that their scores on some paper and pencil tests
> just taken indicate that they have not done very well, or else that they
> scored high in neuroticism, when neither of these things is true. I rec-
> ognize all too well that I am here skating on very thin ice, but I see no
> other way to induce some of the states of anxiety and motivational ten-
> sion which I have to produce in order to carry out my research. The
> procedure I have uniformly followed has been to inform the subjects,

after they have completed the TAT, that a mistake has been made in quoting norms to them for the test taken before the TAT. In this way the state of mind experimentally induced lasts for a very short time, and I have felt that telling them a mistake was made avoids creating the impression that psychologists have purposely been out to trick them. So far no serious results have been reported from the arousal of such short-term emotion.

[Example #2]
An experimenter gave his subject an insoluble task to perform. He repeatedly assured the subject that the task could be solved, intending thus to get him angry.

[Example #3]
A psychologist in an experimental research program was investigating the response of college students to certain kinds of stress situation. In so doing, he had to keep the students unaware of the purpose and plan of the experiment. During the stress, the subjects were exposed to some traumatic experiences, later followed by reassurance and an explanation of the situation.

As these cases suggest, any attempt to develop principles for consent or requirements for psychology would have to come to grips with the use of deception as a research method. When formally adopted by the APA in 1953, principle 4.31–1 was split into two components, the first dealing with stress and harm, the second with deception. The revised 4.31–1 would still require "fully informed" volunteers whenever the danger of serious "after-effects" existed, thus codifying the *concept* of informed consent in psychological research without so *naming* it.[72] However, 4.31–2 would permit withholding of information and deception if methodologically necessitated—and, presumably, only if no danger of serious after-effects prevailed:

> 4.31–1   Only when a problem is significant and can be investigated in no other way is the psychologist justified in exposing research subjects to emotional stress. He must seriously consider the possibility of possible harmful after-effects and should be prepared to remove them as soon as permitted by the design of the experiment. When the danger of serious after-effects exists, research should be conducted only when the subjects or their responsible agents are fully informed of this possibility and volunteer nevertheless.

> 4.31–2   The psychologist is justified in withholding information from or giving misinformation to research subjects only when in his judgment this is clearly required by his research problem, and when the provisions of the above principle regarding protection of the subjects are adhered to.[73]

As we shall see, this issue of deception emerged in the 1960s as a major moral controversy within psychology. The later controversy about deception was chiefly responsible for a shift in psychology from a near-exclusive concern with the ethics of clinical *practice* to a concern that included the ethics of *research*. This shift culminated, in the 1970s, in the development of a special code devoted exclusively to research with human subjects.

Early Discussions of Consent and Deception

The conflict between a principle of consent and a methodology of deception was not to hit psychology full force until the publication of several now celebrated cases, most notably Stanley Milgram's studies of obedience in the early 1960s. (See pp. 174–176.) However, as early as 1953, Irwin Berg pointed to the problem in an essay entitled "The Use of Human Subjects in Psychological Research," published in the *American Psychologist*.[74] Moved by the Nazi atrocities and the Nuremberg Code, which he reprinted in full at the end of his article, Berg mounted a vigorous defense of the principle of consent as essential to the moral conduct of psychological research.

Berg regarded nonadherence to the consent principle as the central problem for research ethics: "When psychological research has aroused public ire, it has probably occurred most often when the principle of *consent* was violated in connection with some cherished cultural value."[75] Although he never referred directly to the problem of deception, Berg drew a negative comparison between psychological experiments in which subjects had been uninformed or coerced and Kinsey's studies of sexual behavior. The former frequently involved less controversial topics than did Kinsey's research, but they, and not Kinsey, had encountered public opposition, presumably because Kinsey's subjects *had* been fully informed and had volunteered.

In 1954, social psychologist W. Edgar Vinacke called explicit attention to moral problems in the deception of experimental subjects in psychological research. "So far as I can tell," wrote Vinacke, "no one is particularly concerned about this," even though, as he saw it, the newly published Ethical Standards of Psychologists had a clear statement of principles on the issue (presumably principles 4.31–1 and 4.31–2).[76] Vinacke's article anticipated many future debates in biomedical and behavioral ethics over whether deceit as a research method was "really" justified: "The issue seems to boil down to the question of whether it is more important to avoid deceiving anyone, or, in the interests of science, to sacrifice a few people in the ultimate expectation of helping many via the knowledge gained."[77] In addition, Vinacke raised the possibility of an APA committee to address issues about human subjects of research and called for empirical inquiry both to compare the effects of deception and full disclosure on research findings and to investigate the reactions of subjects and the public to deceptive research practices.

In the next issue of the *American Psychologist*, Arthur MacKinney referred to Vinacke's call for empirical research on the use of deception and reported on a survey that had been conducted in Minnesota. The survey had assessed the attitudes of about 150 undergraduate students who had participated in experiments involving various levels of deception. MacKinney found little evidence that these subjects "were disturbed about being deceived."[78] Almost as if MacKinney's findings had rebutted Vinacke's concerns, there was little if any subsequent discussion of deception or consent in the psychological literature until after the publication of Milgram's studies. There was a steady rise in the use of deception during this period. A count of the articles in journals in personality and social psychology shows that 18% reported uses of deception in 1948, gradually increasing to 38% by 1963.[79] If in the period from 1954 to 1964 psychologists were relatively silent on the subjects of deception and consent, the next ten years—from 1964 to 1974—witnessed an explosion of commentary and controversy on these subjects. We turn now to an examination of the cases that detonated the debate.

Controversial Cases and Professional Reactions

Psychology has no history of outrages analogous to biomedical experimentation under the Third Reich, but it is not suffering for want of particular projects that inspired heated controversy. Names such as "Milgram's Research" and "Zimbardo's Prison Research" are invoked again and again. Both cases have spawned whole schools of critics and defenders, whose writings often perspicuously illustrate problems of informed consent. In addition to these examples from within psychology, the field was also affected during this period by controversial cases in the social sciences whose methods paralleled those used in psychology and which also involved deception. The two most prominent of these were the "Wichita Jury Study" and Laud Humphreys' "Tearoom-Trade Research." Some of these cases involve no consent, and others consent of questionable quality, a distinction worth keeping in mind when comparing them.

The Wichita Jury Study.[80] The earliest landmark case in the social sciences featured moral problems of confidentiality and privacy more obviously than problems of informed consent, but it contains significant implications for informed consent. In 1954 professors in the social sciences and the Law School at the University of Chicago performed a study on jury deliberations that has since come to be known as the Wichita Jury Study. The researchers secretly recorded the discussions of six separate juries in order to obtain empirical data by which to test frequently voiced criticisms of the jury system and the assumptions about that system implicit in American law. This project generated heated public controversy.

In their defense, the Chicago academicians stressed the beneficial consequences of possessing such data. We should not be left in the dark, they maintained, about the actual operations of an institution so funda-mental to our legal system. Yet the importance of maintaining confiden-tiality in that institution led to questions from the public sector about the justifiability of the methods used to collect the information. The Seventh Amendment to the Constitution guarantees the right of U.S. citizens to a trial by jury in criminal cases, and Senator James O. Eastland echoed the opinion of other commentators when he noted that secret delibera-tion is essential to the jury process as conceived by the framers of the Seventh Amendment. If it became known that secret observational stud-ies might be conducted, this knowledge would tend to constrain and alter the free exchange necessary to a full and fair jury trial. Eastland thought the potentially harmful consequences of recording jury discus-sions also included a constitutional violation. The extent to which his interpretation was shared by other politicians is indicated by 1956 fed-eral legislation explicitly prohibiting the recording of federal grand or petit jury deliberations.

Eastland's appeal to legislative intentions and constitutional guaran-tees rests primarily on a *legal* argument about the protected status of jury secrecy. But there are also ethical issues about consent in social sci-ence research. Researchers often complain that consent alters the phe-nomenon studied to an unacceptable extent. The investigators conduct-ing the Wichita Jury Study therefore never informed the jurors that they were participating in a research project, nor was any form of consent from the juror participants solicited, although consent was obtained in advance from the court and opposing counsel. To the extent that the jurors under investigation believed that their discussions were taking place in private, the recording of those discussions presented familiar moral problems, including lack of respect for autonomy and for privacy.

The Wichita Jury Study was subsequently discussed in the psycholog-ical literature in 1966. In an article reprinted in the *American Psychol-ogist* from the *Columbia Law Review*, Oscar Ruebhausen and Orville G. Brim described the study as an example of invasion of privacy in behav-ioral research, although they did not view the study as the most repre-sentative or the most serious intrusion in the field.[81] Ruebhausen and Brim drew an explicit link between informed consent and the legal-moral obligation to respect the right of privacy. Moreover, theirs is perhaps the first defense in the psychological literature of a consent requirement jus-tified on grounds of autonomy rather than beneficence:

> The right to privacy is, therefore, a positive claim to a status of per-sonal dignity—a claim for freedom, if you will, but freedom of a very special kind. . . . The essence of the claim to privacy is the choice of the individual as to what he shall disclose and withhold, and when he shall do so. Accordingly, the essential privacy-respecting ethic for behavioral research must revolve around the concept of consent. Taken literally, the concept of consent would require that behavioral research refuse to engage in the probing of personality, attitudes, opinions,

beliefs, or behavior without the fully informed consent, freely given, of the individual person being examined.[82]

Reubhausen and Brim proceed to suggest a set of principles for a general code of ethics for behavioral research that would require informed consent "to the fullest extent possible." If consent is impossible without invalidating the research, they suggest procedural mechanisms for ensuring that any invasion of privacy is compatible with the values of the larger community in which the research is conducted.

Milgram's Research on Obedience.[83] It is surprising that Ruebhausen and Brim make no reference in their article to Stanley Milgram's studies of obedience, first published in 1963, because that research quickly assumed a position as the most controversial and instructive case of problems of deception and consent. From 1960 to 1963 Milgram conducted experiments in social psychology that tested ordinary citizens' obedience to and defiance of authority, an interest that Milgram had developed through his study of literature on the Holocaust. Subjects were solicited to participate in "a study of memory and learning" through an advertisement placed in a local newspaper. Subjects of various occupations and levels of education between the ages of 20 and 50 were recruited. The announcement offered $4 (plus 50 cents carfare) for one hour of participation.

In the basic experimental design, two people were taken into the psychology laboratory to participate in what was said quite deceptively to be a "memory experiment." One person was a naive subject who had responded to the newspaper advertisement and was not informed as to the actual objectives or methodology of the research. The other person was a disguised accomplice in the experiment. The authority figure was a third person—the experimenter, who greeted the subjects and instructed them about the study. The naive subject was designated as the "teacher" and the accomplice as the "learner." The experimenter explained only that the study concerned the effects of punishment on the learning process.

The task putatively performed by the learner was a word-pair association. Punishment for a wrong answer had to be given in the form of an electric shock from what appeared to be a technologically advanced and powerful machine. The learner receiving the shock was in an adjacent room, strapped in an "electric chair" apparatus with electrodes fixed to the wrists. The teacher sat before a shock generator ranging in voltage from 15 to 450 volts. The switches varied by increments of 15 volts and were labeled with verbal designators: "Slight Shock," "Moderate Shock," "Strong Shock," "Very Strong Shock," "Intense Shock," "Extreme Intensity Shock," "Danger: Severe Shock," and finally "XXX." The actual subject (the teacher) received a sample shock of 45 volts prior to the experiment.

The study began after the experimenter gave full instructions to the teacher. Whenever the learner failed to designate the correct answer, the teacher was required by the authority (the experimenter) to administer a shock of increasing intensity. The learner, or accomplice, did not actually experience shocks, but the teacher, who repeatedly heard the fake verbal protests of the learner to the electrical shocks, could not know that the learner actually received no shocks. At the 75–volt shock, the learner grunted; at 120 volts he shouted that the shocks were becoming painful; at 150 volts and thereafter, he demanded to be released, and at 270 volts, he let out an agonizing scream. As the voltage increased, his protests became more vehement and emotional. At 300 volts, he fell into a dead silence.

The teachers reacted differently to the learner's responses. When the latter first protested, the teacher frequently asked the experimenter whether to continue. The experimenter adamantly insisted that the experiment must proceed, despite the wishes of the learner. The experimenter stressed that the shocks were painful but not dangerous and that the experiment was important for the advancement of science. The teacher was then torn between following the orders of the authority figure and refusing to continue to inflict pain on the learner. As the voltage was increased, the conflict heightened. For the teachers this conflict was often emotionally intense and gripping. Milgram reported on one case as follows: "I observed a mature and initially poised businessman enter the laboratory smiling and confident. Within 20 minutes he was reduced to a twitching, stuttering wreck, who was rapidly approaching a point of nervous collapse."[84]

Once the teacher either reached the highest voltage lever *or* refused to proceed, the experimental session ended. After the experiment, an interview was held to "debrief" subjects. When the subjects were asked to explain why they had continued to give shocks through the final level, a typical response was, "I wouldn't have done it by myself. I was just doing what I was told." Some subjects were asked at the debriefing to fill out questionnaires to express their feelings about the "memory experiment." All were told that they had been deceived and that the learner had not received any shocks. A reconciliation with the unharmed victim followed. When the experimental series was complete, the subjects received a report of the details of the experimental procedures and results. They also were asked to complete a follow-up questionnaire regarding their participation in the research.

Milgram found that approximately 60% of his subjects were fully obedient to authority: They punished the learner all the way through the most potent shock level ("XXX"). These results had not been expected prior to the experiment, and the research was widely regarded as a significant contribution to social psychology. It was hailed as a discovery not only about conditions under which subjects fail to defy authority, but also about how they transfer responsibility to the authority, using as their excuse—as was often heard during the Nuremberg trials—"I was simply

doing my duty." Critics, however, condemned the research for the allegedly devastating psychological effects on some subjects and for its overt
deception and lack of informed consent. Some critics also complained
that Milgram's conclusions about the nature of obedience were highly
speculative, and were unlikely to be replicated in real-life situations
beyond the laboratory environment.

Within psychology, critical reactions appeared almost immediately
after Milgram's publication of his findings. Among the influential early
commentaries were a 1964 essay by Diana Baumrind in the *American
Psychologist* and a paper by Herbert Kelman delivered at the 1965 APA
convention and published in 1967.[85] Baumrind, who was to remain for
years an outspoken critic of research involving deception, argued that
the emotional disturbance experienced by Milgram's subjects had to be
considered either an actual or a potential harm of real significance. Thus,
her argument was a beneficence-based rather than autonomy-based critique. She intimated that Milgram may have been in violation of principle 4.31–1 of the APA's Ethical Standards, which required that subjects
be fully informed of the possibility of serious after-effects. Her critique
prompted an immediate response from Milgram, who argued that the
subjects in his research were never at risk of injurious effects resulting
from participation.[86]

By contrast to the Baumrind-Milgram exchange, Kelman's agenda was
broader, and was more autonomy-based than beneficence-based. He
acknowledged that honorable people could disagree about the evaluation of Milgram's research and emphasized that his use of deception was
hardly an isolated incident in psychology. Indeed, one of the main
themes of Kelman's article was that since Vinacke had first raised the
issue in 1954, deception had become widely used in studies involving
human subjects. "What concerns me most," wrote Kelman, "is not so
much that deception is used, but precisely that it is used without question. It has now become standard operating procedure in the social psychologist's laboratory."[87]

Kelman discussed several examples of troubling deception research
besides Milgram's studies—for example, research in which subjects had
been misled into doubting their sexual orientation or believing that their
lives were actually in danger. Kelman's concerns were not restricted to
cases in which subjects might experience harmful consequences. Like
Ruebhausen and Brim, he raised questions about deception and consent
that pushed into autonomy territory, beyond beneficence-based, sub-
ject-welfare issues:

> I am equally concerned, however, about the less obvious cases, in
> which there is little danger of harmful effects, at least in the conven-
> tional sense of the term. Serious ethical issues are raised by deception
> per se and the kind of use of human beings that it implies. In our other
> interhuman relationships, most of us would never think of doing the
> kinds of things that we do to our subjects. . . . We would view such

behavior as a violation of the respect to which all fellow humans are entitled.[88]

Humphreys's Tearoom-Trade Research.[89] Kelman's observations about the use of deception in psychology had similar applications in sociology, where a study no less celebrated than Milgram's research emerged in the late 1960s (1965–1968). Sociologist Laud Humphreys was convinced that the public as well as legal authorities and police held dangerous, stereotyped attitudes toward men who commit impersonal sexual acts in public restrooms. "Tearoom sex," as such fellatio in public restrooms is called, is the source of many arrests for "homosexuality" in the United States. Humphreys, who sympathized with the alienation suffered by these men, decided that it was of considerable social importance that they be objectively studied. He therefore set out to discover their motivation for impersonal sexual gratification, as well as their social status.

Humphreys used direct observation and follow-up interviews. He first stationed himself in the so-called tearooms and served as "watchqueen"—the individual who keeps watch and warns by coughing when a police car or stranger approaches. He observed hundreds of acts of fellatio in this role. He gained the confidence of a few of those he observed, revealed his true intentions as a sociologist, and persuaded them to discuss their lives and motives further. But he secretly followed others, recording the license numbers of their cars. A year later, while carefully disguised, Humphreys appeared at their homes, claiming falsely to be a health service interviewer, and interviewed them about their personal affairs.

As he intended, Humphreys's findings eventually cast doubt on numerous stereotypes.[90] However, matters became heated when some members of Humphreys's department at his university objected that his research had unethically violated his subjects' right to privacy and right not to be deceived. The president of Washington University was asked to rescind Humphreys's doctorate. The turmoil over his alleged violations of the autonomy rights of his subjects resulted in furious debates, and even a fistfight among faculty members. Eventually an exodus of approximately half the department members to positions at other universities occurred. Public controversy also erupted. Critics complained that Humphreys failed to respect the right of his subjects to self-determination because most of them had not consented to be studied. The critics argued that the moral wrong entailed by deception cannot be justified by appeals to beneficial consequences for society or social science, no matter the magnitude. A journalist, Nicholas von Hoffman, sharply condemned Humphreys's work as invading "our most private and secret lives."

Neither Humphreys nor self-appointed spokespersons for the group he had studied saw any serious violation of rights, although they admitted that the study involved deception and intrusion into the private lives of nonconsenting subjects. Humphreys argued that the importance of his research easily outweighed any violation of rights that might have been involved. Two sociologists, Irving Louis Horowitz and Lee Rainwater, defended Humphreys in an article that focused on the researcher's right to pursue and to communicate knowledge. To the extent that restrictions on deceptive methods would make studies such as Humphreys's impossible to perform, Rainwater and Horowitz held that those restrictions would infringe on the scientist's right to illuminate still mysterious regions of human behavior.

In 1970 Humphreys's research won the prestigious C. Wright Mills Award for the Study of Social Problems. This award enhanced rather than curtailed the controversy that gathered about the research, and soon the controversy spread to other research as well.

Zimbardo's Mock Prison Research.[91] In 1971 Philip G. Zimbardo, a psychologist at Stanford University, constructed a mock prison environment in the basement of a laboratory at the University. He solicited two dozen male student volunteers from several colleges to act out the roles of prisoners and guards for a daily wage of $15. The experiment was designed to explore the effects of an extreme and rigid institutional situation on individual attitudes and behavior. It had been planned to run for two weeks, but after only six days Zimbardo decided to discontinue the project.

The reason for this premature termination was surprising: The student subjects randomly assigned as guards abused the subjects playing the role of prisoners. As Zimbardo himself put it, "Volunteer prisoners suffered physical and psychological abuse hour after hour for days. . . . Many of the 'prisoners' were in serious distress, and many of the 'guards' were behaving in ways which brutalized and degraded their fellow subjects." Zimbardo claimed that his results showed that the prison environment exerts a powerful effect on the actions and attitudes of those incarcerated, a conclusion that he believed to provide a critical insight into the degrading effects of institutional roles and rules. He cited both the publicity his project attracted in the popular press and the frequency with which government and community officials consulted him about prison reform as evidence that his results reached a wide audience and directly affected public policy. He noted that subjects reported no long-term negative reactions due to the study. Indeed, the majority praised it as a "valuable didactic experience."

Critics disputed Zimbardo's claims about the overall beneficial consequences of his results. They contended that these results revealed nothing about prison environments that had not already been known, while presenting unnecessary risks to subjects. High levels of emotional stress, some physical discomfort, and humiliation and physical degradation at the hands of the guards were all cited in the criticisms.

Unlike the three cases discussed earlier, moral objections to Zimbardo's experiment did not center on intentional deception. The principal question was the more complex one of the relationship between consent and risk. Zimbardo obtained consent through an intentionally abbreviated disclosure; he informed his subjects of his basic purposes and of the possibility that the methods employed would pose certain risks, but did not disclose some of the details of the experimental design. For example, he did not tell his subjects that some of them would be "arrested" by local police as the first step in the simulation study. Moreover, the advance disclosures about risks gave subjects little indication of the intensity of the stress they would experience.

Zimbardo argued that the information he disclosed was not, in context, inadequate. The project staff had had no reason to anticipate such high levels of stress before initiating the study. For example, none of the student profiles, which had been carefully collected in advance, indicated that there might be such reactions. Nonetheless, the need to stop the experiment when it became clear that its stressful effects far exceeded anything the subjects had consented to experience raised a number of significant issues. Questions arose about the extent of the researcher's responsibility both to identify and to disclose all the potential risks before consent can be considered adequate, about the permissible level of risk in research and whether obtaining informed consent can justify very risky or scientifically questionable research, and about whether one can consent to what is uncertain or unknown.

Ethical Principles in the Conduct of Research

The shift of concern from outright deception and the *failure* to obtain consent in the earlier cases to questions about the *quality* of consent in the Zimbardo experiment reflected to some extent a shift already underway during this period in more general discussions of disclosure in psychological research. Although the use of deception was not yet declining (in 1971 47% of the articles published in the *Journal of Personality and Social Psychology* involved deception[92]), concern about the practice was increasing. So was concern about other issues in research ethics that involved consent.

In 1967 M. Brewster Smith, who was later to serve on the committee that drafted the APA's 1973 code of research ethics, published a careful analysis of value conflicts in psychological research with children.[93] Much of the essay was devoted to problems of parental consent. He considered the conditions under which consent is truly informed, under what circumstances explicit parental consent must be obtained, and similar issues. (Interestingly, Smith interpreted principle 4.31–1 as approaching an *absolute* requirement for voluntary consent.[94]) The next year, Herbert Kelman, perhaps the first scholar to address ethical issues in behavioral and social research systematically, published a book on ethical issues in the social sciences in which he reprinted his aforementioned essay on deception.[95] During this period empirical studies of the effects of and alternatives to deception also began to appear.[96]

At the same time, public interest in research ethics and in unearthing and correcting abuses of human subjects began to take shape. As we recount in Chapter 6, the Surgeon General promulgated administrative regulations in 1966 requiring institutional review of research involving human subjects. That same year a government panel on privacy in behavioral research published a report that included a strong statement of support for consent.[97] By 1972, Kelman was arguing vigorously for a principle of consent for psychological research, using language reminiscent of Irwin Berg's arguments in 1953:

> The central norm governing the relationship of investigator and subject is that of voluntary informed consent, and ethical problems generally arise because this norm has been violated or circumvented. Voluntary consent is impossible to the extent that the subjects constitute a captive audience or are unaware of the fact that they are being studied. Informed consent is impossible to the extent that subjects' participation is solicited under false pretenses or they are deceived about the true nature of the research. If investigators were to adhere scrupulously to the norm of consent and related principles, then most of the ethical problems would be avoided or corrected for readily. The question is how such adherence can be facilitated.[98]

In this climate of public and professional controversy, the APA established, in 1966, an ad hoc Committee on Ethical Standards in Psychological Research. It was informally called the Cook Commission, after its chair, Stuart W. Cook, a member of the Committee that had drafted the original 1953 *Ethical Standards of Psychologists*. The Cook Commission was charged with expanding those provisions of the *Ethical Standards* that applied to the conduct of psychological research.[99] The *Ethical Standards* had been revised several times since 1953, most notably in the period 1959 to 1963, when the code had been distilled into 18 general principles, one of which, Principle 16, covered research.[100] Principle 16 preserved the main point of the original principle 4.31–1—that if "a reasonable possibility of dangerous after-effects exists, research is conducted only when the subjects or their responsible agents are fully informed of this possibility and agree to participate nevertheless."[101]

However, there was no longer any specific mention of deception analogous to Principle 4.31–2, and thus the code offered no direct assistance to the membership on what had become a major moral problem for psychology. The code was also relatively unhelpful on another issue that was beginning to rival deception as a problem in research ethics for psychology: widespread use of obligatory student "subject pools," on which experimental psychologists depended heavily.[102] Conflicts about consent were thus at the core of both issues in the drive to develop a research code. The Cook Commission had to address straightforwardly the following dilemmas: (1) Could a principle of *informed* consent be reconciled with a methodological dependence on *deception* that sprang from the belief that naive subjects were necessary to the obtaining of valid results? (2) Could a principle of *voluntary* consent be reconciled with the widespread use of conscripted undergraduates in subject pools? The first problem concerned informed consent, the second free consent.

The Cook Commission used the same empirical and participatory methods developed by the earlier Committee on Ethical Standards.[103] After a pilot survey of 1,000 of the by-then 35,000 members of the APA, a revised questionnaire was sent to a 9,000–member sample asking for descriptions of morally problematic research incidents. Although about 2,000 incidents were subsequently reported in reply, these descriptions were short on examples from such areas as survey research and research with children. As a result, the questionnaire was revised a second time and sent to another sample of 9,000 APA members, this time yielding 3,000 reported incidents. Thus, the Cook Commission had approximately 5,000 case descriptions as a data base for discharging its obligations.

These cases were classified into categories, one of which was informed consent. Each group of research incidents was analyzed by at least two members of the Cook Commission charged with drafting preliminary guidelines on the issue. The process by which these drafts were subjected to public comment and to further comment by the membership is an extraordinary story of professional commitment and procedure. Psychologists with a high degree of exposure to or interest in research ethics, including staff members of research review panels, directors of large research organizations, journal editors, and writers on research ethics were systematically interviewed. Also consulted were professionals in other disciplines, including law, philosophy, sociology, and psychiatry. Drafts of the code were circulated for comment to a variety of professional societies, both within and outside psychology, and over 120 groups responded.

Perhaps most important was an intermediate draft of the code that was circulated to the entire APA membership in 1971. Members were encouraged to communicate their questions and objections. In addition, discussions were scheduled in many of the 1971 meetings of regional psychological associations and at the 1971 APA National Convention, as well as in countless academic psychology departments and other local institutions. Based on an overwhelming response to this 1971 draft, the code was substantially revised.[104] A subsequent (May 1972) draft, which was circulated to the entire APA membership, elicited a much lighter response. The code, in the form it was later formally adopted (in 1972, published in 1973), deviated only slightly from the May iteration.

The 1971 draft included over 22 principles that dealt exclusively with issues of consent and deception.[105] Although some principles were redundant, the proliferation of principles was primarily the result of the abundant detail and specificity with which consent issues and problems were treated. In addition to the major principles creating a prima facie obligation to obtain informed consent and identifying the justified exceptions to this obligation, principles specified (1) the kinds of information that must be disclosed to potential subjects, (2) the kinds of force and threat that are impermissible in consent solicitation, (3) the responsibilities of research assistants regarding consent, and (4) what should be done when there is reason to doubt the subject's competence to give an informed consent.

On the two central issues of deception and subject pools, the 1971 draft took complicated positions. Although the draft recognized that it is a "basic right of human beings to decide for themselves whether and when they will participate as subjects in research,"[106] deviations from a principle of informed consent, including outright deception, were permitted under conditions not substantially different from those outlined in 4.31–1 and 4.31–2. But in the latest version an explicit weighing of the importance of the research against the "costs" to the subject was required. This assessment was to be conducted by an ethics advisory group as well as the investigator:

Principle 5.111

It is unethical to involve a person in research without his prior knowledge and informed consent.

A. This principle may conflict with the methodological requirement of research whose importance has been judged by the investigator (Principle 1.12), with the advice of an ethics advisory group (Principle 1.2), to outweigh the costs to the subject of failing to obtain his informed consent. Conducting the proposed research in violation of this principle may be justified only when:

(1) it may be demonstrated that the research objectives cannot be realized without the concealment,

(2) there is sufficient reason for concealment so that when the subject is later informed, he can be expected to find the concealment reasonable and so suffer no serious loss of confidence in the integrity of the investigator or others involved in the situation,

(3) the subject is allowed to withdraw his data from the study if he so wishes when the concealment is revealed to him,

(4) the investigator takes full responsibility for detecting and removing stressful aftereffects (Principles 1.72 and 1.73) and for providing the subject with positive gain from the research experience (Principles 1.741, 1.742, and 1.743).[107]

Some of the research incidents reviewed by the Cook Commission in formulating this principle illuminate the concerns of the time. Consider, for example, the following two cases, which are representative of dozens of similarly troublesome cases:

[Example 1]

A 'notice of employment' was distributed. When the prospective 'employees' arrived, however, they discovered that it was an experiment and not an employment interview. One subject gave up a half day of work, had his suit cleaned and felt he had been very badly treated.

[Example 2]

A recent case arose in connection with dissertation research in a field setting. The study involved the observation of shoe salesmen's behavior in response to different types of 'customers,' who were collaborators of the researcher. Ethical issues were raised because the salesmen were not aware of participating in the research study and, although no shoes were bought, about 30 minutes of their time was used in each case. No effort was made to remunerate the salesmen or to debrief them after the study was over.[108]

Other incidents were no less dramatic. One, for example, raised issues reminiscent of those found in the Jewish Chronic Disease Hospital case:

In a study comparing effects of LSD with a placebo, the subjects were not told that 'LSD' was involved but rather were told the full chemical name, which would not be recognized by most of the subjects, and the known and suspected effects of LSD were described to subjects in detail. It was felt that using the technical name and describing possible harmful effects was adequate information, and that actually using the term 'LSD' would have caused many subjects to refuse to participate on emotional grounds, while they might be willing if they were specifically told about suspected harmful effects. Since the technical name was the correct one and the suspected effects correctly described, the research was probably covered legally, but ethically I am not so sure.[109]

By comparison to the principles covering disclosure and deception, the statement about subject pools—directed at problems of *free* consent—was more straightforward:

Principle 1.5111

Students should not be required to participate in research as a condition for entering a course or for obtaining grade points or avoiding loss of them, or as an alternative to another onerous task, where that participation requirement is to any extent in the service of research.

A. This principle in no way precludes course requirements for participating in research where the requirement is solely for pedagogic purposes.

B. Where the requirement is both for research and for the pedagogic benefit of the participant, then the participation should be made voluntary by providing equally satisfactory alternative participation opportunities that are designed soley [sic] for pedagogic purposes.

C. It does not suffice to print a research participation requirement in the college catalog or to point it out to the student at the time of registration. This practice does provide the opportunity for a more informed consent but it still has an element of coercion in that the student must deny himself the educational opportunities offered by the course if he chooses not to participate in research designed for research purposes as well as for the student's pedagogic benefit. This problem becomes especially acute to the extent that the course is a requirement for further courses or where equivalent alternative courses are lacking.

D. It does not suffice to allow a choice among a wide variety of research opportunities, while requiring that some must be chosen under threat of academic sanction.[110]

Some of the incidents categorized under the general heading of "types of coercion" reflect more sensitivity and concern about forms of influence than is generally found in the contemporary informed consent literature. The following is an example (although clearly not an example of *coercion*): "In the course of recruiting subjects for an experiment, the graduate student pressed reluctant subjects into participating by arguing that he desperately needed their cooperation if he was to complete his dissertation by an impending deadline."[111]

Predictably, the 1971 draft was heavily criticized in the profession as too confining for the researcher.[112] Two psychologists went so far as to conduct an empirical test of the effects that conformity with the consent principles of the 1971 draft would have on research results. They were unable to replicate the findings of prior studies under these more rigid conditions.[113]

The code as it was finally adopted in 1972 was reduced to ten tidy principles and a preamble, accompanied by an extensive discussion, and case examples. Five principles dealt with issues of disclosure and consent:

> 3. Ethical practice requires the investigator to inform the participant of all features of the research that reasonably might be expected to influence willingness to participate and to explain all other aspects of the research about which the participant inquires. Failure to make full disclosure gives added emphasis to the investigator's responsibility to protect the welfare and dignity of the research participant.
>
> 4. Openness and honesty are essential characteristics of the relationship between investigator and research participant. When the methodological requirements of a study necessitate concealment or deception, the investigator is required to ensure the participant's understanding of the reasons for this action and to restore the quality of the relationship with the investigator.
>
> 5. Ethical research practice requires the investigator to respect the individual's freedom to decline to participate in research or to discontinue participation at any time. The obligation to protect this freedom requires special vigilance when the investigator is in a position of power over the participant. The decision to limit this freedom increases the investigator's responsibility to protect the participant's dignity and welfare.

6. Ethically acceptable research begins with the establishment of a clear and fair agreement between the investigator and the research participant that clarifies the responsibilities of each. The investigator has the obligation to honor all promises and commitments included in that agreement.

7. The ethical investigator protects participants from physical and mental discomfort, harm, and danger. If the risk of such consequences exists, the investigator is required to inform the participant of that fact, secure consent before proceeding, and take all possible measures to minimize distress. A research procedure may not be used if it is likely to cause serious and lasting harm to participants.[114]

As the discussion and analysis that accompanied these principles makes clear, none of them ruled out either deception or the use of subject pools.[115] Indeed, the code's failure to prohibit without qualification certain research activities was severely criticized by a minority of psychologists.[116] Even Principle 7—which, like Principles 4.31–1 and 4.31–2 before it, seemed to require informed consent whenever subjects are at risk—was not interpreted by the Cook Commission as prohibiting the use of deception in Milgram's research: "When such studies can be justified, the investigator incurs a strong obligation to minimize possible psychological damage to the research participants."[117]

The APA's position (or non-position) on research such as Milgram's symbolized the problem of informed consent in psychology by the early 1970s. After almost 20 years of debate and self-study, informed consent was indisputably recognized as a moral ideal for psychological research.[118] At the same time, the view continued to prevail that the strict application of the principle of informed consent would invalidate valuable research findings and would compromise the psychologist's ability to conduct meaningful research.[119] The 1973 code tried to balance these concerns without giving either a clear priority.

American psychology was struggling with what Brewster Smith has called contrasting frames of reference for research ethics. One frame features respect for autonomy, as expressed in informed consent. This frame is, in effect, an autonomy model. The other frame emphasizes issues of welfare and harm—in effect, a beneficence model.[120] As was true of clinical medicine in this same period, a satisfactory balance between these two frames or models had not yet been achieved in psychology's research ethics, and perhaps never will be.[121] However, the discussion had become more sophisticated and astute over the 20–year period of debate, and the groundwork was set for major changes in research practices. In the 1970s and 1980s, both deception and subject pools became progressively less common; at the same time, federally required consent procedures became more prominent, as we shall see in Chapter 6.

Conclusion

In this chapter, as in the previous two, we have looked less at the history of *practices* of consent-seeking than at the history of *values* that underlie practices and public pronouncements. There can be little doubt that a profound qualitative change of outlook on human experimentation has occurred in these values since Nuremberg, so much so that it would be an anachronism even to place the label "informed consent" on research practices and policies in the United States prior to the mid-1960s. Not until the mid-1970s, where we now conclude our history in Chapter 5, did informed consent emerge as a major moral rule for human research in both the biomedical and the psychological sciences. Even then, a cavernous gulf doubtlessly existed between this research *principle* and research *practice*. Yet it is indisputable that something dramatic occurred in research ethics and policies during this period: At the end of World War II, there were virtually no noteworthy formal guidelines or codes governing research with human subjects. But in 1970 Beecher reprinted over 20 guidelines and codes, designed to protect subjects, that had been passed between 1948 and 1968 by major organizations.[122]

Our narrative only begins to address questions about why such a dramatic change occurred and why it did not happen earlier, given some important warnings about inadequacies in research ethics well before Nuremberg.[123] Although Nazi atrocities appear to have been the single most important causal factor in this chain of changes, the full explanation is multi-causal, and in the case of psychology, the experience in Germany had no major direct effect on the developments we have traced. A more thorough history than we have been able to attempt would point to many other social and professional factors as having caused or motivated the changes and would locate the exact lines of causal influence deriving from Nuremberg. Developments in research ethics would have to be placed in a broader context of the rise of biomedical technology, massive new funding for research and a corresponding increase in responsibility for the use of the funds, and an unprecedented new emphasis in American society on individual rights, social equality, and accountability that was prompted in part by the Vietnam War and (later) Watergate. In this respect, our chronicle of events has far more depth than our explanation of those events.

The shifts in values that were occurring in American society fostered an increased sensitivity to the unjust manipulation or exploitation of patients and research subjects, who were often persons of a different social standing than investigators. Some of the cases we have considered sparked moral outrage, based on what appeared to be straightforward exploitation of the vulnerable and defenseless—for example, the mentally retarded, the insane, the institutionalized elderly, captive students, and the poverty-stricken. Often, such subjects were treated as being worth less than others; in extreme instances, as in Nazi maltreatment, they were viewed as utterly worthless except as instrumental to the ends of the investigator. Widespread contemporary concern about the fate of subjects of research was prompted in part by recognition that derelicts, prisoners, prisoners of war, and those of "inferior races" or inferior social status had been treated and still were being treated in some cases as somehow deficient in their humanity and rights.

The history of moral outrage over these events and our subsequent change of moral outlook is not traceable to a single misgiving about the use of subjects or to a basis in the abuse of any single moral principle such as respect for autonomy. Apprehension about exploitation, for example, encompassed uneasiness about coercion, deception, and the imposition of pain and suffering. Nor can any single event be cited as "the cause" of this revolution in perspective, despite the extraordinary impact of each of the cases explored in this chapter.

Nazi Germany is now easy—probably too easy—to dismiss as distant, unrepresentative, and even otherworldly; but Milgram's research, Willowbrook, Tuskegee, and the Jewish Chronic Disease Hospital still serve for many today as models of moral failure that are not easily dismissible as distanced aberrations. Tuskegee continues to serve as a particularly striking example of negligence, insensitivity, and the dangers of harmful intrusions that are unmonitored by policies protective of subjects. The Jewish Chronic Disease Hospital case, too, is an historically instructive example of how a single case can inform and even transform the research community. At the hearings on this case many distinguished investigators testified that Dr. Southam's conduct was not significantly different from prevalent customs in the biomedical research community. Much the same observation was made when Milgram's research was first criticized in social psychology. It is almost unimaginable that even ten years later an appeal to customary practice could have been credibly submitted. Indeed, by 1977, even Milgram was acknowledging that "many regard informed consent as the cornerstone of ethical practice in experimentation with human subjects."[124]

More than Nuremberg, which had no such *immediate* impact, in the later years these cases stimulated discussion and altered viewpoints across the landscape of American research and biomedical ethics. These changing viewpoints were given their most forceful expression in federal regulatory activity, a subject to which we now turn in Chapter 6.

Notes

1. Criticisms in Congress and at NIH are discussed in Chapter 6. For criticism in the popular press, see, for example, J. Lear, "Do We Need New Rules for Experiments on People?" *Saturday Review* (February 5, 1966): 61–70; J. Lear, "Experiments on People—The Growing Debate," *Saturday Review* (July 2, 1966): 41–43;

and W. Goodman, "Doctors Must Experiment on Humans—But What are the Patient's Rights?" *New York Times Magazine* (July 2, 1965): 12–13, 29–33.

2. On historical developments leading to the use of this phrase, see Judith P. Swazey, "Protecting the 'Animal of Necessity': Limits to Inquiry in Clinical Investigation," *Daedalus* 107 (1978): 129–45, and Irving Ladimer, "Human Experimentation: Medico-legal Aspects," *New England Journal of Medicine* 257 (July 4, 1957): 18–24.

3. The first known "code" of research ethics is sometimes said to be that of the American investigator William Beaumont (1785–1853), who established rough guidelines for responsibility in experimentation. His 1833 rules form the oldest known American document on research ethics, and perhaps the oldest code tailored for experimentation to be found anywhere. One of its provisions states that the voluntary consent of the subject is necessary; a second specifies that the project must be abandoned if the subject becomes dissatisfied. See Henry K. Beecher, *Research and the Individual: Human Studies* (Boston: Little, Brown and Co., 1970), 219. Beaumont's treatment of his famous subject, Alexis St. Martin, did not, however, always live up to the high-minded language of his code. See Jesse S. Myer, *Life and Letters of Dr. William Beaumont*, 3rd ed.—repaginated (St. Louis: C. V. Mosby, 1981).

4. But see Percival, Chapter I, Section XII: "It is for the public good, and in an especial degree advantageous to the poor . . . that *new remedies* and *new methods* . . . should be devised. But in the accomplishment of this salutary purpose, the gentlemen of the faculty should be scrupulously and conscientiously governed by sound reason." This passage *does* have implications for the researcher-subject relationship. Thomas Percival, *Medical Ethics; or a Code of Institutes and Precepts, Adapted to the Professional Conduct of Physicians and Surgeons* (Manchester: S. Russell, 1803), 31. The more readily available edition is Chauncey D. Leake, ed., *Percival's Medical Ethics* (Huntington, NY: Robert E. Krieger Publishing Co., 1975), 76.

5. Useful brief accounts of various historical developments earlier than those that we consider are found in A.C. Ivy, "The History and Ethics of the Use of Human Subjects in Medical Experiments," *Science* 108 (July 2, 1948): 1–5; Beecher, *Research and the Individual*, 5–15, and *Experimentation in Man* (Springfield, IL: Charles C Thomas, 1959), 6–8 [This book was issued after publication in the *Journal of the American Medical Association* 169 (January 1959): 461–78]; Donald E. Konold, *A History of American Medical Ethics 1847–1912* (Madison, WI: State Historical Society, 1962), Chapter 3; Gert H. Brieger, "Human Experimentation: History," in Warren T. Reich, ed., *Encyclopedia of Bioethics*, 4 vols. (New York: Free Press, 1978), 2:684–92, and "Some Aspects of Human Experimentation in the History of Nutrition," in National Research Council, *Use of Human Subjects in Safety Evaluation of Food Chemicals: Proceedings of a Conference* (Washington, D.C.: National Academy of Sciences, 1967), 207–15; Joseph V. Brady and Albert R. Jonsen, "The Evolution of Regulatory Influences on Research with Human Subjects," in Robert Greenwald, Mary Kay Ryan, and James E. Mulvihill, eds., *Human Subjects Research* (New York: Plenum Press, 1982), 3–5; Charles R. McCarthy, "Research Policy, Biomedical," in Reich, *Encyclopedia of Bioethics*, 4: 1492–98; Susan Eyrich Lederer, "'The Right and Wrong of Making Experiments on Human Beings': Udo J. Wile and Syphilis," *Bulletin of the History of Medicine* 58 (1984): 380–97, esp. 396; and Stanley J. Reiser, "Human Experimentation and the Convergence of Medical Research and Patient Care," *Annals of the American Academy of Political and Social Science* 437 (May 1978): 8–18.

The earliest "scientific use" of human experimental subjects, as opposed to fortuitous or random observations, generally took the form of auto-experimentation by investigators, sometimes with high risk. Such auto-experimentation included, for example, self-inoculation with gonorrheal pus, intravenous injection of castor oil, the use of carbon tetrachloride as an anesthetic, and self-administration of doses of strychnine that would have been fatal without a charcoal preventative. All were initiated as experiments between 1767 and 1857. (See Ivy, "The History and Ethics of the Use of Human Subjects in Medical Experiments.")

The taking of such risks enhanced an already entrenched image of experimentation as medical quackery. Although an increasing number of scientific successes subsequently promoted acceptance of the idea of methodologically rigorous experimentation involving human subjects, the growth of human subjects research was plagued from the start by public and professional uncertainty regarding the relationship between researcher and subject, stemming in part from the risks involved. The problem of distinguishing the researcher-subject relationship from the physician-patient relationship was an added complication, partially attributable to a lack of consensus regarding fiduciary responsibility, acceptable risk, and appropriate communication between the principals.

Around the late 1930s, experimental research began to be considered an established part of medicine, and even became a routine dimension of hospital practice in Great Britain and the United States. Although researchers were still portrayed by critics as ambitious scientists lacking in humanitarian attitudes toward patients—exploiting them as means to scientific ends (and, thus, as "animals of necessity")—it is fairer to the facts to say that research had simply become tightly linked with various forms of practice, and the very *justification* of research was by then widely conceived in terms of therapeutic goals. See Reiser, "Human Experimentation and the Convergence of Medical Research and Patient Care," esp. 12–13.

6. Smidovich, or Veresaeff (or Veressayev, as he is often referred to in the United States), wrote in the area of research with a special interest in the moral unsoundness of venereal disease research. He examined many published sources in countries around the world, including the United States. Using extensive documentation, he argued that the "zealots of science" had failed to distinguish between "humans and guinea pigs," and were callously disregarding "that consideration" of respect "due to the human being." He recounted staggering instances of "classically shameless" and "criminal" experiments in which subjects were not informed of what was being done to them and indeed were actively deceived about the nature of the investigation. These included numerous experiments involving children abused to the ends of science.

See V. Veresaeff (V. Smidovich), *The Memoirs of a Physician*, trans. Simeon Linden (London: Grant Richards, 1904; a separate edition was New York: Alfred A. Knopf, 1916). [Note: Jay Katz reprinted excerpts from "Veressayev's" book in his *Experimentation with Human Beings* (New York: Russell Sage Foundation, 1972), 284–91. Katz appended the following note: "Wherever possible the references in Dr. Veressayev's book were checked against the original sources; their accuracy was confirmed in every instance." (284)]

7. On Reed and consent generally, see William B. Bean, "Walter Reed and the Ordeal of Human Experiments," *Bulletin of the History of Medicine* 51 (1977): 75–92.

In 1908 Sir William Osler appeared before the Royal Commission on Vivisection, an occasion on which he chose to discuss the subject of Reed's research on yellow fever. When asked by the Commission whether risky research on humans is morally permissible—a view Osler attributed to Reed—Osler answered as follows:

It is always immoral without a definite, specific statement from the individual himself, with a *full knowledge* of the circumstances. Under these circumstances, any man, I think is *at liberty to submit himself to experiments*.

When then asked if "voluntary consent . . . entirely changes the question of morality," Osler replied "Entirely." As recorded by Harvey Cushing, *The Life of Sir William Osler* (London: Oxford University Press, 1940), 794–95. (Italics added.) Brady and Jonsen describe this testimony as reflecting the "usual and customary ethics of research on human subjects at the turn of the century," in "The Evolution of Regulatory Influences on Research with Human Subjects," 4. However, this sweeping historical claim would need more supporting evidence than at present appears to be available.

8. For a brief account of this early legal history, see William J. Curran, "Governmental Regulation of the Use of Human Subjects in Medical Research: The Approach of Two Federal Agencies," *Daedalus* 98 (Spring 1969): 402–405.

Before 1960 there were no state or federal statutes in the United States that regulated research or the involvement of human subjects in research. Any applicable legal principles emerged through the appellate court decisions governing actions for medical malpractice that were discussed in Chapter 4, and through a few isolated cases involving injury from experimental medical techniques. No court actions had been initiated against institutions performing research or against research investigators.

The few early arguably relevant decisions did not distinguish clearly between innovative medical practice and medical experimentation. The courts viewed both innovation and experimentation as unjustified departures from standard practice, although this curb on quackery was directed more at protection of the patient than at restrictions on experimentation. Moreover, these early cases arose in contexts vastly different from those of today's "research."

The first case of historical significance—*Slater* v. *Baker and Stapleton* (England, 1767)—involved a novel technique for healing leg fractures that was used without consent and that deviated sharply from standard practice [95 Eng. Rep. 860 (K.B. 1767)]. *Slater* has been cited as an experimentation case, a malpractice case, and a consent case. A more guarded appraisal is that its essential nature is decidedly mixed and difficult to interpret, as we discuss briefly in Chapter 4. (See pp. 116–117.) The earliest American case of any significance was *Carpenter* v. *Blake* [60 Barb. N.Y. 488 (1871)], which held that if an approved procedure already exists, it can only be departed from at the physician's peril—leaving physicians with virtually no freedom to experiment. *Carpenter* is the paradigm of early restrictions on "experimentation" that attempted to control quackery. The physician in the case did not claim to be engaged in systematic research, which scarcely existed as such, but he did defend against a malpractice charge by claiming that his unorthodox treatment of a dislocated shoulder was not negligence but rather an innovative mode of treatment. The court's response—to the effect that no treatment not approved by a number of respectable practitioners was acceptable—made even honest, scientifically sound experimentation a risky proposition from a legal perspective. Experimentation was categorized in general as a grossly negligent deviation from appropriate practice—an unsurprising conclusion, given both the public image and haphazard reality of research. This state of affairs persisted well into the twentieth century.

However, in 1934 the court in *Brown* v. *Hughes* heralded a relaxation of this rigid stance by rather reluctantly acknowledging that *some* experimentation was necessary for the advance of science, although still equating experimentation with "rash" treatments [94 Colo. 295, 30 P.2d 259 (1934)]. In *Brown* the court appeared to express a slight openness toward deviation from standard practice, referring to the use of "rash or experimental methods" as putting the physician at risk of liability but later acknowledging that only "total abandon" should give rise to liability, or else physicians would not be able to use their learned judgment in the advance of science (see 262–63). Thus, although experiments were viewed as extreme, at least some need for experimentation had begun to be recognized.

In the following year, *Fortner* v. *Koch* [272 Mich. 273; 261 N.W. 762 (1935)] added a new dimension to judicial understanding of the role of human subjects in medical research. In that case, the Michigan Supreme Court recognized (in dictum) the necessity for research involving human subjects in order to achieve medical progress.

By explicitly declaring a disposition to permit reasonable research on consenting human subjects, the court in *Fortner* removed human experimentation from the category of forbidden activities. However, the court was primarily concerned with permitting medical departures that are potentially in the interests of the patient. Therapeutic beneficence thus provided the primary justification for permitting the research. The early cases all dealt with so-called *therapeutic* research—that is, the physician was attempting to cure the particular patient, and was sued for injuries arising from that attempt. Such situations were in part responsible for judicial conservatism regarding experimentation, particularly when accepted treatments are available. The absence of a clear promise of benefit naturally alters the legal issues arising in nontherapeutic research.

The *Fortner* case both required the consent of the subject and limited the amount of acceptable deviation from established practice. This restriction on the permissible degree of *novelty* in therapeutic research was a likely precursor of the subsequent concern in research ethics with the more general issue of the need to balance potential risks to subjects with potential benefits. Thus, in 1935 an influential court had embryonically recognized the importance of what would eventually emerge as the two fundamental categories in the justification of research involving human subjects: an acceptable risk-benefit balance and valid consent.

9. *United States* v. *Karl Brandt, Trials of War Criminals Before the Nuremberg Military Tribunals under Control Council Law No. 10*, Vols. 1 and 2, "The Medical Case" (Military Tribunal I, 1947; Washington, D.C.: U.S. Government Printing Office, 1948–49); reproduced in part in Katz, *Experimentation with Human Beings*, 292–306. See further Leo Alexander, "Medical Science Under Dictatorship," *New England Journal of Medicine* 241 (July 1949): 39–47.

10. Veresaeff had revealed considerable abuse throughout the world. Abuses have been most noticeable in settings in which it was easy to view subjects as enemies or as less than full persons or citizens. For example, physicians in the nineteenth century in the United States placed slaves in pit ovens in order to study heat stroke, poured scalding water over them in an attempt to study typhoid fever, amputated their fingers in order to study the efficacy of anesthesia, and the like. See Martin S. Pernick, "The Patient's Role in Medical Decisionmaking: A Social History of Informed Consent in Medical Therapy," in President's Commission for the Study of Ethical Problems in Medicine and Biomedical and Behavioral Research, *Making Health Care Decisions* (Washington, D.C.: U.S. Government Printing Office, 1982), Vol. 3, 19–21. The Japanese also had not treated certain Koreans much better during occupation in World War II than the Nazis had treated their "subjects."

11. Recorded by Telford Taylor, "Statement," in Alexander Mitscherlich, *Doctors of Infamy: The Story of the Nazi Medical Crimes*, extended edition, trans. Heinz Norden (New York: Henry Schuman, Inc., 1949), xviii, xxv.

12. Andrew C. Ivy, "Statement," in Mitscherlich, *Doctors of Infamy*, xii. During the trial it became apparent that several of the accused had used their positions at the concentration camps to curry favor with the German S.S., whose leader Heinrich

Himmler had strange ideas about "natural" remedies unconnected to medical science—for example, the revival of frozen subjects by placing them in bed between two naked women. However, the actual quality and scientific validity of various of the experiments is an unresolved and controversial matter. See Uristine Moe, "Should the Nazi Research Data Be Cited?" *The Hastings Center Report* 14 (1984): 5–7.

13. For a reprinting of the guidelines, with historical commentary, see Hans-Martin Sass, "Reichsrundschreiben 1931: Pre-Nuremberg German Regulations Concerning New Therapy and Human Experimentation," *Journal of Medicine and Philosophy* 8 (1983): 99–111.

14. Leo Alexander, "Statement," in Mitscherlich, *Doctors of Infamy*, xxxi.

15. Ivy, "The History and Ethics of the Use of Human Subjects in Medical Experiments."

16. Dr. Robert Servatius, "Final Plea for Defendant Karl Brandt," in Katz, *Experimentation With Human Beings*, 304.

17. "Judgment" in *United States* v. *Karl Brandt*, in Katz, *Experimentation With Human Beings*, 305.

18. Principle One provides in part:

> The voluntary consent of the human subject is absolutely essential. . . . [T]he person involved . . . should be so situated as to be able to exercise free power of choice, without the intervention of any element of force, fraud, deceit, duress, over-reaching, or other ulterior form of constraint or coercion; and should have sufficient knowledge and comprehension of the elements of the subject matter involved as to enable him to make an understanding and enlightened decision. This . . . requires that . . . there should be made known to him the nature, duration, and purpose of the experiment; the method and means by which it is to be conducted; all inconveniences and hazards reasonably to be expected; and the effects upon his health or person which may possibly come from his participation in the experiment.

19. In 1946 the American Medical Association's House of Delegates approved a report of its Judicial Council that requires voluntary consent of the subject. This brief guideline predates the Nuremberg Code's publication, but had little historical impact. Its obscurity is not surprising since testimony at Nuremberg was underway, and this testimony was partially responsible for the AMA's guidelines. "Supplementary Report of the Judicial Council," *Journal of the American Medical Association* 132 (1946): 1090. See also American Medical Association, "Principles of Medical Ethics: Opinions and Reports of the Judicial Council." *Journal of the American Medical Association* 167 (June 1958). Special Issue.

20. "Declaration of Helsinki: Recommendations Guiding Medical Doctors in Biomedical Research Involving Human Subjects," adopted by the 18th World Medical Assembly, Helsinki, Finland, 1964 [Published in *New England Journal of Medicine* 271 (1964): 473, and in Katz, *Experimentation With Human Beings*, 312–13]; revised by the 29th World Medical Assembly, Tokyo, Japan, 1975, as reprinted in Robert J. Levine, *Ethics and Regulation of Clinical Research* (Baltimore: Urban & Schwarzenberg, 1981): 287–89, and T.L. Beauchamp and L.W. Walters, eds., *Contemporary Issues in Bioethics*, 2nd ed. (Belmont, CA: Wadsworth Publishing Company, 1982), 511–12.

21. A useful general orientation to the origin, development, and scope of the Helsinki Declaration is found in Ronald R. Winton, "The Significance of the Declaration of Helsinki: An Interpretative Documentary," *World Medical Journal* 25 (July-August

1978): 58–59, and reprinted in *The Medical Journal of Australia* 2 (July 1978): 78–79. For an analysis and a survey of changes introduced in 1975, see D.A.E. Shepherd, "The 1975 Declaration of Helsinki and Consent," *Canadian Medical Association Journal* 115 (December 1976): 1191–92.

22. Declaration of Helsinki, II.5.

23. See Swazey, "Protecting the 'Animal of Necessity'," esp. 133.

24. See Andrew Belsey, "Patients, Doctors and Experimentation: Doubts about the Declaration of Helsinki," *Journal of Medical Ethics* 4 (1978): 182–85.

25. A list of numerous organizations endorsing the Declaration is found in World Medical Association, "Human Experimentation: Declaration of Helsinki," *Annals of Internal Medicine* 65 (1966): 367–68.

26. Beecher, *Experimentation in Man*, 3. See also *Research and the Individual*, xi, for what is, in effect, an identical statement. In the latter work, Beecher lists four "notable papers" predating his own that he believes had already had a significant impact. See 12–13.

27. Beecher, *Experimentation in Man*, 50, 52, 58, and see 15–17, 43–44.

28. Ibid., 50.

29. Irving Ladimer and Donald B. Kennedy, Final Report, Chapter IX. This report is summarized in Curran, "Governmental Regulation," 406–408. Curran was Director of the Institute at the time the report was filed.

30. Irving Ladimer and Robert Newman, eds., *Clinical Investigations in Medicine* (Boston: Boston University Law-Medicine Research Institute, 1963), esp. 236.

31. Irving Ladimer, "Ethical and Legal Aspects of Medical Research on Human Beings," in *Clinical Investigations in Medicine*, esp. 210.

32. Henry K. Beecher, "Ethics and Clinical Research," *New England Journal of Medicine* 274 (June 1966): 1354–60, esp. 1354–55. See also the response to his article published in the same journal, Vol. 275 (October 6, 1966): 790–91, and Beecher's "Some Guiding Principles for Clinical Investigation," *Journal of the American Medical Association* 195 (March 1966): 135–36. Beecher has offered his own account of the historical significance of his 1966 paper in *Research and the Individual*, 13–14.

33. Henry K. Beecher, "Consent in Clinical Experimentation: Myth and Reality," *Journal of the American Medical Association* 195 (1966): 34–35. Beecher had earlier published a more detailed but largely ignored "Editorial" on the "principle of consent" in *Clinical Pharmacology and Therapeutics* 3 (March-April 1962): 141–46.

34. Beecher, "Ethics and Clinical Research," 1355. See also his *Research and the Individual*, e.g., 25, 81.

35. M.H. Pappworth, *Human Guinea Pigs: Experimentation on Man* (Boston: Beacon Press, 1967; London: Routledge and Kegan Paul, 1967), 200, see also 26, 190–94, 205, 215–16.

36. Katz, *Experimentation With Human Beings*, ix.

37. Unless otherwise noted, the facts of this case are drawn from the data reprinted in Katz, *Experimentation With Human Beings*, 9–65.

38. *Hyman* v. *Jewish Chronic Disease Hospital*, 251 N.Y. 2d 818 (1964), 206 N.E. 2d 338 (1965).

39. From Katz, *Experimentation With Human Beings*, 60–61.

40. Beecher, *Research and the Individual*, 89.

41. Some problems were quickly pointed out by Elinor Langer, "Human Experimentation—New York Verdict Affirms Patient's Rights," *Science* (1966): 665–66.

42. Interview with Joseph S. Murtaugh, former Director of the Office of Program Planning, National Institutes of Health, Washington, D.C., March 26, 1971, as reported in Mark Frankel, "The Development of Policy Guidelines Governing Human

Experimentation in the United States: A Case Study of Public Policy-Making for Science and Technology," *Ethics in Science and Medicine* 2: 50. Frankel's Ph.D. dissertation, "Public Policy-Making for Biomedical Research: The Case for Human Experimentation" (George Washington University, 1976), is even more extensive. It will be cited below as "Dissertation." The article will be cited as "The Development of Policy Guidelines."

43. Stephen Goldby, "Experiments at the Willowbrook State School," *Lancet* 1 (April 1971): 749; Paul Ramsey, *The Patient as Person* (New Haven: Yale University Press, 1970), 47–56. Goldby wrote partially from the perspectives of a British legal system that prohibited experiments on children and of the Medical Research Council of Great Britain which held consent by parents and guardians to be invalid. American authors wrote predominantly from personal moral conviction. See also Saul Krugman, "Experiments at the Willowbrook State School", *Lancet* 1 (1967): 966–67, and Saul Krugman, Joan P. Giles and Jack Hammond; "Infectious Hepatitis," *Journal of the American Medical Association* 200 (May 1967): 365–73.

44. Saul Krugman, "Reply to Dr. Goldman," *World Medicine* (November 1971): 25.

45. See editorial comments in *Journal of the American Medical Association* 200 (1967): 406, and Franz Ingelfinger, Editorial Note, *Yearbook of Medicine* (1967–68): 429–30. Krugman's research had been sponsored by the Armed Forces Epidemiological Board, the U.S. Army Medical Research and Development Command, the Health Research Council of the City of New York, and several committees at New York University School of Medicine (including review by its Committee on Human Experimentation). For a detailed list of those who reviewed and approved the proposal, see Krugman's comment in the "Symposium" cited below, 6–7, and 10. Editors at JAMA, NEJM, and the *Journal of Infectious Research* defended the research.

46. See George J. Annas, Leonard H. Glantz, and Barbara F. Katz, *Informed Consent to Human Experimentation* (Cambridge, MA: Ballinger Publishing Co., 1977), esp. 180.

47. Louis Goldman, "The Willowbrook Debate," *World Medicine* (September 1971 and November 1971): 23, 25.

48. Krugman, in *Proceedings of the Symposium on Ethical Issues in Human Experimentation: The Case of Willowbrook State Hospital Research*, Urban Health Affairs Program, New York University Medical Center, 1972, 8. Hereafter "Symposium."

49. The Willowbrook case is discussed in "Symposium," which includes presentations by Saul Krugman, Moshe Tendler, Ellen Isaacs, and Jay Katz. See also Franz Ingelfinger, "Editorial: Ethics of Experiments on Children," *New England Journal of Medicine* 288 (1973): 791–92. Our account is indebted to James J. McCartney's research on the subject, as published in Tom L. Beauchamp and James F. Childress, *Principles of Biomedical Ethics*, 2nd ed. (New York: Oxford University Press, 1983), 317–18.

50. See James H. Jones, *Bad Blood* (New York: Free Press, 1981), Thomas G. Benedek, "The 'Tuskegee Study' of Syphilis: Analysis of Moral Versus Methodologic Aspects," *Journal of Chronic Diseases* 31 (1978): 35–50, esp. 37–38; Charles J. McDonald, "The Contribution of the Tuskegee Study to Medical Knowledge," *Journal of the National Medical Association* 66 (January 1974): 1–11.

51. Jones, *Bad Blood*, Chapter 1; *Final Report of the Tuskegee Syphilis Study Ad Hoc Panel* (Public Health Service, April 28, 1973), 6. See also A.M. Brandt, "Racism and Research: The Case of the Tuskegee Syphilis Study," *Hastings Center Report* 8 (December 1978): 21–29; Benedek, "The 'Tuskegee Study' of Syphilis," 40, 46.

52. Hearings on S. 974, S. 878, and S.J. Resolution 71 before the Subcommittee

on Health of the Senate Committee on Labor and Public Welfare, "Quality of Health Care—Human Experimentation" (1973), 93rd Congress, 1st Session, III, 1035–42. Subjects did receive some treatment through public health officers and health authorities in the state. It was not enough to cure, but enough to render the experiment suspect. See Jones, *Bad Blood*, 69.

53. Jones, *Bad Blood*, 69–71, Chapter 8; Levine, *Ethics and Regulation of Clinical Research*, 51.

54. David J. Rothman, "Were Tuskegee & Willowbrook 'Studies in Nature'?" *Hastings Center Report* 12 (April 1982): 5–7, esp. 7. Cf. Jones, *Bad Blood*, 123. For further confirmation, see Benedek, "The 'Tuskegee Study' of Syphilis," 43.

55. See McDonald, "The Contribution of the Tuskegee Study to Medical Knowledge," esp. 1, 4, 6, and Jones, *Bad Blood*, 179. McDonald, a black physician entirely unsympathetic to the means used in the study, maintained that there had been only two significant studies of the effects of untreated syphilis prior to the late 1950s: Roshan's 1947 "Autopsy Studies in Syphilis" and Gjestland's 1955 "Oslo Study of Untreated Syphilis." He appears to have missed several other studies—for example, a 1929 report published on the Oslo material in German. Also, the Cooperative Clinical Group had published numerous papers on the effects of syphilis, partly treated and untreated. Although McDonald reaches harsh conclusions about the ethics of the experiment—especially its violations of informed consent—he concludes that "In contrast to the opinions of many physicians and syphilologists, it is my opinion that the 'Tuskegee Study,' in spite of its many weaknesses, did make significant contributions to medical knowledge as it pertains to syphilology (4). He also agrees with Gjestland's 1955 comment that "'there is little doubt that the "Alabama Study" is the best controlled experiment ever undertaken in this particular field'" (6). McDonald concludes as follows: "[W]e should not let our present sensitivities obscure the fact that this study has contributed and can continue to contribute a great deal to our knowledge of syphilology" (6). These conclusions are all strongly challenged by Jones in *Bad Blood* (see 258).

56. Jones, *Bad Blood*; McDonald, 179; Benedek, "The 'Tuskegee Study' of Syphilis," 35, 48; David J. Rothman, "Were Tuskegee & Willowbrook 'Studies in Nature'?" 5–7, esp. 5.

57. Jean Heller, "Syphilis Victims in U.S. Study Went Untreated for 40 Years," *New York Times* (July 26, 1972), 1, 8.

58. *Final Report of the Tuskegee Syphilis Study Ad Hoc Panel*, 21–32.

59. Ibid., 21–23.

60. Ibid., 40; see also 14, 29.

61. Ibid., 47.

62. The American Psychological Association had rules regulating the use of animals for research purposes well before it issued its first formal statement on the use of human subjects (which was in its 1953 code). See Irwin A. Berg, "The Use of Human Subjects in Psychological Research," *American Psychologist* [cite missing—apx. 1953–1954].

63. In this history of the development of the 1953 APA ethics code, the Ethical Standards of Psychologists, we draw heavily on three sources: an account by the first chair of the Committee on Ethical Standards for Psychology, Nicholas Hobbs, "The Development of a Code of Ethical Standards for Psychology," *American Psychologist* 3 (1948): 80–84; a history of the period published by APA, "A Little Recent History," *American Psychologist* 7 (1952): 426–28, and Stuart E. Golann, "Ethical Standards for Psychology: Development and Revisions, 1938–1968," *Annals of the New York Academy of Sciences* 169 (1970): 398–405.

64. "A Little Recent History," 426.

65. APA Committee on Ethical Standards for Psychology, "Ethical Standards for Psychology," *American Psychologist* 6 (1951): 427–52.

66. APA Committee, "Ethical Standards for Psychology," 441–42. (Emphasis added.)

67. "Discussion on Ethics," *American Psychologist* 7 (1952): 425–55.

68. "Principles of Professional Ethics: Cornell Studies in Social Growth," *American Psychologist* 7 (1952): 452–55.

69. Ibid., 453.

70. APA Committee, "Ethical Standards for Psychology," 441.

71. The TAT is a standard personality assessment instrument, the Thematic Apperception Test.

72. In a personal communication to the authors, Stuart W. Cook writes as follows: "The concept of informed consent in research was first codified in psychology in 1953. At that time, the American Psychological Association published its first code of ethics. . . . On page 122 of this document you will find Principle 4.31–1." Letter dated 4/19/84. Cook was a member, APA Committee on Ethical Standards for Psychology, 1953 and Chair, Committee on Ethical Standards for Psychological Research, 1973.

73. It should be noted that the language quoted in this chapter is from the full APA document, *Ethical Standards of Psychologists* (1953), 122. In a shorter document also published by APA in 1953, *Ethical Standards of Psychologists: A Summary of Ethical Principles*, principles 4.31–1 and 4.31–2 are combined as one principle, 4.b. Although the language is slightly revised, the substance is unaltered. See 12–13.

74. Berg, "The Use of Human Subjects in Psychological Research," see n.62 above.

75. Ibid., 108.

76. W. Edgar Vinacke, "Deceiving Experimental Subjects," *American Psychologist* 9 (1954): 155.

77. Ibid., 155.

78. Arthur C. MacKinney, "Deceiving Experimental Subjects," *American Psychologist* 10 (1955): 133.

79. J. Seeman, "Deception in Psychological Research," *American Psychologist* 68 (1967): 1025–28.

80. Sources for this case are collected in Katz, *Experimentation With Human Beings*, 67–109.

81. Oscar M. Ruebhausen and Orville G. Brim, Jr., "Privacy and Behavioral Research," *American Psychologist* 21 (May 1966): 423–38 (reprinted from the November 1965 issue of *Columbia Law Review*).

82. Ibid., 426, 430.

83. Sources used for the description of Milgram's research include Robert A. Burt, "The Milgram Experiments: The Rule of Objectivity," *Taking Care of Strangers* (New York: Free Press, 1979); Stanley Milgram, *Obedience to Authority* (New York: Harper & Row Publishers, Inc., 1974), "The Perils of Obedience," *Harper's Magazine* (December 1973), 62–77, "Behavioral Study of Obedience," *Journal of Abnormal Social Psychology* 67 (1963): 371–78, and "Subject Reaction: The Neglected Factor in Ethics of Experimentation," *Hastings Center Report* 7 (October 1977): 19–23; Alan Elms, "Keeping Deception Honest," in T. L. Beauchamp, et al., eds., *Ethical Issues in Social Science Research* (Baltimore: The Johns Hopkins University Press, 1982), 239–42; Barbara Robb, Review of *Obedience to Authority* in *Educational Research* 17: 236–37.

84. Milgram, "Behavioral Study of Obedience," 377.

85. Diana Baumrind, "Some Thoughts on Ethics of Research: After Reading Milgram's 'Behavioral Study of Obedience'," *American Psychologist* 19 (1964), 421–23 and Herbert C. Kelman, "Human Use of Human Subjects: The Problem of Deception in Social Psychological Experiments," initially presented at the meetings of the American Psychological Association in Chicago, September 3, 1965, published in *Psychological Bulletin* 67 (1967), 1–11, and reprinted in Herbert C. Kelman, *A Time to Speak* (San Francisco: Jossey-Bass, Inc., 1968), 208–25.

86. Stanley Milgram, "Issues in the Study of Obedience: A Reply to Baumrind," *American Psychologist* 19 (1964): 848–52. In his later writings, Milgram put forward a more sophisticated defense of his research on grounds that might be called retrospective consent: "The central moral justification for allowing a procedure of the sort used in my experiment is that it is judged acceptable by those who have taken part in it. Moreover, it was the salience of this fact throughout that constituted the chief moral warrant for the continuance of the experiments." (From 199 of Appendix I in his *Obedience to Authority*.)

87. Kelman, "Human Use of Human Subjects," 211. See also Milgram, *Obedience to Authority*, 201.

88. Kelman, "Human Use of Human Subjects," 215.

89. Sources for this account include: Laud Humphreys, *Tearoom Trade: Impersonal Sex in Public Places* (Chicago: Aldine Publishing Co., 1970); Nicholas von Hoffman, "The Sociological Snoopers," *The Washington Post*, B1, col. 1, and B9, col. 5 (January 30, 1970); and Irving L. Horowitz and Lee Rainwater, "Journalistic Moralizers," *Trans-Action* 7 (1970). The latter two sources are both reprinted in *Tearoom Trade*.

90. Fifty-four percent of Humphreys' subjects were married and living with their wives. Only 14% corresponded to stereotypic views of homosexuality.

91. This case is based on Philip G. Zimbardo, "On the Ethics of Intervention in Human Psychological Research: With Special Reference to the Stanford Prison Experiment," *Cognition* (1973), 243–56; Donald P. Warwick, "Types of Harm in Social Research," in *Ethical Issues in Social Science Research*; and P.G. Zimbardo, C. Haney, W.C. Banks, and D. Jaffe, "The Mind as a Formidable Jailor: A Pirandellian Prison," *The New York Times Magazine* (April 8, 1973), section 6: 38–60. All direct quotations are from these sources.

92. Robert J. Menges, "Openness and Honesty versus Coercion and Deception in Psychological Research," *American Psychologist* 28 (1973): 1030–34.

93. M. Brewster Smith, "Conflicting Values Affecting Behavioral Research With Children," *American Psychologist* 22 (1967): 377–82.

94. Ibid., 380.

95. Kelman, *A Time to Speak*, 208–25.

96. See, for example, T.C. Brock and L.A. Becker, "'Debriefing' and Susceptibility to Subsequent Experimental Manipulations," *Journal of Experimental Social Psychology* 2 (1966): 314–23; M.S. Greenberg, "Role Playing: An Alternative to Deception," *Journal of Personality and Social Psychology* 7 (1967): 152–57, and E. Walster, et al., "Effectiveness of Debriefing following Deception Experiments," *Journal of Personality and Social Psychology* 6 (1967): 371–80.

97. As cited in Golann, "Ethical Standards for Psychology: Development and Revisions," 403.

98. Herbert C. Kelman, "The Rights of the Subject in Social Research: An Analysis in Terms of Relative Power and Legitimacy," *American Psychologist* 27 (November 1972): 1001–1002.

99. American Psychological Association, *Ethical Principles in the Conduct of Research with Human Participants* (Washington, D.C.: APA, 1982), 9–14.

100. Golann, "Ethical Standards for Psychology: Development and Revision," 400.

101. "Ethical Standards of Psychologists," *American Psychologist* 18 (1963): 56–60, esp. 59–60.

102. Personal communication, M. Brewster Smith, member of the Cook Commission, 4/11/84. Based on a review of the leading psychological journals in 1971, Robert J. Menges concluded that in as many as 40% of studies, subjects were procured through course requirements, emphasizing the difficulty of obtaining "voluntary informed consent." "Openness and Honesty versus Coercion and Deception in Psychological Research," 1031, 1033.

103. Our account of the development of the research code relies primarily on three sources: William T. McGuire, "Privacy vs. the Goals of the Researcher," in William C. Bier, ed., *Privacy: A Vanishing Value* (New York: Fordham University Press, 1980), 331–47; M. Brewster Smith, "Psychology and Ethics," in Eugene C. Kennedy, ed., *Human Rights and Psychological Research* (New York: Thomas Y. Crowell, Co., 1975), 1–22, esp. 2–6; and American Psychological Association, *Ethical Principles in the Conduct of Research with Human Participants* (1973), especially 3–6.

104. McGuire, "Privacy vs. the Goals of the Researcher," 334.

105. "Ethical Standards for Psychological Research," *APA Monitor* 2 (July 1971): 9–28, specifically principles 1.411, 1.412, 1.413, 1.421, 1.422, 1.423, 1.511, 1.512, 1.513, 1.521, 1.522, 1.523, 1.524, 1.525, 1.531, 1.532, 5.111, 5.112, 5.12, 5.13, 5.21, and 5.22.

106. Ibid., 25.

107. Ibid., 25. Principle 5.111 is identical in this draft to Principle 1.411.

108. Ibid., 25–26.

109. Ibid., 14.

110. Ibid., 14.

111. Ibid., 14.

112. McGuire, "Privacy vs. the Goals of the Researcher," 334.

113. Jerome H. Resnick and Thomas Schwartz, "Ethical Standards as an Independent Variable in Psychological Research," *American Psychologist* 28 (February 1973), 134–39.

114. Ad hoc Committee on Ethical Standards in Psychological Research, *Ethical Principles in the Conduct of Research with Human Participants* (Washington, D.C.: American Psychological Association, Inc., 1973), 1–2.

115. As M. Brewster Smith put it: "[W]e avoided the categorical 'Thou shalt not . . . ,' substituting, in effect, the more cautious 'Thou shalt worry deeply, consult with others sincerely, and be prepared to justify thy decision to thy peers and the public. . . .'" ("Psychology and Ethics," 4.)

116. Ad hoc Committee, *Ethical Principles in the Conduct of Research with Human Participants*, 5–6. See, also, Diana Baumrind, "Metaethical and Normative Considerations Covering the Treatment of Human Subjects in the Behavioral Sciences," in Eugene C. Kennedy, 3rd ed., *Human Rights and Psychological Research*, 37–68.

117. Ad hoc Committee, *Ethical Principles in the Conduct of Research with Human Participants*, 73.

118. Ibid., 9.

119. Ibid., 44.

120. M. Brewster Smith, "Some Perspectives on Ethical/Political Issues in Social Science Research," *Personality and Social Psychology Bulletin* 2 (1976): 445–53, reprinted in Murray L. Wax and Joan Cassell, eds., *Federal Regulations: Ethical Issues*

and Social Research (Washington, D.C.: American Association for the Advancement of Science, 1979), 11–22.

121. Although there are parallels between clinical medicine and research in using these two models, we noted in Chapters 1 and 3 that issues of beneficence take a different turn in clinical medicine than in research. In clinical medicine, the beneficence model features the production of medical benefits and minimization of harms to the patient being treated. In research, although the beneficence model does incorporate issues of welfare and harm to the research subject, it also includes producing the (much disputed) *benefit of generalizable scientific knowledge*. Milgram's early defense of his research is best situtated entirely in this beneficence model for research (see pp. 174–176): His subjects were not injured and new knowledge was gained.

122. Beecher, *Research and the Individual*, Appendix A, esp. 213f.

123. See the sources cited in n. 5 above, esp. Beecher, Brieger, and Lederer.

124. Stanley Milgram, "Subject Reaction: The Neglected Factor in the Ethics of Experimentation," *Hastings Center Report* 7 (October 1977): 19.

6

The Evolution of Federal Policy Governing Human Research

Early developments in the history traced in Chapter 5 began in part as responses to unnecessary and dangerous research. This research often took unfair advantage of subjects' confidence in a physician-patient therapeutic relationship that had never existed or had vanished at the behest of research imperatives. Together with other rules of research ethics, informed consent requirements were adopted to protect individual subjects from harm, exploitation, or injustice. Particularly in biomedical research, harm to subjects was so paramount in many early examples that the harm-prevention purpose and the protection-of-autonomy purpose were intertwined in statements of motivation and justification. This dual purpose contrasts with the principle underlying the case law examined in Chapter 4, which typically has appealed to the right of self-determination as the justifying principle (although the courts frequently did not behave in accordance with their own autonomy-inspired rhetoric).

In this chapter we examine the history of federal policies in the United States that have as their objective the protection of human subjects. This history began to flourish shortly before the period at which Chapter 5 ended: the mid-1960s. During these years, Congress, the Army, and two DHEW (now DHHS) agencies developed an interest in informed consent, partially as a result of the events discussed in Chapter 5. We concentrate on these two agencies, surveying first the developments at the Food and Drug Administration (FDA) and then at the National Institutes of Health (NIH). Both agencies are currently part of the Public Health Service (PHS). However, this was not true of FDA prior to 1968.

The history of informed consent policy at FDA and NIH peaked in importance in the mid-1970s, when the National Commission for the Protection of Human Subjects in effect assumed responsibility for remaining problems and offered an explicit (albeit abbreviated) moral analysis of the guidelines it proposed for national policy. Thus, beginning around 1975—after the full flowering of informed consent in the courts—a more coherent and systematic pattern of federal policy began to emerge for research ethics. This Commission will occupy our attention later in this chapter, just as its eventual successor, the President's Commission (a second federal commission), enjoyed landmark status in Chapter 3.

The examination of research from a moral perspective, begun by these commissions and buttressed by new government regulations issued in 1981, began to shape an otherwise inchoate appeal to autonomy at the federal level into a powerful statement of the purpose and justification of informed consent requirements. The appeal to respect for autonomy grew as this history unfolded, and concern increased over the exploitation of the therapeutic relationship through research. But the proper roles of both beneficence-based and autonomy-based justifications in research ethics remained a matter of controversy throughout this period—and indeed, to the present day.

Early Federal Recognition—Two DHEW Agencies from 1962–1974

The Congress played an active role in the early history of federal involvement, and the Army almost simultaneously (1966) published regulations based on the Nuremberg Code. However, officials at FDA and NIH developed most of the details in the emerging policies that influenced federal concern with informed consent. FDA is a regulatory body. NIH primarily supports and conducts biomedical and behavioral research, while shunning regulatory involvement. These orientations and objectives partially account for some otherwise inexplicable differences in their histories.

An Early NIH Clinical Center Policy

The fact that biomedical research was growing rapidly by mid-century, while remaining largely unregulated, must not be taken to imply that PHS was placidly unconcerned with questions of the ethics of human experimentation. But councils at PHS had no authority to take punitive actions beyond refusals to recommend grants. They could only advise investigators and institutions in extramural research programs, and an assumption generally prevailed at the agency that the professional standards of investigators and applicable law could be trusted to forestall breaches of ethical behavior. Consequently, no legal measures or moral pressures were initiated.

An apparent exception was found at the Clinical Center of the NIH, a research hospital that opened in 1953. Almost all intramural clinical research at NIH is conducted at this center, which operated from the beginning under a set of impressive in-house principles designed to define, in broad terms, the acceptability of human-based research. Procedures to protect subjects through peer review were restricted to "normal" volunteers, nontherapeutic research involving patients, and research that carried unusually high risk. These principles contained a detailed definition of the specific points necessary for obtaining an informed consent. The wording made the subject a partner in the research ("a member of the research team") and required a specific consent agreement to *research* participation in addition to standard *medical* consent. No research study that gave rise to ethical questions was to be approved unless reviewed by a committee composed of representatives of each Institute and the Center staff. The first two research proposals submitted for approval were disapproved on grounds of excessive risk.[1]

This document was the first established policy for the protection of human subjects in a U.S. government health-care facility. Officials at the Center expected these procedures to set the standard for other institutions as well, but this expectation turned out to be a vain hope. The Center's pioneering venture was an isolated and largely ignored event. PHS extramural programs continued to review protocols almost exclusively for scientific merit. Only rarely did questions of ethical merit arise, in part because study sections at NIH had no policies or principles for ethical evaluation of protocols. They also wished to avoid tampering with scientific freedom and judged the scientist and local institutions to be the responsible parties.

A decade after the opening of the Clinical Center, a Law-Medicine Institute study funded by the PHS (see pp. 158–159 in Chapter 5) found little evidence to suggest that the Clinical Center policy had spread to other federal or private institutions. Retrospectively, it appears that a widely shared belief in the value of unregulated scientific research and other presumptions about the professonal integrity of scientific investigators had led the biomedical research community to neglect formal review of research, including peer review within local institutions. However, a series of post-1962 developments in research ethics at the FDA and NIH would change this state of affairs.

FDA Policy Formulation

On October 10, 1962 the U.S. Congress passed the "Drug Amendments of 1962,"[2] which made fundamental changes in federal regulation of the drug industry. In some respects analogous to its predecessors in 1906 (Pure Food and Drugs Act) and 1938 (Food, Drug, and Cosmetic Act), this 1962 change was motivated by influential scientific, journalistic, and congressional reaction to the injuriousness or ineffectiveness of certain drugs. The use of clinical trials and the quality of clinical research were also under investigation.[3] The bill was the direct outgrowth of three years of debate in Senator Estes Kefauver's Subcommittee on Antitrust and Monopoly, which had primarily investigated excessive drug costs, price control, competitive markets, and licensing.

Despite this focus, these drug amendments might never have passed were it not for the infant deformities in Europe produced by the sedative Thalidomide. This gripping example of the effects of a drug (approved for use in Europe but still considered experimental in the United States) that was harmless to the pregnant woman but proved devastating to the fetus had been presented to another congressional subcommittee headed by Senator Hubert Humphrey.[4] Kefauver, Humphrey, and other senators had argued vigorously that loopholes in testing and warning requirements existed at FDA, and procedures for monitoring research protocols and consent procedures had been discussed at their hearings.

The 1962 amendments contained revolutionary instructions for new federal regulations, including provisions governing consent.[5] Bills to require physicians to disclose to their patients that an experimental drug was to be used in treatment had been considered in both the House and the Senate. However, in its deliberations on these amendments the Senate had focused on problems of cost, competition, safety, and efficacy. A so-called "consent requirement" was added at the last moment by Senator Jacob Javits during committee and floor debate in the Senate. This provision required—for the first time in U.S. history—that researchers inform subjects of a drug's experimental nature and receive their consent before starting an investigation, except under circumstances in which researchers "deem it not feasible or, in their professional judgment, contrary to the best interests of such human beings."[6]

This exception involved an uneasy compromise between those, like Javits, who wanted a strong and unqualified consent provision, and those who feared that such a provision might cause undue retardation of an investigation, harm to vulnerable patients who could not consent, and increased legal vulnerability for those engaged in research.[7] Despite the loose wording of the best-interests exceptive clause, the general intention of the consent requirement was not veiled: The Congress served notice that any physician or investigator who used experimental drugs on patients or subjects without an appropriate consent would be in violation of federal law.[8] Senator Javits, together with Senator Carroll of Colorado, had argued vigorously for such legislation based on a Library of Congress research memorandum that found not a single state with a statute that "covered the use of an experimental drug and required the physician to inform the patient of such use."[9]

Javits argued as follows on the Senate floor: "I am for experimentation. I feel deeply that some risks must be assumed in experimentation. But we must hold the balance between . . . the right of the individual to know how his life is being disposed of, at least with his consent, and the virtues of experimentation."[10] Javits proceeded to argue that the job of the Senate was to "weigh in the balance" the obligations to obtain consent and to support experimentation. This view was opposed by some senators on grounds that discretion by physicians in the disclosure of information is needed, and that the moral obligation to disclosure is contingent upon information about the condition of each individual patient.

After Congress passed the new law, the FDA responded by preparing new regulations, which took effect on February 7, 1963. A substantial portion of the regulations was directed exclusively at research design and procedures. These changes reflected a sophisticated reconstruction of old regulations, but consent provisions were poorly developed, simply repeating the vague wording and broad exception in the law. In an important paper (contributed to the 1963 Ladimer-Newman volume mentioned on p. 158), Frances Kelsey—Chief of the Investigational Drug Branch, Division of New Drugs, at FDA—argued that the troubled best-interests "exception" to the requirement to obtain consent could not be validly invoked merely because an investigator believed informed consent would negatively affect the research design or would disturb the patient-physician relationship. Kelsey held that the exception could validly be invoked in only a few extreme cases, usually with special classes of subjects, such as children or in emergency contexts.

However, the matter went unclarified at FDA for the next two years. In 1965, FDA Commissioner George P. Larrick, in a letter to Henry Beecher, obstinately, almost obtusely, refused to offer an interpretation of the consent provisions that budged beyond the literal letter of the law as enacted. This refusal only compounded the vagueness surrounding the policy at FDA, and critics such as William Curran pointed to the objectionable implication that research on the seriously ill and unconscious patient *would be permissible, without consent*, under these guidelines.[11]

On January 17, 1966, James Lee Goddard succeeded Larrick as FDA Commissioner. Beset by numerous reports of experimentation without consent, as well as by the swirl of controversy caused by the Jewish Chronic Disease Hospital case, Goddard determined to resolve the ambiguities surrounding informed consent. He appointed several FDA officials to study the matter and make recommendations. In August 1966, new provisions were published as "Consent for Use of Investigational New Drugs on Humans: Statement of Policy."[12] This event occurred two months after the appearance of Beecher's influential 1966 article. However, because of the short time frame, it is unlikely that Beecher's article affected the wording or the speed of production of the FDA document.

By contrast, the Nuremberg Code and the Declaration of Helsinki were specifically invoked as authoritative general guidelines. Some language from these codes was incorporated almost verbatim. The Declaration's distinction between therapeutic and nontherapeutic research was assimilated as follows: In therapeutic research for patients already undergoing treatment "for either diagnostic or therapeutic purposes," consent was required unless patients could exhibit an "inability to communicate" or unless a therapeutic privilege could be validly invoked. These new regulations also contained requirements for obtaining written consent as well as rules for informing subjects that they might be used as controls, that a placebo might be used, and that—if available—alternative therapies exist.

FDA regulations applied only to experimental drugs, devices, and biologics, and not to all research. For a broader history of regulation in the United States we must shift to NIH, the other federal agency with a history of consent standards that are virtually simultaneous with the changes that occurred at FDA. Subsequent developments at FDA were deeply influenced by central events in this history at NIH.

NIH Policy Formulations

We earlier witnessed the dawning of federal interest in research ethics at the NIH Clinical Center in 1953 and the failure of this event to serve as a precedent for other centers. In conformity with a general skepticism about government-imposed standards and their impact on freedom of research and in acknowledgment that the legally responsible persons were the investigators and their institutions, PHS was at the time content to place responsibility for research ethics on the investigator. The prevailing climate of opinion was that professional judgment should control ethical standards: Presuppositions about the adequacy of professional judgment, as expressed by the professional practice standard in law (see Chapters 2 and 4) and by clinicians in codes (see Chapter 3), were influential in the biomedical community, which during this period drew no very sharp distinctions between researchers and clinicians. There was, then, little perceived need to enable subjects to make well informed, autonomous choices about their involvement in research.

This attitude of deference to professional judgment is perhaps understandable in a context in which the federal government played a minimal role in the funding and regulation of research. But after World War II, NIH grew in an unprecedented manner, and soon became the primary funding source for biomedical research in the United States. As the funding and power of NIH grew, moral problems in research and the need to take responsibility for their resolution became increasingly apparent. During this period of dramatic growth, federally funded research moved from the luxury status of virtually complete freedom from federal regulation to become one of the most heavily regulated of American enterprises. Ethical disputes followed in the wake of a more general concern about federal responsibility to protect the public interest and to monitor the massive sums expended by NIH.

By the mid-1960s, deep concerns abounded about exclusive reliance on the moral character of investigators and about the lack of effective federal monitoring of the conduct of grant recipients. The history to be recounted in the next few pages is a pivotal period during which an awakening over questionable research practices—and not merely medical quackery—first occurred at the federal level in the United States. This history oscillates between a focus on protecting the medical welfare of patients, a concern to protect the public welfare through control and promotion of research, and a desire to enable patients and subjects to make their own—ideally, their own *enlightened*—decisions.

Shannon's Initiatives. Important early developments occurred under the tenacious management of James Shannon, Director of NIH from 1955–1968. As occurs so often in the history under investigation, dramatic and morally unacceptable events prodded federal officials into motion. Shannon, for example, had been disturbed by the events at the Jewish Chronic Disease Hospital and by the actions of a surgeon at a university hospital who unsuccessfully transplanted a chimpanzee kidney into a human being, under partial support by NIH funds. The surgeon reported that the patient had consented, but there had been no prior consultation with other parties, and there was no evidence of possible therapeutic benefit or promise of new scientific information. Shannon learned of these events through the news media, although he was head of the agency that had made the innovative work possible. From his perspective, the adminstrative implications were ominous.[13]

Reports of these events led officials at NIH to conclude that federally funded research could be ethically insensitive, as well as politically explosive, and could be initiated without adequate peer review or consent by patients and subjects. A 1958 conference on law and medicine,[14] Beecher's 1959 article, and a new Administration Manual, issued by DHEW with a section on informed consent,[15] fueled an interest that led to funding for the aforementioned 1960 Law-Medicine study (see p. 158). This study, in turn, had an impact on federal policy developments in the early 1960s. As mentioned above, the study provided strong evidence that adequate consents were not being obtained for research and in general cast doubt on the standards of self-scrutiny of research protocols and procedures used by investigators. The study thus hinted at the need for major policy changes, and officials at NIH were in a mood to agree.

In late 1963, after discussions with the Office of the U.S. Surgeon General, Shannon asked the research resource division at NIH that supported research centers to investigate these problems and make recommendations. An Associate Chief for Program Development, Dr. Robert B. Livingston, was selected to chair this study.[16] His report was submitted in November 1964. It warned of "possible repercussions of untoward events which are increasingly likely to occur" in "unfavorable" circumstances, including events that could "rudely shake" the NIH. It noted the absence of an applicable code of conduct for research, as well as an uncertain legal context.[17] The report also mentioned the furor and press coverage surrounding investigations into the Jewish Chronic Disease Hospital case. The research in this embarrassing case had been funded in part by PHS, and exceptionally close attention was therefore paid at NIH to these events and to the surrounding publicity.[18]

Problems of risk, liability, and the inhibition of research dominated this report; informed consent was no more than a background shadow. Neither the autonomy rights of subjects nor consent was mentioned because neither was the driving concern. Rather, any consent procedure was viewed as providing the subject with an opportunity to avoid risks, whereas the investigator was simultaneously pressured to reduce risks so that patient or subject refusals would be minimized. However, it cannot be said that concern about informed consent was exclusively directed at protection of subjects from risk *rather than* at protection of autonomy. This interpretation is indefensible because informed consent and concern for autonomy were buds on the same stem. Once informed consent began to be advocated, its champions increasingly turned to the protection of autonomy as its goal and justification. But it took years for the issues to be framed explicitly in this way. In the early days consent was more of an aside or an assumption than a central problem needing defense, justification, and policy development.

The Livingston report argued that it would be difficult for NIH to assume responsibility for ethics and research practices without striking an unduly authoritarian posture on requirements for research. The report also noted that there were ethical problems raised by policies in "inhibiting the pursuit of research on man," and added that "NIH is not in a position to shape the educational foundations of medical ethics, or even the clinical indoctrination of young investigators."[19] Shannon was disappointed with this part of the report because he believed that NIH should command a position of increased responsibility.[20] However, he accepted the report and regarded some of its recommendations as "urgent." In early 1965 he asked the U.S. Surgeon General to give "highest priority" to "rapid accomplishment of the objectives" of the basic recommendations. He suggested broad consultation with members of "the legal profession and the clergy" as well as the medical profession and endorsed the idea of "review by the investigator's peers."[21] What should be reviewed and the structure for review were still unspecified.

These events set the stage for further study and debate at PHS—and at FDA, where similar events were occurring simultaneously. During this same period, the World Medical Association adopted the Declaration of Helsinki, which required consent to research, albeit with a notable therapeutic privilege exception. The Medical Research Council of Great Britain quickly endorsed the Helsinki accord. Discussions about stricter controls were also underway in Sweden.[22] Thus, there existed a climate of national and world opinion within which the discussion at PHS took place.[23] In this context, Shannon and Surgeon General Luther Terry reached a joint decision to present these problems to the National Advisory Health Council (NAHC) in September 1965.

The NAHC Response. At this decisive meeting, Shannon argued that the agency should assume responsibility for placing formal controls on the independent judgment of investigators, so as to remove conflict of interest and bias. Specifically, he argued for subjecting research protocols to impartial, prior peer review of the risks of the research and of the adequacy of protections of the rights of subjects.[24] Shannon knew that "consent" could easily be manipulated through the authority of physicians, and there was therefore discussion of how impartiality could be introduced in the consent process as well. The members of NAHC tended to concur with all of these concerns, but doubted that the many fields encompassed by government-supported research could be governed by a single set of procedures or regulations. Nevertheless, within three months, at its meeting on December 3, 1965, NAHC supported a "resolution concerning research on humans" that followed the broad outlines of Shannon's recommendations and that mentioned the importance of securing an informed consent:

> Be it resolved that the National Advisory Health Council believes that Public Health Service support of clinical research and investigation involving human beings should be provided only if the judgment of the investigator is subject to prior review by his institutional associates to assure an independent determination of the protection of the rights and welfare of the individual or individuals involved, of the appropriateness of the methods used to secure informed consent, and of the risks and potential medical benefits of the investigation.[25]

However, there was again no discussion of what would count as an informed consent—no discussion of either its meaning or its criteria.

Two 1966 Statements of Policy. These recommendations were accepted by newly installed Surgeon General William H. Stewart, who issued a policy statement in February 1966 that would become a landmark in the history of informed consent in the United States—as historically important in some respects as *Natanson* or *Canterbury* for case law, two court opinions between which it was chronologically sandwiched. This "Statement of Policy" on "Clinical Investigations Using Human Subjects" compelled institutions receiving federal grant support from PHS to provide prior review by a committee for proposed research with human subjects. The subjective judgment of a principal investigator or program director was no longer sufficient. The three topics required to be reviewed were, as listed above: (1) the rights and welfare of subjects, (2) the appropriateness of methods used to obtain informed consent, and (3) the balance of risks and benefits.[26]

A memorandum that explained this policy and made it effective immediately was sent the same day to the heads of all institutions receiving grant support. The Surgeon General said simply that "the wisdom and sound professional judgment of you and your staff will determine what constitutes the rights and welfare of human subjects in research, what constitutes informed consent, and what constitutes the risks and potential medical benefits of a particular investigation."[27] Questions of the meaning and criteria of informed consent were thus being afforded a *procedural* answer only: Committees would make such determinations. The policy also required a description of the composition of the committee, including the number of members and the professional and public interests represented.

Within five months of the issuance of this policy, the antiquated 1953 Clinical Center document, originally entitled "Group Consideration of Clinical Research," was replaced by a new policy, with a conspicuously updated title: "Group Consideration and Informed Consent in Clinical Research."[28] An ad hoc committee under the Clinical Director had developed the new, intramural policy over the same months the aforementioned extramural "Statement of Policy" on human subjects was formulated. The Clinical Center committee had decided to place a special emphasis on nondiagnostic, nontherapeutic procedures, where both informed consent and peer review seemed of paramount importance.[29]

The new guidelines at the Clinical Center more than any previous government document emphasized the importance of a wide range of informed consent requirements, including an oral explanation readily suited for comprehension by the subject, a detailed disclosure of the study and its hazards, and a list of procedures to be disclosed. Signed consents were required, and allied ethical considerations such as "undue persuasion," "preferential treatment," and "compliance with FDA requirements" were discussed. On balance, the Clinical Center document was the most careful and comprehensive statement issued to this point on the subject of the ethics of research and its integral connection to problems of informed consent. Informed consent was growing in importance, and even began to have some specific content in the research context.

These documents formed the genesis of what has been called the "movement to ethics committees."[30] Peer review was destined to serve as the basis of a string of federal policies governing research ethics and informed consent requirements. These federal initiatives gained endorsement in much of the biomedical community,[31] and were adopted in modified form by the Association of American Medical Colleges as one requirement for the accreditation of medical schools.[32] Over a period of a decade they served as a crude model, which gradually was refined and finally became an accepted part of institutional practices for the protection of human research subjects.[33] Meanwhile, similar requirements were enacted in Great Britain and Sweden.

From the beginning, social and behavioral scientists offered mild opposition to these developments. They foresaw that the provisions concerning informed consent—like the controls on deceptive research promulgated through the professional codes examined in Chapter 5—could have the effect of curtailing or even eliminating certain kinds of research, which would be biased and invalid if informed consent were solicited. The Surgeon General was aware that NIH-supported work in the social and behavioral sciences used methods different from those used in the biomedical field, but he chose at first to minimize these differences and to promulgate a policy that ranged over all research equally.[34]

Despite murmurs, no enduring outcry emerged from the social and behavioral research community, perhaps because much of this research was still being conducted without institutional review. For example, social research funded by the Education and Welfare components of DHEW was not covered under the PHS policy. Because the flow of grants from NIH for social and behavioral research was steady, and because many of the same concerns were surfacing in these areas as in biomedical research,[35] the net result was a blurring of the differences between the biomedical and the behavioral and social sciences and the continued application, in principle, of a uniform set of review requirements for all fields.

In response to the few complaints that did surface from the social and behavioral sciences, the Surgeon General offered a clarification of the policy statement:

> There is a large range of social and behavioral research in which no personal risk to the subject is involved. In these circumstances, regardless of whether the investigation is classified as behavioral, social, medical, or other, the issues of concern are the fully voluntary nature of the participation of the subject, the maintenance of confidentiality of information obtained from the subject, and the protection of the subject from misuse of the findings . . . . [Some procedures] may in some instances not require the fully informed consent of the subject or even his knowledgeable participation.[36]

This statement had the force of blunting criticism from those engaged in social research, but it left unsettled which forms of research might be exempt from the requirements, and why. Beecher's influential 1966 article was published while these requirements were under development and had an immediate impact, although Beecher himself had not argued for stricter federal controls. In retrospect, federal officials were struggling with problems of fairness: They wanted to introduce regulations with teeth that applied to all scientists *equally* but that were not so restrictive as to seriously impede valuable research activities.

A policy revision was issued on May 1, 1969, that contained the most careful of the policy pronouncements to date, including a more thorough treatment of informed consent.[37] The earlier guidelines had been criticized for unclarity about the meaning of the term "informed consent;"[38] this new document was written to remove these objections. However, distinctions between different research methods and the different levels of risk they entail were again blurred. The revision said simply that a person must be free to choose and must receive "a fair explanation of the procedures to be followed, their possible benefits and attendant hazards and discomforts, and the reasons for pursuing the research and its general objectives."[39]

These policy statements contain both a substantive and a procedural approach to ethical issues in research. *Substantively*, only minimal requirements, including those covering consent, were presented. Government officials had determined that they should provide general guidelines, advice, and assistance, while permitting local judgment and supplementary standards to be more concrete and determinative. *Procedurally*, local review was to fill in the gaps by examining the particular protocols and special circumstances of local institutional research. Local review was to decide how to implement national standards and the ethical codes of professional societies. Eugene A. Confrey, Director of the Division of Research Grants, had explicated this policy at a meeting of the Council for International Organizations of Medical Sciences on October 7, 1967. He summarized the strategy as follows: The policy "must be sufficiently general to encompass diversity while avoiding a degree of abstraction that makes it platitudinous, hence vacuous."[40]

This attempt to achieve a uniform package of national standards while permitting broad latitude and diversity at the local review level was an uneasy compromise that yielded protracted controversy. Confusion about how to interpret and implement loosely framed federal standards generated pressure for the introduction of greater coherence and specificity of requirements for review. Gradually it became clear that local institutional review was often haphazard, even irresponsible, and that failures to disclose adequate information to subjects were pervasive.[41] Another and more vigorous policy response was only a matter of time.

The social and behavioral sciences were swept along with the tide, again in the grasp of the model of a "uniform policy" for all DHEW components. But by 1969, complaints began to mount that a *biomedical* model was engulfing the social and behavioral sciences in irrelevant and meaningless criteria and that continued use of the model might seriously impair research in fields such as social psychology. The ideal of a single policy specifying review requirements began to crack, especially around the idea of informed consent requirements that would fit *all* types of social research. These problems came under active consideration at NIH, where new policies were drafted throughout 1970.[42] A policy statement was developed concerning the obligations of and assurances that must be given by institutions sponsoring research,[43] and at the same time lawyers for NIH were investigating whether a signed consent form could operate as a contractual waiver of the physician-researcher's ordinary malpractice liability if the subject was injured.[44]

The Institutional Guide. From the above events emerged a major monograph on the subject of the ethics and regulation of research: *The Institutional Guide to DHEW Policy on Protection of Human Subjects,*[45] first released in 1971. The "Yellow Book," as it was dubbed because of its color, contained detailed considerations of institutional review, developed informed consent requirements, and paid explicit, albeit limited, attention to problems unique to social and behavioral research. Largely the work of one federal official—Donald Chalkley, chief of the Institutional Relations Branch of the Department of Research Grants, NIH— this impressive *Guide* expanded requirements to all programs and activities of DHEW, while retaining the fundamental procedural requirement of committee peer review.

"Informed consent" was defined in the Yellow Book as "the agreement obtained from a subject, or from his authorized representative, to the subject's participation in an activity." The definition enumerated six basic components of informed consent: (1) a fair explanation of procedures, (2) a description of risks and discomforts, (3) a description of benefits, (4) disclosure of alternative procedures, (5) an offer to answer inquiries about the procedures, and (6) an instruction that the subject is free to withdraw consent and discontinue participation at any time. Procedures for documentation of consent were specified, and attention was drawn to the fact that FDA rules governing consent were required by law for all biomedical investigations involving experimental new drugs.[46]

The Yellow Book considered moral problems that arise in research that presents little or no risk to subjects, including social and behavioral research involving personality inventories, interviews, questionnaires, and the use of observation, photographs, taped records, or stored data. It observed that such procedures, even if low in risk, "may constitute a threat to the subject's dignity," may invade privacy, and may therefore be subject to consent, privacy, and confidentiality requirements.[47] Institutional review boards (IRBs, the current official designation for research review committees) were even asked to confirm that the secondary use of data was included in "the scope of the original consent."

Although this new guide seemed to strengthen consent requirements, they were weakened in other respects: Consent could be either oral or written, could be obtained *after* research participation if a complete and prompt debriefing were provided, and could in some cases be considered "implicit in voluntary participation in an adequately advertised activity."[48] These provisions were apparently viewed by the American Psychological Association as acceptable in its 1973 *Ethical Principles in the Conduct of Research with Human Participants*, discussed in Chapter 5. Although reference is made in the introduction to this document to the "new federal regulations" governing research with human subjects, the APA apparently did not believe that federal policies prohibited them from adopting principles that permitted both deception and research without consent in certain circumstances.[49]

The vague implications in previous policy documents that departures from informed consent might be justified were dropped in the Yellow Book. Two paragraphs were added about the physician's right to use discretion in managing information and to invoke the therapeutic privilege even in the research context if there is a "patient/professional relationship" in therapeutic research. *Salgo v. Leland Stanford Jr. University Board of Trustees* (see pp. 125–129) was cited as precedent for the latter exception.[50]

In a speech to a university audience in 1972, Robert Q. Marston, the Director of NIH from 1968 to 1973, praised the developments in research ethics at NIH, but also listed unresolved problems in the composition of review committees, issues of distributive justice in the selection of research subjects, problems of compensation for injury, and problems in assessing whether adequate informed consent had been attained. Marston said he expected to be "initiating changes." He subsequently created a PHS committee charged with examining a broad range of issues in the ethics and regulation of human research. Chaired by Ronald Lamont-Havers, later deputy director of NIH, this committee developed during the next two years draft policies intended to resolve the issues raised in Marston's speech.[51]

In his speech, Marston referred to the importance of the impending Tuskegee Syphilis Report. When the final report was issued (1973), attention was given to the problems of *continuing* review of research proposals that had been previously reviewed by an IRB. The report raised profound questions about whether even the latest federal requirements of informed consent were adequate.[52]

These concerns had also gained the attention of Congress. Senators Jacob Javits and Edward Kennedy pushed to ensure adequate review, including adequate informed consent provisions at NIH. They also jointly introduced legislation to regulate and restrict experimentation that had been undertaken by the Department of Defense. Senator Kennedy had recently assumed the chair of the Subcommittee on Health of the Committee on Labor and Public Welfare, where he joined Senator Mondale in the quest for a National Commission to investigate health science and social policy.

From February through July 1973, Kennedy tirelessly scheduled subcommittee hearings on human experimentation. Willowbrook and Tuskegee were examined, and a number of reservations about the adequacy of present federal guidelines were offered by Bernard Barber, Jay Katz, and others who gave testimony. Much testimony was critical of both past practices of obtaining consent and operative policies governing informed consent.[53] Debates about the ethics of psychosurgery, the use of experimental drugs without consent (and sometimes based on falsified data), research on human fetuses, sterilization of the mentally retarded, and the use of prisoners fanned the flames of controversy.[54] These events, together with Kennedy's earlier hearings on questionable research at the Defense Department, put officials at NIH on notice that the political climate was shifting in a direction supporting legislation. There ensued a further flurry of discussion between NIH officials and concerned members of the House and Senate over the appropriate mechanism for federal regulation of human research.[55]

Two prominent developments emerged from this series of events. First, DHEW converted its grants administration *policies* governing the conduct of research involving human subjects into formal *regulations* applicable to the entire department. Second, Congress passed the National Research Act with a provision creating the National Commission for the Protection of Human Subjects of Biomedical and Behavioral Research. These two events were not unrelated. On the Senate side, Kennedy, with Javits' support, was calling for a permanent, *regulatory* commission independent of NIH to protect the welfare and rights of human subjects. Paul Rogers in the House supported NIH in advocating that the commission be *advisory* only. Kennedy agreed to yield to Rogers if DHEW published satisfactory regulations. This compromise was accepted. Regulations were published on May 30, 1974; on July 12, 1974, P.L. 93–348 was modified to authorize the National Commission as an advisory body.

The new regulations contained an expanded definition of "informed consent," but retained the same "basic elements" found in previous policy statements. These regulations stipulated that "legally effective informed consent" must be obtained by "adequate and appropriate methods" and should ordinarily be documented in writing unless subjects are not placed at significant risk.

Throughout the sections on informed consent, there was a modest shift toward greater stringency. For example, loopholes that might have offered IRBs or investigators a clear opportunity to waive or avoid the documentation of consent were closed, with the exception of one cloudy provision allowing "modified procedures" if "obtaining informed consent would surely invalidate objectives of considerable immediate importance."[56] Furthermore, *all* research was required to undergo review, not merely research that placed subjects at risk. (However, the process of assessment could be different if subjects were not at risk.)

Still, because of time constraints created by the negotiations with Kennedy, the new regulations were, in effect, only modest revisions of the

Yellow Book, and committee review was still primarily aimed at the reduction of risk. By no means was 1974 a high water mark in the now rapidly rising tide of concern about respect for subjects' rights of autonomous choice. Most of the work on these issues by the Lamont-Havers committee was given over for further deliberation to the staff of the National Commission for the Protection of Human Subjects of Biomedical and Behavioral Research.

This Commission was charged with recommending ethical guidelines for the conduct of research involving human subjects to the Secretary of DHEW, the Congress, and the President. It was also asked to identify basic ethical principles that should underlie research.[57] The Congress was clearly dissatisfied with federal guidelines and was puzzled about the ethics of research. Its actions at this time initiated a decade of reports from congressionally funded commissions. Jointly, these commissions issued over 20 volumes on the ethics of research, many dealing in depth with problems of guardian authorization or first-party informed consent. Unlike the earlier period in which the government was prodded into action by controversial cases and scholarly publications, during this period policy makers and scholars would be prodded into action by the multitude of reports and data forthcoming from these federally sponsored commissions.

Later Federal Developments: Two Commissions and New Regulations from 1974–1983

Public outrage over the potential for research on human fetuses (in particular, alleged NIH experimentation on decapitated heads of fetuses), the Tuskegee Study, and other reports of biomedical abuses fueled a climate of uncertainty and increasing hostility toward certain forms of research on humans. The political discussion in Congress had focused, without resolution or clear direction, on such sensitive issues as fetal research, psychosurgery, and experimentation on prisoners. The Congress had overwhelmingly approved creation of the National Commission, and DHEW welcomed it, but with some fears of the havoc that this "ethics commission," as it would pejoratively be dubbed, might wreak.[58]

The National Commission for the Protection of Human Subjects of Biomedical and Behavioral Research: 1974–1978

In its 17 Reports and Appendix volumes,[59] the National Commission pursued issues of autonomy, informed consent, and third-party consent more vigorously than had any previous body. The Commission was charged by Congress to investigate the ethics of research involving various groups of vulnerable subjects, such as prisoners and the mentally handicapped. It also was mandated to examine the IRB system and procedures for informed consent, including parental and guardian authorization. At the same time, it was to propose guidelines whose objective was to ensure that basic ethical principles were instituted in the IRB system and in research involving the above populations.

Late in its deliberations, the Commission developed the following abstract schema of basic ethical principles and the subject areas to which they apply:[60]

Principle of	applies to	Guidelines for
Respect for Persons		Informed Consent
Beneficence		Risk-Benefit Assessment
Justice		Selection of Subjects

In light of this schema—a formal statement of the ethical premises on which the Commission had proceeded—a general strategy was devised for handling problems of research ethics and consent. It provided that the principle of respect for persons—which includes the principle of respect for autonomy for all *autonomous* subjects that are involved—demands *some* form of consent. Under this schema, the *purpose* of consent provisions is not protection from risk, as some earlier federal policies seemed to imply, but rather the protection of autonomy and personal dignity, including the personal dignity of incompetent persons incapable of acting autonomously, for whose involvement a third party must consent.

The Commission viewed the principles listed in its schema as the "basic principles" that it had been charged by Congress to develop. The Commission held that basic principles not only can be "applied" to develop guidelines, but also to properly serve as the *justification* of the guidelines. In this schema, the principle of "respect for persons" included the fundamental imperative "that individuals should be treated as autonomous agents."[61] Hence, more decisively than any previous publication in case law or research ethics, the Commission's volumes reflected the view that the underlying *principle and justification* of informed consent requirements, at least for autonomous persons, is a moral principle of respect for autonomy, and no other. However, because the Commission consumed most of its time on incompetent subjects, problems of third-party or guardian consent were far more emphasized than direct autonomous consent by subjects.

Problems of consent in one form or the other consumed much of the Commission's energies over its four-year existence. Informed consent was eventually analyzed in terms of three necessary conditions: information, comprehension, and voluntariness. This analysis was then applied to problems of obtaining consent from prisoners,[62] the institutionalized mentally handicapped, children, and other groups who may be the subjects of biomedical and behavioral research.[63] Recommendations the Commission made to the Secretary of DHEW on these matters were more detailed and complete than anything DHEW had previously contemplated, and in some cases the formulations of recommended policies involved formidable complexities beyond the powers of an IRB to decipher and make operational. Nonetheless, whole sets of the Commission's recommendations became federal policy with but minor alterations.

The Commission sponsored a study by the Survey Research Center at the University of Michigan to investigate activities of functioning IRBs, including the adequacy of their treatment of problems of informed consent. At the time, little was known about differences among IRBs or about the quality of their performances. This study revealed that the most frequent changes in proposals IRBs returned to investigators for further correction were modifications in the informed consent provisions. The survey also found that most institutions were pleased with the IRB local review system and believed that the established process adequately protected the rights and welfare of subjects. On the basis of these results, the Commission determined to support and expand the use of local review mechanisms, and this strategy formed the groundwork for every set of policy recommendations forwarded by the Commission to the Secretary of DHEW (DHHS).

However, the Michigan study also indicated that almost all changes in informed consent provisions required by IRBs were in consent *forms* rather than in the consent *process*, which the Commission considered vital. The study also indicated that the changes made in forms were often not thorough and did not, for instance, significantly modify the technical language in which investigators tended to write them. Other defects were found in the performance of IRBs in *implementing* standards of informed consent.[64] This led the Commission to pay close attention to the importance of modifying both forms for and practices of informed consent. The Commission published an entire volume (and two appendices) on the IRB system, a volume that perhaps received more attention at NIH than any of the Commission's reports.[65]

The National Commission had a statutory limit, which expired in 1978. In other quarters, governmental activity centering on the regulation of science expanded throughout this period.[66] Consequently, few were surprised when the Secretary of DHEW (DHHS) created a new ethics committee—the "Ethical Advisory Board"—in 1978. This Board, which had been recommended by the National Commission, continued the discussion of the ethics of research at the federal level until 1980; but a Commission that succeeded this Board would later author the only impressive set of publications dealing specifically with informed consent. This was the President's Commission for the Study of Ethical Problems in Medicine and Biomedical and Behavioral Research, already introduced in Chapter 3. We shall return to this Commission after a look at 1981 regulatory activity at DHEW.

Revised Regulations at DHHS: 1981[67]

We have seen that from the start, federal regulatory agencies attempted to formulate a general policy applicable to all research involving human subjects, behavioral as well as biomedical. This model of a uniform policy was never thoroughly studied or well understood. Moreover, the 1974 regulations made no mention of categories of research for which informed consent might be inappropriate—for example, use of pathology samples, records searches, and certain observational studies. Nor was "human subject" defined, and it remained uncertain who counts as a subject of research.

The National Commission had focused largely on biomedical research, with little attention devoted to behavioral and social science research. Although it recommended "expedited review" of some forms of low-risk research, by all accounts (its own included) this Commission paid insufficient attention to distinctive problems in the social and behavioral sciences, especially those of informed consent. One therefore might have expected informed consent in the non-biomedical sciences to figure prominently on the agenda of those responsible for new regulatory initiatives, and this expectation was not doomed to disappointment.

The task of framing the federal response to the recommendations of the National Commission fell to the PHS committee that had been active prior to the creation of the Commission. This committee, now chaired by the Director of the Office for Protection from Research Risks, Charles McCarthy, struggled from the beginning with the problem of how to accommodate the behavioral and social sciences within the regulatory framework. In response to the Office of the Assistant Secretary for Program Planning and Evaluation (DHEW), which was advocating that the non-biomedical sciences be treated independently, the committee considered—and ultimately rejected—the alternative of drafting two separate sets of regulations, one for the behavioral and social sciences and one for the biomedical sciences. The approach that was finally adopted applied the same regulations to all research, regardless of discipline. However, certain kinds of research—including, notably, certain kinds of behavioral and social research—would, under the new regulations, be either entirely exempt from review or eligible for expedited review. The motivation within the Department for creating categories of exempted and expedited research was nearly equally split between the desire to accommodate the behavioral and social sciences and the concern that time-consuming obligations to review all research with human subjects was making it difficult for IRBs to properly review high risk and problematic research.[68]

This strategy of exempting and expediting certain kinds of research was presented for public comment in a notice of proposed rule-making in August 1979.[69] One aspect of the draft rules, the attempt to reconcile

FDA and DHHS regulations, was generally applauded by all affected parties. However, the draft regulations were not well received by some behavioral and social scientists, not only because they objected to the exemptions as not sufficiently broad, but because they objected to the very idea of federal regulation of their activities.[70] Although behavioral and social science research had in fact been covered under federal policy since 1971, this federal constraint had gone relatively unnoticed within the behavioral and social science communities until the 1979 rule-making served to drive the point home. Particularly troublesome, for some, was the proposed application of DHHS rules to all research, and not merely research receiving federal funds. Social researchers responded to the proposed rules by writing to the Office for Protection from Research Risks at NIH, whose officials ultimately accepted the validity of many of these external criticisms.

In the final hours of the Carter administration, on January 13, 1981, DHHS Secretary Patricia Harris signed a new set of regulations applying only to research receiving federal funds. These regulations substantially replaced the 1974 rules. The single most important principle used to make changes in the old regulations was that research presenting little or no harm to subjects should be exempt from full institutional review. For example, forms of educational innovation and testing, survey and interview research, observational research, and research on existing data bases, documents, and records were, under certain circumstances, declared exempt. Research on teeth, hair, and body wastes generally also need not be reviewed. The net effect was a near reversal of the old agency policy for social scientific and low-risk biomedical research. Much behavioral and social research now seemed to be outside the bounds of review, either because it was not federally funded or because broad exemptions had become part of federal regulations.[71]

Investigators conducting research declared exempt from the regulations were no longer federally required to obtain informed consent. For studies not exempt from the regulations, IRBs were permitted to waive consent requirements under certain circumstances. Specifically, the regulations now provided that studies could be approved without satisfying all the consent requirements if the research involved no greater than minimal risk, the rights and welfare of subjects were otherwise protected, the research "could not practicably be carried out" if normal consent provisions were applied, and subjects were supplied with some pertinent information about participation.[72] These provisions appeared to permit various forms of low-risk *deception* research, although this topic was avoided in the regulatory language.[73]

Despite the elimination of some research from review, the intent was not to weaken the moral principle of respect for autonomy in the context of research with human subjects. Rather, the framers of the DHHS rules held that an overenthusiastic and uncritical extension of federally imposed informed consent requirements into every domain of research would render some valuable minimal-risk research impossible and, perhaps more importantly, would introduce unwarranted inefficiency and costs into the review and research process.[74] Moreover, the Office for Protection from Research Risks made it clear that the new regulations were to be regarded as establishing a floor or minimum of protections for human subjects. Institutions were therefore free to increase these protections, including the consent provisions, as they saw fit, but not to reduce protections for any type of applicable research.

The federal commitment to informed consent in research was evidenced in the 1981 regulations in an extensive section on the documentation of informed consent[75] and also in an expanded list of the types of information that must be disclosed and in a new requirement that subjects be given a copy of the consent form.[76] Specifically, investigators were now obligated to give subjects information about the confidentiality of records, an explanation of whether compensation for injury and medical treatment was available, and an explanation of whom to contact for answers to pertinent questions. Moreover, they were required to disclose discoveries made during the course of the research that might affect subjects' continued participation. There were also provisions allowing an IRB to dispense in some cases with the need for signed consent forms and in other cases with written forms altogether. These provisions applied to the minimal-risk research mentioned above, as well as to a small category of circumstances under which a signed form might actually increase some risks for certain subjects—for example, research on drug abuse, homosexuality, syphilis, criminal behavior, and the like.

On balance, the 1981 regulations were well received by the biomedical and the behavioral and social science communities alike. In sharp contrast to the 1979 draft rules, the 1981 regulations provoked a relatively quiet response. Still, the 1981 regulations were subjected to some of the same criticisms that had haunted their predecessors. On the one hand, even sympathetic commentators judged aspects of the consent provisions "formidable" and "egregiously strict."[77] On the other hand, the partial and total exemptions to the regulations were criticized for their lack of strict control.[78] Some state legislatures were moved to make research that was immune to DHHS regulations nonetheless subject to further state requirements, or local review, or both.[79] Many research institutions responded similarly, promulgating policies extending IRB review requirements to non-federally funded research, at least for some cases. Behind the scenes, the Office for Protection from Research Risks gradually renegotiated general assurances under the terms of which virtually all major U.S. research institutions have agreed to satisfy the principle of prior review of all human research.

No federal regulation governing research with human subjects could be expected to satisfy all interested parties or address all outstanding problems. The 1981 regulations left unresolved many issues about informed consent and research, including issues of the adequacy of federal rules and enforcement policies for the protection of subjects' rights. Some unexplored problems began to receive attention in the early 1980s when the new President's Commission cast a broad net over the sea of remaining problems, as we shall now see.

The President's Commission for the Study of Ethical Problems in Medicine and Biomedical and Behavioral Research: 1980–1983

The President's Commission for the Study of Ethical Problems in Medicine and Biomedical and Behavioral Research was authorized in November 1978[80] by the U.S. Congress and was first convened in January of 1980. (See pp. 96–98 above for a general review of this Commission's work.) It was established in part to continue the work initiated by the earlier National Commission for the Protection of Human Subjects, which had left untouched numerous ethical issues about medicine and research. It was also specifically requested by Congress to report every two years on the adequacy of federal rules and implementation procedures with respect to the protection of human subjects.[81]

The President's Commission recognized that the National Commission had paid "considerable attention" to issues of informed consent in research and urged as federal policy many recommendations about informed consent made by its predecessor commission that had lain neglected by federal officials.[82] Indeed, early in its existence the President's Commission corresponded actively with NIH officials, and a number of its suggestions were influential in the changes made in the 1981 DHEW regulations. Regarding consent provisions, the President's Commission took the view that consent need not, under typical conditions, be obtained for research if it involves only the following: (1) observation of behavior in public places free of problems of privacy, (2) review of publicly available information, including analysis of data that contain personally identifiable information, or (3) low-risk questionnaires, interviews, or tests in which an agreement to participate effectively constitutes consent.[83]

The President's Commission never focused on informed consent in its biennial reports on human research regulations and federal policy. Instead these reports concentrated on the adequacy of human subjects rules in federal agencies other than DHHS and on the adequacy of implementation and oversight activities throughout the government.[84] Although the Commission's other reports were mainly directed toward clinical medicine, the Commission was emphatic, and properly so, that the lines distinguishing biomedical practice and research are not always clear.[85] Its studies of informed consent are stated in broadly applicable language that seems likely to have a deep impact on research regulations and on scholars working in biomedical and research ethics.

Conclusion

We have confined attention in this chapter to the United States, where public policies governing informed consent and the protection of human subjects of research have emerged through political developments and regulatory agencies. The U.S. Congress has been perhaps the most actively involved political body in the world in the funding and regulation of research, and we have seen that the bulk of the socially and academically important developments in informed consent in the United States came through either Congress, a federal agency, a congressional commission, or grant support by a federal agency—a generalization that covers at least the period since 1966.

We have but hinted at a broader history that remains to be written of the forces at work in Congress and society leading to the formation of important attitudes that fostered a climate conducive to informed consent requirements. For example, Senator Javits' indebtedness to the New Deal and Senator Kennedy's reasons for holding hearing after hearing on biomedical research (and in one instance for writing proposed regulations for behavioral research) could be connected to many profound socio-economic changes at work during the period we have traced. These changes would include alterations in our conceptions of individual rights as well as political developments such as passage of the Privacy Act and the Freedom of Information Act, which force disclosure of contracts, protocols, and records.[86]

In a 1974 article on drug experimentation, Stephen DeFelice argued that "the informed consent concept is part of a large movement in our society to protect the individual from institutional forces beyond his control."[87] There is much to support this historical thesis that there was a broad social movement to protect the individual from negligence, interference, and abuse, and that informed consent was but a piece of this larger process. Both philosophical ethics and professional ethics for medicine and research often develop from already existent movements, events, and issues in social ethics and politics. Space is too precious to consider these developments here, but any fully adequate history of informed consent would demonstrate that they have considerable explanatory power for events in the period we have examined in this chapter.

Throughout Chapters 5 and 6 we have channeled our *historical* concerns and evidence in the direction of themes in earlier and later chapters that are of direct relevance to a theory of informed consent. We have argued to the conclusion that the principle of respect for autonomy has often been invoked, however obscurely, as the major underlying principle for the justification for informed consent requirements in research. This is not to say that beneficence-based justifications of the consent requirement itself have not played a role in this history. Particularly in early writings, informed consent is treated as a *means of mini-*

mizing risk of harm to subjects. However, we have argued that autonomy-based justifications for the consent provision ultimately triumphed
as the basis of justification in most of the literature on research ethics.
Our claim is not that the goal of enabling autonomous choice for subjects
has been the primary justification underlying the *entire enterprise* of regulations, rules, and practices governing research ethics in general. To the
contrary, reduction of risk and avoidance of unfairness and exploitation
still today serve as the primary justifications for many professional regulatory and institutional controls, and indeed may be the driving motive
behind the general public and scholarly interest in the ethics of research
and in accompanying guidelines on consent. But this qualification does
not impugn our general thesis that protection of autonomy eventually
emerged as the primary justification, in particular, of *informed consent*
provisions, which form only one piece of the social nexus of rules devised
to protect research subjects.

However, dark clouds hover over this historical thesis, and we have
defended it only with attached qualifications. The most important is that
enabling "autonomous choice" or "self-determination" is an obtuse
goal. If mentioned at all in the literature on informed consent, it has
often been buried in vague, general discussion of the importance of protecting the *welfare* and *rights* of subjects. There is often no specific mention of autonomy, self-determination, and the like. If invoked at all, the
concept of autonomy in this literature is generally obscured and the goal
of enabling autonomous choice camouflaged by a different rhetoric, even
when the same set of concerns is at work.

Much the same can be said of the history of informed consent in clinical medicine in Chapter 3. By any fair assessment, enabling autonomous
choice has been one of several imperfectly distinguished and poorly formulated goals in the quest for a satisfactory medical and research ethics,
with little general agreement about how respect for autonomy is to be
understood or expressed. There has also been sparse agreement about
the contexts in which respect for a subject's or patient's decision ought
to extend. Historically, we can claim little beyond the indisputable fact
that there has developed a general, inchoate societal demand for the protection of patients' and subjects' rights, most conspicuously their autonomy rights.

We concluded Chapter 3 with the claim that, as regards informed consent in clinical medicine, "everything changed and nothing changed."
By this paradox we meant that despite a significant shift to include
informed consent in what might be called the *theory* of medical values
and practice—as expressed in medical commentary, medical education,
medical ethics, and the like—the impact of informed consent on medical
practice (its role and presence in day-to-day medical encounters) has
been limited. Although there are no conclusive data, by comparison with
clinical medicine, informed consent in research seems to have had a revolutionary impact on day-to-day activities.

We must, however, be careful not to overdraw the contrast. We do not suggest that the consents obtained from research subjects are necessarily any more meaningful than those obtained from patients or that researchers as a group necessarily take their obligation to solicit informed consent more seriously than do clinicians (although at the aggregate level, we suspect this may be the case). We are merely advancing the hypothesis that research scientists have become more consistently involved than clinicians in the actual business of soliciting consent. Research activities that 20 years ago were conducted without any specific authorization from subjects would now almost automatically require prior "informed consent." This generalization seems less true of clinical medicine, although again one must be cautious in stating such a claim. As we noted in Chapter 3, there is a long tradition of authorization by patients for surgery, which remains today the area in medicine in which "informed consent" is most consistently and scrupulously solicited.

There are many far-reaching social and political reasons why informed consent requirements have more deeply affected human research than the practice of clinical medicine. One immediate factor has doubtlessly been that informed consent in research has been mandated and monitored by federal controls and regulation, through a system of prior review that has linked the funding of research to consent procedures. No similar institutional control exists for clinical medicine. Moreover, as we noted in Chapters 2 and 4, the legal doctrine of informed consent is an after-the-fact legal remedy, with little of the power of the IRB system to influence behavior.

This difference between the research context and the clinical context is, of course, not restricted to issues of informed consent. The research community is in general more regulated than clinically-based physicians. This contrast is illustrated in the activities of the two federal ethics commissions discussed in Chapters 3, 5, and 6. The National Commission, whose focus was on research with human subjects, made specific recommendations to a department of government, which was obligated by the Commission's statutory authority to respond. Many of these recommendations were subsequently enacted into federal regulations. The President's Commission, by contrast, had the same statutory authority as the National Commission to advise government. But the President's Commission had medical care as its focus, and the federal government has little control over the private practice of medicine. The President's Commission produced excellent scholarly reports, urging physicians to adopt a model of shared decisionmaking, but virtually no recommendations requiring a federal response were devised, except for a few in the human subjects area.

The crucial difference is this: In clinical medicine physicians have been *exhorted* to solicit consent, by appeal either to medical ethics or legal self-interest; in research, scientists have in many cases been *compelled by regulation* to obtain informed consent. We believe that the most significant conclusions we have reached in Chapters 3 through 6 all tend to support this way of framing the history of informed consent down to the present day. In Chapter 7 we turn away from history per se, and thus away from the unifying thread found in Chapters 3 through 6. The intent is to move from history to a deeper appreciation and analysis of the conceptual and justificatory uncertainties surrounding both the ideas of informed consent and autonomy.

A logical gap well known to ethical theory may be thought to separate what *has served historically* as the justification of informed consent requirements from what *should* serve as the justification. This gap is an instance of what has been called the fact/value problem, a central problem of justification in modern ethical theory. Another label, "the genetic fallacy," is also sometimes attached to arguments when historical premises alone are deployed: It is said to be fallacious to move from the historical origin of *beliefs* about what is true or justified to claims about what *is* true or justified. This accusation of fallacy relies on a distinction between the context of *origin* or *discovery* and the context of *truth* or *justification*. How X came to be thought of—for example, how a list of informed consent requirements was developed—expresses a context of origin or discovery, whereas appropriate reasons for accepting X as true or justified express the context of truth or justification.

Although we accept this axiom of contemporary logic and ethical theory, we also take the view that any philosophical justification in a theory of informed consent will fail if it remains too distanced from the historical and cultural contexts in which conceptions of informed consent arose and flourished. The concept and the practice of informed consent are social phenomena that cannot be adequately appreciated or evaluated independent of knowledge of the historical forces and context that have given the idea life and meaning. The justificatory bond between informed consent and respect for autonomy is now fixed as a vital part of our moral viewpoint, and we shall not in this book challenge or loosen that bond. What we shall do instead in the next four chapters is provide a philosophical argument in defense of a *particular analysis of both autonomy and informed consent* that we believe is needed to rid these concepts of the pervasive vagueness that always has and to this day still does surround them and their connection.

Our analysis in Chapters 7 through 8 of the concepts of informed consent and autonomy explicates these two concepts in ways that at points we readily admit—in light of the histories we have sketched in Chapters 3 through 6—have a minimum of historical precedent. No inquiry as theoretical as ours in Chapters 7 and 8 could claim merely to mirror what history has already offered, nor should it. It would also be misleading to claim that the analysis of autonomy for which we there argue *is* the sense of the word "autonomy" presently at work in literature on research involving human subjects. Although we believe that our analysis is not inconsistent with what is there presupposed, nothing directly corresponding to our theory is anywhere found in this literature.

We undertake in Chapters 7 and 8, and also in Chapters 9 and 10, a rational reconstruction of the concepts of informed consent and autonomy in order to refine and sharpen what we think historically and in recent literature *should have been meant* in appeals to "informed consent" and "autonomy." At the same time, we draw from what we have learned in Chapters 3 through 6 about what *has been meant*. Our theory is thus informed by history, but not imprisoned by it.

Notes

1. "Group Consideration of Clinical Research Procedures Deviating from Accepted Medical Practice or Involving Unusual Hazard," Memorandum, approved and issued by the Director, NIH, November 17, 1953. See esp. Part III. The first principles and process of review lasted until 1961, when superseded. See also later editions published as *Handbook on the Normal Volunteer Patient Program*. For comment on the first document and the process it initiated, see Irving Ladimer, "Human Experimentation: Medicolegal Aspects," *New England Journal of Medicine* 257 (1957): 18–24, and John C. Fletcher and M. Boverman, "The Evolution of the Role of a Bioethicist in a Research Hospital," in Kare Berg and K.E. Tranoy, eds., *Research Ethics* (New York: Alan R. Liss, Inc., 1983), 131–58.

2. Public Law 87-781, 21 U.S.C. 355, 76 Stat. 780; amending Federal Food, Drug, and Cosmetic Act.

3. See J.H. Young, *The Medical Messiahs: A Social History of Health Quackery in Twentieth Century America* (Princeton, NJ: Princeton University Press, 1967); Louis Lasagna, "1938–1968: The FDA, the Drug Industry, the Medical Profession, and the Public," in John Blake, ed., *Safeguarding the Public: Historical Aspects of Medicinal Drug Control"* (Baltimore: The Johns Hopkins University Press, 1970), esp. 171–73; and William M. Wardell and Louis Lasagna, *Regulation and Drug Development* (Washington, D.C.: American Enterprise Institute, 1975), Chaps. I–II.

4. See Peter Temin, *Taking Your Medicine: Drug Regulation in the United States* (Cambridge, MA: Harvard University Press, 1980), 123–24. The speech cited below by Senator Jacob Javits gives heavy weight to the impact of the Thalidomide "concern."

5. See William J. Curran, "Governmental Regulation of the Use of Human Subjects in Medical Research: The Approach of Two Federal Agencies," *Daedalus* 98 (Spring 1969), and Lasagna, "1938–1968: The FDA, the Drug Industry, the Medical Profession, and the Public."

6. Federal Food, Drug, and Cosmetics Act, Sec. 505(i), 21 U.S.C. 355(i).

7. The debates cited below, and recorded in the *Congressional Record* cited in n. 8, make clear why the Senate needed a compromise. See also Austin Smith, "Legal Considerations in Drug Research," *Clinical Pharmacology and Therapeutics* 4 (1963): 707; Louis Lasagna and W. Wardell, *Regulation and Drug Development*; and Louis L. Jaffe, "Law as a System of Control," in Paul A. Freund, ed., *Experimentation with Human Subjects* (New York: Braziller, 1969), 197–217, esp. 204–205.

8. See "Drug Industry Act of 1962," *Congressional Record* 108 (August 23, 1962): 17395–99, which includes the Library of Congress Memorandum, and statements by Senators Javits and Carroll. See also 17378 (on Thalidomide) and 17391 (on Javits' amendment); Curran, "Governmental Regulation," 412–14; Mark Frankel, "Public Policymaking for Biomedical Research: The Case for Human Experimentation," Ph.D. Dissertation (George Washington University, 1976), hereafter "Dissertation," 148–49.

9. "Drug Industry Act of 1962," 17395.

10. Ibid., 17397, and see 17403–404.

11. See Curran, "Governmental Regulation," 417–19, and Henry K. Beecher, *Research and the Individual: Human Studies* (Boston: Little, Brown, and Co., 1970), 176–78.

12. Part 130—New Drugs, *Federal Register* 31 (August 30, 1966): 11415, par. 130.37, dated August 24, 1966 by Commissioner James L. Goddard. See also Part 130—New Drugs, *Federal Register* 32 (June 20, 1967): 8753–54 and 21 C.F.R. 130.37 (1971).

13. See Keith Reemtsma, et al., "Reversal of Early Graft Rejection after Renal Heterotransplantation in Man," *Journal of the American Medical Association* 187 (1964): 691–96; Mark Frankel, "Dissertation," 146 and "The Development of Policy Guidelines Governing Human Experimentation in the United States: A Case Study of Public Policy Making for Science and Technology," *Ethics in Science and Medicine* 2: 43–59, esp. 48 (hereafter "The Development of Policy Guidelines"). Frankel's work is based in part on an interview with Director Shannon.

14. *Report of the National Conference on the Legal Environment of Medical Science* (University of Chicago and National Society for Medical Research, 1960), esp. Third Session.

15. DHEW, *Grants Administration Manual*, issued as *Grants and Award Programs of the Public Health Service, Policy and Information Statement in Research Grants* (1959).

16. Robert B. Livingston, Memorandum to Shannon on "Moral and Ethical Aspects of Clinical Investigation" (February 20, 1964).

17. Livingston's report indicated that no professional code was adequate or widely accepted in practice, and that many ethical questions were left entirely untouched by existing codes. However, his claim was challenged by the Clinical Director of the National Cancer Institute. See the Memorandum from Clinical Director, NCI (Nathaniel I. Berlin) to Director of Laboratories and Clinics, OD-DIR, "Comments on Memorandum of November 4, 1964 from the Associate Chief of Program Development DRFR, to the Director, NIH" (August 30, 1965), 3.

18. See Robert B. Livingston, Memorandum to Shannon on "Progress Report on Survey of Moral and Ethical Aspects of Clinical Investigation (November 4, 1964), esp. 203. Livingston cited the Ladimer volume as well as the Medical Research Council of Great Britain. See also the interview with Shannon, in Frankel, "The Development of Policy Guidelines," 50; the account of the historical importance of this case at PHS, in Curran, "Government Regulation," 546–48; and Bradford Gray, *Human Subjects in Medical Experimentation* (New York: John Wiley and Sons, 1975), 12.

19. Livingston, Memorandum, 6–7.

20. In the Director's personal copy of the Livingston Report, on file at the NIH, a "NO!!!" is penned in the margin at this point. See also Frankel, "The Development of Policy Guidelines," 50–51. Nathaniel Berlin, in a memo cited below, also disagreed.

21. James A. Shannon, Memorandum and Transmittal Letter to the U.S. Surgeon General, "Moral and Ethical Aspects of Clinical Investigations" (January 7, 1965).

22. Medical Research Council, "Responsibility in Investigations on Human Subjects," *British Medical Journal* 2 (1964): 178.

23. For a brief glimpse of the nature of these discussions, see a memorandum to Shannon from Thomas J. Kennedy, Jr., Chief, DRFR, on "Moral and ethical aspects of clinical research: the experience of the general clinical research centers program" (September 14, 1965).

24. Transcript of the NAHC meeting, Washington, D.C., September 28, 1965.

25. Recommendation to the Surgeon General in a "Resolution Concerning Clinical Research on Humans" (December 3, 1965), transmitted in a Memorandum from Dr. S. John Reisman, the Executive Secretary, NAHC, to Dr. James A. Shannon ("Resolution of Council") on December 6, 1965. Reported in a Draft Statement of Policy on January 20, 1966. A previous resolution in September had been similarly worded, but without mention of informed consent. This first resolution seemed almost entirely concerned with the protection of subject welfare through peer review.

26. U.S. Public Health Service, Division of Research Grants, Policy and Procedure Order (PPO) #129, February 8, 1966, "Clinical Investigations Using Human Subjects," signed by Ernest M. Allen, Grants Policy Officer. The aforementioned Draft Statement of January 21, 1966, was the basis for this formulation. See also Frankel, "Dissertation," 156, and Fletcher and Boverman, "Evolution of the Role of an Applied Bioethicist," 135–36.

27. Memorandum from Surgeon General William H. Stewart, "Clinical Research and Investigation Involving Human Beings" (February 8, 1966). See also: Supplement, April 7, 1966; Revision, July 1, 1966; Clarification, December 12, 1966.

28. "Group Consideration and Informed Consent in Clinical Research at the National Institutes of Health" (July 1, 1966).

29. See Memorandum from James A. Shannon to Institute Directors, et al., "Group Consideration and Informed Consent in Clinical Research at the National Institutes of Health" (July 1, 1966).

30. See William Curran, "Evolution of Formal Mechanisms for Ethical Review of Clinical Research," in N. Howard-Jones and Z. Bankowski, eds., *Medical Experimentation and the Protection of Human Rights* (Geneva: Council for International Organizations of Medical Sciences, 1978), 15; and "Government Regulation," 442ff. See also Curran's "New Public Health Service Regulations on Human Experimentation," *New England Journal of Medicine* 281 (October 1969): 781–82.

31. They were also immediately hailed as a model approach in "Friendly Adversaries and Human Experimentation," *New England Journal of Medicine* 275 (1966): 786.

32. Robert Q. Marston, Director, NIH, "Medical Science, the Clinical Trial, and Society," a speech delivered at the University of Virginia on November 10, 1972, 14 (typescript), hereafter "Speech."

33. See National Commission for the Protection of Human Subjects, IRB Report and Appendices, as cited in n. 59 below.

34. See also the later statement by Surgeon General William H. Stewart, "Memorandum: PHS policy for intramural programs and for contracts when investigations involving human subject are included" (October 30, 1967), addressed to "all Directors who report directly to the Surgeon General."

35. See E.L. Pattullo, "The Federal Role in Social Research, in Tom L. Beauchamp, et al., eds., *Ethical Issues in Social Science Research* (Baltimore: The Johns Hopkins University Press, 1982), 375.

36. "Memorandum," Surgeon General William H. Stewart to Heads of Institutions Receiving Public Health Service Grants (December 12, 1966). See also Stewart's 1967 memorandum above.

37. U.S. Public Health Service, Surgeon General, *Protection of the Individual as a Research Subject: Grants, Awards, Contracts*, (Washington, D.C.: DHEW, PHS, May 1, 1969), 1.

38. See, for example, Curran, "Governmental Regulation," 440f.

39. *Protection of the Individual as a Research Subject*, 3.

40. Eugene A. Confrey, "PHS Grant-Supported Research with Human Subjects," *Public Health Reports* 83 (February 1968): 130.

41. See, for example, the early Memorandum from Donald T. Chalkley, Acting Chief of the Grants Management Branch (NIH-DRG), to the Deputy Director, Division of Research Grants, "Status of Institutional Assurance Mechanism" (September 27, 1968). This memorandum was a part of the historical background of the 1969 policy elaboration, which was also quickly realized to be inadequate. See also the study by Bernard Barber, et al., *Research on Human Subjects: Problems of Social Control in Medical Experimentation* (New York: Russell Sage Foundation, 1973). Tentative conclusions of this discouraging study had been brought to the attention of NIH officials in 1970.

42. For most of these events and their connections, see Frankel's summary, "Dissertation," 166–71. In *Karp* v. *Cooley* the professional practice standard for disclosure received a classic formulation: 493 F.2d 408 (1974), at 419.

43. See Draft Policy, "Protection of Human Subjects: Field Issuance" (July 6, 1970), and DHEW Grants Administration Manual, "Protection of Human Subjects" (April 15, 1971). Of particular importance was the 1963 case *Tunkl* v. *Regents of the University of California*, 60 Cal. 2d 92, 32 Cal. Rptr. 33, 383 P.2d 441 (1963), Annot., 6 A.L.R. 3d 693 (1966).

44. See Joel Mangel, Memorandum: "Contractual exculpation from tort liability— use of an exculpatory clause to avoid liability for negligence" (September 17, 1970).

45. Public Health Service, *The Institutional Guide to DHEW Policy on Protection of Human Subjects*, (Washington, D.C.: Government Printing Office, DHEW Pub. No. (NIH) 72–102, December, 1971). This document was preceded by a DHEW Grants Administration Manual ("Procurement Involving Human Subjects," April 15, 1971) that contained the essentials of the new policy, but without interpretation. (41 C.F.R. Sec. 3-4.55.)

46. Ibid., 7.

47. Ibid., 2–3.

48. Ibid., 7–8.

49. Ad hoc Committee on Ethical Standards in Psychological Research, *Ethical Principles in the Conduct of Research with Human Participants* (Washington, D.C.: American Psychological Association, Inc., 1973), 3.

50. *The Institutional Guide to DHEW Policy on Protection of Human Subjects*, 8. Also cited was the important Canadian case *Halushka* v. *University of Saskatchewan*, 53 D.L.R. (2d) (1965).

51. Initially this committee was composed only of NIH officials. However, NICHD had simultaneously created a small group chaired by Dr. Charles U. Lowe to review special protections for fetal research. The two groups were merged early in 1973, under Lamont-Havers, to become a PHS committee. Dr. Charles McCarthy, a member of the Lamont-Havers committee, provided this information to us in November 1984. See also Fletcher and Boverman, "Evolution of the Role of an Applied Bioethicist," 137.

52. Marston, "Speech," 17–25; *Final Report of the Tuskegee Syphilis Study Ad Hoc Panel* (Public Health Service, April 28, 1973), 7–8.

53. Hearings before the Subcommittee on Health of the Committee on Labor and

Public Welfare," U.S. Senate, "Quality of Health Care—Human Experimentation"
(1973).

54. Regarding falsified data, see "Physicians Who Falsify Drug Data," *Science* 180
(1973): 1038ff. In 1967 FDA had established a six-person investigative group to look
at these charges, headed by Dr. Frances Kelsey. The prisoner research issue had originally been under investigation by Senator Samuel Ervin, whose Subcommittee on
Constitutional Rights was investigating threats to civil liberties posed by federally
funded behavior modification programs. Ervin turned this project over to Kennedy
when the interests of his Subcommittee became deflected by the Watergate scandal.
We are indebted to Barbara Mishkin (personal communication, January 1985) for this
information.

55. These events are recounted in Frankel, "Dissertation," Chapter III. See also a
Memorandum on file at the Office of the Director, NIH, from Charles McCarthy,
"Senate Action Concerning Experimentation Involving Human Subjects" (August 8,
1972).

56. *Code of Federal Regulations*, Title 45, Part 46.10, as printed in *Federal Register*
39 (May 30, 1974): 18919.

57. Public Law 93–348, 88 Stat. 342 (July 12, 1974).

58. Cf. Franz J. Ingelfinger, "Ethics of Human Experimentation Defined by a
National Commission," *The New England Journal of Medicine* 296 (January 1977):
44–45; and Edward Kennedy, *The Congressional Record* (June 29, 1978): S9690.

59. The National Commission for the Protection of Human Subjects of Biomedical
and Behavioral Research: *Report and Recommendations: Research on the Fetus*.
DHEW Publication No. (OS) 76-127 (1976). *Appendix to Report and Recommendations: Research on the Fetus*. DHEW Publication No. (OS) 76–128 (1976). *Report and
Recommendations: Research Involving Prisoners*. DHEW Publication No. (OS) 76-131
(1976). *Appendix to Report and Recommendations: Research Involving Prisoners*.
DHEW Publication No. (OS) 76-132 (1976). *Report and Recommendations: Psychosurgery*. DHEW Publication No. (OS) 76-0001 (1977). *Appendix to Report and Recommendations: Psychosurgery*. DHEW Publication No. (OS) 77-0002 (1977). *Disclosure of Research Information Under the Freedom of Information Act*. DHEW
Publication No. (OS) 77-0003 (1977). *Report and Recommendations: Research Involving Children*. DHEW Publication No. (OS) 77-0004 (1977). *Appendix to Report and
Recommendations: Research Involving Children*. DHEW Publication No. (OS) 77-
0005 (1977). *Report and Recommendations: Research Involving Those Institutionalized as Mentally Infirm*. DHEW Publication No. (OS) 78-0006 (1978). *Appendix to
Report and Recommendations: Research Involving Those Institutionalized as Mentally
Infirm*. DHEW Publication No. (OS) 78-0009 (1978). *Report and Recommendations:
Institutional Review Boards*. DHEW Publication No. (OS) 78-0008 (1978). *Appendix
to Report and Recommendations: Institutional Review Boards*. DHEW Publication No.
(OS) 78-0009 (1978). *Report and Recommendations: Ethical Guidelines for the Deliv-
ery of Health Services by DHEW*. DHEW Publication No. (OS) 78-0010 (1978).
*Appendix to Report and Recommendations: Ethical Guidelines for the Delivery of
Health Services by DHEW*. DHEW Publication No. (OS) 78-0011 (1978). *The Belmont
Report: Ethical Guidelines for the Protection of Human Subjects of Research*. DHEW
Publication No. (OS) 78-0012 (1978). *Appendices A and B to The Belmont Report:
Ethical Guidelines for the Protection of Human Subjects of Research*. DHEW Publica-
tion Nos. (OS) 78-0013 and 78-0014 (1978).

60. The National Commission, *The Belmont Report: Ethical Principles and Guidelines for the Protection of Human Subjects of Research* (The National Commission for
the Protection of Human Subjects of Biomedical and Behavioral Research, April 18,
1979), 4–20.

61. Ibid., 3–4. See also Joseph V. Brady and Albert R. Jonsen (two Commissioners), "The Evolution of Regulatory Influences on Research with Human Subjects," in Robert Greenwald, Mary Kay Ryan, and James E. Mulvihill, eds., *Human Subjects Research* (New York: Plenum Press, 1982), 3–18, esp. 6f, 10ff.

62. See the National Commission, *Report and Recommendations: Research Involving Prisoners*, esp. vii, 3, 6, 8, 16–19.

63. Perhaps the clearest example is found in *Report and Recommendations: Research Involving Those Institutionalized as Mentally Infirm*, Chapter 5. Other sources are referenced in n. 59.

64. See the National Commission, *Report and Recommendations: Institutional Review Boards*, Chapter 2; *Report and Recommendations: Research Involving Children*, 43–46. Our presentation of information in this paragraph is also indebted to explanations of the data provided by Bradford H. Gray, Robert A. Cooke, and Arnold S. Tannenbaum, "Research Involving Human Subjects," *Science* 201 (September 22, 1978): 1094–1101; and Bradford H. Gray and Robert A. Cooke, "The Impact of Institutional Review Boards on Research," *Hastings Center Report* 10 (February 1980): 36–41.

65. See the National Commission, *Report and Recommendations: Institutional Review Boards*, esp. 1–54.

66. See Donald S. Frederickson, "The Public Governance of Science," *Man and Medicine* 3 (1978): 77–88.

67. Our account of the development of the 1981 federal regulations, as well as the political developments bringing about the National Commission, is based on unpublished information provided in personal communication with Dr. Charles McCarthy, Director of the Office for Protection from Research Risks, NIH, November 1984.

68. Personal communication, Dr. Charles McKay, Associate Director, Office for Protection from Research Risks, NIH and Dr. Charles McCarthy, Director, November 1984.

69. DHEW, Office of the Secretary, "Proposed Regulations Amending Basic HEW Policy for Protection of Human Subjects," *Federal Register* 44 (August 14, 1979): 45 CFR Part 46, 47688–98.

70. The most outspoken such critic was Ithiel De Sola Pool; see, for example, "The New Censorship of Social Research," *Public Interest* 59 (1980): 57–65, and Carol Levine, "Update," *IRB: A Review of Human Subjects* 1 (1979): 7. See also E.L. Pattullo and Judith P. Swazey, "Social Scientists and Research Review: Two Views," *Hastings Center Report* 10 (1980): 15–19; Carol Levine, "Social Scientists Form Committee to Protest Regulations," *IRB: A Review of Human Subjects Research* 1 (December 1979); E.L. Pattullo, "Modesty is the Best Policy: The Federal Role in Social Research," in Beauchamp, et al., *Ethical Issues in Social Science Research*, 373–90; and Murray L. Wax, "Overseeing Regulations or Intimidating Research," *IRB: A Review of Human Subjects Research* 3 (April 1981): 8–10.

71. DHHS, Office of the Secretary, "Final Regulations Amending Basic HHS Policy for the Protection of Human Research Subjects," *Federal Register* 46 (January 26, 1981): 45 CFR Part 46, S 46.101–124, 8386–91. The federal government retained the right to withhold funds from any institution that failed materially to protect the rights of subjects, regardless of the source of funding. See S 46.123, par. B

72. DHHS, "Final Regulations," S 46.116(c)-(d).

73. See Rebecca S. Dresser, "Deception Research and the HHS Final Regulations," *IRB: A Review of Human Subjects Research* 3 (April 1981): 3–4.

74. DHHS officials also believed that informed consent requirements were inappropriate for certain methodologies—for example, simple telephone interviews—

that were common outside the research context. These officials also regarded the rules as unenforceable requirements.

75. DHHS, "Final Regulations," S 46.117. Documentation of informed consent was distinguished from procedures for soliciting consent. Emphasis was placed on these procedures; documentation could be waived under some (comparatively easily met) circumstances.

76. DHHS, "Final Regulations," S 46.116(a), 46.116(b), and 46.117(b2).

77. William J. Curran, "New Ethical-Review Policy for Clinical Medical Research," *New England Journal of Medicine* 304 (April 1981): 953.

78. Robert M. Veatch, "Protecting Human Subjects: The Federal Government Steps Back," *Hastings Center Report* 11 (June 1981): esp. 9. For a heavily qualified endorsement from within the social science community, see Murray L. Wax and Joan Cassell, "From Regulation to Reflection: Ethics in Social Research," *The American Sociologist* 16 (1981): 224–29.

79. See discussion of the New York and California statutes (both enacted *before* the 1981 regulations) in "Note, Ensuring Informed Consent in Human Experimentation," *North Carolina Law Review* 58 (1979): 137.

80. Title III of Public Law 95-622, enacted November 9, 1978, codified at 42 U.S.C., Ch. 6A. A "sunset" date for the Commission was first set at December 31, 1982, and later extended by Public Law 97-377 to March 31, 1983.

81. President's Commission for the Study of Ethical Problems in Medicine and Biomedical and Behavioral Research, *Protecting Human Subjects* (Washington, D.C.: Government Printing Office, 1981), 1.

82. See, for example, Ibid., 2, 66, 74f.

83. Letter of September 18, 1980, from Morris B. Abram, Chairman of the President's Commission, to HHS Secretary Patricia Harris. See "Update," *IRB: A Review of Human Subjects Research* 2 (November 1980), 9; and Alexander M. Capron, "Reply," *IRB: A Review of Human Subjects Research* 3 (April 1981): 10–12.

84. President's Commission, *Protecting Human Subjects* and *Implementing Human Research Regulations* (Washington, D.C.: Government Printing Office, 1983).

85. President's Commission, *Summing Up* (Washington, D.C.: U.S. Government Printing Office, 1983), 17ff, 30ff, 43ff.

86. During the 1970s it became apparent that a right-to-know movement had taken hold in the United States, especially in matters of consumer protection. The belief that citizens in general have a right to know about significant risks is reflected in a diverse set of laws and federal regulations. These include The Freedom of Information Act; The Federal Insecticide, Fungicide, and Rodenticide Amendments and Regulations; The Motor Vehicle and School Bus Safety Amendments; The Truth-in-Lending Act; The Pension Reform Act; The Real Estate Settlement Procedures Act; The Federal Food, Drug, and Cosmetic Act; The Consumer Product Safety Act; and the Toxic Substances Control Act.

87. Stephen L. DeFelice, "An Analysis of the Relationship between Human Experimentation and Drug Discovery in the United States," *Drug Metabolism Reviews* 3 (1974): 175.

III

A THEORY
OF INFORMED
CONSENT

7

The Concept of Autonomy

At this point we move from historical analysis to conceptual analysis, from the history of informed consent to its nature. This shift requires us to analyze the concept of autonomy and its relationship to informed consent. As the histories in Chapters 3 through 6 indicate, informed consent is rooted in concerns about protecting and enabling autonomous or self-determining choice by patients and subjects. Accordingly, in the present chapter we provide a theory of autonomous action that is adequate to express what is respected or protected by informed consent. In Chapter 8 this analysis of the nature of *autonomy* provides the essential foundation for our analysis of the nature of *informed consent*.

Autonomy and Informed Consent

We begin by introducing two significant distinctions: (a) between autonomous persons and autonomous actions, and (b) between substantially autonomous actions and those that are less than substantially autonomous. The goal of a *substantially autonomous action* will later play a prominent role in our presentation of informed consent.

Distinguishing Persons and Their Actions

Consents and refusals are actions. As we shall see in Chapter 8, informed consents are acts of autonomous authorizing—and, in the case of refusals, of declining to authorize. Somewhat paradoxically, autonomous actions can be performed not only by by *autonomous persons*—those who generally, but not always, act autonomously—but also (on some occasions) by *nonautonomous persons*—those who generally, but not always, fail to act autonomously. Autonomous persons are the kinds of persons who qualify to choose and consent precisely because they are autonomous. The nonautonomous person—for example, a one year old or a severely demented person—is usually not the right type of agent to qualify; he or she is not a person whose choices, consents, or refusals ought to be treated as binding.

Theories of autonomy seem typically to be theories of the autonomous person, as exemplified by the following thoughtful portrait of the autonomous person or "particular personality ideal" drawn by Stanley Benn:

> To be a chooser is not enough for autonomy, for a competent chooser may still be a slave to convention, from his milieu. He assesses situations . . . by norms . . . absorbed unreflectively.
>
> The autonomous man is the one . . . whose life has a consistency that derives from a coherent set of beliefs, values, and principles, by which his actions are governed. . . .
>
> The principles by which the autonomous man governs his life make his decisions consistent and intelligible to him as his own; for they *constitute* the personality he recognizes as the one he has made his own.[1]

Benn's theory features, as he puts it, a *"kind* of agent": The autonomous person is consistent, independent, in command, resistant to control by authorities, and the source of his or her basic values and beliefs. The person's life as a whole expresses self-directedness.

One of the problems with such a theory of the autonomous person is that few choosers, and also few choices, would be autonomous if held to such standards. Benn has correctly emphasized that his theory presents an aspirational *ideal* of autonomy that distinguishes what he calls "normal choosers" from ideal choosers. This status as an ideal theory makes his account too enriched for our purposes. The theory is elevated above what generally is and should be meant in moral and legal theory by expressions such as "respect for autonomy" and "exercise of autonomy," which are broad enough terms in ordinary language and in our theory to include "normal choosers" and their choices. It would follow from an exclusive reliance on Benn's analysis of autonomy that we need not honor and respect *as autonomous* most of the prudent and responsible choices made most of the time by normal choosers. An autonomous choice would presumably also have to conform to an autonomous person's elected life plan—a starkly rigorous requirement—in order to satisfy his ideal standard.[2]

Theories of the autonomous person need not be so demanding, of course. A plausible account of the autonomous person could, for example, be restricted to the enumeration of certain capacities for and patterns of recurrent autonomous action: resistance to social conformity, reflectiveness, understanding and insight, resistance to manipulations attempted by others, and the like. Unfortunately, there is no widespread agreement at present regarding the definitive characteristics of the autonomous person, just as there is no agreement regarding the characteristics of autonomous action.

The distinction between the capacities of persons and their particular actions has been ignored in the literature on informed consent, with unfortunate results that have eventuated in complaints such as the following by William Thompson, in a discussion of tests of patients' abilities to understand disclosed information:

[General findings] that patients often fail to remember and perhaps fail to understand what they have been told—are interesting and important, but do not resolve the basic question of patients' *capacity* to exercise informed consent. People's failure to understand a *particular disclosure* may result from inadequacies in that disclosure rather than inadequacies *in the patient*. Hence these studies do not tell us whether patients are capable of understanding when properly informed. . . . [Last two italics added.][3]

It is always an open question whether an autonomous person with the capacity to give an informed consent actually has, in any specific instance, given an informed consent, in the sense of making an autonomous choice to authorize or refuse an intervention. The *capacity* to act autonomously is distinct from *acting* autonomously, and possession of the capacity is no guarantee that an autonomous choice has been or will be made. (The capacity to do A may only be *definable* in terms of "A," but the capacity is distinct from all instances of A, just as all dispositions are distinct from their exercise.) An autonomous person who signs a consent form without reading or understanding it is *qualified* to give an informed consent, but has failed to do so. Similarly, if an autonomous person acts in a way he or she did not intend—for example, by accidentally signing form *x* when he or she meant to sign form *y*—then the act of signing *x* is not autonomous, although it is the act of an autonomous person.

It is a common pattern in contexts of informed consent for autonomous persons to fail—for a wide variety of reasons—to give informed consents, even when their acts are formally certified or recognized as informed consents *because* they are acts of autonomous persons. The autonomous person may fail to act autonomously in a specific situation if ill in a hospital, overwhelmed by new information, ignorant, manipulated by a clever presentation of data, and so on.

This helps explain why autonomous actions are examined in this book rather than autonomous persons. Our primary interest is in the nature of informed consent—*what* an informed consent *is*—rather than problems of *from whom* consent should be or may be obtained. Our view is that informed consents and informed refusals are particular actions; the goal of informed consent requirements is to enable patients and subjects to perform these actions, that is, to make substantially autonomous choices about whether to authorize a medical intervention or research involvement.

Degrees of Autonomous Action

Throughout a long history of reflection on autonomy, there has been a recurrent temptation to analyze personal autonomy in terms of two implicit models: (1) a *freedom* model, and (2) an *authenticity* model. The freedom model is employed in dazzlingly diverse ways by writers such as Immanuel Kant, various German and British Idealists, and Isaiah Berlin. The analysis of autonomy in terms of authenticity—"one's own" actions, character, beliefs, and motivation—is developed in no less diverse ways by such writers as Benn, Gerald Dworkin, and various writers in the existentialist tradition. In both models, theories are often dependent on analogies to the autonomy of political states, where "autonomy" has variously referred to popular sovereignty, citizen participation, independent nationhood, nongovernance by alien forces, control by citizens, and the like. However, other theories try to develop an account divorced from a background in political theory.

Our analysis is indebted to these influential theories, but we depart from them in major ways. We analyze autonomous action as follows:

X acts autonomously only if X acts
1. intentionally,
2. with understanding, and
3. without controlling influences.

We believe, but do not here *argue*, that these three conditions are the basic conditions of autonomous action. Whether each condition in 1–3 is a *necessary* condition of autonomous action—as we believe—and whether they are jointly *sufficient* conditions—a more difficult thesis to sustain—are not matters on which we shall speculate in detail, because such claims would need far more argument than can be attempted here. In the above schema we have construed these conditions as necessary but without any mention of their sufficiency, a problem to which we return in the concluding section. Until we reach that section we shall assume only that each of these conditions is necessary.

The first condition, the condition of intentionality, is not a matter of degree: Acts are either intentional (and therefore potentially autonomous) or nonintentional (and therefore nonautonomous). By contrast, the conditions of understanding and lack of controlling influences (which we refer to as the condition of noncontrol, that is, noncontrol by the influences of others) can both be satisfied to a greater or lesser extent. Thus, actions can be autonomous by degrees, as a function of different levels of satisfaction of these two conditions. The conditions of understanding and noncontrol may be placed on a broad continuum from fully present to wholly absent, as represented by the diagram in Figure 1, which uses the language of *substantial* satisfaction of the conditions. For reasons discussed later, we designate this point on the continuum as a watershed for autonomous actions of the sort that qualify as informed consents.

The hypothetical construct of a *fully* autonomous action—represented by the left-most extremes of the two parts of the diagram in Figure 1— graphically depicts the idea of degrees of autonomy. A fully or ideally autonomous action is an intentional action that is fully understood and completely noncontrolled by the influences of others: Lack of under-

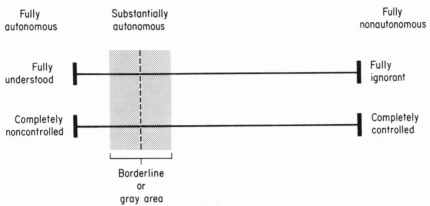

Fig. 1. Degrees of autonomy of intentional actions

standing and control by others do not prevail in any degree. But as the conditions constituting an autonomous action are stripped away by degrees from this hypothetical circumstance, pieces of the interlocking machinery are eroded and the resultant action increasingly becomes less autonomous. With sufficient stripping, the behavior becomes nonautonomous.

The claim that actions are autonomous by degrees, rather than categorically autonomous or nonautonomous, may at first seem a surprising thesis. Yet it is a direct consequence of the conditions that define autonomous action. A person can thoroughly understand an abundance of relevant information at a moment of action or can have only limited understanding. The more information the person understands, the more enhanced are the possibilities for autonomy of action. The form of control exerted by the influence attempts of others also affects the degree to which an action is autonomous. It is noncontroversial, for example, that there are degrees of threats and degrees of abilities to resist threats. Our claim is merely the corollary that some threats render actions more nonautonomous than others.

Another corollary of the degrees thesis, and of our analysis in terms of the three necessary conditions of autonomous action, is that there are *both* different conditions under which *and* different degrees in which autonomous action may be enhanced or compromised. Thus, a person can satisfy one or more of our three conditions, while failing to satisfy another. For example, a person may be fully controlled by a robber's threat of severe harm in yielding his or her money, yet may understand perfectly the nature and implications of the action taken, and may intend to take it. Such an act of compliance would *not*, however, be autonomous, because the condition requiring lack of control by others—like each of the conditions 1–3—is a necessary condition of autonomous action; and it is not satisfied under the circumstances, not even by degrees. A coerced action is not made any more autonomous if the person's understanding is improved. Thus, if any one of the three conditions is unsatisfied, the act is *non*autonomous. If, however, this is not the case—that is, the act is intentional and there is neither full ignorance nor full control by others, then the degree of autonomy that can be ascribed to an action is correlated with the degrees to which the understanding and noncontrol conditions are fulfilled.

Although this analysis of acts as "autonomous by degrees" is, we believe, conceptually correct, there are also contexts in which it is necessary to establish thresholds above which all acts are *treated as* autonomous and below which all acts are treated as nonautonomous. The decision how and where to draw this line is invariably based on moral and policy considerations, and no sharp line can be drawn purely on conceptual grounds to distinguish autonomous from nonautonomous action. As we shall see, in informed consent contexts we should look neither for *full* autonomy nor merely for *some evidence* of autonomy. The proper threshold is the general goal of *substantially* autonomous action.

Substantially Autonomous Actions

Literature on informed consent overflows with statements that subjects and patients are not qualified to "really understand" that to which they consent.[4] Such statements frequently imply that "full autonomy" is the only instance of real autonomy, and that if a patient or subject cannot exhibit full understanding and full independence from the control of others, then his or her decisions are not informed consents.

Such statements are premised on faulty and unargued assumptions about "real" or "true" autonomy. Like Benn's theory, these assumptions are expressions of *ideal* rather than normal or adequate degrees of autonomy. Such aspirational objectives are worthy ideals, but falling short of them is an inevitable reality. This is true of informed consent, and of virtually all comparably consequential decisions and actions in life. To chain informed consent to *fully or completely* autonomous decisionmaking stacks the deck of the argument and strips informed consent of any meaningful place in the practical world, where people's actions are rarely, if ever, fully autonomous.

As our history of informed consent in Chapters 3 through 6 suggests, consent requirements did not arise with the hope of enabling people to make decisions about health care or research participation that were *more* autonomous than decisions of comparable consequence made in other arenas of life. Much of the initial impetus came from concern that people were *less* able to act autonomously as patients and subjects than elsewhere. Assuming comparable capacity for decisionmaking, one's appreciation of information and independence from controlling influences in the informed consent setting need not outstrip one's information and independence in making a financial investment, hiring a building contractor, or accepting a job offer. The goal, realistically, is that such consequential decisions are *substantially autonomous*—that is, near the fully autonomous end of the continuum.

In Figure 1, substantially autonomous acts are somewhere between midpoint and fully autonomous, represented symbolically by the dotted line (the middle of the "borderline" area). Any exact placement of this line risks the criticism that it is "arbitrary," because the range for placement is wide, and controversy over any attempt at precise pinpointing is a certainty. Yet the label "arbitrary" is too quick, because the placing of threshold points marking substantially autonomous decisions can be carefully reasoned, if not precisely located, in light of specific goals. We believe that substantial autonomy is a reasonable and achievable goal—an appropriate threshold—for decisionmaking and participation in research or medical interventions, no less and no more than elsewhere in life. The criteria of substantiality for any particular action or type of action will be treated throughout this book as a matter that can only be addressed in a particular context, rather than pinpointed through a general theory. We use the model of substantiality as a standard that patients and subjects might realistically satisfy, and that professionals are morally bound to assist them to satisfy if informed consents should be obtained.

It is a separate issue whether this criterion of substantial autonomy should be the only source for distinguishing consents or refusals that are "valid" from those treated as "invalid." There may be compelling policy or moral justifications in some contexts for adopting consent requirements that establish a threshold below the level of substantial autonomy, in effect treating *less than substantially* autonomous consents as *valid* or, more precisely, *effective* consents. Some of these issues are considered later, but at this point we must turn to the prior matter of analyzing the three conditions in our theory of autonomous action. In Chapters 8 through 10, these will serve, by augmenting the analysis, as conditions of *informed consent*, just as they serve here as the conditions of *autonomous action*.

Three Conditions of Autonomous Action

The Condition of Intentionality

Intentionality is a conceptually necessary condition of autonomous action and in its own right one of the most important concepts in the history of philosophy. Although he never used the word "autonomy," eighteenth-century philosopher Thomas Reid had already seen the vast importance of intention for a theory of what counts as *one's action*:

> Every man knows infallibly that what is done by his conscious will and intention, is to be imputed to him . . . and that whatever is done without his will and intention, cannot be imputed to him with truth. . . . If he intended and willed it, it is his action in the judgement of all mankind. But if it was done without his knowledge, or without his will and intention, it is as certain that he did it not. . . . What I never conceived nor willed, I never did.[5]

The Nature of Intentional Action. But what does it mean to act "intentionally," and is Reid's sweeping characterization correct? Clearly a mere *act of intending*, as when we intend to take our medicine but never get around to it, does not qualify as an *intentional action*. We can intend many things without *acting* on such an intention. "Pure intending," as Donald Davidson has called it,[6] can occur without any practical action or consequence other than the act of intending. Only if action occurs with an intention to perform the action is there an intentional action.

Such intentional actions are not events that merely happen to people. As intentional, they cannot be accidents and cannot be performed inadvertently or by mistake. Nor can it be that another agent uses physical force to push the person into "doing" it. Instead, the actor must have the sense that he or she makes the act happen, that he or she is its author or agent. But even under this description, the scope of the concept is too broad and the meaning too inspecific. The psychological and philosophical literatures abound with diverse analyses of intentional action that treat the notion as synonymous or co-extensive with actions variously described as volitional, deliberate, self-regulated, self-controlled, willed, freely-willed, reasoned, goal-directed, planned, or instrumental. To complicate matters further, the law offers a substantial literature on intentional action that addresses related problems such as criminal *mens rea* and tortious intent.[7]

Despite the diffuse character of the literature, certain core themes are widely shared in contemporary treatments of intentional action in philosophy and psychology. Chief among these is that intentional acts require plans: the integration of cognitions into a blueprint for action. An action plan is a map or representation of the strategies and tactics proposed for the execution of an action.[8] The relationship between intentional action and action plans is straightforward. For an act to be intentional, it must correspond to the actor's conception—his or her plan—of the act in question (although a planned outcome might not materialize).

Imagine, for example, that Toi intends to chop an onion. Toi's plan for chopping an onion entails executing a highly routinized sequence of actions, chief of which is a series of peeling and chopping movements. Note that Toi need not have deliberated about or reflected upon her onion-chopping plan—an actor need not be consciously aware of all or even any of the behavioral steps in the plan, although if there is a deviation or slip in the execution of the plan, that difference may come to the actor's attention.[9] Now imagine that on the way to the cutting board the onion falls from Toi's hand into a working food processor, and the onion is chopped. It might in some ironic sense be said that Toi "chopped" the onion, yet she did not do so intentionally, even though she wanted and intended to chop the onion. Whatever action or behavior was performed, Toi was aware that it did not correspond to *the way* she intended—planned—to do it. Her "chopping" of the onion was, as it turns out, accidental.

This example illustrates how an actor's intention in the action of doing X includes a conception of how X is to be done. Whether a given act, X, is intentional, depends on whether in performing X the actor could, upon reflection, say, "I did X as I planned," and in that sense, "I did the 'X' I intended to do." This is true of even basic actions like moving one's arm, as contrasted with accidental movements such as having one's arm jolted.

In our account of intentional action, the importance of the contrast between an unplanned doing of something and an intentional doing is paramount. Things that agents do by accident are but one subclass of the larger class of unintentional doings. Other candidates include things that persons do inadvertently, certain habitual behaviors, and instances of so-called occurrent coercion in which a person is physically forced by another to do something. However, the most prevalent and relevant kind of unintentional doing—and the kind that offers the most intuitive and informative contrast to intentional action—is the doing of something by accident.

In a heavily condensed formulation, we can say that intentional action is action *willed in accordance with a plan*, whether the act is wanted or not. Consider the following case of accidental behavior, which is not intentional because it fails to satisfy this condition: A man who intends to follow a physician's prescribed dosage opens a medicine cabinet, takes out a prescription bottle, and devours four pills. By accident, the man takes a fatal overdose. It was not his intention to deviate from doctor's orders and certainly not to kill himself. He did both, but he did not do them intentionally, even though he acted intentionally in devouring four pills.

Many questions remain about the cognitive events or processes that are required for intentional action, as do questions about the conditions under which—both phylogenetically across species and developmentally within species—the kind of mental life necessary for intentional action emerges.[10] Fortunately, such issues about the details of intentional action can be sidestepped here, because the relevant problems can all be handled, for our purposes, under the discussion of the condition of understanding. There is in general a close correspondence between understanding that one is doing "X" and doing "X" intentionally.[11] In Chapter 9 we argue that in informed consent contexts the association between intentionality and understanding is even closer than in many other contexts of autonomous action. This view has led us to be briefer in this volume in our examination of intentionality than in our analysis of the other two conditions of autonomous action (which are examined in Chapters 9 and 10).

Wanting, Willing, and Acting Intentionally. For a theory of informed consent, a central problem about intentionality is whether special kinds of wants or desires are necessary conditions of intentional action. It could be argued that foreseen acts the actor does not want or desire to perform are not intentional. Alvin Goldman uses the following example in an attempt to prove that such actions are unintentional:[12] Imagine that he, Goldman, is taking a driver's test. The desired act is that of convincing the examiner that he is a competent driver. While driving, Goldman comes to an intersection that requires a right turn. He extends his arm to signal for a turn even though he knows it is raining and thus that, in signaling for the turn, his hand will get wet. According to Goldman, his signaling for a turn is an intentional act. It is a means to achieving his goal of convincing the examiner that he is a competent driver. By contrast, his getting a wet hand is a *nonintentional* act, a mere "incidental by-product" of his plan of action. (For this reason, some philosophers prefer to say that it was an event or occurrence, not an act at all.[13])

In our view, getting the hand wet *is* intentional. It is willed in accordance with a plan in the minimal sense of not being accidental, inadvertent, habitual, and the like, and this fact is for us (unlike Goldman) sufficient for saying that it is intentional.[14] There is nothing about the nature of intentional acts, as opposed to accidental occurrences, that rules out aversions or what one desires to avoid. In this case, Goldman's motivation for getting his hand wet may reflect *conflicting* wants and desires, and in the most straightforward sense of "want," Goldman does not want a wet hand; but this does not render the act of getting the hand wet less autonomous.[15] As Reid suggests, it is something the person did with his "conscious will and intention." Goldman could say to his wife that in sticking his arm out the window he did not act intentionally to shrink his shirt, which was an accident, but he cannot say with credibility that it was an accident that his now ruined shirt got wet. In short, causing the shrinking of the shirt was accidental, but not the getting of the shirt wet.

Goldman's analysis raises profound questions about the individuation of actions that we cannot hope to resolve here. Whether anticipated but undesired events such as wet arms obtained in signaling turns should be considered (1) separate acts ("the hand's getting wet" being a separate event from "the signaling for a turn"), (2) different ways of describing the intended act, or (3) simply a consequence of the intended act is a thorny philosophical problem that we will by-pass through our aforestated thesis that what the person does intentionally must have been willed in accordance with a plan, although not necessarily wanted. Let us now explore the claim that an intentional action is an action willed in accordance with a plan, even though it may not be wanted.

Some intentional acts are wanted or desired for their own sake, and not for the sake of something else. For example, a lover of swimming may want to swim for the sake of the experience of swimming and not, as may be the case for another person, for the sake of a tanned or fit body. Let us call wanting something for its own sake *intrinsic* wanting. Other intentional acts are wanted not for their own sake but for the sake of something else. In such cases, the actor believes them to be the means to a goal wanted in the primary sense. Let us call wanting for the sake of something else *instrumental* wanting. Only if at least one of these two forms of wanting is involved would Goldman consider an act intentional.

However, other intentional acts are not wanted in either of these two senses. An actor may view these acts as, *ceteris paribus*, altogether *undesirable* or *unwanted*. They are performed only because they are entailed in the doing of other acts that are wanted. One could say that such acts are foreseen, "wanted acts" in the sense that the actor wants to perform them in the circumstances more than he or she wants not to perform them. But it is better to overthrow the language of wanting altogether and to say, as Hector Castañeda puts it, that they are *tolerated* acts.[16] They are not so undesirable as to cause the actor to choose against performing the desired act that entails them. In such a situation, both kinds of acts—the desired act and the otherwise undesired act—are, as we analyze action, *intentional*. Let us call such intentional actions ones of "tolerating" rather than "wanting."

Consider the following three examples, which illustrate the three forms of intentional action, two forms of wanting and one of tolerating: (1) John has always liked facial scars on men. He particularly likes sharp, jagged scars over the cheekbone, although, as with many aesthetic preferences, John is unable to explain why he likes them. John decides he wants just such a scar on his own face and enlists the services of a plastic surgeon. Here John intrinsically wants the scar; he intentionally consents to *surgery*, and he intentionally consents to being *scarred* by surgery. (2) Harry is involved in a personal injury suit in which he is trying to recover for lacerations to his face and neck suffered in an automobile accident. Harry is counting on the money in the settlement to reduce some outstanding gambling debts; he worries that the scar on his face is healing too well. He decides to enlist the services of a plastic surgeon to freshen the wound to make it jagged and sharp. Here, Harry wants the scar instrumentally; he intentionally consents to *surgery* and he intentionally consents to *being scarred* by surgery. (3) Don has skin cancer on his right cheek. He is eager to have surgery until his physician informs him that, despite use of the best technique, he will be left with a sharp, jagged scar. Don is horrified at the prospect of disfigurement and desperately wants to avoid being scarred. Nevertheless, after becoming convinced that there is no meaningful way that he could consent to surgery but refuse the scarring, and after considering the alternative of refusing surgery, Don intentionally consents to *surgery*, and in so doing he intentionally consents to *being scarred* by surgery. Although his consenting to a facial scar is a tolerating and not a wanting of the scarring, the intentional act of consenting to the scarring is no less Don's *own* act than is his consenting to surgery. Don, then, intentionally consents to being scarred by surgery.

This last sentence has an intuitive ring of oddity. It seems strange to insist that Don intends to be scarred, just as Harry and John intend to be scarred. This oddity has led Goldman, John Searle, and others to interpret intentional action more narrowly than we have.[17] The model of wanting, as we may call it, is the only model that applies to intentional actions for them, so that tolerated actions cannot be intended. By its very presuppositions, such analysis cannot accommodate, *as intentional*, tolerated acts such as getting one's hand wet and consenting to scarring. By contrast, we have interpreted intentional actions more broadly to include any action willed in accordance with a plan, including tolerated as well as wanted acts.

We are thus using a *model of willing* rather than a *model of wanting* to capture the breadth of intentional action. In Don's case, for example, while it may seem odd to say that he intentionally consented to being scarred by surgery, it seems still more odd to say that Don's consent to being scarred was unintentional or was a nonintentional act, as Goldman prefers to say. For those who find both a model of willing and a model of wanting awkward, the following reformulation may prove more appealing: Don intentionally consents to *surgery* that he knows will cause him to have a facial scar. The important matter is that a person's willing acceptance of tolerated outcomes is properly describable as intentional.[18]

Still, there is something unsettling and odd about this conclusion. Don's intention in undergoing surgery does not seem to be that of being scarred; indeed, the scarring is a reason against undergoing the surgery. We seem to be saying that Don intends to be scarred and intends not to be scarred. It seems self-contradictory to say that Don intends to minimize the scarring and at the same time say that he intends the scarring. From the physician's perspective, it appears that the doctor intends to scar Don but will do his best not to scar him, almost as if he intends not to carry out his intention. Can the doctor hope not to do what he intends to do? Can Don?

The way out of these problems is the following: While we do treat "willing" and "intending" as synonymous, it is not our claim that "being willing" is synonymous with "acting intentionally." Acting under the condition of being willing is only one kind of intentional or willed action.

In other cases, one is not merely willing to do something but positively eager to do it. Whether done from a condition of being willing or being eager is irrelevant to its being intentional; the act is intentional in both cases. Thus, "Don intends to be scarred" can be read as "Don is willing to be scarred" in this case; and "Don intends to minimize the scarring" can be read as "Don is eager to see that the scarring be kept to a minimum." Don acts intentionally in authorizing the surgery and intends, quite consistently, both of the above.

Acts that can be described as intentional consents involving acts of toleration are common in informed consent settings. Undesirable consequences or risks of harm that attend particular procedures generally fall into this category. Case law hinges almost entirely on whether disclosures about undesirable outcomes or risks have been made, and, if not, whether they represent tolerable outcomes under the circumstances or whether knowledge of them would have altered the patient's intentions and behavior. Consider, for example, the case of *Bang v. Charles T. Miller Hospital*: Mr. Bang did not intend to consent to sterilization, which was an outcome of prostate surgery, a surgery to which he *did* in fact give his formal, intentional consent.[19] (Under negligence theory the physician-plaintiff would not have prevailed if it could have been demonstrated that sterilization is a *tolerable*—even if undesirable—outcome of prostate surgery, but only if such an outcome would not cause a reasonable person to refuse consent.) If Mr. Bang had consented with an understanding of the inevitability of sterilization, then the infertility would have been a tolerable outcome and his consent to that outcome would have been an intentional act of toleration.

Are There Degrees of Intentional Action? Because our theory of autonomy is based on the concept of degrees of autonomy, the following question might be raised: Are all intentional acts equal in degree of intentionality? That some acts are *more intended* or *more intentional* has an intuitive appeal, yet it is impossible, we believe, to support this intuition by a theory. It is unclear what (if anything) would make actions more or less intentional, although there are two not entirely implausible grounds for explicating the idea of degrees of intentional action. These are *mindfulness of willing* and *correspondence with an action plan*. According to the first—mindfulness of willing—acts are more or less intentional, according to how emphatically the will is at work in expressing them. Less intentional actions are in some degree automatically executed, with little if any cognitive awareness. More intentional actions, by contrast, require what Miller, Galanter, and Pribram call emphatic inner speech, a real "effort of the will."[20] This effort may involve deliberate planning, careful monitoring, perhaps even written notes for the act to be successfully conceived and executed. For example, when a person is first learning to drive a car, every act of learning to control and react requires concentration, deliberation, and active internal awareness. However, once the person has become an accomplished driver, the same acts of steering, engaging the passing lights, and the like can be performed automatically—in effect, mindlessly.

A second possible way of explicating the notion of degrees of intention is through the degree of correspondence between an action and an action plan that prefigures *what* the actor intends to do and *how* he or she intends to do it. The more closely the action corresponds to the action plan, one might argue, the more it can be said that the action the person did perform was the action the person intended to perform. (One can, of course, ditch or modify an action plan in mid-stream, in which case a new action plan is the test model for assessing correspondence.) This degree of correspondence between the action performed and the action plan depends not only on the sheer number of discrepancies from the plan—a quantitative consideration—but also on the importance of each discrepancy—a qualitative consideration. An action can deviate from an action plan in trivial ways that have no significant effect on the action's character, but an action can also deviate from an action plan in major ways, so that the act is almost unrecognizable as the act intended under the action plan.

However intuitively attractive the idea of degrees of intentional action may be, it is a theory to be avoided. Acts are either intentional or non-intentional, not somehow on a continuum. As Jay Wallace has pointed out to us, one can say, perfectly correctly, that actions can be more or less *deliberate* without having to say that they are more or less *intentional*. The extent to which an intentional act is deliberate may well be measured by criteria of consciousness, reflectiveness, and correspondence to an action plan. But even comparatively nondeliberate acts, such as automatically breaking or flipping a light switch, may still be intentional in exactly the same respects as deliberate actions like consenting to surgery. All things considered, then, it seems best to avoid succumbing to the tempting idea of degrees of intentional action.

It is unlikely, in any event, that consents and refusals would fail of substantial autonomy because they fail the two grounds just discussed. Acts that did fail these grounds would also likely fail to satisfy the condition of understanding, a subject to which we now turn.

The Condition of Understanding

An action cannot be autonomous if the actor fails to have an understanding of his or her action. This condition is of special importance for a theory of informed consent. Clinical experience suggests that patients and subjects exhibit wide variability in their understanding of information about diagnoses, procedures, risks, prognoses, and the like. Although some patients and subjects are calm and attentive, others are nervous, anxious, or distracted in ways that affect understanding. The quality of autonomous decisionmaking may therefore differ dramatically, in accordance with how well a person understands.

But what does it mean for a person to understand? There is no consensus answer or approach to this question in philosophy or psychology, where there is a surprisingly brief history of discussion.[21] Some of the great classic works in epistemology, including Locke's *An Essay Concerning Human Understanding* and Hume's *An Enquiry Concerning Human Understanding*, are by title treatises on "the understanding"; but these works are more focused on ideas, belief, perception, mental concepts, processes of knowing, and the like than on the analysis of understanding. "Understanding" primarily refers in these writings to the intellect or to faculties of knowledge and judgment. Although many contributions in past and present epistemology are directly pertinent to the analysis of understanding, we endorse a quip by Arthur Danto: "Think how much we understand in comparison with how dark the concept of understanding remains to this day!"[22]

It is questionable whether in psychology the understanding of understanding is more advanced than in philosophy. The central question in psychology has been *how* people understand or comprehend human communications, with the emphasis on cognitive and neurophysiological processes. Major discussions have, for example, focused on the structures of memory and knowledge involved in word recognition, sentential understanding, and discourse interpretation,[23] as well as on the effect of stress and neuropsychological factors on learning. Work on these and other topics has relied on operational definitions of key terms, in almost total isolation from conceptual and comprehensive experimental treatments of the nature of understanding—although, as we shall see in Chapter 9, some of this work is relevant to problems in informed consent that pertain to the understanding of disclosed information.

Some writers have a ready explanation for why psychology has failed to advance analysis of the concept of understanding. They surmise that this task is primarily philosophical; to refer to a "theory of understanding," without being careful about which *kind* of theory, is to conjure up false expectations and confusions. From their perspective, philosophy is the discipline that provides analysis of the *meanings of terms* such as "understand"; psychology is the field that provides a theory of learning about *how we come to understand*. We reject this dichotomy in our examination of understanding. We do not seek simply an analysis of the word "understand," nor an explanation of how empirically we come to understand. Rather, we treat what it is to understand—the demands that must be satisfied in order for it to be true to say that someone understands something.

The Uses of "Understand." Numerous problems must be faced before any such analysis can be successful. "Understand" is a word with several uses, as the following sentences illustrate: "I understand his motives,"

"I understand English," "I understand that the sun is at the center of the universe," "I understand the history of the period," "I understand the word 'leopard'," "I understand the truths of mysticism," "I understand how to pray," "I understand that you have been faithful," "I understand you completely," and "I understand what you are saying."

In the sentence, "I understand how to pray," "understand" entails "competence," as we analyze that term in Chapter 8. Unlike most of the uses in the sentences in the above list, to understand in this sense is to have a practical competence or know-how, and the word is used to express one's possession of it. This can be called "understanding *how* (to do something)," which is equivalent to knowing how.

By contrast, there is a second use of "understand": Sentences like "I understand that you have been faithful" and "I understand that the sun is at the center of the universe" are straightforward propositional knowledge claims. This can be called "understanding *that* (some proposition is true)." Here the analysis of understanding is reducible to the analysis of knowledge—for example, knowledge as justified true belief (or some variant of this analysis). One form of understanding of relevance to this volume is understanding that "I am being asked to consent to this intervention." This is one kind of "understanding that."

Other acts of understanding have to do with human communications, and this takes us to a third use of "understand." Here one does not have to *believe* information in order to understand it. The sentences "I understand what you are saying" and "I understand you completely" do not imply that one believes that what is said is true, only that one apprehends what has been said. This can be called "understanding *what* (has been asserted)." "Understanding what" is correctly analyzable as "understanding that" if the understanding is *that* "proposition p has been asserted." This fact we can acknowledge, only to set it aside. The important point for our purpose—the analysis of autonomy and informed consent—is that the typical pattern of understanding in informed consent settings is for patients or subjects to come to understand *that* they must consent to or refuse a particular proposal by understanding *what* is communicated in an informational exchange with a professional.

Although this pattern of communication is typical of contexts of informed consent, the full pattern is not essential for understanding. As we shall see in Chapter 8, a consent can be based on substantial understanding quite independent of any professional exchange or disclosure. For both our theory of autonomous action and our theory of informed consent, the kind of understanding at issue is a special case of propositional understanding or "understanding that." Specifically, it is a person's understanding that his or her action is an action of a certain description with consequences of a certain description. Thus, we need an account that can identify the conditions under which a person understands the nature and implications of his or her actions. More colloquially, we need a way of analyzing the question, so frequently asked in both psychiatric and informed consent situations, "Do you understand what you are doing?" This question is usually translatable as, "Do you have justified beliefs about the consequences of what you are doing?"

Understanding One's Action. What does it mean to understand that one is performing a certain act? Thus far, this kind of understanding has been treated in the context of informed consent largely through law and psychiatry, which appeal to criteria governing competence and insanity determinations. Understanding has been given a narrow compass in these fields that is unsuitable for our purposes. On the other hand, the problems confronting any complete analysis of this kind of understanding are vast. In this volume, we offer but a modest proposal by comparison to that vast literature. Our analysis is intended to convey only the distinguishing characteristics of understanding one's action.

Starting with the polar extreme of *full* or *complete* understanding, let us say, as a tentative hypothesis, that a person has such total understanding of an action if the person correctly apprehends all the propositions or statements that correctly describe (1) the nature of the action, and (2) the foreseeable consequences and possible outcomes that might follow as a result of performing and not performing the action. So interpreted, *full* understanding does not amount to *omniscience*, because this criterion demands only *foreseeable* present and future events, not all such events. However, there are two dangers here, both worth careful attention.

First, it might be argued that our definition is *not demanding enough*: In one perfectly reasonable sense of "understand" we do demand omniscience, or at least more than mere foreseeability. For example, if workers exposed to carcinogens in the workplace have no reason to believe that the chemicals they handle are dangerous, and know everything about the chemicals that is known by anyone at the time, then they know the foreseeable consequences and yet do not understand what they are doing to themselves in handling the materials. Similarly, both patients and surgeons who know all there is to know about the consequences of a surgical procedure in light of available information know the foreseeable consequences, but if there are unforeseen, unknowable consequences that would count as entirely compelling reasons not to perform the surgery, then there is an important respect in which patients and surgeons do not understand what they are doing. Our definition is clearly not broad enough to capture this sense of "understand," especially as an account of *full* or *complete* understanding.

Our way of handling this first problem is to set it aside. The restricted sense of "understand" we shall operate with is tied to an *evidentiary standard* of what it is to understand—a justified belief standard rather than a justified *true*-and-*full* belief standard. We shall return to this point momentarily.

Second, the reverse kind of objection might be made against our definition, namely that requiring apprehension of *all* correct and foreseeable descriptions of an action and its possible consequences is *too demanding* a standard, one far too removed from any ordinary or conventional understanding of human actions. A person's apprehension of many descriptions of this sort would make no contribution whatever to the person's understanding of the act, at least not in any sense relevant to the personal or social meaning(s) of the action. For example, most human actions involve bodily movements; act descriptions will be available of chemical and atomic processes attending them. But these descriptions may be entirely irrelevant to understanding the action. Therefore, it seems that in analyzing *full or ideal* understanding, the tentative characterization we have given is too broad.

We accept this second caution and so would reformulate the definition as follows: A person has a *full* or *complete* understanding of an action if there is a fully *adequate* apprehension of all the *relevant* propositions or statements (those that contribute in any way to obtaining an appreciation of the situation) that correctly describe (1) the nature of the action, and (2) the foreseeable consequences and possible outcomes that might follow as a result of performing and not performing the action. To the extent that this ideal is less than satisfied, an action is based on less than *full* understanding, and thus is less than a fully autonomous action.

Several problems attend any attempt to evaluate the extent to which a person's understanding of an action deviates from this ideal of full understanding. First, a list or count of the *number* of relevant act-descriptions the person fails to understand will not necessarily express the actual extent of the person's understanding of his or her action. In our discussion of intentional action we noted that not all discrepancies between action plans and actual actions are of equal importance. This is also true of act-descriptions. Some act-descriptions are irrelevant, trivial, and others vital. Even if a person understands many descriptions of his or her act, the failure to understand just *one* description, if it is important enough, can substantially compromise understanding. For example, in the aforementioned real-life case of Mr. Bang, the adequacy of his understanding of his act of consent apparently turned on a single act-description, namely, that his consent involved a consent to sterilization. In Chapter 9 we propose, as a partial explication of the threshold of substantial understanding, a criterion in the informed consent context for distinguishing relatively important act-descriptions from relatively unimportant ones.

How to make this distinction between trivial and important act-descriptions is only a piece of the larger problem of understanding one's action. Another unsettled problem concerns what it means for someone to apprehend or appreciate an act-description *adequately*, whether it is trivial or important. For example, many patients who consent to major surgery understand that as a consequence of their consent they will suffer postoperative pain. Many "understand" that they will experience the pain, but their projected expectations of the pain may be seriously inadequate.[24] In some situations patients simply cannot, in advance, adequately appreciate the real nature of the pain, just as some of the students in the Zimbardo mock-prison study discussed in Chapter 5 could not have appreciated in advance the actual intensity of the stress that would be involved in the experiment. Even with prior personal experience it is often difficult to appreciate or anticipate the depth of projected stress and pain.

In such situations there is a respect in which patients and subjects *correctly apprehend* the act-description, "If I consent to this procedure, I will have severe pain." But there is also a respect in which their apprehension or understanding of the act-description is *less than correct*; this deficiency occurs to the extent that their conception inadequately reflects what pain, stress, and the like *are*, how they feel, how they take over the person's responses, and so on. This problem is compounded by the inevitable variation in tolerance of pain and stress, both between individuals and within the same individual over time.

Ignorance and False Beliefs. Other problems for our account of what it means to understand one's action are posed by the issue of false beliefs. Consider John Stuart Mill's much discussed example, in which a man wants to cross what he believes to be an *intact* bridge.[25] Unfortunately, this belief in intactness is false. The bridge is out. Assuming the state of the bridge is *foreseeable*, the man's understanding of the action of walking across the bridge is less than complete because it fails to include at least one relevant act-description, namely, that if he attempts to cross the bridge he will fall in the river.

The relationship of demonstrably false beliefs to autonomous action is relatively straightforward. To the extent that a person's understanding of a proposed action is based on false beliefs about that which would otherwise be relevant to an understanding of the action, performance of that action is less than fully autonomous (even if he or she is "responsible" for the false beliefs on which he or she acts). Of course, some false beliefs are more important as descriptions of the action than others, and these must be given more weight in an assessment of their impact on autonomy. We must also take account of the probabilities involved in belief. If a person believes that a medical treatment will be effective in a particular case, it does not turn out to be the case that the person had a false belief about the general efficacy of the treatment merely because it proves to be ineffective in that case. If the person did not understand the inherently probabilistic character of the judgment of effectiveness— believing, for example, that the treatment always works—then the person would have proceeded on a false belief about efficacy. But we would not want to say that no action is autonomous if the actor is surprised by the outcome.

Even a superficial discussion of the roles of true and false propositions as bases of action surpasses our objectives. But we must consider one problem: Little analytic probing is required to show that it is often difficult to provide *evidence* of truth or falsity or to achieve *intersubjective agreement* about the truth or falsity of beliefs, and that these difficulties present major problems for informed consent. Consider the following three act-descriptions: (1) "If I consent to this blood transfusion I will burn in hell." (2) "I know that 50% of the patients with my problem do not survive this type of surgery. I am a fighter, and if I consent to this surgery, I *will* survive." (3) "Nothing good can come of my consenting to this procedure, because no matter what new skills and coping styles I might develop, I will never want to live as a quadriplegic." Each of these beliefs could be central and even decisive for a person's decision to consent to or refuse medical treatment. Yet they may be viewed by others, including those seeking consent, as highly questionable, poorly reasoned, or patently false.

All other things being equal, does the holding of such beliefs diminish understanding and thus autonomy? There is no answer to this question that will be free of heavy qualification. One approach to the probabilities and inherent uncertainties that attend many beliefs is to adopt an *evidential* standard for evaluating the acceptability of a belief statement. Rather than invoking a standard of truth or correctness, this approach asks whether, under the circumstances, the person holding the belief is *justified in believing* that it is true—and therefore, if appropriate, *warranted in asserting* to another *that* it is true. This justified-belief standard captures the common-sense conception of reasonable (even if not true) belief and assertion that underlies ordinary social agreements about what is veridical.

There is, of course, more than one standard of evidence, and significant epistemological problems surround what counts as evidence and therefore as justified belief. All evidence gathering must be done within the context of some theory that governs what counts as the facts or as evidence. No evidence is ever independent of the theory that it presupposes, and two or more theories may put forward competing standards of evidence. Yet the criteria for theory-assessment may themselves be in dispute, and there may be no higher-level rules for assessing the criteria in the competing theories.

A justified belief standard provides little assistance, then, in making judgments about the acceptability of particular beliefs if there is little or no agreement on the criteria for determining the *justifiability* of such beliefs. If the justifiability of a belief or the warrant for its assertion is inherently and unavoidably contestable, there may be no adequate grounds for determining whether a given belief compromises understanding, and whether it prevents the person from acting autonomously. While this is a major problem in epistemology of indisputable relevance to discussions of informed consent, it does not provide a sufficient reason to preclude adoption of a justified belief standard for assessing the quality of a person's *understanding*. This is the standard that we shall hereafter adopt.

Accurate Interpretation and Effective Communication. As noted earlier, understanding one's action—a form of "understanding *that*"—is often heavily dependent in informed consent contexts on "understanding what"—for example, understanding what is being disclosed by a professional seeking consent. If a person claims to understand *that* something, X, is the case, evidence for the truth of X must be shown. But in claiming to understand *what* someone said in asserting the truth of X, one must only show that communication of X has occurred, not that what has been communicated, X, is true. In order to understand in a circumstance of communication, one's formulation or representation of what is said must be substantially *accurate* but not necessarily *believed.* If what is communicated and understood is false, that fact too is irrelevant, because it is irrelevant whether one believes it or is justified in believing it. The only vital condition of understanding here can be stated in two words: *accurate interpretation.* Usually such accurate interpretation occurs in the form of effective communication, which is generally analyzable in terms of having justified beliefs about others' statements and intentions. We shall see when we study understanding in Chapter 9 that in many consent situations effective communication is *without peer as the most important form of understanding.*

"Understanding," explicated as accurate interpretation, resembles some analyses of the German word "Verstehen" (to understand), which has received intense attention in writings on the philosophy of history in discussions of the understanding of the actions and motives of other persons. One understands in this sense if and only if one can penetrate and accurately interpret the past inner functioning of another's mind, reliving the person's experiences and rethinking the person's thoughts by a process of inference. As Patrick Gardiner puts it, the claim is that understanding consists in taking a "psychological X-ray photograph," or reconstructing what must have occurred, just as a master detective reconstructs the moves and motives of a criminal.[26]

Although sometimes excessively elevated in importance in German philosophy, this verstehen theory provides a useful insight. To understand what someone has said is often to establish a *correspondence* between one's interpretation or representation of the statement and what the person meant to say. To the extent that such an assumed correspondence is inaccurate, the hearer does not accurately interpret or understand (what has been said). How to explicate the nature of this correspondence or accurate interpretation has proved elusive, to say the least, eventuating in metaphorical appeals to what it might mean for a language or a mind to "picture" a state of affairs. This problem exceeds the range of our discussion. We can nonetheless take the ideas of correspondence, accurate interpretation, and effective communication to be basic. They should provide an adequate basis for our understanding of understanding here and in the expanded discussion in Chapter 9.

The Condition of Noncontrol

A fundamental condition of personal autonomy is that actions, like the actions of autonomous states, are free of—that is, independent of, not governed by—controls on the person, especially controls presented by others that rob the person of self-directedness. The close connection between this condition and autonomy is semantically obvious in that autonomy, self-governance, and self-determination are all treated in dictionaries as synonymous with independence from control by others. As the third condition of autonomous action in our theory, *noncontrol* has equal standing with intentionality and understanding. However, it differs from these other two conditions by not being measured as a positive presence, but in terms of the negative condition of not being controlled by others. "Noncontrol," then, entails that there are not external controls on the action; this independence from control is its relevance for a theory of autonomous action.

In analyzing the condition of noncontrol, we use *influence* and *resistance* to influence as basic concepts in the analysis. Control is exerted through influences in our analysis, but not all influences are controlling. Many influences are resistible, and some are even trivial in their impact on autonomy. Influences come from many sources, and take many forms: Threats of physical harm, promises of love and affection, economic incentives, reasoned argument, lies, and appeals to emotional weaknesses are all influences. They can vary dramatically in degree of influence actually exerted.

These problems of control are often addressed in the literature on informed consent through the concept of voluntariness, which is sometimes treated as synonymous with autonomy. The role and importance of "voluntariness" for informed consent is emphatic and unconditional in the lead principle of the Nuremberg Code (see pp. 153–158):

> 1. The voluntary consent of the human subject is absolutely essential.
> This means that the person involved should have legal capacity to consent; should be so situated as to be able to exercise free power of choice, without the intervention of any element of force, fraud, deceit, duress, overreaching, or other ulterior form of constraint or coercion. . . .

Literature on informed consent tends to treat acting *voluntarily* (or voluntary action) as synonymous with acting *freely* (or free action). However, caution is in order about these terms, and likewise about the related notions of acting *intentionally* (intentional action) and acting *willfully* (willed action). We use "willing" and "intending" synonymously, in accordance with our previous analysis of acting intentionally.[27] Both should be sharply distinguished from "control" and "noncontrol": Nonintentional actions are not necessarily controlled by the influences of others; and an *act* can be completely noncontrolled by the influences of others and still be nonintentional. For example, if a person accidentally signs the wrong consent form, this is an unintentional act of signing (some prefer to say that it is an act of signing mistakenly), but not necessarily an act controlled by others.

Conversely, if a person's actions are entirely controlled by others, these actions may still be intentional, as when a victim at gunpoint intentionally hands over possessions to a robber. A person coerced by such a threat is obviously controlled; the threat deprives the person of freedom, normal opportunities, and voluntary choice—to invoke some of the more time-honored terminologies. Although the coerced person is deprived of the ability to act *autonomously*, the person is not thereby deprived of the ability to act *intentionally*. That is, the person may respond to the threat with an intentional action, albeit one completely controlled by the influence of another person. We can say, without conceptual confusion, that a person who is entirely controlled in performing an act may nevertheless *act intentionally* in performing it.

In some literatures acting voluntarily and willing or intending are taken as near synonyms, whereas in our theory acting intentionally is distinguished sharply from acting in the absence of controlling influences. The word "voluntariness" is sometimes defined so broadly as to be virtually synonymous with both autonomy and freedom of the person. Joel Feinberg, for example, analyzes voluntariness and voluntary choice in terms of the absence of psychological compulsion, the presence of adequate knowledge, and the absence of external constraints.[28] Were we to adopt Feinberg's analysis, the voluntariness condition would become the parent or generic term for autonomous actions. It would be *the* rather than *a* condition of autonomy. In other treatments, "voluntariness" has been loosely related to ideas about agency, authorship, nonsubjection to authority, privacy, personal command, authenticity, and choice—all commonly associated with autonomy no less than voluntariness.

These many confusing associations surrounding the term "voluntariness" are too much, we believe, to combat successfully through a conceptual analysis that attempts to tidy up its meaning, and hence we avoid the word entirely. We substitute a conception of noncontrol that does not have the history and connotation that burdens the terms "freedom," "voluntariness," and "independence."

The Nature of Control and Noncontrol. We also choose the word "control" because it can be shaped in meaning by an account of the nature of control and influence more readily than can terms such as "constraint," "restraint," "rule," "governance," and other terms that are used to express ways of powerfully affecting behavior. Words like "constrain" and "restrain," for example, imply that force, compulsion, or coercion must be at work, but this analysis is distinct from the one that we shall develop of influence and control. One advantage of coining a new technical term like "noncontrolled" is the relative ease with which it can be defined without obstructive, counterintuitive associations.

What, then, do we mean by the terms "controlled act" and "noncontrolled act"? We can begin to address this question by examining the polar extreme of a *completely* or *fully* noncontrolled act. Such acts have either (1) not been the target of an influence attempt, or (2) if they have been the target of an attempt to influence, it was either not successful or it did not deprive the actor in any way of willing what he or she wishes to do or to believe. Thus, a person can be *influenced* without in any way being *controlled* by the influence agent, because the person acts on the basis of what he or she wills rather than on the basis of subjection to the influence agent's will and ends.

By contrast, completely controlled acts are entirely dominated by the will of another; they subject the actor to serve as the means to the other's ends and in no respect to serve the actor's own ends. Person A's action controls an action X of person B if A gets B to do X through irresistible influences that would work even if B, left to his or her own ends, in no way wanted to do X. If a doctor orders a reluctant patient to take a drug, and coerces the patient to compliance, then the patient is under the will of the doctor and is fully controlled. If, by contrast, a physician merely persuades a patient to take a drug that the patient is at first reluctant to take, then the patient wills to take it and is not under the will of the doctor.

There are many in-between cases: For example, suppose the physician has made it clear that he or she will be upset with the patient if the patient does not take the drug, and the patient is intimidated. Although the patient is not convinced that it is the best course to take the medication, which would not be accepted if the physician merely offered it as an option, the patient agrees to take the drug because it appears that acceptance will foster a better relationship with the doctor than could otherwise prevail. Here the patient performs the action to a significant extent on the basis of what is willed to personal ends, but only under a heavy *measure* of control by the physician's role, authority, and indeed prescription. Unlike the first case, the patient does not find it overwhelmingly difficult to resist the physician's proposal, but, unlike the second case, it is nonetheless awkward and difficult to resist this rather "controlling" physician. The physician's recommendation is not *ir*resistible, simply *difficult* to resist.

From Control to Noncontrol. Not all influences are controlling, and not all that are controlling are *equally* controlling. Some facilitate choice and are welcomed by persons on whom they operate. In our analysis, there are three *main* categories or forms of influence: coercion, manipulation, and persuasion (hence the title of Chapter 10). However, as Figure 2 exhibits, manipulation is the only form of influence that rests on a continuum. Coercion and persuasion are not continuum concepts: Coercion is always controlling, but not by degrees; persuasion is never controlling and involves no degree of noncontrol. Manipulation, by contrast, *is* controlling or noncontrolling and admits of degrees. This analysis involves

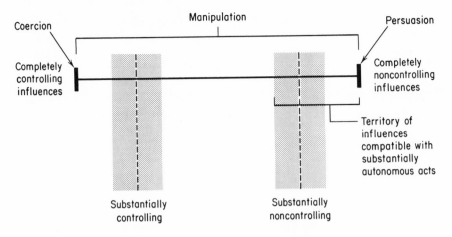

Fig. 2. The continuum of influences from controlling to noncontrolling

some theoretical reform of ordinary conceptions of these notions and so bears further discussion.

Coercion, the most frequently mentioned form of influence in philosophical and legal literature, might be thought to rest in a broad region near one end of the continuum of influences, from influences that wholly control the person to less controlling influences (see Figure 2). But this is an incorrect depiction. Coercive interventions always entirely compromise autonomy by wholly controlling action. At the opposite extreme are forms of noncontrolling influence that do not govern the person, but rather facilitate choice. They can be resisted and it is always up to the person's decision to accept or reject these forms of noncontrolling influence. Persuasion is the most notable example. When persuaded by another, one willingly acts or accepts a belief as one's own. Other forms of influence such as deception, indoctrination, seduction, and the like are forms of manipulation. Some manipulative strategies can be as controlling as coercion or as noncontrolling as persuasion; other manipulations fall somewhere between these endpoints.

This description of a continuum from control to noncontrol that is coextensive with manipulation follows from our earlier discussion of degrees of autonomy. Our primary concern in treating informed consent is with the *extent* to which any form of influence or particular influence renders an action less than substantially noncontrolled and therefore outside the territory of influences compatible with substantially autonomous acts. The dotted lines and shaded areas on Figure 2 represent the ambiguity involved in establishing thresholds for substantial control and noncontrol. There are no definitive criteria for distinguishing with exactitude acts that are substantially noncontrolled from acts that are only slightly more controlled—or for that matter, for distinguishing influences that leave the person substantially noncontrolled from influences that move toward more control.

Distinctions between the three main categories are not sufficiently refined or refinable to permit all influences to be sharply distinguished and classified as either manipulative or persuasive or coercive. We provide definitions of coercion, manipulation, and persuasion that serve to highlight the distinctions between the categories and to permit proper classification of most cases. However, these definitions are not sufficiently rigorous to withstand all counterexamples presenting "hard cases," and we do not systematically defend our definitions against others that have appeared in the philosophical, legal, and social scientific literatures.

Subjective vs. Objective Interpretations of the Basic Categories. Both objective and subjective interpretations of these categories of influence are possible, but our analysis relies predominantly on a subjective interpretation. Individuals are subjectively influenced in different ways, some persons being far more resistant to particular influence attempts than others. What manipulates or coerces one person may not manipulate or coerce another, even if the same manipulation attempt is directed at both equally. *Being manipulated*, then, is an inherently subjective event, one relative to the person's response. However, the terms "manipulation" and "manipulative acts" are often used, correctly, in a nonsubjective sense. In ordinary language, an act directed at a large audience, such as a television advertisement, may be properly described as a manipulation, or as manipulative, even if it succeeds in manipulating only a small portion of those at whom it is directed.[29]

A fanciful example will exhibit what is at stake in choosing between an objective and a subjective analysis: Imagine that a mischievous daughter wants to go on a date with a boy her mother intensely dislikes. The mother refuses permission. The daughter then produces a caged mouse and says, "Either I go out on the date or I will let the mouse loose in the house." Most mothers, let us suppose, would not be much troubled by the mouse, although terribly upset with the daughter. A typical parental reaction would be to seize the caged mouse and assert dominion over the daughter. However, *this* mother, as the daughter well knows, has a severe, psychologically crippling mouse phobia and will yield to any request when faced with the alternative of a mouse about the house. This mother is *coerced* by the daughter's threat into consenting to the giving of permission for the date, even though the average person (or reasonable person, or rational person, or normal person, or most persons) would not be so coerced in the circumstances.

Because the average (or normal, reasonable, etc.) person would find the mouse threat resistible, the daughter's action is not one of coercion on an *objective interpretation* of the category. The notion of "objectivity" is here tied to average (normal, etc.) reactions (see pp. 32–33 for an analysis of "objective" in this sense). If the average (normal, reasonable, etc.) person would be able to resist, then on an objective interpretation no threat is coercive, no matter its effect on any *particular* person. This account is unsatisfactory for our purposes, because the subjective impact on the individual is the decisive matter in determining the extent to which the person's action is autonomous. The mother's giving permission for the date *would be coerced* and therefore nonautonomous on our analysis, even if no one else in the world would be successfully threatened in this circumstance by the presence of an uncloistered mouse.[30]

In Chapter 10 we shall explore further the relevance of this distinction between objective and subjective interpretations, as they impact on our understanding of informed consent.

Definitions of the Three Forms of Influence. Our basic definitions, which will be expanded in Chapter 10, of the major categories of influence may now be stated: *Coercion* occurs if one party intentionally and successfully influences another by presenting a credible threat of unwanted and avoidable harm so severe that the person is unable to resist acting to avoid it. For a threat to be coercive, it is necessary (but not sufficient) either that both parties know that the person making the threat has the power and means to make it good or that the person threatened believes the other party to have the power, a belief of which the other party is aware. The threatened outcome of harm may be of many types: physical, psychological, economic, legal, and so on.

Manipulation is a catch-all category that includes any intentional and successful influence of a person by noncoercively altering the actual choices available to the person or by nonpersuasively altering the person's perceptions of those choices. The essence of manipulation is getting people to do what the manipulator intends by one of these two general means. Some scholars have regarded the absence of manipulation as essential for informed consent. Jeffrie Murphy, for example, holds that the reason for securing informed consent is to respect autonomy, "which means in this context making sure that he [the subject] is not merely *used* or *manipulated.*" He contends that "The information required for informed consent is that level of information which is necessary in order to eliminate or at least radically reduce the possibility of the subject's being *manipulated* by the physician."[31] Murphy discusses only informational manipulation, whereby the structure or perception of choices available to a patient is altered by managing information so that the person does what the physician intends. Although we would deny that informational manipulation exhausts the scope of manipulation, we do agree with Murphy that this form of manipulation is a major problem for informed consent.

Finally, *persuasion* is restricted to influence by appeal to reason. Persuasion is the intentional and successful attempt to induce a person, through appeals to reason, to freely accept—as his or her own—the beliefs, attitudes, values, intentions, or actions advocated by the persuader. Persuasion is always a nonclandestine form of interpersonal influence; the persuader openly puts forward reasons for accepting or adopting what is advocated. All choices made and acts performed on the basis of persuasion are noncontrolled, and, if the other conditions of autonomous action are satisfied, autonomous.

An appeal advanced in a storm of double-talking rhetoric that attempts to induce agreement or consent by making a person confused or disoriented does not qualify as an appeal to reason; it is an attempt to manipulate by altering perceptions through means other than reason. Similarly, manipulation, and not persuasion, occurs if an influence agent creates or otherwise brings about contingencies that subsequently come to function as reasons for another to act as he or she desires. We will expand on these themes in Chapter 10.

Although there is no need for informed consent requirements that would circumscribe persuasion per se, in many contexts in which informed consent is solicited, persuasion is difficult to distinguish from various forms of manipulation. (Similarly, it is often difficult—but also necessary—to distinguish certain more controlling forms of manipulation from coercion, which is always completely controlling.) For example, when information must be presented to patients and subjects, the presentation itself will contain, to varying degrees, nonsubstantive elements like tone, manner and order, word choice, time and setting, and the appearance, style, and character of the presentation agent. These need not be, but could be, potentially manipulative, as can the substantive content of an argument.

In general, it is not possible to specify with precision where persuasion ends and some types of manipulation begin. These concepts are too illformed; and ordinary language, philosophy, and the social sciences all fail to provide exact boundaries. Fortunately, we have no need to stipulate such precise boundaries. More important is to be able to distinguish substantially noncontrolling influences, as distinct from all other forms of influence. People generally choose and act in the face of competing wants, needs, familial interests, legal obligations, persuasive arguments, and the like. Many of these factors are influential without being to any substantial degree controlling. From the perspective of informed consent, we need only establish general criteria for the point at which substantial noncontrol is imperiled. This task too is reserved for Chapter 10.

Is Authenticity a Necessary Condition?

Thus far we have presented three conditions of autonomous action. But are they actually sufficient, and might not some other condition(s) be necessary?

It does not take much ingenuity to imagine cases in which a person acts intentionally, understands what he or she is doing, is not controlled by the influence attempts of others, and yet acts in a manner that seems less than autonomous. Various actions performed under the influence of drugs, serious depression, or psychiatric disorder are obvious candidates. David L. Jackson and Stuart Youngner studied the decisions of patients in an intensive care unit and concluded that little "true autonomy" is to be found in the choices of these patients. They found the patients to suffer from deep ambivalence about treatment, depression, emotionally colored thinking, and hidden psychiatric problems.[32]

Authenticity as Reflective Acceptance

The question these examples place before us is whether our theory of autonomy can account for such cases without adding at least one more condition as necessary for a proper analysis of autonomous action. While we cannot here hope to resolve the "borderline" or "hard" cases, such as those described by Jackson and Youngner, we can at least enhance the plausibility of our theory of autonomous action by considering the leading candidate for position as an additional condition, which is *authenticity*. An authenticity condition would require actions to be consistent with a person's reflectively accepted values and behavior in order to be autonomous. Authenticity in this usage requires that actions faithfully represent the values, attitudes, motivations, and life plans that the individual personally accepts upon due consideration of the way he or she wishes to live.

We noted earlier (p. 237) that an authenticity *model* of autonomy has deeply influenced current thinking about autonomy. This model of autonomy, in one of its garbs, underlies the following description by Ruth Macklin:

> To be autonomous in this sense is to have a "self-legislating will," as Kant described it. The autonomous agent is one who is self-directed, rather than one who obeys the command of others. These descriptions of autonomy all presuppose the existence of an authentic self, a self that can be distinguished from the reigning influences of other persons or alien motives.[33]

The authentic part of the self presumably has unique importance as the repository of the person's reflective preferences, as contrasted with desires and aversions on which one has not reflected or identified with. According to some accounts, unless such reflective values are in place, the actions of the self are not truly one's own; one is not acting as "one's own person." Therefore, only actions motivated by such values can be truly autonomous.

Authenticity is the most important condition in Gerald Dworkin's influential theory of autonomy. For him authenticity need not involve the actual invention or authorship of one's motivation or one's principles; one has only to *accept or identify with* preferences, behavior, motivation, and the like.[34] It makes no difference how one comes to have desires—for example, one might be socialized or conditioned to have them—but only whether on reflection one accepts them, and thus makes them one's own. Desires that are not reflectively accepted are not authentic. For example, a person may have a habit-induced desire to smoke a cigarette, while simultaneously desiring *not* to desire to smoke the cigarette. His desire to smoke is therefore not authentic: "It is the attitude a person takes towards the influences motivating him which determines whether or not they are to be considered 'his'," and therefore to be considered the motives of an autonomous agent.[35]

Now, is a new or substitute condition such as this vision of authenticity needed for the account of autonomous action we have presented? We think not, at least not in this form. Those who defend authenticity as a condition have raised vital points about reflective preferences and about ownership of values, but they also have reached an overly demanding conclusion about autonomous action. If conscious, reflective identification with one's motivation were made a necessary condition of autonomous action, a great many intentional, understood, uncontrolled actions that *are* autonomous in our theory would be rendered *non*autonomous by the authenticity theory.

But, it may be asked, is our presentation and interpretation *fair* to the theories in question, or are we distorting their logic? As a way of answering this question, consider a few everyday actions: actions like stopping at red lights, praying before meals, standing up when the national anthem is played, ordering sandwiches on whole wheat rather than white bread, purchasing instead of stealing goods, and the like. Often the agents involved will have reflected on whether they wish to accept or identify with the complex psychohistorical and sociocultural motivational structures that underlie such actions. Just as often, however, no such reflection or identification will have taken place. In many cases, the actors are unaware of the motivational or conditioning history that underlies and prompts their actions, and have made no reflective identification with the origins of their actions. If so, their actions must be declared not to be authentic, and so nonautonomous on the theory now under investigation.

Even very deliberate actions may fail of authenticity. In choosing to vote for a political candidate, for example, Ms. X may have spent weeks and even months in following a campaign, sorting out the issues, and making careful judgments about the quality of the competing candidates. Let us suppose she has sharpened her grasp of many issues, has reflected diligently over the issues found in televised debates, and has even revised some features in her political philosophy. Yet many of the fundamental values that play a role in her final choice—such as capitalism and fiscal conservatism—may have never been reflectively accepted, remaining in effect uncritical cultural assumptions of which Ms. X is barely aware. It seems both incorrect and unwise to label Ms. X's choice less than substantially autonomous. Ms. X's choice, like the other actions described above, are, in general, intentional, well understood by the actor, and not controlled by the influence attempts of others.[36] Thus, in every ordinary, conventional, and we think acceptable sense they are the actor's *own actions.*

One test, and perhaps the most important test of the adequacy of an analysis of autonomy is how well the analysis would function in the moral life, where it will inescapably be connected to the principle of *respect* for autonomy. The problem with adding authenticity, as interpreted thus far, as a condition of autonomous action is *not* that this condition fails to show any insight into the distinction between persons who readily conform to their culture's patterns and those who live a relatively independent, reflective life; of course such an insight is present. The problem is that an account of autonomous action that follows the conception of these proponents of authenticity would result in morally unacceptable judgments regarding which actions are *worthy of respect as autonomous* and which are not. The "as autonomous" condition on this formulation is essential: We are not suggesting that only autonomous actions are worthy of respect. Our point is that the authenticity condition will considerably narrow the scope of actions protected by a principle of respect *for autonomy* because the range of autonomous actions is severely restricted.

If authenticity were made a necessary condition of autonomous actions, many familiar acts of consenting and refusing would fail to qualify as autonomous, and thus would not qualify for protection from interference by the principle of respect for autonomy. The refusal of blood transfusions, for example, by a Jehovah's Witness who had never reflectively considered whether he wished to identify with the beliefs underlying the refusal would fail to qualify as autonomous, and this person's preferences might then be *validly* overruled because there is no autonomy in them to be respected. Although some protections might be afforded to such a person by appeal to *other* moral principles, such as a general principle of respect for persons or a utilitarian principle, the subtraction of autonomy from such acts of consent and refusal would inevitably lower the status of these acts in the moral life. Moreover, the importance of the principle of respect for autonomy would itself be diminished, because its utility in guiding moral conduct in everyday interactions would be reduced.[37]

To see how an authenticity criterion can be morally perilous if applied in contexts of informed consent, consider Bruce Miller's use of Dworkin's analysis:

> If a refusal of treatment is a free action, but there is reason to believe that it is not authentic or not the result of effective deliberation then the obligation of the physician is to assist the patient to effectively deliberate and reach an authentic decision.[38]

Because Miller is relying on an authenticity account of autonomy, his rule implies that no refusal by a patient that had not been reached by *authentic* values would qualify as autonomous and therefore would not be protected by the principle of respect for autonomy. Although the rule is presumably intended by Miller merely to require physicians to *help* patients reach a point where they can make autonomous decisions, it risks resulting in more physician unwillingness to accept patient refusals than would be morally tolerable.

Possible Reformulations of the Authenticity Condition

But suppose the defender of authenticity shifts ground in retreat to a less ominous criterion that is more narrowly drawn. There are two possible ways to develop such a less demanding criterion. The first is to require as a condition of autonomous action only *stability* or *consistency* in the values underlying choice, rather than *reflective acceptance* of the values. We believe the effect of this revision would still be to render nonautonomous many choices that are worthy of respect as autonomous. True, if a person is acting out of character it would be irresponsible of a professional not to probe for an explanation of the behavior, as it may signal that the person is not acting autonomously. However, people frequently act in ways that represent departures from their "stable" values. Some of these acts are autonomous. The values of such persons can be in transition, or their values can be poorly formed or irrelevant to a particular situation.

Sometimes there is a straightforward desire to act out of character, in order to have a novel experience or for the effect behaving unexpectedly will have on others. At other times, and particularly in informed consent contexts, new and unfamiliar circumstances, problems, and choices may generate apparently or actually anomalous actions that are out of character simply because the surrounding events are unprecedented in the actor's experience. It seems to us morally inappropriate to deny such acts—which can be well informed, intentional, and independent of control by others—protection from interference under the principle of respect for autonomy. In such circumstances, we must be especially careful not to place undue restrictions on what it means for a choice to be *one's own*.

The second—and more promising—way to develop a narrower criterion of authenticity is to require as a condition of autonomous action only *nonrepudiation* in the values underlying choice, not *reflective acceptance* of them.[39] This position is negative rather than positive: Values and motives are authentic if and only if the agent does *not* reflectively repudiate or abjure them. This position has the advantage of meeting our problem about an authenticity condition's rendering most of our ordinary intentional and informed actions nonautonomous and thus not worthy of an important form of respect. On this new condition, unreflected-upon motives and values will be *authentic* unless the agent repudiates those motives or values by consciously judging them inauthentic. Otherwise the person's values and motives stand as authentic.

This new condition is substantive and far from trivial in light of our account because it holds that intentional, noncontrolled, and well understood events that the person reflectively *repudiates* are *not* autonomous. This set of actions would presumably not be large, but would certainly include classic and important cases of "weaknesses of the will"—for example, acts of taking drugs or acts of infidelity where the person repudiates the driving desire or value while nonetheless acting on it.

This seems to us by far the most appealing form of authenticity as a candidate for status as a condition of autonomous action. Certainly there is an intuitive ring of plausibility to the idea that actions from repudiated motives are not performed autonomously. Some of the most intriguing illustrations of the thesis that actions done from repudiated motives are nonautonomous come from clinical examples of phobic and compulsive behavior. In an attempt to capture the struggle experienced by patients who act in ways that harm them although they sincerely desire not to do so, Richard Ferrell and others have analyzed "volitionally disabled" behavior as intentional but "unvoluntary." Consider one of their cases:

> A young woman had a long history of obsessional traits dating to childhood. . . . Eventually she developed a germ phobia which resulted in hand-washing rituals and this culminated in nearly ceaseless hand-washing to the extent that she used several bars of soap per day until the skin on her hands began to break down. . . . She viewed the situation as a disaster and passionately wished it were different but felt powerless to do anything about it.[40]

Many psychiatric and nonpsychiatric cases relevantly resembling this one present a challenge for a theory of autonomy like ours because the acts of handwashing seem to be intentional, noncontrolled, and done with understanding. While the authenticity condition may seem confirmed by such examples, and therefore preferable to ours, if one moves from examples like the compulsive handwasher—whose actions seem definitely to be nonautonomous—to more commonplace examples of repudiated action, the relevance of nonrepudiation for a theory of autonomous action becomes less clear. If a woman repudiates her motivations for being a housewife—which are lack of nerve, fear of failure in the business world, and so on—and yet goes on being a housewife quite intentionally, without being controlled, and with understanding, are the acts or commitment involved in being a housewife *non*autonomous? Again, what should we say about the corporate executive who repudiates her avarice and greed—who tries repeatedly but unsuccessfully to become more spiritual and less material in her desires—but goes on being a corporate executive so as to earn the high salary she wishes she did not want but does want? Are her actions as a corporate executive *nonautonomous*?

There are also problems about allowing a person's values and motives to stand as authentic *unless* repudiated. For example, in the case of the compulsive handwasher described above, what if the woman, instead of repudiating her desires, had never reflectively considered her values and motives at all? Would it not seem odd to describe the motives underlying her compulsive actions as "authentic"? Reaching still further, would her handwashing behavior be *autonomous unless* repudiated? Similar questions can be raised about the heroin addict. Is the heroin addict's drug-related behavior authentic (and autonomous) unless repudiated? One reason why our theory and all theories known to us of authenticity and autonomy will be inadequate to fully handle such cases has to do with the unknowns, on the one hand, of what really is or belongs to the self (here one needs theories of the self and of self-identity), and on the other hand, of the correct explanation of human behavior in terms of its causes and underlying reasons.

This second reformulation of authenicity, then, will not be an easy one to fashion free of problems, and it is far from clear that such a condition is needed for a theory of autonomous action. More promising, we believe, than authenticity (as nonrepudiation) would be a reformulation of our condition of noncontrol to include not only independence from control *by others*, but also independence from control by neurotic compulsions, addictions, and related self-alienating psychiatric disorders. How to fashion such a reformulation awaits numerous answers to the aforementioned unknowns about the nature of the self and need have no bearing on the theory of informed consent to be developed in Chapter 8. Accordingly, we can leave it an open possibility that something like an expanded condition of noncontrol or some nonrepudiation condition *may* be necessary for a theory of autonomous action.

Conclusion

No doubt our theory of autonomy, presented in the brief form of a single chapter, has not adequately expressed the nature and scope of our three conditions and has not come to grips with alternative possibilities. The behavior that accompanies some psychiatric disorders, for example, will not be easy to interpret or to classify by reference to our descriptions of these conditions. We do not deny that our three conditions need further refinement. This refinement we welcome. Indeed, we have already noted our view that no comprehensive theory of autonomous action—for example, one capable of handling the problems posed by multiple personalities, manic depressives, anorexics, heroin addicts, and the like—can be fashioned independent of a satisfactory theory of the self that is capable of distinguishing alien forces on the self from the core self or "real" self.

Fortunately, for our purposes, no further conditions beyond intentionality, understanding, and noncontrol are needed for the analysis of informed consent, the subject of Chapter 8.

Notes

1. Stanley I. Benn, "Freedom, Autonomy, and the Concept of a Person," *Proceedings of the Aristotelian Society* LXXVI (1976): 123f.

2. Benn distinguishes his *ideal* theory of autonomy from *ordinary* capacities of thinking, evaluating, and resisting, which he says belong to the theory of *autarchy* rather than autonomy. Ibid., 124.

3. William C. Thompson, "Psychological Issues in Informed Consent," in President's Commission for the Study of Ethical Problems in Medicine and Biomedical and Behavioral Research, *Making Health Care Decisions* (Washington, D.C.: U.S. Government Printing Office, 1982), Vol. 3, 86.

4. See, for example, the influential statement in Franz J. Ingelfinger, "Informed (But Uneducated) Consent," *New England Journal of Medicine* 287 (August 1972): 465–66.

5. *The Works of Thomas Reid*, ed. Sir William Hamilton, 3rd ed., 2 vols. (Edinburgh: MacLachlan and Stewart, 1852), 2:524–25. Reid is discussing, in part, the conditions under which persons can be held responsible. We shall not address the complicated relationship between intention, autonomy, and responsibility. However, we can say the following: From the fact that a person acts neither intentionally nor autonomously in performing a particular action, it does not follow that the person is *not responsible* for what was done. If a man shoots his beloved wife thinking her shadowy figure that of a burglar, although the man did not intentionally and autonomously shoot his wife, he must bear some responsibility for the killing. Questions of autonomy and intention are best kept separate from those of responsibility, however intimately they are connected at some level.

6. Donald Davidson, "Intending," in his *Essays on Actions and Events* (New York: Oxford University Press, 1980), 83–89.

7. For a basic introduction to the law of intent, see William L. Prosser, *The Law of Torts*, 4th ed. (St. Paul: West Publishing Co., 1971), the classic handbook of torts. The criminal law is even more complicated; see, for example, Charles E. Torcia, *Wharton's Criminal Law*, 14th ed. (1978), Vol. I, 136–40.

8. See, for example, George A. Miller, Eugene Galanter, and Karl Pribram, *Plans and the Structure of Behavior* (New York: Holt, Rinehart, and Winston, 1960); and Alvin I. Goldman, *A Theory of Human Action* (Englewood Cliffs, NJ: Prentice-Hall, 1970).

9. In psychology, integrated knowledge structures, usually called schemas or scripts, are used to describe the initiation and performance of complex action

sequences such as chopping an onion or flying a plane. Schemas and scripts are constructs that represent how individuals organize related information when they are
engaged in such cognitive processes as perception, understanding, memory, or information retrieval. Consider, for example, Donald A. Norman's recently proposed theory of action and schema construction, "Categorization of Action Slips," *Psychological Review* 88 (1981): 1–15. In complex action sequences, detections of slips or
deviations from the plan are sometimes difficult tasks. As Norman puts it, "The task
is non-trivial, for the specification of the intention is at a considerably different level
than are the mechanics of the act." Ibid., 11.

10. See, for example, J.S. Bruner, "The Organization of Action and the Nature of
Adult-Infant Transaction"; V. Reynolds, "Behavior, Action and Act in Relation to
Strategies and Decision-making"; and Peter C. Reynolds, "The Primate Construc-
tional System: The Theory and Description of Instrumental Object Use in Humans
and Chimpanzees," all in Mario von Cranach and Rom Harre, eds., *The Analysis of
Action: Recent Theoretical and Empirical Advances* (Cambridge: Cambridge University Press, 1982), 313–28, 329–42, and 343–86, respectively. See also Charles R.
Gallistel, "Motivation, Intention, and Emotion: Goal Directed Behavior from a Cog-
nitive-Neuroethological Perspective," in Michael Frese and John Sabini, eds., *Goal
Directed Behavior: The Concept of Action in Psychology* (Hillsdale, NJ: Lawrence Erlbaum Associates, 1985), 55–61. For a classic discussion, see Edward C. Tolman, *Pur-
posive Behavior in Animals and Men* (New York: The Century Co., 1932).

11. One can understand that one is doing "X" and still not be doing it intentionally
(when, for example, "X" is done with awareness but by accident), but if one *does*
perform "X" intentionally, one must understand that "X" is what one is doing. However, if "X" = "Y", it does not follow that "Y" was done intentionally. One can intentionally (and with understanding) write a book without understanding that one is writing its publisher's chief commercial failure of the decade. The latter one certainly
does not intend.

12. Goldman, *A Theory of Human Action*, 49–85. It is unintentional because it fails
to satisfy one of the conditions in Goldman's definition of intentional action. Specifically, in Goldman's theory an act is intentional only if the actor believes either that
the act is on the same level as the desired act, or that it will generate the desired act.
In the language of Goldman's theory, his getting his hand wet is a "foreseen but level-
indeterminate" act, not a "foreseen but undesired act."

13. We are avoiding the difficult problem of determining whether something like
Goldman's hand getting wet is an act, intentional or unintentional, rather than a mere
event or effect of another act. We follow John Searle in thinking that we cannot reliably distinguish in many situations between acts, consequences, and events. John R.
Searle, "The Intentionality of Intention and Action," *Cognitive Science* 4 (1980): 65.
Also, just under the surface in all the examples in this section is a dispute in action
theory over the proper description and individuation of actions. For example, the suicide case discussed previously could be approached as a *single act* with multiple,
appropriate descriptions: The act of taking the pills, the act of committing suicide,
and the act of swallowing could all be considered different descriptions of the *same
act*. Alternatively, each of these accounts could be treated as descriptions of *different
acts* that are in some way related—for example, one act could be the means to next.
The "single act, multiple descriptions" position has been ably defended by Donald
Davidson. See, for example, "Actions, Reasons, and Causes," *Journal of Philosophy*
LX (1963): 686 and "The Logical Form of Action Sentences," in Nicholas Rescher,
ed., *The Logic of Decision and Action* (Pittsburgh: University of Pittsburgh Press,
1967), 84. For a vigorous critique of this position, and a defense of the "different
acts" approach, see Goldman, *A Theory of Human Action*, 1–20.

14. We are here assuming what is implicit in the example—that the act of getting one's hand wet was foreseen by Goldman and not inadvertent and that it was not brought about by another agent moving Goldman's hand into the rain. One other possibility—that Goldman's putting his hand out the window was merely the product of habit—is also ruled out by the example. We do not of course, believe our analysis is sufficient to *refute* Goldman's position. A far more substantial argument would be needed to do so.

15. See, for example, Hector-Neri Castañeda, "Intensionality and Identity in Human Action and Philosophical Method," *Nous* 13 (1979): 235–60; Miller, Galanter, and Pribram, *Plans and the Structure of Behavior*, 62–63; William James, *The Principles of Psychology*, Vol. II (New York: H. Holt and Co., 1890), 560–62.

16. Castañeda, "Intensionality and Identity in Human Action and Philosophical Method," 255.

17. Goldman, *A Theory of Human Action*, 49–85; John R. Searle, *Intentionality* (Cambridge: Cambridge University Press, 1983), 79–111. Searle does not use the language of wants, goals, and desires in his analysis of intentional action. Instead, he uses the concept of the "conditions of satisfaction of the intention" to evaluate the intentionality of acts and outcomes; see esp. 103.

18. If the reader prefers the position that tolerated *actions*, as we have called them here, are really tolerated *events*, *outcomes*, or *consequences* rather than acts, we readily concede that the above line of argument can be completely recast using this language. We are not concerned to take a position on this problem of action theory. (See n. 13.) The only conclusion on which we must not yield is our claim that one can intentionally consent to what is knowingly tolerated. It would be incorrect to interpret our examples so that the event of undergoing a disfiguring surgical procedure is not a candidate for being an intentional act of the agent because it is merely something that *happens* to the agent, by contrast to the signaling case, in which the toleration of getting one's hand wet is an alternative way of describing an act that is clearly intentional. In our example the two cases are directly parallel: Don's consenting to the scarring is an alternative way of describing an act that is clearly intentional—Don's act of consenting to surgery that scars.

19. *Bang* v. *Charles T. Miller Hospital*, 251 Minn. 427, 88 N.W. 2d 186 (1958). (This was, in fact, a battery case.) Sterilization is not necessarily an outcome of all prostate surgery, but it was an inevitable outcome of the specific procedure selected by Mr. Bang's surgeon.

20. Miller, Galanter, and Pribram, *Plans and the Structure of Behavior*, 71.

21. Much the same can be said of the law, as well. The *law* of informed consent—and law generally—focuses on knowledge and foreseeability, and never addresses understanding unless a question of competence arises. The law is usually directed not toward the person whose understanding is in question but toward the information-giver, the person in power. Duties to give information are readily enforceable in law, whereas it is considered difficult or impossible—and therefore unfair—to require a physician, or a police officer giving Miranda warnings, or someone procuring a contract, to ensure that the other party actually understands. If understanding is questionable in certain cases, as for example in installment contracts with low-income purchasers, more disclosure is usually required.

22. A.C. Danto, *Analytical Philosophy of Knowledge* (Cambridge: Cambridge University Press, 1968), 152.

23. See, for example, Robert J. Sterberg and Janet S. Powell, "Comprehending Verbal Comprehension," *American Psychologist* 38 (August 1983): 878–93; Richard J. Harris and Gregory E. Monaco, "Psychology of Pragmatic Implication: Information Processing Between the Lines," *Journal of Experimental Psychology: General* 107

(March 1978): 1–22; and G.B. Flores D'Arcais and R.J. Jarvella, eds., *The Process of Language Understanding* (New York: John Wiley & Sons, 1983).

24. See *Dixon* v. *Peters*, No. 8214SC754 N.C. App (filed Sept. 6, 1983) for an illustration of ambiguities in levels or kinds of understanding. In this case, the issue is whether the plaintiff "understood" the risk of scarring in a hair transplant procedure.

25. John Stuart Mill, *On Liberty*, 4th ed., in *Collected Works of John Stuart Mill*, Vol. XVIII (Toronto: University of Toronto Press, 1977), 294–95.

26. Patrick Gardiner, *The Nature of Historical Explanation* (Oxford: Oxford University Press, 1961), 128.

27. This formulation is intended to embrace even the acts of persons who are incapable of acting in accordance with their own desires. Thus, the acts of persons suffering from certain psychiatric illnesses—compulsions, eating disorders, addictions— are, on our account, both *intentional* and *willed* acts. Whether they are nonvoluntary, free, and so on is another matter. The same problem is present for action done under hypnotic suggestion: Mr. S may intend to do X *because of* hypnotic suggestion, and thus he performs an intended action. Compare Richard B. Ferrell, et al., "Volitional Disability and Physician Attitudes Toward Noncompliance," *Journal of Medicine and Philosophy* 9 (1984): 333–51, esp. 340. However, such actions do pose important and as yet unresolved problems for a theory of autonomy, problems we return to in the final pages of this chapter.

28. Joel Feinberg, *Social Philosophy* (Englewood Cliffs, NJ: Prentice-Hall, 1973), esp. 48.

29. The law, in general, requires both *intent to influence* (or its legal equivalent) and that the attempt *succeed* before liability will be imposed for fraudulent misrepresentation, duress, undue influence, and other legal forms of deception and overreaching.

30. The law would recognize the daughter's act as coercive simply because the daughter *knew* that her mother would be so affected. The reason an objective standard is applied is generally because imposing a subjective standard would be unfair: No one can, in general, anticipate who will or will not be *subjectively* influenced. But if actual knowledge is involved, no such problem of fairness arises, and imposing liability is appropriate under the circumstances.

31. Jeffrie G. Murphy, *Retribution, Justice, and Therapy* (Boston: D. Reidel Publishing Co., 1979), 186, 191.

32. David L. Jackson and Stuart Youngner, "Patient Autonomy and 'Death with Dignity': Some Clinical Caveats," *The New England Journal of Medicine* 301 (August 1979): 404–408; and "Commentary: Family Wishes and Patient Autonomy," *Hastings Center Report* 10 (October 1980): 21–22. For a similar thesis, see Mark Siegler, "Critical Illness: The Limits of Autonomy," *Hastings Center Report* 7 (October 1977): 12–15.

33. Ruth Macklin, *Man, Mind, and Morality: The Ethics of Behavior Control* (Englewood Cliffs, NJ: Prentice-Hall, 1982), 57.

34. Dworkin acknowledges that personal choice and decision have much to do with moral autonomy, but he insists that they enter "late in the game," after one has, for example, significant moral obligations that one did not simply invent or choose. See his "Moral Autonomy," in H. Tristram Engelhardt, Jr. and Daniel Callahan, eds., *Morals, Science, and Sociality* (Hastings-on-Hudson, N.Y.: The Hastings Center, 1978), 160–71. See also Robert Young, "Autonomy and Socialization," *Mind* 89 (1980): 576.

35. Gerald Dworkin, "Autonomy and Behavior Control," *Hastings Center Report* 6 (February 1976): 25. Dworkin's analysis was developed independently of, but is sim-

ilar to Harry Frankfurt's well-known treatment of higher-order desires, which is partially motivated by the objective of showing what is distinctive about human persons.
(See n. 39.) The most distinctive capacity of the human species, Frankfurt argues, is
that persons can want to be different from what they are; they can engage in reflective
self-evaluation manifested in higher-order desires. In Dworkin's analysis, any influences on the person not assimilated at the higher level, *as* the person's, are not
authentic, and therefore are not autonomous. Inauthentic influences have never been
made the person's own, no matter how long they have been part of the person or how
comfortable the person is with the desires.

36. Although an action like praying before meals may not currently be controlled
by the influence attempts of others, it is likely that at some earlier point in the person's history of socialization, this action was the subject of influence attempts. This
conditioning history presumably accounts, at least in part, for the person's current
motivational structure, yet the person may never have reflected upon or identified
with the structure.

37. Thus, we reject authenticity, in the form of second-level identification, as a
condition of autonomy, because we believe it is too demanding as a condition of
autonomous action. However, it may not be too demanding as a necessary condition
of autonomous *persons*, particularly in a theory of morally autonomous persons, a matter too involved to be pursued here. Dworkin's emphasis on the authentic *self* is indic-
ative that he is not thinking of choices and actions, but of persons.

38. Bruce Miller, "Autonomy and the Refusal of Life Saving Treatment," *Hastings
Center Report* 11 (August 1981): 22.

39. This idea was brought to our attention through an unpublished paper by Harry
G. Frankfurt, although we are unsure that our formulation accurately reflects his set-
tled views. For his earlier work, see "Freedom of the Will and the Concept of a Per-
son," *Journal of Philosophy* 68 (1971): 5–20, and "Identification and Externality," in
Amelie O. Rorty, ed., *The Identities of Persons* (Berkeley: University of California
Press, 1976), 239–51. See also n. 30 above.

40. Ferrell, et al., "Volitional Disability and Physician Attitudes Toward Noncompliance," 344. Ferrell, et al., provide an analysis of volitional ability and disability
that draws heavily on prior work by Bernard Gert and Timothy Duggan. See Duggan
and Gert, "Voluntary Abilities," *American Philosophical Quarterly* 4 (1967): 127–35,
and "Free Will as the Ability to Will," *Nous* 13 (1979): 197–217.

8

The Concepts of Informed Consent and Competence

Covered by the account of autonomous action in Chapter 7, we now turn to analysis of the concepts of informed consent and competence. We argue that "informed consent" has two distinct senses or general uses. In the first sense, an informed consent is a special kind of autonomous action: an autonomous authorization by a patient or subject. The second sense of "informed consent" is analyzable in terms of rules governing informed consent in public policy and institutional contexts.

The policy dimensions of this second sense of informed consent require that attention also be paid to the concept of competence, especially the competence to consent. Competence is analyzed in later parts of the chapter in terms of criteria of autonomous *persons*, as distinct from autonomous *actions*. Judgments of competence, we argue, primarily serve a gatekeeper function by identifying persons from whom it is appropriate to obtain informed consents.

Two Concepts of Informed Consent

Legal, philosophical, regulatory, medical, and psychological literatures have generally discussed informed consent in terms of its "elements." The following elements have been identified as the concept's analytical components:[1]

1. *Disclosure*
2. *Comprehension*
3. *Voluntariness*
4. *Competence*
5. *Consent*

The fifth element is labeled "consent" in only a few analyses. Some commentators omit it entirely as an element; others prefer to call this element *decision*,[2] and still others prefer to emphasize *shared decisionmak-*

ing or *collaboration*[3] as a substitute for the consent of a patient or subject. Whatever the precise formulation, the fifth element refers to the final stage in the act of giving an informed consent.

Disagreements such as those over the proper label for "consent" are minor, and there is otherwise more agreement than disagreement over the appropriateness of these five elements. Indeed, there may be more consensus on this analysis of informed consent into its elements than on any other topic in the literature on informed consent. These elements are also extensively used in this literature as the conditions in a *definition* of informed consent—or, as some prefer to say, as the conditions in a definition of *valid* consent.[4] According to this mode of definition, X is an informed consent if and only if some of the elements 1–5 above are conditions that are satisfied in the circumstances. Precisely which of the five elements is used varies from theory to theory. Transformation of all five elements into a definition of informed consent yields the following:

Action X is an informed consent by person P to intervention I if and only if:
1. P receives a thorough *disclosure* regarding I,
2. P *comprehends* the disclosure,
3. P acts *voluntarily* in performing X,
4. P is *competent* to perform X, and
5. P *consents* to I.

Although this schema is at first glance an attractive definition of informed consent, and one that is faithful to the uses of the term in such practical contexts as clinical medicine and law, the list of conditions in this analysis is biased by the special concerns of medical convention and malpractice law. Conditions 1–5 are less suitable as conditions in a conceptual analysis or definition of informed consent than as a list of the elements of informed consent as they have emerged in institutional or regulatory settings in which consent requirements appear in policies. This approach to the definition of informed consent also unjustifiably escalates into prominence the special orientations of both medicine and law toward *disclosure* and *responsibility* for patients and subjects.

To take but one instance of the kind of bias at work in this form of definition, the U.S. Supreme Court in *Planned Parenthood of Central Missouri* v. *Danforth* found cause to reflect on the meaning of "informed consent": "One might well wonder . . . what 'informed consent' of a patient is . . . [We] are content to accept, *as the meaning*, the giving of information to the patient as to just what would be done and as to its consequences."[5] This definition is strikingly similar to definitions provided by physicians in the national survey discussed in Chapter 3 (see pp. 98–99), where the focus was also exclusively on disclosure. Yet, this is a profoundly inadequate conception of the general *meaning* of "informed consent," one tainted by an implicit assumption of medical authority and by an unrelieved legal focus on the theory of liability, which delineates not a meaning but a *duty*.

There is nothing about the nature of an informed consent per se that requires disclosure as a necessary condition, and certainly nothing that would *orient* its *meaning* around disclosure. A person otherwise knowledgeable about a proposed intervention—a physician undergoing a procedure, for example—could give a well informed consent without any disclosure whatever.[6] Other conditions in the above list of conditions are not necessary for similar reasons. For example, consider element 4, competence: Some persons who are *legally* incompetent (which is often the referent of element 4) may give informed consents, and in some instances *psychologically* incompetent persons (also often the referent of element 4) may be able to do so. We return to this problem in the final section of this chapter.

The transformation of the above five-fold set of elements into a definition of informed consent thus raises as many problems and confusions as it offers insights. There is no necessary association between these elements and logical conditions. That is, there is no necessary connection between an analytical listing of the hallmark characteristics of informed consent and the logically necessary and sufficient conditions of informed consent that govern its meaning. Neither is there a necessary association between the *logical conditions* of informed consent and *normative requirements* (duties and the like) governing the obtaining of consent, although the two have often been uncritically conflated.[7] To assert that some condition—for example, voluntariness—*must* be present could be either a *normative* claim or could be a purely *logical* (conceptual) claim.[8] Our task in the following pages is the purely logical one of providing a conceptual analysis of informed consent.

Analyzing Informed Consent

What, then, is an informed consent? This question about the logical conditions of informed consent should be approached in the same spirit as the treatment of the logical conditions of autonomous action in Chapter 7. Answering this question is complicated because there are two common, entrenched, and starkly different meanings of "informed consent." That is, the term is analyzable in two profoundly different ways—not because of mere subtle differences of connotation that appear in different contexts, but because two different *conceptions* of informed consent have emerged from the histories traced in Chapters 3 through 6 and are still at work, however unnoticed, in literature on the subject.

In one sense, which we label *sense₁*, "informed consent" is analyzable as a particular kind of action by individual patients and subjects: an autonomous authorization. In the second sense, *sense₂*, informed consent is analyzable in terms of the web of cultural and policy rules and requirements of consent that collectively form the social practice of informed consent in institutional contexts where *groups* of patients and subjects must be treated in accordance with rules, policies, and standard practices. Here, informed consents are not always *autonomous* acts, nor are they always in any meaningful respect *authorizations*.

In analyzing these two concepts—sense₁ and sense₂—we will rely more on our theory of autonomous action (in Chapter 7) and our historical analyses of informed consent (see Chapters 3 through 6) than on either ordinary language subtleties of the term "informed consent" or on beliefs pervasive in society about consent in medical settings. We have already noted how physicians interpreted the term "informed consent" in a recent survey. In that same survey, the responses from a sample of the American public were even more discouraging. When asked "What does the term informed consent mean to you?", one of the most popular answers from the public was that informed consent means that patients agree to treatment by letting the doctor do whatever is "necessary," "best," or "whatever he sees fit." Twenty-one percent of respondents said that they have no understanding of the term.[9] Such responses form an inadequate basis for a conceptual analysis of informed consent as that notion has emerged in modern medicine and research. The settings for the actual practice of obtaining consents also provide an unreliable basis, because the implicit understanding is often that "informed consent" means no more than the empty formality, as health professionals sometimes put it, of "consenting the patient"—that is, obtaining a signature on a consent form.[10]

With these cautions in mind, we can turn to more controlled methods of analyzing these two concepts of informed consent that rely only in part on their historical foundations.

Sense₁: Informed Consent as Autonomous Authorization

Just as choices, consents, and refusals are species of the larger category of *actions*, so informed consents and informed refusals are, in sense₁, species of the larger category of *autonomous* actions. However, it is mistaken to say that informed consent in this sense is *synonymous* with autonomous choice (or action). It is likewise wrong to hold that the conditions of informed consent are identical to the conditions of autonomous choice (or action). An informed consent is a specific kind of autonomous choice (or action), an autonomous authorization by patients or subjects.

Jon Waltz and T.W. Scheuneman, in an influential early article (discussed in Chapter 4), define informed consent in terms of two elements or conditions: "the dual elements of *awareness* and *assent*." They require in addition that there be an "absence of such duress" as would render the assent "inoperative."[11] Their proposal is apparently that informed consent should be analyzed as an uncoerced willingness to undergo a procedure regarding which the patient or subject has adequate information (predominantly, in their analysis, through a disclosure of risks and consequences). On the basis of the information the assent occurs. This analysis is a foray in the right direction. The term "assent" is a synonym for one general meaning of "consent," and "awareness" points to the "informed" component; to assent is to agree with or acquiesce in an opinion or to comply with an arrangement. This strikes close to what occurs in giving an informed consent.

However, the idea of an informed consent suggests that a patient or subject does more than express agreement with, acquiesce in, yield to, or comply with an arrangement or a proposal. He or she actively *authorizes* the proposal in the act of consent.[12] John may *assent* to a treatment plan without authorizing it. The assent may be a mere submission to the doctor's authoritative order, in which case John does not call on his *own* authority in order to give permission, and thus does not authorize the plan. Instead, he acts like a child who submits, yields, or assents to the school principal's spanking and in no way gives permission for or authorizes the spanking. Just as the child merely submits to an authority in a system where the lines of authority are quite clear, so often do patients.

Accordingly, an informed consent in sense$_1$ should be defined as follows: An informed consent is an autonomous action by a subject or a patient that authorizes a professional either to involve the subject in research or to initiate a medical plan for the patient (or both). Following the analysis of *substantial* autonomy in Chapter 7, we can whittle down this definition by saying that an informed consent in sense$_1$ is given if a patient or subject with (1) substantial understanding and (2) in substantial absence of control by others (3) intentionally (4) authorizes a professional (to do I).

It follows analytically from our analysis in Chapter 7 that all substantially autonomous acts satisfy conditions 1–3; but it does not follow from that analysis alone that all such acts satisfy 4. The fourth condition, then, is what distinguishes informed consent as one *kind* of autonomous action. (Note also that the definition restricts the kinds of authorization to medical and research contexts.) A person whose act satisfies conditions 1–3 but who refuses an intervention gives an *informed refusal*. The conditions of this latter kind of action are identical to 1–4 above, except that the fourth condition is the converse, a nonauthorization or refusal to authorize.

The Problem of Shared Decisionmaking. This analysis of informed consent in sense$_1$ is deliberately silent on the question of how the authorizer and the agent(s) being authorized *arrive at an agreement* about the performance of "I." Recent commentators on informed consent in clinical medicine, notably Jay Katz and the President's Commission (see Chapter 3), have tended to equate the idea of informed consent with a model of "shared decisionmaking" between doctor and patient. The President's Commission titles the first chapter of its report on informed consent in the patient-practitioner relationship "Informed Consent as Active, Shared Decision Making," while in Katz's work "the idea of informed consent" and "mutual decisionmaking" are treated as virtually synonymous terms.[13]

There is of course an historical relationship in clinical medicine between medical decisionmaking and informed consent. The emergence of the legal doctrine of informed consent was instrumental in drawing attention to issues of decisionmaking as well as authority in the doctor-patient relationship. Nevertheless, it is a confusion to treat informed consent and shared decisionmaking as anything like *synonymous*. For one thing, informed consent is not restricted to clinical medicine. It is a term that applies equally to biomedical and behavioral research contexts where a model of shared decisionmaking is frequently inappropriate. Even in clinical contexts, the social and psychological dynamics involved in selecting medical interventions should be distinguished from the patient's *authorization*.

In Chapter 9 we endorse Katz's view that effective communication between professional and patient or subject is often instrumental in obtaining informed consents (sense$_1$), but we resist his conviction that the idea of informed consent entails that the patient and physician "share decisionmaking," or "reason together," or reach a consensus about what is in the patient's best interest. This is a manipulation of the concept from a too singular and defined moral perspective on the practice of medicine that is in effect a moral program for changing the practice. Although the patient and physician *may* reach a decision together, they need not. It is the essence of informed consent in sense$_1$ only that the patient or subject *authorizes autonomously*; it is a matter of indifference where or how the proposal being authorized originates.

For example, one might advocate a model of shared decisionmaking for the doctor-patient relationship without simultaneously advocating that every medical procedure requires the consent of patients. Even relationships characterized by an ample slice of shared decisionmaking, mutual trust, and respect would and should permit many decisions about routine and low-risk aspects of the patient's medical treatment to remain the exclusive province of the physician, and thus some decisions are likely always to remain subject exclusively to the physician's authorization. Moreover, in the uncommon situation, a patient could autonomously authorize the physician to make *all* decisions about medical treatment, thus giving his or her informed consent to an arrangement that scarcely resembles the sharing of decisionmaking between doctor and patient.[14]

Authorization. Because authorization is central to our account of informed consent in sense$_1$, it seems appropriate that we provide an analysis of the notion of authorization. Because to do so with thoroughness would require its own volume, our analysis must be brief: In authorizing, one both assumes responsibility for what one has authorized and transfers to another one's authority to implement it. There is no informed consent unless one *understands* these features of the act and *intends* to perform that act. That is, one must understand that one is assuming responsibility and warranting another to proceed.

To say that one assumes responsibility does not quite locate the essence of the matter, however, because a *transfer* of responsibility as well as of authority also occurs. One's authorization gives another both permission to proceed and the responsibility for proceeding. Depending on the social circumstances, X's having authorized Y to do I generally signifies either that X and Y *share* responsibility for the consequences of I or that the responsibility is entirely X's (assuming, of course, that Y executes I in a non-negligent and responsible fashion). Thus, the crucial element in an authorization is that the person who authorizes uses whatever right, power, or control he or she possesses in the situation to endow another with the right to act. In so doing, the authorizer assumes some responsibility for the actions taken by the other person. Here one could either authorize *broadly* so that a person can act in accordance with general guidelines, or *narrowly* so as to authorize only a particular, carefully circumscribed procedure.

Sense₂: Informed Consent as Effective Consent

By contrast to sense₁, sense₂, or *effective* consent, is a policy-oriented sense whose conditions are not derivable solely from analyses of autonomy and authorization, or even from broad notions of respect for autonomy. "Informed consent" in this second sense does not refer to *autonomous* authorization, but to a legally or institutionally *effective* (sometimes misleadingly called *valid*) authorization from a patient or a subject. Such an authorization is "effective" because it has been obtained through procedures that satisfy the rules and requirements defining a specific institutional practice in health care or in research.

We saw in Chapters 3 through 6 that the social and legal practice of requiring professionals to obtain informed consent emerged in institutional contexts, where conformity to operative rules was and still is the sole necessary and sufficient condition of informed consent. Any consent is an informed consent in sense₂ if it satisfies whatever operative rules apply to the practice of informed consent. Sense₂ requirements for informed consent typically do not focus on the autonomy of the act of giving consent (as sense₁ does), but rather on regulating the behavior of the *consent-seeker* and on establishing *procedures and rules* for the context of consent. Such requirements of professional behavior and procedure are obviously more readily monitored and enforced by institutions.

However, because formal institutional rules such as federal regulations and hospital policies govern whether an act of authorizing is effective, a patient or subject can autonomously authorize an intervention, and so give an informed consent in sense$_1$, and yet *not effectively authorize* that intervention in sense$_2$.

Consider the following example. Carol and Martie are nineteen-year-old, identical twins attending the same university. Martie was born with multiple birth defects, and has only one kidney. When both sisters are involved in an automobile accident, Carol is not badly hurt, but her sister is seriously injured. It is quickly determined that Martie desperately needs a kidney transplant. After detailed discussions with the transplant team and with friends, Carol consents to be the donor. There is no question that Carol's authorization of the transplant surgery is substantially autonomous. She is well informed and has long anticipated being in just such a circumstance. She has had ample opportunity over the years to consider what she would do were she faced with such a decision. Unfortunately, Carol's parents, who were in Nepal at the time of the accident, do not approve of her decision. Furious that they were not consulted, they decide to sue the transplant team and the hospital for having performed an unauthorized surgery on their minor daughter. (In this state the legal age to consent to surgical procedures is twenty-one.)

According to our analysis, Carol gave her informed consent in sense$_1$ to the surgery, but she did not give her informed consent in sense$_2$. That is, she autonomously authorized the transplant and thereby gave an informed consent in sense$_1$ but did not give a consent that was effective under the operative legal and institutional policy, which in this case required that the person consenting be a legally authorized agent. Examples of other policies that can define sense$_2$ informed consent (but not sense$_1$) include rules that consent be witnessed by an auditor or that there be a one-day waiting period between solicitation of consent and implementation of the intervention in order for the person's authorization to be effective. Such rules can and do vary, both within the United States by jurisdiction and institution, and across the countries of the world.[15]

Medical and research codes, as well as case law and federal regulations, have developed models of informed consent that are delineated entirely in a sense$_2$ format, although they have sometimes attempted to justify the rules by appeal to something like sense$_1$. For example, disclosure conditions for informed consent are central to the history of "informed consent" in sense$_2$, because disclosure has traditionally been a *necessary* condition of effective informed consent (and sometimes a *sufficient* condition!). The *Salgo* court spoke of a "full disclosure of facts" as "*necessary* to an informed consent," and the U.S. Supreme Court defined "informed consent" *entirely* in terms of disclosure.[16] The legal doctrine of informed consent, as examined in Chapters 2 and 4, is pri-

marily a law of disclosure; satisfaction of disclosure rules virtually con-
sumes "informed consent" in law.[17] This should come as no surprise,
because the legal system needs a generally applicable informed consent
mechanism by which injury and responsibility can be readily and fairly
assessed in court. These disclosure requirements in the legal and regulatory contexts are not conditions of "informed consent" in sense₁;
indeed disclosure may be entirely irrelevant to giving an informed consent in sense₁. If a person has an adequate *understanding* of relevant
information without benefit of a disclosure, then, as we saw earlier, it
makes no difference whether someone *disclosed* that information.

Other sense₂ rules besides those of disclosure have been enforced.
These include rules requiring evidence of adequate comprehension of
information and the aforementioned rules requiring the presence of
auditor witnesses and mandatory waiting periods. Sense₂ informed consent requirements generally take the form of rules focusing on disclosure, comprehension, the minimization of potentially controlling influences, and competence. Examples of such sense₂ requirements can be
found in the Federal Regulations discussed in Chapter 6. The last sub-
section of the 1966 FDA Regulations, for instance, provides the following formal definition of informed consent:

> 'Consent' or 'informed consent' *means* that the person involved has
> legal capacity to give consent, is so situated as to be able to exercise
> free power of choice, and is provided with a *fair* explanation of all
> material information concerning the administration of the investigation
> drug, or his possible use as a control, as to enable him to make an
> understanding decision as to his willingness to receive said investiga-
> tional drug. This latter element *requires* that before the acceptance of
> an affirmative decision by such person the investigator should make
> known to him. . . . [a long list of items to be disclosed follows][18]

This definition was adapted by FDA officials from parts of the Declaration of Helsinki and the Nuremberg Code. The first principle of the
Nuremberg Code requires "voluntary consent," the meaning of which
is explicated as follows:

> This *means* that the person involved should have legal capacity to give
> consent; should be so situated as to be able to exercise free power of
> choice. . . . and should have sufficient knowledge and comprehension
> of the elements of the subject matter involved as to enable him to make
> an understanding and enlightened decision. This latter element
> *requires* that before the acceptance of an affirmative decision by the
> experimental subject there should be made known to him. . . . [a long
> list follows][19]

In the subsequent 1971 "Institutional Guide to DHEW Policy on Protection of Human Subjects"—the "Yellow Book"—the following abbreviated definition is provided:

> Informed consent *is* the agreement obtained from a subject, or from his authorized representative, to the subject's participation in an activity.
>
> The basic elements of informed consent are . . . [a list of six types of *disclosure* to be made follows][20]

The above definitions of the term "informed consent" express the present-day mainstream conception in the federal government of the United States. They are also typical of international documents and state regulations, which all reflect a sense$_2$ orientation. These documents derive from some conviction—perhaps based on a social consensus—about the requirements or practices needed to enable effective authorizations in the special set of circumstances found in institutions dedicated to health care and research.

Although most formal definitions of informed consent in sense$_2$ have been forged from contexts of public policy and law, definitions of informed consent rooted more in moral theory than in law or public policy can also fall into the sense$_2$ class. The following legally-indebted definition—offered by Albert Jonsen, Mark Siegler, and William Winslade and designed for the teaching of medical ethics in medical schools and health care institutions—is illustrative:

> Informed consent is defined as the willing and uncoerced acceptance of a medical intervention by a patient after adequate disclosure by the physician of the nature of the intervention, its risks and benefits, as well as of alternatives with their risks and benefits.[21]

The Relationship Between Sense$_1$ and Sense$_2$

A sense$_1$ "informed consent" can fail to be an informed consent in sense$_2$ by a lack of conformity to applicable rules and requirements. Similarly, an informed consent in sense$_2$ may not be an informed consent in sense$_1$. The rules and requirements that determine sense$_2$ consents need not result in autonomous authorizations at all in order to qualify as informed consents. For example, under a North Carolina statute a signed consent form *constitutes* "valid consent" (informed consent in sense$_2$) so long as a reasonable person would have understood the information in its disclosed form, even if the patient in fact did not understand; moreover, if the patient had not been informed at all, but a reasonable person would have consented *if* informed, then the patient's "uninformed" consent is valid.[22]

Such peculiarities in informed consent law have led Jay Katz to argue that the legal doctrine of "informed consent" bears a "name" that "promises much more than its construction in case law has delivered." He has argued insightfully that the courts have, in effect, imposed a mere duty to warn on physicians, an obligation confined to risk disclosures and statements of proposed interventions. He maintains that "This judicially imposed obligation must be distinguished from the *idea* of informed consent, namely, that patients have a decisive role to play in the medical decisionmaking process. The idea of informed consent, though alluded to also in case law, cannot be implemented, as courts have attempted, by only expanding the disclosure requirements." By their actions and declarations, Katz believes, the courts have made informed consent a "cruel hoax" and have allowed "the idea of informed consent . . . to wither on the vine."[23]

The most plausible interpretation of Katz's contentions is through the sense₁/sense₂ distinction. If a physician obtains a consent under the courts' criteria, then an informed consent (sense₂) has been obtained. But it does not follow that the courts are using the *right* standards, or *sufficiently rigorous* standards in light of a stricter autonomy-based model—or "idea" as Katz puts it—of informed consent (sense₁).[24] If Katz is correct that the courts have made a mockery of informed consent and of its moral justification in respect for autonomy, then of course his criticisms are thoroughly justified. At the same time, it should be recognized that people can proffer legally or institutionally effective authorizations under prevailing rules even if they fall far short of the standards implicit in sense₁.[25]

Sense₁ as a Model for Sense₂. Despite the differences between sense₁ and sense₂, a definition of informed consent need not fall into one or the other class of definitions. It may conform to both. Many definitions of informed consent in policy contexts reflect at least a strong and definite reliance on informed consent in sense₁. Although the conditions of sense₁ are not logically necessary conditions for sense₂, we take it as morally axiomatic that they *ought* to serve—and in fact have served—as the benchmark or model against which the moral adequacy of a definition framed for sense₂ purposes is to be evaluated. This position is, roughly speaking, Katz's position.

A defense of the moral viewpoint that policies governing informed consent in sense₂ *should* be formulated to conform to the standards of informed consent in sense₁ is not hard to express. We have argued in earlier chapters that the goal of informed consent in medical care and in research—that is, the purpose behind the obligation to obtain informed consents—is to enable potential subjects and patients to make autonomous decisions about whether to grant or refuse authorization for medical and research interventions. Accordingly, embedded in the reason for having the social institution of informed consent is the idea that institutional requirements for informed consent in sense₂ *should* be intended to maximize the likelihood that the conditions of informed consent in sense₁ will be satisfied—although we did not claim in Chapters 3 through 6 that historically they *have always* been so intended.

How informed consent in sense₁ might function as a normative standard for informed consent in sense₂ deserves at least brief explication.

First, there is no way to decide rationally that a set of consent requirements in sense$_2$ is morally acceptable only if at least some particular percentage of the authorizations that follow from them—60% or 70% or 80% or 100%—satisfy the conditions of informed consent in sense$_1$. However, a comparative, pragmatic justification can be offered: A set Y of consent requirements in sense$_2$ is morally preferable to any set Z if, all other things being equal, (1) Y results in more informed consents (in sense$_1$) than Z, (2) Y results in fewer "false negatives"—that is, fewer informed consents in sense$_1$ will fail to meet the formal requirements of informed consent in sense$_2$—than Z, and (3) Y results in fewer "false positives" than Z—that is, fewer authorizations that are not substantially autonomous will meet its formal requirements as informed consents in sense$_2$.

Here we need to reintroduce the distinction (discussed at the end of Chapter 6) between requirements that *have* served in institutional and policy contexts and those that *should* be operative in such contexts. Our book is not the appropriate forum for discussing the precision with which the standards in sense$_2$ *should* conform to the conditions of sense$_1$ in order to have a morally adequate standard for sense$_2$, but this moral matter is so vital that it deserves at least brief attention.

A major problem at the policy level, where rules and requirements must be developed and applied in the aggregate, is the following: The obligations imposed to enable patients and subjects to make authorization decisions must be evaluated not only in terms of the demands of a set of abstract conditions of "true" or sense$_1$ informed consent, but also in terms of the impact of imposing such obligations or requirements on various institutions with their concrete concerns and priorities. One must take account of what is fair and reasonable to require of health care professionals and researchers, the effect of alternative consent requirements on efficiency and effectiveness in the delivery of health care and the advancement of science, and—particularly in medical care—the effect of requirements on the welfare of patients. Also relevant are considerations peculiar to the particular social context, such as proof, precedent, or liability theory in case law, or regulatory authority and due process in the development of federal regulations and IRB consent policies.

Moreover, at the sense$_2$ level, one must resolve not only which requirements will define effective consent; one must also settle on the rules stipulating the conditions under which effective consents must be obtained. In some cases, hard decisions must be made about whether requirements of informed consent (in sense$_2$) should be imposed at all, even though informed consent (in sense$_1$) *could* realistically and meaningfully be obtained in the circumstances and could serve as a model for institutional rules. For example, should there be any consent requirements in the cases of minimal risk medical procedures and research activities?

The problem of how to develop a morally acceptable set of requirements for informed consent in sense$_2$ recalls the discussion in Chapter 1 of the need to balance competing moral principles and obligations in implementing policy or institutional rules. This need to balance is not a problem for informed consent in sense$_1$, which is not policy oriented. Thus, it is possible to have a *morally acceptable* set of requirements for informed consent in sense$_2$ that deviates considerably from the conditions of informed consent in sense$_1$. However, the burden of moral proof rests with those who defend such deviations since the primary moral justification of the obligation to obtain informed consent is respect for autonomous action.

Beyond Health Care and Research. One potential objection to our analysis of informed consent—in both sense$_1$ and sense$_2$—is that it is too narrow: Why confine the concept of informed consent to *medical* procedures and *research* projects? A wide variety of consents have nothing to do with medicine or research. All classical contractarian political theories, for example, employ some notion of voluntary and informed consent as the essential basis of the legitimacy or validity of government: The people authorize by their free acts of consent that a government obtain sovereignty. Many commonplace actions also qualify as informed consents. For example, in one wedding ceremony, the bride and groom are explicitly asked to give their "informed consent to marry. . . . " In short, informed consent in this first sense could be applied to autonomously authorizing appliance repairs, withdrawing money from a checking account, hiring an agent, and hundreds of other daily activities.

We do not deny, of course, that the concept of informed consent could be broadened to mean *any* authorization that is substantially autonomous. But we do deny that this is a plausible reading of what the term has meant in any significant document on the subject of informed consent. We noted from the outset that our analysis is to be consonant with the historical development of the concept of informed consent, as presented in Chapters 3 through 6. The meaning that emerges from this history is restricted to research and medical care. For example, in contexts other than medicine and research (contracts and leases, e.g.), where the idea of a consent that is informed has been put to some serious work, the language that is used is almost always something like "express written consent" rather than "informed consent."

Practical Purposes of Sense$_1$. In the remainder of this book we focus on the conditions of informed consent in sense$_1$. However, our objective is not to present an *ideal* model of informed consent. Quite the contrary. In delineating informed consent in sense$_1$ in terms of *substantial* rather than *full* autonomy, as in Chapter 7, we have already rejected the view that it is never possible to obtain "true" informed consents. Many circumstances in medical care and research permit substantially autonomous authorizations, and in many settings they are now obtained.

The conditions of informed consent in sense₁ can be used to serve two practical purposes. First, because informed consent in this sense is an evaluative standard for informed consent in sense₂, a more detailed analysis of sense₁ should make it easier for deliberative bodies such as courts, commissions, hospital ethics committees, professional organizations, and IRBs to assess the moral adequacy of requirements of informed consent in sense₂. Policy makers should be able to determine what existing sense₂ requirements accomplish, how well they accomplish it, and how to implement desirable changes. Second, the conditions elaborated in Chapters 9 and 10 provide a blueprint for situations in which it is appropriate or morally desirable to obtain substantially autonomous authorizations. A better understanding of informed consent in sense₁ is also useful, of course, for those who wish to *exceed* operative policy or legal requirements at the sense₂ level.

In Chapters 9 and 10 we analyze the demands of two conditions of informed consent in sense₁ in order to show what can be done to increase the likelihood that these conditions will be satisfied. We do not consider the problem of *competence* in either chapter. This may appear surprising in the face of the substantial attention and prominence given to standards of competence in informed consent literature. But Chapters 9 and 10 are exclusively about informed consent in sense₁, and competence is not in any conventional respect a sense₁ problem. In sense₁, if a patient's consent is sufficiently autonomous, then it is irrelevant whether the person giving the authorization is competent in the light of some legal policy or psychiatric standard. However, this is not true of informed consent in sense₂, where competence has enjoyed a justifiably central role in specifying *from whom* consent may and must be solicited. One problem is who in the circumstance counts as a legitimate authority for the purpose of consent. Because these issues are frequently treated at the policy level almost exclusively as problems of competence, we turn in conclusion to a brief discussion of competence as it functions in sense₂ requirements.

Competence to Consent: The Gatekeeping Concept

Thus far we have argued that conditions of autonomous action, together with a condition of authorization, define informed consent in sense₁ and that these conditions can and often do serve as the model in terms of which policy requirements of informed consent (in sense₂) are formulated and evaluated. In this section we argue that the characteristics of the autonomous *person* play a similar role for requirements that govern competence to consent.

In legal and policy contexts, reference to *competent* persons is, of course, more common than reference to *autonomous* persons. In these contexts competence functions as a gatekeeping concept for informed consent in sense$_2$. That is, competence judgments function to distinguish persons from whom consent *should* be solicited from those from whom consent need not or should not be solicited. Although the reference is generally to competent persons, judgments regarding from whom consent rightly should be solicited are necessarily normative judgments whose underlying moral rationale is rooted in the concept of autonomous persons. This rationale is as follows: If a person is *autonomous* and situated in a context in which consent is appropriate, it is a prima facie moral principle (derived from the basic principle of respect for autonomy) that informed consent should be sought from the person. By contrast, if a person is *nonautonomous* and situated in a context in which consent is required, it is a prima facie moral principle (*not* derived from the principle of respect for autonomy, but rather from beneficence) that some mechanism for the authorization of procedures or decisions other than obtaining the person's consent should be instituted.

Thus, gatekeeping by allowing autonomous persons—competent persons—to give informed consent and not allowing nonautonomous persons—incompetent persons—to give informed consent is accomplished by an appeal to the moral principle that autonomous persons are *rightfully* the decisionmakers. Gatekeeping of this description is not the only framework for determining who is competent and who incompetent, and therefore who should and should not be solicited to give an informed consent. But classically this perspective *has been* a deeply embedded model governing what we earlier in this chapter called the "element" of competence, as that element appears in treatments of informed consent in policy and legal contexts.

We shall expand on the relationship between autonomous persons and competence as we proceed, but we need first to examine the general concept of competence and its specific application to contexts of informed consent.

The Nature and Degrees of Competence

The special commitments of medicine, law, psychiatry, philosophy, psychology, and other professions have led to competing perspectives on competence that are in many instances incompatible. Some have claimed that there is not and likely never will be a consensus *definition* of competence.[26] This view is short-sighted: A core meaning of the word "competence" ranges over all the many contexts in which it is applied. That meaning is the *ability to perform a task*.[27] By contrast to this invariable *meaning* of "competence," the *criteria* of particular competences do vary across contexts because the criteria are necessarily relative to specific tasks. The set of criteria for someone's being a competent magician is necessarily different from the set of criteria for someone's being a competent baker or a competent animal trainer.

Judgments of incompetence are therefore impossible to understand unless a task is assumed or specified. If X says, "Y is incompetent," an appropriate query is, "Y is incompetent to do what?" To manage legal affairs? To recognize a friend? To remember facts? To decide whether to undergo a medical procedure? The description of persons as *generally* incompetent is not an exception and should not avoid reference to *particular* tasks; rather, this category assumes numerous particular tasks that the generally incompetent person is unable to perform. These tasks are those encompassing the ordinary affairs of life, such as making purchases, authorizing another to act on one's behalf, protecting one's property, and the like. Confusion pervades much of the literature on competence because authors glide uncritically between criteria of *general* competence and criteria of such *specific* task-oriented competences as the competence to decide while in agonizing pain whether to undergo a specific medical procedure that carries a risk of a particular type and degree.

The concept of "specific incompetence" has been invoked in law and policy to reduce the risk that vague generalizations about vague criteria of competence will function to exclude persons who are in fact competent from undertaking the relevant tasks, including giving an informed consent or refusal. It has begun to be appreciated that a person can be incompetent to perform some tasks, while competent at the same time to perform other tasks. For example, some patients are capable of understanding simple low-risk procedures but not technologically complicated high-risk procedures. A person can also lack the relevant abilities and so be incompetent to do something at one point in time, and yet be competent to perform the same task at another point in time. A manic-depressive correctly judged incompetent to consent to or refuse treatment during an acute manic phase might nonetheless be competent at other times. These are clear indications of how a term like "competent to consent" can, without the requisite specificity, seriously mislead.[28]

Competence is further complicated because it is a continuum concept. Persons may be judged more or less competent to the extent they possess a certain level of ability or number of abilities. For example, an experienced surgeon is likely to be more competent to consent to surgery than a frightened young soldier. We can often say not only that a person X is competent to consent, but also that X is *more or less* competent to consent than Y—or even that X is more or less competent to consent to intervention I than X is competent in other areas, or that X is probably more competent to consent to I now than he or she will be at some later time.

Like the continua developed in Chapter 7 to explicate autonomous action, the continuum of competence ranges without discernible breaks from full competence through various levels of partial competence to full incompetence. For practical and policy reasons cut-offs must be stationed on this continuum in order to establish that any person at or below the threshold point lacks a sufficient measure of abilities, and so is to be treated as incompetent,[29] and that everyone on the "competence side" is to be treated as competent. All gatekeeping requirements for informed consent (sense$_2$) function by establishing or presuming thresholds. While it is obviously untrue that all competent individuals are equally competent or all incompetent persons equally incompetent, the function of competence determinations is to sort persons into these two basic classes, and thus to treat persons as *either* competent *or* incompetent.

Naturally, it is often a difficult *evaluative* matter how and where the cut-off distinguishing competence from incompetence should be situated. We shall now explore the various ways in which such judgments are normative.

Normative Functions of the Concept of Competence

If the label "incompetent" is placed on a patient or subject, a train of coercive events is potentially set in motion. The label "competence" commonly functions to denote persons whose consents, refusals, and statements of preference will be accepted as binding, while "incompetence" denotes those who are to be placed under the guidance and control of another. The competent person must be dealt with as his or her own person; that person's will, and not the will of another, must prevail as the source of authorization or refusal. If such a *competent* person cannot make an informed choice merely because of eliminable ignorance, the information required to remove ignorance must be supplied; similarly, if the competent person is in danger of control by the exertion of family pressures, then steps should be taken to ease the family pressures. But in the case of the *incompetent* person, matters are starkly different because information will be provided to a third party authorized to decide on the incompetent's behalf, and the decision will be reached by that party.

Where the cut-off line should be situated on the continuum of ability that divides competence from incompetence is a normative question with several levels. Establishing the *requisite abilities* is a first level of evaluation; then *thresholds for each of those abilities* must be fixed. Still a third normative dimension is present if a *test* of competence is used to determine who passes and who fails. Thus, selection of each of the following three distinguishable components always involves normative judgments:

1. the relevant abilities,
2. a threshold level of the abilities in (1), and
3. an empirical test for (2).

Empirical judgments that a person *is* competent or incompetent cannot be made without such evaluations as their presupposition. That is, it is an empirical question whether someone has the requisite level of abilities, but this question can only be asked and answered if the evaluative dimensions (#1 and #2, at least) have already been fixed and can be presupposed in the empirical search.

The selection of abilities, thresholds, and tests will depend on moral and policy questions closely related to the concerns that shape the selection of requirements for informed consent in sense$_2$. Central issues include the number of moral principles to be balanced and the weight to be given to each principle in different circumstances. In determinations of the competence of patients and subjects, the evaluative tradeoff is usually between two principles—the principle of respect for autonomy, on the one hand, and that of beneficence on the other.

Those who give priority in such evaluations to the medical welfare of patients (under what we have called the beneficence model) over respect for their autonomy will argue for a conservative or stringent set of abilities, thresholds, and tests of competence to consent. By contrast, those committed to the priority of the principle of respect for autonomy (the autonomy model) over that of health and safety will likely argue for a more liberal or less stringent set of standards of competence that will result in more patients and subjects being classified as agents whose authorizations and refusals ought to be honored. Conflicts based on these competing moral commitments should come as no surprise. They are simply one further instance of the clash that can occur between the moral principles of autonomy and beneficence that we have had occasion to point to in virtually every previous chapter.

A wide variety of standards of competence to consent has been suggested in the literature. These tests are strikingly diverse, and some are far more difficult for patients and subjects to qualify under than others. The more demanding tests require a higher level of skill at a defined task (a threshold problem), or an increased number of tasks and skills (a requisite-abilities problem). Some tests require only the simple ability to evidence a preference. Others require abilities to understand information and to appreciate one's situation. Still others make it extremely difficult for many people to qualify as competent to give a consent. For example, a person may be required to (1) show an accurate understanding of a procedure, (2) weigh its risks and benefits, *and* (3) make a prudent decision in the light of such knowledge.[30]

Psychological Competence, Legitimate Authority, and Autonomous Persons

Standards of competence to consent tend to focus on *psychological* skills or capacities, and competence to consent is often placed under the generic category of "psychological competence." Theories of autonomous persons are often expressed in terms of such psychological traits and abilities, namely, the cognitive skills and character traits that define the autonomous person. However, psychological theories and the model of the autonomous person will only take us so far in an analysis of competence to consent. Even if agreement existed as to precisely which psychological properties define the autonomous person, the question of who is competent to give an informed consent would still not be entirely resolved. *Social* criteria of qualification in addition to purely *psychological* criteria are almost invariably involved. Some persons who satisfy threshold psychological conditions of competence to consent will not be considered by society as able to give valid authorizations, either in general or for a specific intervention or action. Usually this restriction is believed justified because these individuals belong to a *class* of persons not permitted by law, policy, or social convention to assume responsibility for the consequences of their decisions (even if *some* class members may possess sufficient psychological abilities).

It would be misleading, of course, to plunge a sharp wedge between the "psychological" and the "social" criteria defining competence to consent. Social criteria assigning responsibility for one's actions are often merely easy and convenient markers for more complex attributes of character. For example, age has conventionally been used as a rough operational measure of maturity, with established thresholds floating from ages 21 to 18 to 16, and sometimes even lower for specific purposes. Here the broadly applicable social criterion of age has replaced a related but more complex set of psychosocial criteria such as maturity, experience, and good judgment. A modern trend of requiring individual assessment of the competence of minors for specific purposes, including consent to some types of health services, is but one of many indicators that support this interpretation.[31]

The requisite social criteria of competence to consent may vary considerably from one community or culture to another. In some tribal societies only village chiefs are believed competent to consent, and in some traditional Eastern societies mentally healthy adults in their twenties and thirties may not be viewed as competent to consent to such events as marriage. Matters are not rigidly fixed in our own society. Willard Gaylin has argued that judgments of a child's *competence* to consent are and should be affected by what is *at stake* for the child. If the risks stemming from a medical intervention are low, whereas the potential gain in health is high, we will and should be less sanguine, he argues, about treating a child's refusal as competent and therefore honoring it. But should the child elect the intervention, we are likely to be, and should be, more generous. In Gaylin's view, this is not an ad hoc maneuver or a sham because competence judgments are connected by their very nature to judgments about experience, maturity, responsibility, *and* welfare.[32] The President's Commission proposed a similar sliding risk-benefit scale, to be applied to adults as well as to children: As an intervention increases the risks *or* the benefits for persons, the level of ability required for a judgment of competence to choose or refuse the intervention should be increased; and as the consequences for wellbeing become less substantial, the level of capacity required for competence should be decreased.[33]

Proposals like that of the President's Commission make it clear that the model of the autonomous person is not the *only* force at work when standards of competence to give an informed consent in sense$_2$ are in question. The welfare of patients and subjects, broad social interests in ensuring good outcomes, and cultural views about responsibility and authority all figure as countervailing forces. But if the role of these forces in forming competence standards for informed consent is challenged, the reference point for criticism and reconstruction is most plausibly the model of the autonomous person. Perhaps nowhere is this conflict more obvious than in the continuing debate about the competence of children to consent to treatment, but here the major underlying problems are usually not about the validity of the standard of the autonomous person but rather about its applicability.

Conclusion

Building on the historical and conceptual foundations in Chapters 1 through 7, we have now provided an answer to the question, "What *is* an informed consent?" Central to an adequate answer is the distinction we have drawn between two concepts, or two senses, of informed consent. Informed consent in sense$_1$ is defined in terms of the conditions of a particular kind of autonomous action: an autonomous authorization. Whether an attempted authorization actually authorizes is determined by whether the act *is* an *autonomous* authorization. By contrast, an informed consent in sense$_2$ is defined in terms of *effective* authorization, where the nature and acceptability of authorizations are established by operative informed consent rules in a particular policy system. These rules or requirements of informed consent in sense$_2$ are developed in institutional contexts in which "gatekeeper" requirements, such as competence standards, are essential.

In examining the similarities and differences between the two senses of "informed consent," we have maintained that in neither sense is the concept merely an abstract ideal disconnected from the real world of informed consent practices. One of the purposes of analyzing sense$_1$ is to assist those who wish to obtain substantially autonomous consents even if there is no obligation to do so under existing sense$_2$ rules. We have noted that the conditions of informed consent in sense$_1$ can function as model standards for fashioning the institutional and policy requirements of sense$_2$. We have also argued that inevitable deviations from sense$_1$ conditions in the establishing of sense$_2$ rules may be morally acceptable, depending on the realities of consent-seeking in sense$_2$ settings. However, because the primary moral justification of the obligation to obtain informed consent is the principle of respect for autonomy, whether a particular set of requirements for informed consent in sense₂ is morally acceptable or morally preferable must depend in large measure on the extent to which it serves to maximize the likelihood that the conditions of informed consent in sense₁ will be satisfied.

In the remaining two chapters we attempt to make the standards of informed consent in sense₁ more workable and more accessible to policy makers and professionals than our analysis has thus far made possible.

Notes

1. Representative sources from a wide variety of disciplines include Robert Levine, "The Nature and Definition of Informed Consent in Various Research Settings," *Appendix: Vol. I, The Belmont Report* (Washington, D.C.: DHEW Publication No. (OS) 78–0013, 1978), (3–1)–(3–91), esp. (3–3)–(3–9); T. Beauchamp and J. Childress, *Principles of Biomedical Ethics*, 2nd ed. (New York: Oxford University Press, 1983), 70; Margaret A. Somerville, as prepared for the Law Reform Commission of Canada, *Consent to Medical Care* (Ottawa: Law Reform Commission, 1979), 11ff, 24; President's Commission for the Study of Ethical Problems in Medicine and Biomedical and Behavioral Research, *Making Health Care Decisions*, Vol. 1, Chapter 1, esp. 38–39; Alan Meisel and Loren Roth, "What We Do and Do Not Know About Informed Consent," *Journal of the American Medical Association* 246 (November 1981): 2473–77; Charles W. Lidz and Alan Meisel, "Informed Consent and the Structure of Medical Care," in President's Commission, *Making Health Care Decisions*, Vol. 2, 317–410, esp. 318; Martha P. Stansfield, "Malpractice: Toward a Viable Disclosure Standard for Informed Consent," *Oklahoma Law Review* 32 (1979): 871–74; and the National Commission for the Protection of Human Subjects of Biomedical and Behavioral Research, *The Belmont Report* (Washington, D.C.: DHEW Publication No. (OS) 78–0012, 1978), 10.

2. Meisel, Roth, and Lidz, in particular. (See n. 1.)

3. Jay Katz and the President's Commission, in particular. (See n. 13.)

4. For the language of *valid* consent, see Charles Culver and Bernard Gert, *Philosophy in Medicine: Conceptual and Ethical Issues in Medicine and Psychiatry* (New York: Oxford University Press, 1982), 42–63; and June Fessenden-Raden and Bernard Gert, *A Philosophical Approach to the Management of Occupational Health Hazards* (Bowling Green, Ohio: Social Philosophy and Policy Center, 1984), Chapter IV, esp. 12.

5. 428 U.S. 52, 67 n.8 (1976). (Italics added.)

6. Some courts have acknowledged that disclosure of information already known to the patient is unnecessary. The 1972 case of *Cobbs* v. *Grant* (502 P.2d 1) is an early example.

7. For an analysis that conflates *definitional conditions* with both *requirements* and *elements*, see Charles W. Lidz, et al., *Informed Consent: A Study of Decisionmaking in Psychiatry* (New York: The Guilford Press, 1984), 3–5.

8. The logical claim about the *concept* of informed consent that voluntariness *must* be present entails that an act could not *be* an act of informed consent unless it was performed voluntarily. From this conceptual claim that voluntariness is a necessary (logical) condition of "informed consent," it is tempting to glide to a *normative*

requirement: Voluntariness must be present in the consent context because not compromising a person's voluntariness is a moral or legal requirement governing the obtaining of informed consents. Informed consent *requirements* could, in this way, be made to correspond to each of the above *elements*; that is, there could be disclosure requirements, comprehension requirements, noninfluence requirements, competence requirements, and the like. These requirements would then be the requirements that must be satisfied for any consent to be *valid*. In this chapter, we provide only a conceptual analysis of informed consent (sense$_1$ and sense$_2$), including an analysis of the demands of the conditions of sense$_1$. We do not address requirements governing what morally and legally must be done in obtaining informed consents sense$_2$.

9. President's Commission, *Making Health Care Decisions*, Vol. 1, 18–19.

10. See Charles W. Lidz and Loren H. Roth, "The Signed Form—Informed Consent?" in Robert F. Boruch, et al., eds., *Solutions to Ethical and Legal Problems in Social Research* (New York: Academic Press, 1983), 145–57.

11. Jon R. Waltz and T.W. Scheuneman, "Informed Consent to Therapy," *Northwestern University Law Review* 64 (1970): 643.

12. Authorization is needed because of the kind of proposal tendered to the person. Typically proposed in informed consent contexts is that a professional do something, or refrain from doing something, that directly and personally affects a patient or subject and that the professional cannot *rightfully*, by reference to the principle of respect for autonomy, do (or not do) on his or her authority alone. Frequently, the proposal cannot with moral sanction be implemented without the patient's or subject's authorization or permission. Thus, mere assent or agreement is insufficient.

13. President's Commission, *Making Health Care Decisions*, Vol. 1, 15 and Jay Katz, *The Silent World of Doctor and Patient* (New York: The Free Press, 1984), 87 and "The Regulation of Human Research—Reflections and Proposals," *Clinical Research* 21 (1973): 785–91. Katz does not provide a sustained analysis of joint or shared decisionmaking, and it is unclear precisely how he would relate this notion to informed consent. At times, Katz links informed consent to individual self-determination and the (implicit) decisionmaking authority of patients (see *The Silent World*, xvii, 85ff, 99, and 102), and at times he mentions the role of authorization; but more frequently the notion of shared authority or decisionmaking serves as virtually the sole criterion. See, for example, *The Silent World*, 86 and 87: "Yet, the idea of informed consent demands joint decision making between physician and patient, a sharing of authority. . . . The idea of informed consent—of mutual decision making—remains severely compromised."

14. Katz holds that the delegation of decisionmaking authority to the physician is compatible with his view of shared decisionmaking. Personal communication, January 1985. As we mentioned in the Preface, it remains an open and essentially normative question what role informed consent *ought* to play in clinical medicine. That is, under what conditions—for what procedures and under what circumstances—ought physicians to be obligated to obtain specific authorizations from patients? It is equally unclear how this important question is to be answered by those who appeal to a model of shared or joint decisionmaking between patient and physician.

15. William Curran studied the differences between European and North American countries and found substantial differences in the practices and policies of what is permitted to count as an informed consent. In general, he found that European policies are more cautious than those in North America. William Curran, "Evolution of Formal Mechanisms for Ethical Review of Clinical Research," in Norman Howard-Jones and Zbigniew Bankowsi, eds., *Medical Experimentation and the Protection of Human Rights* (Geneva: Council for International Organizations of Medical Sciences, 1979), esp. 13.

16. *Salgo* v. *Leland Stanford Jr. University Board of Trustees,* 317 P.2d 170 (1957) (italics added); *Planned Parenthood of Central Missouri* v. *Danforth,* 428 U.S. 52, 67 n.8 (1976).

17. See *Wilkinson* v. *Vesey,* 295 A.2d 676, 685 (1972).

18. *Federal Register* 31 (1966), 11415 (italics added).

19. Nuremberg Trials, *United States* v. *Karl Brandt, Trials of War Criminals Before the Nuremberg Military Tribunals under Control Council Law No. 10* (Military Tribunal I, 1947; Washington, D.C.: U.S. Government Printing Office, 1948–49), Principle 1 (italics added).

20. National Institutes of Health/Public Health Service, "The Institutional Guide to DHEW Policy on Protection of Human Subjects" (Washington, D.C.: DHEW Publication No. (NIH) 72–102, 1971), 7 (italics added).

21. Albert R. Jonsen, Mark Siegler, and William J. Winslade, *Clinical Ethics: A Practical Approach to Ethical Decisions in Clinical Medicine* (New York: Macmillan Publishing Co., 1982), 69.

22. North Carolina General Statutes, Section 90–21.13 (1975), (Cumulative Supplement, 1984). Similar statutes making signed consent forms presumptively valid exist in a number of states.

23. Jay Katz, "Disclosure and Consent," in A. Milunsky and G. Annas, eds., *Genetics and the Law II* (New York: Plenum Press, 1980), 122, 128.

24. We have already noted that Katz's "idea" of informed consent—as the active involvement of patients in the medical decisionmaking process—is different from our sense₁.

24. We have already noted that Katz's "idea" of informed consent—as the active involvement of patients in the medical decisionmaking process—is different from our sense$_1$.

25. Alan Stone provides another instructive example of the need to distinguish sense$_1$ and sense$_2$. He argues that "informed consent is a legal fiction which in reality serves three social policy goals that have no relation to individual autonomy or freedom of choice." This comment is more provocative and misleading than is merited because of Stone's failure to distinguish between sense$_1$ and sense$_2$. Stone apparently means to argue that federal and institutional policies rarely, if ever, are adequate to insure autonomous decisionmaking and are generally motivated by quite different "policy goals." (In Stone's analysis, these goals include banning forms of research, compensating injured patients and subjects, and turning the doctor-patient relationship into a more contractual one.) One can agree with Stone that informed consents in sense$_1$ are rarely obtained and that this is lamentable, while at the same time noting that effective consents in sense$_2$ are *commonly obtained,* however flawed they may be by the standards of sense$_1$. Alan A. Stone, "The History and Future of Litigation in Psychopharmacologic Research and Treatment," in D.M. Gallant and Robert Force, eds., *Legal and Ethical Issues in Human Research and Treatment: Psychopharmacologic Considerations* (New York: SP Medical & Scientific Books, 1978), esp. 32, and also his "Informed Consent: Special Problems for Psychiatry," *Hospital and Community Psychiatry* 60 (1979): 321–27.

26. See Loren Roth, Alan Meisel, and Charles W. Lidz, "Tests of Competency to Consent to Treatment," *American Journal of Psychiatry* 134 (1977): 279–85, esp. 284; and Meisel, "What It Would Mean to be Competent Enough to Consent to or Refuse Participation in Research: A Legal Overview," in Natalie Reatig, ed., *Proceedings of the Workshop on Empirical Research on Informed Consent with Subjects of Uncertain Competence,* (Rockville, MD: National Institute of Mental Health, January 12, 1981), 32–71.

27. Our definition is indebted to Culver and Gert, *Philosophy in Medicine,* Chapter 3.

28. See *Rennie* v. *Klein,* 462 F.Supp. 1131 (D.N.J. 1978).

29. See Daniel Wikler, "Paternalism and the Mildly Retarded," *Philosophy and Public Affairs* 8 (Summer 1979): 377–92, and reissued as "The Bright Man's Burden," in Ruth Macklin and Willard Gaylin, eds., *Mental Retardation and Sterilization* (New York: Plenum Press, 1981), 149–66. Wikler's analysis requires a distinction between a *relativist* conception of competence (people are more or less competent) and a *threshold* conception (people above the threshold are equally competent).

30. See Roth and Meisel, "What We Do and Do Not Know About Informed Consent;" Paul S. Appelbaum and Loren Roth, "Competency to Consent to Research: A Psychiatric Overview," *Archives of General Psychiatry* 39 (August 1982): 951–58; Roth, Meisel, and Lidz, "Tests of Competency to Consent to Treatment;" Ruth Macklin, "Some Problems in Gaining Informed Consent from Psychiatric Patients," *Emory Law Journal* 31 (Spring 1982): 360–68; Paul S. Appelbaum, Stuart A. Mirkin, and Alan L. Bateman, "Empirical Assessment of Competency to Consent to Psychiatric Hospitalization," *American Journal of Psychiatry* 138 (September 1981): 1170–76; Paul S. Appelbaum and Loren H. Roth, "Involuntary Treatment in Medicine and Psychiatry," *American Journal of Psychiatry* 141 (February 1984): 202–205.

31. For a discussion of a broad range of issues on the subject of children and competence to consent, see Gary B. Melton, Gerald P. Koocher, and Michael J. Saks, eds., *Children's Competence to Consent* (New York: Plenum Press, 1983).

32. See Willard Gaylin, "The Competence of Children: No Longer All or None," *Hastings Center Report* 12 (April 1982): 33–38, esp. 35. For similar reasoning with an adult patient, see *Lane* v. *Candura* 376 N.E. 2d 1232 (Mass. App. 1978), and Virginia Abernethy, "Compassion, Control, and Decisions about Competency," *American Journal of Psychiatry* 141 (1984): 53–58, esp. 56.

33. President's Commission, *Making Health Care Decisions*, Vol. 1, 60.

9

Understanding

In Chapter 8, we argued that for an act to be an informed consent (sense$_1$), it must be an authorization that is intentional, substantially non-controlled, and based on substantial understanding. In this chapter the condition of understanding, and indirectly the conditions of intentionality and authorization, are shown to have important implications for the practice of obtaining informed consents. Our objective is to make informed consent in sense$_1$—and not merely in sense$_2$—meaningful to the actual experiences of soliciting and giving consent.

We begin by arguing that the condition of substantial understanding has a special place in the pragmatic context of consent solicitation that makes it more central than the conditions of intentionality and authorization. We then consider criteria of substantial understanding, building on the general analysis of understanding already provided in Chapter 7 (see pp. 248–255). This topic leads to problems about the relationship between criteria of understanding and standards of *disclosure*—the topic under which many matters in this chapter have traditionally been discussed. We conclude with a discussion of ways to increase the likelihood that the understanding condition will be satisfied in the context of consent solicitation.

The purpose of this chapter and the subsequent chapter is *not* to propose legal reforms or generally applicable social policies for consent (sense$_2$ rules or requirements); the purpose is to analyze understanding as a condition of informed consent in sense$_1$ and to suggest strategies for increasing the likelihood that this condition will be satisfied. Many of our proposals are demanding, by comparison to existing law and policy, and some may be judged feasible requirements or policies in a narrow range of consent contexts. However, we believe many of these strategies can and should be broadly implemented. Sense$_1$ informed consents, we maintained in Chapter 8, can be obtained extensively, once the fable of a *fully* informed consent has been demythologized. This lesson has no better application than to the content of the present chapter.

298

Understanding and Authorizing

Central to our arguments is the following thesis: Acts of consenting to medical and research procedures—signing forms, saying "o.k.," and the like—rarely fail to be informed consents in sense$_1$ because they fail to satisfy *only* the condition of intentionality or the condition of authorization. If these conditions are unsatisfied, almost invariably there are problems with satisfying the condition of substantial understanding as well. Conversely, if there are no problems with the condition of substantial noncontrol, the securing of adequate understanding *generally* (not always) turns out to be sufficient to secure sense$_1$ informed consents. The reason is that if the condition of substantial understanding is adequately satisfied, the conditions of intentionality and authorization usually present no problem, because they too have been adequately satisfied.

This connection between understanding and the other conditions is neither logical nor causal. One can produce far-fetched imaginative cases—accidental slips of the tongue in response to a request for consent, e.g.—where the understanding condition is satisfied and intentionality or authorization is not; but such problems virtually never arise in actual informed consent contexts. The central place of understanding is perhaps clearest by comparison to the condition of intentionality. Although it is possible to generate many examples of understanding what one is doing while one is not doing it intentionally (e.g., behavioral accidents, slips of the tongue, and mistakes), as a pragmatic matter this rarely (if ever) occurs when the act in question is the giving or refusing of consent. It is hard to imagine a plausible scenario in which a patient's consent to surgery "x" would be unintentional if the patient adequately understood that what he or she was doing was consenting to surgery "x."[1] The same can be said of the condition of authorization. It is highly unlikely that a person could have a correct understanding that he or she is performing an act of authorization and not, in fact, be authorizing (unless, of course, sense$_2$ rules of authorization were the relevant rules). Thus, as a contingent matter of fact, if a person has an adequate understanding that his or her act Z is an act of consenting, act Z is almost invariably an act of authorization.[2]

Because of this special relationship between understanding and intentionality and authorization, if the understanding condition of informed consent in sense$_1$ has been satisfied, there is good reason to believe an act of consenting to a medical or research procedure is an autonomous authorization (assuming that the substantial noncontrol condition is also satisfied). This explains why we can afford, in this chapter, to focus almost exclusively on understanding: Its proper satisfaction generally evidences satisfaction of three of the four conditions of informed consent (in sense$_1$), and the final of the four is treated in Chapter 10.

Criteria of Substantial Understanding

We must now confront the problem of the criteria of substantial understanding: What does it mean for a person to have a substantial understanding of the act of consenting or refusing? A definitive answer to this
question would require a comprehensive theory or account of the nature
of understanding that surpasses our resources and needs, and our efforts
must thus be far less ambitious. In Chapter 7 (pp. 251–253), we presented a formulation of *full* (or complete) understanding that will suffice
to launch our discussion here: X has a full understanding of X's action if
X apprehends with full adequacy all the relevant propositions or statements that correctly describe (1) the nature of the action, and (2) the
foreseeable consequences and possible outcomes that might follow as a
result of performing and not performing the action. Our task now is to
put this abstract account to work by giving meaning to the criterion of
substantial (as opposed to full) understanding.

Literature on informed consent is noteworthy in that its treatment of
issues of understanding (or, as it is often called, "comprehension") is
almost exclusively preoccupied with the question of how much a person
must understand about a proposed intervention—in particular, how
much about risks, alternatives, and the like. This literature neglects
almost altogether the fact that persons must understand not only *what*
they are authorizing but, more basically, *that* they are authorizing. We
begin by discussing what it means to say that unless a person has a substantial understanding of his or her act as an act of authorization, the act
is not an informed consent (sense$_1$), even if the person has a substantial
understanding of the proposed intervention.

Understanding That One Is Authorizing

A common but mistaken presumption is that patients and subjects generally understand when they "consent" (perhaps an effective informed
consent in sense$_2$) that they are performing acts of authorization. It is a
no less common but mistaken presumption that those who solicit consent, at least in clinical contexts, understand consent as an authorization.
This matter is vital for informed consent in sense$_1$, and, depending on
the context, for sense$_2$ as well. One who failed to understand an act of
authorizing *as* an act of authorizing would not have given an informed
consent, and courts could presumably invalidate a signed consent
because the patient did not appreciate the fact that his or her act was
one of authorizing.

Here we may recall the recent national survey of physicians and members of the general public reviewed in Chapter 3 (pp. 98–99), in which
only a minority of physicians associated informed consent with the
patient's giving permission or authorization. The majority defined

informed consent as informing patients about conditions and treatments, and *not* as patients' authorizing interventions. This interpretation was mirrored in the responses from the general public when asked what the term "informed consent" meant to them. Among the most popular answers were that "informed consent" means that patients agree to treatment by letting the doctor do whatever is "necessary," "best," or "whatever he sees fit."[3] Similar understandings of the act of consenting have been documented in clinical populations. For example, in a study of 200 cancer patients, 28% believed that "if patients are given consent forms they must sign them";[4] and in a survey of 400 new mothers who had consented to genetic screening for their newborns, 12% said they did not understand that they could have refused the screening test.[5]

It is relatively easy to point to cases involving an inadequate understanding of consent as an act of authorization. It is more difficult to be precise about what a person must understand to have a *substantial* understanding of the nature of his or her act as one of authorization. For *full* understanding the person must have a complete understanding of *all* the relevant propositions that correctly describe the nature and implications of the person's action as an authorization, as entailed by the authorization condition of informed consent (in sense$_1$, as described in Chapter 8.)

Under this general requirement, X must understand, at a minimum, that by consenting, X has given a specific agent, Y, express permission to do something, R. In most cases, X must also understand that X's express permission is required for Y to do R.[6] This is the permission-giving and transfer-of-control function of authorization (see pp. 279–280). Finally, X must understand which among the certain and possible consequences of R are X's responsibility (by virtue of X's having consented to R) and which, if any, remain Y's responsibility. As we noted in Chapter 8, these implications for assumption of responsibility may vary; they may result from general operative norms or conventions,[7] or from a negotiated arrangement between the person seeking consent and the person giving it. Whatever the terms, X must understand them.[8]

Depending on the complexity of the situation, an understanding of all propositions relevant to these two elements of authorization—permission giving and division of responsibilities—may be easily obtainable. The requisite understanding may thus be relatively simple and, because there may not be much to understand, there may be little difference between a person's having a *full* understanding of his or her act as an act of authorization and the person's having only a *substantial* understanding.

However, this uncomplicated understanding is less likely to be found in the case of understanding *that which* is being authorized. Medical procedures and research protocols can be highly complex and will generally admit of many more correct and relevant descriptions than will the act of authorization. Here the difference between a criterion of substantial understanding—by contrast to full understanding—is most applicable and most in need of explication.

Understanding What One Is Authorizing

The discussion in Chapter 7 of substantially autonomous action applies directly to analysis of action based on substantial understanding. Substantial understanding is not an immutable concept whose criteria are fixed and knowable with precision. Substantial understanding is merely a rough benchmark on the continuum of understanding between midpoint and full understanding. (See Figure 1 in Chapter 7.) The exact placement of this line is necessarily a matter of judgment, but not just any judgment will suffice.

One key to the analysis of substantial understanding is found in a point already made in Chapter 7. Not all the relevant descriptions of an action are equally important. In Chapter 7, the term "relevant description" was explicated broadly, to include propositions that contribute in any way—even a minor way—to one's apprehension of a situation. The condition of substantial understanding demands apprehension of all the *material* or *important* descriptions—but not all the *relevant* (and certainly not all *possible*) descriptions. Thus, a person could be wholly ignorant of relatively trivial or unimportant but nevertheless relevant propositions about R (or, for that matter, about the nature of authorization) and still give an informed consent (in sense₁) to R. To require understanding of *every* relevant description of R, no matter how trivial, would be to require full understanding, not merely substantial understanding. In Chapter 7 we rejected the criterion of full understanding as too demanding for informed consent and as generally beyond the level of understanding that accompanies most actions, even consequential actions, in ordinary life. Even professionals who make disclosures do not have this depth of understanding.

What distinguishes relatively important descriptions of R from relatively unimportant descriptions? Perhaps the most important general criterion is the extent to which the description is *material to the person's decision* to authorize R. This criterion has a long tradition in the law, where it has been applied in the legal doctrine of informed consent to fashion and evaluate disclosure duties of physicians.[9] As we apply it to informed consent (in sense₁), a person must understand those propositions about R and about authorizing R that are germane to the person's evaluation of whether R is an intervention the person should authorize.

This criterion is entirely *subjective*. In Chapter 7, we argued that both those acts that a person intrinsically or instrumentally wants to perform and those consequences or acts that the person is willing to tolerate are based not only on immediate beliefs and desires, but also on longstanding and long-range goals and values. These uniquely personal attributes are complicated products of personal history and social environment. They deeply affect how the individual evaluates various act descriptions. A description that one person, because of his or her history or values, might consider material to the decision to consent to R might be viewed by another person as entirely immaterial.

"Material description" is, in our usage, identical in meaning to "*important* description," and is distinct from both *relevant* description and *full* understanding. A material description is or would be viewed by the actor as worthy of consideration in the process of deliberation about whether to perform a proposed action. There is no need to demonstrate that, taken either alone or in combination with other propositions, understanding this proposition would *causally* affect the outcome of the person's decision whether to act—that is, would serve as either a necessary or sufficient condition of the decision. Information can be material for a person's deliberation even if it makes no causal difference to the outcome. For example, a patient might want to know whether a major scar would occur from a procedure, although—as it turns out—the person would elect the procedure whether or not it left an ugly scar. Yet the person is still glad to have the information about the scar, and it is certainly material to the person's understanding of what is being authorized. To make causal efficacy a necessary condition of materiality would be far too narrow a conception, despite the somewhat venerable place of this criterion in law. Even were it possible to identify reliably the causally decisive propositions in the decision process, more propositions than the causally necessary or sufficient propositions usually need to be available in order that one or several may turn out to be of causal significance.[10]

Consider a case in which a pregnant woman, Gretchen, faces a high risk of neonatal death if her baby is delivered vaginally. Let us stipulate that, given Gretchen's values and psychohistory, no propositions about the nature or implications of Caesarean section other than propositions about the implications for her baby's life are going to have a causal effect on her decision to consent to a C-section delivery. However, we can further stipulate that Gretchen considers, reflects upon, and deliberates using many other propositions about the proposed C-section in coming to grips with her decision to consent. For example, she ponders the length and placement of the incision, the expected level of post-operative pain and discomfort, the increased risk of Caesarean section in subsequent pregnancies, and the like.

These aspects of the nature and implications of Caesarean delivery are worthy of consideration in the process of deliberation, from Gretchen's perspective. She *values* her *understanding* of them and would be upset to discover, after the fact, that she had consented to the C-section in ignorance of them—even though she would not claim that her understanding, or failure to understand, these facts would have caused her to change her mind or have streamlined the decision process. Thus, Gretchen views these propositions about C-section delivery as *material* to her decision, although not causally relevant or decisive. Her viewing of them as material *makes* them material. Moreover, Gretchen can draw a sharp distinction between these propositions and other sorts of considerations that she views as immaterial to her decision—for example, the type of sutures to be used or the numbers of layers of fat and muscle to be incised. Note that these are nevertheless *relevant* propositions about C-sections for an understanding of C-sections, although they are not *material* to Gretchen.

Gretchen's evaluations of the materiality of different propositions about C-section delivery are not intrinsic to the nature of such surgery. They are rooted in Gretchen's values, needs, and interests. Other women facing the same decision might hold a completely different set of propositions to be material, even if they, like Gretchen, would not be causally affected by any propositions except those about the impact on neonatal outcomes, and even if many propositions relevant to an understanding of the procedure and outcome were not for them material.

Consider another pregnant woman, Margaret, in the same situation as Gretchen. Margaret is an olympic-class marathon race walker. Throughout her pregnancy, Margaret has continued to walk about 10 miles per day, although her pace necessarily slowed as her pregnancy progressed. For several months, Margaret has been looking forward to a national race, to be held a month after her due date. Although Margaret has no illusions about a good finish—she expects to be in less than top condition because of her pregnancy—she has eagerly anticipated her participation. Margaret would consider the proposition that a C-section would compromise her ability to participate in a walking race, one month postpartum, as definitely material to her deliberations. By contrast, Gretchen might consider the effects of C-section on race walking to be as immaterial to her decision as the color of her obstetrician's eyes.

Margaret and Gretchen share the view that certain aspects of authorizing a C-section that are not causally relevant to their decisions are nevertheless worthy of consideration and should be understood. Other women may view as material only those propositions that have a direct causal effect on their decisions. Our point is not that a set of material propositions cannot be identical with the set of causally necessary propositions, but merely that they need not be; and neither set need be identical with the set of relevant propositions. Subjective, personal assessment rather than causal outcome is the appropriate criterion of materiality. We shall argue later that this subjective criterion of materiality is the most important, but not the only, criterion for substantial understanding and for informed consent in sense$_1$.

Standards of Understanding and Disclosure

Thus far, our discussion has focused on the kinds of understanding required for informed consent (in sense$_1$), without regard for how this understanding is to be acquired. So long as the understanding is substantial, it makes no difference whether this understanding is self-taught, reflects prior experiences and history, is derived from a videotape, or finds its inspiration in divine revelation. Of course, the reality of informed consent in clinical medicine and research is that a patient or subject cannot usually achieve substantial understanding without the aid of the professional(s) seeking consent. If the patient or subject knows little about the intervention, the most efficient—and, often, the only— way for the person to achieve an adequate understanding of the intervention is to have the professional disclose information.

As we noted in Chapters 2 and 4, the topic of appropriate standards for professional disclosure has generated more commentary and controversy than any other issue about informed consent. In the remainder of Chapter 9, we reformulate this problem: Our question is not the traditional one, "What should professionals be obligated to disclose to subjects and patients when soliciting consent?" Instead, remodel the problem as follows: If patients and subjects are ignorant or inexperienced, what can professionals do to facilitate obtaining informed consents based on substantial understanding? That is, how can professionals *enable* patients and subjects to make informed autonomous choices?

In the discussion that follows, we concentrate first on classic problems defining the scope of professional disclosures. In subsequent sections, we consider factors that influence the effectiveness of information exchanges between those seeking and those giving consent.

The Inadequacy of Conventional Disclosure Standards

A starting point for promoting substantial understanding is to reject the two operative disclosure standards in informed consent law (see Chapter 2). The professional practice standard and the reasonable person standard may both be appropriate for a legal doctrine of informed consent (in sense$_2$), and even for an institutional policy (in some sense$_2$ form), but these standards will contribute little to consent practices if the goal is the obtaining of informed consents in sense$_1$.[11]

The reasons for this claim are uncomplicated: Under the professional practice standard, disclosure is determined by the customary rules or traditional practices of the relevant professional community. What professionals customarily disclose may fail to include some or even all of the information that patients or subjects would find material to their consent decisions. In contrast to this standard, the "materiality" of a piece of information in the reasonable person standard is central to the question of whether it must be disclosed. However, materiality is determined by reference to a hypothetical "objective" reasonable person, without regard to the interests, values, or concerns of the particular patient or subject in question. Thus, again, the disclosed information may fail to contain some or all of the information material to the person from whom consent is being sought.

The third disclosure standard introduced in Chapter 1—the subjective standard—is the most adequate of the three legal standards from the perspective of informed consent in sense$_1$.[12] Disclosure duties in the subjective standard are not judged by reference to the informational needs of the "community" or "objective" reasonable person, but by reference to the specific informational needs of the individual patient or subject.[13] In the discussion that follows we draw heavily on the ideals established by the subjective standard, without making any claim whatever about the adequacy of *legal* standards *qua* legal. However, we caution that even appropriate use of the subjective standard of *disclosure* is not by itself likely to lead to satisfaction of the condition of substantial *understanding*, for reasons we will now detail.

From Disclosure to Communication: A Subjective Standard of Understanding

What should a professional disclose in order to obtain consents based on substantial understanding? At first glance it might appear that any attempt is doomed to failure. On the one hand, because there are no intersubjective criteria for distinguishing material from immaterial information, any stock disclosure—such as might appear on a mimeographed list of "what all patients need"—is inappropriate. Yet if the subjective standard is adopted, it is often difficult, if not impossible, for a physician or a researcher to guess correctly what would be material to a prospective patient or subject, especially a complete stranger.

If the professional cannot discern what information would be material to whom, one path would be to try to disclose everything. This strategy would entail disclosing to all prospective patients or subjects every *relevant* (not merely *material*) proposition about the proposed act of consenting to R that the professional can identify, in the hopes of satisfying most, if not all, of everyone's informational needs and interests. However, as a practical matter, this strategy fails feasibility and is not desirable even from the patient's point of view. Professionals would have to make inordinately lengthy, and in large measure useless, disclosures in order to describe medical and research procedures in terms of all conceivably relevant characteristics, implications, risks, and consequences. Moreover, no matter how comprehensive the disclosure, there is no guarantee that everyone's interests and needs will be served. Finally, as we shall discuss later in this chapter, because of certain problems with information overload, overdisclosure is as likely under most circumstances to lead to inadequate understanding as is underdisclosure.

Given these problems, are there practical and realistic guides for structuring professional disclosures of relevance to informed consent (in sense₁)? The answer is affirmative; but the solution lies not in reformulations of conventional or proposed legal disclosure standards, but rather in the adoption of a different approach to understanding and informed consent—an approach that focuses more broadly on issues of communication, while dispensing with abstract and disembodied issues about proper *standards* of disclosure. Disclosure is the lawyer's entre to the world of informed consent; but it is a back-fence gate to that world, and a narrow one at that.

From the perspective of informed consent (in sense₁), disclosure standards requiring a specified quantum of information are not only insufficient, but present an entirely misleading approach to the issues. Such disclosure standards are not adequate to protect autonomous decision-making, because the emphasis on disclosure is the wrong emphasis. The central question is not merely, "What facts should the professional provide?" but "What should the professional ask and say?" and, as we shall see shortly, "How should the professional act?" Traditional questions about adequate disclosures need to be reformulated as questions about effective communication (see Chapter 7, p. 255). This entails use of a subjective standard of understanding.

The key to effective communication is to invite active participation by patients or subjects in the context of an informational exchange. Ordinarily, the professional soliciting consent has but a narrow window from which to view the values and informational needs of others. Professionals would do well to end their traditional preoccupation with disclosure and instead ask questions, elicit the concerns and interests of the patient or subject, and establish a climate that encourages the patient or subject to ask questions. This is the most promising course to ensure that the patient or subject will receive information that is personally material— that is, the kind of description that will permit the subject or patient, on the basis of his or her personal values, desires, and beliefs, to act with substantial autonomy.

Core Disclosures and Shared Understanding: An Objective Standard

This subjective approach to substantial understanding does not altogether obviate the traditional idea of professional "disclosure." In the absence of a disclosure initiated by the professional, how could patients or subjects, who often know virtually nothing about the object of choice, begin to formulate their concerns, let alone ask meaningful questions?

Moreover, how can there be shared understanding between the parties if the professional seeking consent never puts forward what he or she views as important, but is instead only responding to questions initiated by the patient or subject? The professional's own perspective, opinions, and recommendations are often essential for the patient's or subject's deliberation, as well as for mutual understanding. Even if not essential, they are almost always highly valued and material.

Professionals should disclose to those from whom they seek consent some core set of facts or propositions akin to the disclosures currently required by courts and regulations that stipulate specific kinds of disclosures. From the perspective of informed consent in sense$_1$, "core disclosures" are guided by three considerations: (1) those facts or descriptions that patients or subjects usually consider material in deciding whether to refuse or consent to the proposed intervention or research, (2) what the professional believes to be material about the proposed intervention or research, including the professional's recommendation, if there is one, and the reasons why the patient or subject should take the professional's advice, and (3) what needs to be said to establish the purpose of seeking consent and the nature and implications of consent as an act of authorization.[14] In many cases, the content for disclosure specific to (1) and (2) will overlap. This overlap is to be expected; the professional will be interpreting consideration (1), and it is natural for the professional to think that patients or subjects will consider material many of those items considered material by the professional. By contrast, (3) will generally identify different information for disclosure (of the sort discussed on pp. 300–302).[15]

Although we support continuation of the tradition of core disclosures by professionals, from the perspective of informed consent in sense$_1$, the content of this disclosure and its relative role in the consent process must depart significantly from conventional disclosure practices. Such a core disclosure should only serve to *initiate* the communication process necessary for substantial understanding. The communication should not stop at this point and should not flow only unilaterally if there is to be informed consent in sense$_1$. Specific and clear statements should make explicit the professional's willingness to engage in a two-way discussion.

The Idea of Sharing an Understanding. If properly structured, core disclosures can initiate the dialogue necessary for substantial understanding. Without a core disclosure, a completely individualized approach, such as that proposed by the subjective standard for disclosure, runs the risk that ignorant patients and subjects will be made solely responsible for processing and evaluating the information provided—a highly unsatisfactory outcome.

This issue points to one of the potential limitations of an entirely patient- or subject-centered approach to understanding and consent.

Thus far we have argued that the substantial understanding condition of sense$_1$ informed consent demands that a person's understanding of a proposed intervention (R) include those propositions about R and the authorization of R that the person views as material to a decision to authorize R. Although this is the central criterion for evaluating the adequacy of a person's understanding, it is not the sole standard. Sometimes the set of propositions a person views as material to his or her decision to authorize R is not sufficiently comprehensive to ensure that the "R" the person intends to authorize is, by an *objective* account, the *same* R the person being authorized believes he or she has been given permission to implement.

Suppose, for example, that the only proposition material to Carol's decision to consent to a hysterectomy is whether her husband wants her to consent. Once she has established her husband's preference, Carol is not interested in knowing or considering anything else—not the nature of the procedure, its consequences and risks, *nothing*. Under such a circumstance, as far as Carol is concerned she understands all the propositions that are material to her decision whether to authorize a hysterectomy. One would be hard pressed to argue, however, that she has given an informed consent to a hysterectomy if all she understands about her decision is what her husband wants her to do. Indeed, for all we know, Carol thinks her husband wants her to have a diagnostic test or surgery on the rectum when he asks her to consent to a "hysterectomy"; or she may have no idea at all what the procedure is.

In order to avoid such pitfalls there must sometimes be an *extrasubjective component* to the knowledge base necessary for substantial understanding, but how to describe this knowledge base for a particular context like informed consent is problematic. Packages of minimum objective "facts" or "truths" that must be understood seem unpromising. As a practical matter, the most efficient strategy is to operationally define this extrasubjective component of substantial understanding in terms of the already existing extrasubjective core disclosure discussed earlier. Under this conception, not only must X understand those propositions about authorizing R that X views as material to a decision whether to consent, but also that X understands what Y (the professional) believes about various matters. Specifically, X should understand (1) what an informed professional in Y's position would judge to be of value for most patients or subjects in deciding whether to authorize R, (2) what a professional in Y's position judges that most patients or subjects view as material for authorizing R and (3) what it means for X's consent to R to be an authorization. As a result of this procedural approach to the *objective* requirement for substantial understanding, X and Y come to share an understanding about the terms of the authorization and the nature of what is authorized (R).

Although this *shared* understanding is not conceptually necessary for substantial understanding (other criteria for the extrasubjective component could be developed), its importance cannot be overemphasized. This approach recognizes that an informed consent includes many of the features of a valid contract, chief of which is that the parties agree to the essential elements of the arrangement. Without agreement about the essential features of the R being authorized, there can be no assurance that X's informed consent to "*R*" is indeed to R and not to r, and thus no assurance that X is giving an informed consent to the proposed intervention. It is generally Y, not X, who will implement R; if X and Y have different conceptions (R and r) of the proposed intervention, and the differences have implications for what is actually to be implemented, generally *only* Y's, and *not* X's, conception will be effected.

We are not arguing that X and Y must have an *identical* understanding about what it means to authorize R in order to have a *shared* understanding. But X and Y must at least share an understanding that is sufficiently broad and objective to assure each party that the same R is under consideration. Sometimes this shared understanding can accommodate significant disagreements between the parties. Recall our discussion in Chapter 7 of the distinction between "understanding that" and "understanding what" (see pp. 249–251). Understanding what another person says (or believes) does not require believing that what the other says is true. Thus, that party Y believes that Q is true is compatible with a shared understanding of Q with X, even if X believes Q is false.

The Problem of False Beliefs and Inherently Contestable Beliefs. The problem of false beliefs and inherently contestable beliefs (see pp. 253–254) presents an interesting challenge to these claims. X may believe the proposition "I will certainly survive intervention R." By contrast, Y may hold as true a different proposition about R, for example, that there is a 90% probability that X will survive R. For X and Y to share an understanding, it is not necessary that X change his or her belief to accept Y's proposition as true, or vice versa. Instead, it is sufficient that X and Y understand each other. That is, X should be able to say honestly "I understand you believe there is a 10% chance that I will not survive R, whereas I believe there is no chance."

But this analysis is predicated on the assumption that X's proposition about survival qualifies as an inherently *contestable* belief. If this were not the case, and X simply held a *false* belief material to the decision to consent, then X's consent would be based on less than substantial understanding and thus would not qualify as an informed consent in sense₁. Again we see that not everything can be subjective when it comes to understanding: In a situation of disclosure a person has to understand true and material statements *as true*. The obligation to ensure a person's understanding in the informed consent context should also include an obligation to disabuse an individual of even a resolutely held false belief.

This obligation would apply to informed refusals no less than to informed consent.[16]

Consider the following actual case in which a false belief figured prominently in a patient's refusal of medical treatment:

> A 57–year-old woman was admitted to hospital because of a fractured hip. . . . During the course of the hospitalization, a Papanicolaou test and biopsy revealed stage 1A carcinoma of the cervix. . . . surgery was strongly recommended, since the cancer was almost certainly curable by a hysterectomy. . . . the patient refused the procedure.
>
> The patient's treating physicians at this point felt that she was mentally incompetent. Psychiatric and neurological consultations were requested to determine the possibility of dementia and/or mental incompetency. The psychiatric consultant felt that the patient was demented and not mentally competent to make decisions regarding her own care. This determination was based in large measure on the patient's steadfast 'unreasonable' refusal to undergo surgery. The neurologist disagreed, finding no evidence of dementia. On questioning, the patient stated that she was refusing the hysterectomy because she *did not believe* she had cancer. 'Anyone knows', she said, 'that people with cancer are sick, feel bad and lose weight', while she felt quite well. The patient continued to hold this view despite the results of the biopsy and her physicians' persistent arguments to the contrary.[17]

Although in this case the patient and the physicians "share an understanding," in the sense that the patient understands that the physicians are telling her she has cancer and the physicians understand that the patient does not believe that what they are saying is true, this is not an *acceptable* "shared understanding." Unlike the example of faith and survival probabilities described above, the patient's belief is not inherently contestable. In the light of overwhelming medical evidence to the contrary, the patient is simply *unjustified* in believing she does not have cancer. So long as the patient persists in holding this false belief, and so long as this belief is material to her decision, the patient cannot give an informed refusal (in sense$_1$).

In this particular case, the patient was eventually persuaded of the falsity of her belief. The outcome is a testament both to the social and psychological complexities inherent in achieving effective communication in many consent situations and to the complexities involved in expressing the physician's duties to accept refusals: A critical complicating factor in the case was the patient's social history. She was a poor white from Appalachia with a third-grade education. The fact that her treating physician was black was the major reason for her false belief that she had no cancer. Discussions with another physician (who was white) and with her daughter resulted in a change in belief. Subsequently the patient consented to and successfully underwent a hysterectomy.[18]

Open Withholding of Information

Implicit in the previous sketch of a core disclosure, and in the appeal to effective communication, is the assumption that professionals will respond to questions and concerns of their patients and subjects as fully as they are able. However, sometimes, particularly in research, professionals are not willing to share certain relevant items of knowledge with the patient or subject. Instead, they may prefer to make a forthright acknowledgment that they are purposely withholding certain information.

In biomedical research, the paradigmatic example is the clinical trial in which potential patient-subjects are informed that they cannot be told the treatment they are to receive. In behavioral and social science research, there are similar examples of blinded randomizations to experimental treatments requiring that information about assignment be withheld from potential subjects. These subjects are sometimes informed that they cannot be told the purpose or the specific topic of the research, and in some cases they are asked to consent to studies after being informed that the research procedures will be intentionally deceptive.

Is such withholding of information compatible with informed consent? The central issue is whether potential subjects or patients who understand that they are being kept partially ignorant about a particular intervention or research project can nonetheless give informed consents (in sense$_1$) to that project or intervention. The answer to this question again requires resort to a subjective criterion. Any answer must be based on the subject's ability to judge the materiality of the information being withheld. Subjects are not always in a good position to make such a judgment, and it is sometimes difficult to assess whether unknown or unseen events or information is likely to be important or trivial. Generally, this depends on the kind and amount of information being withheld.

Consider the following actual case: The Glaucoma Laser Trial is evaluating two different treatments for glaucoma, drug therapy and laser therapy.[19] All subjects receive both treatments simultaneously, one in each eye. Random assignment procedures are used to determine which eye receives which treatment. Thus, the only information being withheld from potential subjects at the time of the consent decision is whether it will be their right or left eye that will first receive the laser treatment. Here potential subjects can have an adequate understanding of the information being withheld from them and thus are in a good position to judge for themselves how material the withheld information is likely to be for their decisions. Doubtless, few potential subjects will consider it material to know which eye gets which therapy. Those for whom it is material which eye gets which therapy will be in a good position to make the judgment to refuse research participation if they wish.

Of course, potential subjects are not *always* in a good position to evaluate the likely materiality of the withheld information. Consider another
actual case of a study examining the extent to which disclosing the side
effects and complications of seizure medications affects patients'
reported experience of adverse reactions (through suggestion).[20] Potential subjects are told that if they agree to participate in the study they
will be randomly assigned to one of two different kinds of drug information sessions with their physicians. Although potential subjects are
reassured that whatever educational condition they are assigned to they
will not receive less information than their physicians normally provide
(which is true), they are never told *how* the two conditions are different.
To do so would seriously jeopardize the validity of the study. Thus, if a
potential subject in this study were to ask the investigator how the two
educational sessions are different or what the basic research question is,
the investigator could only answer, "I'm sorry. I can't tell you that. If I
did, it would spoil the study."

By contrast to the glaucoma trial, it is more difficult in this study for
potential subjects to evaluate the materiality of what is withheld. One
consolation is that potential subjects who are troubled by any uncertainty or gap in their understanding can, *ceteris paribus*, refuse to participate. However, this safeguard does not address conceptual and epistemological problems of whether the resultant refusals or consents are
substantially autonomous.

The resolution of these problems depends at least in part on an analysis
of the intervention or arrangement to which one is consenting. For
example, in the side-effect-suggestibility study described above, if the
subject cannot confidently evaluate the materiality of withheld information, such that it remains doubtful whether the subject has a substantial understanding of the proposed research project, the subject may not
be able to give a sense$_1$ informed consent to participation in that particular research project. But the subject may nonetheless be able to give
an informed consent to participate in research being conducted by the
investigator, under the guarantees and terms of ignorance that have been
discussed, provided that the subject has an understanding of that which
is material to her or his decision to authorize the professional to proceed
under the specified conditions.

It is often dilemmatic whether informed consents can be given under
the condition of an open withholding of information, but certainly it
would be precipitous to maintain that patients and subjects can never
give informed consents merely because they lack some *relevant* descriptions. They may, in the end, have every *material* description needed to
autonomously authorize a professional to proceed with some general
arrangement, even if they are not in a position to authorize some *specific*
research or medical intervention.

Understanding Through Effective Communication

We are now in a position to defend our claim in Chapter 7 that "understanding what"—that is, understanding as effective communication—is often without peer as the most important sense of understanding in many consent situations.

The reasons for this claim are perhaps by now obvious. First, insofar as professionals are frequently the primary source of information available to patients and subjects, it is critical that the latter be able to understand *what* the professional is saying, both in the core disclosure and in the professional's response to questions. Second, even if the subject's or patient's general understanding of the situation does not depend heavily on the professional's disclosure, unless the professional is understood, there is no guarantee that the parties have the same intervention in mind—the "shared understanding" just described. Finally, unless the professional understands messages from the patient or subject, the professional cannot provide satisfactory responses to questions, and thus the patient or subject is unlikely to obtain the information needed to make a substantially autonomous choice. Unless the professional understands the patient or subject, it would also be difficult to identify and help modify false beliefs and confusions.

We are not arguing that effective communication or shared understanding is a necessary condition of the patient's or subject's giving a sense$_1$ informed consent. As noted elsewhere, our account of informed consent is indifferent *how* substantial understanding is achieved. However, as a practical matter, effective communication and shared understanding—including the professional's understanding—are frequently the most available and critical means to the end of understanding by the patient or subject.

Earlier we referred to "setting a climate" for communication. Without the proper climate, a request from a professional that the patient or subject ask for information is as likely to result in "an embarrassed silence" as to elicit the desired result of a meaningful exchange.[21] Patients find it difficult to approach physicians with questions or concerns, and even when they do not understand their physicians, many still do not ask questions.[22] The extent to which this passive attitude characterizes research subjects is less clear. However, at least in clinical contexts and in settings such as Milgram's obedience research discussed in Chapter 5, in which the investigator is viewed with deference as an authority, one of the major obstacles to achieving understanding is reticence on the part of patients and subjects to articulate their informational needs and to acknowledge their ignorance.

In Chapter 10, we discuss how constraints inherent in the *role* of patient (and, under some conditions, the role of subject) make autonomous action difficult. Factors that are so characteristic of the role of patient, such as deference and fear of displeasing the physician or of appearing to waste the physician's time, can inhibit patients and subjects from initiating or even participating in active informational exchanges with physicians.

Stephen Bochner's astute observations about the "culture of the medical consultation" can be borrowed to illustrate a social situation that might be called the "culture of the consent solicitation."[23] From Bochner's perspective, a medical consultation—a consent solicitation may be substituted—is like any other stylized social encounter. It has its own set of rules and assumptions about how to behave, rules about the goals of the encounter, about who can say what to whom when, and so on. We have previously outlined such rules as they would operate in contexts of informed consent (in sense$_1$). Because of the imbalance of relevant experience and power between the professional and the patient or subject, these rules are generally more familiar to, and often controlled by, the professional. The professional's job is to teach the rules—that is, to teach the culture of the consent solicitation—to the patient or subject, as one function of the "core disclosure": The professional is to teach the rules of the culture by explicitly disclosing what is expected of the person (and what is expected of the professional as well).[24]

Successful teaching may require more than disclosing, however. Because some of the behaviors expected of the patient or subject—like asking questions or expressing concerns—are likely to be new and awkward, the professional may be successful only if illustrations, examples, and words of encouragement and support are supplied.[25] Non-verbal behavior is also important. The extralinguistic and contextual properties of communication are increasingly being recognized as central to a communication's effectiveness.[26] Even body posture and the seating position of doctor and patient have been shown to affect the mutuality of their exchange.[27] At the very least, it is important that the professional appear unhurried and courteous and that discussions occur in environments that admit of sufficient privacy and leisure for genuine discussion—for example, not in the hallway, or while fidgeting to leave, or just before the proposed procedure is to begin.

Moreover, nothing about sense$_1$ informed consent demands that its conditions be satisfied in a single sitting or setting.[28] The process of obtaining informed consent may properly take place over time, in numerous encounters. Empirical evidence suggests that in the clinical context the more informed consent is part of a participatory process that extends over time, the greater the degree of patient involvement in communication and decisionmaking.[29] Moreover, in sense$_1$ informed consent, only a limited role should probably be accorded to the classic consent form or written disclosure statement. Unless the proposed intervention or research participation is either simple or already within the experience of the prospective patient or subject, it is unlikely in many settings that a written communication alone, even if well written and augmented with an opportunity to ask questions, will allow for the effective communication of information generally required for substantial understanding.

Communication and the Understanding of Information

Much of our argument thus far has been aimed at showing that the adequacy of a subject's or patient's understanding may ultimately depend both on the adequacy of the person's understanding of disclosed information and on the adequacy of the professional's grasp of the person's questions and responses. Various factors may compromise understanding of both sorts. We cannot here cover all imaginable difficulties or barriers to effective communication, but we need at least to examine the important categories of factors whose negative effects can be prevented or at least minimized in the solicitation of consent.

Problems of Language, Inference, and Background Knowledge

It is a widely recognized principle of human communication that mutual understanding is heavily dependent on the extent to which the communicants share a background in a language and area of knowledge.[30] Language communities are defined both linguistically (e.g., as English speaking) and culturally (e.g., the family unit, social class, generation, ethnicity, occupational group, etc.). Proper interpretation is facilitated if, in addition to being culturally similar, persons have a prior history of interpersonal interaction. We take it as axiomatic that communicants dissimilar in respects relevant to the subject of their communication, or strangers, are less likely to understand each other. This is true not only because they use different words and have different beliefs, but because they are not likely to draw the same *inferences* from the same linguistic message and context. For example, when people speak they consistently leave out information that may be central to their intended message, but which they presume can readily be inferred by the listener.[31] This presumption is often safe so long as the speaker and the listener are of a relevantly similar language community, but it is also a presumption that can turn out to be mistaken. The more the speaker and listener deviate from a shared language, the less can the hearer's inferential structure be reliably depended on to supply the missing information.

While these generalizations have an air of the obvious about them, this process of inference is absolutely central to human communication.[32] Parties to a communication are constantly hypothesizing, often in unnoticed ways, about what the other is saying—trying to form justified beliefs about what the other believes. These hypotheses represent the hearer's attempts to correctly infer what the speaker means or intends to say.

The implications of these comments for informed consent in medicine and research are profoundly important. Professionals and their subjects and patients are often very dissimilar. The stereotypic scenario involves a white, upperclass male professional in his thirties soliciting consent from an elderly, poorly educated, Black or Hispanic woman. Unless the professional is sensitive to the linguistic usage and ordinary assumptions about meaning and inference that underlie the patient's or subject's attempts at communication, the professional can easily fail to understand the patient's or subject's intended meaning well enough to respond with the desired information when questions are asked.

Sometimes even the "obvious" problem of a formal language barrier can be unintentionally overlooked. In a study of how patients and physicians negotiate treatment decisions after the finding of an abnormal Pap smear, Sue Fisher reports on the case of Lucy, a 42–year-old, bilingual Mexican-American:

> When the doctor and patient met to discuss treatment options, he informed her that the extent of her lesion had not been visualized, told her that she needed to have a conization biopsy as the next diagnostic step, and talked about a hysterectomy. . . . While he [the doctor] was on the phone, Lucy turned to me [the researcher-observer] and asked, in Spanish, if the doctor had said he was going to take out her uterus. I explained, in Spanish, the difference between a conization biopsy and hysterectomy and confirmed that the doctor had been talking about removing her uterus. She asked if that would be necessary and I suggested that she ask the doctor.
>
> Two things particularly struck me about our exchange. First, because Lucy spoke English so well, both the doctor and I assumed she understood it equally well. She did not. . . . I was also struck by the consequences of the exchange. At the next opportunity . . . the patient requested information that . . . affected the treatment performed. [Lucy was treated with conization biopsy only.][33]

Miscommunications of this order are less likely to occur if the professional and patient or subject are more similar in background.[34] However, even if professional and subject or patient are of the same educational and social class, communication maybe ineffective because of the special vocabularies of medicine and research. The difficulties introduced by medical and scientific jargon, particularly in consent forms—and the frequency of such difficulties—have been well documented in the informed consent literature.[35] These difficulties are not restricted to the use of uniquely scientific terms; ordinary English words like "control" and "history" take on special meanings in these contexts that untutored lay persons do not usually understand. For example, in one study a parent

A THEORY OF INFORMED CONSENT

of an ill child told the interviewer that the physicians said they would "admit her for a work-up, whatever that means." The parent did not understand that this term indicated that the child was to be hospitalized.[36]

The problem runs deeper than remembering to avoid the use of undefined technical terms. While it is helpful to explain to a patient that a myocardial infarction "is the same as a 'heart attack,'" this change of vocabulary does not, by itself, guarantee any advance in effective communication. Although both physician and patient are likely to have a concept of heart attack, these concepts may be starkly different. Recent research indicates that lay persons' theories of disease and the meanings they give to specific illnesses are often stunningly different from standard medical definitions and conceptions on such dimensions as symptomology and etiology, consequences for patients, and whether the illness is acute or chronic.[37]

Here we may recall the case described earlier of the patient who refused treatment because she did not believe she had cancer. This woman's false belief must be situated within *her* beliefs about the diagnosis and symptomology of cancer (e.g., "Anyone knows . . . that people with cancer are sick, feel bad and lose weight.")[38] In terms of the patient's representation of cancer, there is insufficient evidence to confirm a diagnosis; by contrast, under the physician's representation the diagnosis is a virtual medical certainty. Effective communication may require the professional and patient or subject to come to grips with each other's differing hypotheses and representations. If the patient's or subject's representation is unjustified—as in this case—it must be modified if a sense₁ informed consent is to be obtained.

Problems with understanding sometimes occur not because the patient or subject is operating with meanings different from the professional's, but because the patient or subject has *no* relevant interpretations of meaning. That is, the person's knowledge base is too impoverished to interpret the information provided by the professional. Because new information is understood through old information, communications about alien or completely novel situations or concepts are extremely difficult to process.[39] In the jargon of the cognitive sciences, the hearer does not have the conceptual database, cognitive constructs, or categories from which to make the appropriate interpretations.[40]

This is not to say that people cannot comprehend alien information or that people can never communicate with each other if they share but a modest amount of background enculturation. Such a conclusion would foreclose the possibility of sense₁ informed consent in many (if not most) important situations. The educational and psychological literatures offer several suggestions for successful communication of novel, alien, and specialized information to lay persons.[41] One strategy is to draw analogies between the novel information and more ordinary events with which the patient or subject is likely to be familiar. Better still is for the professional to help the patient or subject draw his or her own analogies—that is, to assist the person in making the connections necessary for the information to be meaningful. A simple example is the following: "Have you ever had novacaine or some similar pain killer for a dental procedure? Do you remember what your mouth felt like when the novacaine started to wear off? That's about how your leg would feel all the time if . . . ''

Visual materials can also be useful. What cannot be adequately conveyed in words sometimes can be easily communicated in pictures—for example, the differences in mutilation between a simple and a modified mastectomy. Occasionally, effective communication requires the use of linguistic or cultural interpreters who are able to bridge the world views of professional and patient or subject. As simple as these strategies may seem in the abstract, they are lessons still to be taught and learned in vast segments of the world of medicine and research.

Risk and Uncertainty

Many problems of understanding and communication come together in an area of special relevance to informed consent—the comprehension and assessment of information about risks and probabilities. It is widely agreed that people have problems processing information about risks and that these problems introduce inferential errors and disproportionate exaggeration of risks in the making of choices.[42]

Inferential Errors and Formulation Effects. Inferential errors in deliberations that involve risk information are not unique to patients, subjects, or "laypersons" in general.[43] There is ample evidence that even the experts often succumb to the power of a vivid and rich example in ways that "distort" their assessments of the riskiness of certain events. Indeed, some biases are so ubiquitous in the human experience that—as Daniel Kahneman and Amos Tversky suggest—it may be "psychologically unfeasible" to expect decisionmakers to resist acting in accord with them.[44] One of the more troublesome of these biases for informed consent is the so-called "framing" or "formulation" effect.[45] It has been widely appreciated that people's choices between risky alternatives can be predictably influenced by the way the risk information is presented or framed.[46] Whether the proverbial glass is described as half *empty* or half *full* establishes a frame of reference against which risky outcomes and contingencies are viewed as either losses or gains.

Formulation effects have been demonstrated in several empirical studies involving assessment of medical risk information.[47] For example, in one study samples of radiologists, outpatients with chronic medical problems, and graduate students in business were asked to make a hypothetical choice between two alternative therapies for lung cancer—surgery and radiation therapy.[48] The preferences of all three groups were markedly affected by whether the information about outcomes was framed in terms of probability of survival or probability of dying. When the outcomes were framed in terms of probability of survival, only 25% chose radiation over surgery. However, when the outcomes were framed in terms of probability of death, 42% preferred radiation. The authors attribute the result to the fact that the risk of perioperative death, which has no analogue in radiation therapy, looms larger in the mortality frame than in the survival frame.

One obvious implication is that in exploiting these formulation effects, professionals have the power with which to manipulate decisions about treatment or research without resorting to deception, a subject to which we return in Chapter 10. But the more relevant question for our purposes is how these formulation effects affect autonomy when they are not intentionally manipulated—when they occur "without anyone being aware of the impact of the frame on the ultimate decision."[49] Kahneman and Tversky have pointed out that formulation effects violate a basic principle of rational choice in modern decision theory, the principle of invariance, which requires that preferences between prospects not depend on the manner in which the prospects are formulated, provided that the alternative formulations contain identical or equivalent information.[50]

This violation is not in itself a problem for autonomous action in that there is no requirement of rationality in our theory. Our concern is not with the quality of the reasoning behind the choice but with understanding, intentionality, and absence of control by others. Formulation effects do not diminish the autonomy of acts merely because they reduce the rationality of choice and acts. But formulation effects can diminish autonomy and keep acts from being sense₁ informed consents if they compromise any one of our three conditions—most likely the condition of understanding, of course.

Although the robustness of formulation effects has been well established, it is not clear *why* they have such a pervasive impact on choice. It is possible that formulation effects are successful at least in part because they result in a person's failing to *understand* generally material descriptions of the prospects. Kahneman and Tversky have, for example, speculated that framing effects are more like perceptual illusions in their tenacious grip on deliberation and preference than like computational errors.[51] If a person comes to "see" the options of surgery or radiation in terms of probabilities of survival, this framing may keep the person from simultaneously being able to "see" or understand the risk of death. Thus, if a survival frame prevents a person from understanding that there will be a risk of death on the operating table, and this act-description would otherwise be material to the person's decision, then, on our theory, the person's choice of surgery would be based on less than substantial understanding and would not qualify as a sense₁ informed consent.

Framing effects do not invariably diminish understanding in ways that render acts less than substantially autonomous. We are merely speculating as to how formulation effects may be mediated through understanding. In some cases, framing effects may not have a blinding impact. In other cases, the propositions to which the person is blinded may not be material to the person's decision. Nevertheless, because the power and precise nature of framing effects are difficult to ascertain in concrete cases, the prudent course for professionals seeking sense₁ informed consents is to provide patients and subjects with *both sides* of the story—the half-full and the half-empty presentations, the mortality and the survival frames—in the hopes of avoiding the gaps in understanding that framing effects may produce.[52]

In discussions of risk assessment and judgments under uncertainty, questions of understanding *what* has been stated or claimed should not be conflated either with questions about understanding *that* something is true or with questions of value and subjective preferences. As an illustration of how these problems can easily be run together, consider the following argument by William Thompson, who asks us to imagine a situation similar to the notorious experiment (see pp. 161–162) conducted in

> the Jewish Chronic Disease Hospital in Brooklyn, in which experimenters injected live cancer cells subcutaneously into patients as part of a study of people's ability to reject foreign cells. For argument's sake, let us assume that the injections pose no risk to subjects but that learning the injections contain cancer will cause subjects to greatly overestimate the dangers posed by the experiment. Under such circumstances should potential subjects be told the injections contain cancer cells? This disclosure is one that will make a difference to the decision of many subjects, hence disclosure is essential to protecting their autonomy. But the disclosure protects their autonomy at the price of their objectivity. Subjects' assessments of the risks of physical injury posed by the experiment will be more accurate if they are not told about the cancer.[53]

Thompson takes this disclosure to be an example of how "an 'accurate' disclosure can produce an inaccurate understanding."[54] But an assessment needs to be made of what is meant by the subject's "greatly overestimating" the dangers of the experiment. While the word "cancer"—like a formulation effect—could serve to put blinders on the subjects, leaving them with an inadequate understanding on which to base their refusals, alternative explanations are equally plausible. Indeed, the subjects could have an entirely justifiable assessment of the risks and still be profoundly negatively affected by a disclosure that the experiment includes the injection of cancer cells.[55] Refusing to participate because the injection contains cancer cells does not necessarily entail any "overestimate" or misunderstanding of the dangers posed by the experiments. For example, subjects may justifiably dispute the truth value of the scientific claim of "no risk." They may reason that "We're not going to take *any* chances. Who knows what could be wrong with your scientific theories?"

Alternatively, even if subjects did not dispute the truth value of the claim that the injections pose no risk of cancer, the involvement of live cancer cells could still result in refusals to participate. A potential subject, Mary, might say, "Look, I understand what you're saying and I believe you. I *really* do believe that there is absolutely no risk of contracting cancer from these injections, and I'm not in the least worried about any health risks. It just doesn't feel right to me to have those injections. I can't explain it better than that. I just don't like the idea of it." Some may want to label Mary's decision "irrational." Certainly she is not very articulate, but by our theory this defect does not disqualify her decision from status as substantially autonomous. Note that Mary is not laboring under any "misunderstanding" about the risk, and thus the condition of substantial understanding is unaffected. What Mary lacks is any "objective reason" for her refusal, but such is not demanded.

Understanding Numeric and Non-Numeric Expressions of Probability. Although formulation effects and related inferential errors may pose the most interesting theoretical problems, simple inabilities to interpret numeric probabilistic information—percentages, odds, ratios, rates, and other problems linked to poor arithmetic skills and training—can also compromise a patient's or subject's understanding in a consent situation.[56] It can be meaningless to disclose that the "risk is between 0.2% and 0.3%," unless this information is translated into simple and familiar concepts and relationships, such as "This risk means that out of every 1000 patients who have this surgery, 2 to 3 will get (the problem) and 997 to 998 will not." There is some evidence that by more effective presentations people can *learn* to understand and use base-rate information, but the task can be arduous.[57]

Numeric probabilistic information can also be augmented with a non-numeric expression of probability. However, because there is considerable intersubjective and contextual variability in the different meanings people attach to common phrases of probability (e.g., rarely, very likely, improbable, possible, high chance, etc.), exclusive reliance on such expressions or on anecdotal examples is undesirable.[58] The patient's or subject's assessment of the meaning of these expressions may be very distant from the professional's. The prudent course for professionals seeking sense₁ informed consent may be to express probabilities in both numeric *and* non-numeric terms, while at the same time assisting the patient or subject to assign meaning to the probabilities through comparison with more familiar risks and prior experiences.

It should be noted that there is nothing about the condition of substantial understanding that requires people to apply Bayes theorem or any other rule or procedure to arrive at the precise probability (e.g.,

31%, 43%, etc.) that, based on available diagnostic and base rate information, they have a certain disorder or will experience a side effect or complication.[59] All that is generally required is that patients and subjects have an appreciation of their personal risk of harm and possible benefit that is sufficiently accurate for justified belief. Thus, for example, from the perspective of substantial understanding, it is appropriate but not always necessary that a patient understand that the likelihood that cardiac surgery will cause the patient to have a stroke is about .01% to .03%. Instead, it is sufficient that the patient understand the risk is "small," where "small" is given content by analogy to some event of comparable probability and significance with which the patient is familiar. Not acceptable is for the patient to interpret the probabilities to mean that there is virtually no chance a stroke will be suffered because this belief would constitute a misleading distortion.

Problems of Information Overload, Stress, and Illness

A major obstacle to satisfying the condition of substantial understanding and thus obtaining sense$_1$ informed consents is the fact that human beings can process only limited amounts of information. From the perspective of substantial understanding, information overload can be as significant as information underload.

In most consent contexts, information must be retained in short-term memory long enough to be given meaning, generally by relating it to old information, and to be evaluated in terms of its importance to the consent decision. However, even in the best of circumstances, there are significant constraints on the amount of information that can be retained. For example, one rule of thumb in literature on cognition holds that people can retain in short-term memory only about seven independent "chunks" or units of information. (The amount of information in a chunk is affected by familiarity and meaningfulness.)[60] Without care on the part of the professional, many discussions of proposed research or medical treatment will far outstrip this limited capacity.

Several factors conspire to make information overload a pressing problem in many consent situations. One factor is the aforementioned problem of novel and alien information. Information overload is exacerbated if patients and subjects are presented with unfamiliar terms and information that they cannot meaningfully organize. One strategy that professionals can use to combat this problem is to assist patients and subjects in meaningfully grouping information by dividing and organizing it into preannounced categories—for example, "I am going to tell you about the purpose of the research, what your involvement would be like, the risks of participation, and then the benefits. First, the purpose of the study."[61]

The problem of information overload is also exacerbated by the time pressures impinging on many informed consent discussions, particularly those involving physicians. Common sense would suggest, and learning studies bear out, that lack of time to assimilate information negatively affects comprehension. We have already noted that nothing inherent in sense₁ informed consent requires the process to be accomplished in a single encounter. Provision of sufficient time to process information and creative use of written information and audiovisual aids may be particularly helpful in achieving substantial understanding. These materials could even be given to patients or subjects to review in detail at their own convenience.[62]

Another feature of the problem of information overload for informed consent is that information exchanged between professional and patient or subject is often not the only information vying for the patient's or subject's attention. Although theories of and research in comprehension and short-term memory generally assume that attention is being paid to the information under examination, competing demands are often present on attentional capacities that can affect understanding. In consent solicitation contexts, patients and subjects may be bombarded by many kinds of informational inputs, of which the information exchanged in consent discussions is but one part, and the capacity to attend to and process information may be compromised by powerful distractions like anxiety, fear, and pain. Those who are hospitalized are especially vulnerable. Upon admittance, the patient is removed from usual patterns of activities and concerns. Familiar family and friends are restricted or entirely forbidden and replaced by a host of new faces. Strange food, noises, sights, procedures, and sensations abound. In such a situation, a large part of one's attentional capacity is likely to be given over toward adapting to and making sense of this environmental chaos, with little attention reserved for disclosed information. At the same time, hospitalized patients, and others diagnosed as ill, often struggle with feelings of anxiety and the discomfort accompanying fear of the unknown. It is well established that anxiety has a predictably powerful negative effect on many cognitive tasks, including attention and recall.

In addition to generalized anxiety concerning the unknown, fear often attends contemplation of an intervention likely to carry substantial risks. An important decision may entail psychological conflict. The conflicts are likely to intensify as the decisionmaker becomes aware of the risk of suffering serious losses from the course of action selected. Simultaneous opposing tendencies to accept and to reject a given course of action may be present, leading one to experience hesitation, vacillation, ambivalence, fear, uncertainty, and acute emotional distress, especially if required to choose between two alternatives both of which are known to have unpleasant consequences.[63] This description is appropriate for many contemporary medical decisions.

Even mild stress that occurs when a decisionmaker anticipates slight losses or uncertain risks may have discernible effects on cognitive processes. Irving Janis and Leon Mann have studied how decisional conflict and attention to and appraisal of information relevant to the decision are mediated in different patterns of coping, in accordance with the stress of decisionmaking.[64] These coping patterns are essentially attention-directing strategies that enable an individual to make a decision while preserving energy to deal with other problems. Two factors are critical: The person must believe there is sufficient time to make an adequate decision and the person must believe there are viable or genuine alternatives. If these factors are not present, the problem of information overload is generally solved by shortcutting the attention paid to information, thereby compromising understanding.

Both of these factors—time in which to make a decision and the belief that there are alternatives—are typical features in informed consent situations that professionals frequently can manage for the better, but often do not. In many clinical situations, especially in surgery, consent is formally solicited and information given immediately prior to treatment, when there is little time to make a decision. By this point the patient has already made a decision for surgery, perhaps by default. A major behavioral commitment to taking some action is made merely by voluntarily entering the hospital. It is not surprising that a typical response in such a situation is to distance oneself from information that challenges the original decision for surgery—including, paradigmatically, the kinds of risk information typically included in a core consent disclosure. This style of coping with acute decisional stress helps explain why many patients' capacity for remembering the risks of treatment is lower than for any other category of information.[65] Who would want, on the eve of surgery after having disrupted one's life, gathered one's courage, and entered the hospital, to change one's mind? And thus who would want to pay attention to information that challenges the wisdom of the decision?

Predisposition to treatment is of course only one of several barriers to substantial understanding among the sick. Physical illness in itself is an attention-stealing distraction. In the above discussion, fear, anxiety, and uncertainty can all be regarded as the causes of distraction from optimum information processing and also as stressors that may have physiological consequences that further reduce cognitive abilities. In general, the cognitive functions that are most susceptible to disruption by illness and other stressors are those that are actively involved in linguistic communication: the facility to store, recall, and dismiss information in active memory, the maintenance of vigilance in attentive focus, and the ability to suppress distractions. Weakening of these functions by physical problems may have a disastrous effect on complex cognitive activity because the more complex cognitive acts entailed in giving meaning to novel information are built on the basic functions.

Pain is another example of an acute internal distractor. The relief of intense pain can become an immediate and overriding concern, one that can cause an individual to opt for treatment without adequate under- standing. Coronary bypass surgery, orthopedic surgery, and many other forms of surgery are directed at the relief of pain. Commonly a point emerges at which the pain is no longer worth enduring. At this point the benefits of surgery will seem overwhelmingly obvious to the patient, especially to desperate patients. Risks will quickly recede in significance. Pain can constrain the choices of such patients not only because of its immediate intensity, it can also interfere with the efficient and effective processing of information. Balancing risks against benefits may no longer be possible with anything like understanding. At the same time, treat- ments for pain, most notably narcotics and analgesics, frequently defeat clear thinking.

In addition, many disease states directly affect intellectual function and communication (e.g., Wernicke-Korsakoff psychosis and transient global amnesia). It is necessary to distinguish categories of illness that result in chronic changes in intellectual function, language function, or memory from those in which there may be rapid reversibility of intellec- tual function (metabolic encephalopathy), language function (transient ischemic attack), or memory (transient global amnesia). In the latter cases a patient or subject may have impaired cognitive functioning one hour but not the next. Psychiatric illnesses present different but no less formidable challenges.[66]

Some patients or subjects with adequate understanding may be treated as unable to give an informed consent because they are unable to com- municate in normal ways. But in some instances innovative and primi- tive, yet adequate levels of communication can be developed. Examples include the patient with "locked in" syndrome who has learned to com- municate through eyeblinks and the patient with a pure motor aphasia who can respond to yes-no questions with a shake of the head.

The major question for both the chronic and reversible cases is whether the patient's or subject's understanding and ability to commu- nicate are sufficiently compromised to preclude substantial understand- ing. Compromised abilities to comprehend or communicate should not be automatically equated with an inability to give sense$_1$ informed con- sent, as our discussion of competence in Chapter 8 indicated. (See pp. 287–293.)

Confirmation of Substantial Understanding

A professional can never be certain that a patient or subject has an understanding adequate to make a substantially autonomous choice. However, a professional can often make a reasoned assessment of the person's understanding. We conclude this chapter with a brief review of several techniques that might be used to improve the evidentiary base for making such determinations.

The technique that has been discussed most frequently in the informed consent literature is the application of reading-ease formulas to written consent materials.[67] But the *readability* of a consent form or disclosure statement, taken by itself, says nothing about *understanding*, even if it stands to reason that readability facilitates understanding. Moreover, these written documents generally play only a minor or bolstering role for sense₁ informed consent. We shall here simply pass over the intricacies of problems surrounding the readability and comprehensibility of written documents and turn instead to more promising strategies for assessing understanding.

Recognition Tests for Disclosed Information. Several studies of informed consent have attempted to assess patient or subject comprehension of disclosed information through the administration of multiple choice and true/false knowledge tests, referred to as recognition tests.[68] Using recognition tests to confirm understanding is, however, problematic. Unlike reading ease formulas, no standardized recognition tests have been readied for consent settings, and the development of valid recognition tests is fraught with conceptual and methodological difficulties. For example, recognition tests frequently fail to distinguish *comprehension* of disclosed information from *acceptance* of the information (as true, false, or conditionally true, at a specified level of probability). Asking a research subject, "Which of these statements best describes the purpose of a research project?" will not necessarily elicit the same response as asking, "Which of these statements best describes what Dr. X told you is the purpose of the project?" The second question directly addresses the issue of recognition of what was disclosed. The first question does not, assessing instead research subjects' personal beliefs about the purpose of the research; these beliefs may or may not have been influenced by the purpose as described in the investigator's disclosure. Sometimes the issues of comprehension (of disclosed information) and acceptance (of the disclosed information as true) have been confused in a single "comprehension test." For example, in one study of information retention in normal volunteers, a true/false format for a recognition test included both the item "I was told I could get an ulcer" (recognition of disclosed information) and the item "This drug is safer than other drugs for arthritis" (evaluative belief).[69]

Recognition tests are designed to measure comprehension of some domain of information or facts presented by the professional. Even the best recognition tests reveal little about the quality of the communication between professional and patient or subject, and relatively little about the overall adequacy of the patients' or subjects' understanding. For example, suppose a research subject can correctly recognize on a true/false or multiple-choice item that he or she was told gastrointestinal ulceration is a risk of research participation. We still know nothing about how the research subject understood the risk—what meaning the subject gave to it—and perhaps most importantly, whether the subject's personal meaning corresponded to the meaning intended by the investigator (e.g., as "gastrointestinal ulceration" is defined in standard medical sources). Recognition tests are also rarely able to identify whether a patient or subject holds any material false beliefs that the test is not designed to detect but that could nevertheless prevent the person from being able to give a sense$_1$ informed consent.

Still, an abiding skepticism about testing is not warranted by these warnings. Recognition tests can contribute to assessing understanding, if they are well constructed and if they are used as screening devices to identify patients and subjects who may be confused about disclosed information at a time in the consent process when there is still opportunity for professionals to help clarify apparent misconceptions. Recognition tests used in this way can become a standardized mechanism for gathering feedback, which we will now argue is the most important strategy available to professionals for confirming understanding.

"Feedback" Testing. The "feedback loop"—as it is sometimes designated in the communications literature—is simultaneously the best method available for assessing understanding in the context of interpersonal communication and for achieving it. We offer no precise definition for "feedback": It refers to any information in the context of interpersonal communication that provides the respective parties with data about the extent to which they understand one another. Feedback can be unintentional and unsolicited, as when a person's quizzical facial expressions give the professional "feedback" that the person is confused or distressed by what is being discussed. However, in the sense we use the term, "feedback" is expressly sought.

Strategies for securing feedback can be made formal parts of the consent process, as in the case of structured recognition or open-ended recall tests.[70] One specific strategy that has been recommended for consent contexts is to have patients or subjects restate in their own words what has been disclosed to them by professionals, followed by professional feedback as to the correctness of their interpretations.[71] Opportunities for feedback can also be integrated informally into the general dynamic of the exchange. For example, a professional can preface the reformulation of a patient's or subject's question or comment with directive phrases like "I hear you saying that," or "I think you are saying. . . . " Such informal communication strategies help establish the expectation that the patient or subject, as well as the professional, will be checking perceptions and assessing the quality of the communication.

The feedback the professional gets from the patient or subject functions as the basis of the professional's judgment about the adequacy of the person's understanding. At the same time, feedback is an essential part of the mechanism for achieving understanding. If feedback suggests confusion or misunderstanding, the parties can try again, and the cyclical feedback loop process can continue until the parties are mutually satisfied that substantial understanding—effective communication—has been achieved.

This discussion of feedback fits easily into our earlier analysis of understanding. There we discussed the probabilistic character of understanding in the context of interpersonal communication—understanding what—and likened the process of this kind of understanding to a string of hypotheses. Professionals and subjects and patients cannot be assured that they have understood one another—especially in the case of persons already known to suffer problems of comprehension—without some form of checking. That is, there must be exchanges that test what each thinks the other intends to say.[72] Feedback permits the parties to expose their hypotheses about the nature and meaning of the communication to mutual confirmation.

Conclusion

We began this chapter with the warning that our discussion would have demanding implications for professional conduct that far exceed current legal and regulatory disclosure requirements. Our shift from a focus on disclosure to a focus on effective communication is not simply a call for more or different information. It is a call for a different way of viewing and structuring the process of soliciting consent; the emphasis for the professional is on assisting the patient or subject to have a substantial understanding of what is at stake in the consent decision, a responsibility generally not dischargeable by the competent recital of a string of pertinent facts or the handing out of a well-conceived consent form. By contrast to the more conventional approaches, we have suggested numerous strategies professionals can use to increase the likelihood that substantial understanding will be achieved—of which only one, albeit an important one, is providing a core disclosure.

We make no normative claim that what we have proposed here ought to be, or even could be, turned into enforceable requirements for the legal doctrine of informed consent or into regulatory constraints. We do not even claim that professionals must always conduct themselves in accordance with the strategies suggested in this chapter. Our expedients may not be maximally expedient: A substantial amount of that scarcest of resources—both the professional's time *and* the subject's or patient's time—would be demanded to execute some of these strategies. For many less consequential procedures and interventions it may not be warranted to require whatever it takes to achieve substantial understanding.

This question, however, is about the proper role of informed consent in health care and research, and thus about informed consent in sense$_2$ as well as in sense$_1$. As we noted in Chapter 8, at the sense$_2$ level there must be a complex balancing of policy objectives, moral considerations, and the interests of various parties in the setting of consent requirements. Our concern in this chapter and in Chapter 10 is not with informed consent in sense$_2$, but with informed consent in sense$_1$, where substantial understanding is a necessary, and thus nonnegotiable, condition. In this chapter, we have attempted to explicate both what this condition demands in the actual practice of consent solicitation and what professionals can do to promote its satisfaction. We move now from the condition of substantial understanding to the condition of substantial noncontrol.

Notes

1. One among the possible exceptions would involve occurrent coercion (see n. 10 in Chapter 10 and also p. 242 in Chapter 7). If Mr. Jones takes Mrs. Jones's hand and forcibly makes her sign a consent form the "act" is unintentional but understood. However, even in this kind of example, Mrs. Jones is not likely to understand herself as having consented to anything. Other possible exceptions may be found among psychiatric patients or the neurologically impaired.

2. There is no logical relationship between understanding and authorization. By this we mean that substantial understanding is neither a sufficient nor a necessary condition of authorization and authorization is neither a sufficient nor a necessary condition of substantial understanding. Perhaps the most controversial component of this claim is that substantial understanding is not a necessary condition of authorization. We are asserting that a person can authorize something, that is, a person can perform an act that is recognizable by applicable social convention as an act of authorization, without having an adequate understanding of his or her act and without doing so intentionally—e.g., by signing a consent form hurriedly or by mistake. As we argued in Chapter 7, what makes an act of authorization is its conformity to operative social conventions or rules about transfer of permission, reponsibility, etc., and the behaviors accepted as making or symbolizing this transfer (e.g. handshakes, signatures, nods of the head, etc.), *not* what the person intends or understands. These conventions or rules regarding authorization may be formal institutional policies, as in the legal doctrine of informed consent sense$_2$; but they need not be. They may be informal but culturally well-intended verbal and nonverbal behaviors, as in responding "yes" to a request for permission or in giving a specific hand signal in a special context (e.g. an Indian chief authorizing warriors to attack).

3. Louis Harris, et al., "Views of Informed Consent and Decisionmaking: Parallel Surveys of Physicians and the Public," in President's Commission for the Study of Ethical Problems in Medicine and Biomedical and Behavioral Research, *Making Health Care Decisions* (Washington, D.C.: U.S. Government Printing Office, 1982), Vol. 1, 17–18.

4. Barrie R. Cassileth, et al., "Informed Consent: Why Are Its Goals Imperfectly Realized?" *New England Journal of Medicine* 302 (April 1980): 896–900.

5. Ruth R. Faden, et al., "A Survey to Evaluate Parental Consent As Public Policy for Neonatal Screening," *American Journal of Public Health* 72 (1982): 1347–51.

6. We are purposely ambiguous as to the sense in which X's express permission is "required" for Y's performance of R; it may be morally required but not required by convention, required by an institutional policy but not by law, etc.

7. These, in fact, may be the norms or requirements that define informed consent in sense₂ in the specific context, although they need not be. For example, federal regulations governing research with human subjects require institutions to have clear policies about responsibility and compensation for research-related injuries, which institutions are also required to disclose to potential subjects as part of the consent seeking process. In contexts in which there are no conventions controlling division of responsibility, for example, when informed consent sense₂ does not exist, the terms by which responsibilities are to be assigned can be privately arranged by the relevant parties.

8. One approach to explicating the meaning of an act or a concept, for example, an authorization, is in terms of its basic elements or primitives. However, we do not attempt in this volume to do anything like a thorough analysis of authorization in terms of primitives. To do so would require fitting our analysis within some wider theory of the representation of meaning, for example, Robert Schank's Conceptual Dependency Theory—see, Robert Schank and Robert Abelson, *Scripts, Plans, Goals, and Understanding* (Hillsdale, N.J.: Lawrence Erlbaum Associates, 1977), esp. 11–17.

9. Materiality is a fundamental but not readily quantifiable threshold concept in the law of evidence. A material fact or issue is one of sufficient relevance and significance to put before the judge and jury for consideration, but not necessarily to meet the standard of proof in the case. Materiality has innumerable legal applications, but it has never been well-defined. It was explicitly applied to informed consent disclosure by Jon R. Waltz and T.W. Scheuneman in their influential article, "Informed Consent to Therapy," *Northwestern Law Review* 628 (1970): 640. Their formulation was adopted almost verbatim by the *Canterbury* court, 464 F.2d 772, 788 (DC Cir. 1972). Waltz and Scheuneman defined a material risk this way: "When a reasonable person, in what the physician knows or should know to be the patient's position, would be likely to attach significance to the risk or cluster of risks in deciding whether or not to undergo the proposed therapy."

10. For an example of just how difficult it would be to identify reliably the causally decisive propositions, see Paul S. Appelbaum and Loren H. Roth, "Treatment Refusal in Medical Hospitals," in President's Commission, *Making Health Care Decisions*, Vol. 2, 469, 472.

11. It is not clear what happens when one adds to either the reasonable person standard or the professional practice standard an affirmative obligation to ask the patient whether he or she wants a more detailed explanation, as was done in an Oregon state statute to the professional practice standard, Oregon Revised Statutes, 1977, Section 677–097. In the legislation in Oregon it is doubtful that the effect on informational exchange will be as we envision it because of the sparse character of the wording. However, the potential exists for making both standards more compatible with informed consent sense₁ through modifications like those implemented by the Oregon legislature.

12. For legal commentary favoring this standard as appropriate for a legal doctrine of informed consent, see Alexander M. Capron, "Informed Consent in Catastrophic Disease Research and Treatment," *University of Pennsylvania Law Review* 123

(1974): 340–438, esp. 370, 413–14, 429; L.W. Kessenick and P.A. Mankin, "Medical Malpractice: The Right to be Informed," *University of San Francisco Law Review* 8 (1973): 261–81; Marcus Plant, "An Analysis of Informed Consent," *Fordham Law Review* 36 (1968); N. Jan Almquist, "When the Truth Can Hurt: Patient-Mediated Informed Consent in Cancer Therapy," *UCLA-Alaska Law Review* 9 (1980): 191–94; Richard E. Simpson, "Informed Consent: From Disclosure to Patient Participation in Medical Decisionmaking," *Northwestern University Law Review* 76 (1981): 172–207; and Leonard L. Riskin, "Informed Consent: Looking for the Action," *University of Illinois Law Forum* 1975 (1975): 580–90. Roughly this standard has been promoted as a moral standard for medical practice by Charles Culver and Bernard Gert, *Philosophy in Medicine: Conceptual and Ethical Problems in Medicine and Psychiatry* (New York: Oxford University Press, 1982), Chapter 3.

13. This is the standard preferred by most physicians in the national survey discussed in Chapter 3, see Harris, et al., "Views of Informed Consent and Decisionmaking," 303.

14. As we noted earlier, conventional disclosures, particularly in clinical medicine, focus almost exclusively on the proposed intervention, without mention of information that would enable the patient or subject to understand informed consent as an act of authorization. Until such time as the purpose and nature of informed consent are more widely understood, substantial understanding will not be achieved unless a patient or subject is explicitly informed that without express permission there will be no intervention or research participation and that the professional will abide by his or her decision.

15. In Chapter 8 we discuss the relationship between sense$_1$ informed consent and models of doctor-patient decisionmaking, such as the model of shared decisionmaking advocated by Katz and the President's Commission. We are not here arguing that all decisions about medical management and treatment should be made by patients solely on their own. We are also taking no position on which medical interventions morally or legally require explicit informed consent. This is a sense$_2$ question about the proper role for informed consent in clinical medicine. We are concerned only with situations in which the aim is to secure sense$_1$ informed consent. For such circumstances, we are suggesting that physicians be obligated to tell patients that the purpose of informed consent is to permit patients to make decisions about whether to authorize treatment.

16. For a very different problem about and context for false belief—and one where informed consent is not likely to be achieved—see Ebun O. Ekunwe and Ross Kessel, "Informed Consent in the Developing World," *Hastings Center Report* 14 (1984): 22–24. For an extension of these problems into the domain of *irrational* false belief, see Jay Katz, "The Right to Treatment—An Enchanting Legal Fiction?" *University of Chicago Law Review* 36 (1969): 755–83.

17. Ruth R. Faden and Alan I. Faden, "False Belief and the Refusal of Medical Treatment," *Journal of Medical Ethics* 3 (1977): 133.

18. Ibid., 135.

19. Curtis Meinert, personal communication, January 1985.

20. Kimberly Quaid, "The Effects of Disclosure Standards on Patients' Knowledge and Belief," personal communication, January 1985.

21. Stephen Bochner, "Doctors, Patients and their Cultures," in David Pendleton and John Hasler, eds., *Doctor-Patient Communication* (London: Academic Press, 1983), 137.

22. See, for example, Candace West, " 'Ask Me No Questions . . . ': An Analysis of Queries and Replies in Physician-Patient Dialogues," in Sue Fisher and Alexandra D.

Todd, *The Social Organization of Doctor-Patient Communication* (Washington, D.C.: Center for Applied Linguistics, 1983), 75–106; Philip Ley, "Patients' Understanding and Recall," in David Pendleton and John Hasler, *Doctor-Patient Communication*, 93–94; Debra L. Roter, "Patient Participation in the Patient-Provider Interaction: The Effects of Patient Question-Asking on the Quality of Interaction, Satisfaction and Compliance," *Health Education Monographs* 5 (1977): 281–315; Debra L. Roter, "Patient Question-Asking in Physician-Patient Interaction," *Health Psychology* 3 (1984): 395–410; David Pendleton and Stephen Bochner, "The Communication of Medical Information in General Practice Consultations as a Function of Patients' Social Class," *Social Science and Medicine* 14A (1980): 669–73; B. Svarstad, "Physician-Patient Communication and Patient Conformity with Medical Advice," in D. Mechanic, ed., *The Growth of Bureaucratic Medicine* (New York: Wiley, 1976), 220–38; and W. Stiles, S. Putnam, and M. Jacobs, "Verbal Exchange Structure of Initial Medical Interviews," *Health Psychology* 1 (1982): 315–36.

23. Bochner, "Doctors, Patients, and their Cultures," 127–38.

24. See Albert B. Robillard, Geoffrey M. White, and Thomas W. Maretzki, "Between Doctor and Patient: Informed Consent in Conversational Exchange," in Fisher and Todd, *The Social Organization of Doctor-Patient Communication*, 107–133, for an analysis of the sociolinguistics of a single consent solicitation.

25. Bochner uses the language of modeling desired patient behaviors by taking "the patient through the actual paces of requesting and receiving health-related information." ("Doctors, Patients and their Cultures," 137.)

26. See, for example, Marga Kreckel, "Communicative Acts and Extralinguistic Knowledge," in Mario von Cranach and Rom Harre, eds., *The Analysis of Action* (Cambridge: Cambridge University Press, 1982), 267–308; and Howard S. Friedman, "Nonverbal Communication in Medical Interaction," in Howard S. Friedman and M. Robin DiMatteo, eds., *Interpersonal Issues in Health Care* (New York: Academic Press, 1982), 51–66.

27. P. Pietroni, "Non-verbal Communication in the General Practice Surgery," in B. Tanner, ed., *Language and Communication in General Practice* (London: Hodder and Stoughton, 1976).

28. There is also nothing in sense₁ informed consent that requires that the person who provides the patient or subject with information about R necessarily be the person who will be authorized to do R. For example, if the agent to be authorized has poor communication and education skills, it may be perfectly appropriate and even preferable to delegate this task to another, for example, a professional health educator.

29. Charles W. Lidz and Alan Meisel, "Informed Consent and the Structure of Medical Care," in President's Commission, *Making Health Care Decisions*, Vol. 2, 317–410, esp. 391.

30. See, for example, Bochner, "Doctors, Patients and their Cultures"; Harry C. Triandis, "Culture Training, Cognitive Complexity and Interpersonal" in R.W. Brislin, Stephen Bochner, and W.J. Lonner, eds., *Attitudes: Cross-Cultural Perspectives on Learning* (New York: Wiley/Halsted, 1975); B. Bernstein, *Classes, Codes and Control, Vol. 1: Theoretical Studies Towards a Sociology of Language* (London: Routledge & Kegan Paul, 1970); and Marga Kreckel, "Communicative Acts and Extralinguistic Knowledge."

31. Robert Schank and Robert Abelson, *Scripts, Plans, Goals, and Understanding* (Hillsdale, N.J.: Lawrence Erlbaum Assoc., 1977), esp. 22. Here and throughout this section what we say about speakers and listeners would apply as well to writers and readers.

32. See Richard J. Harris and Gregory E. Monaco, "Psychology of Pragmatic Implication: Information Processing Between the Lines," *Journal of Experimental Psychology: General* 107 (1978): 1–22.

33. Sue Fisher, "Doctor Talk/Patient Talk: How Treatment Decisions are Negotiated in Doctor-Patient Communication," in Fisher and Todd, *The Social Organization of Doctor-Patient Communication*, 147.

34. See, for example, Pendleton and Bochner, "The Communication of Medical Information in General Practice Consultations as a Function of Patients' Social Class."

35. See, for example, T.M. Grundner, "On the Readability of Surgical Consent Forms," *New England Journal of Medicine* 302 (1980): 900–902; G.R. Morrow, "How Readable Are Subject Consent Forms?" *Journal of the American Medical Association* 244 (1980): 56–58; and B. Gray, et al., "Research Involving Human Subjects," *Science* 1094 (1978): 201.

36. Barbara Freeman, et al., "Gaps in Doctor-Patient Communication: Doctor-Patient Interaction Analysis," *Pediatric Research* 5 (1971): 300, as cited in Bernard Barber, *Informed Consent in Medical Therapy and Research* (New Brunswick, NJ: Rutgers University Press, 1980), 88, see also 85–91.

37. See, for example, Daniel Meyer, Howard Levanthal and Mary Gutman, "Common Sense Models of Illness: The Example of Hypertension," *Health Psychology* 4(1985): 115–35, and Aaron V. Cicourel, "Hearing is Not Believing: Language and the Structure of Belief in Medical Communication," in Fisher and Todd, *The Social Organization of Doctor-Patient Communication*, 221–39.

38. See p. 311. We are here taking the patient's statements at face value. Given the facts of the case, it is possible that the patient's defense of her belief in terms of the absence of symptomology was merely a socially acceptable response intended to cover up her real reasons—for example, that no black person could competently make such a diagnosis, etc.

39. Schank and Abelson, *Scripts, Plans, Goals and Understanding*, 67.

40. See, for example, C.H. Frederikson, "Representing Logic and Semantic Structure of Knowledge Acquired from Discourse," *Cognitive Psychology* 7 (1975): 371–458; Janice M. Keenan, "Psychological Issues Concerning Implication," *Journal of Experimental Psychology: General* 107 (1978): 23–27; G.A. Kelly, *The Psychology of Personal Constructs* (New York: Norton, 1955); and O.J. Harvey, D.E. Hunt, and H.M. Schroder, *Conceptual Systems and Personality Organization* (New York: Wiley, 1961).

41. E.B. Huert and C.M. MacLeod, "Cognition and Information Processing in Patient and Physician," in G.C. Stone, F. Cohen, and N.E. Adler, eds., *Health Psychology* (San Francisco: Jossey-Bass, Inc., 1979), 303–32.

42. The most widely cited work in this area has been done by Amos Tversky and Daniel Kahneman. See, for example, the following jointly authored articles: "Choices, Values and Frames," *American Psychologist* 39 (1984): 341–50; "Judgment Under Uncertainty: Heuristics and Biases," *Science* 185 (1974): 1124–31; "The Framing of Decisions and the Psychology of Choice," *Science* 211 (1981): 453–58; and Daniel Kahneman and Amos Tversky, "Prospect Theory," *Econometrica* 47 (1979): 263–92. See also, Daniel Kahneman, Paul Slovic and Amos Tversky, eds., *Judgment Under Uncertainty: Heuristics and Biases* (New York: Cambridge University Press, 1982); Paul Slovic, Baruch Fischhoff, and Sarah Lichtenstein, "Behavioral Decision Theory," *Annual Review of Psychology* 28 (1977): 1–39; and Richard Nisbett and Lee Ross, *Human Inferences: Strategies and Shortcomings of Social Judgment* (Englewood Cliffs, NJ: Prentice-Hall, 1980).

43. For a general review, see Baruch Fischhoff, Sarah Lichtenstein, Paul Slovic, et al., *Acceptable Risk* (Cambridge: Cambridge University Press, 1981).

44. Kahneman and Tversky, "Choices, Values and Frames," 344.

45. Ibid., 346.

46. See, for example, Tversky and Kahneman, "The Framing of Decisions and the Psychology of Choice."

47. S.E. Eraker and H.C. Sox, "Assessment of Patients' Preferences for Therapeutic Outcome," *Medical Decision Making* 1 (1981): 29–39; Barbara McNeil, et al., "On the Elicitation of Preferences for Alternative Therapies," *New England Journal of Medicine* 306 (May 1982): 1259–62.

48. McNeil, et al., "On the Elicitation of Preferences."

49. Kahneman and Tversky, "Choices, Values and Frames," 346.

50. Ibid., 343.

51. Ibid.

52. See, for example, Baruch Fischhoff, Paul Slovic, and Sarah Lichtenstein, "Knowing What You Want: Measuring Labile Values," in T. Wallston, ed., *Cognitive Processes in Choice and Decision Behavior* (Hillsdale, N.J.: Erlbaum, 1980), 117–41.

53. William C. Thompson, "Psychological Issues in Informed Consent," in President's Commission, *Making Health Care Decisions*, Vol. 3, 102–103.

54. Ibid., 102.

55. In fairness to Thompson, he appears quite sensitive to the debate about rationality, inferences, facts and values (see "Psychological Issues in Informed Consent," 87–89). It may be either an overreading on our part or an oversight on his that accounts for our interpretation of this example.

56. Despite the presumably universal exposure to percentages in the public schools—see K. Kramer, *The Teaching of Elementary School Mathematics* (Boston: Allyn and Bacon, Inc., 1966)—observation and research indicate that students have difficulty in learning the subject, and their grasp does not improve as they move through the public school system. In an early study, it was found that 90% of ninth graders could not readily calculate a number when a percentage of that number is given (W.S. Guiler, "Difficulties in Percentage Encountered by Ninth Grade Pupils," *Journal of Elementary Schools* 46 (1946): 563. The more recent National Assessment of Educational Progress also found that both school children and adults had limited ability to manipulate percentages in problems, including both transformation of fractions into their equivalent percentages and the problems mentioned from the Guiler study, T.P. Carpenter, T.G. Coburn, R.E. Reys, and J.W. Wilson, "Results and Implications of the NAEP Mathematics Assessment: Secondary School," *Math Teacher* 68 (1975): 453–70.

57. See, for example, Nesbitt and Ross, *Human Inferences*, 273–96.

58. See, for example, G.D. Bryant and G.R. Norman, "Expressions of Probability: Words and Numbers," *New England Journal of Medicine* 302 (1980): 411; Carpenter, Coburn, Reys, and Wilson, "Results and Implications of the NAEP Mathematics Assessment: Secondary School"; R.H. Simpson, "Stability in Meaning of Quantitative Terms: A Comparison over 20 Years," *Quarterly Journal of Speech* 49 (1963): 146–51; Sarah Lichtenstein and J.R. Newman, "Empirical Scaling of Common Verbal Phrases Associated with Numerical Probabilities," *Psychological Science* 10 (1967): 563–64.

59. For an illustration of how Bayes Theorem could be applied to a patient's assessment of disclosed risk information, see Thompson, "Psychological Issues in Informed Consent," 90.

60. For example, if presented with a meaningless list of letters (e.g., X, K, A, Y, N, Q, B, T, etc.), most subjects can only remember seven. However, if subjects are presented with the letters (C, A, T, D, O, G, T, O, P, B, O, X, P, I, T, N, O, D, R, U, T)

most can remember 21 letters—those of the seven three-letter words. Subjects are able to chunk the letters into meaningful units, in this case, words, and thus increase the information that can be held in memory. See, for example, R.L. Klatzky, *Human Memory Structure and Processes*, 2nd ed. (San Francisco: W.H. Freeman and Co., 1980).

61. Philip Ley, "Memory for Medical Information," *British Journal of Social and Clinical Psychology* 18 (1979): 245–55, and Lynn C. Epstein and Louis Lasagna, "Obtaining Informed Consent: Form or Substance," *Archives of Internal Medicine* 123 (1969): 682–88.

62. G. Morrow, et al., "A Simple Technique for Increasing Cancer Patients' Knowledge of Informed Consent to Treatment," *Cancer* 42 (1978): 793.

63. Irving L. Janis and Leon Mann, *Decision Making* (New York: The Free Press, 1977).

64. Ibid.

65. See, for example, G. Robinson and A. Merav, "Informed Consent: Recall by Patients Tested Post-Operatively," *The Annals of Thoracic Surgery*, 22 (1976): 209–12; J.H. Bergler, et al., "Informed Consent: How Much Does the Patient Understand?", *Clinical Pharmacology and Therapeutics*, 27 (1980): 435–40; Barbara Rimer, et al., "Informed Consent: A Crucial Step in Cancer Patient Education," *Health Education Quarterly* 10 (1984): 30–42; and Barrie Cassileth, et al., "Informed Consent—Why Are its Goals Imperfectly Realized?", *The New England Journal of Medicine*, 302 (1980): 896–900.

66. Compare Charles Culver, F. Ferrell, and Ronald Green, "ECT and Special Problems of Informed Consent," *American Journal of Psychiatry* 135 (May 1980): 586–91.

67. Some of the more widely used formulas include the Fry Readability Scale and the Dale-Chall Formula. See, for example, Philip Ley, "The Measurement of Comprehensibility," *Journal of the Institute of Health Education*, 10 (1973): 23–29; Tom M. Grunder, "Two Formulas For Determining the Readability of Subject Consent Forms," *American Psychologist* 33 (1978): 773–75; and Philip Ley, "Giving Information to Patients," in J.R. Eiser, ed., *Social Psychology and Behavioral Medicine* (Chichester, NY: Wiley and Sons, 1982), 339–75.

68. Sometimes these tests have been administered during or shortly after consent solicitation, thus serving as measures of comprehension at the time consent was given or refused, whereas in other studies, tests have been administered as long as six months after consent was solicited and thus are measures of long-term memory only, telling us little about the adequacy of consent at the time it was obtained. See Alan Meisel and Loren H. Roth, "Toward an Informed Discussion of Informed Consent," *Arizona Law Review* 25 (1983): 288–89, 292–95.

69. M. Hassar and M. Weintraub, " 'Uninformed' Consent and the Wealthy Volunteer: An Analysis of Patient Volunteers in a Clinical Trial of a New Anti-Inflammatory Drug," *Clinical Pharmacology and Therapeutics* 20 (1976): 379–386.

70. In a recognition test the respondent "recognizes" the correct response from among the alternatives given. In a free recall test, no answers are provided; the respondent must "recall" the answer from an otherwise unprompted memory base.

71. R.B. Stuart, "Protection of the Right to Informed Consent to Participate in Research," *Behavioral Therapy* 9 (1978): 73–82.

72. For moral problems of comprehension in research with the elderly and an attempt to resolve these problems by the use of testing, see Harvey A. Taub and Marilyn T. Baker, "A Reevaluation of Informed Consent in the Elderly: A Method for Improving Comprehension Through Direct Testing," *Clinical Research* (1984): 17–21.

10

Coercion, Manipulation, and Persuasion

Disclosing, informing, and comprehending are the most widely discussed topics in traditional commentary on informed consent. But remaining independent of control by others is equally important for autonomous decisionmaking. Many important life decisions are made in contexts replete with competing claims and interests, social demands and expectations, and express attempts by others to direct an outcome. These influences on individuals are often unavoidable and may even be desirable, but some interfere with or deprive persons of autonomous choice. Our task in this chapter is to distinguish influences that are compatible with substantial autonomy from influences that are not.

We began work on this project in Chapter 7, with a general analysis of the condition of noncontrol, which required that we distinguish coercion, manipulation, and persuasion. We argued that coercive influences are never compatible with substantially autonomous action, but that all persuasive influences and some manipulative influences permit substantial autonomy (see Figure 2, p. 259). It follows that informed consents (in sense₁) can be obtained only if the persons consenting are subjected either to no influence, to persuasive influences, or to certain kinds of manipulative influences that do not preclude autonomous decision making.

This abstract conclusion offers no more guidance than other general pronouncements in the informed consent literature that require voluntariness or the absence of coercion and undue influence.[1] If our position on noncontrol and informed consent is to be meaningful and of practical import, a more complete analysis must be presented of the distinguishing characteristics or hallmarks of persuasion, coercion, and manipulation that are compatible and incompatible with substantial autonomy, as they are likely to appear in informed consent contexts. Complex questions surround the characteristics of subtle, minor manipulations, a subject that will absorb much of our energy later in this chapter. We begin, how-

337

ever, with coercion. Because coercion has no place in informed consent (in sense₁, and almost certainly no place in sense₂ either), we proceed quickly to persuasion. The overlap and interplay between persuasive and manipulative influences then leads to a core problem: manipulations that are compatible with substantial autonomy.

Our task throughout is less to undertake a detailed theoretical analysis of each of the three categories of influence—coercion, manipulation, and persuasion—than to identify and examine the problems that some forms of influence—manipulation, in particular—pose for informed consent.

Coercion

Much of the informed consent literature leaves the unmistakable impression that coercion is a major problem for informed consent, both in clinical medicine and in research. For example, both the American Psychological Association and Henry Beecher have pointed to the "subtle coercion" involved in the use of students and laboratory personnel as research subjects,[2] and many others have identified what they believe to be either subtle or blatant forms of coercion in the case of consent by prisoners used as research subjects.[3] Willard Gaylin has contended that medicine generally enjoys wide institutional privileges of coercion,[4] and Franz Ingelfinger, in his influential article "Informed (but Uneducated) Consent," asserted that "some element of coercion" is present in many transactions in which the investigator-physician asks a patient to become involved in an experiment.[5] Ingelfinger gave eloquent expression to the potential for coercion in the plight of the patient-subject:

> Incapacitated and hospitalized because of the illness, frightened by strange and impersonal routines, and fearful for his health and perhaps life, he is far from exercising a free power of choice when the person to whom he anchors all his hopes asks, "Say, you wouldn't mind, would you, if you joined some of the other patients on this floor and helped us to carry out some very important research we are doing?" When "informed consent" is obtained, it is not the student, the destitute bum, or the prisoner to whom, by virtue of his condition, the thumb screws of coercion are most relentlessly applied; it is the most used and useful of all experimental subjects, the patient with disease.[6]

Despite this concern about coercion in informed consent contexts, the influences adverted to by these commentators are not, strictly speaking, coercive. In the continuum of influences we developed in Chapter 7, coercion is an extreme form of influence by another person that completely controls a person's decision. In the writings of the authors just cited, "coercion" is often used in a broader, and more judgmental, sense to designate any kind of pressure or influence that takes unfair advantage or unfairly or inappropriately compromises the quality of autonomy in a patient's or subject's consent, but without necessarily controlling the consent. Some accounts of coercion even define it in terms of *morally impermissible* influences.[7]

These analyses of "coercion" are all wide of the mark of our use. Our claim that coercion has no place in informed consent (sense₁) depends on the premise that coercion deprives the person of autonomous choice, and thus is incompatible with informed consent. This thesis is not that such a deprivation is necessarily immoral. The severe threats often presented by legal sanctions, including those that prohibit various health behaviors, may be coercive, but the issue of their *justifiability* is a separate matter.[8] In short, we use "coercion" in a more restricted, specific, and less judgmental sense than the term is used in many other contexts.[9]

The Nature of Coercion

Coercion can result either by compelling someone to do something he or she does not want to do or by preventing someone from doing something he or she wants to do. In either case, the will of another dominates, so that the coerced person's "choice" is not his or her own but effectively that of the other. In Chapter 7 we proposed the following definition: Coercion occurs if one party intentionally and successfully influences another by presenting a credible threat of unwanted and avoidable harm so severe that the person is unable to resist acting to avoid it. The three critical features in this definition, at least for our purposes, are that

1. the agent of influence must *intend* to influence the other person by presenting a severe threat,
2. there must be a credible *threat*, and
3. the threat must be *irresistible*.

For the threat to be credible, either both parties must know that the person making the threat can make it good, or the one making the threat must successfully deceive the person threatened into so believing. A mere perception of coercion in the mind of a patient or subject, and the person's subsequent conduct correlative to the perception, is not sufficient for coercion. The intentions of the influence agent to threaten are essential. Ignoring this vital point has led to many needless debates over the coercion of consent.

This brief definition does not deviate significantly from some other influential analyses of coercion and will prove adequate to serve our needs in this volume. At the same time, it should be acknowledged that this definition does not fully reflect the rich literature on coercion in philosophy and political theory in which crucial distinctions have been introduced and various elements in this general conception qualified, reconstructed, and criticized.[10] Only two substantive controversies in this literature need to be engaged because of their relevance for issues of informed consent. These are (1) whether offers as well as threats can be coercive, and (2) whether all threats are coercive.

Threats and Offers

The first issue can be dispatched quickly.[11] The dominant position in the philosophical literature conceives coercion exclusively in terms of threats of severe negative sanctions. For example, Bernard Gert takes the firm position that if a person acts to secure an offered good, no matter how attractive or overwhelming the offer, coercion is not involved.[12] In Robert Nozick's pioneering analysis of coercion, he similarly implies that only threats can be coercive, in part because he believes that people shun threats but welcome offers.[13] We accept this analysis. The essence of coercion is control of a person's behavior by the negative sanction of presenting a threat.[14] Even if an offer is made in a setting in which it is abnormally attractive—for example, money or freedom for deprived prisoners—it is manipulative rather than coercive. (See pp. 357–359.)

To maintain that large or attractive offers coerce would in the end make a mockery of the concept of coercion—unless, of course, the offer is merely a disguised threat. By this expanded definition, anyone who intentionally and successfully influenced another by presenting an offer so attractive that the person was unable to resist it would have coerced the other person. Thus, attracting a professional athlete to move from one team to another through a fat contract would have to be declared coercive. If attractive contracts are declared "coercive," the requirement that the coerced decision not be the chooser's own but effectively that of the influence agent is substantially diluted, and thus the central meaning of coercion is lost in the shuffle.

Nonetheless, some kinds of offers have long been viewed by numerous writers as inherently coercive instruments or circumstances. Among the best known examples in recent years have been irresistible offers made to prisoners to become research subjects. Beecher was among the earliest to denounce such practices as coercive and as involving bribery inconsistent with obtaining informed consent:

> Whenever coercion could operate, however subtly, the consent of volunteers must be suspect. This applies especially to civil prisoners and other captive groups, such as medical students. . . .
> The prospect of an award of extreme benefit to the [prisoner] subject such as a great reduction in time of imprisonment or parole or pardon could constitute a bribe greater than the human spirit could be expected to support, with clear violation of the necessary requirements of the principle of consent.[15]

We would agree that if a prison official said, "We will not allow you to leave when your time is up unless you become an experimental subject," this would constitute a threat and would be coercive. However, the offer described by Beecher is a genuine offer, not a veiled threat. A distinction should be drawn between being coerced to imprisonment and being coerced in prison: Many prisoners may in fact *not* be free to consent because of coercion within the prison, but this coercion does not follow from the bare fact of their being coercively imprisoned. An offer to prisoners may not be one that they reasonably can be expected to resist, and it may even be exploitative, but we shall see later that these are problems of manipulation, not coercion.

We do not mean to suggest that, because such offers are not instances of coercion, it is morally legitimate to use them to induce prisoners to be research subjects. Indeed, the offer condemned by Beecher may be a morally impermissible manipulation, but it is not a threat and not coercive as described. Questions of the moral justifiability of the offer are separate matters.

A Subjective Criterion of Resistibility

Are all threats coercive? A negative answer to this question is implied in our basic definition of coercion: Only threats so severe that the person threatened *cannot resist* acting to avoid them are coercive. As with attractive offers, threats that are resistible may qualify as manipulations, but not as coercion.

A second question now arises: resistible by what standard? Unlike Gert and others, we rely on a subjective analysis that focuses on how coercion of a particular individual occurs. An influence that coerces one person may fail to coerce another, even if the threats to both are equally severe, and are so perceived by both. In a successful threat, the will of the influence agent controls and the other person's "choice" conforms; but whether the person who attempts control will succeed depends heavily on the sujective response of the person at whom the attempt to coerce is directed.

Consider the following schema:

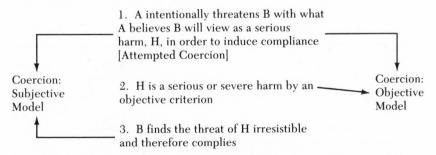

If condition 1 is satisfied, the result is attempted coercion. According to an *objective* interpretation (used by Gert and others), 1 and 2 are jointly sufficient for coercion; but according to our *subjective* analysis, condition 2 is entirely irrelevant and is replaced by 3; 1 and 3 are then jointly sufficient for coercion.[16] Thus, on our analysis, coercion occurs only if the person who is the target of the coercion finds the threat irresistible. Some threats will coerce virtually all persons, whereas others will coerce only a few persons; but either way, a judgment of coercion must await a case-by-case analysis, depending ultimately on the subjective responses of those at whom attempted coercion is directed.

Many difficult cases remain difficult under this conception of coercion. Consider the following example: Sometimes fecund women in work environments such as chemical plants and zinc smelters, where exposure to mutagenic and teratogenic chemicals may be serious, encounter a company policy that suddenly makes their jobs off limits to them because of their child-bearing potential. The intentional aim of the policy, sometimes designated "protective exclusion," is to protect the actual or potential fetus from harm (and the company from liability for harm). Some fertile women workers have "elected" to undergo what have been called "voluntary" sterilizations, rather than yield their well-paying positions. Such policies are coercive if the company intends to present a threat to their workers in adopting them. But can it reasonably be said that the policy as designed coerces the women *to be sterilized* if the company never specifically intended (or even imagined) that women would respond to the exclusionary policy by being sterilized? (See condition 1 in the schema.) Moreover, can it reasonably be said that the threat of a loss (or perhaps transfer) of position is not resistible by a worker? (See condition 3 above.)

A related problem is that a criterion of "subjective irresistibility", like any subjective criterion, is difficult to implement in practice. We offer no suggestions as to how to measure or test whether a given threat would prove irresistible to any particular individual. Such assessments doubtless have to be made for policy purposes on the basis of evidence and predictions about how *most* people would respond to a given threat under the circumstances—an *objective* criterion—and how the individual in question may differ in relevant abilities, life experiences, and values from most people. Fortunately, from the perspective of $sense_1$ informed consent, we need not linger on the practical problem posed by our subjective account of coercion. Whether a threat actually is irresistible for an individual or hovers around the edge of irresistibility is not a distinction of relevance, because no threat of either magnitude is compatible with substantial autonomy and thus with informed consent. As we shall see in the section on manipulation of options, only threats and punishments at the other end of the continuum, those that are relatively *resistible*, allow choices to be substantially noncontrolled.

Public or institutional policies of general application—such as those governing permissible treatment of prisoners or the institutionalized mentally or physically disabled—must of course deal with an aggregate population within which it would be difficult if not impossible to determine how threats subjectively affect particular individuals. In some of these populations the likelihood of subjective coercion may be great, the risks to the population high, and the resources needed for evaluation on a case-by-case basis prohibitive. For these reasons, policies determined on a subjective criterion would generally be unworkable, and a balancing of the interests involved suggests the advisability of an objective criterion, perhaps along lines already suggested by Gert.[17]

In such *policy* contexts, coercive threats may have to be distinguished from noncoercive threats by the irresisibility to the average, or ordinary, or reasonable person under the circumstances—an objective standard. For *policy* purposes a credible threat that a person on this objective model cannot be expected to resist thus *is a coercive act* (as suggested by the above schema).

This approach facilitates policies of informed consent in *sense₂*, but of course our analysis is directed at informed consent in *sense₁* (autonomous authorization). Some manipulated consents obtained near the level of coercion, and certainly ones that do not satisfy the criterion of substantial absence of control by others, may be allowed in policies dealing with aggregate populations to qualify as "informed consents." But they can never be acceptable under the criterion of substantial autonomy.

Consider the following example of the use of an objective criterion: During World War II some United States Air Force pilots were used at the Mayo Clinic in high-stress, potentially fatal experimental tests of cockpit pressures produced by new and faster jets. All pilots in the experiment were classified as "volunteers." An objective criterion would require that the system by which pilots were recruited for this experimental protocol present the offer to participate in the experiment in a way resistible by the average military pilot (not merely the average person in society at large, as the pressures in both circumstances are quite different). Any intentional threat of a sanction, such as disgrace or ostracism, that is not resistible by the average military pilot in the circumstances would constitute coercion, even if *some* pilots did in fact find the threats resisitible. Conversely, any pilot who consented because severely threatened beyond his ability to resist would *not be coerced, according to this objective analysis*, because the average pilot (or most pilots) did find the sanctions resistible.

This formulation makes apparent the tradeoff in adopting an objective criterion: What is gained in ease and sureness of application is lost in those few persons who are *in fact subjectively coerced* but cannot be viewed as coerced on a purely objective criterion. Weak and vulnerable persons, subject to coercive threats that would not faze a "reasonable person", would *not* be coerced on this criterion, a central reason we have accepted a subjective criterion.

"Coercive Situations"

An important question for the analysis of coercion is, "Can there be non-intentional, situational coercion?" Although our definition of "coercion" requires that coercion be intentional on the part of a coercer, some situations seem to force persons to act in ways they would not otherwise act, with the same effectiveness as the intentional interventions of others. Sometimes people unintentionally make other persons feel "threatened," and sometimes *situations,* such as illness and economic necessity, present "threats" of serious harm that a person feels compelled to prevent at all costs. Such circumstances are sometimes called "coercive situations." We will preserve this label for them; but do these felt "threats," when acted on, amount to instances of *coercion* in our sense?

Two examples will make this problem clearer. First, our earlier example of using prisoners in experimentation is again applicable in this context, if we assume that a prisoner is left without any viable alternative to participation in research because of the awfulness of the alternatives in the circumstance or because of what may appear to be threats presented by prison officials. As Alvin Bronstein, Director of the National Prison Project, puts the problem for informed consent, "You cannot create [a prison] institution in which informed consent without coercion is feasible."[18]

Second, economic necessity is often used to illustrate the problem:[19] In circumstances of severe economic deprivation, a person might accept a job or sign a contract that the person would refuse under less stringent economic circumstances. The prospect of starvation if an objectionable job offer is rejected seems to "coerce" no less than an intentional threat by an employer or businessman to fire an otherwise unemployable person unless the person agrees to be transferred to an objectionable job. The psychological *effect* on the person forced to choose may be identical, and the person can appropriately say in both cases, "I had no choice; it would have been crazy to refuse." Moreover, if, as virtually everyone agrees, a contract signed under another's threat is invalid (and the "consent" behind the signing an invalid consent), can we not say that a person who signs a contract in a "coercive situation" has signed an invalid contract (and given an invalid consent)?

In both coercion and "coercive situations," the person *does not act freely*; in the above examples, the person is not free to be an experimental subject, to take the job, or to sign the contract. The person is tightly constrained by circumstances, without any viable alternative; natural necessities such as eating simply cannot be set aside. It does not follow, however, that persons in such "coercive situations" do not act *autonomously*. In our analysis, the person who takes a job or signs a contract in order to avoid starving can be described as *not free* because of the constraints in the "coercive situation." A great many consenting surgery candidates of all types are persons left without meaningful choices in just this respect: To survive they have no meaningful choice but to elect the surgery. But this loss of freedom cannot be equated with a loss of autonomy: Such persons may have carefully deliberated about their situations and reached a decision under totally noncoercive circumstances, in our sense of "coercion." We consider it a serious confusion to move from a correct claim about a deprivation or loss of freedom caused by desperate circumstances to a (fallaciously drawn) conclusion that there has been a loss of autonomy because of a coercive situation. (We do, of course, recognize that a theory of action is needed to cover this claim.)

Natural, environmental, and circumstantial threats, such as those presented by disease, are not in the relevant sense *controlling*. To say that they are controlling would be to say that any severe pressure of any type is coercive. In a true situation of coercion, what *controls*, and thus deprives one of autonomy, is the will of another person, substituted for one's own will or desire, where the presented option is avoidable and the coercee wishes to avoid it. If *intent* to threaten is *not* present, one may of course feel just as *forced* to a choice and may just as heartily wish to avoid it, but because the option is not intentionally presented by another person, it neither substitutes another's will for one's own will nor forces an *eliminable* choice. In a "coercive situation," no one is in control of the unintentional or situational "threat" that is presented; but a truly coerced act is always one in which the choice is forced and is eliminable by the coercer. A consent under coercion, then, does not qualify as an informed consent (sense₁) not simply because one is constrained or compelled to the "choice," but also because one's choice is being caused or controlled by another.

The view we are defending is analogous to a centuries-old pattern of reflection in law about the causation of harm. (See Chapter 2, pp. 34–35.) Most would agree that harm can be caused by natural events such as snakebites and earthquakes; but in law the notion of *responsibility* for harm is analytically linked to the concept of the *causation* of harm. The law is not concerned with the causation of harms of all forms, but only with the ascription of causal responsibility for harmful outcomes. Only human agents—not pets, environmental threats, or human incompetents—can be, in the relevant sense, responsible.[20] In our analysis of coercion, we analogously restrict the notions of "control" and "coercion" to the intentional acts of others for which they are responsible and which they could eliminate.

Our analysis has implications for the soliciting of informed consents in sense₁. It anticipates that many patients and subjects facing or experiencing severe harms and influences of many types and from many sources may nevertheless be able to give informed consents in the face of extraordinarily difficult *but not coercive* pressures.[21] If we concluded that the "threats" created or introduced by serious illness needing therapy were coercive, we would be forced to conclude that many patients who choose, after thorough deliberation, for or against therapies are not acting autonomously. To reach the conclusion that, as a general rule, substantial autonomy is not possible for persons beset by severe illness would be to eliminate the possibility of informed consent precisely where it is often most important, and where the health professional may have a profoundly important moral obligation to patiently discuss treatment and research options in order to receive a well-considered informed consent (in sense₁).

The paradigm is the case of the presumptively dying patient. The principle of beneficence will generally enjoin the clinician to offer an intervention with lifesaving potential, even if the person is incapable of resisting the offer of the proposed intervention because of the "threat" of death. Despite the horribly pressured nature of such circumstances, we believe it is possible for at least some patients to give informed consents in sense₁.

Persuasion

Surprisingly, coercion has been a recurrent topic in the informed consent literature, while the relationship between persuasion and informed consent has been largely ignored. Yet persuasion is a ubiquitous form of interpersonal influence that figures prominently in the consent decisions of most, if not all, patients and subjects. We have already stated our position that persuasion, properly understood, poses no problem for informed consent in sense₁. (See pp. 261–262.) Indeed, it is the model form of influence in informed consent contexts: It can enable and even facilitate substantially autonomous authorizations.

The Nature of Persuasion

There has been and continues to be confusion on this matter in literature on informed consent. A typical approach to persuasive influence in this literature is Richard Warner's discussion of "When is consent free?":

> . . . The degree of freedom of a choice is determined by (1) the extent to which it is directly motivated by the person's ideal self-image, and (2) the extent to which the choice is *not* influenced by the indirect sources of motivation—family, friends, the hospital staff, and economic considerations.
>
> Ideally, then, a person who is to give consent should be presented with the relevant information and left completely free to make up his mind. . . .

> So, to keep your choice as free as possible, we should (a) try to make
> sure that we do not influence you in any other way besides presenting
> the information, and (b) present the information in a way that is "neu-
> tral"—that reflects as little personal bias as possible for one alternative
> as opposed to another.[22]

A variant of this same thesis is found in an article on Willowbrook that
we discussed in Chapter 5: Louis Goldman believes "an 'explanation'
easily shades into 'persuasion'—and from there to 'coercion' is by no
means a giant step."[23]

Both statements depart as far from our usage of "persuasion," as does
the title of the once bestseller *The Hidden Persuaders*. It is a *giant* step
from persuasion to both biased manipulative maneuvering and coercion.
The step to coercion moves across the full continuum of influence from
noncontrol to control (as we developed the continuum in Chapter 7).
Moreover, Warner seems to hold that *persuading* someone to consent is
less objective or more biased than an *explanation* that simply discloses
the facts without a persuasive, argued analysis; he suggests that explanation is more acceptable than persuasion because persuasion, like coercion, is a form of influence that intrinsically limits autonomy. This
account is entirely incompatible with our definition of persuasion, and
also, we believe, harbors an incorrect vision of the health professional's
proper role in many consent situations.

Frequently in clinical situations, professionals would be morally
blameworthy if they did not attempt to persuade their patients to consent to interventions that are medically necessitated. Reasoned argument in defense of an option is itself information, and as such is no less
important in ensuring understanding than disclosure of facts. The real
challenge to the professional is often to *restrict* influence attempts to
explanation and persuasion, so as to secure a true nonmanipulated
informed consent from the patient or subject.[24] Thus, an adequate
understanding of the *nature and boundaries* of persuasion can be critical
to proper consent solicitation, but this is no grounds for objecting to persuasion per se.

In Chapter 7 we defined "persuasion" as the intentional and successful
attempt to induce a person, through appeals to reason, to freely
accept—as his or her own—the beliefs, attitudes, values, intentions, or
actions advocated by the persuader. This definition excludes a number
of distinctions often introduced in the analysis of persuasion: (1) A distinction is sometimes drawn between "rational" and "nonrational" persuasion, for example, and Warner and Goldman may be implicitly relying
on such a distinction in stating their claims. Because our definition of
persuasion restricts the category to influence by appeals to reason, "persuasion" in this definition is necessarily rational persuasion. (2) In Chap-

ter 5 (see p. 209) we noticed that NIH once used a category of "undue persuasion." While we would recognize a general category of "undue influence," which includes all coercion and some manipulation, there can be *no* "undue persuasion" in our categorization, at least not in the sense of unduly *controlling*. (3) We also do not recognize what Paul Appelbaum and Loren Roth label "forceful persuasion" as a form of persuasion. This is a form of influence in which persistent and sometimes misleading language is used. They cite, as an example, an intern who does not accept a patient's refusal of an x-ray; the intern insists that he "absolutely must have the film and that he [the patient] could not refuse it." The patient then agrees. In our categories, neither nonrational nor forceful "persuasion" qualifies as a form of *persuasion*, because both are forms of *manipulation*.[25]

In the process of persuasion there is a respect in which we can say that a person is *caused* to believe something by the influence of the persuader. Suppose that person X's persuasive influence is necessary and sufficient for Y's belief, and in that respect is the causal condition of the belief. It would be mistaken to infer from the existence of such a causal relation that persuasion is incompatible with autonomous choice and absence of control by others or that bias or undue or nonrational influence is somehow at work. If a person is persuaded, an *autonomous act* of acceptance is *caused by* pointing out to the person a motive or reason for acceptance. The meaning of "cause" is quite different here than in the earlier analysis of coercion where "causation" was analyzed in terms of *causal control*. Here there is no control, in our sense, but only the presentation of a motive or reason.

This point is central. In persuasion, the influence agent must bring to the persuadee's attention *reasons* for acceptance of the desired perspective. In paradigmatic cases of persuasion, these reasons are conveyed through written or spoken language, by use of structured argument and reasoning. However, reasons can also be conveyed through nonverbal communication—through, for example, visual evidence—and by artful questioning and structured listening, as with certain forms of insight therapies[26] or the use of the Socratic method.[27] In both the Socratic method and insight therapies, A helps B discover the reasons why B should accept a viewpoint; A elicits reasons from B, rather than simply telling or showing B what the reasons are. Depending on the specifics of the process, the Socratic method and insight therapies may involve heavy doses of what we shall refer to later as self-persuasion, in addition to the interpersonal, persuasive effects of the influence agent.

As with "coercion," our definition of "persuasion" does not fully reflect the rich literature on this topic, particularly in psychology.[28] However, this definition is sufficient to serve our needs in this volume, if augmented by the following discussion of the distinguishing marks of persuasion in social interaction.

Warnings and Predictions

One central feature of persuasion, according to our definition, is that the reasons that comprise the persuasive appeal exist *independent* of the persuader. If the influence agent creates or in some way has control over the contingencies that the agent offers as "reasons," the influence is no longer strictly persuasive, but rather manipulative or even coercive.

James Tedeschi has proposed a classification scheme for influence strategies that supports this point.[29] Tedeschi distinguishes between two broad categories of influence—those in which the influence agent has control over positive and negative reinforcements and those in which the agent has no control over reinforcements but does have control over relevant *information* about reinforcements. In the first category, the powerful influence agent can use threats and offers to bring about the desired response; that is, the agent can manipulate or coerce. In the second category, the agent can only influence by sharing with the influenced person his or her information about likely outcomes; the agent can warn about negative outcomes that the influence agent does not control but knows about, or the agent can predict positive consequences, which again the agent does not control. Insofar as the influence attempt is restricted to warnings and predictions, it is persuasive; insofar as it includes threats or offers it spills over into manipulation and possibly into coercion.

Paradigmatic cases can be cited to distinguish threats from informational warnings and also to distinguish offers from mere predictions of good outcomes.[30] For example, if a psychiatrist attempts to influence a psychiatric outpatient to seek voluntary commitment by making it clear that unless the patient does so the psychiatrist will seek an involuntary commitment, persuasion is not involved, despite any use of reasoned argument, because a threat rather than an informational warning is presented. However, if the doctor explains to the patient that certain behaviors are likely to induce his family to commit him and points out that voluntary commitment is less onerous, persuasion can be at work. Similarly, it is persuasion if a doctor attempting to influence a patient to consent to eye surgery correctly tells the patient that without surgery the patient will go blind. But, if the doctor tells a patient that unless the patient consents to surgery the doctor will turn the patient over to the police, and the patient is an escaped felon sentenced to life, the doctor is not trying to persuade the patient through an informational warning but rather is attempting to coerce the patient into consenting by threatening a loss of liberty.

Reason and Justified Belief

A reliance on "reasons" in the persuasive appeal is central to our account. There are, however, questions about what counts as a reason—

in particular, whether persuasion should be restricted in some way to "good reasons" and, if so, what distinguishes a good reason from a bad one.

Subjectively Held Reasons and Justified Belief. These questions revive some problems discussed in Chapters 2, 4, and 9 about subjective and objective standards: Is it persuasion if a professional believes that the reasons offered in a conversation with a subject or patient are bad reasons, but knows that the person at whom the message is directed believes they are good reasons? For example, a physician may believe it is a bad reason for a heart patient to consent to drug therapy, while eliminating cardiac surgery, if the patient's reason is that drugs do not leave a scar. Is it irrelevant whether anyone other than the patient believes such a reason to be a good reason? If the patient values the medical treatment chiefly for this reason—and this is the patient's only real interest in choosing medication over surgery—then is it not a good reason for the patient if offered in a persuasive communication?

We accept only a *partially* subjective interpretation of what counts as a good reason. The determinative criterion is whether persuadees are influenced by what they, in the light of their values and preferences, consider to be good reasons. Our definition of persuasion does not require that the persuader must believe that the reasons offered for consideration are good reasons.[31] But it does seem essential to require that persuaders believe that what they are saying about "X," in an attempt to persuade, is *true* of "X," or at least *warranted by the evidence.* Thus, the reasons advanced must only be believed by the persuader to have these qualities.

This observation is critical to our understanding of persuasion and prevents the analysis of a good reason from being entirely subjective, because not any reason accepted by the persuadee as a good reason qualifies as good. Persuasion cannot involve appeal to reasons or arguments that the influence agent believes are false, invalid, or otherwise indefensible—even if the target of the appeal, the patient or subject, believes them to be justified. In the eye surgery example cited earlier, assume that the physician knew—correctly—that blindness was *not* the inevitable consequence of refusing surgery. Assume further that the physician knew that the patient believed—falsely—that if surgery was not performed, blindness would necessarily result. Any attempt by the physician to influence the patient to consent to surgery by an appeal to the "consequence of inevitable blindness" would be manipulation rather than persuasion. By contrast, in our other example, the physician who influenced the patient to choose drug therapy over heart surgery may be said to have used persuasion, so long as the physician believed the determinative reason—the absence of a scar—to be true, though unwise, and treated it accordingly in their communication.

Intentional appeals to "false beliefs" and attempts to confuse or distort perceptions have no place in persuasion. Paradigmatically, persuasion succeeds by *improving*, and not by undermining, a person's understanding of his or her situation—a core difference between our view and Warner's, as quoted earlier. In our analysis, then, the messages that comprise a persuasive communication are restricted to statements that the persuader believes to be warranted by the evidence, although the persuader need not find these statements to be good or sufficient reasons for the person influenced to use as the substantive basis for a decision.

Appeals to Reason and Emotion. Perhaps the most important, and also the most elusive, characteristic of persuasion is the criterion that it influences by *appeal to reason*. Despite analysis since the earliest epochs of Western philosophy, it remains unsettled what "reason" is, apart from some general faculty or process of the mind. In studies of reason or reasoning in contemporary psychology, reason tends to be similarly explicated in terms of cognition or thought, by contrast to emotion or affect.[32] Both perspectives suggest that central questions about appeals to reason may be resolvable not by what the influence agent said or did, but rather by how or through what psychological processes the person responded to and was affected by the influence—for example, through some dominantly cognitive process or with primarily emotive reactions and motivations such as hate, fear, disgust, or embarrassment.

The role of the various psychological processes potentially involved in the context of persuasion is illustrated by a prominent debate in the social psychological literature of the 1960s and early 1970s about "fear appeals." "Fear appeals" is a term given to a form of persuasive communication in which failure to adopt a recommended attitude or action is associated with negative consequences. Thus, fear appeals attempt to influence by issuing warnings. Sometimes misleadingly called "threatening" communications, they have been used extensively in public health contexts to induce people to have chest x-rays, to quit smoking, to brush their teeth, or to be immunized against tetanus. In clinical contexts, fear appeals can play a prominent role in consent solicitations if there is a discussion of the harms and risks of not consenting to the recommended treatment. In Chapter 3 we encountered such a use of fear appeals in the writings of the French medieval physician Henri de Mondeville: "The method by which the surgeon can compel the obedience of his patients, is to explain to them the dangers of disobedience. He may exaggerate these if the patient has a bold and hardy spirit."[33]

Although now largely a dead issue in the psychological literature, at one time controversy flourished about the nature of fear appeals, the conditions under which they are effective, and the psychological processes through which they work.[34] Two major rival explanations were put forward—Irving Janis's Fear-Drive Model and Howard Leventhal's Parallel Response Model.[35] Janis argued that fear appeals succeed in influencing by arousing a negative emotional state (fear) that drives the subject to adopt a recommended action as a means of reducing the fear. Leventhal rejected the claim that the arousal of fear is a necessary condition of successful influence when threatening communications are used. He argued for a cognitive model in which such warnings can produce *both* feelings of fear *and* beliefs that one is endangered. According to Leventhal, acceptance of the recommended action is more likely to occur if cognitions (e.g., beliefs that one is endangered) rather than emotions (e.g., fear) are the dominant responses.

This disagreement between Janis and Leventhal can be reinterpreted in terms of our framework (by admittedly taking some liberty with the originals) as follows. The Leventhal position is that fear appeals influence by appeal to reason, through straightforward persuasion. By contrast, the Janis position holds that fear appeals influence by inducing negative emotions that cause the person to act in ways that may have nothing to do with reason. At the time, the weight of empirical evidence seemed to support Leventhal's model.[36] However, the hypotheses in Janis's model were far from conclusively falsified.[37] It seems likely that both models, in more sophisticated form, can account for some portion of psychological reality: "Fear appeals" seem to be successful in certain circumstances by overwhelming the person with fear and panic—totally bypassing reason—and in other circumstances by convincing the person of the need to take protective action and respond accordingly.

We are, of course, arguing that influence by appeal to reason—persuasion—is in principle distinguishable from influence by appeal to emotion. The challenge to professionals in consent solicitation is to distinguish in particular cases which responses are likely to be provoked and to take care not to overwhelm the person with frightening information, particularly if the person is in a psychologically vulnerable or compromised state.

To move modestly beyond these issues, Stanley Benn has correctly argued that the essence of persuasion is that it induces change by convincing a person through the merit of the reasons put forward, but he oversteps when he argues that persuasion is necessarily *impersonal* in the sense that the reasons or "substance of the argument" are persuasive regardless of who advances them or how they are presented.[38] Appeals to reason are not solely restricted to the substance or linguistic content of the arguments advanced. Judgments about the credibility and expertise of the person presenting an argument can appropriately affect reasoned judgments about the correctness of the premises and the soundness of the argument. Similarly, the same arguments may be more persuasive if the reasons are presented by a professional speaker than by an inexperienced amateur; small variations in the precise language used, the order of presentation, and other communication skills all may affect the persuasiveness of an argument without altering its informational substance.

Finally, acceding to an argument simply because one *likes* the influence agent or finds the agent physically attractive—for example, a lover encouraging his partner to quit smoking—may be distinguished from accepting an argument because the influence agent is an *expert*—for example, a physician recommending surgery. However, there is nothing inherently contrary to reason about acceding to an influence agent's argument simply because one likes the agent or finds the agent attractive. Even if the person influenced is ignorant of the influence agent's argument, disagrees with it, or does not understand it, the person influenced may have his or her own reason for adopting what the influence agent is advocating. This reason may even be the influencee's desire to make the influencer happy or to secure his or her affection or approval. Such cases are not instances of persuasion per se; instead, they can be called "self-persuasion." Although self-persuasion is conceptually outside the bounds of social influence and issues of control by others, we include self-persuasion in our discussion because of its intimate connection with both persuasion and the kind of personal deliberation and decisionmaking that occur in the context of informed consent.[39]

Self-Persuasion

In classic instances of self-persuasion, a person does not find the *reasons or arguments* of an influence agent persuasive or convincing. However, the influence agent's intervention does provoke personal thoughts in the influencee, and these self-generated reasons succeed in persuading the person to adopt precisely what the influence agent advocates. In this convenient coincidence, there is a causal connection between the influence agent's intervention and the influencee's response; yet the influence agent did not prevail through the specific appeals to reason that had been put forward.

Consider the following example, which is doubtless typical of many consent situations. In seeking consent for cardiac surgery, a surgeon advances a string of arguments about pain control, increased function, decreased risk of future periods of incapacitation, and the like. The patient consents to surgery not for any of these reasons, but because the physician's discussion reminds the patient of the experience of a friend whose unabated cardiac problems contributed to the friend's recent and extremely unpleasant divorce.

In many consent solicitations, novel arguments in the personal internal dialogue of the patient or subject, and not the arguments put forward by the professional, may in the end be determinative. This outcome obviously raises no issue of control by others and is also generally compatible with the aforementioned view that patients' and subjects' understanding of their situations should be, if anything, improved rather than compromised by professional attempts to influence consent decisions through persuasion.[40] To the extent that understanding is intentionally compromised by an influence attempt, the intervention fails to be purely persuasive, and instead shades into the region of our last major category of social influence, manipulation.

Manipulation

The effect of manipulation on autonomous action is a darker area of human interaction than either coercion or persuasion. As noted in Chapter 7 (see Figure 2, p. 259), some manipulative influences are controlling, whereas others are compatible with parts of the continuum of influence that permit autonomous action. By the nature of the continuum, the influences that are compatible with autonomy are so as a matter of degree. One puzzle for the continuum analysis is to understand the place of minor manipulative influences on the continuum. These manipulations either limit autonomy in inconsequential ways or do not limit autonomy at all. They are especially important because only minor manipulations are compatible with informed consent (in sense$_1$).

The Nature and Types of Manipulation

Analysis of the relationship between manipulation and sense$_1$ informed consent is made particularly difficult by the fact that, unlike both coercion and persuasion, manipulation is not a distinctive kind of social influence. Manipulation is a label for a class of influence strategies whose common feature is that they are neither instances of persuasion nor instances of coercion. As expressed in Chapter 7, we define manipulation as any intentional and successful influence of a person by noncoercively altering the actual choices available to the person or by nonpersuasively altering the other's perception of those choices.

Using the term "manipulation" in this general and comprehensive sense requires its liberation from connotations of immorality or unfairness. "Manipulation" is often analyzed as necessarily immoral,[41] perhaps because it is assumed that a manipulative influence necessarily constrains a person, making the person do what he or she does not wish to do. Sometimes it is said that manipulation uses another person to the manipulator's own ends, thus necessarily violating Kant's fundamental moral maxim against exploitation (which is a *categorical* imperative).[42] But we make no such presumptions. The moral character of offering an incentive that noncoercively alters a person's choices—for example, a retirement-bonus incentive program that makes early retirement attractive—differs markedly from the moral character of an act of deception that tricks a person into doing something he or she would not otherwise do; yet we

use manipulation as the generic term ranging over both.[43] Questions of
the moral justifiability of manipulation are separate matters, just as they
were for coercion.

Manipulative influences fall into three different, and for us basic categories or types. First, there is *manipulation of options*, in which options
in the person's environment are modified by increasing or decreasing
available options or by offering rewards or threatening punishments.
Second, there is *manipulation of information*, in which the person's perception of these options is modified by nonpersuasively affecting the person's understanding of the situation. Third, there is *psychological manipulation*, in which a person is influenced by causing changes in mental
processes other than those involved in understanding. These types of
influence differ in their nature but not necessarily in the measure of their
impact on autonomous action. We begin with manipulation of options.

Manipulation of Options

Manipulation of options involves the direct modification of the options
available to a person with the intent, which is successful, of modifying
the person's behavior or beliefs. For example, the manager who gets an
employee to transfer to a new position by increasing the person's salary
manipulates the person by presenting an attractive new offer, thereby
directly modifying his or her options. If the manager induced the previous occupant of the position to retire by reducing the person's salary,
that too is an environmental manipulation because it makes the option
of continued employment less attractive.

There are several methods by which this kind of manipulation can be
effected. The manipulator can decrease or increase the *number* of
options open to a person, with the effect of modifying behavior. Alternatively, the manipulator can, by punishing or threatening to punish
behavior not preferred by the manipulator or rewarding or offering to
reward the behavior intended by the manipulator, change the ordinary
or expected structure of available options. In practice, all of these methods are often used jointly in order to bring about a relative advantage
for the manipulator's preferred outcome.

In informed consent contexts, a common combination of these types is
the following: The manipulator simultaneously creates a new option such
as the "opportunity" to participate in research or to receive a new medical treatment, and gerrymanders the reward structure so that the option
presented is clearly preferable. For example, the manipulator could offer
incentives to consent such as free medication or could indicate that emotional support will be withdrawn from the person if consent is withheld.
Some minimal element of manipulation is inevitable in the consent-solicitation process. The very making of the proposal requiring a consent

from the patient or subject is an offer to do something with the intent to influence and modify behavior. Thus, the offer is an attempted manipulation.

The central issues, from our perspective, turn on how to differentiate those proposals that are compatible with substantial autonomy from those that are not. Our concern is over which kinds of accompanying manipulations—threats, punishments, rewards and offers—permit a patient or subject to give an informed consent (sense$_1$) and which kinds deprive the person of that opportunity.

Manipulation Through Threats and Offers. Manipulation through threats or actual punishments is conceptually similar to coercion, in that both categories of influence involve attempts to affect choice and action by imposing or by threatening to impose harmful consequences. The only difference between coercion and manipulation through threats and punishments is a matter of *degree.* In coercion, the harms are so severe that the influencee cannot resist acting to avoid them (the threat is irresistible). If the harms are not this severe and the influencee *can* resist (the threat is resistible) but *does not* resist, then manipulation and not coercion has taken place.

Thus, this kind of manipulation using threats includes all intentional attempts at coercion in which it turns out that the influencee could resist the threat but does not. This category of manipulation also includes intentional attempts to bring about desired responses through lesser threats or punishments that the influence agent never intended or expected to be *irresistible,* but expected might not be resisted. Although manipulation through threats and punishments can have a profound effect on choice and action, some threats are so inconsequential as to be entirely compatible with substantial noncontrol and therefore with informed consent sense$_1$. Later in this section we will propose a simple rule of thumb for identifying these minor threats.

The most difficult and complex of all problems about autonomy and manipulation is not that of punishment and threat but rather is the effect of rewards and offers. This category of social influence refers to the intentional use of rewards, and offers of rewards, to bring about a desired response. For example, during the Tuskegee Syphilis experiments various methods were used to stimulate and sustain the interest of subjects in continued participation. They were offered free burial assistance and insurance, free transportation to and from the examinations, and a free stop in town on the return trip; they were rewarded with free medicines and free hot meals on the days of the examination. The deprived socio-economic condition of these subjects made them easy targets for such manipulation. (See pp. 165–167 in Chapter 5.)

As we use the terms, an "offer" is a presentation, overture, or approach of reward, as in "a sum of money offered," but we shall sometimes use only the word "reward" as shorthand for both offers and rewards, reserving "offer" largely for contexts in which an offer has been made but no reward received or awarded. Rewards will also be understood to include both increased positive outcomes—for example, money given—and decreased negative outcomes—for example, amelioration of the effects of disease or reduction in workload. A reward, then, may function merely to secure an additional good, to remove or reduce an existing harm, or both.

Welcome and Unwelcome Offers. Like both coercion and manipulation through threat, the impact on autonomy of manipulation through offers is analyzable through a criterion of resistibility. However, threats and offers are relevantly different in a critical respect: It is reasonable to assume that (except in certain cases of overdetermination) the influencee finds the manipulation attempt *unwelcome* in the case of a threat and wants to resist it. By contrast, in the case of manipulation through rewards, depending on the terms and the circumstances, the influencee may not only wish not to resist the offer but may actively *welcome* the offer. If the offer is welcomed by the manipulatee, there is no issue of *control* by others, even though there has been an *influence.* The manipulatee's act is entirely autonomous because it proceeds from the dictates of his or her own will. The implications for informed consent are immediate: So long as an offer is welcomed by the person influenced, it is completely compatible with informed consent (in sense₁).

Of course, much turns on what we mean by an offer's being "welcome." A welcome offer is one the person influenced wants to *receive,* but not necessarily to *accept.* There may be overriding reasons why the influencee wants to reject it; but this matter is distinct from how the influencee feels about receipt of the offer, which he or she may welcome even knowing that rejection is a foregone conclusion. For example, a university professor may solicit job offers with the intent of rejecting the offers, welcoming them only as a means to improve present salary and position. Again, an economist may welcome an offer to serve as a paid consultant to a prestigious government contractor, even though an already overcrowded schedule may be reason to reject or at least question the prudence of accepting the offer.

One might find an offer welcome or unwelcome for many reasons. We cannot here delve into the complex morass of human motivations that would *cause* such welcoming, although we certainly acknowledge its relevance to the matter of influence. Instead, we propose the following rule of thumb: If the influencee finds an offer welcome, and is not simultaneously under some different and controlling influence causing acceptance or rejection of the offer, then the influencee is capable of acting autonomously in response to the offer.

Situations of Desperate Need. One of the implications of this position

is that so long as the offer is welcome, the influencee can act automo-
mously under even the greatest of circumstantial pressures. The most
problematic cases will be analogous to those earlier discussed under the
topic "coercive situations." We shall label cases pertinent to the problem of manipulation "situations of desperate need." To say that a person
"desperately needs" something will mean that without it there is a
strong probability that the person (or some loved one, etc.) will be seriously harmed.

Consider two cases, which we shall label case (A) and case (B). First,
case (A): Carol and Mary have both consented to participate in a public
opinion survey in which they will be interviewed every four months for
the next two years on the role of women in society. They will be paid
$25 for each completed interview. Carol is a financially secure lawyer,
earning a six-digit salary; Mary is a $9,000 a year receptionist receiving
food stamps to help feed her five children, who have never been to a
dentist because of the lack of family funds. Although the $25 payment
(the reward) obviously means something very different to Mary than to
Carol, this fact alone does not render Mary's consent less autonomous
than Carol's consent.

To make the situation in case (A) unambiguous, we stipulate that in
this instance Mary has no interest whatever in refusing the research. She
desperately needs to earn extra money and she sees being interviewed
on an interesting topic as a comparatively pleasant and attractive way to
do so. Thus, her consent to participation is what Mary wills and wants to
do in the circumstances. "The imposition of the researcher's will upon
her own" would be a far-fetched description of the actual circumstances.
True, it may be her financial situation that is causing Mary to will or want
as she does. In this sense she may not be *free* to say no to an opportunity
to earn $150 (see pp. 344–346). But this state of affairs is independent
of the researcher's offer, and this particular offer—the researcher's
manipulation—is not itself "controlling" Mary's decision to consent.
The offer, we recall, is *welcomed*.

Now, consider case (B): The conclusions we just reached change dramatically if we alter the facts of case (A) in several ways so that Mary
receives an offer that she does *not* welcome. Instead of a series of interesting interviews in pleasant surroundings, suppose the research
involves painful and invasive medical procedures—liver biopsies, myelograms, repeated venipunctures, new drugs not yet on the market, and
much more that is equally distasteful. The compensation remains the
same: $25 for each day-long session in the hospital for six sessions. This
time Carol sneers at the offer and refuses to participate. Mary, however,
is desperate and still consents. Mary has no more desire to submit to
these procedures than does Carol. Indeed, Mary finds the whole prospect frightening, horrifying. She has had several previous surgeries and
one frightening experience with a bad drug. Mary wishes desperately

that she had never received such an offer because once it is made, she feels she must accept, whereas beforehand she would never have been faced with such a tragic "choice."

In this second case the manipulator has a control over Mary's choice in a way that is not parallel to the research-interview situation. In both cases (A) and (B), Mary is not free to choose otherwise because of the constraints on her. However, in case (A) Mary's consent remains substantially under her control and independent of control by the investigator, while in case (B) her consent does not. This judgment that *control* by others occurs in (B), and therefore that there is a *deprivation of autonomy*, turns in important ways on our subjective criterion of controlling influence. Had another person, Susie, *welcomed* the offer made in case (B), then, unlike Mary, Susie would not have been controlled and could respond autonomously in electing to accept the offer.

To some the idea of a welcome offer to persons in desperate need may seem inherently exploitative. But this need not be the case. In 1722 several inmates of the Newgate Prison volunteered to be subjects in an experiment on smallpox innoculation as an alternative to hanging.[44] It might at first seem that they were controlled, but more plausibly this is a case of a welcome offer to persons in desperate need. The facts of the outcome indicate just how welcome: These condemned men all survived and were released.

Problems of Exploitation. This example is not intended as an implicit denial that problems of exploitation are in the foreground of cases closely resembling those we have just presented. Taking unfair advantage of vulnerable subjects certainly can occur in such cases. While cases (A) and (B) above focus on problems of autonomy and control, rather than moral concerns, the latter are often voiced about offers to subjects, especially if offers to alleviate harm are made to those already in coercive situations. These issues are primarily about *justice* rather than respect for autonomy. (See Chapter 1, pp. 14–16.) They include the just allocation in society of the burden of research risks, as well as wider issues about social arrangements that permit persons in desperate financial circumstances to go unaided and to be subjected to exploitation. These valid concerns for research ethics present a range of moral problems well beyond our subject.

One final comment is in order about case (B) and our thesis about *degrees* of autonomy. Case (B) involves a situation in which an offer made to a person in desperate need is both unwelcome and difficult to resist. Although problems with resisting offers are easy to understand in such cases, a person need not be in a desperate or even needy circumstance to find an unwelcome offer difficult to resist.[45] For example, a civic-minded person already overburdened with obligations to community and charity groups may find an offer from the mayor to chair yet another citizens' task force unwelcome and yet also hard to resist, perhaps

because the person has difficulty refusing opportunities to assume community leadership. However, in general, offers of "mere goods"—that
is, offers that add goods to one's life without functioning directly to alleviate harms one faces—are far easier to resist than offers of rewards that
promise to remove currently suffered harms or threatened harms.

The relationship between this general rule and autonomous action is
straightforward. The extent to which any unwelcome offer compromises
autonomy is a function of the ease or difficulty the manipulatee finds in
attempting to resist the offer. Because rewards of "mere goods" are generally easier to resist than rewards that stand to alleviate harms, they are
also generally more compatible with autonomous action than are harm-
alleviating goods. There will, however, be some exceptions to this
generalization.

Implications for Consent Solicitation. It follows from the argument thus
far that certain circumstances of manipulation of options—some offers
and rewards, and even some threats and punishments—are compatible
with substantial noncontrol and thus with informed consent. We have no
magical formulae for establishing the threshold that demarcates these
"compatible" manipulations. Nonetheless, we believe the following generalizations to be defensible: First, any offer that is welcomed by the
influencee is compatible with substantial noncontrol, and thus with
sense₁ informed consent. Second, any threat or unwelcome offer is compatible with sense₁ informed consent if it can be *reasonably easily
resisted* by the person manipulated. Under this formulation, if a manipulatee yields to a threat or unwelcome offer this may signify only that
the manipulatee has no *overriding* interest in resisting. The behavior of
yielding does not in itself prove that the manipulatee found the threat or
offer difficult to resist.

Here, as with coercion, we are proposing a *subjective* criterion of level
of resistance. This subjective criterion has implications for the rule of
thumb we proposed earlier to the effect that unwelcome offers of mere
goods are usually more easily resisted, and therefore are more compatible with consent, than unwelcome offers of goods that would alleviate
or remove harms. From a subjective perspective, what is valued as a
"mere good" by one person may be viewed by another as the means to
alleviate a significant harm. Subjective evaluation is thus inherent in the
assessment of what *counts* as goods and harms, as well as in the assessment of their *magnitudes.* A committed young scientist may find the offer
of $500 to falsify data very unwelcome, but depending on personal attri-
butes and circumstances, the scientist may not find the offer easily resistible. Whether we can correctly say that the scientist's acceptance of the
offer is less than substantially autonomous will depend entirely on that
person's desires and structure of resistance. (Piling so much on the
notions of "resistance" and "resistibility" without a deeper analysis of

these terms admittedly leaves a certain incompleteness, but this is a complicated psychological and philosophical problem that we do not here have the resources to consider.)

Because of inherent difficulties in interpreting whether a specific offer is welcome and, if not, whether it is easily resistible, the safest course for professionals wishing to secure sense$_1$ informed consents is either to avoid altogether making any such proposals to potential subjects or patients or to restrict proposals to only those offers that are reasonably foreseeable as welcomed or easily resistible. The paradigmatic case is relatively risk-free nontherapeutic research in which the offer of rewards and incentives to encourage potential subjects to consent to participate is often welcomed, although it also could be easily resisted. A lively debate has evolved over the kinds of incentives, particularly monetary incentives, that may be offered to different kinds of research subjects; but this debate usually turns more on the problem of "due" and "undue" inducements than on the topics we are examining. In our analysis, the proper application of subjective criteria to these research cases would require substantial information about the subjects themselves. Depending on the heterogeneity of the subjects, we may decide that a manipulative monetary reward is compatible with sense$_1$ informed consent for some subjects, but not for others.

For policy rules governing informed consent in sense$_2$, objective criteria would no doubt generally have to be employed—for example, rules expressing how ordinary or average or prudent persons would view the offer and whether they would find it easily resistible. Consider how this objective approach and the above analysis would apply to an actual case presented by Harold Gamble:[46] It was the policy of an academic department to offer extra credit as an incentive to students to consent to participate in faculty research projects. Students could earn up to a 5% increase in grade points, after a grade curve for test scores had been established. Under no circumstances could these extra-credit points result in a change of grade from a "B" to an "A". Extra-credit points of up to the same value could be earned through other activities, including short papers, special projects, book reports, and brief quizzes on additional readings.

Using the conclusions reached thus far, we would characterize this policy as an instance of manipulation through the offer of goods that most, but not all, students would welcome. Because the reward is "extra-credit" points, this proposal offers students an opportunity to secure a good, and not a highly desirable good at that, because the extra-credit points can never be used to secure an "A." Moreover, it seems reasonable to expect average students who find the offer unwelcome to be able to resist the proposal. Thus, we conclude that—as a policy matter—student authorizations can be treated in this case as informed consents (in sense$_2$), although occasionally a student may not give a sense$_1$ informed consent because, by reference to the subjective criterion, the student will be controlled by the manipulation.

Our conclusion differs sharply from Gamble's, who maintains that this policy may be "subtly coercing" students into consenting. Although he admits that it would be difficult to show that the offer of extra-credit points is coercive, he seems to think that because the benefit offered is somehow uniquely attractive to students, students may not be consenting freely. In applying objective criteria of welcomeness and resistibility, we see no basis for reaching the judgment that the reward as offered is controlling, and we suspect that on all but rare occasions students will remain substantially independent of control.

Manipulation of Information

The manipulation of information is a deliberate act that successfully influences a person by nonpersuasively altering the person's understanding of the situation, thereby modifying perceptions of the available options. The manipulator does not change the person's actual options; only the person's perception is modified as a result of the manipulation. Thus, informational manipulation affects what a person believes. There is an intimate connection between informational manipulation and the condition of understanding discussed in Chapter 9 because this form of manipulation can affect autonomy by reducing understanding.

A Rule for Identifying Minor Informational Manipulations. Informational manipulations that are not sufficiently controlling to render acts less than substantially autonomous are compatible with informed consent (in sense$_1$). These minor informational manipulations cannot, however, be distinguished from more controlling manipulations by appeal to a "subjective resistibility" criterion such as the criterion discussed for manipulation of options. Most informational manipulations require by their very nature that the manipulatee be kept in partial ignorance or in confusion. Sometimes it is even necessary that the person be completely unaware that he or she is in any respect the subject of an influence attempt. The manipulator's clandestine activities preclude the manipulatee from either consciously acceding to or resisting the influence attempt, thereby voiding any test of potential resistibility.

A more appropriate rule of thumb for distinguishing minor informational manipulations is to appeal to the requirements of substantial understanding discussed in Chapter 9; so long as an informational manipulation does not cause a person to fail to satisfy the condition of substantial understanding, the manipulation is compatible with sense$_1$ informed consent. In Chapter 9 we argued that substantial understanding in the context of informed consent requires that a person satisfy both an objective criterion—generally based on some core disclosure made by the professional (see pp. 307–310)—and a subjective criterion composed of all the relevant beliefs that are material to the patient's or subject's evaluation whether to authorize a particular arrangement. (See pp. 302–304.) So long as an informational manipulation does not compromise the person's ability to satisfy either the subjective criterion of substantial understanding, the objective criterion, or both, and thus does not interfere with the understanding condition, the manipulation is compatible with substantial noncontrol and with informed consent (sense$_1$).

As a practical matter, it is not likely that many informational manipulations would be judged compatible with sense$_1$ informed consent. Although professionals can make educated and sometimes quite accurate guesses about the likelihood that a given manipulation would affect information considered material by a particular patient or subject, such determinations are delicate and difficult. The most prudent course for a professional seeking to obtain sense$_1$ informed consents is obviously to refrain altogether from engaging in informational manipulation. (Although there may be consent contexts in which lying and other forms of informational manipulation by professionals are justifiable, such manipulations nevertheless cannot result in sense$_1$ informed consents.) Credulity is likely to be greater in "ordinary" health care and research contexts than in contexts where skepticism and resistance are expected under the rules of the game—for example, advertising and commerce generally. In comparison to many commercial transactions, health care contexts exhibit an imbalance of knowledge and power; these contexts are often imbued with a background of credibility, trust, and dependency. Thus, attempted informational manipulations are more likely to be both successful and more controlling in health care contexts.

Deception. Deception is the most common form of informational manipulation and the core of our concern. Deception uses such intentional strategies as lying, withholding of information, true assertion that omits a vital qualification, and misleading exaggeration in order to cause persons to believe what is false. A blatant, and we hope highly atypical, example of manipulation using deception was discussed in Chapter 5, where we saw that subjects in the Tuskegee study consented to painful spinal taps after physicians told them, falsely, that the taps were a "special free treatment" (see pp. 165–167 above). Although deception usually involves language, manipulation by deception may also be effected through other modes of communication, such as the misleading packaging of products in oversized, half-filled containers. Such packaging manipulates the information that consumers use to make a choice by inducing them to make incorrect inferences based on their observations and expectations, rather than by employing or failing to employ language. Another example is the practice, common among plastic surgeons, of showing prospective patients "before and after" pictures of former patients. If a surgeon picks a case of unusually successful surgery—beyond realistic expectations for this particular patient—with the intent to deceive the patient as to possible outcomes, this act is deceptive if successful. Many advertisements attempt, of course, precisely this strategy.

Most recent commentary on deception as a problem for informed consent has focused more on the research context than the clinical context. We saw in Chapter 3 that there is a venerable tradition in medicine of intentionally withholding information from patients, but this practice has traditionally been defended as a way to make the patient take an optimistic attitude of hope rather than as a way to manipulate consent. Such practices certainly can manipulate consent decisions, but the kind of manipulation in clinical practice that is probably most difficult to discover, pinpoint, and describe is the subtle slanting, misrepresentation, or omission of information that leaves a patient critically ignorant (sometimes, but not always, intentionally).

This problem has been discussed by Edmond Cahn and Jay Katz, who have written about "the witting and unwitting manipulation of disclosure" that occurs in order to "engineer consent" by trading on fear and ignorance in patients. Katz cites as an example the problem of consent to "unnecessary surgery": Consent is obtained by representing an elective procedure—such as hysterectomy for fibroid tumors—as, without qualification, the medically indicated procedure for avoiding cancer.[47] Any physician who knowingly uses such a technique to induce consent or compliance engages in a potentially controlling manipulation that can easily deprive the patient of making a substantially autonomous choice (depending, of course, on the patient's full complement of beliefs).

Another example of deception as a clinical issue is placebo therapy: The clinician employs deception in order to heal through the suggestibility effect of "fake" interventions such as sugar pills or pseudo-surgery. It is difficult to determine whether or to what extent this or any kind of deception is currently a significant problem for informed consent in clinical contexts. Deception of patients in the solicitation of consent is not much discussed in the professions, nor is it now as publicly defended as it has been in the past (see Chapter 3).[48] The major exception to this general lack of commentary is the theme, especially in the legal literature, of the potential for abuse of the therapeutic privilege (see Chapter 2, pp. 37–38). One recurrent concern in this literature is that clinicians will use the therapeutic privilege to withhold information, not merely to avert significant harm to patients but as a convenient means of manipulating patients into consenting to their recommendations.[49]

As we discussed in Chapter 5, there is a continuing and lively debate in psychology about deception of human subjects and the role of informed consent.[50] The central issue is the necessity in certain circumstances of a choice between scientific validity and truthful or complete disclosure. If this tradeoff involves a consent-solicitation procedure that causes potential subjects to believe what is false, about either something material to them or something that would otherwise be required in a core disclosure, resulting authorizations would not be informed consents (in sense$_1$). The classic example is Stanley Milgram's obedience experiments (see Chapter 5, p. 174), in which subjects were deceived about virtually every aspect of the study to which they were consenting. By our criteria, these consents did not satisfy the conditions of informed consent in sense$_1$. Much the same can be said about Laud Humphreys's "tearoom trade" research (see Chapter 5, p. 177), in which deception was blatant.

Also problematic from the perspective of informed consent are the "little" deceptions sometimes employed in the recruitment of subjects. For example, potential subjects are told that invasive research procedures "sting a little" or are "uncomfortable," when in fact most people find them unambiguously painful. This practice is doubtless found in clinical contexts as well. Consider, for example, the case of Mr. Berkey (Chapter 4, p. 128), who consented to undergo a myelogram after having been led to believe (falsely) that a myelogram was similar to an electromyogram. In most such instances, the false beliefs induced are likely to be far from trivial to subjects and patients.

Although deception is doubtlessly the most common strategy used to induce a person to believe what is false or otherwise compromise a person's understanding, deception does not exhaust the category of informational manipulation. Also qualifying as informational manipulations are such interventions as (1) intentionally overwhelming a person with excessive information so as to induce confusion and a reduction of understanding, (2) intentionally provoking or taking advantage of fear, anxiety, pain, or other negative affective or cognitive states known to compromise a person's ability to process information effectively (see pp. 323–326), and (3) intentionally exploiting framing effects by presenting information in a way that leads the manipulatee to draw certain predictable inferences (see pp. 319–322).[51] The effects of these interventions on autonomy can be assessed, like the effects of deception, in terms of the extent to which they compromise the person's ability to satisfy the condition of substantial understanding. However, unlike deception, the processes by which these interventions compromise understanding are sometimes unclear and frequently complex. As such, these informational manipulations may encompass strategies and effects that overlap with our final major category of manipulation—psychological manipulation.

Psychological Manipulation

It is difficult to give a precise characterization of what should be meant by "psychological manipulation." Like the category of manipulation itself, psychological manipulation is a catch-all classification that includes any intentional act that successfully influences a person to belief or behavior by causing changes in mental processes other than those involved in understanding. We would include under this broad heading such diverse strategies as subliminal suggestion, flattery and other appeals to emotional weaknesses, and the inducing of guilt or feelings of obligation,[52] all of which can successfully influence a person to act as the manipulator intends.[53]

One form of psychological manipulation of particular relevance to informed consent contexts is a strategy, practiced adeptly by many salespersons, called "low-balling."[54] This tactic typically involves revealing certain less favorable aspects of a proposal to a person only after the person has made an initial decision to accept the proposal. Low-balling can involve lying, although it need not. The central feature of low-balling is that it always involves *withholding* information at a point in an intentionally ordered interaction. However, unlike most ordinary uses of withholding to deceive and manipulate, in low-balling the withheld information is always revealed to the one manipulated *before* he or she makes an irrevocable commitment to the decision. The low-balling phenomenon is particularly instructive for the relationship between autonomy and manipulation, because it has been demonstrated that low-balling works best when manipulatees perceive their decisions to be volitional.[55]

Consider as an example a salesperson concluding negotiations with a customer for the purchase of a set of automobile tires. After a quarter of an hour of discussion, the customer agrees to purchase two Blimpo-brand tires for $150. After the sales clerk has written up the first half of a receipt and has the VISA credit card in hand, he remarks that the $150 price does not include three forms of tax, and then casually mentions that charges for mounting the tires and balancing the wheels are extra, as is the cost of an extended warranty policy highly recommended for these tires. The total charge for all goods and services, including sales tax, is $202.50, and the clerk wonders if the customer still wants the Blimpo tires and, if so, which of the additional services is desired, if any.

Low-balling is a good example of the overlap between informational manipulation and psychological manipulation. Although low-balling involves the manipulation of information, it does not work simply by rendering the manipulatee ignorant of material information, thereby compromising the manipulatee's understanding of the situation. Instead, ignorance is used to initiate certain psychological processes that are difficult to reverse even after the ignorance condition is removed.[56] Specifically, the low-ball effect is thought to be mediated by the effects of psychological commitment. People have a strong psychological tendency to continue with an active decision, especially if an agreement has been reached, even after becoming aware that the decision is more costly to execute than was originally thought. The specific cognitive or motivational mediators of this tendency are unclear, but several explanations have been proposed, including the creation of perceptions of social obligations or responsibility and the strain and work associated with decisionmaking. Whatever the explanation, the low-ball effect involves complex psychological processes, and thus psychological manipulation as well as information manipulation.

Robert Cialdini and his associates have recently studied low-balling as a compliance technique in a series of social-psychological experiments. One of their experiments illustrates the applicability of this procedure for manipulating decisions to consent. In this study, 63 undergraduate students were asked to participate in a psychological experiment through the use of a low-ball or a control procedure. In the low-ball procedure, the students were asked whether they were willing to be research subjects in an experiment. The requirements for participation were at that point partially described. If a student agreed to participate, then he or she was informed that the experiment was being run at 7:00 a.m., and was asked again whether he or she was willing to participate. In the control procedure, students were given the complete disclosure (including information about the 7:00 a.m. starting time) before they were asked to agree to participate. As expected, students in the low-ball condition were significantly more likely than the control students to consent to participate in the research. Fifty-three percent of the students in the low-ball condition actually appeared at the appointed time as compared to only 24% of the students who received the non-low-balled disclosure.[57]

Many influence strategies like low-balling that combine elements of psychological and informational manipulation are commonly used in sales, fund raising, recruiting, advertising, and the like. The so-called "contrast principle" is another example: An expensive item is shown first, so that anything by comparison will appear to be a real bargain, or a real estate agent shows dilapidated, overpriced housing so that decent housing appears, by contrast, a bargain.[58] Low-balling may also be used frequently to increase the likelihood that people will consent to medical interventions and research participation. In survey research, for example, one strategy for recruiting subjects is to withhold details about the number or length of follow-up interviews until the subject has agreed to participate in the initial round of interviewing.

It can be a tedious and thorny chore to decide whether psychological manipulations like low-balling are compatible with substantial noncontrol in specific cases. Here, as with manipulation of options, the relevant criterion is whether the manipulation is easily resistible by the manipulatee. Whereas some psychological manipulations, like successful subliminal suggestion, are obviously difficult if not impossible to resist, the effect on autonomy of other kinds of psychological manipulations is much harder to predict. People vary dramatically in their vulnerability to different psychological manipulations. Moreover, the same person can find the same manipulation differentially resistible, depending on other aspects of the person's state of mind, such as tiredness or confusion. For these reasons, rather obviously, the prudent course for professionals seeking sense$_1$ informed consents is again to avoid the use of psychological manipulation altogether.

The Problem of Role Constraints

We have already argued that nonintentional, situational factors can neither coerce nor otherwise control actions so as to compromise autonomy, no matter how desperate the person's circumstance. However, there is an area of influence or constraint on action of particular relevance to informed consent where the distinctions between the intentional and unintentional begin to intermingle and may be indistinguishable, or at least may be too heavily entangled to be distinguished. We refer to this prickly problem as "the problem of role constraints."

A person's *role* can carry with it certain expectations for behavior and consequent intentional actions that function to limit or constrain that person's autonomous expression. Constraint does *not* occur exclusively because other persons intentionally structure particular encounters with that person in manipulative ways; it also occurs because social or cultural arrangements and expectations for the role the person assumes can function as constraints on autonomous expression. Hospitals, boot camps, and prisons fit this description in various degrees in the roles they assign to patients, inductees, and prisoners. Franz Ingelfinger's case of soliciting consent to be involved in research from unwary patients (see pp. 238–239)—which he mistakenly labels "coercion"—is a typical hospital-based example: The researcher intentionally makes a *manipulative offer* to a patient who is already in a passive and dependent role. However, sometimes the researcher may be entirely oblivious to the offer's *being manipulative*, but it nonetheless has the same effect as any intentional manipulation. On many other occasions, patients are constrained by numerous role expectations, and are themselves unaware of the constraints involved.

In taking this view, there is a risk of letting an all-too-hazy notion of role constraints obscure altogether the possibilities for autonomous action. In some respects *all* our actions are shaped and constrained by social experience. The possibility of a confrontation with police and courts constrains behavior every day. If one understands the entire fabric of social experience in terms of social roles and expectations—a venerable sociological tradition—role constraints might be said to operate pervasively to limit or (depending on one's point of view) altogether undermine any capacity for autonomous action. John Stuart Mill seems to have come to this conclusion about the expectations and constraints generally operative in nineteenth-century British society. However, the *general* circumstance of social and role constraint should be distinguished from *particular* cases or contexts of role constraint. We use the notion of role constraint to capture situations in which people in roles such as that of the hospitalized patient do not act as they would *prefer* to act, and *would otherwise* act, were they not under the peculiarly intense and often oppressive pressures and constraints inherent in the dependent role in which they are circumstanced.

Examples of this inchoate notion of role constraint are found in the constraints of autonomous action inherent not only in the patient role, but in the prisoner role, the student role, and the employee role. The distinguishing feature of these roles is that they place one in a position of relative powerlessness, with authority figures in complementary roles of power and control. Part of adjusting to a constraining role is learning to be generally passive—that is, learning to let authority control and even dictate one's actions in ways one ordinarily would not permit another to do.

Consider a case in which Marc, hospitalized for disc surgery, wants to discontinue the antidepressant medication he has been taking for the past few days. When his physician first suggested—shall we say "prescribed?"—that he take the drug, Marc readily agreed. His physician's arguments seemed sound to him, namely that his depressed mood could be contributing to his poor progress and, moreover, that the drug could also help with Marc's migraine headaches, which have been particularly severe since the surgery. However, Marc has discovered that he intensely dislikes the side effects of the drug, particularly the constant sensation of dryness in the mouth. The drug also seems to have disturbed his sleep; but, most importantly, Marc has come to resent the implication, symbolized by this treatment, that his mental state or attitude is responsible for his continued pain. Marc now realizes that he feels more angry than depressed and wants the medication discontinued.

When Marc's physician makes rounds, Marc tries to explain to his doctor how he feels. She listens with an authoritative look and quickly dismisses his concerns. "Try it for a few more days," suggests the doctor, "I really think it's helping you." Marc waits another two days and tries again. This time Marc explicitly says he no longer wants to take the drug. His doctor's response remains unchanged. "I know you don't like the dry-mouth sensation, but it really is important that you take the drug." She then tells Marc she will stop by tomorrow and hastens from the room. A half-hour later, the nurse comes in with the antidepressant and Marc takes the pill.

If Marc so strongly wants the medicine discontinued, why does he not boldly refuse to take the pill with the same ease that he would stop taking a prescription drug at home or refuse to increase his life insurance when his agent urges a new policy? Is his taking the pill under these circumstances an act correctly described as substantially autonomous, or has the act somehow been deprived of substantial autonomy? There are no simple answers to these questions, and no very safe generalizations across the many possible cases. To some extent, Marc may be afraid of the consequences if he refuses the medicine; that is, he may believe that if he does not take his medicine, he will suffer punitive responses. Specifically, Marc may be afraid that his doctor will be angry with him or that the hospital staff will mistreat him if he becomes a "problem patient." Marc may simply believe that whether he takes the pill is not an event he can control or has any right to control, even though he must actively place the pill in his mouth. Marc may believe that he must have his physician's permission to stop the medicine, that this is not something that he, as the patient, can decide on his own, no matter how strongly he feels. Marc has learned that giving up this kind of control is part of being a patient. It is something the role *demands*, and he is subject to significant rejection if he deviates from the directed path.

Considerable evidence indicates that patterns of passivity characterize behavior in authoritarian relationships like the doctor-patient relationship, particularly in the case of hospitalized patients. For example, in summarizing the findings of their recent participant observation study of consent and medical decisionmaking, Charles Lidz and Alan Meisel conclude as follows:

> In general the physician was clearly the dominant actor in terms of making decisions about what treatments, if any, a patient was to have. Both doctors and patients saw the process this way:
>
>   (a) The doctor's ordinary role, in practice, was to decide what was to be done and to inform the patient of that decision. Ordinarily this information came in the form of a recommendation; though depending on the treatment involved or the personalities of the doctor of the patient, it might be better characterized along a spectrum running from an "order" at one end to a neutral disclosure of alternatives at the other end.
>
>   (b) The patient's ordinary role, in practice, was to acquiesce in the doctor's recommendation. Patients played a more active role when the doctor presented alternatives without placing any preference on them. Sometimes patients objected to a recommendation; occasionally they vetoed it. But on the balance the typical patient role was one of passive acquiescence.[59]

Lidz and Meisel's observations are consistent with the psychosocial literature on "good-patient" and "bad-patient" role behavior among the hospitalized.[60] The good-patient and bad-patient roles are alternative coping responses to the loss of control and depersonalization that for many typify the experience of hospitalization.[61] Good patients are cooperative, undemanding, and respectful: "The hospitalized (good) patient regards pleasing the doctor and nurse by behaving properly as a chief role obligation. For the patient 'behaving properly' means doing what one is told and not making trouble.''[62] Being a good patient may, in some cases, not be compatible with acting autonomously. By contrast, the "bad-patient" role has often been described as a behavioral pattern in which the patient insists on exerting his or her autonomy. The bad-patient role is likened to a consumer-rights role, with the patient insisting on his or her right to criticize and to be informed.[63]

Good-patient behavior is generally thought to be conducive to hospital structure and functioning and as a result is encouraged and rewarded by the staff. Bad-patient behavior, which includes complaints and demands for attention as well as petty acts of mutiny, is viewed as dysfunctional from the perspective of hospital operations, and generates such negative staff reactions as condescension, psychiatric referrals, ignoring of complaints, and overmedication.[64] Not surprisingly, most patients become good patients.[65]

There are conceptual problems in analyzing this notion of role constraints. Even more problematic in such cases than distinguishing intentional, manipulative treatments from situational factors is distinguishing both from generalized effects of role-based expectations on behavior. As we have already acknowledged, all social roles and environments have inherent constraints, as defined by prevailing normative conventions. Massive variance also abounds in people's abilities to resist or defy role and social conventions. The operative notion in control through role expectations is that certain roles are peculiarly *defined* by their passivity and their dependency on powerful authority figures. Although people in such roles can respond to proposals in terms of their wants and preferences, many are more likely to respond compliantly, almost without regard for even strong personal preferences. People in dependent roles believe that they are supposed to behave compliantly, even if, relevant to a specific proposal, those with power have made no specific threats or promises. As a result, people in these roles have less opportunity (*ceteris paribus*) to act autonomously than people not in these roles.

A tough question is how a person's being in a constraining role affects the autonomous character of any specific action the person takes while in that role. This problem is in some respects analogous to unresolved issues about the *authenticity* of actions, as discussed in Chapter 7 (see pp. 262–268). For example, if a person acts from blind obedience to authority while in a dependent role, the extent to which the action is, in fact, authored by the person or the self is questionable. Here again—as with problems of authenticity—nothing short of a full theory of the self may be required in order to resolve the many thorny ambiguities presented by such situations. Nevertheless, from the undisputed fact that the patient role has inherent constraints, it would be absurd to suggest that every decision a person makes while in that role is nonautonomous, or even that the person's actions are *necessarily* rendered less autonomous by the patient role. Because the effects of role constraints are so diffuse, so variable in subjective effect from individual to individual, and frequently so completely intermingled with intentional manipulative interventions, it is not possible to specify defining characteristics or threshold criteria that identify when the intentional features of role con- straints function to push acts over the line of substantial noncontrol. From the perspective of informed consent, the best that can be done is to identify as at high risk those role relationships that are characterized by a pattern of socialized and constantly reinforced passivity. The hope would be for professionals seeking to obtain informed consents (sense$_1$) to counteract or mitigate the generalized effects of role manipulation without destroying the valuable and functional parts of structured role relationships.

To this end, we have already suggested in Chapter 9 that professionals could include in their core disclosures a discussion of the purpose of soliciting informed consent and the significance and binding character of consents and refusals. This discussion could serve to counteract mis- impressions and false associations subjects and patients may have about role expectations. More importantly, an explicit discussion of *the purpose and import of informed consent* should help overcome the inclination that many people have to yield compliantly to proposals from powerful authority figures. This tendency is to view such proposals as de facto orders or to view compliance as necessary to secure a desired outcome that the power figure controls.

In addition to this core disclosure, as we proposed in Chapter 9, spe- cial efforts may be needed to secure informed consent (sense$_1$) from groups that have been indentified as particularly vulnerable to the effects of role constraints and who are thus both more easily manipulated and more likely to hold false beliefs about the consequences of refusing to comply with professionals' requests. For example, in clinical contexts, there is evidence that certain populations of patients are particularly dependent and vulnerable to manipulations of all sorts. Groups broadly identified include the frail, the elderly, the poor, the poorly educated, the retarded, the seriously ill, and the hospitalized.[66] In nonclinical pop- ulations, major concern has thus far centered on the institutionalized, prisoners, and others in total institutions, where both role manipulation and straightforward manipulation of options are thought to be endemic, ubiquitous, and inseparable.[67] For groups such as these, it may, for exam- ple, prove helpful to have the person soliciting consent be someone who does not have means-ends control over the individual from whom con- sent is sought, or to have a family member, friend, or professional advo- cate present during all consent discussions.[68]

The proper application of such strategies for limiting the effects of role constraints and manipulative interventions depends on the exercise of sound situational judgment. We do not suggest that these strategies need to be employed in every instance in which the goal is to obtain sense$_1$ informed consent and the professionals seeking consent are in positions of authority or power.

Conclusion

From a practical perspective, our discussion of the condition of substantial noncontrol and the specific influences categorized as coercion, persuasion, and manipulation is neither as precise nor as complete as we would like. As mentioned previously, in many cases determinations as to whether a particular influence is compatible with substantial noncontrol will not be obvious and will require experienced judgment and extensive knowledge of the situation and the person giving consent. This will be particularly true if the determination rests on an interpretation of subjective criteria, such as subjective resistibility or materiality of information.[69] For these reasons, we have advocated that the prudent course for professionals seeking sense$_1$ informed consents is to eschew altogether the use of psychological and informational manipulation and to restrict offers of rewards to proposals that likely will be welcomed by the patient or subject. By contrast, we have set no restrictions on the use of persuasion, which is an acceptable form of influence in informed consent contexts.

In many respects, our conclusions are less demanding of professionals than the program for professional conduct presented in Chapter 9. Still, the condition of substantial noncontrol is not likely to be met, and thus informed consents (sense$_1$) not obtained, unless professionals pay careful attention to the specifics of their conduct when they make consent proposals. This is especially true for consents solicited from patients and subjects who are vulnerable to manipulative interventions.[70]

We have acknowledged throughout that the conditions of sense$_1$ informed consent—understanding, intentionality, authorization, and independence from control by others—are often difficult to satisfy, in both medical care and research contexts. Yet ours is not an ideal-state theory of informed consent. Quite the contrary: We reject the tendentious thesis that it is never possible to obtain "true" informed consents. It is, of course, a matter of empirical speculation how often in medical care and research informed consents in sense$_1$ are in fact obtained, but with sufficient effort on the part of professionals, we are confident that such consents can be obtained frequently, and for some procedures even routinely. Under what conditions the effort required to obtain sense$_1$ informed consents is justified remains an open question. However, this problem of justification moves beyond the question of autonomy and informed consent that has absorbed us in this book.

Notes

1. See, for example, Code of Federal Regulations, 45 CFR 46, Protection of Human Subjects, revised March 9, 1983, 9; President's Commission for the Study of Ethical Problems in Medicine and Biomedical and Behavioral Research, *Deciding to Forego Life-Sustaining Treatment* (Washington, D.C.: U.S. Government Printing Office, 1983), 45–46.

2. Henry K. Beecher, *Experimentation in Man* (Springfield, IL: Charles C.Thomas, 1959), 18, and "Editorial: Some Fallacies and Errors in the Application of the Principle of Consent in Experimentation," *Clinical Pharmacology and Therapeutics* 3 (March-April 1962): 144–45; American Psychological Association, "Ethical Standards for Psychological Research," *APA Monitor* 2 (1971): 14 (as discussed above in Chapter 5, pp. 182–185).

3. See, for example, Beecher, *Experimentation in Man*, 19–20; Carl Cohen, "Medical Experimentation in Prisoners," *Perspectives in Biology and Medicine* (Spring 1979): 357–72; and Richard Singer, "Consent of the Unfree: Medical Experimentation and Behavior Modification in the Closed Institution, Part II," *Law and Human Behavior* 1 (1977): 105–22, esp. notes.

4. Willard Gaylin, "On the Borders of Persuasion: A Psychoanalytic Look at Coercion," *Psychiatry* 37 (1974): 1–8. See also Peter Breggin, "Coercion of Voluntary Patients in an Open Hospital," *Archives of General Psychiatry* 10 (1964): 173–81, esp. 174–75.

5. Franz J. Ingelfinger, "Informed (But Uneducated) Consent," *New England Journal of Medicine* 287 (1972): 466.

6. Ibid.

7. For a spread of definitions that conform to this description, see Jeffrie G. Murphy, *Retribution, Justice, and Therapy* (Boston: D. Reidel Publishing Co., 1979), 193–94; Vinit Haksar, "Coercive Proposals: Rawls and Gandhi," *Political Theory* 4 (1976): 65–79; John D. Hodson, *The Ethics of Legal Coercion* (Boston: D. Reidel Publishing Co., 1983), xiii; and Richard T. DeGeorge, *Business Ethics* (New York: Macmillan Publishing Co., 1982), 192.

8. For the thesis that there is "a moral use of coercion" based on the protection of "health as a moral value," see Edmund D. Pellegrino, "Autonomy and Coercion in Disease Prevention and Health Promotion," *Theoretical Medicine* 5 (1984): 83–91.

9. For example, "coercion" is often used loosely in the psychological literature. See Mary John Smith, *Persuasion and Human Action* (Belmont, CA: Wadsworth Publishing Co., 1982), 9–11, and James T. Tedeschi, "Threats and Promises," in Paul Swingle, ed., *The Structure of Conflict* (New York: Academic Press, 1970), 155–91. Similarly, the term "coercive power" is used to refer to the ability of the influence agent to punish failures to comply, regardless of the severity of the punishment, see J.R.P. French, Jr. and B.H. Raven, "The Bases of Social Power," in Dorwin Cartwright, ed., *Studies in Social Power* (Ann Arbor, MI: University of Michigan Press, 1959), 150–67, and B. Raven, "Social Power and Influence," in I.D. Steiner and M. Rischenbein, eds., *Current Studies in Social Psychology* (New York: Holt, 1965).

10. A basic distinction made in the coercion literature that we do not develop here is that between *occurrent* coercion and *dispositional* coercion. See, for example, Michael D. Bayles, "A Concept of Coercion," in J. Roland Pennock and John W. Chapman, eds., *Coercion: Nomos XIV* (New York: Aldine, 1972), 17. Not including occurrent coercion as the *paradigm* of coercion is attacked in Virginia Held, "Coercion and Coercive Offers," in Pennock and Chapman, *Coercion: Nomos XIV*, 49–62, esp. 50–54.

In occurrent coercion, a person is physically forced to behave as he or she otherwise would not. For example, if a woman does not want to consent to a mastectomy for breast cancer but her husband grabs her hand and physically forces her to sign the consent form, she has been "occurrently coerced." If, however, the husband induced the wife to sign the consent by threatening to leave her, this would be an instance of dispositional coercion, which achieves compliance by *threatening* harm or sanction. Although physical force would be necessary to carry out the sanction, in dispositional coercion behavioral compliance is not brought about by the application of physical force. Our analysis excludes occurrent coercion and is concerned solely with dispositional coercion. There is controversy about the relationship of occurrent coercion to *actions*, in contrast to *behaviors*. The root of this problem is found in the debate in action theory over whether actions are by definition voluntary. If there are no involuntary acts, then occurrent coercion can compel only behaviors and not actions, because there is no meaningful way in which an occurrently coerced response can be "voluntary."

One of the problems with this debate is, of course, how to define "voluntary" (see Chapter 7, pp. 256–257). For a discussion of the general problem of coercion and the action/behavior distinction see Bernard Gert, "Coercion and Freedom," in Pennock and Chapman, *Coercion: Nomos XIV*, 32; Norman S. Care and Charles Landesman, "Introduction," *Readings in the Theory of Action* (Bloomington: Indiana University Press, 1968).

Occurrent coercion is rarely a problem for informed consent, but occurrent coercion has been an issue for the coercion of medical treatment generally; see, for example, Martin S. Pernick, "The Patient's Role in Medical Decisionmaking: A Social History of Informed Consent in Medical Therapy," in President's Commission for the Study of Ethical Problems in Medicine and Biomedical and Behavioral Research, *Making Health Care Decisions* (Washington, D.C.: U.S. Government Printing Office, 1982), Vol. 3, 3, 23; and two papers by Paul S. Appelbaum and Loren H. Roth, "Involuntary Treatment in Medicine and Psychiatry," *American Journal of Psychiatry* 141 (1984): 53–58, and "Treatment Refusal in Medical Hospitals," in President's Commission, *Making Health Care Decisions*, Vol. 2, 462, 466.

11. For more detailed discussion of whether offers can be coercive, see, for example, David Zimmerman, "Coercive Wage Offers," *Philosophy and Public Affairs* 18 (1981): 121–45; David Lyons, "Welcome Threats and Coercive Offers," *Philosophy* 50 (1975): 427; Held, "Coercion and Coercive Offers," 55; Donald McIntosh, "Coercion and International Politics," in Pennock and Chapman, *Coercion: Nomos XIV*, 243–71; Theodore Benditt, "Threats and Offers," *Personalist* 58 (1977): 382–84; and Christian Bay, *The Structure of Freedom* (Stanford: Stanford University Press, 1958), Chapters 3 and 4.

12. Gert, "Coercion and Freedom," 36–37.

13. Robert Nozick, "Coercion," in Sidney Morgenbesser, Patrick Suppes, and Morton White, eds., *Philosophy, Science and Method: Essays in Honor of Ernest Nagel* (New York: St. Martin's Press, 1969), 440–72.

14. See, for example, Nozick, "Coercion"; Bayles, "A Concept of Coercion"; Gert, "Coercion and Freedom"; and Alan P. Wertheimer, "Political Coercion and Political Obligation," in Pennock and Chapman, *Coercion: Nomos XIV*, 213–43; H.J. McCloskey, "Coercion: Its Nature and Significance," *Southern Journal of Philosophy* 18 (1980): 335–51, esp. 340–41.

15. Beecher, "Editorial," 144–45.

16. As we noted in Chapter 4, the law also generally requires condition 3 before criminal or civil liability is imposed for any number of activities, including some that employ coercive force, threats, or deception. Cf. also McCloskey, "Coercion," 341–42.

17. Gert analyzes what he refers to as "coercion in the narrow sense" in terms of threatening evil presented by one person to another, where the evil is sufficient to constitute an unreasonable incentive for the other to act to avoid it. Gert defines an incentive as unreasonable "if it would be unreasonable to expect any rational man in that situation not to act on it." (Gert, "Coercion and Freedom," 34–35). Thus, for Gert, the line distinguishing minor evils (we prefer the term "harms") and evils that are severe enough to induce coerced acts is drawn in terms of what it would be reasonable to expect a "rational person" to resist.

Let Q stand for any rational person on Gert's formulation. On a slight modification of Gert's analysis, the "rational person" could be replaced by appeal to the *ordinary* or *average* person, paradigms that approximate the legal fiction of the "reasonable person" discussed in Chapters 2, 4, and 9. Such a reasonable person model seems to us preferable to Gert's, largely because rationality is too elusive and contested a concept to be satisfactory.

As Gert ("Coercion and Freedom," 34, n. 7) points out, his definition of coercion (as well as our subjective account) makes an appeal to Stanley Benn's concept of "an irresistible temptation." See Benn's "Freedom and Persuasion," *Australasian Journal of Philosophy* 45 (1967): 267.

18. Alvin Bronstein, "Remarks," in National Academy of Sciences, *Experiments and Research with Humans: Values in Conflict* (Washington, D.C.: National Academy of Sciences, 1975), 131. For a contrasting claim, see Deborah G. Johnson, "Prisoners and Consent to Experimentation," *Archives for Philosophy of Law and Social Philosophy* 68 (1978): 167–78.

19. See B.C. Postow, "Coercion and the Moral Bindingness of Contracts," *Social Theory and Practice* 4 (1976): 75–92; McCloskey, "Coercion," 340–41; and June Fessenden-Raden and Bernard Gert, *A Philosophical Approach to the Management of Occupational Health Hazards* (Bowling Green, OH: Social Philosophy and Policy Center, 1984), 14–15.

20. For an insightful analysis of the language of causation and harm, see Joel Feinberg, *Harm to Others*, Vol. I in his *The Moral Limits of the Criminal Law* (New York: Oxford University Press, 1984), esp. Chapter 1, 118–25, 171–86, and "Harm and Self-Interest," in P.M.S. Hacker and J. Raz, eds., *Law, Morality and Society: Essays in Honor of H.L.A. Hart* (Oxford: Clarendon Press, 1977), 45f. See also H.L.A. Hart and A.M. Honore, *Causation in the Law* (Oxford: Clarendon Press, 1959), 17–48, for an analysis of the subtleties in the general language of "cause." (Note, also, that our analysis of agents and coercion assumes that the coercer is *not* coerced.)

21. Jeffrie Murphy has argued that certain individuals subjected to severe situational pressures are unable to give informed consents, not because they were coerced, but because the pressure destroyed their capacity for psychological control. See Murphy, "Consent, Coercion and Hard Choices," 86.

22. Richard Warner, *Morality in Medicine: An Introduction to Medical Ethics* (Sherman Oaks, CA: Alfred Publishing Co., 1980), 28–29 (emphasis added). Contrast this position with that of Albert R. Jonsen, Mark Siegler, and William J. Winslade, who assert (without supporting argument) that "It is the *obligation* of physicians to try to persuade patients to follow a course designed to achieve" goals that ameliorate illness. *Clinical Ethics: A Practical Approach to Ethical Decisions in Clinical Medicine* (New York: Macmillan Publishing Co., 1982), 99 (emphasis added).

23. Louis Goldman, "The Willowbrook Debate," *World Medicine* 29 (September 1971): 23.

24. Persuasion is not always the only influence strategy appropriate to professionals. We shall see later that certain manipulations are also compatible with sense$_1$

informed consent. Also, there will be circumstances in which a professional is morally justified in using influence interventions that are still more controlling. However, this would not result in the obtaining of informed consents (in sense$_1$).

25. Appelbaum and Roth, "Treatment Refusal in Medical Hospitals," 443; see also 452, 462.

26. Donald Warwick and Herbert Kelman, "Ethical Issues in Social Intervention," in G. Zaltman, ed., *Processes and Phenomena of Social Change* (New York: Wiley, 1973), 409.

27. See, for example, William J. McGuire, "A Syllogistic Analysis of Cognitive Relationships," in Martin J. Rosenberg and Carl I. Hovland, eds., *Attitude Organization and Attitude Change* (New Haven: Yale University Press, 1960), 65–111.

28. Our understanding of persuasion—which restricts persuasion to influence that operates only through appeal to reason—runs counter to the broad and sometimes inconsistent use of the term in psychology. In the psychological literature, very little, if any, distinction is made between psychological manipulation (even in its most subtle forms) and persuasion. Distinctions sometimes have been made in psychology between rational and nonrational persuasion, but the bases for the distinctions have not neatly followed those outlined in philosophy. Although the focus in psychology has been on motivational and cognitive processes as they affect the internalization of new beliefs, persuasion has traditionally been defined broadly as synonymous with any kind of attitude change, often without regard to the psychological processes by which this change is brought about. For examples of different approaches to persuasion in psychology, see Smith, *Persuasion and Human Action*, 7; Richard E. Petty and John T. Cacioppo, *Attitudes and Persuasion: Classic and Contemporary Approaches* (Dubuque, IA: William C.Brown Co., 1981), 4; and Gerald R. Miller, "On Being Persuaded: Some Basic Definitions," in Michael E. Roloff and Gerald R. Miller, eds., *Persuasion: New Directions in Theory and Research* (Beverly Hills, CA: Sage Publications, 1980), 12–14.

What we call persuasion shares features with what psychologists French and Raven call "informational power." Although subjective feelings are not dispositive on this point, there is evidence that when people are influenced through the use of informational power (persuasion), they are likely to perceive themselves as in control—they believe that they are acting autonomously. See Judith Rodin and Irving Janis, "The Social Influence of Physicians and Health Care Practitioners," in Howard S. Friedman and M. Robin DiMatteo, eds., *Interpersonal Issues in Health Care* (New York: Academic Press, 1982), 39.

29. Tedeschi, "Threats and Promises."

30. Although in most instances it is relatively easy to distinguish threats from warnings, hard cases are ineliminable. For a careful analysis of ambiguities in the conditions distinguishing threats from warnings, see Nozick, "Coercion," 453-56. Nozick considers a case in which an employer tells his employees that if they vote to unionize his factory in an upcoming election he will close the factory. Four versions of the case are presented, each illustrating different subtleties in the threat/warning distinction.

31. Here we disagree with Benn, who holds that (rational) persuasion is limited to cases where the persuader uses only arguments that he or she finds persuasive ("Freedom and Persuasion," 32).

32. The distinction between cognition and affect is currently under active examination in psychology; see, for example, Howard Levanthal, "The Integration of Emotion and Cognition," in M. Clark and S. Fiske, eds., *Affect and Cognition: The 17th Annual Carnegie Symposium on Cognition* (Hillsdale, NJ: Erlbaum, 1982).

33. Henri de Mondeville, from passages in Mary Catherine Welborn, "The Long

Tradition: A Study in Fourteenth-Century Medical Deontology," in Chester R. Burns, ed., *Legacies in Ethics and Medicine* (New York: Science History Publications, 1977), 213.

34. See, for example, Kenneth L. Higbee, "Fifteen Years of Fear Arousal: Research on Threat Appeals," *Psychological Bulletin* 72 (1969): 426–44.

35. Irving L. Janis, "Effects of Fear Arousal on Attitude Change: Recent Developments in Theory and Research," in L. Berkowitz, ed., *Advances in Experimental Social Psychology* (New York: Academic Press, 1967), 167–222; and Howard Levanthal, "Fear Appeals and Persuasion: The Differentiation of a Motivational Construct," *American Journal of Public Health* 61 (1971): 1208–24, and "Findings and Theory in the Study of Fear Communications," in Berkowitz, *Advances in Experimental Social Psychology*, 119–86.

36. See, for example, Ronald W. Rogers and C. Ronald Mewborn, "Fear Appeals and Attitude Change," *Journal of Personality and Social Psychology* 34 (1976): 54–61.

37. Howard Penn Krisher, Susan A. Darley, and John M. Darley, "Fear-provoking Recommendations, Intentions to Take Preventive Actions, and Actual Preventive Actions," *Journal of Personality and Social Psychology* 26 (1973): 301–308.

38. Benn, "Freedom and Persuasion," 265–66, n. 8.

39. In social psychology, it is increasingly recognized that people are frequently not influenced by the reasons presented by the persuader but by self-generated reasons (cognitions) *prompted* by the persuader's arguments. To the extent that these self-generated cognitions are favorable to the persuader's position, the position will be adopted. See, for example, Richard E. Petty, "The Role of Cognitive Responses in Attitude Change Processes," in Richard E. Petty, Thomas M. Ostrom, and Timothy C. Brock, eds., *Cognitive Responses in Persuasion* (Hillsdale, NJ: Lawrence Erlbaum, Assoc., 1981), 135–39.

40. A professional's persuasive intervention may provoke in the patient or subject self-generated reasons that turn out to be determinative (for the influencee), but that are nevertheless *false* beliefs. Thus, the professional's intervention may be the "cause" of the patient's or subject's consenting based on less than substantial understanding. However, as long as this state of affairs is, from the professional's perspective, an *unintended* outcome, one cannot properly attribute the patient's or subject's failing to give a sense₁ informed consent to a failure to satisfy the condition of substantial noncontrol; only the condition of substantial understanding is affected.

41. Our account of manipulation (or, perhaps more precisely, our use of the term) thus differs substantially from a standard philosophical account of manipulation requiring the use of deception or trickery to change another's intentions or actions. In philosophical literature "manipulation" generally carries a nefarious connotation of immorality. Ruth Macklin's characterization is representative: "To manipulate people is to 'handle them,' a figurative image calling to mind the way a puppeteer pulls the strings of his marionettes." Ruth Macklin, *Man, Mind and Morality* (Englewood Cliffs, NJ: Prentice-Hall, 1982), 12. Similarly, Richard T. DeGeorge defines "manipulation" as "playing upon a person's will by trickery or by devious, unfair, or insidious means." He takes all manipulation to be (at least prima facie) immoral. DeGeorge, *Business Ethics*, 192.

42. Jeffrie G. Murphy takes this view. See his *Retribution, Justice, and Therapy* (Boston: D. Reidel Publishing Co., 1979), 186, 191.

43. This morally neutral approach to manipulation is a centerpiece of Donald Warwick and Herbert Kelman's essay on the ethics of social intervention. Our analysis of manipulation is indebted to their treatment, although we depart from Warwick and

Kelman on several crucial points. For example, they see two basic kinds of manipulation—*environmental* manipulation and *psychic* manipulation—whereas we divide manipulation into three basic types—manipulation of options, manipulation of information, and psychological manipulation. See Warwick and Kelman, "Ethical Issues in Social Intervention," 403.

44. Henry K. Beecher, *Research and the Individual: Human Studies* (Boston: Little, Brown and Company, 1970), 6.

45. It must be remembered that ours is a subjective standard of irresistibility, and so we must admit even the very rare case where an unwelcome offer of a mere good is not only difficult to resist but absolutely irresistible. No psychological theory known to us precludes the possibility that an unwelcome offer of a mere good could be irresistible to a manipulatee. Consider, for example, a scrupulous and high-minded government official who is offered a bribe to "overlook certain irregularities" in the federal audit of a large corporation. The official happens also to be an avid collector of Chinese porcelain; indeed, her passion knows no bounds. Although the official covets many pieces that she does not own, there is one treasure, in particular, that she desires above all else in her life. It is this very treasure that the official is offered in this unwelcome offer of bribery.

It seems possible that the official's will to resist could be destroyed, overwhelmed, shattered—her resistance completely broken down—by the attractiveness of the offer. When the adjective "irresistible" is used as a synonym for "necessary," "compulsory," "resistless," "choiceless," and the like, the reference is to a certain effect on the will, and there is no reason why the unwelcome offer of a mere good *could not* have precisely this effect.

46. Harold F. Gamble, "Students, Grades and Informed Consent," *IRB* 4 (May 1982): 7–10.

47. Jay Katz, *The Silent World of Doctor and Patient* (New York: Free Press, 1984), 113–14. For case material illustrative of precisely this point, see Sue Fisher, "Doctor Talk/Patient Talk: How Treatment Decisions are Negotiated in Doctor-Patient Communication," in Sue Fisher and Alexandra D. Todd, *The Social Organization of Doctor-Patient Communication* (Washington, D.C.: Center for Applied Linguistics, 1983), 135–57.

48. Witness, for example, the furor and controversy surrounding a celebrated case of deception and placebo therapy involving drug dependency in a pain patient; see Loren Pankrantz, "Self-Control Techniques as an Alternative to Pain Medication," *Journal of Abnormal Psychology* 84 (1975): 165–68.

49. See, for example, Charles W. Lidz and Alan Meisel, "Informed Consent and the Structure of Medical Care," in President's Commission, *Making Health Care Decisions*, Vol. 2; Alan Meisel, "The Exceptions to the Informed Consent Doctrine," *Wisconsin Law Review 1979* (1979): 413–88.

50. See, for example, Alan C. Elms, "Keeping Deception Honest: Justifying Conditions for Social Scientific Research Stratagems," in Tom L. Beauchamp, et al., eds., *Ethical Issues in Social Science Research* (Baltimore, MD: The Johns Hopkins Press, 1982), 232–45.

51. See William C. Thompson, "Psychological Issues in Informed Consent," in President's Commission, *Making Health Care Decisions*, Vol. 3, esp. 85–99.

52. See ibid., 105–107 for a discussion of techniques for inducing guilt and feelings of reciprocity or obligation as they might apply to informed consent. This last influence strategy—inducing feelings of reciprocity—shares some common features with what French and Raven, in "The Bases of Social Power," call "referent power." This is the kind of power one has to influence another because the other finds the influence

agent benevolent, likable, admirable, etc. Judith Rodin and Irving L. Janis have pointed to referent power as an underutilized but potentially very important kind of influence for health care professionals to use in helping their patients. See Rodin and Janis, "The Social Influence of Physicians and Other Health Care Practitioners As Agents of Change," 37–49, and Irving L. Janis, "Problems of Short-Term Counseling" and "Helping Relationships: A Preliminary Theoretical Analysis," both in Janis, ed., *Counseling on Personal Decisions* (New Haven, CT: Yale University Press, 1982), 1–36. Whether, or under what conditions, the use of referent power by physicians compromises their patients' autonomy of action is unclear.

53. Perhaps the most extreme form of social influence—brainwashing—combines elements of psychological manipulation with coercion, punishment, and informational manipulation. In programs of "brainwashing," sometimes called "coercive persuasion" (see, for example, Willard Gaylin, "On the Borders of Persuasion: A Psychoanalytic Look at Coercion," *Psychiatry* 37 (1974): 1–9), overt severe threats of harm have been used to induce behavioral compliance. This use of coercion should be distinguished from the use, common in brainwashing, of physical deprivation and suffering that are not used as a threat to induce compliance, but as a mechanism for weakening the person's psychological and physical abilities to resist ideological conversion or total psychological dependence. This physical and psychological deprivation makes it unnecessary for subsequent commands to be accompanied by threats; that is, it makes it unnecessary for subsequent acts to be coerced.

54. Robert B. Cialdini, et al., "Low-Ball Procedure for Producing Compliance: Commitment then Cost," *Journal of Personality and Social Psychology* 36 (1978): 463–78, esp. 464.

55. Ibid.

56. Low-balling is closely related to another technique for inducing compliance, known as the foot-in-the-door technique. A long-time favorite of social psychologists, this procedure involves increasing compliance with a request by first inducing compliance with an initial smaller, but different, request. See J.L. Freedman and S.C. Fraser, "Compliance with Pressure, the Foot-in-the-Door Technique," *Journal of Personality and Social Psychology* 4 (1966): 195–202; P. Pliner, et al., "Compliance without Pressure, Some Further Data on the Foot-in-the-Door Technique," *Journal of Experimental Social Psychology* 10 (1974): 17–22; and Mark Snyder and Michael R. Cunningham, "To Comply or Not Comply: Testing the Self-Perception Explanation of the 'Foot-in-the-Door' Phenomenon," *Journal of Personality and Social Psychology* 31 (1975): 64–67. Although the robustness of the foot-in-the-door technique has recently been called into question, it is thought to involve the same or similar psychological mediators as low-balling, except that this technique does not involve any manipulation of information. See Robert D. Foss and Carolyn B. Dempsey, "Blood Donation and the Foot-in-the-Door Technique: A Limiting Case," *Journal of Personality and Social Psychology* 37 (1979): 580–90, and Cialdini, et al., "Low-Ball Procedure for Producing Compliance," 467–68.

Behavioral scientists have recommended another, related form of psychological manipulation as a means to increase the number of "volunteers" as blood donors. It has been suggested that solicitees first be asked for a large commitment, after which one can retreat to all "smaller requests." See R.M.A. Oswaldt, "Review of the Experimental Manipulation of Blood Donors Motivation," in D.J. Osborne, M.M. Gruneberg, J.R. Eiser, eds., *Research in Psychology and Medicine*, Vol. II (New York: Academic Press, 1979), 44–51.

57. Cialdini, et al., "Low-Ball Procedure for Producing Compliance," 10.

58. Robert B. Cialdini, *Influence: How and Why People Agree* (New York: William Morrow and Co., 1984).

59. Lidz and Meisel, "Informed Consent and the Structure of Medical Care," 391–92.

60. See J. Lorber, "Good Patients and Problem Patients: Conformity and Deviance in a General Hospital," *Journal of Health and Social Behavior* 16 (1975): 213–25; R.L. Coser, *Life in the Ward* (East Lansing, MI: Michigan State University Press, 1962); and D.L. Tagliacozzo and H.O. Mauksch, "The Patient's View of the Patient Role," in E.G. Jaco, ed., *Patients, Physicians, and Illness* (New York: Free Press, 1972).

61. Shelley E. Taylor, "Hospital Patient Behavior: Reactance, Helplessness, or Control?" in Friedman and DiMatteo, *Interpersonal Issues in Health Care*, 209–32.

62. Ibid., 213.

63. Ibid., 214; see also n. 60.

64. Ibid., 226.

65. See n. 60.

66. See, for example, Louis Harris, et al., "Views of Informed Consent and Decisionmaking: Parallel Surveys of Physicians and the Public," in President's Commission, *Making Health Care Decisions*, Vol. 2, 187–88, 204–208; Lidz and Meisel, "Informed Consent and the Structure of Medical Care," 342–43; Diana Axelsen and Ray A. Wiggins, "An Application of Moral Guidelines in Human Clinical Trials to a Study of Benzodiazepene Compound as a Hypnotic Agent Among the Elderly," *Clinical Research* 25 (1977): 1–7; and Sandra Berkowitz, "Informed Consent, Research and the Elderly," *The Gerontologist* 18 (1978): 237–43.

Historically, the notion that role manipulation is inherent in the doctor-patient relationship can be traced to Talcott Parsons' analysis of the "sick role." According to Parsons, one of the defining marks of the sick role is that ill persons comply with technically competent medical advice. In addition, they are generally exempted from ordinary role and task obligations. *Essays on the Social Situation of Mental Patients and Other Inmates* (Garden City, NJ: Anchor Books, 1961).

67. See Erving Goffman's classic study, *Asylums,* for an analysis of the effects of institutionalization on deindividuation, conformity, and obedience (Garden City, NY: Anchor Books, 1961). See Richard Singer, "Consent of the Unfree," for an interpretative review of the literature on the extent to which the prisoner role permits individuality and voluntary choice in the context of a contemporary American prison.

68. Under "professional advocate" we would include patient advocates or ombudsmen, attorneys, religious leaders, and in some instances social service professionals. We do not include mere "auditor witnesses" who need not bear any special supportive relationship to the person making the consent decision.

69. Complicating the picture further is the inevitability in many circumstances of "overdetermined" consents, in the sense that more than one kind of influence is individually sufficient to bring about the consent and two or more such individually sufficient conditions are present in the circumstances. For example, a person might be both persuaded to consent to involvement in research and manipulated to do so, if reasoned argument is combined with a manipulative presentation. In an overdetermined situation, the person will consent even if one of the two forms of influence were to vanish. It may be precipitous—and perhaps even wrong in some cases—to hold that the consent is less than substantially autonomous.

70. Particularly troublesome are cases in which the only influence strategies employed by the professional soliciting consent are persuasion and easily resistible manipulations, but the person's consent decision is simultaneously being heavily manipulated by family members or friends. Such situations may represent paradigm examples where actions that cannot qualify as informed consents sense$_1$ should be accepted as informed consents sense$_2$.

Index